INDIGENOUS PEOPLES
IN INTERNATIONAL LAW

Indigenous Peoples
in International Law

SECOND EDITION

S. James Anaya

OXFORD
UNIVERSITY PRESS

2004

OXFORD
UNIVERSITY PRESS

Oxford   New York
Auckland   Bangkok   Buenos Aires   Cape Town   Chennai
Dar es Salaam   Delhi   Hong Kong   Istanbul   Karachi   Kolkata
Kuala Lumpur   Madrid   Melbourne   Mexico City   Mumbai   Nairobi
São Paulo   Shanghai   Taipei   Tokyo   Toronto

First published in 1996 by Oxford University Press, Inc.
198 Madison Avenue, New York, New York 10016

www.oup.com

First issued as an Oxford University Press paperback, 2000

Oxford is a registered trademark of Oxford University Press

Library of Congress Cataloging-in-Publication Data
Anaya, S. James.
Indigenous peoples in international law / S. James Anaya.—2nd ed.
p.   cm.
Includes bibliographical references and index.
ISBN-13 978-0-19-517350-5

1. Indigenous peoples—Legal status, laws, etc.   I. Title.
K3242 .A96 2004
342.08'72—dc22   2003023353

To Jana, Andrea, and Emilio

Preface

This book endeavors to identify the contours and general content of international law's treatment of indigenous peoples as a particular subject of concern. Its focus is on the relevant trends within the international system that concern groups identified as "indigenous"—generally understood as groups that are descended from the original or longtime inhabitants of lands now dominated by others—and on providing a normative framework by which to understand and evaluate those trends. This second edition maintains the central contention of the first: that international law, although once an instrument of colonialism, has developed to support the resilient efforts of indigenous groups worldwide to survive and flourish as distinct peoples on their ancestral or traditional lands. This movement in international law has been grudging and imperfect, falling short of indigenous peoples' full aspirations; yet it is in marked contrast with legal and policy regimes originating in the past that sought to do away with or suppress indigenous identities, as this book endeavors to show. The contemporary international regime concerning indigenous peoples is identified here as arising within international law's human rights program, which was instituted in earnest with the United Nations Charter and which has moved international law away from an exclusively state-centered orientation.

This second edition includes developments within international law's human rights program that have occurred since publication of the first edition in 1996. It is not necessarily comprehensive of all relevant developments; rather, the effort here is to provide an updated overall picture of the rights and status of indigenous peoples in international law. Included are the most significant developments, such as the establishment of the United Nations Permanent Forum on Indigenous Issues; several decisions by U.N. treaty-monitoring bodies, International Labour Organization committees, the Inter-American Commission on Human Rights, and the Inter-American Court of Human Rights; and ongoing discussions around efforts within the United Nations and the Organization of American States to articulate declarations on indigenous rights—developments all of which generally confirm the normative and institutional trends identified in the first edition.

Although the shortcomings and mistakes in this book are mine alone, I could not have written it without the perspectives I have gained and support I have received from many colleagues, friends, and loved ones, and from the indigenous nations and communities with which I have had the privilege of working over the years. I am especially grateful to my friends and colleagues at the University of Arizona, Robert Williams, Jr., and Luis Rodríguez-Piñero, for encouraging me and helping me to sharpen my ideas; and Toni Massaro, dean of the college of law, for her constant, unfailing support for my and others' work on indigenous issues. I am also fortunate to have received guidance in various ways from Natalia Alvarez, Gudmunder Alfredsson, Arthur Bonfield, Julian Burger, Ward Churchill, Bartolomé Clavero, Robert Clinton, Robert T. Coulter, Todd Crider, Erica Daes, Carlos Deocón, Vine DeLoria, Jr., Dalee Sambo Dorough, Ingmar Egede, Richard Falk, Julie Ann Fishel, Charles Hale, John Henricksen, Moira Gracey, Claudio Grossman, Benedict Kingsbury, Will Kymlicka, Hurst Hannum, Robert Hershey, Richard Hughes, Darlene Johnston, Kenneth Kress, Thomas Luebben, Oren Lyons, Theodore Macdonald, Patrick Macklem, David Maybury-Lewis, Glenn Morris, Hermann Pünder, Chandra Roy, Deborah Schaaf, Martin Scheinin, Elsa Stamatopoulou, Rodolfo Stavenhagen, Rennard Strickland, Steven Tullberg, Burns Weston, Siegfried Wiessner, Gerald Wilkinson, and David Weissbrodt. My thanks also go to Marina Hadjioannou, who assisted with the research for this second edition of the book, and to Sandy Davis, whose hard work contributed to pulling together the manuscript for this edition. Several of my students at the University of Iowa, where I wrote the first edition, and at the University of Arizona, where I completed this edition, also contributed to research and other necessary tasks, for which I am grateful.

I cannot express the depth of my gratitude for the insights and motivation I have gained from Carrie and Mary Dann and other members of the Western Shoshone Nation, the people of the Mayangna community of Awas Tingni in Nicaragua, leaders and members of Maya communities in Belize, Brooklyn Rivera and Armstrong Wiggins of the Miskito people in Nicaragua, José Abeyta of Isleta Pueblo, Floyd Hicks of the Fallon Paiute-Shoshone Tribe, Abadio Green and other leaders of the National Indigenous Organization of Colombia, and the many other indigenous individuals, peoples, and organizations with which I have been fortunate to work. Much of what I have to say in this book is due to them, although I do not here speak for them.

Finally, I am thankful to my family for all they have done—in ways they often do not know—to support me in this work.

Tucson, Arizona   S. J. A.
February 2004

Contents

INDIGENOUS PEOPLES
IN INTERNATIONAL LAW

Introduction

Half a millennium ago, people living on the continents now called North and South America began to have encounters of a kind they had not experienced before. Europeans arrived and started to lay claim to their lands, overpowering their political institutions and disrupting the integrity of their economies and cultures. The European encroachments frequently were accompanied by the slaughter of the children, women, and men who stood in the way. For many of the people who survived, the Europeans brought disease and slavery. Similar patterns of empire and conquest extended to other parts of the globe, resulting in human suffering and turmoil on a massive scale.[1]

As empire building and colonial settlement proceeded from the sixteenth century onward, those who already inhabited the encroached-upon lands and who were subjected to oppressive forces became known as indigenous, native, or aboriginal. Such designations have continued to apply to people by virtue of their place and condition within the life-altering human encounter set in motion by colonialism. Today, the term *indigenous* refers broadly to the living descendants of preinvasion inhabitants of lands now dominated by others. Indigenous peoples, nations, or communities are culturally distinctive groups that find themselves engulfed by settler societies born of the forces of empire and conquest. The diverse surviving Indian communities and nations of the Western Hemisphere, the Inuit and Aleut of the Arctic, the Aboriginal people of Australia, the Maori of Aotearoa (New Zealand), Native Hawaiians and other Pacific Islanders, the Saami of the European far North, and many of the minority or nondominant tribal peoples of Africa and Asia are generally regarded, and regard themselves, as indigenous. They are *indigenous* because their ancestral roots are embedded in the lands in which they live, or would like to live, much more deeply than the roots of more powerful sectors of society living on the same lands or in close proximity. Furthermore, they are *peoples* to the extent they comprise distinct communities with a continuity of existence and identity that links them to the communities, tribes, or nations of their ancestral past.[2]

3

In the contemporary world, indigenous peoples characteristically exist under conditions of severe disadvantage relative to others within the states constructed around them. Historical phenomena grounded on racially discriminatory attitudes are not just blemishes of the past but rather translate into current inequities. Indigenous peoples have been deprived of vast landholdings and access to life-sustaining resources, and they have suffered historical forces that have actively suppressed their political and cultural institutions. As a result, indigenous peoples have been crippled economically and socially, their cohesiveness as communities has been damaged or threatened, and the integrity of their cultures has been undermined. In both industrial and less-developed countries in which indigenous people live, the indigenous sectors almost invariably are on the lowest rung of the socioeconomic ladder, and they exist at the margins of power.[3]

Some indigenous groups were not severely affected, if at all, by colonization or its legacies until well into the twentieth century. Isolated tribal peoples in the Amazon, for example, lived mostly unaffected by outside forces until fairly recently. In much of the Arctic, indigenous peoples were mostly left to continue lifestyles built around harvesting abundant wildlife resources within vast territorial domains. But even the most isolated indigenous groups are now threatened by encroaching commercial, government, or other interests motivated by prospects of accumulating wealth from the natural resources on indigenous lands or by strategic military concerns. History is repeating or threatening to repeat itself in the name of modernization, development, and security.

In the face of tremendous adversity, indigenous peoples have long sought to flourish as distinct communities on their ancestral lands, and they have endeavored to roll back inequities lingering as the result of historical patterns of colonization. Armed resistance, diplomacy, and law have been tools in this quest for survival. Over the last several years especially, in conjunction with efforts through domestic or municipal arenas of decision making, indigenous peoples have appealed to the international community and looked to international law as a means to advance their cause.[4]

International law is a universe of authoritative norms and procedures—today linked to international institutions—that are in some measure controlling across jurisdictional boundaries. The central contention of this book is that international law, although once an instrument of colonialism, has developed and continues to develop, however grudgingly or imperfectly, to support indigenous peoples' demands.

This book stands at the intersection of international law, indigenous peoples, and concern over the circumstances that have placed them in nondominant positions relative to other segments of humanity. Despite the usage already identified and adopted here, the term *indigenous* can in some ways be understood to refer to all but the most transient or migratory segments of humanity. The European nationalities that spawned colonialism are certainly, in a literal sense, indigenous to their homelands. And the dominant settler populations that were born of colonial patterns have created societies that many might now describe as indigenous to the place of settlement. It even may be said that recently migrating populations are in the process of becoming part of the dominant "indigenous" receiving society or laying down roots that will, over time, establish their own distinctive "indigenous" connections with the place of migration. Within international law and institutions, however, the term *indigenous*, or similar terms such as *native* or *aboriginal*, just as in the domestic legal regimes of many countries, has long been used to refer to a particular subset of humanity that represents a certain common set of experiences rooted in historical subjugation by colonialism, or something like colonialism.[5] Today, indigenous peoples are identified, and identify themselves as such, by reference to identities that predate historical encroachments by other groups and the ensuing histories that have wrought, and continue to bring, oppression against their cultural survival and self-determination as distinct peoples.[6] Numerous processes of decision within the international system have focused on the common set of ongoing problems that are central to the demands of these groups, such that there are discernible patterns of responses and normative understandings associated with the rubric of *indigenous peoples*. The aim of this book is to synthesize these international processes, especially insofar as they reveal a contemporary regime of international law on the subject.

This work relies upon many decisions, written instruments, and procedures, although its aim is not to exhaustively catalogue all such items within the domain of international law that are relevant to the subject of indigenous peoples. Since the first edition of this book, others have provided extensive documentation of international developments concerning indigenous peoples, making information about these developments now fairly easily accessible.[7] Rather, this book's purpose is to provide an account of relevant developments that reveals the contours and general content of international law's treatment of indigenous peoples as a distinct subject of concern. The focus here is on taking stock of the trends within the international system concerning indigenous peoples and on providing a normative framework by which to understand and evaluate those trends.

This work takes as a fundamental premise that no area of international law can be merely described as if it were reducible to a set of rules with fixed meaning. As the distinguished jurist Rosalyn Higgins has observed, "International law is not rules. It is a normative system . . . harnessed to the achievement of common values—values that speak to all of us."[8] While there are formal "sources" of international law—namely, treaties, custom, and general principles of law—these sources, and the procedures that engage them, must be evaluated and interpreted in light of the values that speak *to all of us*, and with attention to the realities of a changing world of diverse contexts in which previously unheard, and unheard of, groups wield increasing influence, if only by the force of their words, ideas, and passion. Analysis of international law is thus more aptly about process in connection with norms and values than about rules alone. This view contrasts with that which finds international law only in what states have already agreed upon in written texts or clearly consented to through already well-established patterns of behavior. Such an understanding of international law is far too narrow, for it misses the importance of recent and ongoing multifaceted processes of decision that have enacted and are continuing to enact change in the normative system that functions within the international domain. So to assert here that international law is developing (imperfectly and grudgingly) in ways that support indigenous peoples demands is to engage in a normative interpretation of observable processes of decision that goes beyond what may have already been said or written down.

Part I of this book sketches the development of international law and its treatment of indigenous peoples over time, identifying the emergence in recent years of new norms and activity within the law's burgeoning human rights program. Attention to international law's diverse temporal manifestations and evolutionary character is essential to understanding the contemporary movement in favor of indigenous peoples' demands and the tensions inherent in that movement. Among efforts to use international law in favor of indigenous peoples in the last few decades, a frequently invoked strain of argument has been within the classical state-centered framework of international law that developed in Europe from the seventeenth century onward along with the institution of the modern state. Within this frame of argument indigenous groups have been referred to as "nations" and identified as having attributes of "sovereignty" that predate and, at least to some extent, should trump the sovereignty of the states that now assert power over them. The rhetoric of nationhood is used to posit indigenous peoples as states, or something like states, within a post-Westphalian world of separate, mutually exclusive political communities. Advocates for indigenous peoples point to a history in which "original" sovereignty of indigenous communities over defined territories has been illegitimately taken from them or suppressed. The international law rules that developed in the nineteenth century relating to the acquisition and transfer of territory by and among states are invoked to demonstrate the illegitimacy of the assault on indigenous sovereignty. But while appealing to many, this strain of argument must confront international law's strong historical doctrinal tendency, precisely at its height in the nineteenth century, to view as unqualified for statehood non-European indigenous peoples and to instead favor the consolidation of power over them by the European states and their colonial offspring. It is also strongly resisted by contemporary international norms of state sovereignty that have survived robustly from historical doctrine and by existing political configurations that favor the sovereignty of already widely recognized states to the exclusion of any competing sovereignty.

International law's embrace of human rights, however, engenders a discourse that is an alternative to the state-centered, historical sovereignty one, a discourse that has yielded results within the international system for indigenous peoples. Indigenous peoples have seized upon the institutional and normative regime of human rights that was brought within the fold of international law in the aftermath of World War II and the adoption of the United Nations Charter. Much like the moral discourse engaged in by pre-nineteenth-century theorists who are associated with the early development of international law and who questioned the legality of colonial patterns, the contemporary human rights discourse has the welfare of human beings as its subject and is concerned only secondarily, if at all, with the interests of sovereign entities. Within the human rights framework, indigenous peoples are groups of human beings with fundamental human rights concerns that deserve attention. Historical events are indeed relevant, but that relevance is in the extent to which history accounts for conditions of *present-day* oppression and inequities that affect the lives of indigenous human beings and their communities.

Responding to indigenous peoples' demands is a human rights imperative that is now widely recognized within the international system. And with this recognition has come a sustained level of international institutional activity focused upon indigenous peoples' concerns and a corresponding body of norms that build upon long-standing human rights precepts. This regime is in tension with notions of state sovereignty that continue as central to the international system and that generally blunt international concern over human rights, and it challenges the human rights system's traditional focus on the rights of individuals rather than on the collective rights of groups. Nonetheless, an indigenous rights regime has developed, and it continues to develop, within international law's human rights program in ways that are in some measure favorable to indigenous peoples' demands.

Part II of the book describes the structure and content of contemporary international norms concerning indigenous peoples, emphasizing their grounding and linkages with the principle of self-determination and other human rights standards of general applicability. The principle or right of self-determination, which is strongly embedded in abstract terms in major international legal instruments, including the United Nations Charter, is central to the chorus of indigenous peoples' demands within the international arena. But independently of the subjective meaning attached to the principle by indigenous peoples, a common tendency has been to understand self-determination as wedded to attributes of statehood, with "full" self-determination deemed to be in the attainment of independent statehood, or at least in the right to choose independent statehood.

For obvious reasons, this tendency has impeded widespread explicit affirmation that self-determination, as a principle of international law, applies to indigenous peoples.

An alternative understanding of self-determination, however, emerges from taking seriously the principle's grounding within the human rights, as opposed to states rights, framework of international law. International human rights texts that affirm self-determination, and authoritative processes that have been responsive to self-determination demands, point to core values of freedom and equality that are relevant to all segments of humanity, including indigenous peoples, in relation to the political, economic, and social configurations with which they live. Under a human rights approach, attributes of statehood or sovereignty are at most instrumental to the realization of these values—they are not themselves the essence of self-determination. And for most peoples—especially in light of cross-cultural linkages and other patterns of interconnectedness that exist alongside diverse identities—*full* self-determination, in a real sense, does not require or justify a separate state and may even be impeded by establishment of a separate state. It is a rare case in the post-colonial world in which self-determination, understood from a human rights perspective, will require secession or the dismemberment of states. For many groups, however, some change in existing structures of governance or other measures short of secession are needed to bring about and ensure an atmosphere in which they may live and develop freely, under conditions of equality, in all spheres of life. And such measures are typically required for indigenous peoples, to be enacted according to their own preferences, as now widely recognized among international actors.

The contemporary international concern for indigenous peoples effectively is based upon the identification of a long-standing sui generis set of deviations from the self-determination standard, deviations that result from a common set of historical and contemporary factors. Attention is needed to correct the legacies of the past and the conditions of the present that impede indigenous self-determination and to ensure indigenous self-determination for the future. Building upon self-determination's core values and related human rights principles, a still developing body of international norms elaborates upon the elements of self-determination for the indigenous peoples genre and marks the objects of corrective measures. These norms derive from existing written instruments and their interpretation by authorized institutions, and from ongoing consensus-building processes among states, indigenous peoples, and other actors. They fall roughly within the following categories: nondiscrimination, which precludes inferior treatment of indigenous individuals or attributes of indigenous group identity; cultural integrity, which applies contextually to protect all aspects of the vast diversity of indigenous cultural patterns; lands and natural resources, a set of prescriptions based on recognition of indigenous modalities of land and resource tenure that originate apart from formal state property regimes; social welfare and development, entitlements aimed at defeating the conditions of economic disadvantage that are characteristic of indigenous peoples; and self-government, the political dimension of self-determination which simultaneously requires both spheres of autonomy for indigenous regulatory institutions and effective means of indigenous participation in the larger political order.

It is generally assumed that these norms, like indigenous self-determination more generally, will ordinarily be applied within the frameworks of existing states. At the same time, these norms are accompanied by a corresponding duty on the part of states to take the measures necessary to fully implement them, through channels of decision making that involve indigenous peoples themselves. This duty is to be realized through all relevant state institutions acting within their respective spheres of competency, and it may require reforms that reach even constitutional dimensions.

While international norms concerning indigenous peoples are to be implemented by state actors through mostly local decision making, international institutions monitor and promote that implementation through a series of specific procedures. These international procedures, the subject of part III of this book, range from information gathering to the adjudication of complaints against states that are accused of failing to uphold their duty of implementation. The relatively new Permanent Forum on Indigenous Issues, a U.N. institution, is developing methods for ongoing monitoring of conditions concerning indigenous peoples, adding to the monitoring work that has been going on for some time through the U.N. Working Group on Indigenous Populations. Several other institutions, which are not specifically or exclusively concerned with indigenous peoples, have adapted their procedures to address indigenous peoples demands while simultaneously invoking and further developing relevant norms. All these procedures are aimed at overcoming or blunting political, economic, and other forces that all too frequently function within domestic arenas to impede state measures that would bring about compliance with international norms. Existing configurations of power and doctrine that strongly favor state authority over that of international institutions, along with factors of international institutional capacity, render these procedures weak in their ability to bring about prompt and concrete results in specific problems situations. Nonetheless, international institutions and procedures that engage the concerns of indigenous peoples are important elements in ongoing efforts to consolidate norms of indigenous self-determination and to see those norms effectively implemented.

While advancing understanding about these multiple dimensions of international law as it concerns indigenous peoples is the principle aim of this book, this study also casts light on the nature of international law itself and its capacity to change, and to be an agent of change. As an examination of the international dynamics surrounding indigenous peoples' demands reveals, such capacity exists, even while being limited by configurations of power and doctrine that are weighted in history.

Notes

1. The devastation of the early European contact has been extensively documented. *See, e.g.*, David Batstone, *From Conquest to Struggle: Jesus of Nazareth in Latin America* 14 (1991) (describing the conquest of Central and South America, and observing that "[t]he magnitude of genocide committed by the Spanish conquistadors against the indigenous people . . . is staggering"); John F. Guilmartin, Jr., "The Cutting Edge: An Analysis of the Spanish Invasion and Overthrow of the Inca Empire," in *Transatlantic Encounters: Europeans and Andeans in the Sixteenth Century* 40, 44 (Kenneth J. Andrien & Rolena Adorno eds., 1991) (describing the 1536–1537 Spanish siege of Cusco, in which Hernando Pizarro "ordered all captured Indian women killed; he also ordered the right hands of several hundred captured male noncombatants cut off, after which they were released to spread fear and demoralization"); Francis Jennings, *The Founders of America: How Indians Discovered the Land, Pioneered in It, and Created Great Classical Civilizations; How They Were Plunged into a Dark Age by Invasions and Conquest; and How They Are Reviving* 135 (1993) (explaining that "[m]ilitary conquest was accomplished by familiar European techniques of massacre, devastation, terrorism, and resultant demoralization of native peoples"); David S. Trigger, *Whitefella Comin': Aboriginal Responses to Colonialism in Northern Australia* 20 (1992) (describing nineteenth-century conflicts between white settlers and aboriginal people in Australia, including "vicious killings of Aboriginal men, women and children"). *See also* Julian Burger, *Report from the Frontier: The State of the World's Indigenous Peoples* 36–46 (1987) and sources cited therein.

2. A study by the United Nations contains the following definition:

> Indigenous communities, peoples and nations are those which, having a historical continuity with pre-invasion and pre-colonial societies that developed on their territories, consider themselves distinct from other sectors of the societies now prevailing in those territories, or parts of them. They form at present non-dominant sectors of society and are determined to preserve, develop and transmit to future generations their ancestral territories, and their ethnic identity, as the basis of their continued existence as peoples, in accordance with their own cultural patterns, social institutions and legal systems.

U.N. Subcommission on Prevention of Discrimination and Protection of Minorities, *Study of the Problem of Discrimination against Indigenous Populations*, U.N. Doc. E/CN.4/Sub.2/1986/7/Add. 4, para. 379 (1986).

3. *See* Burger, *supra* note 1, at 17–31 (describing "life at the bottom" for indigenous peoples worldwide in terms of employment, health, discrimination, and social marginalization). *See also, e.g.*, Ronet Bachman, *Death and Violence on the Reservation: Homicide, Family Violence, and Suicide in American Indian Populations* (1992) (documenting social ills and economic barriers faced by Indians in the United States and attributing them to long-standing patterns of oppression); Royal Commission on Aboriginal Peoples, *Public Hearings: Exploring the Options—Overview of the Third Round* (1993) (discussing myriad problems faced by aboriginal people in Canada and the need for "healing"); Jon C. Altman & John Nieuwenhuysen, *The Economic Status*

of Australian Aborigines (1979); George Psacharophoulos & Harr A. Patrinos, "Indigenous People and Poverty in Latin America," *Finance and Development*, Mar. 1994, at 41 ("[T]here is no question that the indigenous people of Latin America live in conditions of extreme poverty, with children unable to keep up with their non-indigenous counterparts").

4. *See infra* chapter 2, notes 42–54 and accompanying text.

5. *See Working Paper by the Chairperson-Rapporteur, Mrs. Erica-Irene A. Daes, on the Concept of "Indigenous People,"* U.N. Doc. E/CN.4/Sub.2/AC.4/1996/2 (1996) (surveying historical and contemporary practice).

6. *Cf.* Benedict Kingsbury, "'Indigenous Peoples' in International Law: A Constructivist Approach to the Asian Controversy," 92 *Am. J. Int'l L.* 414, 457 (1998) (arguing for a flexible approach to understanding the concept of "indigenous peoples" that emphasizes the commonality of "experiences, concerns and contributions made by groups in many different regions"). *See generally Note by the Chairperson-Rapporteur of the Working Group on Indigenous Populations, Ms. Erica-Irene Daes, on Criteria Which Might Be Applied When Considering the Concept of Indigenous Peoples,* U.N. Doc. E/CN.4/Sub.2/ AC.4/1995/3 (1995).

7. Especially noteworthy are Patrick Thornberry's and Fergus Mackay's detailed descriptions and analyses of global and regional instruments and decisions that concern indigenous peoples. *See* Patrick Thornberry, *Indigenous Peoples and Human Rights* (2002); Fergus Mackay, *Los derechos de los pueblos indígenas en el sistema internacional* (1999). *See also Human Rights of Indigenous Peoples* (Cynthia Price Cohen ed., 1998); Maivân Clech Lâm, *At the Edge of the State: Indigenous Peoples and Self-Determination* (2000); Siegfried Wiessner, "The Rights and Status of Indigenous Peoples: A Global Comparative and International Legal Analysis," 12 *Harv. Hum. Rts. J.* 57 (1999).

8. Rosalyn Higgins, *Problems and Process: International Law and How We Use It* 1–3 (1994).

I

DEVELOPMENTS OVER TIME

1

The Historical Context

Like all systems of law, international law is the product of historical as well as modern elements. International law especially is rooted in jurisprudential strains originating in classical Western legal thought, although today it is increasingly influenced by non-Western actors and perspectives. The subject of indigenous peoples is not new to this genre of law but has figured with varying degrees of prominence in the legal discourse and practice related to international law's evolution over centuries. Discussions of indigenous peoples have appeared frequently in major treatises and published lectures contributing to the development of international law since the dawn of systemic European encroachment on distant lands half a millennium ago. This chapter discusses the historical threads of legal thought and official behavior that relate to the development of international law prior to the middle part of the twentieth century. It is not intended as a comprehensive history of international law and its treatment of indigenous peoples but is, rather, an effort to provide a contextual backdrop for assessing international law as it concerns *today's* indigenous peoples, the principal focus of this book.

This historical backdrop demonstrates the evolving character and role of international law in relation to the patterns of empire and conquest that engulfed indigenous peoples. What we now call international law can be traced to the natural law philosophies of Renaissance European theorists, which were in some measure, although not entirely, sympathetic to indigenous peoples' existence as self-determining communities in the face of imperial onslaught. International law, however, shed its naturalist frame as it changed into a state-centered system, strongly grounded in the Western world view; it developed to facilitate colonial patterns promoted by European states and their offspring, to the detriment of indigenous peoples. An understanding of the steps in this historical evolution contributes to an appreciation of the dynamic nature of international law over time, and it provides a frame of reference for assessing the character and course of international law as it now develops relative to indigenous peoples.

The Early Naturalist Frame

The advent of European exploration and conquest in the Western Hemisphere following the arrival of Christopher Columbus brought on questions of the first order regarding the relationship between Europeans and the indigenous peoples they encountered. Within a frame of thinking traditionally linked to the rise of modern international law, prominent European theorists questioned the legality and morality of claims to the "New World" and of the ensuing, often brutal, settlement patterns. Enduring figures in this discussion were the Dominican clerics Bartolomé de las Casas (1474–1566) and Francisco de Vitoria (1486–1547).[1] De las Casas gained notoriety as an ardent defender of the people indigenous to the Western Hemisphere who became known to the world as (the other) Indians. De las Casas, having spent several years as a Roman Catholic missionary among the Indians, gave a contemporaneous account of the Spanish colonization and settlement, vividly describing the enslavement and massacre of indigenous people in the early sixteenth century in his *History of the Indies.*[2] De las Casas was particularly critical of the Spanish *encomienda* system, which granted Spanish conquerors and colonists parcels of lands and the right to the labor of the Indians living on them.[3]

Francisco de Vitoria, primary professor of theology at the University of Salamanca, joined de las Casas in confirming the essential humanity of the Indians of the Western Hemisphere. Never having traveled across the Atlantic, however, Vitoria was less concerned with bringing to light Spanish abuses against the Indians than with establishing the governing normative and legal parameters. Vitoria held that the Indians possessed certain original autonomous powers and entitlements to land, which the Europeans were bound to respect.[4] At the same time, he methodically set forth the grounds on which Europeans could be said validly to acquire Indian lands or assert authority over them.[5] Vitoria's lectures on the Indians established him among the often cited founders of international law.[6] His prescriptions for European encounters with indigenous peoples of the Western Hemisphere contributed to the development of a system of principles and rules governing encounters among all peoples of the world.[7] Vitoria's influence on later theorists is evident in the seventeenth-century work of Hugo Grotius, the most prominent of the "fathers" of international law.[8]

The early European jurisprudence concerned with indigenous peoples and associated with the early development of international law was the legacy of medieval European ecclesiastical humanism.[9] This jurisprudence perceived a normative order independent of and higher than the positive law or decisions of temporal authority.[10] Conceptions about the source of higher authority, characterized as natural or divine law, varied. For Vitoria and other Spanish school theorists, God figured prominently as the source of legal authority, and law merged with theology.[11] Grotius moved toward a secular characterization of the law of nature,[12] defining it as a "dictate of right reason" in conformity with the social nature of human beings.[13] This perceived higher authority, whatever its source, provided the jurisprudential grounds for theorists to conceive of and examine norms from a fundamentally humanist, moral perspective, and to withhold the imprimatur of law from acts of earthly sovereigns found to violate the moral code. Thus the early international law theorists were prepared to confront official practices and declare unlawful even the acts of monarchs when these acts were at odds with the perceived natural law. Further, the naturalist theorists viewed the law applying to sovereigns as part of an integrated normative order encompassing all levels of human interaction.[14]

The view of a suprasovereign normative order applying across all levels of humanity had been encouraged by a politically complex medieval Europe, in which the king's realm was but one among a maze of loyalties. The relationship of monarchs to large rural populations had been mediated from below by independent lords and sublords, while from above the pope and emperor asserted universalist claims to which the king was theoretically subordinate.[15] In the Europe of the high Middle Ages, sovereignty and political loyalties were fragmented, resulting in shifting and overlapping political communities.[16] Against this backdrop of evolving political interdependencies and the perception of a normative order applying throughout humanity, theorists discerned rights and duties as applying beyond limited denominations of human association such as "nation," "state," or "kingdom."

Within this historical jurisprudential frame, the threshold question for determining the rights and status of the American Indians was whether they were rational human beings. In his published lectures, *On the Indians Lately Discovered* (1532),[17] Vitoria answered this question in the affirmative. He surmised that the Indians

> are not of unsound mind, but have, according to their kind, the use of reason. This is clear, because there is a certain method in their affairs, for they have polities which are orderly arranged and they have definite marriage and magistrates, overlords, laws, and workshops and a system of exchange, all of which call for the use of reason; they also have a kind of religion.[18]

From this premise, Vitoria rejected the view that papal donation to the Spanish monarchs provided a sufficient and legitimate basis for Spanish rule over Indian lands in the Western Hemisphere. Pope Alexander VI had purported to grant the Spanish monarchs all territories discovered by their envoys that were not already under the jurisdiction of Christian rulers.[19] And the Spanish monarchy had viewed this donation as establishing legal title to New World lands, in addition to entrusting the Spanish crown with the mission of converting Indians to Christianity.[20] Invoking precepts informed by "Holy Scripture," Vitoria held that the Indians of the Americas were the true owners of their lands, with "dominion in both public and private matters."[21] Neither emperor nor pope, he said, possessed lordship over the whole world.[22] Further, Vitoria maintained that discovery of the Indians' lands alone could not confer title in the Spaniards "anymore than if it had been they who had discovered us."[23]

While unambiguously rejecting title by discovery or papal grant, Vitoria found more palatable the argument that the Spaniards could legitimately assume authority over Indian lands for the Indians' own benefit. Although Vitoria found the Indians sufficiently rational to possess original rights and dominion over lands, he entertained the view that they

> are unfit to found or administer a lawful State up to the standard required by human and civil claims. Accordingly they have no proper laws nor magistrates, and are not even capable of controlling their family affairs; they are without any literature or arts, not only the liberal arts, but the mechanical arts also; they have no careful agriculture and no artisans; and they lack many other conveniences, yea necessaries, of human life. It might, therefore, be maintained that in their own interests the sovereigns of Spain might undertake the administration of their country, providing them with prefects and governors for their towns, and might even give them new lords, so long as this was clearly for their benefit.[24]

Vitoria pondered this view with ambivalence. He said, "I dare not affirm it at all, nor do I entirely condemn it."[25] Nonetheless, the argument articulated but not adopted by Vitoria to justify Spanish administration over Indian lands was a precursor to the trusteeship doctrine later adopted and acted upon by nineteenth-century states.[26] Of more generally foreboding significance, implicit in Vitoria's pejorative characterization of American Indians was the measurement of cultural expression and social organization by the European standard: Although they met some standard of rationality sufficient to possess rights, the Indians could be characterized as "unfit" because they failed to conform to the European forms of civilization with which Vitoria was familiar.

Against the backdrop of this Eurocentric bias, Vitoria ultimately constructed a theory of just war to justify Spanish claims to Indian lands in the absence of Indian consent. Within the early naturalist frame, Indians not only had rights but obligations as well.[27] According to Vitoria, under the Roman *jus gentium*,[28] which he viewed as either "natural law or . . . derived from natural law,"[29] Indians were bound to allow foreigners to travel to their lands, trade among them, and proselytize in favor of Christianity.[30] In his lecture, *On the Indians, or On the Law of War Made by the Spaniards on the Barbarians*,[31] Vitoria concluded that the Indians' persistent interference in Spanish efforts to carry out these activities could lead to "just" war and conquest. Vitoria counseled, however, against sham assertions of "imaginary causes of war."[32]

Thus Vitoria articulated a duality in the normative construct deemed applicable to European contact with non-European indigenous peoples. On the one hand, the American Indians were held to have rights by virtue of their essential humanity. On the other hand, the Indians could lose their rights through conquest following a "just" war, and the criteria for determining whether a war was "just" were grounded in a European value system.[33] The essential elements of this normative duality were advanced by other important European theorists of the period associated with the beginnings of international law, including Francisco Suárez (1548–1617), Domingo de Soto (1494–1560), Balthasar Ayala (1548–1584), and Alberico Gentilis (1552–1608).[34]

Writing a century after Vitoria, Grotius continued in this vein, although without specifically addressing the rights of American Indians. In his famous treatise, *On the Law of War and Peace* (1625), Grotius, like Vitoria, rejected title by discovery as to all lands inhabited by humans, "even though the occupant may be wicked, may hold wrong views about God, or may be dull of wit. For discovery applies to those things which belong to no one."[35] Further, Grotius affirmed that the ability to enter into treaty relationships is a necessary consequence of the natural rights of *all* peoples, including "strangers to the true religion": "According to the law of nature this is no degree a matter of doubt. For the right to enter treaties is so common to all men that it does not admit of a distinction arising from religion."[36] Grotius likewise endorsed the concept of just war,[37] but in keeping with his secularized conception of the law of nature, he discarded the Christian mission as alone constituting grounds for war or conquest.[38] Grotius identified three broad "justifiable causes" for war: "defence, recovery of property, and punishment."[39]

Modern scholarship has established that in affirming the rights of indigenous peoples to land and an autonomous existence, these early theorists influenced the development of policies and legal prescriptions handed down by European sovereigns—although those policies and prescriptions were not always followed.[40] This early affirmation of rights also can be seen reflected in the ensuing pattern of treaty making between the European powers and indigenous peoples.[41] It has equally been established, however, that the theory of just war, colored by a European world view, provided enduring support for patterns of colonization and empire that exerted control over indigenous peoples and their lands.[42]

The Early Modern State System and the Law of Nations

The emergence of the modern system of states in Europe prompted a revision of the framework within Western legal discourse for the treatment of indigenous peoples. The era of the independent territorial state began in earnest with the Treaty of Westphalia in 1648, which ended the Thirty Years War and the political hegemony asserted by the Roman Catholic Church.[43]

Along with the rise of the modern state came a marked evolution in naturalist thinking. European theorists transformed the concept of natural law from a universal moral code for humankind into a bifurcated regime comprised of the natural rights of individuals and the natural rights of states. This transformation has been called "the most important intellectual development of the seventeenth century subsequent to Grotius."[44] The English philosopher Thomas Hobbes (1588–1679), in his major work, *Leviathan* (1651), posited that individuals lived in a warlike state of nature prior to joining civil society, represented by the state.[45] Hobbes considered the state analogous to the individual as a holder of natural rights.[46] Prominent theorists, including Samuel Pufendorf (1632–1694) and Christian Wolff (1679–1754), accepted Hobbes's vision of humanity as a dichotomy of individuals and states, and they began developing a body of law focused exclusively on states under the rubric the "law of nations."[47]

The post-Westphalian concept of the law of nations approached its full expression in the writing of the Swiss diplomat Emmerich de Vattel (1714–1769), an avowed disciple of Wolff.[48] In his treatise, *The Law of Nations, or The Principles of Natural Law* (1758),[49] Vattel elaborated the idea of a discrete body of law concerned exclusively with states. Against the backdrop of a system of European state-societies, each of which claimed autonomy, he defined the "*Law of Nations*" as "*the science of the rights which exist between Nations or States, and of the obligations corresponding to these rights.*"[50] Vattel adhered to the rhetoric of natural law and its presumptive universality but viewed natural law as having distinct consequences when applied to states as opposed to individuals.[51] He developed a complex construct of the natural law of states, to which he added the positive law of treaties and custom among states.[52]

The individual/state dichotomy underlying Vattel's construct has powerfully affected the tradition of Western liberal thought. In contrast to the views of earlier naturalist theorists, the individual/state framework acknowledges the rights of the individual on the one hand and the sovereignty of the total social collective on the other. But it is not alive to the rich variety of intermediate or alternative associational groupings actually found in human cultures, nor is it prepared to ascribe to such groupings any rights not reducible either to the liberties of the citizen or to the prerogatives of the state.

Instead, the theory and jurisprudence associated with the individual/state dichotomy assumes that the state embodies the paragon of human association and aspiration. This assumption is reflected in the Hobbesian theoretical justification for the state that Vattel adopted and set forth in his *Law of Nations*:

> The end or aim of civil society is to procure for its citizens the necessities, the comforts, and the pleasures of life, and in general their happiness; to secure to each the peaceful enjoyment of his property and a sure means of obtaining justice; and finally to defend the whole body against all external violence.

It is now easy to form a just idea of a perfect State or Nation; all of its acts must concur in obtaining the end we have just pointed out.

When men, by the act of associating together, form a State or Nation, each individual agrees to procure the common good of all, and all together agree to assist each in obtaining the means of providing for his needs and to protect and defend him. It is clear that these reciprocal agreements can only be fulfilled by maintaining the political association. The whole Nation is therefore bound to maintain it.[53]

Vattel's use of *Nation* and *State* as interchangeable terms throughout his work manifests a related and pervasive assumption that these two conceptual categories coincide. The concept of nationhood emerged in Europe to acknowledge, validate, and designate politically conscious groupings that were consolidated by monarchical rule and bound by common cultural, sociological, and ethnic characteristics.[54] Statehood developed as a reference to the post-Westphalian political community and attendant bureaucracy, whose dominant organizing characteristic was territory.[55] Statehood and nationhood converged as mutually reinforcing concepts and political phenomena, hence the term *nation-state*.[56] The conceptual convergence of the nation and state was effectively a corollary of the individual/state perceptual dichotomy. Thus, Vattel, while using both of the terms *nation* and *state*, did not acknowledge their distinctiveness as conceptual categories by distinguishing their rights and duties.

Beyond confining group autonomy rights to the categories of nation or state, the jurisprudential framework articulated by Vattel further advanced the theoretical primacy of the state by embracing notions that were precursors to the modern doctrine of state sovereignty. Vattel asserted that "Nations [are] free and independent of each other, in the same manner as men are naturally free . . . [and accordingly] each Nation should be left in the peaceable enjoyment of that liberty which she inherits from nature."[57] Because nations are "free, independent and equal," according to Vattel, each should be left alone to judge its own obligations, particularly in regard to its own citizenry.[58] Vattel further held that the "general and common right of nations over the conduct of any sovereign state is only commensurate to the object of that society which exists between them."[59]

Vattel thus articulated the foundation for the doctrine of state sovereignty, which, with its corollaries of exclusive jurisdiction, territorial integrity, and nonintervention in domestic affairs, developed into a central precept of international law.[60] Unlike many exaltations of state sovereignty in later international discourse, however, Vattel did not appear to view the state in isolation from its theoretical human underpinnings. Vattel's injunction of noninterference and exclusive jurisdiction was based upon idealized notions of the state as corresponding to the autonomous nation and embodying civil society, formed consensually by individuals in their own interests of comfort and self-preservation. For Vattel the state was free, independent, and equal *as a result* of the natural rights of its individual constituents. And the state's attributes of sovereignty were a means of maximizing the interests of the corresponding nation, a group of more or less homogeneous individuals joined in social compact. Vattel's affirmations of sovereign equality and independence of states, therefore, were in effect naturalist prescriptions based upon an assessment of human interests, however misguided that assessment may have been.[61]

In any case, inasmuch as the normative construct envisioned by Vattel was wedded to the individual/state perceptual dichotomy, an assessment of their place within the dichotomy would be crucial to applying that construct in the context of indigenous peoples. To enjoy any rights as distinct communities, indigenous peoples would have to be regarded as nations or states. Otherwise, indigenous peoples would be conceptually reduced to their *individual* constituents, presumably in a state of nature, and their rights of *group* autonomy would not be accounted for. Moreover, as a matter of definition, indigenous peoples could not enjoy rights or duties under the "Law of Nations" unless they qualified as nations or states, or, perhaps more accurately, nation-states.

The very idea of the nation-state would always make it difficult for non-European aboriginal peoples to qualify as such. The concept of the nation-state in the post-Westphalian sense is based upon European models of political and social organization whose dominant defining characteristics are exclusivity of territorial domain and hierarchical, centralized authority.[62] By contrast, indigenous peoples of the Western Hemisphere and elsewhere, at least prior to European contact, typically have been organized primarily by tribal or kinship ties, have had decentralized political structures often linked in confederations, and have enjoyed shared or overlapping spheres of territorial control.[63] As an example of life in the state of nature, Hobbes had described "the savage people in many places of the Americas" who "except the government of small Families . . . have no government at all; and live at this day in that brutish manner."[64] This characterization resembles that advanced earlier by Vitoria, even though for Vitoria the existence and content of indigenous peoples' rights was not directly a function of whether or not they qualified as states.[65]

Vattel himself defined states broadly to include all "political bodies, societies of men who have united together and combined their forces, in order to procure their mutual welfare and security."[66] Vattel clearly believed at least some non-European aboriginal peoples qualified as states or nations with rights as such. Bringing into question European expansionism in the Americas, Vattel remarked: "Those ambitious Europeans States which attacked the American Nations and subjected them to their avaricious rule, in order, as they said, to civilize them, and have them instructed in the true religion—those usurpers, I say, justified themselves by a pretext equally unjust and ridiculous."[67]

Even Vattel's broad definition of the state or nation, however, is conditioned by a basic prejudice favoring the values behind European political and social organization. This European perspective is evident in Vattel's distinction between the "civilized Empires of Peru and Mexico" (evidently referring to the Incas and the Aztecs) and the North American "peoples of those vast tracts of land [who] rather roamed over them than inhabited them."[68] As to the former, "conquest . . . was a notorious usurpation, [while] the establishment of various colonies upon the continent of North America might, if done within just limits, have been entirely lawful."[69] Vattel seemed to distinguish between forms of indigenous society by accepting a Lockean natural law duty to cultivate the soil.[70] Although he did not hold expressly that a society based upon sedentary pursuits was a prerequisite for statehood, he did accept the view that cultivating land established a greater right to the land than did hunting or gathering. Later theorists expanded upon the distinction between sedentary and hunter-gatherer societies as a basis for denying indigenous peoples not only land rights but also status as nations or states subject to international law.[71]

Vattel's ambiguity on the status of indigenous peoples was compounded by his statements on the condition of political communities falling under the authority of others. On the one hand Vattel held that a state does not lose its sovereignty or independent status by placing itself under the protection of another as long as it retains its powers of self-government.[72] On the other hand Vattel stated, almost as if to beg the question, that once "a people . . . has passed under the rule of another, [it] is no longer a State, and does not come directly under the Law of Nations. Of this character were the Nations and the Kingdoms which the Romans subjected to their Empire."[73]

The ambiguities and tensions brought on by the state-centered law of nations were reflected in the United States Supreme Court's early decisions on the American Indians, decisions figuring prominently in the fabric of international jurisprudence concerning indigenous peoples. These decisions came half a century after Vattel's writing, at a time when the young country, founded on natural law visions of civil society, had yet to reconcile the anomalous existence of the Indians within its asserted boundaries. Three decisions, each written by Chief Justice John Marshall, were substantially framed by the question of the status of indigenous peoples within the Vattellian version of international law.

Divergent tendencies appear in these early nineteenth-century U.S. Supreme Court decisions.[74] One tendency viewed tribal societies as not qualifying as nations or states and hence as without full rights to group autonomy or ancestral lands. This tendency dominated in the first of the Marshall trilogy, *Johnson v. M'Intosh*,[75] in which Marshall, following Vattel's preference for sedentary peoples, described the Indians as

fierce savages, whose occupation was war, and whose subsistence was drawn chiefly from the forest. To leave them in possession of their country, was to leave the country a wilderness; to govern them as a distinct people was impossible, because they were as brave and high-spirited as they were fierce, and were ready to repel by arms every attempt on their independence.[76]

Reasoning from this characterization of the Indians, Marshall justified upholding superior U.S. title to Indian lands on the basis of discovery alone:

> However extravagant the pretension of converting the discovery of an inhabited country into conquest may appear; if the principle has been asserted in the first instance, and afterwards sustained; if a country has been acquired and held under it; if the property of the great mass of the community originates in it, it becomes the law of the land, and cannot be questioned.[77]

Marshall's acceptance of the "pretension" of discovery, however, was equivocating. Marshall, whose jurisprudence incorporated natural law and the law of nations,[78] suggested that he was not necessarily endorsing the diminishment of Indian rights in favor of the European discoverer merely on the basis of discovery; rather, he was deferring to U.S. assertions of title by discovery as required by the limits of domestic judicial competency: "However this restriction may be opposed to natural right, and to the usages of civilized nations, yet, if it be indispensable to that system under which the country has been settled, and be adapted to the actual conditions of the two people, it may, perhaps, be supported by reason, and certainly cannot be rejected by Courts of justice."[79]

Marshall's ambiguity continued in a different course in a second case, *Cherokee Nation v. Georgia*,[80] in which he likened the Indian tribes to "domestic dependent nations. . . . Their relationship to the United States resembles that of a ward to his guardian."[81] This characterization followed Marshall's holding that the Cherokee people did not qualify as a "foreign state" under the provision of Article III of the U.S. Constitution, a provision entitling a foreign government to invoke the Supreme Court's original jurisdiction. Marshall's designation of qualified nationhood outside the scope of Article III, however, did not clearly identify the tribes as inherently inferior or as having a status necessarily outside the scope of the law of nations. Marshall's narrow interpretation of the term *foreign state* as used in Article III of the Constitution rested substantially on the Constitution's specific reference elsewhere to "Indian tribes" and the particular treaty relationship between the Cherokee and the United States.[82] Marshall stressed that the Indians "acknowledge *themselves*, in their treaties, to be under the protection of the United States."[83] This characterization of relationships between the tribes and the United States is consistent with a view of the tribes as nations or states possessing the prerogative under the law of nations to consent to the protection of another sovereign.

Marshall again wrote for the Court in *Worcester v. Georgia*,[84] another case involving the Cherokee, and seemingly settled on the view that native tribes within the boundaries of the United States qualified as polities subject to the law of nations. Marshall emphasized the common reference to the tribes as "nations" and, citing Vattel, compared them to the "[t]ributary and feudatory states" of Europe,[85] which Vattel held to rank among sovereign states subject to the law of nations despite their having assented to the protection of a stronger power. Accordingly, Marshall applied principles clearly identifiable with the teachings of the early international legal theorists. Marshall upheld the "original natural rights" of Indians over their lands, which they could not lose by discovery alone.[86] *Voluntary* cession and *actual* conquest, as with other nations of the world, were the bases for gauging whether an Indian tribe had been divested of its rights.[87] And in the absence of actual conquest, the United States' protectorate over the tribes was a matter of treaty relationship, not unilateral imposition.[88]

In *Worcester*, Marshall clarified, or perhaps revised, his earlier statements on the effects of European discovery of Indian lands. Marshall discussed the European practice whereby the first power among them to lay claim to Indian land had the sole right of acquiring it from the Indians, and the Indians could not convey rights in the land to others. Marshall characterized this principle, the "discovery doctrine," not only as a limitation for the Indians but also as "a restriction which those European potentates imposed on themselves."[89] According to Marshall, the principle "regulated the right given by discovery among the European discoverers, but could not affect the rights of those already in possession, either as aboriginal occupants, or as occupants by virtue of a discovery made before the memory of man."[90] Marshall suggested that the discovery principle, based upon consent among states representing only a subset of humanity, was distinct from the natural rights accruing to the Indians independently of the will of states. The distinction is consistent with the view of the classical theorists that the positive customary law is subordinate to the law of nature.

Marshall's assessment in *Worcester* of the status of Indian tribes, although sui generis, no doubt was influenced by the character of the tribe involved in that case, the Cherokee Nation. With several of their leaders educated in Christian missionary schools, the Cherokee had adopted Western forms of governance and land use and had otherwise borrowed heavily from Anglo-American or European ways.[91] In *Johnson v. M'Intosh*, Marshall had declined to discuss the merits of arguments that would deny rights to Indians because of nonsedentary or non-European ways.[92] But in *Worcester* Marshall stressed the "national character" and self-governing capacity of the Cherokee,[93] and he described the Cherokee as "a distinct community, occupying its own territory, with boundaries accurately described."[94] It can thus be said that the Cherokee for Marshall approximated the description of political community that Vattel and other Western theorists of the period seemed most comfortable in denominating nations or states. Certainly many, if not most, Indian tribes were unlike the Cherokee and instead remained closer to what Marshall saw in *Johnson v. M'Intosh* as societies "whose subsistence was drawn chiefly from the forest. To leave them in possession of their country was to leave the country a wilderness."[95]

Wheaton, the Supreme Court reporter and a friend of Marshall, stated what Marshall declined to adopt expressly. In his classic treatise, *Elements of International Law* (1846), Wheaton discussed the Marshall decisions concerning the rights of "Indian nations,"[96] apparently placing Indian peoples like the Cherokee among the subjects of the law of nations, which by then was also called international law. At the same time, Wheaton excluded from the subjects of international law "an unsettled horde of wandering savages not yet formed into civil society. The legal idea of the state necessarily implies that of the habitual obedience of its members to those persons in whom superiority is vested, and a fixed abode, and definite territory belonging to the people by whom it is occupied."[97]

Wheaton thus signaled the ensuing dominance of the political and jurisprudential tendency to deny indigenous peoples status, and hence protection, under international law unless they fit within narrow categories of political and social organization and land use.[98] To see indigenous peoples as "states" would in the end prove all too difficult for Western eyes.

The Positivists' International Law

Not long after the Marshall decisions, international law abandoned consideration of indigenous peoples as political bodies with rights under international law, yielding to the forces of colonization and empire as Western colonizers consolidated indigenous lands within their respective spheres of political hegemony and control. The major premises of the late-nineteenth- and early-twentieth-century positivist school ensured that the law of nations, or international law, would become a legitimizing force for colonization and empire rather than a liberating one for indigenous peoples.

The first of these major premises, which had been expressed by Vattel and reflected in Marshall's Supreme Court opinions, was that international law is concerned only with the rights and duties of states. A second and related premise, also derived from Vattel's framework, was that international law upholds the exclusive sovereignty of states, which are presumed to be equal and independent, and thus guards the exercise of that sovereignty from outside interference.[99] The positivist formulation, however, parted company with Vattel's view that the law of nations embraces natural law and presumptively applies universally to all self-governing political bodies. Accordingly, a third premise at the core of the positivist school was that international law is law *between* and not *above* states, finding its theoretical basis in their *consent*.[100] And a fourth premise—the culmination of earlier tendencies to conceptualize the state in narrow terms—was that the states that make international law and possess rights and duties under it make up a limited universe that excludes a priori indigenous peoples outside the mold of European civilization.[101] Positivism drove this fourth premise to a theory of recognition under which statehood for international law purposes depended upon recognition by nineteenth-century European and European-derived states.[102]

These premises meant that Indian tribes and other indigenous peoples, not qualifying as states, could not participate in the shaping of international law, nor could they look to it to affirm the rights that had once been deemed to inhere in them by natural or divine law. States, on the other hand, both shaped the rules of international law and enjoyed rights under it largely independently of natural law considerations. It followed that states could create doctrine to affirm and perfect their claims over indigenous territories as a matter of international law and treat the indigenous inhabitants according to domestic policies, shielded from uninvited outside scrutiny by international law itself. State sovereignty, originally conceived of to advance human interests, would be a conceptual means by which international law could enter into complicity with inhumane forces.

Late-nineteenth- and early-twentieth-century theorists relied upon the positivist construct of international law to provide the imprimatur of law for conditions of dubious legitimacy. The construct not only upheld the territorial bases of the American states but also limited the parameters of international concern over the ongoing colonization of Africa and other non-European territories.

The British publicist John Westlake, in his *Chapters on the Principles of International Law* (1894), provided one of the most complete expositions of the positivistic justification for the categorical exclusion of indigenous peoples as subjects of international law. Westlake distinguished between "civilised and uncivilised humanity" and viewed "international society" as limited to the civilized.[103] In no uncertain terms, he deemed European-style government and sedentary lifestyle the test of "civilisation."[104] Westlake's rationale for imposing the requirement of European-style government is extravagant and worth quoting at length:

> When people of the European race come into contact with American or African tribes, the prime necessity is a government under the protection of which the former may carry on the complex life to which they have been accustomed in their homes, which may prevent that life from being disturbed by contests between different European powers for supremacy on the same soil, and which may protect the natives in the enjoyment of a security and well-being at least not less than they enjoyed before the arrival of the strangers. Can the natives furnish such a government, or can it be looked for from the Europeans alone? In the answer to that question lies, for international law, the difference between civilisation and want of it. . . . The inflow of the white race cannot be stopped where there is land to cultivate, ore to be mined, commerce to be developed, sport to enjoy, curiosity to be satisfied. If any fanatical admirer of savage life argued that the whites ought to be kept out, he would only be driven to the same conclusion by another route, for a government on the spot would be necessary to keep them out. Accordingly international law has to treat such natives as uncivilised.[105]

Westlake's rationalization effectively admitted that international law was an instrument of the "white" and powerful colonizer. Not being among the "civilised" and powerful forces of colonization, indigenous peoples could not look to international law to thwart those forces. Indigenous peoples' rights had no place in the discussion. According to Westlake:

> When again men like Victoria, Soto and Covarruvias maintained the cause of the American and African natives against the kings and peoples of Spain and Portugal, they were not so much impugning the title of their country as trying to influence its conduct, they were the worthy predecessors of those who now make among us the honourable claim to be "friends of the aborigines." Then and now such men occupy a field to which international law may be said to invite them by keeping itself within its own limits. Even those who, in accordance with the modern tendency, make rights instead of law their starting point, can hardly avoid admitting that rights which are common to civilised and uncivilised humanity are not among those which it is the special function of international right to develop and protect. . . .
>
> . . . This is true, and it does not mean that all rights are denied to such natives, but that the appreciation of their rights is left to the conscience of the state within whose recognized territorial sovereignty they are comprised, the rules of the international society existing only for the purposes of regulating the mutual conduct of its members.[106]

Through the early part of this century, the major international law publicists repeated the view that indigenous peoples had no status or rights in international law. The later writers, apparently more confident in this view's acceptance, dispensed with the lengthy rationalization that Westlake devoted to it. Among the later publications was the 1924 edition of W. E. Hall's *A Treatise on International Law*, which saw the exclusion of indigenous peoples from international law's subjects as simply a necessary result of the positivist conception of international law as law by the states and for the states of European origin:

> It is scarcely necessary to point out that as international law is a product of the special civilisation of modern Europe, and forms a highly artificial system of which the principles cannot be supposed to be understood or recognised by countries differently civilised, such states only can be presumed to be subject to it as are inheritors of that civilisation.[107]

In the 1920 edition of the noted jurist Lassa Oppenheim's *International Law*, the basis for excluding indigenous peoples from among the subjects of international law was reduced to their subjective nonrecognition by those within the "Family of Nations." According to Oppenheim's treatise, "As the basis of the Law of Nations is the common consent of the civilised States, statehood alone does not imply membership of the Family of Nations. . . . Through recognition only and exclusively a State becomes an International Person and a subject of

International Law."[108] Oppenheim's influential work thus embraced what became known as the constitutive theory of recognition of statehood, by which
statehood does not exist in international law until the moment of recognition.[109]

Given the circularity of describing the members of the "Family of Nations"
(the states with "international personality") as those states recognized by the
Family of Nations, Oppenheim's treatise was driven to list them.[110] Prominent
among the privileged few were the "old Christian States of Western Europe"
and "the body of Christian States which grew up outside Europe," including "the
American States which arose out of colonies of European States."[111] Oppenheim
further included the two "non-Christian" states of Turkey and Japan, while excluding "such states as Persia, Siam, China, Abyssinia, and the like" because
they had failed to "raise their civilisation to the level of that of the Western"
states.[112] Eliminating whatever ambiguity remained about the status of Indian
tribes and similar indigenous peoples, Oppenheim's treatise added expressly,
echoing words previously heard, that the law of nations does not apply "to organized wandering tribes."[113]

Some positivist theorists of the period went beyond merely excluding indigenous peoples from among the subjects of international law in order to maintain their vision of international law as law made *by* states and *for* states, to the
effective exclusion of indigenous peoples' territorial or sovereign rights. Despite
the views of earlier theorists contemporaneous with a practice of treaty making
between indigenous peoples and European powers, positivist theorists argued
that the European states and their offspring within the "Family of Nations" *never
had* considered the aboriginal peoples capable of possessing rights on the international plane. The American jurist Charles Hyde, for example, explained that
"[a]t the time of European explorations in the Western Hemisphere in the fif-
teenth and sixteenth centuries. . . . States were agreed that the native inhabitants possessed no rights of territorial control which the European explorer or
his monarch was bound to respect."[114] Hyde accordingly concluded that "[t]he
American Indians have never been regarded as constituting persons or States of
international law."[115]

By deeming indigenous peoples incapable of enjoying sovereign status or
rights in international law, international law was thus able to govern the patterns
of colonization and ultimately to legitimate the colonial order, with diminished
or no consequences arising from the presence of aboriginal peoples. For international law purposes, indigenous lands prior to any colonial presence were
considered legally unoccupied or *terra nullius* (vacant lands).[116] Under this fic-
tion, discovery was employed to uphold colonial claims to indigenous lands and
to bypass any claim to possession by the natives in the "discovered" lands.[117] In
order to acquire indigenous lands, a colonizing state need not pretend conquest
where war had not been waged, nor rely upon the rules of war where it had.[118]
Instead, the positivist doctrines of effective occupation of territory and recognition

of such occupation by the "Family of Nations" provided the legal mechanism for consolidating territorial sovereignty over indigenous lands by the colonizing states.[119] An indigenous community's right to govern itself in its lands, as well as any right not to be conquered except in a "just war," was simply considered outside the competency of international law.

Likewise, treaties with American tribes and other indigenous peoples could simply be ignored for the purposes of international law.[120] Westlake went so far as to hold that treaties with indigenous groups by which they ceded lands could not establish a state's title to territory because the "uncivilised tribes" did not comprehend the full attributes of territorial sovereignty.[121] He thus justified a diminished status for indigenous treaties and rights in their lands while purporting to scrutinize the basis of colonial claims. Further, while acknowledging such diminished rights and suggesting the desirability of treaty relations with tribal groups to promote stability, Westlake characterized those rights, even if under treaty, as creating only moral obligations beyond the scope of international law.[122]

A somewhat dissenting strain of legal thought of the late nineteenth-early twentieth centuries was reflected in the work of the British publicist M. F. Lindley. Lindley continued the perception of a hierarchy of political and social organization in which the highest forms corresponded with European societies and their offspring.[123] But he argued that non-European "backward" peoples with a certain minimum of organization did qualify as "political societies," such that their territories could be acquired only by the rules ordinarily applicable to members of the "International Family."[124] For Lindley, unlike Westlake and others, the historical practice of treaty making between acknowledged members of the "International Family" and certain indigenous groups supported such a view. But while Lindley held that mere occupation could not confer legal title to the territory of indigenous peoples sufficiently organized as political societies, he maintained that their territories could be acquired by wars of conquest regardless of any underlying moral issue: "[O]nce a Conquest has become a *fait accompli*, International Law recognizes its results."[125]

Whatever the merits of Lindley's analysis, by the early part of the twentieth century states had largely abandoned treaty making with tribal peoples and had mostly consolidated control over indigenous peoples' lands in the Americas and elsewhere with little or no outside scrutiny, aided by the imprimatur of legality supplied by the positivist frame. The dominance of the positivists' approach to indigenous peoples and their rights is reflected in international tribunal decisions of the 1920s and 1930s.

In 1926 an international arbitration tribunal ruled that Great Britain could not maintain a claim for the "Cayuga Nation" as such, but only for the Cayuga Indians living in Canada on the basis of their British nationality.[126] In taking this position, the tribunal declared resolutely that an Indian "tribe is not a legal unit of international law."[127] The tribunal cited Hyde, among others, for the proposition that Indians never *had* been considered subjects of international law.[128] And in the subsequent edition of his work, Hyde completed the bootstrap to support that position by citing the Cayuga Indians decision.[129]

A second relevant international arbitration in 1928 involved competing claims to the Island of Palmas between the United States and the Netherlands.[130] The United States' claim was derived from Spain, which had based its title primarily upon prior discovery. The tribunal ruled in favor of the Netherlands because of its effective occupation and display of authority on the island. The tribunal discussed various treaties the Dutch had entered into with native rulers but considered them only as "facts" relevant to the Netherlands' assertion of sovereignty.[131] The tribunal stated that such *"contracts between a State . . . and native princes of chiefs of peoples* not recognized as members of the community of nations . . . are not, in the international law sense, treaties, or conventions capable of creating rights and obligations."[132]

A third case concerned a 1933 ruling on the legal status of Eastern Greenland by the Permanent Court of International Justice.[133] Although acknowledging the indigenous Inuit ("Eskimo") population in Eastern Greenland, the court considered the territory's legal status as framed by the competing claims to sovereignty asserted by Norway and Denmark.[134] Norway's assertion that parts of Greenland had been *terra nullius* at relevant times was trumped only by a finding that Denmark had effectively established sovereignty recognized by others within the exclusive community of states. Neither the Inuits' presence nor their efforts at driving away Nordic settlers had any bearing upon the territory's status.[135] This case, like the *Island of Palmas* case, illustrates the operation of the positivists' international law, which affirmed sovereignty built upon colonialism to the exclusion of the sovereignty of indigenous peoples.

Trusteeship Doctrine and Its "Civilizing" Mission

As colonizing states and their offspring consolidated power over indigenous lands, many such states adopted trusteeship notions akin to those proposed earlier by Vitoria as grounds and parameters for the nonconsensual exercise of authority over indigenous peoples.[136] Although it represented an element of humanistic thought toward indigenous peoples, nineteenth- and early-twentieth-century trusteeship doctrine was rooted in the same Western philosophy that underlay the positivist construct of international law, which viewed non-European aboriginal peoples and their cultures as inferior. Pursuant to this philosophy, associated with the now infamous school identified as "scientific racism," the objective of trusteeship was to wean native peoples from their "backward" ways and to "civilize" them.[137]

Among the colonial powers of the nineteenth century, Great Britain was a leader in devising special administrative regimes over native peoples with the objective of reengineering their cultural and social patterns in line with European conceptions of civilized behavior. In 1837, a special committee of the British House of Commons concluded that such a policy was required by the "obligations of conscience to impart the blessings we enjoy,"[138] as well as by practical considerations: "[W]e have abundant proof that it is greatly for our advantage to have dealings with civilized men rather than with barbarians. Savages are dangerous neighbors and unprofitable customers, and if they remain as degraded denizens of our colonies they become a burden upon the State."[139]

The British policy, and its premise of indigenous inferiority, is reflected in the following excerpt of a letter by Prime Minister Lord John Russell, written on August 23, 1840, to Sir George Gipps, the governor of New South Wales, Australia:

> Between the native, who is weakened by intoxicating liquors, and the European, who has all the strength of superior civilization and is free from its restraints, the unequal contest is generally of no long duration; the natives decline, diminish, and finally disappear. . . .
>
> The best chance of preserving the unfortunate race . . . lies in the means employed for training their children. The education given to such children should consist in a very small part of reading and writing. Oral instruction in the fundamental truths of the Christian religion will be given by the missionaries themselves. The children should be taught early; the boys to dig and plough, and the trades of shoemakers, tailors, carpenters, and masons; the girls to sew and cook and wash linen, and keep clean the rooms and furniture.[140]

The United States, among other countries, followed the British lead in a firm embrace of trusteeship doctrine in its domestic law and policy. In the late nineteenth century, a vast government bureaucracy emerged under the U.S. commissioner of Indian affairs to consolidate and manage the system of reservations, pueblos, rancherias, and settlements that were home to the surviving Indian people within the country's external boundaries. In 1868, the Indian commissioner wrote of his task:

> What, then, is our duty as the guardian of all the Indians under our jurisdiction? To outlaw, to pursue, to hunt down like wolves, and slay? Must we drive and exterminate them as if void of reason, and without souls: Surely, no.
>
> It is beyond question our most solemn duty to protect and care for, to elevate and civilize them.[141]

Pursuant to its "civilizing" mission, the Indian Office assumed virtually despotic powers over Indian people through the early part of the twentieth century, even though judicial doctrine supported the view that the tribes continued to possess inherent sovereign powers. With most Indian people rendered dependent on government programs for their subsistence, government officials effectively supplanted or eliminated autonomous structures of tribal governance. On the reservation, the government "Indian agent was the new taskmaster bringing a multitude of new programs foreign to Indian ideas of the proper role of man in his society."[142] Government programs designed to break Indian culture ran in collusion with those of Christian missionary institutions.[143]

Similarly, in Canada the Indian Act of 1876 consolidated and imposed a system of pervasive government control over Indian peoples and their lands.[144] In Brazil, legislation established Indians as wards of the state and set in motion government programs to manage their affairs and facilitate their adoption of Euro-Brazilian ways.[145] In Venezuela, the 1915 Mission Act delegated to the Catholic Church the task of "civilizing" the Indians and persuading them to live in established settlements.[146] In this same vein, the 1853 Constitution of Argentina established in Congress the power to "maintain peaceful relations with the Indians, and to promote their conversion to Catholicism."[147]

Trusteeship notions were internationalized through a series of conferences and related efforts aimed at regulating continued European penetration into Africa and the Pacific. Most notable in this respect was the first Berlin Conference on Africa, which concluded in 1885 with the signing of a document intended to set the basic parameters for what has been dubbed the "scramble for Africa."[148] Under article VI of the General Act, the signatory powers agreed to "bind themselves to watch over the preservation of the native tribes, and to care for the improvement of the conditions of their moral and material well-being," with the ultimate purpose of "instructing the natives and bringing home to them the blessings of civilization."[149] In 1888 the Institute of International Law, a consortium of international jurists dedicated to developing and clarifying international law, adopted a statement on the conditions required for a state to secure good title to occupied territory. Article VI of the statement identifies among these conditions the existence of a local authority that complies with "the duty of watching over the conservation of the aboriginal populations, their education, and the amelioration of their moral and material condition."[150] The international character of trusteeship was further enhanced and its scope broadened by the 1919 Covenant of the League of Nations adopted at the close of World War I. Under the Covenant, all League members committed to "undertake to secure the just treatment of the native inhabitants of territories under their control."[151]

In his 1926 work Lindley argued that the trusteeship doctrine as advanced by the Berlin General Act and the Covenant had become widely accepted and hence should be understood as part of general international law.[152] Lindley held that even if indigenous peoples were not themselves considered full subjects of international law, states could become obligated vis-à-vis each other as a matter of general international law for the benefit of native peoples over which they exercised control.[153] Although somewhat grounded in international practice of the period, Lindley's proposition was in tension with state sovereignty principles that strongly tended to shield states from international scrutiny over matters deemed within their domestic realm.

Yet even to the extent that they made their way into international law and established indigenous peoples as limited objects of international concern, conceptions of trusteeship—rooted in negative regard for indigenous cultural attributes—translated into more of a justification for colonial patterns than a force against them. Pursuant to the civilizing mission, government and Christian church agents proceeded through the early part of the twentieth century to break down indigenous forms of political and social organization, disrupt communal landholdings, and suppress cultural practices.[154] Hence the civilizing mission—against the backdrop of the dominant positivist frame of international law that effectively diminished indigenous peoples' rights—ultimately facilitated the acquisitive forces that wrested control over indigenous peoples and their lands.

Thus, whether through the doctrine of trusteeship or the positivist legal construction that denied sovereign status to indigenous peoples, international legal discourse and related decision processes developed historically to support the forces of colonization and empire that have trampled the capacity of indigenous peoples to determine their own course under conditions of equality. Early affirmations of indigenous peoples' rights succumbed to a state-centered Eurocentric system that could not accomodate indigenous peoples and their cultures as equals.

However, just as international law once moved away from natural law thinking that was to some extent supportive of indigenous peoples' survival as distinct autonomous communities, international law is again shifting. But this time the shift is in retreat from the orientation that would divorce law from morality and deny international rights to all but states, or that would regard non-Westernized peoples as necessarily inferior. As the following chapter seeks to demonstrate, this latest shift, although fraught with tension, carries a reformed body of international law concerning indigenous peoples.

Notes

1. *See generally* Antonio E. Pérez Luño, *La polémica sobre el Nuevo Mundo—Los clásicos españoles en la Filosofía del Derecho* (2d ed. 1995); *La escuela de Salamanca y el Derecho Internacional en América* (Araceli Mangas Martín ed., 1993); Greg C. Marks, "Indigenous Peoples in International Law: The Significance of Francisco de Vitoria and Bartolomé de las Casas," 13 *Austl. Y.B. Int'l L.* 1 (1992); Glenn T. Morris, "In Support of the Right of Self-Determination for Indigenous Peoples under International Law," 29 *German Y.B. Int'l L.* 277, 284–88 (1986).

2. Bartolomé de las Casas, *History of the Indies: Selections* (Andrée Collard ed. and trans., 1971).

3. De las Casas's attack on the *encomienda* system and other aspects of Spanish colonization is described in Lewis Hanke, *The Spanish Struggle for Justice in the Conquest of America* (1949), and in Leslie C. Green & Olive Dickason, *The Law of Nations and the New World* 201–14 (1989). For a critical view of de las Casas's engagement with the Spanish colonial activity, see Bartolomé Clavero, *La destrucción de las Indias, ayer y hoy* 11–52 (2002). Although the Spanish viewed *encomienda* labor as a form of serfdom that did not give actual ownership of the laborers to the Spanish settlers, in practice it differed little from slavery. *See* Ronald Sanders, *Lost Tribes and Promised Lands* 128–32 (1978). *See also* Green & Dickason, *supra* at 185–87. Apart from the *encomienda* system, slavery was an accepted practice where indigenous peoples were "raided" from not yet colonized territories and brought back to labor in Spanish settlements. Slave raiding became more prevalent as local indigenous populations died off under harsh conditions of labor. Sanders, *supra* at 131.

4. *See infra* notes 17–23 and accompanying text.

5. *See infra* notes 27–33 and accompanying text.

6. *See, e.g.*, Arthur Nussbaum, *A Concise History of the Law of Nations* 79–84 (rev. ed. 1954) (identifying Vitoria as "a most distinguished figure" related to "the history of the law of nations"). *See also* Harold Damerow, "A Critical Analysis of the Foundations of International Law" 23–29 (1978); Marks, *supra* note 1; Myres S. McDougal et al., "Theories about International Law: A Prologue to a Configurative Jurisprudence," 8 *Va. J. Int'l L.* 188, 215–27 (1968).

7. *See* Nussbaum, *supra* note 6, at 82 (identifying Vitoria's contribution to prescriptions concerning commerce and to the law of war).

8. Grotius relied heavily on Vitoria in his 1608 work, *The Freedom of the Seas*. Hugo Grotius, *The Freedom of the Seas* (Carnegie Endowment for International Peace ed. 1916) (Ralph van Deman Magoffin trans. of 1633 ed.).

9. *See* Green & Dickason, *supra* note 3, at 163–73; Nussbaum, *supra* note 6, at 38–39. Medieval scholasticism, in which the philosophy of Thomas Aquinas looms large, synthesized an Aristotelian view of natural law as inherent in the innate rationalism of human nature with the divine law of Christian theology. Under the scholastic synthesis of these two traditions, natural law is viewed as the rational, albeit imperfect, human manifestation of God's eternal law. A more extensive discussion of the role of Aristotelian natural law in medieval scholasticism and the works of Thomas Aquinas is presented in Walter Ullmann, *Principles of Government and Politics in the Middle Ages* 231–79 (1961).

10. *See* Nussbaum, *supra* note 6, at 61–114; Damerow, *supra* note 6, at 23–29; McDougal et al., *supra* note 6, at 215–27.

11. *See* Nussbaum, *supra* note 6, at 72–73, 79–101.

12. For Grotius even God was subject to the law of nature: "The law of nature, again, is unchangeable—even in the sense that it cannot be changed by God. . . . Just as even God, then, cannot cause that two times two should not make four, so He cannot cause that that [*sic*] which is intrinsically evil be not evil." Hugo Grotius, *The Law of War and Peace* 40 (Classics of International Law ed. 1925) (Francis W. Kelsey trans. of 1646 ed.). *See generally* Hersch Lauterpacht, "The Grotian Tradition in International Law," 23 *British Y.B. Int'l L.* 1, 8–9 (1946).

13. Grotius, *The Law of War and Peace, supra* note 12, at 38–39; *see* Lauterpacht, *supra* note 12, at 7.

14. *See* McDougal et al., *supra* note 6, at 217–24 (discussing the various levels of emphasis the natural law theorists applied to units of human interaction other than territorial communities).

15. *See* Stuart Hall, "The State in Question," in *The Idea of the Modern State* 6–7 (Gregor McLennan et al. eds., 1984); Andrew Vincent, *Theories of the State* 85 (1987).

16. Vincent describes political society in the Middle Ages as "criss-crossed with overlapping groups and conflicting loyalties and bodies of rules." Vincent, *supra* note 15, at 15. The feudal system, the dominant political order of medieval Europe,

> tended to have a fragmenting effect on political organization. It was essentially a complex and rather loose structure of contractual or mutual obligations existing throughout a complex social hierarchy. . . . The monarch was in no special sovereign position; he was part of and reliant upon the community of the realm and was consequently under the law, not the source of it. . . . Many of the more significant groups—the large estates, the clergy, guilds and nobility—generated their own systems of rules and courts.

Id. at 14. For a political and social history of the period spanning roughly from 1300 to 1550, marking the decline of the feudal system toward the dawn of the modern state, see Daniel Waley, *Later Medieval Europe: From Saint Louis to Luther* (2d ed. 1985).

17. Published in Francisco de Victoria, *De indis et de ivre belli relectiones* (Classics of International Law Series, 1917) (translation by J. Bate based on Iaques Boyer ed., 1557; Alonso Muñoz ed., 1565; & Johann G. Simon ed., 1696) (using the Latin version of his name, "Victoria") [hereinafter *De indis*].

18. *Id.* at 127.

19. The text of this papal donation, known as bull *Inter caetera* (1493), is in *European Treaties Bearing on the History of the United States and Its Dependencies to 1648*, at 61–63 (Francis G. Davenport ed., 1967).

20. *See* Hanke, *supra* note 3, at 25–27; Green & Dickason, *supra* note 3, at 4–6. The papal bull *Inter caetera* was relied upon in the *Requerimiento*, a decree issued by Spain's King Ferdinand in 1512. The *Requerimiento* expressly invoked the papal donation as it ordered the "idolatrous Indians" to acknowledge "the Church as the Ruler and Superior of the whole world and the high priest called the Pope, and in his name the King and Queen Juana in his stead as superiors, lords, and kings of these islands and in this Tierra Firme by virtue of said donation." The decree was intended to be read to Indians encountered by Spanish conquistadors, and it imposed severe penalties on indigenous peoples who did not immediately acknowledge its precepts: "[W]e shall take you and your wives and children and shall make slaves of them . . . and we shall take away your goods, and shall do all the harm and damage that we can, as to vassals who do not obey." *See* Hanke, *supra* note 3, 31–36 (quoting and discussing the *Requerimiento*). As Hanke observes, the *Requerimiento* was "read to trees and empty huts when no Indians were to be found. Captains muttered its theological phrases into their beards on the edge of sleeping Indian settlements, or even a league away before starting the formal attack,

and at times some leather-lunged Spanish notary hurled its sonorous phrases after the Indians as they fled into the mountains." *Id.* at 34.

21. *De indis, supra* note 17, at 127–28.

22. *Id.* at 132–38.

23. *Id.* at 139.

24. *Id.* at 161.

25. *Id.* at 160.

26. *See infra* notes 136–53 and accompanying text (discussing trusteeship doctrine).

27. *Compare* Felix S. Cohen, "The Spanish Origin of Indian Rights in the Law of the United States," 31 *Geo. L.J.* 1 (1942). While Cohen presents a pioneering discussion of Vitoria's work as an affirmation of Indian rights, he did not mention or come to grips with the parts of Vitoria's lectures that discussed the duties of the Indians and the Spanish recourse to war against them under certain circumstances.

28. The Latin term *jus gentium* as used by classical-era scholars often has been translated in modern times as the "law of nations," as it was in the 1917 translation of Vitoria's sixteenth-century work. As Nussbaum points out, however, it was not until "the seventeenth century that *jus gentium* began to assume the significance of a technical term for the law among independent states." Nussbaum, *supra* note 6, at 13–15. The body of Roman law to which the term originally applied was concerned with the rights and duties of *people* throughout the Roman Empire. *Id.* For detailed discussions on the Roman *jus gentium*, see Juan Iglesias, *Derecho Romano* (12th ed., 1999); Fernando Bentancourt, *Derecho Romano Clásico* (1995).

29. *De indis, supra* note 17, at 151.

30. *Id.* at 153.

31. Published in *De indis, supra* note 17.

32. *Id.* at 156.

33. Professor Robert Williams, Jr., has taken an especially critical view of the Renaissance European theory of just war, particularly as articulated by Vitoria on the basis of the Roman *jus gentium* and biblical passages, calling it a highly "Eurocentrically and Christianocentrically understood consensus of the whole world in harmony with the West's vision of reason and truth." Robert A. Williams, Jr., *The American Indian in Western Legal Thought: The Discourses of Conquest* 107 (1990). *See also* Robert A. Williams, Jr., "The Medieval and Renaissance Origins of the Status of the American Indian in Western Legal Thought," 57 *S.C. L. Rev.* 1, 76–85 (1983).

34. *See generally* Green & Dickason, *supra* note 3, at 48–54, 198 (discussing Gentili, Suárez, and Ayala); Nussbaum, *supra* note 6, at 84–101 (discussing Suárez, Ayala, and Gentilis). Lewis Hanke points out that Bartolomé de las Casas had a uniquely limited view among sixteenth-century Spanish theorists of the grounds that might justify the use of force and conquest. In his highly sympathetic portrayal of the Dominican missionary, Hanke stresses that de las Casas denied that the objective of converting American Indians to Christianity could alone justify war against them. Hanke, *supra* note 3, at 72–77. *See also* Green & Dickason, *supra* note 3, at 202. Hanke concedes, nonetheless, that de las Casas, in addition to wholeheartedly embracing the Christian evangelizing mission, joined in the premise that war against the Indians might be permissible under certain conditions. Hanke, *supra* note 3, at 178.

35. Grotius, *The Law of War and Peace, supra* note 12, at 550. In his 1608 work, *The Freedom of the Seas*, Grotius, citing Vitoria, affirmed the universality of rights and obligations on the grounds that

> God was the founder and ruler of the universe, and especially that being the Father of all mankind, He had not separated human beings, as He had the rest of living things, into different species and various divisions, but had willed them to be of one race and to be known by one name; that furthermore He had given them the same origin, the same structural organism, the ability to look each other in the face, language too, and other means of communication, in order that they all might recognize their natural social bond and kinship.

Grotius, *Freedom of the Seas, supra* note 8, at 1–2.

36. Grotius, *The Law of War and Peace, supra* note 12, at 397.

37. *Id.* at 169–85.

38. Although he argued that the punishment of those who behave impiously or who engage in religious persecution is justified, Grotius asserted that "wars cannot justly be waged against those who are unwilling to accept the Christian religion." *Id.* at 516. Grotius, following in the tradition of Bartolomé de las Casas, *see supra* note 34, presented two arguments in support of his claim that war should not be waged against those who "refused to embrace the Christian religion when proffered to them." First, he asserts that because Christianity is insusceptible to "purely natural arguments," nonbelievers have reason initially to resist the faith. Second, he relies on Christian scriptures that dictate that conversion should not be compelled by fear or threat of punishment. Grotius, *The Law of War and Peace, supra* note 12, at 516–17.

39. *Id.* at 171.

40. Felix Cohen makes the case that Spanish law in the late sixteenth century and afterward ultimately provided a humane basis for the treatment of indigenous peoples, notwithstanding the conspicuous failure of Spanish settlers to observe it. Cohen, *supra* note 27, at 12–13. He cites the Spanish Laws of the Indies, which commanded that the granting of lands to Spanish settlers could not prejudice or injure the Indians. Cohen characterizes the Laws of the Indies as holding Indians in a legally equal position to that of Spanish settlers. *Id.*

Likewise, Hanke notes that in 1542 Emperor Charles V of Spain abolished the slavery-like *encomienda* system and instituted the "New Laws." Hanke, *supra* note 3, at 83, 91–92. Hanke characterized the New Laws and the regulations that accompanied them as "so sweeping and so strongly in favor of the Indians that Las Casas himself might well have drafted them." *Id.* at 91. The enactment of the New Laws was met with outrage by Spanish colonists in the Americas, who were obliged in certain circumstances to relinquish Indian laborers held on *encomiendas. Id.* But the Spanish officials sent to enforce the New Laws in Mexico suspended many of the more far-reaching provisions in response to the widespread protests. In Peru, the viceroy sent to enforce the New Laws was decapitated in an ensuing revolt. In 1545, caving in to a vigorous campaign waged against the New Laws in the Spanish court, Charles V revoked a significant provision of the New Laws, preserving the *encomienda* system. *Id.* at 95–105. *See also* Robert N. Clinton, "The Proclamation of 1763: Colonial Prelude to Two Centuries of Federal-State

Conflict over the Management of Indian Affairs," 69 *B.U. L. Rev.* 329 (1989) (discussing the seventeenth- and eighteenth-century British policy of acknowledging preexisting Indian territorial rights in North America).

41. A wealth of contemporary scholarship exists detailing the patterns of treaty making between European and non-European indigenous peoples since the sixteenth century. *E.g.*, Felix S. Cohen's *Handbook of Federal Indian Law* 50–59 (Renard Strickland et al. eds., 2d ed. 1989) (discussing early treaties with native peoples of North America); Robert Clinton, *supra* note 40, at 331–53 (discussing eighteenth-century boundary and peace treaties involving indigenous groups in colonial North America); Howard Berman, "Perspectives on American Indian Sovereignty and International Law, 1600–1776," in *Exiled in the Land of the Free: Democracy, Indian Nations, and the U.S. Constitution* 128–29, 193 (Oren Lyons & John Mohawk eds., 1992) (discussing treaties involving Indian nations in northeastern North America); Malcolm Shaw, *Title to Territory in Africa: International Legal Issues* 31–48 (1986) (discussing treaties with native peoples of Africa); C. H. Alexandrowicz, *An Introduction to the History of the Law of Nations in the East Indies* 3–11, 12 n.B (1967) (citing treaties between indigenous peoples of the Indian subcontinent and Portugal, the Dutch East Indies Company, the English East Indian Company, and other parties during the seventeenth, eighteenth, and nineteenth centuries).

42. *See, e.g.*, Hanke, *supra* note 3, at 133–46 (discussing the waging of numerous "just wars" in Mexico, Nicaragua, Peru, Chile, and the Philippines throughout the sixteenth century); C. H. Alexandrowicz, *supra* note 41, at 234, 239 n.G (noting that the breach of a treaty was identified as grounds for "just war" in treaties and negotiations between Western European powers and East Indian peoples and was invoked by the English East India Company when it resorted to war against Tippoo Sultan in the late eighteenth century).

43. *See* Leo Gross, "The Peace of Westphalia, 1648–1948," in *International Law in the Twentieth Century* 25, 33–46 (Leo Gross et al. eds., 1969) (discussing the transformative impact of the Peace of Westphalia on European society and on conceptions of international law); J. H. Shennan, *Liberty and Order in Early Modern Europe: The Subject and the State, 1650–1800*, at 3 (1986).

44. Damerow, *supra* note 6, at 29.

45. Hobbes characterized the state of nature—life outside of civil society—as a state of war, in which life is "solitary, pooor, nasty, brutish, and short." Thomas Hobbes, *Leviathan* 89 (Richard Tuck ed., 1991) (1651). For Hobbes, the commonwealth forms when people

> confer all their power and strength upon one Man, or upon one Assembly of men, that may reduce all their Wills, by plurality of voices, unto one Will; which is as much as to say, to appoint one Man, or Assembly of men, to beare their Person. . . . This is more than Consent, or Concord; it is a reall Unitie of them all, in one and the same Person, made by Covenant of every man with every man. . . . This done, the Multitude so united in one Person, is called a "COMMON-WEALTH," in latine CIVITAS.

Id. at 120. The *state of nature* and *natural law* were not used interchangeably but were discrete terms for Hobbes. Hobbes defined "natural law" as a dictate of right reason, with "reason" referring not to inherently true principles but to a method of deductive thinking. *See* Norberto Bobbio, *Thomas Hobbes and the Natural Law Tradition* 118–19 (Daniela Gobetti trans., 1993).

46. Hobbes stated:

[E]very Soveraign hath the same Right, in procuring the safety of his People, that any particular man can have, in procuring his own safety. And the same Law, that dictateth to men that have no Civil Government, what they ought to do, and what to avoyd in regard of one another, dictateth the same to Common-wealths, that is, to the Consciences of Soveraign Princes, and Soveraign Assemblies; there being no Court of Naturall Justices, but in the Conscience onely.

Thomas Hobbes, *supra* note 45, at 244 (footnote omitted).

47. Damerow, *supra* note 6, at 32.

48. The relationship between Vattel's work and that of his predecessor Christian Wolff is described by Nussbaum, *supra* note 6, at 156–58.

49. Emmerich de Vattel, *The Law of Nations, or The Principles of Natural Law* (Classics of International Law Series, 1916) (Charles G. Fenwick trans. of 1758 ed.).

50. *Id.* at 3 (emphasis in original).

51. *Id.* Preface at 5a. Vattel elaborated:

[T]he *Law of Nations* is in its origin merely the *Law of Nature applied to Nations.* Now the just and reasonable application of a rule requires that the application be made in a manner suited to the nature of the subject; but we must not conclude that the Law of Nations is everywhere and at all points the same as natural law, except for a difference of subjects, so that no other change need be made than to substitute Nations for individuals. A civil society, or a State, is a very different subject from an individual person, and therefore, by virtue of the natural law, very different obligations and rights belong to it in most cases. The same general rule, when applied to two different subjects, cannot result in similar principles, nor can a particular rule, however just for one subject, be applicable to a second of a totally different nature. Hence there are many cases in which the natural law does not regulate the relations of States as it would those of individuals. We must know how to apply it conformably to its subjects; and the art of so applying it, with a precision founded upon right reason, constitutes the Law of Nations as a distinct science.

Id. at 4.

52. *Id.* at 8–9; *see* Damerow, *supra* note 6, at 33–48 (explaining the categories of law identified by Vattel as comprising the law of nations).

53. Vattel, *supra* note 49, at 13.

54. *See* David Beetham, "The Future of the Nation State," in *The Idea of the Modern State*, *supra* note 15, at 208–09 (discussing European nationhood in terms of "characteristics of culture and historical identity").

55. *See* Shennan, *supra* note 43, at 3 (describing the post-Westphalian state as "organized around an impersonal, centralized and unifying system of government resting

on law, bureaucracy and force"); Vincent, *supra* note 15, at 19 ("Primarily a State exists in a geographically identifiable territory over which it holds jurisdiction.").

56. David Beetham observes that "[t]he nation-state, then, is a historical product, not a fact of nature. It embodies two distinct ideas of sovereignty: sovereignty as the idea of the state's supreme and independent jurisdiction over a given territory; and sovereignty as the idea that the source of legitimacy for that jurisdiction derives from the people who constitute the nation." Beetham, *supra* note 54, at 209.

57. Vattel, *supra* note 49, at 6.

58. *Id.* at 7, 20. *See* Richard Falk, "The Theoretical Foundations of Human Rights," in *Human Rights in the World Community* 31, 32 (Richard P. Claude & Burns H. Weston eds., 2d ed. 1992) (discussing Vattel).

59. Vattel, *supra* note 49, at 8.

60. *See* J. L Brierly, *The Law of Nations: An Introduction to the International Law of Peace* 37–38 (6th ed. 1963) (linking the doctrine of state sovereignty to Vattel); Francis S. Ruddy, *International Law in the Enlightenment: The Background of Emmerich de Vattel's "Le Droit des gens"* 97–123 (1975) (similarly analyzing Vattel); Ian Brownlie, *Principles of Public International Law* 287 (6th ed. 2003) (identifying sovereignty as the "basic constitutional doctrine" of international law).

61. *See* Nussbaum, *supra* note 6, at 157–58. *See also* Brierly, *supra* note 60, at 37 (characterizing Vattel's view as a "misleading deduction from unsound premises").

62. *See* Shennan, *supra* note 43, at 3; Stuart Hall, *supra* note 15, at 7–9; Vincent, *supra* note 15, at 45–47.

63. *See generally* Duane Champagne, *Social Order and Political Change: Constitutional Governments among the Cherokee, the Choctaw, the Chickasaw, and the Creek* (1992) (describing social organization of various groups of North American Indians).

64. Hobbes, *supra* note 45, at 89.

65. *See supra* notes 18–23 and accompanying text.

66. Vattel, *supra* note 49, at 3.

67. *Id.* at 116.

68. *Id.* at 38.

69. *Id.*

70. Vattel held that

[e]very Nation is . . . bound by the natural law to cultivate the land which has fallen to its share. . . . Those who still pursue this idle mode of life . . . [of seeking] to live upon their flocks and the fruits of the chase . . . occupy more land than they would have need of under an honest system of labor, and they may not complain if other more industrious Nations, too confined at home, should come and occupy part of their lands.

Id. at 37–38. This view, anticipating the modern law and economics movement, reflects the highly influential theory of property rights earlier advanced by John Locke. Locke identified property as the individual appropriation of generally available resources: "'[T]is the taking any part of what is common, and removing it out of the state Nature left it in, which *begins Property*." Thus ownership is established through labor: "God . . . commanded Man to Labour . . . to subdue the Earth, *i.e.* improve it for the benefit of life, and therein lay something out upon it that was his own, his labour." The natural world is envisioned as "lying waste," awaiting the labor of man to transform it into valuable and productive property. John Locke, *Two Treatises of Government* 309, 312 (Peter Laslett ed., 2d ed. 1970). Locke specifically cited the Indians of the Americas as not engaging in sufficient labor to perfect a property interest in the lands they occupied. *Id.* at 313–15. Vattel's rendering of the Lockean view was later interpreted in a major treatise on American law as follows:

> Erratic tribes of savage hunters and fishermen, who have no fixed abode, or sense of property, and are engaged constantly in the chase or in war, have no sound or exclusive title either to an indefinite extent of country, or to seas and lakes, merely because they are accustomed, in search of prey, to roam over the one, or to coast the shores of the other. Vattel had just notions of the value of these aboriginal rights of savages, and of the true principles of natural law in relation to them. . . . The colonists have not deviated from the precepts of the law of nature, in confining the natives within narrower limits.

3 James Kent, *Commentaries on American Law* 312–13 (14th ed. 1896).

71. *See infra* notes 104–22 and accompanying text.

72. Vattel, *supra* note 49, at 11–12.

73. *Id.* at 12.

74. The early Marshall Indian law decisions have been discussed repeatedly in the extensive scholarly literature concerning the rights of indigenous North Americans. Much of this literature has invoked the Marshall decisions to demonstrate early legal recognition of indigenous peoples' sovereign rights, *e.g.*, John H. Clinebell & Jim Thomson, "Sovereignty and Self-Determination: The Rights of Native Americans under International Law," 27 *Buff. L. Rev.* 669, 693–94 (1978); or it has cited Marshall to demonstrate the historical diminution of such rights by the dominant legal and political culture, *e.g.*, Ward Churchill, "The Earth Is Our Mother: Struggles for American Indian Land and Liberation in the Contemporary United States," in *The State of Native America: Genocide, Colonization, and Resistance* 139, 142–43 (Annette Jaimes ed., 1992). Such contradictory approaches result from adherence to one or the other of divergent strains of thought in the Marshall decisions.

75. 21 U.S. (8 Wheat.) 543 (1823). This case involved a property dispute between two parties both claiming title to a tract of land. The Court held that the defendant's title, granted by the United States, was superior to the plaintiff's title, which he received when he purchased the land from an Indian tribe. According to the discovery doctrine articulated by the Court, the United States had exclusive rights to acquire full title to lands by purchase or conquest.

76. 21 U.S. at 590.

77. *Id.* at 591.

78. *See* Robert K. Faulkner, *The Jurisprudence of John Marshall* (1968).

79. 21 U.S. at 592. This aspect of *Johnson* is discussed further in chapter 5, *infra*, notes 75–78 and accompanying text.

80. 30 U.S. (5 Pet.) 1 (1831). *Cherokee Nation* involved an effort by the Cherokee to invoke the original jurisdiction of the Supreme Court to enjoin the state of Georgia

from executing and enforcing its state laws over Cherokee territory recognized by treaty with the United States. The Cherokee filed a motion to enjoin before the Supreme Court around the same time of the arrest on Cherokee territory and prosecution under Georgia law of Corn Tassel, a Cherokee tribal member, for the murder of another Cherokee. After the motion was filed, Georgia defied a writ of error by the Supreme Court and hanged Corn Tassel, asserting that the Supreme Court lacked jurisdiction over the matter. The Supreme Court ultimately denied the motion for injunction on jurisdictional grounds. *See* David H. Getches et al., *Federal Indian Law: Cases and Materials* 101–04 (4th ed. 1998).

81. 30 U.S. at 17.

82. *Id.* at 16–17. Justice Marshall wrote the plurality opinion among the six justices participating in the case. Justices Baldwin, Johnson, and McLean concurred in the decision that the Cherokee were not a "foreign state" for the purposes of Article III of the U.S. Constitution. But Justices Baldwin and Johnson wrote separate opinions each denying that Indian tribes possessed any sovereignty at all. Justice Thompson, on the other hand, wrote a dissenting opinion, joined by Justice Story, taking the position that the Cherokee Nation was a foreign state both under international law and U.S. constitutional law. In writing for the Court, Marshall took a middle road by describing the tribes as "domestic dependent nations," and he suggested that the status of tribes under international law, or the law of nations, was a matter distinct from the Article III question.

83. *Id.* at 17 (emphasis added).

84. 31 U.S. (6 Pet.) 515 (1832). *Worcester* involved the arrest of several missionaries for violating Georgia law that required non-Indians to obtain licenses from the state governor to live in Cherokee territory. The Supreme Court overturned the convictions, holding that Georgia law had no force on Cherokee territories as established by treaty with the United States.

85. *Id.* at 560–61.

86. *Id.* at 559.

87. *Id.* at 541–63.

88. *Id.* at 546–62.

89. *Id.* at 559.

90. *Id.* at 554.

91. *See* William G. McLoughlin, *Cherokees and Missionaries, 1789–1839*, at 124–49 (1984); William G. McLoughlin, *Cherokee Renascence in the New Republic* 350–89 (1986); William L. Anderson, *Cherokee Removal, Before and After* 4–5 (1991).

92. "We will not enter into the controversy, whether agriculturists, merchants, and manufacturers, have a right, on abstract principles, to expel hunters from the territory they possess, or to contract the limits." 21 U.S. at 588.

93. *Worcester*, 31 U.S. at 555–56.

94. *Id.* at 556.

95. *Johnson*, 21 U.S. at 590.

96. Henry Wheaton, *Elements of International Law* 50–51 (8th ed. 1866).

97. *Id.* at 26.

98. Following this tendency, the U.S. federal government eventually asserted more and more authority over Indian tribes:

Beginning in 1871, Congress embarked on a sequence of new policies that marked the end of meaningful self-government. Tribes were defined out of the Treaty Power (1871); prohibited from making contracts without the consent of the secretary of interior (1871); forced to submit to a federally organized Indian police force (1875); made subject to a code of oppressive rules drafted and executed by the Bureau of Indian Affairs, which sought to regulate their family, religious and economic affairs (1882); and, finally, tribal territories were subdivided without regard for tribal law (1884).

Russel Lawrence Barsh & James Youngblood Henderson, *The Road: Indian Tribes and Political Liberty* 62 (1980) (footnotes omitted). Faced with the perceived limits of its domestic judicial competency to reverse the federal encroachments, the Supreme Court sustained them. *See, e.g.,* United States v. Kagama, 118 U.S. 375 (1886) (upholding congressional power to legislate federal prosecution of crimes committed by Indians on reservations and thus infringe on internal tribal resolution of disputes); Lone Wolf v. Hitchcock, 187 U.S. 553 (1903) (affirming power of Congress unilaterally to abrogate Indian treaties); *see generally* Charles F. Wilkinson, *American Indians, Time, and the Law: Native Societies in a Modern Constitutional Democracy* 24–26 (1987) (identifying *Kagama* and *Lone Wolf* as progenitors of a jurisprudential trend away from the Marshall cases). Moreover, as positivism came to overpower natural law thinking, as discussed subsequently, the rights of the nineteenth-century states—derived from the European practice of discovery—found sanction in international law, and the natural law possessory rights recognized by Marshall did not. Similarly, in domestic legal discourse the discovery doctrine came to be construed as providing the discoverer rights superior to the original occupancy rights of the Indians. *See, e.g.,* Kent, *supra* note 70, at 384–87. The Supreme Court reverted to a trend toward reliance on discovery and unaccomplished conquest as a way of justifying the wresting of Indian rights, rejecting, implicitly if not explicitly, Marshall's final assessment of the legal status of Indian tribes. *See, e.g.,* Tee-Hit-Ton Indians v. United States, 348 U.S. 272, 279 (1954) ("This [diminished] position of the Indian has long been rationalized by the legal theory that discovery and conquest gave the conquerors sovereignty and ownership of the lands there obtained" [*citing* Johnson v. M'Intosh, 21 U.S. (8 Wheat.) 543].). In United States v. Rogers, 45 U.S. (4 How.) 567 (1846), Chief Justice Taney altogether reconstructed the history of Indian-European contact set forth by Marshall in *Worcester.* According to Taney, "The native tribes, who were found on this continent at the time of its discovery have never been acknowledged or treated as independent nations by European governments, nor regarded as the owners of the territories they respectively occupied." 45 U.S. at 571.

99. *See, e.g.,* John Westlake, *Chapters on the Principles of International Law* 110 (1894); William E. Hall, *A Treatise on International Law* 65 (Alexander P. Higgins ed., 8th ed. 1924).

100. *See* Damerow, *supra* note 6, at 76–81 (discussing the positivist school); Brierly, *supra* note 60, at 51 (same).

101. *See infra* notes 103–07 and accompanying text.

102. *See* C. H. Alexandrowicz, *supra* note 41, at 9–10; *see also infra* notes 108–13 and accompanying text.

103. Westlake, *supra* note 99, at 136–38.

104. *Id.* at 141–45. Westlake, however, conceded that the precolonial "countries" of "Mexico and Peru," apparently referring to the Aztecs and Incas, had characteristics ranking them as states rather than "uncivilised tribes." *Id.* at 146. He thus reflected Vattel's distinction between "the empires of Peru and Mexico" and the hunter-gatherer tribes of North America. Vattel, *supra* note 49, at 38. But unlike Vattel, he took no care to deem the conquest of the Aztecs and Incas as a "notorious usurpation."

105. Westlake, *supra* note 99, at 141–43.

106. *Id.* at 136–38.

107. Hall, *supra* note 99, at 47. In Hall's view, in order to be subjects of international law,

> states outside European civilisation must formally enter into the circle of law-governed countries. They must do something with the acquiescence of the latter, or of some of them, which amounts to an acceptance of the law in its entirety beyond all possibility of misconstruction. It is not enough consequently that they shall enter into arrangements by treaty identical with arrangements made by law-governed powers, nor that they shall do acts, like sending and receiving permanent embassies, which are compatible with ignorance or rejection of law.

Id. at 47–48. Citing European dealings with China, Hall's eighth edition acknowledged a tendency of European states to conduct relations with entities "which are outside the sphere of international law" in accordance with its rules. *Id.* Hall reasoned, however, that such dealings in themselves could not fairly or possibly be assumed to establish acceptance into the family of "law-governed," "civilised" states. *Id.* at 48–49. Acceptance was at least a matter of reciprocity: "European states will be obliged, partly by their sense of honor, partly by their interests, to be guided by their own artificial rules in dealing with semi-civilised states, when the latter have learned enough to make the demand, long before a reciprocal obedience to those rules can be reasonably expected." *Id.* at 48.

108. 1 Lassa F. L. Oppenheim, *International Law* 134–35 (Ronald F. Roxburgh ed., 3d ed. 1920). Oppenheim further explained,

> As this basis is the common consent of the civilised States, there are three conditions for the admission of new members into the circle of the Family of Nations. A State to be admitted must, first, be a civilised State which is in constant intercourse with members of the Family of Nations. Such State must, secondly, expressly or tacitly consent to be bound for its future international conduct by the rules of International Law. And, thirdly, those States which have hitherto formed the Family of Nations must expressly or tacitly consent to the reception of the new member.

Id. at 32.

109. *See* Brownlie, *supra* note 60, at 87–88 (discussing the "constitutive" theory of recognition).

110. *See* Oppenheim, *supra* note 108, at 188–91.

111. *Id.* at 33.

112. *Id.* at 34–35.

113. *Id.* at 126.

114. 1 Charles C. Hyde, *International Law Chiefly as Interpreted and Applied by the United States* 163–64 (1922).

115. *Id.* at 19. This conclusion is further promoted by Alpheus Snow's 1918 work, *The Question of the Aborigines in the Law and Practice of Nations*, which was commissioned by the U.S. Department of State. Alpheus Snow, *The Question of the Aborigines in the Law and Practice of Nations* 16 (1972 ed.).

116. *See, e.g.*, Oppenheim, *supra* note 108, at 383–84.

117. *See, e.g.*, Hyde, *supra* note 114, at 163–71; Westlake, *supra* note 103, at 155–60.

118. *See, e.g.*, Hyde, *supra* note 114, at 175 ("If the inhabitants of the territory concerned are an uncivilized people, deemed to be incapable of possessing a right of property and control, the conqueror may, in fact, choose to ignore their title, and proceed to occupy the land as though it were vacant.").

119. *See. e.g.*, Oppenheim *supra* note 108, at 384; Hall, *supra* note 99, at 125–26. The use of these doctrines in the context of indigenous peoples is identified in Gudmundur Alfredsson, "International Law, International Organizations, and Indigenous Peoples," 36 *J. Int'l Aff.* 113 (1982).

120. *See, e.g.*, Oppenheim, *supra* note 108, at 337 ("Cessions of territory made to private persons and to corporations by native tribes or by States outside the dominion of the Law of Nations do not fall within the sphere of International Law, neither do cessions of territory by native tribes made to States which are members of the Family of Nations.").

121. Westlake. *supra* note 99, at 143–45.

122. *Id.* at 145, 149–55.

123. *See* Mark F. Lindley, *The Acquisition and Government of Backward Territory in International Law* 21–23 (1926) (discussing the attributes of "political society"). Lindley, for example, distinguished between the indigenous tribes of New Zealand, with which the British crown had dealt through treaty, and the Australian "Aboriginal tribes, forming probably the least-instructed portion of the human race in all the arts of social life." *Id.* at 41. Lindley held that "there appeared to be no political society to deal with" among the latter, and hence "[o]ccupation was the appropriate method of" acquiring the lands they inhabited. *Id.*

124. *Id.* at 45–46.

125. *Id.* at 47.

126. Cayuga Indians (Great Britain) v. United States, VI R. Int'l. Arb. Awards 173 (1926). The claim was based on obligations Great Britain had undertaken toward the Cayuga Indians in an 1814 treaty with the United States.

127. *Id.* at 176.

128. *Id.*

129. Hyde, *supra* note 114, at 25, n.1.

130. Island of Palmas (U.S. v. Neth.), II R. Int'l. Arb. Awards 831 (1928).

131. *Id.* at 858.

132. *Id.* (emphasis in original).

133. Legal Status of Eastern Greenland (Den. v. Nor.), 1933 P.C.I.J. (ser. A/B) No. 53.

134. *Id.* at 46–47.

135. *See id.*

136. *See supra* notes 24–25 and accompanying text (discussing Vitoria).

137. *See generally Imperialism* 1–40 (Philip D. Curtin ed., 1971) (excerpts from original nineteenth-century texts explaining the inherent inferiority of nonwhite cultures and races through pseudoscientific reasoning).

138. House of Commons, Select Committee on Aboriginal Tribes, *Report* (1837) (as quoted in Barsh & Henderson, *supra* note 98, at 86).

139. *Id.*

140. Letter from Lord John Russell to Sir George Gipps, Aug. 23, 1840, reprinted in Snow, *supra* note 115, at 29.

141. Indian Commissioner Nathaniel G. Taylor writing on the question "Shall our Indians be civilized?" in the *Annual Report of the Commissioner of Indian Affairs,* Nov. 23, 1868, reprinted in *Documents of United States Indian Policy* 123, 126 (Francis Paul Prucha ed., 2d ed. 1990).

142. S. Lyman Tyler, *A History of Indian Policy* 88 (1973).

143. *See generally* Petra T. Shattuck & Jill Norgren, *Partial Justice: Federal Indian Law in a Liberal Constitutional System* 78–84 (1991); Michael C. Coleman, *Presbyterian Missionary Attitudes toward American Indians, 1837–1893* (1985); Evelyn Hu-DeHart, *Missionaries, Miners & Indians: Spanish Contact with the Yacqui Nation of Northwestern New Spain* (1981).

144. Act of April 12, 1876, chap. 18, 1876 Can. Stat. 43. The act vested in the office of the superintendent general of Indian affairs comprehensive powers of management of the land, property, and social relations of the indigenous peoples. These powers governed a regime in which all Indian lands were subject to subdivision at the authorization of the superintendent general; the regime also established a fee system wherein title was granted and conveyances made only with his approval. The act statutorily created the terms of both Indian status and band membership. *See generally* Bradford W. Morse "Aboriginal Peoples and the Law," in *Aboriginal Peoples and the Law: Indian, Métis and Inuit Rights in Canada* 1–5 (Bradford W. Morse ed., 1989).

145. The 1916 Civil Code of Brazil mandated that "[t]he savages shall remain subject to the tutelary regimen established by special laws and regulations which shall cease as they become adapted to the civilization of the country." Codigo Civil do Brasil art. 6. Article 6 was implemented by Decree No. 5464 issued in 1928, which created four categories of Indians based on their degree of assimilation into Brazilian society, as demonstrated by location and type of residence and religious and social practices. Rights of property ownership and civil law capacity were derived from the level of integration attained. *See* Stephen Conn, "Inside Brazilian Indian Law: A Comparative Perspective," in *Indigenous Law and the State* 269–73 (Bradford W. Morse & Gordon R. Woodman eds., 1988) (surveying Brazilian Indian law and the administration of the state guardianship of indigenous peoples); Cecilia Medina, *The Legal Status of Indians in Brazil* (1977) (describing the effect of Brazilian Indian law on the legal and societal status of the state's indigenous people).

146. The 1915 law and related official action sanctioning the role of the Catholic church is discussed in Mary Watters, *A History of the Church in Venezuela: 1810–1930,* at 215–16 (1933).

147. Const. Arg. (1853) chap. IV, art. 67 (15).

148. *See The Scramble for Africa: Documents on the Berlin West African Conference and Related Subjects 1884–1885*, at 291 (R. J. Gavin & J. A. Betley comp., trans., & eds., 1973).

149. General Act of the Conference of Berlin art. VI, reprinted in *The Scramble for Africa, supra* note 148, at 291. *See also* Lindley, *supra* note 123, at 333 (citing similar provisions in the concluding acts of subsequent conferences).

150. 10 Institut de Droit International, *Annuaire* (1888–89) 203 (translation from Snow, *supra* note 115, at 174–75).

151. Covenant of the League of Nations art. 23(a).

152. Lindley, *supra* note 123, at 324–36. *But see* South West Africa (Phase 2), 1966 I.C.J. 61, 34–35 (declining to recognize the juridical character of such trusteeship obligations operative in the late nineteenth and early twentieth centuries, other than those arising directly from the League of Nations mandates system).

153. Lindley, *supra* note 123, at 324–27.

154. David A. Nock, *A Victorian Missionary and Canadian Indian Policy: Cultural Synthesis vs. Cultural Replacement* (1988); Luis N. Rivera, *A Violent Evangelism: The Political and Religious Conquest of the Americas* (1992); Watters, *supra* note 146.

2

Developments within the Modern Era of Human Rights

The preceding chapter demonstrated that the normative discourse and related patterns of official behavior in international law have long had implications for the status and rights of peoples who are indigenous to lands subject to colonization and its legacies. Shaped by Western perspectives and political power, international law developed a complicity with the often brutal forces that wrested lands from indigenous peoples, suppressed their cultures and institutions, and left them among the poorest of the poor.

Within the past decades, however, there have been significant advancements in the structure of world organization and shifts in attendant normative assumptions. These changes have engendered a reformed system of international law, and the reformed system, in turn, has provided fertile ground for social forces to further alter, and eventually reverse in many ways, the direction of international law where it concerns the indigenous peoples of today. This chapter begins by discussing briefly the contemporary international legal system, identifying its move away from state-centered positivism and its growing concern for individuals and groups about precepts of world peace and human rights. The chapter goes on to describe developments within the modern human rights frame and their culmination in a new generation of conventional and customary international law concerning indigenous peoples.

The Contemporary International Legal System

The character of international law has evolved with shifts in the ordering of political power and the burgeoning of international institutions that constitute themselves on precepts of a peaceful and just world order. On one hand, the principles, norms, and procedures that fall within the rubric of international law remain substantially state-centered, and the rhetoric of state sovereignty continues as central to international legal discourse. On the other hand, the community of states whose sovereignty international law is deemed to uphold has extended far beyond the European "family." International law has reacquired its presumptive universality and thus theoretically welcomes within the global community of states all those fulfilling the criteria of statehood. The constitutive theory of statehood, by which statehood for the purposes of international law depends upon positive recognition, has given way to a dominant declarative theory, by which statehood presumptively exists by virtue of certain objective criteria, independently of acts of recognition.[1]

In practical terms, recognition by a preponderance of actors on the international plane remains crucial to a state's capacity to invoke or benefit from the principles and procedures of international law. Whether judged by the objective criteria of statehood or by the phenomenon of recognition, however, the international community of states has expanded such that the countries of Africa, Asia, Latin America, the Caribbean, and the Pacific, many of which were born since the mid-twentieth century, now comprise a majority. With this embrace of non-European cultures and perspectives, Eurocentric precepts increasingly are undermined in global decision making. Also significant is the demise of the cold-war-era East-West cleavage that divided the world's states ideologically and politically, a cleavage that, like past perceived or actual rifts in humanity, undermined the very idea of a globally operative, politically neutral body of law.

In addition to achieving greater inclusiveness and an enhanced universalist posture in terms of states, international law increasingly addresses and is shaped by nonstate actors and perspectives. Individuals, international organizations, transnational corporations, labor unions, and other nongovernmental organizations participate in procedures that shape the content of international law.[2] In turn, individuals and certain associational entities have been made subjects of international norms or included as participants in treaty-governed international processes.[3] Accordingly, international tribunals and publicists in general hold that "international personality" is no longer limited to states.

International law, furthermore, has been made to include a burgeoning and influential transnational discourse concerned with achieving peace and a minimum of human suffering.[4] This modern discourse of peace and human rights, which tempers positivism in international law, represents in significant measure the reemergence of classical-era naturalism, in which law was determined on the basis of visions of *what ought to be*, rather than simply on the basis of *what is*, and which contextualized the state as an instrument of humankind rather than its master.[5] This discourse, carried out by scholars, advocates, and government representatives at various levels of decision extending into the international plane, and increasingly free from Western cultural biases, seeks to define norms not by mere assessment of state conduct but rather by the prescriptive articulation of the expectations and values of the *human* constituents of the world community. By directly addressing the concerns of human beings, moreover, this discourse expands the competency of international law over spheres previously reserved to the asserted sovereign prerogatives of states.

The United Nations and other international organizations that emerged in the aftermath of the two world wars have been both a manifestation of and an impetus for the changing character of international law.[6] The multilateral treaties that are the constituent instruments of the world's major intergovernmental organizations largely mark out the parameters for the contemporary international legal system. These parameters have both substantive and procedural aspects. In both, there are elements of the traditional state-centered framework as well as nonstatist, normative ones that influence the framework and work to reform it.

The United Nations Charter, most notably, embraces substantive statist precepts by including among the organization's founding principles respect for the "sovereign equality" and "territorial integrity" of member states and for nonintervention into their domestic affairs.[7] By specifying that *member* states are the beneficiaries of sovereignty principles, furthermore, the Charter promotes a kind of constitutivism in the international legal framework. Although membership ostensibly is open to all "peace-loving states" willing and able to meet the obligations under the Charter,[8] membership remains an act of positive recognition, and often a highly political one. Under the Charter, the sovereignty of member states is empowered and, necessarily, any claim of conflicting sovereignty on the part of some nonmember entity is undermined.

While affirming such elements of the state-centered framework, however, the Charter establishes among the organization's purposes the promotion of "equal rights and self-determination of peoples,"[9] "respect for human rights and for fundamental freedoms for all without distinction as to race, sex, language, or religion"[10] and "conditions of economic and social progress and development."[11] The Charter, moreover, emphasizes peace and world security as the organization's ultimate objectives.[12]

In setting the procedural parameters for U.N. activity, the Charter upholds the state-centered system by limiting voting in the General Assembly and in the other major U.N. organs to member states,[13] and by limiting access to the International Court of Justice to states and certain designated U.N organs and affiliate agencies acting with at least the acquiescence of member states.[14] The Charter further bows to the *realpolitik* of world affairs of earlier times by designating five World War II–era superpowers as permanent members of the Security Council, whose membership is otherwise rotating, and by allowing each such permanent member veto power.[15]

The Charter, however, in addition to requiring that all member states be "peace loving," commits them to "take joint and separate action in co-operation with the Organization" for the achievement of the Charter's moral objectives.[16] The mere existence of the General Assembly and other forums established or authorized by the Charter vastly encourages that cooperation. Further, although limiting formal U.N. membership to states, the Charter engenders meaningful levels and forms of nonstate participation in the organization's deliberative processes. The Charter allows for nongovernmental organizations to affiliate with the U.N. Economic and Social Council, the parent body of the United Nations' human rights and social policy organs.[17] With such affiliation, numerous nongovernmental organizations have been permitted various forms of participation in U.N. forums concerning human rights and social issues.[18] Lower-level U.N. policy-making organs, furthermore, include experts acting in their individual capacities. The U.N. Secretariat, which has significant powers of initiative under the Charter, itself provides an important source of nonstate influence, particularly in matters of human rights.[19]

Thus, through the pervasive U.N. system as well as through similarly devised organizations at the regional level, statist conceptions are upheld but are made to contend with humanistic precepts and moral objectives in the authoritative multilateral processes that comprise and shape international law. And these processes are influenced not only by reformist tendencies among states but also by nonstate actors.

The humanistic precepts that are founding principles of the United Nations and other major international organizations have been grounds for the creation of an extensive and still developing body of norms concerned directly with the welfare of human beings. Under the rubric of "human rights," these norms and accompanying oversight procedures, established or reflected in multilateral treaties and other authoritative instruments such as U.N. General Assembly resolutions,[20] more or less regulate *all* states as to their own citizens.[21] The international human rights movement, which has engaged states as well as nonstate actors, has taught that sustained and coordinated international concern over the safeguarding of particular human interests is capable of rendering state claims of exclusive sovereignty or jurisdiction over such interests with diminished force in today's international law.[22]

While the international human rights movement has been a leading factor in the expansion of international law's scope and in the moderation of the doctrine of sovereignty, it also has promoted the demise of international law's historical linkage to the pervasive individual/state perceptual dichotomy of human organization. Within Western thought since the eighteenth century, rights have been thought of and articulated mostly in terms of the *individual's* demands of freedom, equality, participation, and economic and physical security vis-à-vis the state, or in terms of the *state's* sovereign prerogatives.[23] Although Western individualism and statism continue as pervasive forces, authoritative discussion of human rights has become increasingly attentive to values supportive of human beings' associational and cultural patterns that exist independently of state structures.[24] Accordingly, concepts of group or collective rights have begun to take hold in the articulation of human rights norms and in adjudicative or quasi-adjudicative procedures of international human rights organs.

In sum, international law—the body of principles, norms, and procedures that today function across national boundaries—remains state-centered, but it is now pulled at by a discourse directly concerned with individuals and even groups. Notions of state sovereignty, although still very much alive in international law, are ever more yielding to an overarching normative trend defined by visions of world peace, stability, and human rights. This trend, promoted by modern international institutions and involving nonstate actors in multilateral settings, enhances international law's competency over matters at one time considered within states' exclusive domestic domain.

The expanding opening in international law for concern with nonstate entities on humanistic grounds in part entails a resurfacing of the naturalist framework that the early classical theorists invoked to enjoin sovereigns with regard to the treatment of indigenous peoples,[25] but it is an opening increasingly free of the bounds of Eurocentric perspectives. This opening, forged by the modern human rights movement, has been the basis for international law to revisit the subject of indigenous peoples and eventually become reformulated into a force in aid of indigenous peoples' own designs and aspirations.

The Initial Model within the Modern Human Rights Frame

The concern within the international system for peoples or populations identified as indigenous has arisen as part of a larger concern for those segments of humanity that have experienced histories of colonization and continued to suffer the legacies of those histories. In the post–United Nations Charter world of the middle part of the twentieth century, the political theory that supported colonialism by European powers had long been discredited and had faded in light of the major contending political theories of the time: Western democracy, Marxism, and variations thereof. Despite the divergence of mid-twentieth-century political theory that polarized geopolitical forces, the international community viewed colonialism and its legacies with certain shared precepts. Whether viewed through the lens of Marxism or Western democratic theory, colonial structures were regarded negatively for depriving people of self-government in favor of administration that was ultimately controlled by the peoples of the colonizing states for their own benefit.

At the close of World War II the international system had instituted the United Nations Charter and incorporated human rights precepts among its foundational elements. The reformed system joined the revolutionary movements that fought colonialism where it continued to exist in its classical form and urged self-government in its place.[26] The regime of decolonization prescriptions that were developed and promoted through the international system, however, largely bypassed indigenous patterns of association and political ordering that originated prior to European colonization. Instead, the population of a colonial territory as an integral whole, irrespective of precolonial political and cultural patterns, was deemed the beneficiary unit of decolonization prescriptions.

Thus the implementation of the Charter–based decolonization regime did not entail a reversion to the status quo of political or social ordering prior to the historical processes that culminated in colonization. Rather, it led to the creation of altogether new institutional orders, viewed as appropriate to implementing self-government. General Assembly Resolution 1514 of 1960 confirmed the norm of independent statehood for colonial territories with their colonial boundaries intact, regardless of the arbitrary character of most such boundaries.[27] Under the companion Resolution 1541 and related international practice, self-government was also deemed implemented for a former colonial territory if it became associated or integrated with an established independent state,[28] as long as the resulting arrangement entailed a condition of equality for the people of the territory concerned and was upheld by their freely expressed wishes.[29]

A corollary to the focus on the colonial territorial unit was what became known as the "blue water thesis," which developed effectively to preclude from decolonization procedures consideration of enclaves of indigenous or tribal peoples living within the external boundaries of independent states.[30] While state sovereignty over distant or external colonial territories was eroding in the face of normative precepts deployed internationally, it remained relatively steadfast over enclave indigenous groups and worked to keep them outside the realm of international concern. In 1949, the U.N. General Assembly adopted a resolution recommending that the Economic and Social Council conduct a study on the "social problem of the aboriginal populations and other under-developed social groups of the American Continent."[31] Subsequent action within the Economic and Social Council, however, effectively barred any such study unless requested by affected states, and no request was made.[32]

A measure of international concern did eventually take hold, within the human rights frame and parallel to the decolonization movement, toward members of groups identified as indigenous and living within independent states. The major embodiment of the mid-twentieth-century deployment of the international human rights program in the specific context of indigenous populations is International Labour Organization (ILO) Convention No. 107 of 1957.[33] The ILO, a specialized agency predating but now affiliated with the United Nations, developed Convention No. 107 and its accompanying Recommendation 104[34] following a series of studies and expert meetings signaling the particular vulnerability of indigenous workers.[35] Although representing elements of nonstate influence within the international system, these studies and expert meetings proceeded with no apparent participation on the part of indigenous peoples' own designated representatives.

While identifying members of indigenous groups as in need of special measures for the protection of their human rights, Convention No. 107 reflects the premise of assimilation operative among dominant political elements in national and international circles at the time of the convention's adoption.[36] The universe of values that promoted the emancipation of colonial territories during the middle part of the last century simultaneously promoted the assimilation of members of culturally distinctive indigenous groups into the dominant political and social orders that engulfed them. Assimilation and rights of full citizenship were used to bring within the fold of self-government indigenous groups living in independent and newly independent states. Precepts of self-government and human rights largely remained conditioned by a perceptual dichotomy between individual/state that had Western origins and by the attendant idea of a culturally homogenous independent nation-state.[37] Nation building was a corresponding policy (de facto if not in theory in the case of Marxist systems) of breaking down competing ethnic or cultural bonds, a policy engaged in even by, or perhaps especially by, newly independent states.[38] To the extent the international community valued cultural diversity, it was largely the diversity existing *among* the different states and colonial territories, not the diversity that might exist wholly *within* them.

The thrust of Convention No. 107 of 1957, accordingly, is to promote improved social and economic conditions for indigenous populations generally, but within a perceptual scheme that does not seem to envisage a place in the long term for robust, politically significant cultural and associational patterns of indigenous groups. Convention No. 107 is framed in terms of *members* of indigenous populations and their rights as equals within the larger society.[39] Indigenous *peoples* or *groups* as such are only secondarily, if at all, made beneficiaries of rights or protections. The convention does recognize indigenous customary laws and the right of collective land ownership. Such recognition, however, is posited as transitory and hence is overshadowed by a persistent deference and even preference for national programs of integration and noncoercive assimilation. The following provisions illustrate the convention's tenor and thrust:

Article 2

1. Governments shall have the primary responsibility for developing co-ordinated and systematic action for the protection of the populations concerned and their progressive integration into the life of their respective countries.

. . . .

3. The primary objective of all such action shall be the fostering of individual dignity, and the advancement of individual usefulness and initiative.

. . . .

Article 3

1. So long as the social, economic and cultural conditions of the populations concerned prevent them from enjoying the benefits of the general laws of

the country to which they belong, special measures shall be adopted for the protection of the institutions, persons, property and labour of these populations.

2. Care shall be taken to ensure that such special measures of protection—

(a) are not used as a means of creating or prolonging a state of segregation, and

(b) will be continued only so long as there is need for special protection and only to the extent that such protection is necessary.

The philosophy toward indigenous peoples reflected in Convention No. 107 also manifested itself at the international level in mid-twentieth-century programs promoted by the Inter-American Indian Institute, which was established in 1940.[40] The institute, which became a specialized agency of the Organization of American States (OAS), organized a series of periodic conferences and otherwise acted as an information and advisory resource for OAS member states. Like ILO Convention No. 107, the initial policy regime adopted by the institute embraced programs aimed at enhancing the economic welfare of indigenous groups and promoting their integration into the larger social and political order.[41]

ILO Convention No. 107 and Inter-American Indian Institute programs that were developed within the international human rights frame of the middle part of the last century have been much maligned for their assimilationist or integrationist elements. Nonetheless, with these programs the subject of people identified by their indigenousness vis-à-vis majority or dominant populations established a foothold in the international system through the conceptual and institutional medium of human rights. That foothold and the language of human rights became the basis for a much enhanced international concern for indigenous peoples and a reformed normative regime regarding them.

The Contemporary Indigenous Rights Movement

The international system's contemporary treatment of indigenous peoples is the result of activity over the last few decades. This activity has involved, and substantially been driven by, indigenous peoples themselves. Indigenous peoples have ceased to be mere objects of the discussion of their rights and have become real participants in an extensive multilateral dialogue that also has engaged states, nongovernmental organizations (NGOs), and independent experts, a dialogue facilitated by human rights organs of international institutions.

During the 1960s, armed with a new generation of men and women educated in the ways of the societies that had encroached upon them, indigenous peoples began drawing increased attention to demands for their continued survival as distinct communities with historically based cultures, political institutions, and entitlements to land.[42] Indigenous peoples articulated a vision of themselves different from that previously advanced and acted upon by dominant sectors.[43]

In the 1970s indigenous peoples extended their efforts internationally through a series of international conferences and direct appeals to international intergovernmental institutions.[44] These efforts coalesced into a veritable campaign, aided by concerned international nongovernmental organizations and an increase of supportive scholarly and popular writings from moral and sociological, as well as juridical, perspectives.[45] The proliferation of scholarly literature helped establish indigenous peoples' demands as legitimate among influential intellectual and elite circles. Among the major developments in this movement was the International Non-Governmental Organization Conference on Discrimination against Indigenous Populations in the Americas, in Geneva, which was organized as a project of the NGO Sub-Committee on Racism, Racial Discrimination, Apartheid and Colonialism. The 1977 Conference, attended by indigenous peoples' representatives from throughout the Western Hemisphere, contributed to forging a transnational indigenous identity that subsequently expanded to embrace indigenous peoples from other parts of the world.[46] The conference also helped establish a pattern of coordination among indigenous peoples from throughout the world in the formulation and communication of their demands, a pattern that has continued through subsequent numerous international meetings.[47]

Following the 1977 conference, indigenous peoples' representatives began appearing before U.N. human rights bodies in increasing numbers and with increasing frequency, grounding their demands in generally applicable human rights principles.[48] Indigenous peoples have enhanced their access to these bodies as several organizations representative of indigenous groups have achieved official consultative status with the U.N. Economic and Social Council, the parent body of the U.N. human rights machinery.[49] Indigenous peoples also have invoked procedures within regional human rights bodies, particularly those associated with the Organization of American States.[50]

Indigenous peoples' contemporary efforts internationally build on the initiative of the Council of the Iroquois Confederacy in the 1920s. Deskaheh, speaker of the council, led an attempt to have the League of Nations consider the Iroquois's long-standing dispute with Canada. Although Deskaheh found support among some League members, the League ultimately closed its door to the Iroquois, yielding to the position that the Iroquois grievances were a domestic concern of Canada and hence outside the League's competency.[51] In more recent years, however, benefiting from an international system in which assertions of domestic jurisdiction are less and less a barrier to international concern over issues of human rights, indigenous peoples have been successful in attracting significant attention to their demands at the international level.

The heightened international concern over indigenous peoples generated through years of work was signaled by the U.N. General Assembly's designation of 1993 as "The International Year of the World's Indigenous People"[52] followed by the proclaiming of an "International Decade" on the same theme.[53]

Probably the most important development linked with the International Decade was the establishment of a "Permanent Forum on Indigenous Issues" within the U.N. Economic and Social Council, which met for the first time in May 2002.[54] With this heightened international concern for indigenous peoples has come a reformulated understanding of the contours of general human rights principles and their implications in this context. And grounded upon this reformulated understanding there is a new—though still developing—generation of international law concerning indigenous peoples.

ILO Convention No. 169 of 1989

The ILO Convention on Indigenous and Tribal Peoples, Convention No. 169 of 1989,[55] is a central feature of international law's contemporary treatment of indigenous peoples' demands. Convention No. 169 is a revision of the ILO's earlier Convention No. 107 of 1957, and it represents a marked departure in world community policy from the philosophy of integration or assimilation underlying the earlier convention. With indigenous peoples increasingly taking charge of the international human rights agenda as it concerned them, Convention No. 107 of 1957 came to be regarded as anachronistic. In 1986, the ILO convened a "Meeting of Experts" which included representatives of the World Council of Indigenous Peoples, a loose confederation of indigenous groups from throughout the world. The meeting recommended the revision of Convention No. 107, concluding that

> the integrationist language of Convention No. 107 is outdated, and that the application of this principle is destructive in the modern world. In 1956 and 1957, when Convention No. 107 was being discussed, it was felt that integration into the dominant national society offered the best chance for these groups to be part of the development process of the countries in which they live. This had, however, resulted in a number of undesirable consequences. It had become a destructive concept, in part at least because of the way it was understood by governments. In practice it had become a concept which meant the extinction of ways of life which are different from that of the dominant society. The inclusion of this idea in the text of the Convention has also impeded indigenous and tribal peoples from taking full advantage of the strong protections offered in some parts of the Convention, because of the distrust its use has created among them. In this regard, it was recalled that the Sub-Commission's Special Rapporteur had stressed in his study . . . the necessity of adopting an approach which took account of the claims of indigenous populations. In his opinion, the policies of pluralism, self-sufficiency, self-management and ethnodevelopment appeared to be those which would give indigenous populations the best possibilities and means of participating directly in the formulation and implementation of official policies.[56]

The discussion on the revision of the convention proceeded at the 1988 and 1989 sessions of the International Labour Conference, the highest decision-making body of the ILO. The annual conference consists of representatives of worker and employer organizations as well as of states. Special arrangements were made to allow representatives of indigenous groups limited participation in the deliberations of the conference committee designated for the revision. At the close of the 1989 session, the full Labour Conference adopted the new Convention No. 169 and its shift from the prior philosophical stand.[57] The convention came into force in 1991 with the ratifications by Norway and Mexico.[58]

The basic theme of Convention No. 169 is indicated by the convention's preamble, which recognizes "the aspirations of [indigenous] peoples to exercise control over their own institutions, ways of life and economic development and to maintain and develop their identities, languages and religions, within the framework of the States in which they live."[59] Upon this premise, the convention includes provisions advancing indigenous cultural integrity,[60] land and resource rights,[61] and nondiscrimination in social welfare spheres;[62] and it generally enjoins states to respect indigenous peoples' aspirations in all decisions affecting them.[63]

Upon adoption of Convention No. 169 by the International Labour Conference in 1989, several advocates of indigenous peoples' rights expressed dissatisfaction with language in Convention No. 169, viewing it as not sufficiently constraining of government conduct in relation to indigenous peoples' concerns.[64] Criticism was leveled at several of the convention's provisions that contain caveats or appear in the form of recommendations, and at the underlying assumption of state authority over indigenous peoples.[65] Much of this criticism, however, was couched in highly legalistic terms and worst-case scenario readings of the convention without much regard to overall context. The overriding reason for disappointment appeared to be a grounded simply in frustration over the inability to dictate a convention in terms more sweeping than those included in the final text.

Convention No. 169 can be seen as a manifestation of the movement toward responsiveness to indigenous peoples' demands through international law and, at the same time, the tension inherent in that movement. Indigenous peoples have demanded recognition of rights that are of a collective character, rights among whose beneficiaries are historically grounded communities rather than simply individuals or (inchoate) states. The conceptualization and articulation of such rights collides with the individual/state perceptual dichotomy that has lingered in dominant conceptions of human society and persisted in the shaping of international standards. The asserted collective rights, furthermore, challenge notions of state sovereignty, which are especially jealous of matters of social and political organization within the presumed sphere of state authority.

The resulting difficulties in the development of Convention No. 169 manifested themselves especially over the debate on the use of the term *peoples* to identify the beneficiaries of the convention. As in other international contexts in which indigenous rights have been discussed, advocates pressed for use of the term *peoples* over *populations* to identify the beneficiary groups.[66] The former is generally regarded as implying a greater and more positive recognition of group identity and corresponding attributes of community. State governments, however, resisted use of the term *peoples* because of its association with the term *self-determination* (e.g., the phrase "self-determination and equal rights of peoples" of the United Nations Charter) which in turn has been associated with a right of independent statehood. The issue was all the more complicated because indigenous peoples generally have invoked "a right of self-determination" as an expression of their desire to continue as distinct communities free from oppression, while in virtually all instances denying aspirations to independent statehood.[67]

The peoples/populations controversy was in the end resolved by an unhappy compromise, which allowed use of the term *peoples* in the new convention, but with the following provision added to the text: "The use of the term 'peoples' in this convention shall not be construed as having any implications as regards the rights which may attach to the term under international law."[68] Furthermore it was agreed that the following appear in the record of the committee proceedings leading to the convention: "It is understood by the Committee that the use of the term 'peoples' in this Convention has no implication as regards the right to self-determination as understood in international law."[69]

The International Labour Office has taken the position that the qualifying language regarding the use of the term "peoples . . . did not limit the meaning of the term, in any way whatsoever" but rather simply was a means of leaving a decision on the implications of the usage of the term to procedures within the United Nations.[70] In any event, the qualifying language in the convention reflects an aversion on the part of numerous states to expressly acknowledge a right to self-determination for indigenous groups out of fear that it may imply an effective right of secession. Thus, while the development of Convention No. 169 promoted a reformed discourse on indigenous rights, express usage of the term *self-determination* in this connection continued to raise controversy.

It is nonetheless evident that the normative concept underlying indigenous peoples' self-determination rhetoric took hold to a substantial degree in Convention No. 169.[71] Even the qualified usage of the term *peoples* implies a certain affirmation of indigenous group identity and corresponding attributes of community. Whatever its shortcomings, moreover, Convention No. 169 succeeds in affirming the value of indigenous communities and cultures, and in setting forth a series of basic precepts in that regard. Although the convention "contains few absolute rules [it] fixes goals, priorities and minimal rights" that follow generally from indigenous peoples' articulated demands.[72] The convention, furthermore, is grounds for the invocation of international scrutiny over the particularized concerns of indigenous groups pursuant to the ILO's fairly well-developed mechanisms for implementing the standards expressed in ILO conventions.[73] Since the convention was adopted at the 1989 Labour Conference, indigenous peoples' organizations and their representatives increasingly have taken a pragmatic view and expressed support for the convention's ratification. Indigenous peoples' organizations from Central and South America have been especially active in pressing for ratification. Indigenous organizations from other regions that have expressed support for the convention include the Saami Council, the Inuit Circumpolar Conference, the World Council of Indigenous Peoples, and the National Indian Youth Council.

New and Emergent Customary International Law

ILO Convention No. 169 is significant to the extent it creates treaty obligations among ratifying states in line with current trends in thinking prompted by indigenous peoples' demands. The convention is further meaningful as part of a larger body of developments that can be understood as giving rise to new customary international law with the same normative thrust. Since the 1970s, the demands of indigenous peoples have been addressed continuously in one way or another within the United Nations and other international venues of authoritative normative discourse. The extended multilateral discussion promoted through the international system has involved states, nongovernmental organizations, independent experts, and indigenous peoples themselves. It is now evident that states and other relevant actors have reached a certain new common ground about minimum standards that should govern behavior toward indigenous peoples, and it is also evident that the standards are already in fact guiding behavior. Under modern theory, such a controlling consensus, following as it does from widely shared values of human dignity, constitutes customary international law.

Norms of customary international law arise—or to use the now much favored term *crystallize*—when a preponderance of states and other authoritative actors converge on a common understanding of the norms' contents and generally expect future behavior in conformity with those norms. Customary law is "generally observed to include two key elements: a 'material' element in certain past uniformities in behavior and a 'psychological' element, or *opinio juris*, in certain subjectivities of 'oughtness' attending such uniformities in behavior."[74] The traditional points of reference for determining the existence of a customary norm are patterns of communicative behavior involving physical episodic conduct. Such episodic conduct is illustrated by Professor D'Amato:

> [A] courier of state X delivers an unwelcome message to the king of state Y. The king imprisons the messenger. State X responds by sending another courier (obviously a reluctant one) who delivers the message that unless Y returns

the first courier safe and sound X will sack and destroy the towns of Y. If Y releases the first courier with an apology and perhaps a payment of gold, a resolution of the issue in this manner will lead to a rule that official couriers are entitled to immunity against imprisonment.[75]

Under traditional analysis, the content of the emergent rule and the required subjectivities of normative expectation (the so-called *opinio juris*) are inferred from the episodic conduct.

Today, however, interactive patterns around concrete events are not the only—or necessarily required—material elements constitutive of customary norms. With the advent of modern international intergovernmental institutions and enhanced communications media, states and other relevant actors increasingly engage in prescriptive dialogue. Especially in multilateral settings, explicit communication of this sort may itself bring about a convergence of understanding and expectation about rules, establishing in those rules a *pull toward compliance*—to use the terminology of Professor Thomas Franck[76]—even in advance of a widespread corresponding pattern of physical conduct.[77] It is thus increasingly understood that explicit communication among authoritative actors, whether or not in association with concrete events, is a form of practice that builds customary rules.[78] Of course, conforming conduct will strengthen emergent customary rules by enhancing attendant subjectivities of expectation.[79]

There has been a discernible movement toward a convergence of reformed normative understanding and expectation on the subject of indigenous peoples; under the theory just sketched, this movement is constitutive of customary international law. Relevant norm-building international practice, which has been substantially driven by indigenous peoples' own efforts, has entailed information gathering and evaluation, discussion and articulation of policies and norms, and the reporting of domestic initiatives against the backdrop of the developing norms.

A watershed in relevant U.N. activity was the 1971 resolution of the Economic and Social Council authorizing the U.N. Sub-Commission on Prevention of Discrimination and Protection of Minorities (now the Sub-Commission on the Promotion and Protection of Human Rights) to conduct a study on the "Problem of Discrimination against Indigenous Populations."[80] The resulting multivolume work by special rapporteur José Martínez Cobo[81] was issued originally as a series of partial reports from 1981 to 1983.[82] It compiled extensive data on indigenous peoples worldwide and made a series of findings and recommendations generally supportive of indigenous peoples' demands.[83] The Martínez Cobo study became a standard reference for discussion of the subject of indigenous peoples within the U.N. system. Moreover, it initiated a pattern of further information gathering and evaluative work on the subject by experts working under the sponsorship of international organizations.

An example of such further expert work on the subject of indigenous peoples was the 1981 Conference of Specialists on Ethnocide and Ethnodevelopment in Latin America, sponsored by the U.N. Educational, Scientific and Cultural Organization. The conference, held in San José, Costa Rica, adopted a declaration affirming the "inalienable right of Indian groups" to consolidate their cultural identity and to "exercise. . . self-determination."[84] Later expert seminars convened by the United Nations on various aspects of indigenous peoples' concerns, and reaching conclusions emphasizing this same theme, have included the participation of persons named by indigenous peoples' organizations.[85]

Upon the recommendation of the Martínez Cobo study and representatives of indigenous groups that attended the 1977 NGO Conference, the U.N. Human Rights Commission and the Economic and Social Council approved in 1982 the establishment of the U.N. Working Group on Indigenous Populations.[86] The working group is an organ of the Sub-Commission on the Promotion and Protection of Human Rights, which is composed of individuals who act in the capacity of independent human rights experts rather than government representatives. Since its creation, the working group has met annually in weeklong sessions. The working group's original mandate was to review developments concerning indigenous peoples and to work toward the development of corresponding international standards.[87] The scope of the working group's activity subsequently was expanded to include a study on treaties between indigenous peoples and states and another on indigenous cultural and intellectual property.[88] The working group is itself composed of five rotating members of the sub-commission. Through its policy of open participation in its annual sessions, however, the working group has become an important platform for the dissemination of information and exchange of views among indigenous peoples, governments, nongovernmental organizations, and others.

The working group's most groundbreaking work has been pursuant to its standard-setting mandate, which was refined when in 1985 the sub-commission approved the group's decision to draft a declaration on the rights of indigenous peoples for adoption by the U.N. General Assembly.[89] In 1988, the working group chair produced the first complete draft of the declaration, which substantially reflected proposals submitted by indigenous peoples' representatives.[90] Discussion of the declaration proceeded at subsequent sessions of the working group until it had completed, in 1993, its final revision of the draft for consideration by its parent bodies within the United Nations. In 1994 the sub-commission adopted the working group draft and submitted it to the U.N. Commission on Human Rights,[91] which subsequently established its own, ad hoc working group to work on the declaration.[92]

Through the process of drafting a declaration, the sub-commission's Working Group on Indigenous Populations engaged states, indigenous peoples, and others in an extended multilateral dialogue on the specific content of norms concerning indigenous peoples and their rights.[93] By welcoming commentary and proposals by indigenous peoples for over a decade, the working group provided an important means for indigenous peoples to promote their own conceptions about their rights within the international arena. As the drafting process proceeded in the group, more and more governments responded with their respective pronouncements on the content of indigenous peoples' rights. Virtually every state of the Western Hemisphere eventually came to participate in the working group discussion on the declaration. Canada, with its large indigenous population, took a leading role. States of other regions with significant indigenous populations also became active participants, especially Australia and New Zealand. The Philippines, Bangladesh, and India are just three of the other numerous states that at one time or another made oral or written submissions to the sub-commission working group in connection with the drafting of the declaration.

The development of ILO Convention No. 169 was an effective extension of the standard-setting discussion in the sub-commission working group, although indigenous groups participated less fully, given the formal ILO structure in which the drafting of Convention No. 169 took place.[94] Most of the states active in the working group's proceedings also took on visible roles in the committee of the International Labour Conference that drafted Convention No. 169. The United States, although it participated minimally in the working group's standard-setting activity, contributed notably to the ILO process.[95] Representatives of a total of thirty-nine governments participated in the conference committee, in addition to the worker and employee delegates who are part of the "tripartite" system of governance in the ILO.[96] The ILO treaty revision process accelerated the international discussion of indigenous peoples' rights by focusing it on the adoption of a normative instrument within a fairly short time frame.

With the increase in international attention to indigenous peoples' rights has come an expanding core of common opinion on the content of those rights, a core of opinion substantially shaped by indigenous peoples' contemporary demands and supported by years of official inquiry into the subject. This core of common opinion is reflected at least partly in the text of Convention No. 169, which was approved by the drafting committee by consensus[97] and adopted by the full conference by an overwhelming majority of the voting delegates.[98] None of the government delegates voted against adoption of the text, although a number abstained.[99] Government delegates who abstained, however, expressed concern primarily about the wording of certain provisions or about perceived ambiguities in the text, while in many instances indicating support for the core precepts of the new convention.[100]

Their trepidation about the text of Convention No. 169 was in large part a result of the limitations of language within the prevailing frame of international legal rhetoric. Within this prevailing frame, as indicated earlier,[101] words used to signify group identity or entitlements raise already heightened sensitivities about state sovereignty, often overshadowing the consensus on underlying normative precepts. For example, a number of states that abstained from voting in favor of adoption of Convention No. 169 at the 1989 Labour Conference expressed concern about the use of the term *territories* in the convention. The term *territories* is used there to signify indigenous peoples' interests in the total environment of the areas in which they live.[102] While not disagreeing with the specific meaning attached to the term in the convention, some governments expressed fear that its usage would imply a competing sovereignty, given the traditional usage of the term *territory* in association with independent statehood.[103] Yet despite such rhetorical sensitivities, which made a small minority of governments abstain from voting in favor of the convention, no government recorded outright rejection of the essential principles represented in the text. In fact, several of the abstaining governments indicated support for the convention's basic thrust by reporting domestic initiatives generally consistent with the convention.[104]

Since the convention was adopted in 1989, government comments directed at developing an indigenous rights declaration in the U.N. sub-commission working group, the sub-commission itself, and the U.N. Commission on Human Rights generally have affirmed the basic precepts set forth in the convention, and indeed the comments indicate an emerging consensus that accords even more closely with indigenous peoples' demands.[105] During the last several years discussions within the Commission on Human Rights working group on the declaration have continued to reflect divergent views among indigenous and state representatives about certain aspects of the draft declaration that was developed by the sub-commission working group. Nonetheless, these same discussions have helped to consolidate consensus about certain core principles that are reflected in the draft.[106] Furthermore the Draft United Nations Declaration on the Rights of Indigenous Peoples, which was adopted by the full body of independent experts who constitute the sub-commission, stands in its own right as an authoritative statement of norms concerning indigenous peoples on the basis of generally applicable human rights principles; and it is also a manifestation of the movement in a corresponding consensual nexus of opinion on the subject among relevant actors. The extensive deliberations leading to the draft declaration, in which indigenous peoples themselves played a leading role, enhance the authoritativeness and legitimacy of the draft.

The draft U.N. declaration goes beyond Convention No. 169, especially in its bold statements in areas of indigenous self-determination,[107] land and resource rights,[108] and rights of political autonomy.[109] It is clear that not *all* are satisfied with *all* aspects of the draft declaration developed by the sub-commission working group. Some indigenous peoples' representatives have criticized the draft for not going far enough, while governments typically have held that it goes too far. Nonetheless, a common ground of opinion exists among experts, indigenous peoples, and governments about indigenous peoples' rights and attendant standards of government behavior, and that widening common ground is in some measure reflected in the sub-commission draft.

This common ground also is reflected in government and other authoritative statements made in the context of ongoing parallel efforts to develop a declaration on indigenous peoples' rights within the Organization of American States. In 1989, the OAS General Assembly resolved to "request the Inter-American Commission on Human Rights to prepare a juridical instrument relative to the rights of indigenous peoples."[110] Pursuant to this task, the Inter-American Commission on Human Rights developed a Proposed American Declaration on the Rights of Indigenous Peoples, [111] after having consulted and gathered comments from governments and indigenous peoples from throughout the Americas about the nature and content of the rights to be included in the proposed instrument.[112] Subsequently, the OAS General Assembly established, as an organ of the Permanent Council's Committee on Juridical and Political Affairs, a working group of OAS member status to study the commission's proposed declaration.[113] This working group has met on several occasions with the participation of representatives of indigenous peoples from throughout the Western Hemisphere.[114] Although reflecting a range of views over multiple areas of concern to indigenous peoples, the written and oral commentary on the proposed American declaration substantially confirms the core of consensus evident in the procedures surrounding the draft U.N. declaration and ILO Convention No. 169.[115]

Further norm-building activity that draws from this consensus is under way within the African region. In November 2003 the African Commission on Human and Peoples' Rights, an expert body affiliated with the African Union, adopted a resolution "[r]ecognizing the standards in International law for the promotion and protection of the rights of minorities and indigenous peoples,"[116] and establishing a new working group to promote "the rights of indigenous populations/communities in Africa."[117] The working group is mandated to collect information and investigate the situations of indigenous peoples, and to make proposals on "appropriate measures and activities to prevent and remedy violations of the human rights and fundamental freedoms of indigenous populations/communities."[118] The establishment of this working group is an important development in favor of discerning and applying the normative regime attached to the concept of indigenous peoples in a region in which the concept has been hotly contested.[119]

Other international initiatives, as well as already developed normative instruments, contribute to a new generation of international consensus on indigenous peoples' rights.[120] The consensus on the need to recognize and protect the cultural integrity of indigenous peoples is reflected in, and further advanced by, specific references to indigenous children in various articles of the Convention on the Rights of the Child, an international treaty that has been ratified by almost all of the world's states. In particular, article 30 of the convention affirms:

In those States in which ethnic, religious or linguistic minorities or persons of indigenous origin exist, a child belonging to such a minority or who is indigenous shall not be denied the right, in community with other members of his or her group, to enjoy his or her own culture, to profess and practise his or her own religion, or to use his or her own language.[121]

In yet another development, the state parties to the Amazonian Cooperation Treaty agreed in 1989 to establish a Special Commission on Indigenous Affairs with the objective of "[e]nsuring the effective participation by each Amazonian Country's indigenous populations in all phases of the characterization of indigenous affairs," especially in regard to development programs.[122] The commission subsequently adopted a work plan giving priority to the recognition and protection of indigenous land and resource rights. A larger segment of the indigenous peoples of the Western Hemisphere benefit by the creation of an Indigenous Peoples' Fund, pursuant to a convention signed at the Second Summit Meeting of Ibero-American Heads of State in 1992.[123] The fund is to address the development needs of indigenous peoples in countries of Latin America and the Caribbean, in accordance with decision-making procedures that include representative indigenous organizations.

In 1991 the World Bank adopted a revised policy directive in view of the pervasive role the bank plays in financing development projects in less-developed countries where many of the world's indigenous people live.[124] Much of the discussion within international institutions about indigenous peoples has focused not just upon the potential benefits of development programs aimed specifically at indigenous groups but also upon the damaging effects of many industrial development projects that have taken place in areas traditionally occupied by indigenous groups.[125] The World Bank adopted Operational Directive 4.20 after a period of expert study that helped reshape attitudes within the bank toward greater programmatic action concerning indigenous peoples affected by bank-funded projects, action in line with contemporary trends in thinking about their rights.[126]

Resolutions adopted at the 1992 U.N. Conference on Environment and Development include provisions on indigenous people and their communities. The Rio Declaration,[127] and the more detailed environmental program and policy statement known as Agenda 21,[128] reiterates precepts of indigenous peoples' rights and seeks to incorporate them within the larger agenda of global environmentalism and sustainable development.[129] Resolutions adopted at subsequent major U.N. conferences—the 1993 World Conference on Human Rights, the 1994 U.N. Conference on Population and Development, the World Summit on Social Development of 1995, the Fourth World Conference on Women of 1995, and the World Conference Against Racism of 2001—similarly include provisions that affirm or are consistent with prevailing normative assumptions in this regard.[130]

In its 1989 resolution "on the Position of the World's Indians," the European Parliament expressed its concern over the conditions faced by indigenous peoples and called on governments to secure indigenous land rights and enter consultations with indigenous groups to develop specific measures to protect their rights.[131] Elaborating upon these and related themes, the European Parliament adopted another resolution in 1994, on "Measures Required Internationally to Provide Effective Protection for Indigenous Peoples."[132] The 1994 resolution holds that indigenous peoples have the "right to determine their own destiny by choosing their institutions, their political status and that of their territory."[133] In the same vein, the European Commission, the executive organ of the European Union, released in 1998 a "Working Document on support for indigenous peoples in the development co-operation of the Community and Member States."[134] This document promotes a series of development programs for the benefit of indigenous peoples which are to be based upon their full participation and informed consent, with the objective of establishing conditions by which these peoples are able to maintain control over their own economic, social, and cultural development.

More generally emphasizing the underlying need for international attention and cooperation to secure indigenous peoples in the full enjoyment of their rights are the following: the 1972 resolution of the Inter-American Commission on Human Rights identifying patterns of discrimination against indigenous peoples and stating that "special protection for indigenous populations constitutes a sacred commitment of the States"[135]; the Helsinki Document 1992—The Challenge of Change, adopted by the Conference on Security and Cooperation in Europe, which includes a provision "[n]oting that persons belonging to indigenous populations may have special problems in exercising their rights"[136]; article 8(j) of the Convention on Biological Diversity, which affirms the value of traditional indigenous knowledge in connection with conservation, sustainable development, and intellectual property regimes[137]; parts of the Vienna Declaration and Programme of Action adopted by the 1993 United Nations Conference on Human Rights, urging greater focus on indigenous peoples' concerns within the U.N. system[138]; the 1997 Charter of Civil Society for the Caribbean Community, by which Caribbean states "recognise the contribution of the indigenous peoples to the development process and undertake to continue to protect their historical rights . . . culture and way of life"[139]; and the OAS Inter-American Democratic Charter of 2001, which links promoting the rights of indigenous peoples with the strengthening of democracy.[140]

The foregoing demonstrates a substantial level of international concern for indigenous peoples, along with a certain convergence of international opinion about the content of indigenous peoples' rights. This convergence of opinion carries subjectivities of obligation and expectation attendant upon the rights, regardless of any treaty ratification or other formal act of assent to the norms articulated. The discussion of indigenous peoples and their rights as promoted through international institutions and conferences has proceeded in response to demands that indigenous groups have made over several years and upon an extensive record of justification.[141] The pervasive assumption has been that the articulation of norms concerning indigenous peoples is an exercise in identifying standards of conduct that are *required* to uphold widely shared values of human dignity. Accordingly, indigenous peoples' rights typically are regarded as, and can be demonstrated to be, derivative of previously accepted, generally applicable human rights principles.[142] The multilateral processes that build a common understanding of the content of indigenous peoples' rights, therefore, also build expectations that the rights will be upheld.

Furthermore, the sense of obligation that attaches to newly articulated norms concerning indigenous peoples is properly viewed as being of a legal and not just moral character. Traditionally, there has been a distinction between subjectivities of *moral* as opposed to *legal* obligation or expectation, with only the latter qualifying as *opinio juris*, the essential psychological component of customary law. This distinction between moral and legal obligation is a product of the positivist thinking that prevailed in international legal discourse at the turn of the century. Under such thinking, it was possible for a state to violate widely shared and followed moral precepts while not infringing upon international law.[143] However, contemporary international law now includes broad moral precepts among its constitutional elements, particularly within the rubric of human rights. The United Nations Charter and the constituent texts of the major regional intergovernmental organizations, along with an infusion of normative discourse within authoritative processes of decision over the last several decades, have firmly established an obligation to uphold human rights as a matter of general international law.[144] The *legal* character of the obligation can thus be seen to attach to all the subjectivities of obligation that surface within the realm of human rights.[145]

The consequent demise of the traditional distinction between moral and legal subjectivities for the purposes of identifying customary law is evident in contemporary jurisprudential studies. For Miguel D'Estéfano, state practice builds customary law where it is a response to "an idea of justice and humanity."[146] Professor Meron finds *opinio juris* in a subjective belief that a practice follows from "compelling principles of humanity."[147] Similarly, Professors McDougal, Laswell, and Chen hold that "subjectivities of oughtness [*opinio juris*] required to attend . . . uniformities of behaviour may relate to many different systems of norms, such as prior authority, natural law, reason, morality, or religion."[148]

Thus, insofar as there is both a pattern of communicative behavior regarding the content of indigenous peoples' rights and a convergence of attendant subjectivities of obligation or expectation, as is evident in recent developments, there is customary international law. The claim here is not that each of the authoritative documents referred to can be taken in its entirety as articulating customary law but that the documents represent core precepts that are widely accepted and, to that extent, are indicative of customary law.

This assertion was adopted and promoted by the Inter-American Commission on Human Rights in prosecuting the *Case of the Mayagna Awas Tingni Community v. Nicaragua*[149] before the Inter-American Court of Human Rights, in relation to norms concerning indigenous land rights. The commission relied on several of the documents referenced here to argue to the court that, as a matter of customary international law, indigenous peoples have property rights in conformity with their traditional land tenure.[150] The Court itself did not explicitly adopt this position; however, in ruling that Nicaragua had violated the property rights of the Awas Tingni Community by failing to protect the community's land tenure, the court applied an "evolutionary interpretation" of the property rights provision of the American Convention of Human Rights and invoked the same concepts of indigenous land rights that are reflected in numerous international instruments.[151] In his separate opinion concurring in the judgment the Court, Judge Sergio Ramírez specifically cited ILO Convention No. 169 and the drafts of the U.N. and OAS declarations to identify "an ever broader and more robust consensus" on the rights of indigenous peoples, which, he emphasized, should guide the court's interpretation of the American Convention.[152] Thus, although not as explicitly as did the inter-American commission, the inter-American Court contributed to the *opinio juris* related to developing customary international norms of indigenous land rights, while simultaneously demonstrating that those norms, and the *opinio juris* underlying them, are at least partly grounded in previously articulated and accepted human rights norms of general applicability, such as the right to property. Other international bodies have likewise contributed to the development of customary international norms concerning indigenous peoples, by reinforcing those norms through interpretation of human rights treaties of general applicability.[153]

The existence of customary norms concerning indigenous peoples and their pull toward compliance is confirmed especially by statements that governments make about relevant domestic policies and initiatives before international bodies concerned with promoting indigenous peoples' rights. The government practice of reporting on domestic policies and initiatives has been a regular feature of the U.N. sub-commission working group's activity under its mandate "to review developments pertaining to . . . the human rights and fundamental freedoms of indigenous populations."[154] In addition, several governments made statements on domestic developments during the negotiation of ILO Convention No. 169 and upon its submission for a record vote.[155] Within these and other contexts of international multilateral discourse,[156] more and more states have entered the discussion of developments concerning indigenous peoples, affirming a pattern of responsiveness to indigenous peoples' demands.[157]

The written and oral statements of governments reporting domestic initiatives to international bodies are doubly indicative of customary norms. First, the accounts of government conduct provide evidence of behavioral trends by which the contours of underlying standards can be discerned or confirmed, notwithstanding the persistent difficulties among governments and others in agreement on normative language for inclusion in written texts. Second, because the reports are made to international audiences concerned with promoting indigenous peoples' rights, they provide strong indication of subjectivities of obligation and expectation attendant upon the discernible standards.

Illustrative are the following statements to the 1993 World Conference on Human Rights in Vienna under the agenda item "Commemoration of the International Year of the World's Indigenous People."

Statement of Colombia on Behalf of the Latin American and Caribbean Group

In Latin America there exists a process of recognizing the role played by indigenous cultures in the definition of our identity, a process which takes the form of State measures, through constitutional and legislative means, to accord respect to indigenous cultures, the return of indigenous lands, indigenous administration of justice and participation in the definition of government affairs, especially as concerns their communities.

Within the framework of State unity, this process is characterized by the consecration in some constitutions of the multiethnic character of our societies.[158]

Statement on Behalf of the Delegations of Finland, Sweden and Norway

In the Nordic countries, the Sami people and their culture have made most valuable contributions to our societies. Strengthening the Sami culture and identity is a common goal for the Nordic governments. Towards this end, elected bodies in the form of Sami Assemblies, have been established to secure Sami participation in the decision making process in questions affecting them. Cross border cooperation both between Sami organizations and between local governments in the region has also provided a fruitful basis for increasing awareness and development of Sami culture.[159]

Statement by the Delegation of the Russian Federation

[W]e have drawn up a stage-by-stage plan of work.

At the first stage we elaborated the draft law entitled "Fundamentals of the Russian legislation on the legal status of small indigenous peoples" which was adopted by the Parliament on June 11, 1993.

This Law reflects . . .

collective rights of small peoples in bodies of state power and administration, in local representative bodies and local administration;

legitimized ownership rights for land and natural resources in regions where such peoples traditionally live;

guarantees for the preservation of language and culture.

The next stage consists in elaborating the specific mechanism for the implementation of this law. Work is underway on draft laws on family communities and nature use.[160]

Made over a decade ago, these are the kind of statements that continue to be uttered by state representatives in numerous international forums. These and other such statements that are made without reference to any treaty obligation manifest the existence of customary norms. Evident in each of these statements is the implied acceptance of certain normative precepts grounded in general human rights principles. And because the developments reported in these statements are independently verifiable, despite continuing problems not reflected in the government accounts, it is evident that the underlying standards are in fact guiding or influencing behavior. Over the last several years, numerous states have enacted constitutional provisions or laws that more or less reflect the developing international consensus about indigenous peoples' rights.[161] A great deal remains to be done to see these constitutional provisions and laws fully implemented, just as for many indigenous peoples the emerging international customary norms remain an ideal distant from reality. In any case, customary norms of international law are reinforced by conforming domestic laws and related practice—even more so when states hold their domestic acts out to the international community as correct; on the other hand, nonconforming domestic practice does not undermine the apparent direction of the international norm building except to the extent the nonconformity is held out and eventually accepted as legitimate under the international regime.[162]

As customary international norms take shape around a certain consensus of what counts as legitimate in relation to indigenous peoples, the specific contours of these norms are still evolving and remain somewhat ambiguous. Yet a lack of perfect uniformity in the relevant practice and opinion does not negate the norms' existence in some form. Despite imprecision in the outer contours of a new generation of internationally operative norms, their core elements increasingly are confirmed and reflected in the extensive multilateral dialogue and processes of decision focused on indigenous peoples and their rights. Even though imprecise and still evolving, common understandings about the rights of indigenous peoples— understandings that can be characterized as customary international law—are sufficiently crystalized to mark the parameters of any discussion or decision in the international arena in response to the demands of indigenous peoples.

The contemporary international law of indigenous peoples, which includes ILO Convention No. 169 and customary law, is a dramatic manifestation of the mobilization of social forces through the human rights frame of the contemporary international system. Indigenous peoples themselves have been at the helm of a movement that has challenged state-centered structures and precepts which have continued within international law and global organization. This movement, although fraught with tension, has resulted in a heightened international concern over indigenous peoples and a constellation of internationally accepted norms generally in line with indigenous peoples' own demands and aspirations.

Notes

1. *See generally* Ian Brownlie, *Principles of Public International Law* 85–101 (6th ed. 2003) (discussing theories of recognition of statehood).

2. *See generally* Jonathan I. Charney, "Transnational Corporations and Developing Public International Law," 1983 *Duke L.J.* 748; W. Feld, *Nongovernmental Forces and World Politics: A Study of Business, Labor and Political Groups* (1972); Krysztof Skubiszewski, "Forms of Participation of International Organizations in the Law-Making Process," 18 *Int'l Org.* 790 (1964); Nigel S. Rodley, "The Work of Non-Governmental Organizations in the World Wide Promotion and Protection of Human Rights," *United Nations Bulletin of Human Rights,* No. 90/1 (1991), at 90–93.

3. For an excellent discussion of the participants in the post-United Nations Charter international legal system, including participants other than states, *see* Rosalyn Higgins, *Problems and Process: International Law and How We Use It* 39–55 (1994). *See also* Wolfgang Friedmann, *The Changing Structure of International Law* (1964); Manuel Rama-Montaldo, "International Legal Personality and Implied Powers of International Organizations," 44 *Brit. Y.B. Int'l L.* 111 (1970); *Restatement of the Law (Third): The Foreign Relations Law of the United States,* sec. 101, at 22 (regarding international law's applicability to individuals); *id.* sec. 219, at 140 (legal status of international organizations).

4. *See generally International Human Rights in Context: Law, Politics, Morals* (Henry J. Steiner & Philip Alston eds., 2d ed. 2000); *Human Rights in the World Community: Issues and Action* (Richard P. Claude & Burns H. Weston eds., 2d ed. 1992); *New Directions in Human Rights* (Ellen Lutz et al. eds., 1989); Vernon Van Dyke, *Human Rights, Ethnicity, and Discrimination* (1985). This discourse is encouraged by a reassertion of moral argument, akin to historical natural law method, in modern jurisprudence concerning both international and domestic processes of decision. *See generally* George W. Paton, *A Textbook of Jurisprudence* 106–17 (David P. Derham ed., 3d ed. 1964) (surveying modern natural law theories). Examples of contemporary, influential jurisprudential studies that draw upon the natural law approach to influence authoritative decision making are Carlos Santiago Nino, *The Ethics of Human Rights* (1991); Ronald Dworkin, *Law's Empire* (1986); and Lon Fuller, *The Morality of Law* (rev. ed. 1977).

5. *See supra* chapter 1, notes 1–42 and accompanying text (discussing natural law theorists of the late Middle Ages and early Renaissance).

6. *See generally United Nations, Divided World: The UN's Roles in International Relations* (Adam Roberts & Benedict Kingsbury eds., 2d ed. 1993).

7. U.N. Charter art. 2, paras. 1, 4, 7.

8. *Id.* art. 4.

9. *Id.* art. 1, para. 2.

10. *Id.* art. 1, para. 3.

11. *Id.* art. 55.

12. *See id.* art. 1, para. 1; preamble.

13. *See id.* arts. 18 (General Assembly), 27 (Security Council), 67 (Economic and Social Council), 89 (Trusteeship Council).

14. *See id.* arts. 93, 96; Statute of the International Court of Justice, June 26, 1945, arts. 34, 35, 65 T.S. No. 993, 3 Bevans 1179.

15. *See* U.N. Charter art. 23, para. 1.

16. *Id.* art. 56.

17. *Id.* art. 71.

18. *See generally* Pei-heng Chiang, *Non-governmental Organizations at the United Nations: Identity, Role, and Function* (1981); Philip Taylor, *Nonstate Actors in International Politics: From Transregional to Substate Organizations* (1984).

19. *See* David Bowett, *The Law of International Institutions* 87 (4th ed. 1982).

20. For a compilation of human rights instruments developed through U.N. and related processes, see United Nations, *Human Rights: A Compilation of International Instruments*, U.N. Doc. ST/HR/1/Rev.6, U.N. Sales No. E.02.XIV.4 (vol. 1, pts. 1 & 2) (2002). Extensive international human rights regimes also have been developed through the Organization of American States, the Council of Europe and the Organization of African Unity. These regimes are summarized in Burns Weston, Robin Lukes, & Kelly Hnatt, "Regional Human Rights Regimes: A Comparison and Appraisal," in *Human Rights in the World Community, supra* note 4, at 244.

21. It is generally agreed that there is now a minimal corpus of human rights guarantees that is binding on all states as a matter of customary international law. Mark W. Janis, *An Introduction to International Law* 253–61 (4th ed. 2003); Tom J. Farer, "The United Nations and Human Rights: More Than a Whimper, Less Than a Roar" 9 *Hum. Rts. Q.* 550 (1987). *See also* Filartiga v. Peña-Irala, 630 F.2d 876 (2d Cir. 1980) (right against torture as customary international law). For a description of the methodology and institutions for the enforcement of human rights norms, see *Guide to International Human Rights Practice* (Hurst Hannum ed., 3d ed. 1999). *See also* chapters 5 and 6, *infra* (discussing implementation procedures for human rights norms for the benefit of indigenous peoples).

22. *See Human Rights in the World Community, supra* note 4, at 3–5; Mark Janis, *supra* note 21, at 253–85; Erica-Irene Daes, *Status of the Individual and Contemporary International Law: Promotion, Protection, and Restoration of Human Rights at the National, Regional, and International Levels*, U.N. Sales No. E.91.XIV.3, at 21 (1992).

23. *See supra* chapter 1, notes 51–53 and accompanying text.

24. *See generally The Rights of Peoples* (James Crawford ed., 1988) (an anthology of perspectives on peoples' and group rights within the international human rights frame). The burgeoning attention to groups and group rights in international legal discourse is highlighted by the *International Journal on Group Rights*, published by Martinus Nijhoff Publishers.

25. *See supra* chapter 1, notes 10–14 and accompanying text.

26. Chapters XII and XIII of the U.N. Charter created a trusteeship system similar to but with results more effective than the system of mandates under the League of Nations, the failed attempt at world organization that preceded the U.N. at the close of World War I. U.N. trusteeship was established for the territories detached from the powers defeated in World War II with the objective of moving the territories to self-governing or independent status. Of far greater scope and impact has been the program pursuant to Chapter XI of the Charter, entitled "Declaration on Non-Self-Governing Territories," establishing special duties for U.N. members "which have or assume responsibilities for the administration of territories whose peoples have not yet attained a full measure of

self-government." U.N. Charter art. 73. Under article 73 of Chapter XI, such members commit themselves:

> a. to ensure, with due respect for the culture of the peoples concerned, their political, economic, social, and educational advancement, their just treatment, and their protection against abuses;
>
> b. to develop self-government, to take due account of the political aspirations of the peoples, and to assist them in the progressive development of their free political institutions, according to the particular circumstances of each territory and its peoples and their varying stages of advancement . . .
>
> . . . .
>
> e. to transmit regularly to the Secretary-General for information purposes, subject to such limitation as security and constitutional considerations may require, statistical and other information of a technical nature relating to economic, social, and educational conditions in the territories for which they are respectively responsible.

Id. The General Assembly created a list of territories subject to the reporting requirement of article 73(e) of Chapter XI and developed a committee structure to deliberate upon the reports with a view toward promoting Chapter XI policies. After a period of resistance by colonial powers, the General Assembly became increasingly engaged in promoting decolonization on the basis of Chapter XI and related Charter principles. *See* Robert E. Riggs & Jack C. Plano, *The United Nations: International Organization and World Politics* 193–98 (2d ed. 1994) (discussing U.N. procedures under Chapter XI).

27. *See* Declaration on the Granting of Independence to Colonial Countries and Peoples, G.A. Res. 1514(XV), Dec. 14, 1960, para. 5, U.N. GAOR, 15th Sess., Supp. No. 16, at 66, U.N. Doc. A/4684 (1961) ("Immediate steps shall be taken, in . . . Non-Self-Governing Territories . . . to transfer all powers to the peoples of those territories."); Malcolm Shaw, *Title to Territory in Africa: International Legal Issues* 93 (1986) (discussing the arbitrary character of colonial boundaries in Africa in terms of the ethnic composition of the indigenous populations, boundaries that were left intact through decolonization).

28. Under Resolution 1541, a territory ceases to be non–self-governing by "(a) [e]mergence as a sovereign independent State; (b) [f]ree association with an independent State; or (c) [i]ntegration with an independent State." Principles Which Should Guide Members in Determining Whether or Not an Obligation Exists to Transmit the Information Called for in Article 73(e) of the Charter of the United Nations (Declaration on Non-Self-Governing Territories), G.A. Res. 1541(XV), Dec. 15, 1960, principle 6, U.N. GAOR, 15th Sess., Supp. No. 16, at 29, U.N. Doc. A/4684 (1961). Ofuatey-Kodjoe concludes that G.A. Res. 1541 is generally reflective of international practice in the application of the principle of self-determination to the colonial territories. W. Ofuatey-Kodjoe, *The Principle of Self-Determination in International Law* 115–28 (1977).

29. *See* G.A. Res. 1541, *supra* note 28 ("Free association should be the result of a free and voluntary choice by the peoples of the territory concerned.").

30. The blue water, or salt water, thesis was developed in opposition to efforts by certain colonial powers (particularly Belgium and France) to expand the scope of the

obligations and procedures of Chapter XI of the U.N. Charter, which concerns non-self-governing territories, to include enclave indigenous populations. Ofuatey-Kodjoe, *supra* note 28, at 119. These states argued that the "primitive" communities living within the frontiers of many states were in relevant respects indistinguishable from the peoples living in colonial territories, an argument apparently advanced for self-serving ends to diffuse the political momentum coalescing against colonialism. Gordon Bennett, *Aboriginal Rights in International Law* 12–13 (1978). Latin American states especially opposed the expansive interpretion of Chapter XI and eventually prevailed in securing the more restrictive interpretation, which effectively limited Chapter XI procedures to overseas colonial territories. *Id.* The blue water thesis was incorporated into G.A. Res. 1541, *supra* note 28, which states in relevant part:

Principle IV

Prima facie there is an obligation to transmit information in respect of a territory which is geographically separate and is distinct ethnically and/or culturally from the country administering it.

Principle V

Once it has been established that such a *prima facie* case of geographical and ethnical or cultural distinctness of a territory exists, other elements may then be brought into consideration. These additional elements may be, *inter alia*, of an administrative, political, juridical, economic or historical nature.

31. G.A. Res. 275(III) (1949).

32. *See* U.N. ESCOR, 11th Sess., 397th mtg., July 24, 1950, U.N. Doc. E/SR.397 (1950). The initiative for a study foundered in the face of opposition by affected states. *See id. See also* Hurst Hannum, "New Developments in Indigenous Rights," 28 *Va. J. Int'l L.* 649, 657–58 (1988).

33. Convention (No. 107) Concerning the Protection and Integration of Indigenous and Other Tribal and Semi-Tribal Populations in Independent Countries, June 26, 1957, International Labour Conference, 328 U.N.T.S. 247 (entered into force June 2, 1959) [hereinafter ILO Convention No. 107].

34. Recommendation (No. 104) Concerning the Protection of Indigenous and Other Tribal and Semi-Tribal Populations in Independent Countries, International Labour Conference, June 26, 1957, *International Labour Conventions and Recommendations, 1919–1991*, at 636 (1992).

35. Professor Hannum recounts the history of ILO activity leading to the adoption of ILO Convention No. 107 as follows:

As early as 1921, the ILO carried out a series of studies on indigenous workers. In 1926, it established a Committee of Experts on Native Labour, whose work led to the adoption of a number of conventions and recommendations concerning forced labor and recruitment practices of indigenous groups. A second Committee of Experts on Indigenous Labour first met in 1951. It encouraged states to extend legislative provisions to all segments of their population, including indigenous communities, and called for improved education, vocational training, social security, and protection in the field of labor for indigenous peoples. Finally, in 1953, the ILO published a comprehensive reference book, entitled *Indigenous Peoples: Living and Working Conditions of Aboriginal Populations in Independent Countries*, which provided a survey of indigenous populations throughout the world and a summary of national and international action to aid these groups.

Hannum, *supra* note 32, at 652–53 (footnotes omitted).

36. The adoption of ILO Convention No. 107, for example, corresponds to the "termination" period in the United States during which federal policy was to promote the assimilation of Indian cultures by terminating federal recognition of their tribal status. *See generally* David H. Getches et al., *Federal Indian Law: Cases and Materials* 204–224 (4th ed. 1998).

37. This perceptual dichotomy and its historical implications for indigenous peoples is discussed in chapter 1, *supra* notes 43–71 and accompanying text.

38. *See* Rodolfo Stavenhagen, *The Ethnic Question: Conflicts, Development, and Human Rights* 5–6, U.N. Sales No. E.90.III.A.9 (1990).

39. The first article of the convention states: "This Convention applies to . . . *members* of tribal or semi-tribal populations." Convention No. 107 art. 1, para. 1 (emphasis added).

40. *See* Convention Providing for the Creation of an Inter-American Indian Institute, Nov. 1, 1940, T.S. No. 978, 3 Bevans 661.

41. Rodolfo Stavenhagen characterizes the periodic conferences sponsored by the institute as establishing the parameters for an ideology justifying the assimilationist policies that many governments vigorously pursued. Rodolfo Stavenhagen, "La Situación y los derechos de los pueblos indígenas de América," 52 *América Indígena*, Nos. 1–2, at 89 (1992). As indigenous peoples themselves consolidated a movement that rejected the assimilationist approach in the 1980s and 1990s, see *infra* notes 42–54 and accompanying text, the institute's influence and activities diminished and it entered a period of virtual inactivity.

42. In the United States, for example, several young Indians, among them college graduates, appeared uninvited at the 1961 Conference on Indian Policy organized with the help of the University of Chicago Anthropology Department. They issued a statement declaring "the inherent right of self-government" of Indian people and that they "mean to hold the scraps and parcels [of their lands] as earnestly as any small nation or ethnic group was ever determined to hold on to identity and survival." Moreover, the young activists used the conference as a springboard for the creation of the National Indian Youth Council and with it a new form of Indian advocacy connected with the larger civil rights movement. Later developments included the formation of other Indian activist organizations, including the American Indian Movement and its international arm, the International Indian Treaty Council.

43. Important elements of this process included widely read works by indigenous authors, *e.g.*, Vine Deloria, Jr., *Custer Died for Your Sins* (1969) (Vine Deloria is Standing Rock Sioux); Ramiro Reinaga, *Ideología y Raza en América Latina* (1972) (Ramiro Reinaga is Quechua).

44. An extensive, analytical account of indigenous peoples' efforts internationally beginning in the 1970s is in Bice Maiguashca's paper, "The Role of Ideas in a Changing World Order: The Case of the International Indigenous Movement, 1975–91," which was delivered at the conference, Changing World Order and the United Nations System, in Yokohama, Japan, March 24–27, 1992. *See also* Ronald Niezen, *The Origins of Indigenism: Human Rights and the Politics of Indigenism* 29–52 (2003); Franke Wilmer, *The Indigenous Voice in World Politics: Since Time Immemorial* (1993) Alison Brysk, *From Tribal Village to Global Village: Indian Rights and International Relations in Latin America* (2000).

45. *See generally* Bernadette Kelly Roy & Gudmundur Alfredsson, "Indigenous Rights: The Literature Explosion," 13 *Transnat'l Persp.* 19 (1987).

46. For a description and analysis of the origins of the indigenous rights movement and the emergence of a transnational indigenous identity, *see* Niezen, *supra* note 44, at 29–93.

47. Indigenous peoples' representatives at the conference drafted and circulated a draft Declaration of Principles for the Defense of the Indigenous Nations and Peoples of the Western Hemisphere. The declaration, reprinted in the appendix, *infra*, became an early benchmark for indigenous peoples' demands upon the international community. Other important international conferences in the 1970s and 1980s were the periodic conferences of the Inuit Circumpolar Conference and the World Council of Indigenous Peoples. The Fourth General Assembly of the World Council of Indigenous Peoples, held in Panama in 1984, developed a declaration of principles, which is reproduced in the *Report of the Working on Indigenous Populations at its Fourth Session*, Annex 3, U.N. Doc. E/CN.4/Sub.2/1985/22 (1985) [hereinafter *1985 Working Group Report*], and also in the appendix, *infra*. Bice Maiguashca identifies this declaration and the declaration produced at the 1977 NGO conference in Geneva as constituting the core of "the indigenous counter-hegemonic project." Maiguashca, *supra* note 44, at 16. Another important declaration was the one produced and signed by indigenous NGOs from throughout the world in attendance at the 1985 and 1987 sessions of the U.N. Working Group on Indigenous Populations, which declaration appears in U.N. Doc. E/CN.4/Sub.2/1987/22, Annex 5 (1987), and in the appendix, *infra*. *See also* Proposed Universal Declaration on Indigenous Rights by the Assembly of First Nations (Canada), reprinted in U.N. Doc. E/CN.4/Sub.2/AC.4/1989/5 (1989). With increasing frequency over the last several years, indigenous peoples have organized international conferences on an *ad hoc* basis or in association with other international events. One such conference was the World Conference of Indigenous Peoples on Territory, Environment and Development, held in Kari-Oca village, Brazil, in May 1992, in anticipation of the U.N.-sponsored World Conference on Environment and Development. The Kari-Oca conference produced a multifaceted declaration on development strategies; culture, science, and intellectual property; and on indigenous rights generally.

48. *See generally Rethinking Indian Law* 139–76 (National Lawyers Guild ed., 1982) (discussing indigenous peoples' efforts of the late 1970s–early 1980s within the U.N. Commission on Human Rights and its Sub-Commission on Prevention of Discrimination and Protection of Minorities). *See also infra* notes 86–93 and accompanying text (discussing indigenous peoples' participation in the U.N. Working Group on Indigenous

Populations, which was created in 1982); *infra* chapter 7, notes 28–66 and accompanying text (discussing cases involving indigenous individuals and groups before the U.N. Human Rights Committee pursuant to the complaint procedures of the Optional Protocol to the International Covenant on Civil and Political Rights).

49. These organizations today include the Aboriginal and Torres Strait Islander Commission, American Indian Law Alliance, Asian Indigenous and Tribal Peoples Network, Assembly of First Nations–National Indian Brotherhood, Asociación Kunas Unidos por Napguana, Association of Indigenous Peoples of the North, Siberia and Far East of the Russian Federation (RAIPON), Cherokee Nation of New Jersey, the Consejo Indio de Sud-América (CISA), Four Directions Council, Grand Council of the Crees (of Québec), Indian Law Resource Center, Indian Movement Tapaj Amaru, Indigenous World Association, International Indian Treaty Council, International Organization of Indigenous Resources Development, Inuit Circumpolar Conference, Jigyansu Tribal Research Centre, Link-Up Queensland Aboriginal Corporation, National Aboriginal and Islander Legal Services Secretariat, National Congress of American Indians, National Indian Youth Council, the Saami Council, Native American Rights Fund, Shimin Gaikou Centre, Citizens' Diplomatic Centre for the Rights of Indigenous Peoples, Society for Threatened Peoples, and the World Council of Indigenous Peoples. Standards for formal accreditation with the Economic and Social Council are specified in *Arrangements for Consultation with Non-Governmental Organizations*, E.S.C. Res. 1296(XLIV), May 23, 1968, U.N. ESCOR, 44th Sess., Annex, U.N. Doc. E/4485 (1968).

50. *See infra* chapter 7, notes 67–157 and accompanying text (discussing cases brought by or on behalf of indigenous peoples before the Inter-American Commission on Human Rights and the Inter-American Court of Human Rights). The use of international human rights procedures by indigenous peoples was encouraged by the publication in 1984 of *Indian Rights, Human Rights: Handbook for Indians on International Human Rights Complaint Procedures*, a small book written with the nonlawyer in mind. This publication by the Indian Law Resource Center (which now has offices in Helena, Montana, and Washington, D.C.) was subsequently published in Spanish and widely distributed throughout the Americas.

51. *See* Akwesasne Mohawk Counselor Organization, *Deskaheh: Iroquois Statesman and Patriot* (1984); Niezen, *supra* note 44, at 31–36.

52. G.A. Res. 45/164 (Dec. 18, 1990). *See generally* "Inauguration of the 'International Year of the World's Indigenous People,'" 3 *Transnat'l L. & Contemp. Probs.* 165 (1993) (a compilation of related statements before the U.N. General Assembly by the U.N. secretary-general, indigenous peoples' representatives, and others).

53. G.A. Res. 48/163 (Dec. 21, 1993) (proclaiming the "International Decade of the World's Indigenous People" commencing Dec. 10, 1994).

54. *See* ECOSOC Res. E/RES/2000/22 (July 28, 2000) (establishing the Permanent Forum); *Report of the First Session of the Permanent Forum on Indigenous Issues*, U.N. Doc. E/2002/42/Supp. 43 (Wilton Littlechild, Rapporteur). The Permanent Forum is discussed in chapter 6, *infra*.

55. Convention No. 169 Concerning Indigenous and Tribal Peoples in Independent Countries, June 27, 1989, International Labour Conference (entered into force Sept. 5, 1991), reprinted in the appendix, *infra* [hereinafter ILO Convention No. 169].

56. *Report of the Meeting of Experts*, para. 46, reprinted in part in *Partial Revision of the Indigenous and Tribal Populations Convention, 1957 (No. 107)*, Report 6(1), International Labour Conference, 75th Sess. at 100–18 (1988). The study of the special rapporteur referred to is the study of José Martínez Cobo conducted under the auspices of the U.N. Sub-Commission on Prevention of Discrimination and Protection of Minorities, which is discussed *infra* notes 80–83 and accompanying text.

57. For detailed descriptions of the process leading to the adoption of ILO Convention No. 169 and analyses of the convention's provisions, see Lee Swepston, "A New Step in the International Law on Indigenous and Tribal Peoples: ILO Convention No. 169 of 1989," 15 *Okla. City U. L. Rev.* 677 (1990); Russell L. Barsh, "An Advocate's Guide to the Convention on Indigenous and Tribal Peoples," 15 *Okla. City U. L. Rev.* 209 (1990).

58. Subsequent ratifications include those of Argentina, Bolivia, Brazil, Colombia, Costa Rica, Denmark, Ecuador, Fiji, Guatemala, Honduras, Netherlands, Norway, Paraguay, Peru, and Venezuela.

59. Convention No. 169, *supra* note 55, fifth preambular para. The principal aspects of the convention are described further in chapters 3 and 4, *infra*, in a synthesis of conventional and customary international norms concerning indigenous peoples.

60. *E.g.*, *id.* art. 5 ("[T]he social, cultural, religious and spiritual values and practices of these peoples shall be recognised and protected."). *See also infra* chapter 4, notes 17–88 and accompanying text (discussing the norm of indigenous cultural integrity as reflected, *inter alia*, in Convention No. 169).

61. Convention No. 169, *supra* note 55, pt. 2 (land). The principal land rights provisions of ILO Convention No. 169 are discussed *infra* chapter 4, at text accompanying notes 104–17.

62. *Id.* pt. 3 ("Recruitment and Conditions of Employment"), pt. 4 ("Vocational Training, Handicrafts and Rural Industries"), pt. 5 ("Social Security and Health"), pt. 6 ("Education and Means of Communication"). *See also infra* chapter 4, notes 150–80 and accompanying text (discussing the rights of social welfare and development).

63. *E.g.*, *id.*, art. 7(1):

The peoples concerned shall have the right to decide their own priorities for the process of development as it affects their lives, beliefs, institutions and spiritual well-being and the lands they occupy or otherwise use, and to exercise control, to the extent possible, over their own economic, social and cultural development. In addition, they shall participate in the formulation, implementation and evaluation of plans and programmes for national and regional development which may affect them directly.

64. Representatives of indigenous peoples' organizations expressed such dissatisfaction to the International Labour Conference upon completion of the drafting of Convention No. 169. *See* Statement of Ms. Venne, representative of the International Work Group for Indigenous Affairs (speaking on behalf of indigenous peoples from North and South America, the Nordic countries, Japan, Australia, and Greenland), International Labour Conference, Provisional Record 31, 76th Sess. at 31/6 (1989) [hereinafter 1989 ILO Provisional Record 31].

65. *E.g.*, Convention No. 169, *supra* note 55, art. 8(1) ("In applying national laws and regulations to the peoples concerned, *due regard* shall be had to their customs or customary laws"); art. 9(1) (*"To the extent compatible with the national legal system and with internationally recognised human rights, the methods customarily practised by the peoples concerned for dealing with offences committed by their members shall be respected."*); art. 10(1) ("In imposing penalties laid down by general law on members of these peoples *account shall be taken* of their economic, social and cultural characteristics.") (emphasis added).

66. *See, e.g.*, comments of the Indigenous Peoples' Working Group of Canada, in International Labour Office, *Partial Revision of the Indigenous and Tribal Populations Convention, 1957 (No. 107)*, Report 4(2A), International Labour Conference, 76th Sess. at 9, (1989) ("Indigenous and tribal peoples are distinct societies that must be referred to in a precise and acceptable manner. Continued use of the term 'populations' would unfairly deny them their true status and identity as indigenous peoples."). The position in favor of use of the term *peoples* was advanced by the worker delegates in the committee deliberations leading to Convention No. 169. *See Report of the Committee on Convention 107*, International Labour Conference, Provisional Record 25, 76th Sess. at 25/6–8 (1989) [hereinafter 1989 ILO Provisional Record 25]. An example of indigenous peoples' advocacy in this regard in other international settings is the Statement by the Inuit Circumpolar Conference presented to the 1989 session of the U.N. Working Group on Indigenous Populations, Aug. 1, 1989, at 1, stating that "Inuit and other indigenous peoples worldwide are not and have never been mere 'populations.'"

67. *See, e.g.*, Statement by the National Coalition of Aboriginal Organizations, Australia, during the 75th session of the International Labour Conference, June 13, 1988, at 2:

> [W]e define our rights in terms of self-determination. We are not looking to dismember your States and you know it. But we do insist on the right to control our territories, our resources, the organisation of our societies, our own decision-making institutions, and the maintenance of our own cultures and ways of life.

68. Convention No. 169, *supra* note 55, art. 1(3).

69. 1989 ILO Provisional Record 25, *supra* note 66, at 25/7, para. 31. Some government representatives, however, continued to express reservations about even the qualified use of what they perceived to be a term of art that might be read to undermine the territorial integrity of a state with indigenous communities dwelling within its exterior borders. *Id.* at 25/7–8, paras. 36–42.

70. Statement of Lee Swepston of the International Labour Office to the U.N. Working Group on Indigenous Populations, July 31, 1989.

71. *See generally infra* chapter 3 (discussing the principle of self-determination and its application in the context of indigenous peoples).

72. Swepston, *A New Step*, *supra* note 54, at 689.

73. For a description of the ILO's norm implementation machinery, see *infra* chapter 6, notes 47–57 and accompanying text; chapter 7, notes 1–27 and accompanying text.

74. Myres McDougal et al., *Human Rights and World Public Order: The Basic Policies of an International Law of Human Dignity* 269 (1980) (footnote omitted). *Cf.*

Art. 38(1)(a) of the Statute of the International Court of Justice describing "international custom, as evidence of a general practice accepted as law."

75. Anthony D'Amato, "The Concept of Human Rights in International Law," 82 *Colum. L. Rev.* 1110, 1130 (1982).

76. *See* Thomas M. Franck, "Legitimacy in the International System," 82 *Am. J. Int'l L.* 705 (1988) (a jurisprudential study concerned with identifying the elements that establish in international norms the "compliance pull").

77. *See* McDougal et al., *supra* note 74, at 272 ("[I]t is easily observable that such organizations, especially the United Nations and affiliated agencies, play an increasingly important role as forums for the flow of explicit communications and acts of collaboration which create peoples' expectations about authoritative community policy.").

78. *See id.* at 272–73; Bin Cheng, "United Nations Resolutions on Outer Space: Instant International Customary Law?" 5 *Indian J. Int'l L.* 23, 45 (1965) (stating that the common belief of states that they are bound to a rule is the "only one single constitutive element" and conforming actual conduct merely provides evidence of the rule's existence); H.W.A. Thirlway, *International Customary Law and Codification* 56 (1972) ("The *opinio necessitatis* in the early stages is sufficient to create a rule of law, but its continued existence is dependent upon subsequent practice accompanied by *opinio juris*, failing which the new-born rule will prove a sickly infant and fail to survive for long."). Accordingly, Professor Brownlie defines the "material sources of custom" to include "diplomatic correspondence, policy statements, press releases . . . comments by governments on drafts produced by the International Law Commission, . . . recitals in treaties and other international instruments, a pattern of treaties in the same form, practice of international organs, and resolutions relating to legal questions in the United Nations General Assembly." Brownlie, *supra* note 1, at 6.

The International Court of Justice, in Military and Paramilitary Activities (Nicar. v. U.S.), 1986 I.C.J. 4 (June 27), relied primarily on United Nations resolutions to discern the applicable rules of customary international law. *See also* TOPCO/CALASIATIC v. Libyan Arab Republic, International Arbitration Tribunal, Merits (1977), 17 *I.L.M.* 1 (1978) (René Dupuy, arbitrator) (finding applicable customary law in part on the basis of patterns of voting on U.N. General Assembly resolutions). For an insightful analysis of the relationship between resolutions by international institutions and customary international law, see Rosalyn Higgins, "The Role of Resolutions of International Organizations in the Process of Creating Norms in the International System," in *International Law and the International System* 21 (W. Butler ed., 1987).

Professor Sohn observes that government practice in negotiating the text of an international instrument may itself generate customary law, even in advance of formal adoption or ratification of the instrument: "The Court is thus willing to pay attention not only to a text that codifies preexisting principles of international law but also to one that crystallizes an 'emergent rule of customary law.'" Louis B. Sohn, "'Generally Accepted' International Rules," 61 *Wash. L. Rev.* 1073, 1077 (1986), citing Continental Shelf Case (Tunisia/Libyan Arab Jamahiriya), 1982 I.C.J. 18, 38. *See also* Louis B. Sohn, "Unratified Treaties as a Source of Customary International Law," in *Realism in Law-Making: Essays on International Law in Honour of Willem Riphagen* 231 (A. Bos & H. Siblesz eds., 1986); Michael Akehurst, "Custom as a Source of International Law," 47 *Brit. Y.B.*

Int'l L. 1, 15–16 (1974–75); Jorge Castañeda, *Legal Effects of United Nations Resolutions* 169–77 (Alba Amoia trans., 1969); Grigorii Ivanovich Tunkin, *Theory of International Law* 114–15 (1974) (William Butler trans., 1974); Theodor Meron, *Human Rights and Humanitarian Norms as Customary Law* 41 (1989).

79. *See generally* Joseph Gabriel Starke, *Introduction to International Law* 38–39 (10th ed. 1989) (describing how the recurrence of a usage develops *opinio juris*, that is, "an expectation that, in similar future situations, the same conduct or the abstention therefrom will be repeated").

80. E.S.C. Res. 1589(L), May 21, 1971, U.N. ESCOR, 50th Sess., Supp. No. 1, at 16, U.N. Doc. E/5044 (1971).

81. U.N. Sub-Commission on Prevention of Discrimination and Protection of Minorities, *Study of the Problem of Discrimination against Indigenous Populations*, U.N. Doc. E/CN.4/Sub.2/1986/7 & Adds. 1–4 (1986) (José Martínez Cobo, special rapporteur) [hereinafter Martínez Cobo Study].

82. The original documents comprising the study are, in order of publication: U.N. Docs. E/CN.4/Sub.2/476/Adds.1–6 (1981); E/CN.4/Sub.2/1982/2/Adds.1–7 (1982); and E/CN.4/Sub.2/1983/21/Adds.1–7 (1983).

83. *See* Martínez Cobo Study, *supra* note 81, Add. 4, U.N. Sales No. E.86.XIV.3 (vol. 5: Conclusions and Recommendations).

84. Declaration of San José, UNESCO Latin American Conference, Dec. 11, 1981, paras. 2, 3, UNESCO Doc. FS 82/WF.32 (1982), reprinted in the appendix, *infra*.

85. These include seminars organized by the U.N. Technical Advisory Services on racism and indigenous-state relations (Geneva, 1989), indigenous self-government (Greenland, 1991), the role of indigenous peoples in sustainable development (Chile, 1992), indigenous land rights and claims (Canada, 1996), indigenous journalism (Spain, 1998), indigenous research and higher education (Costa Rica, 1999), indigenous peoples and resource extraction companies (Geneva, 2001), and multiculturalism and indigenous peoples in Africa (Tanzania, 2000; Mali, 2001; Botswana, 2002). The reports of these seminars are, respectively, in *Report of the United Nations Seminar on the Effects of Racism and Racial Discrimination on the Social and Economic Relations Between Indigenous Peoples and States*, U.N. Doc. E/CN.4/1989/22, HR/PUB/89/5 (1989) (Ted Moses, special rapporteur); *Report of the Meeting of Experts to Review the Experience of Countries in the Operation of Schemes of Internal Self-Government for Indigenous Peoples*, U.N. Doc. E/CN.4/1992/42 (1991); *Report of the United Nations Technical Conference on Practical Experience in the Realization of Sustainable and Environmentally Sound Self-Development of Indigenous Peoples*, U.N. Doc. E/CN.4/Sub.2/1992/31 (1992); *Report of the Expert Seminar on Practical Experiences Regarding Indigenous Land Rights and Claims*, U.N. Doc. E/CN.4/Sub.2/AC.4/1996/6/Add.1, 4 (1996); *Report of the Workshop of Indigenous Journalists*, U.N. Doc. E/CN.4/Sub.2/AC.4/1998/6 (1998); *Report of the Workshop on Research and Higher Education Institutions and Indigenous Peoples*, U.N. Doc. E/CN.4/Sub.2/AC.4/1999/5/Add.1 (1999), *Report on the Seminar on "Multiculturalism in Africa: Peaceful and Constructive Group Accommodation in Situations Involving Minorities and Indigenous Peoples,"* U.N. Doc., E/CN.4/Sub.2/AC.5/2000/WP.3 (2000); *Report of the Second Workshop on Multiculturalism in Africa: Peaceful and Constructive Group Accommodation in Situations Involving Mi-*

norities and Indigenous Peoples, U.N. Doc. E/CN.4/Sub.2/AC.5/2001/3 (2001); *Workshop on Indigenous Peoples, Private Sector Natural Resource, Energy and Mining Companies and Human Rights*, U.N. Doc. E/CN.4/Sub.2/AC.4/2002/3 (2002); *Report of the Third Workshop on Multiculturalism in Africa: Peaceful and Constructive Group Accommodation in Situations Involving Minorities and Indigenous Peoples*, U.N. Doc. E/CN.4/Sub.2/AC.4/2002/4 (2002).

86. Human Rights Commission Res. 1982/19 (Mar. 10, 1982); E.S.C. Res. 1982/34, May 7, 1982, U.N. ESCOR, 1982, Supp. No. 1, at 26, U.N. Doc. E/1982/82 (1982).

87. *Id.*, paras. 1–2.

88. *See* ECOSOC Decision 1992/256 (July 20, 1992) (authorizing the appointment of Irene E. Daes as the special rapporteur to conduct a study on the "protection of the cultural and intellectual property of indigenous people"); ECOSOC Decision 1988/134 (May 27, 1988) and ECOSOC Res. 1989/77 (May 24, 1989) (authorizing the appointment of Miguel Alfonso Martínez as the special rapporteur to conduct a study on "treaties agreements and other constructive arrangements between States and indigenous populations").

89. Sub-Commission on Prevention of Discrimination and Protection of Minorities Res. 1985/22 (Aug. 29, 1985).

90. *Universal Declaration on Indigenous Rights: A Set of Preambular Paragraphs and Principles*, U.N. Doc. E/CN.4/Sub.2/1988/25, at 2 (1988). After comments by governments and indigenous peoples' representatives, the chair revised the draft in 1989. *See First Revised Text of the Draft Universal Declaration on the Rights of Indigenous Peoples*, U.N. Doc. E/CN.4/Sub.2/1989/33 (1989).

91. The working group's final draft was published in an annex to the *Report of the Working Group on Indigenous Populations on Its Eleventh Session*, U.N. Doc. E/CN.4/Sub.2/1993/29, Annex 1 (1993) [hereinafter *1993 Working Group Report*]. After the draft was submitted to a technical review, *see Technical Review of the Draft United Nations Declaration on the Rights of Indigenous Peoples*, U.N. Doc. E/CN.4/Sub.2/1994/2 (1994), it was adopted without changes by the full sub-commission by its resolution 1994/45 of August 26, 1994. The draft declaration appears in an annex to the sub-commission resolution as the "Draft United Nations Declaration on the Rights of Indigenous Peoples," U.N. Doc. E/CN.4/1995/2, E/CN.4/Sub.2/1994/56, at 105 (1994) [hereinafter Draft United Nations Declaration], and it is reprinted in the appendix, *infra*. By the same resolution 1994/45 the sub-commission submitted the draft declaration to the Commission on Human Rights for its consideration.

92. The Commission on Human Rights, by its resolution 1995/32 of March 3, 1995, decided

> to establish, as a matter of priority and from within existing overall United Nations resources, an open-ended inter-sessional working group of the Commission on Human Rights with the sole purpose of elaborating a draft declaration, considering the draft contained in the annex to resolution 1994/45 of 26 August 1994 of the Sub-commission on Prevention of Discrimination and Protection of Minorities, entitled draft "United Nations declaration on the rights of indigenous peoples" for consideration and adoption by the General Assembly within the International Decade of the World's Indigenous People.

An annex to the commission's resolution 1995/32 establishes a procedure for "organizations of indigenous people" to be accredited to participate in the commission's drafting working group. Although the procedure is designed to provide for greater participation by individuals and groups than that ordinarily allowed in the commission's proceedings, it will likely result in a lower level of access to the drafting process than that which indigenous peoples have enjoyed in the sub-commission's working group. The latter working group has allowed virtually any person who attends its meetings to participate in its deliberations, without prior accreditation.

93. A listing of the participants at the working group meetings and a summary of the discussion is included in the reports that correspond to each of the annual working group sessions. *See, e.g., Report of the Working Group on Indigenous Populations on Its Twelfth Session,* U.N. Doc. E/CN.4/Sub.2/1994/30, at 4–8 (1994) [hereinafter *1994 Working Group Report*]; *1993 Working Group Report, supra* note 91, at 4–7.

94. *See* Swepston, *A New Step, supra* note 57, at 684–85 (discussing indigenous participation in the drafting procedures). For a description of the International Labour Organization's system of governance, see Bowett, *supra* note 19, at 140–43 (4th ed. 1982); Nicolas Valticos, *International Labor Law* 27–42 (1979).

95. *See generally* government statements summarized in *Report of the Committee on Convention No. 107, International Labour Conference, Provisional Record* 32, 75th Sess. (1988); 1989 ILO Provisional Record 25, *supra* note 66.

96. 1989 ILO Provisional Record 25, *supra* note 66, at 25/1, n.1.

97. *Id.* at 25/24–25/25.

98. The vote was 328 in favor, 1 against, with 49 abstentions. The opposing vote was cast by the employer delegate from the Netherlands. International Labour Conference, Provisional Record 32, 76th Sess. at 32/17–32/19 (1989) [hereinafter 1989 ILO Provisional Record 32].

99. Among the delegates recording votes in favor of the convention were representatives of the governments of ninety-two states; the government delegations of twenty states recorded abstentions. *Id.*

100. Peru's statement is typical of the views expressed by the abstaining governments:

Given the importance of this subject for Peru, our delegation participated actively in the revision of Convention No. 107 with a view to updating the text and improving it on a multilateral basis to promote the rights of indigenous and native populations and to guarantee these rights in the various countries. We also wished to ensure that, within the international community these populations would be able to develop fully and transmit their cultural heritage.

In my country, there is very progressive legislation along these lines and I must highlight the fact that most of the criteria laid down in the new Convention are already contained in our legal instruments. However, the work which has taken place within this tripartite forum—at an international level—has been of considerable significance and receives our full support.

In this context, after the prolonged negotiations which led to a consensus text, our delegation nevertheless felt bound to express reservations with respect to the use in the Convention of some terms which could lead to ambiguous

interpretations and create difficulties with our laws in force, on some points of
the highest importance. These reservations are laid down in paragraph 156 of
the report of the Committee.

Id. at 32/12. The part of the committee report cited reflects Peru's concern over the use of
the term *territories* and other language that "might imply the right to accord or deny
approval and thereby lead to concepts of sovereignty outside the Constitution." 1989 ILO
Provisional Record 25, *supra* note 66, at 25/22. *See also, e.g.*, Statement of the Government Delegate of Argentina, 1989 ILO *Provisional Record* 32, *supra* note 98, at 32/12
(concurring in the "pluralistic view of the new Convention" and endorsing "national legislation which recognises the cultural and social identity of indigenous peoples and the
granting of land" to them, while at the same time expressing difficulty with use of the
term *peoples* to refer to the subject groups and with the inclusion of the words *consent* and
agreement in art. 6, para. 2). Notably, despite the initial position of its government on
Convention No. 169, Peru subsequently ratified the convention. Additionally, in Argentina—another state that abstained in the vote on Convention No. 169 at the 1989 Labour
Conference—also eventually ratified the convention.

101. *See* notes 66–70 *supra* and accompanying text.

102. ILO Convention No. 169, *supra* note 55, art. 13, para. 2.

103. *See, e.g.*, Statement of the government delegate of Peru, 1989 ILO *Provisional
Record* 32, *supra* note 98, at 32/12 (stressing "the fact that most of the criteria laid down
in the new Convention are already contained in [Peru's] legal instruments," while emphasizing earlier statement expressing concern over use of the term "territories").

104. *See infra* note 155.

105. *See* summaries of government comments delivered at the 1993 and 1994 ses-
sions of the U.N. sub-commission working group, which appear, respectively, in 1993
Working Group Report, supra note 91; 1994 *Working Group Report, supra* note 93.
Written comments on the proposed declaration appear verbatim or are summarized in
*Analytical Compilation of Observations and Comments Received Pursuant to Sub-
Commission Resolution 1988/18*, U.N. Doc. E/CN.4/Sub.2/1989/33/Adds.1–3 (1989);
*Analytical Commentary on the Draft Principles Contained in the First Revised Text of
the Draft Declaration on the Rights of Indigenous Peoples*, U.N. Doc. E/CN.4/Sub.2/
AC.4/1990/1 & Adds.1–3 (1990); *Revised Working Paper Submitted by the Chairper-
son/Rapporteur*, U.N. Doc. E/CN.4/ Sub.2/1991/36 (1991). *See also Report of the working group established in accordance with Commission on Human Rights Resolution 1995/
32*, U.N. Doc. E/CN.4/2000/84/ (Dec. 6, 1999) (Oct. 18–29, 1999, session) [hereinafter
"Report of the 1999 session of the Commission working group on the indigenous declaration"]; *Report of the working group established in accordance with Human Rights Commission resolution 1995/32*, U.N. Doc. E/CN.4/2001/95, paras. 62–109 (Feb. 6, 2001)
(Nov. 20–Dec. 1, 2000, session) [hereinafter "Report of the 2000 session of the Commission working group on the indigenous declaration"].

106. The evolution of the debate can be observed by comparing the Report of the
1999 session of the Commission working group on the indigenous declaration, *supra*
note 105, with the *Report of the working group established in accordance with Commission on Human Rights Resolution 1995/32*, U.N. Doc. E/CN.4/1997/102 (Dec. 10,

1996) [hereinafter "Report of the 1996 session of the Commission working group on the indigenous declaration"].

107. *See* Draft United Nations Declaration, *supra* note 91, art. 3 (discussed *infra* chapter 3, notes 85–98 and accompanying text).

108. *Id.* arts. 25–30. *See infra* chapter 4, notes 118–19 and accompanying text (government commentary on land rights in connection with working group procedures).

109. *Id.* arts. 31–38. *See infra* chapter 4, notes 189–91 and accompanying text (discussing the "right to autonomy or self-government" articulated in article 31 of the draft declaration).

110. AG/RES.1022(XIX-0/89). The proposal for a new OAS legal instrument on indigenous rights is described in *Annual Report of the Inter-American Commission on Human Rights, 1988–89*, O.A.S. Doc. OEA/Ser.L/V/II.76, Doc. 10, at 245–51 (1989).

111. Proposed American Declaration on the Rights of Indigenous Peoples, approved by the Inter-American Commission on Human Rights on Feb. 26, 1997, at its 1333rd session, 95th regular session, published in *Annual Report of the Inter-American Commission on Human Rights*, O.A.S. Doc. OEA/Ser.L/V/II.95, Doc. 7 rev. (March 14, 1996) reprinted in the appendix, *infra*.

112. This commentary is summarized in Report on the First Round of Consultations Concerning the Future Inter-American Legal Instrument on Indigenous Rights, published in *Annual Report of the Inter-American Commission on Human Rights, 1992–1993*, O.A.S. Doc. OEA/Ser.L/V/II.83, Doc. 14, corr. 1, at 263 (1993).

113. *See* OAS General Assembly Resolution 1610 (XXIX-O/99). *See also* General Assembly Resolution 1708 (XXX-O/00) (renewing the mandate of the working group).

114. *See Special Meeting of the Working Group to Prepare the Draft American Declaration on the Rights of Indigenous Peoples, Washington, D.C., April 2–6, 2001, Report of the Chair*, OEA/Ser.K/XVI, GT/DADIN/doc. 23/01 rev. 1 (2001); *Special Session of the Working Group to Prepare the Draft American Declaration on the Rights of Indigenous Peoples, 11–15 March, 2002, Washington, D.C., Report of the Rapporteur*, OEA/Ser.K/XVI, GT/DADIN/doc.83/02 (2002); *Special Session of the Working Group to Prepare the Draft American Declaration of the Rights of Indigenous Peoples, Washington, D.C., February 24–28, 2003, Report of the Rapporteur*, O.A.S. Doc. OEA/Ser.K/XVI, GT/DADIN/doc.138/03 (2003).

115. A manifestation of this consensus can be found in a document prepared by the president of the working group on the OAS draft declaration, comparing proposals by representatives of indigenous peoples and of states. *Working Document Comparing the Original Draft of the Inter-American Commission on Human Rights, Proposals by the States and by the Indigenous Representatives, as well as the Proposed Draft by the Chair of the Working Group to Prepare the Draft American Declaration on the Rights of Indigenous Peoples*, O.A.S. Doc. OEA/Ser.K/XVI, GT/DADIN/doc. 53/02 (2002).

116. Resolution on the Adoption of the "Report of the African Commission's Working Group on Indigenous Populations/Communities," African Commission on Human Rights, Banjul, Nov. 20, 2003, preambular para. 3.

117. *Id.* para. 4.

118. *Id.*

119. For example, Miguel Alfonso Martínez attracted criticism for asserting, in his U.N.-sponsored study on treaties, that the concept of indigenous peoples with few exceptions is inappropriate in the African and Asian contexts because all the major population groups there underwent similar histories of colonialism and all can be considered indigenous. *See Study on treaties, agreements and other constructive arrangements between States and indigenous populations: final report submitted by the Special Rapporteur, Mr. Miguel Alfonso Martínez,* U.N. Doc. E/CN.4/Sub.2/1999/20, paras. 78–91 (1999).

120. For a detailed discussion of measures adopted by international and regional institutions concerning indigenous peoples, *see* Fergus Mackay, *Los derechos de los pueblos indígenas en el sistema international* (1999); Patrick Thornberry, *Indigenous Peoples and Human Rights* (2002); Russel Lawrence Barsh, "Indigenous Peoples in the 1990s: From Object to Subject of International Law?" 7 *Harv. Hum. Rts. J.* 33, 43–74 (1994); Siegfried Wiessner, "The Rights and Status of Indigenous Peoples: A Global Comparative and International Legal Appraisal," 12 *Harv. Hum. Rts. J.* 57 (1999).

121. Convention on the Rights of the Child, G.A. res. 44/25, annex, 44 U.N. GAOR Supp. (No. 49) at 167 U.N. Doc. A/44/49 (1989), entered into force Sept. 2, 1990. For a discussion of the convention and relevant U.N. procedures, see Patrick Thornberry, *Indigenous Peoples and Human Rights* 225–41 (2002).

122. Resolution of the Third Meeting of Ministers for Foreign Affairs of the State Parties to the Treaty for Amazonian Co-Operation Setting Up a Special Commission in Indigenous Affairs, Mar. 7, 1989.

123. Convenio Constitutivo del Fondo para el Desarrollo de los Pueblos Indígenas de América Latina y el Caribe, concluded at the Summit Meeting of Ibero-American Heads of State, Madrid, Jul. 24, 1992 (entered into force Aug. 4, 1993).

124. *See generally* Shelton Davis & William Partridge, "Promoting the Development of Indigenous People in Latin America," *Finance and Development,* Mar. 1994, at 38, 39 (discussing the role of the World Bank and other international financial agencies).

125. *See* Julian Burger, *Report from the Frontier: The State of the World's Indigenous Peoples* 1–5 (1987) (discussing the impact of development projects on indigenous lands, especially in parts of the developing world).

126. A discussion of the dynamics leading to the adoption of World Bank Operational Directive 4.20 is in Michael Cernea, *Sociologists in a Development Agency: Experiences from the World Bank* 19–21 (World Bank Environment Department, May 1993, Washington, D.C.). The following provisions of Operational Directive 4.20 indicate its essential thrust:

6. The bank's broad objective towards indigenous people, as for all the people in its member countries, is to ensure that the development process fosters full respect for their dignity, human rights, and cultural uniqueness.

. . .

8. The Bank's policy is that the strategy for addressing the issues pertaining to indigenous peoples must be based on the *informed participation* of indigenous peoples themselves. Thus, identifying local preferences through direct consultation, incorporation of indigenous knowledge into project approaches,

and appropriate early use of experienced specialists are core activities for any project that affects indigenous peoples and their rights to natural and economic resources. (Emphasis added.)

At the time of this writing, the Bank is in the process of revising its Operational Directive 4.20. It is evident that the discussions on this revision are being influenced by the normative trends discussed here, even while concerns are raised about the proposed revisions that might weaken mandatory Bank procedures regarding development programs affecting indigenous peoples. *See* World Bank, Summary of Consultations with External Stakeholders Regarding the World Bank Indigenous Peoples Policy (Draft PO/BP 4.10), Internal Report, Apr. 18, 2002 (updated Oct. 7, 2002); World Bank, *Approach Paper on Revision of OD 4.20 on Indigenous Peoples.* For a critical perspective of the World Bank's revision, see Fergus McKay, "Universal Rights or a Universe unto Itself? Indigenous Peoples' Human Rights and the Work Bank's Draft Operational Policy 4.10 on Indigenous Peoples," 17 *Am. U. L. Rev.* 527 (2002).

127. Rio Declaration on Environment and Development, U.N. Conference on Environment and Development, Rio de Janeiro, June 13, 1992, principle 22, U.N. Doc. A/CONF.151/26 (vol. 1), Annex 1 (1992).

128. Agenda 21, U.N. Conference on Environment and Development, Rio de Janeiro, June 13, 1992, U.N. Doc. A/CONF.151/26 (vols. 1, 2, & 3), Annex 2 (1992).

129. Especially pertinent is Chapter 26 of Agenda 21, *id.*, vol. 3, at 16, reprinted in the appendix, *infra.* Chapter 26 is phrased in nonmandatory terms; nonetheless, it carries forward normative precepts concerning indigenous peoples and hence contributes to the crystallization of consensus on indigenous peoples' rights. Chapter 26 emphasizes indigenous peoples' "historical relationship with their lands" and advocates international and national efforts to "recognize, accomodate, promote and strengthen" the role of indigenous peoples in development activities. *Id.*, art. 26.1.

130. *See* Vienna Declaration and Program of Action, U.N. Doc. A/CONF.157/23 (1993), adopted by the World Conference on Human Rights (Vienna, June 14–25, 1993), at paras. 20 (declaration), 28–32 (program of action); Programme of Action adopted at the International Conference on Population and Development, Cairo, Sept. 5–13, 1994, paras. 6.21–6.27, U.N. Doc. ST/ESA/SER.A/149, U.N. Sales No. E.95.XIII.7 (1995); Copenhagen Declaration on Social Development, in *Report of the World Summit for Social Development (Copenhagen, March 6–12, 1995)*, U.N. Doc. A/CONF.166/9 (1995), chap. 1, Res. 1., Annex I, at paras. 26(m), 29, commitments 5(b), 4(f), 6(g); *Programme of Action of the World Summit for Social Development, id.*, Annex II, paras. 12(i), 19, 26(m), 32(f) & (h), 35(e), 38(g), 54 (c), 61, 67, 74(h), 75(g); Beijing Declaration, in *Report of the Fourth World Conference on Women (Beijing, 4–15 September 1995)*, U.N. Doc. A/CONF.177/20 (1985), chap. 1, Res. 1, Annex I, para. 32; Platform of Action, *id.*, Annex II, paras. 8, 32, 34, 58(q), 60(a), 61(c) 83(m)(n)(o), 89, 106(c)(y), 109(b)(j), 116, 167(c), 175(f); Declaration, in *Report of the World Conference Against Racism, Racial Discrimination, Xenophobia and Related Intolerance* (Durban, South Africa, Aug. 31–Sept. 8, 2001), U.N. Doc. A/CONF.189/12, chap. 1, preamble, paras. 13–14, 22–24, 39–45, 73, 103; Programme of Action, *id.*, paras. 15–23, 78(j), 203–09; Political Declaration in *Report of the World Summit on Sustainable Development*

(Johannesburg, South Africa, August 26–September 4, 2002), U.N. Doc. A/CONF.199/ 20 (2002), chap. 1, Res. 1, para. 25; Plan of Implementation of the World Summit on Sustainable Development, *id.*, Res. 2, paras. 7(e)(h)(g); 37(f), 38 (i), 40(d)(r), 42(e), 43(b), 44(h)(j)(k)(l), 45(h), 46(b), 53, 54(h), 63, 64(d), 70 (c), 109(a).

It should be noted that, from the point of view of the indigenous representatives participating in these conferences, the provisions of these resolutions have not provided sufficient affirmation of rights of the indigenous people. Particularly notable is the dissatisfaction of the indigenous representatives at the Durban conference on racism. *See* "Press Release: Protest of Indigenous Peoples must be taken seriously: World Conference must withdraw discriminating articles from final resolution," issued by the Society for Threatened Peoples on Sept. 4, 2001. Nevertheless, despite the shortcomings of the Durban Declaration, it should not overlooked that it includes provisions that reinforce the norms reflected in ILO Convention Num. 169 and the draft declarations of the United Nations and of the OAS, in a way similar to the resolutions of the other conferences.

131. Resolution on the Position of the World's Indians, European Parliament, 1989, reprinted in *Review of Developments Pertaining to the Promotion and Protection of Human Rights and Fundamental Freedoms on Indigenous Peoples*, U.N. Doc. E/CN.4/ Sub.2/AC.4/1989/3, at 7 (1989).

132. Resolution on Action Required Internationally to Provide Effective Protection for Indigenous Peoples, Feb. 9, 1994, Eur. Parl. Doc. PV 58(II) (1994), reprinted in the appendix, *infra*.

133. *Id.*, para. 2.

134. See *Working Document of the Commission on Support for Indigenous Peoples in the Development Co-operation of the Community and Member States*, SEC (98) 773 final (May 11, 1998) (promoting new ways of cooperation between the Union and member states, and indigenous peoples); EU Development Council Resolution on Indigenous Peoples within the Framework of the Development Cooperation of the Community and Member States, 13461/98 (affirming indigenous peoples' rights, including self-development, and calling for integrating indigenous peoples' concerns into the Union's existing procedures and guidelines for development co-operation). Since 1999, the rights of indigenous peoples constitute a thematic priority within the European Initiative for Democracy and Human Rights. *See* Council Regulation (EC) No. 975/1999 of 29 Apr. 1999 (laying down the requirements for the implementation of development cooperation operations which contribute to the general objective of developing and consolidating democracy and the rule of law and to that of respecting human rights and fundamental freedoms, *Official Journal* L 120, pp. 1–8, art. (1)(d)); Council Regulation (EC) No 976/1999 of 29 Apr. 1999 (laying down the requirements for the implementation of Community operations, other than those of development cooperation, which, within the framework of Community cooperation policy, contribute to the general objective of developing and consolidating democracy and the rule of law and to that of respecting human rights and fundamental freedoms in third-world countries, *Official Journal* L 120, pp. 8–14, art. 3 (a)(d)). *See also Communication from the Commission to the Council and the European Parliament: The European Union's Role in Promoting Human Rights and Democratisation in Third Countries*, COM(2001), 252 final (May 8, 2001), at 15, 17, 28 (proposing "Combating Racism and Xenophobia and Discrimination Against Indigenous Peoples" as a thematic priority

of the European Initiative); *Communication from the Commission to the Council: Review of progress of working with indigenous peoples*, COM (2002) 291 final (June 16, 2002) (assessing the progress of the EU policies with indigenous peoples).

135. Resolution on Special Protection for Indigenous Populations, Inter-American Commission on Human Rights, Dec. 28, 1972, O.A.S. Doc. OEA/Ser.P,AG/doc.305/73, rev. 1, at 90–91 (1973).

136. Helsinki Document 1992—The Challenges of Change, July 10, 1992, para. 6(29), reprinted in U.N. GAOR, 47th Sess., at 65, U.N. Doc. A/47/361 (1992).

137. Convention on Biological Diversity, art. 8(j), UNCED, Rio de Janeiro, June 5, 1992, U.N. Doc. UNEP/Bio.Div/N7INC.5/4 (1992) (entered into force Dec. 29, 1993). Implementation of the convention includes periodic meetings of state parties (Conferences of the Parties), as well as a number of technical committees and working groups on specific issues covered by the convention. The issue of indigenous traditional knowledge has been object of a specific focus by the Conference of the Parties. *See* Decision III/14 (Implementation of article 8.j), *Report of the Third Meeting of Conference of the Parties to the Convention on Biological Diversity*, U.N. Doc. UNEP/CBD/COP/3/38 (1997), Annex 2, at 90–93; Decision IV/9 (Implementation of article 8.j and related provisions), *Report of the Fourth Meeting of the Conference of the Parties to the Convention on Biological Diversity*, U.N. Doc. UNEP/CBD/COP/4/27 (1998), Annex, at 111–14; Decision V/16 (Article 8.j and related provisions), *Report of the Fifth Meeting on the Conference of the Parties to the Convention on Biological Diversity*, U.N. Doc. UNEP/CBD/COP/5/23 (2000), Annex III, at 141–43; Decision VI/10 (Article 8.j and related provisions), *Report of the Six Meeting on the Conference of the Parties to the Convention on Biological Diversity*, U.N. Doc. UNEP/CBD/COP/6/20 (2002), Annex I, at 151–169. Following a workshop on traditional knowledge and biological diversity (Spain, 1992), the Conference of the Parties decided to create an ad hoc working group on article 8(j). As of this writing, this working group has held two meetings (Spain, 2000; Canada, 2002). In addition, the Conference of the Parties decided to establish a technical expert group in order to develop a thematic focal point within the convention's general clearing-house mechanism on issues related to article 8(j) and related provisions. This expert group met in Bolivia in 2003. The reports and conclusions of these meetings are found in *Report of the Workshop on Traditional Knowledge and Biological Diversity*, U.N. Doc. UNEP/CBD/TKIP/1/3 (1997); *Report of the first meeting of the Ad Hoc Open-ended Inter Sessional Working Group on Article 8(j) and Related Provisions of the Convention on Biological Diversity*, U.N. Doc. UNEP/*CBD*/COP/5/5 (2000); *Report of the Ad Hoc Open-ended Inter-Sessional Working-Group on Article 8(j) and Related Provisions of the Convention on Biological Diversity on the work of its second meeting*; U.N. Doc. UNEP/CBD/COP/6/7 (2002); *Report of the Ad Hoc Technical Expert Group on Traditional Knowledge and the Clearing House Mechanism*, U.N. Doc. UNEP/CBD/AHTEG/TK-CHM/1/3 (2003).

138. Vienna Declaration and Programme of Action, World Conference on Human Rights, Vienna, June 25, 1993, pt. 1, para. 20; pt. 2, paras. 28–32, U.N. Doc. A/CONF.157/23 (1993).

139. Charter of Civil Society for the Caribbean Community, adopted by the Conference of the Heads of Government of the Caribbean Community (CARICOM) in its 8th meeting (San Juan, Antigua and Barbuda, Feb. 19, 1997).

140. Inter-American Democratic Charter, issued at Lima, Sept. 11, 2001, by the OAS General Assembly, AG/doc.8 (XXVIII-E/01).

141. *See supra* notes 42–54, 80–96, and accompanying text.

142. *See infra* chapters 3 and 4.

143. *See supra* chapter 1, notes 100–06 and accompanying text (discussing the character of international law under late-nineteenth and early-twentieth-century positivist school).

144. *See supra* notes 9–12, 20–22.

145. *See* Filartiga v. Peña-Irala, 630 F.2d 876 (2d. Cir. 1980) (United States court of appeals decision holding that U.N. Charter obligation to uphold human rights applies to those human rights whose content is generally understood).

146. Miguel A. D'Estéfano, 1 *Esquemas del derecho internacional público: Primera parte* 13 (1986) (translation from Spanish is my own).

147. Meron, *supra* note 78, at 53.

148. McDougal et al., *supra* note 74, at 269. *See also* Brownlie, *supra* note 1, at 26–27 (discussing considerations of humanity that may function as a source of law).

149. The Case of the Mayagna (Sumo) Awas Tingni Community v. Nicaragua, Inter-Am. Ct.H.R. (Ser. C) No. 79 (Judgment on merits and reparations of Aug. 31, 2001), published in abridged version in 19 *Ariz. J. Int'l & Comp. Law* 395 [hereinafter "*Awas Tingni* case"]. The author is a lawyer for the indigenous community in this case and assisted the Inter-American Commission of Human Rights during the proceedings before the Inter-American Court. For further analysis of the case, *see infra* chap. 4, notes 124–33 and accompanying text, and chapter 7, notes 127–57 and accompanying text.

150. *Final Written Arguments of the Inter-American Commission on Human Rights, submitted to the Inter-American Court of Human Rights in the Case of the Awas Tingni Mayagna (Sumo) Indigenous Community Against the Republic of Nicaragua, August 10, 2001*, para. 64, published in 19 *Ariz. J. Int'l & Comp. L.* 325 (2002). The commission effectively advanced this position again in its report finding the United States in violation of its human rights obligations in relation to the Western Shoshone people and their rights to lands and natural resources in the Case of Mary Dann and Carrie Dann v. United States, Case No. 11.140, *Inter-Am. Comm. H.R., Report No. 75/02* (Dec. 27, 2002). The commission affirmed the existence of "general international legal principles applicable in the context of indigenous human rights" and articulated the content of such principles on the basis of many of the same developments referenced here. *Id.*, para. 130. The author was counsel to the petitioners in this case, which is discussed further in chapters 4 and 7.

151. *Awas Tingni* case, *supra* note 149, paras. 148–49.

152. *Separate Concurring Opinion of Judge Sergio Ramírez, id.*, paras. 5–10.

153. For an analysis of the relevant jurisprudence of the U.N. Human Rights Committee in relation to the International Covenant on Civil and Political Rights, see *infra* chap. 3, notes 99–100 and accompanying text; chap. 4, notes 41–58 and accompanying text. For an analysis of the jurisprudence of the U.N. Committee on the Elimination of Racial Discrimination in relation to the International Convention on the Elimination of All Forms of Racial Discrimination, see *infra* chap. 4, notes 11, 17, and accompanying text; chapter 6, notes 73–87 and accompanying text.

154. E.S.C. Res. 1982/34, *supra* note 86. *See* discussion of "Review of Developments Pertaining to the Promotion and Protection of Human Rights and Fundamental Freedoms of Indigenous Populations," which appears in reports of the U.N. subcommission working group, *e.g.*, 1993 Working Group Report, *supra* note 91; 1994 Working Group Report, *supra* note 93. *See also* various statements of governments given orally at the working group sessions, on file at the Office of the High Commissioner for Human Rights in Geneva. Written government submissions on domestic developments appear, *inter alia*, in U.N. Doc. E/CN.4/Sub.2/AC.4/1989/2 & Add.1 (1989) (information received from Australia, Brazil, Canada, and Venezuela); U.N. Doc. E/CN.4/Sub.2/AC.4/1990/4 (1990) (information received from Bangladesh); U.N. Doc. E/CN.4/Sub.2/AC.4/1991/4 (1991) (information received from Colombia).

155. *See, e.g.*, government statements made to the conference committee that drafted Convention No. 169, summarized in 1989 ILO Provisional Record 25, *supra* note 66, at 25/2–25/3; government statements to the plenary of the Labour Conference upon the convention's submission for a vote in 1989 ILO Provisional Record 31, *supra* note 64, at 31/12–31/17; 1989 ILO Provisional Record 32, *supra* note 98, at 32/11–32/12. The statements reflect a clear trend of programmatic reforms generally in line with the convention, even among states whose governments abstained from voting in favor of its adoption. *See id.* "Several Government members referred to recent enactments of legislation . . . and noted that their legislation went beyond the provisions contained in the proposed Convention." 1989 ILO Provisional Record 25, *supra* note 66, at 25/2. Among the abstaining governments that reported on such domestic developments were the governments of Bangladesh, Brazil, Argentina, and Peru. 1989 ILO Provisional Record 32, *supra* note 98, at 32/11–32/12. The government delegate from Bangladesh, for example, even while expressing reservations about the need to revise the ILO Convention, reported on "recent legislation passed by the Parliament with a view to further strengthening the rights of tribal peoples and the machinery to enable them to manage their own affairs and preserve their socio-cultural heritage and separate identity." *Id.*

156. Such other contexts include the U.N. General Assembly at the inauguration of the International Year of the World's Indigenous People in December 1992 and at the inauguration of the International Decade in December 1994; the U.N.-sponsored World Conference on Human Rights in Vienna, June 14–25, 1993, particularly under its agenda item, "Commemoration of the International Year of the World's Indigenous People"; and, increasingly, the annual sessions of the U.N. Human Rights Commission and its Sub-Commission on Prevention of Discrimination and Protection of Minorities.

157. For example, the report of the 1991 session of the sub-commission working group, states:

Several Governments reported that their countries had experienced political changes and indigenous peoples have benefitted from the new constitutional reforms and enactment of legislation. Indigenous representatives participated in the drafting process or were consulted. As some indigenous representatives stated, even at this stage, new laws are being proposed or have been adopted which recognize the right to self-determination of indigenous peoples and their right to land, acknowledge the jurisdiction of indigenous peoples in their own territories, suggest mechanisms for dealing with the settlement of land claims, and recognize the right to education and health care.

Report of the Working Group on Indigenous Populations on Its Ninth Session, U.N. Doc. E/CN.4/Sub.2/1991/40 (1991), at 12.

158. Declaración de Colombia en Nombre del Grupo Latinoamericano y del Caribe en la Conmemoración del Año Internacional de las Poblaciones Indígenas (Tema 8), Conferencia Mundial de Derechos Humanos (June 18, 1993) (translation from Spanish is my own).

159. H. E. Ambassador Haakon B. Hjelde, Head of the Norwegian Delegation, Statement on Behalf of the Delegations of Finland, Sweden and Norway to the World Conference on Human Rights in Vienna (June 18, 1993).

160. Z. A. Kornilova, Statement by Member of the Delegation of the Russian Federation at the World Conference on Human Rights on Agenda Item 8, "International Year of the World's Indigenous People" (June 18, 1993).

161. The following works identify and discuss the numerous constitutional and legislative reforms in the Americas over the last several years: Bartolomé Clavero, *Derecho indígena y cultura constitutional en América* (1994); *Derecho Indígena* (Magdalena Gómez, ed. 1997); *The Challenge of Diversity—Indigenous Peoples and Reform of the State in Latin America* (Willem Assis et al. eds., 2000); Donna Lee Van Cott, *The Friendly Liquidation of the Past: The Politics of Diversity in Latin America* (2000); Ama Llunku & Abya Yala, *Constituyencia indígena y código ladino por América* (2000). Relevant parts of the constitutions and legislation of several Latin American countries are reproduced in *Derechos de los Pueblos Indígenas* 399–436 (Josu Legarreta et al. eds., 1998. *See also infra* chapter 5 (discussing developments in numerous countries).

162. *See* Meron, *supra* note 78, at 57–60.

II

CONTEMPORARY
INTERNATIONAL NORMS

3

Self-Determination:
A Foundational Principle

As demonstrated in the preceding chapter, international norms have developed in the specific context of indigenous peoples over the last several years, including those articulated in International Labour Organization Convention No. 169 on Indigenous and Tribal Peoples, as well as those now discernible as customary international law. These norms arise within international law's modern human rights frame, and hence they derive largely from more broadly applicable human rights standards that are well established in international law. By the same token, the broadly applicable human rights principles and norms, which are included in several multilateral treaties and other written instruments that have been promulgated by the United Nations and regional institutions, are in themselves relevant to indigenous peoples' efforts to survive and flourish under conditions of equality. Generally applicable human rights principles combine with developments specifically concerning indigenous peoples to establish the applicable normative regime. This regime includes a series of interrelated norms that address indigenous peoples' concerns, along with a duty on the part of states to take the steps necessary to implement these norms. Part II of this book is an effort to define the structure and core elements of this contemporary normative regime that concerns indigenous peoples, beginning with its foundations in the principle of self-determination.

No discussion of indigenous peoples' rights under international law is complete without a discussion of self-determination, a principle of the highest order within the contemporary international system. Indigenous peoples have repeatedly articulated their demands in terms of self-determination, and, in turn, self-determination precepts have fueled the international movement in favor of those demands.

Affirmed in the United Nations Charter[1] and other major international legal instruments,[2] self-determination is widely acknowledged to be a principle of customary international law and even *jus cogens*, a peremptory norm.[3] Mention of self-determination within contemporary political discourse has at times raised the specter of destabilization and even violent turmoil. And indeed, as many have observed, self-determination rhetoric has been invoked in the world of late in association with extremist political posturing and ethnic chauvinism.[4] Furthermore, a number of states have resisted express usage of the term *self-determination* in articulating indigenous peoples' rights.[5] But notwithstanding rhetorical extremism or aversion to express invocation of the *term self-determination*, the *concept* underlying the term entails a certain nexus of widely shared values. These values and related processes of decision can be seen as a stabilizing force in the international system and as foundational to international law's contemporary treatment of indigenous peoples.

In the following pages, self-determination is identified as a universe of human rights precepts concerned broadly with peoples, including indigenous peoples, and grounded in the idea that all are equally entitled to control their own destinies. Self-determination gives rise to remedies that tear at the legacies of empire, discrimination, suppression of democratic participation, and cultural suffocation. This chapter defines the principle of self-determination generally and identifies its particular significance for indigenous peoples in light of contemporary developments.[6]

The Character and Scope of Self-Determination

The concept of self-determination derives from philosophical affirmation of the human drive to translate aspiration into reality, coupled with postulates of inherent human equality.[7] Scholars have often cited the normative precepts of freedom and equality invoked in the American revolt against British rule and the overthrow of the French monarchy as progenitors of the modern concept of self-determination.[8] The core values associated with self-determination, however, clearly are not solely within the province of the history of Western thought. In his concurring opinion in the *Namibia* case before the International Court of Justice, Judge Ammoun identified equality as a central precept of self-determination and linked it with "[t]wo streams of thought . . . established on the two opposite shores of the Mediterranean, a Graeco-Roman stream represented by Epictetus, Lucan, Cicero and Marcus Aurelius; and an Asian and African stream, comprising the monks of Sinai and Saint John Climac, Alexandria with Plotinus and Philo the Jew, Carthage to which Saint Augustine gave new lustre."[9]

The term *self-determination* gained prominence in international political discourse around World War I.[10] President Woodrow Wilson linked the principle of self-determination with Western liberal democratic ideals and the aspirations of European nationalists.[11] Lenin and Stalin also embraced the rhetoric of self-determination in the early part of this century, while viewing self-determination in association with Marxist precepts of class liberation.[12] World War II gave rise to the United Nations, and "self-determination of peoples" was included in the United Nations Charter among the organization's founding principles.[13] The international human rights covenants hold out self-determination as a "right" of "[a]ll peoples,"[14] as do the African Charter on Human and Peoples' Rights[15] and the Helsinki Final Act.[16]

For a period in history, international law was concerned only with the rights and duties of independent sovereigns, disregarding the face of humanity beyond the sovereign.[17] Under the modern rubric of human rights, however, international law increasingly is concerned with upholding rights deemed to inhere in human beings individually as well as collectively.[18] Extending from core values of human freedom and equality, expressly associated with peoples instead of states, and affirmed in a number of international human rights instruments, the principle of self-determination arises within international law's human rights frame and hence benefits human beings *as human beings* and not sovereign entities as such.[19] Like all human rights norms, moreover, self-determination is presumptively universal in scope and thus must be assumed to benefit all segments of humanity.[20]

While human beings fundamentally are the beneficiaries of the principle of self-determination, the principle bears upon the institutions of government under which human beings live. Self-determination is extraordinary as a vehicle for coalescing international concern for the essential character of government structures, a concern that may extend to the point of enjoining them to yield authority or territory. When first articulated as a principle of international relations around World War I, self-determination justified the breakup of the German, Austro-Hungarian, and Ottoman empires and served as a prescriptive vehicle for the redivision of Europe in the wake of the empires' downfall.[21] In its most prominent modern manifestation within the international system, self-determination has promoted the demise of colonial institutions of government and the emergence of a new political order for subject peoples.[22] Also, the international community through the United Nations declared illegitimate, on grounds of self-determination, South Africa's previous governing institutional order, with its entrenched system of apartheid.[23]

In each of these contexts, values linked with self-determination constituted a standard of legitimacy against which institutions of government were measured. Self-determination is not separate from other human rights norms; rather, self-determination is a configurative principle or framework complemented by the more specific human rights norms that in their totality enjoin the governing institutional order. As discussed below, this framework concerns both the procedures by which governing institutions develop and the form they take for their ongoing functioning.

Implications of the Term *Peoples*

Although self-determination presumptively benefits all human beings, its linkage with the term *peoples* in international instruments[24] indicates the collective or group character of the principle. Self-determination is concerned with human beings, not simply as individuals with autonomous will but more as social creatures engaged in the constitution and functioning of communities. In its plain meaning, the term *peoples* undoubtedly embraces the multitude of indigenous groups like the Maori, the Miskito, and the Navajo, which comprise distinct communities, each with its own social, cultural, and political attributes richly rooted in history.[25]

Many, however, have interpreted the use of the term *peoples* in this connection as restricting the scope of self-determination; the principle of self-determination is deemed only concerned with "peoples" in the sense of a limited universe of narrowly defined, mutually exclusive communities entitled a priori to the full range of sovereign powers, including independent statehood. This approach has encouraged controversy over whether indigenous peoples are "peoples" entitled to self-determination.

There are three dominant variants of this restrictive approach regarding the term *peoples*, each of them problematic. One variant holds that self-determination only applies to the populations of territories that are under conditions of classical colonialism.[26] This view focuses on the international decolonization regime that resulted in independent statehood for colonial territories as integral units. This approach correctly identifies decolonization as a manifestation of the principle of self-determination, but it goes too far in effectively equating the scope of self-determination with the scope of decolonization procedures.[27] Limiting self-determination's applicability to the peoples in territories of a classical colonial type denies self-determination's relevance to all segments of humanity and thus undermines the principle's human rights character.

A second variant holds that the "peoples" entitled to self-determination include the aggregate populations of independent states, as well as those of classical colonial territories.[28] The proposition that self-determination is concerned with the "peoples" of both states and colonial territories substantially approaches a conception of self-determination as a human rights principle benefiting all segments of humanity. The difficulty is in the underlying view that *only* such units of human aggregation—the *whole* of the population of an independent state or a colonial territory entitled to independent statehood—are beneficiaries of self-determination. This conception renders self-determination inapplicable to the vast number of substate groups whose claims represent many of the world's most pressing problems in the postcolonial age.[29] And by effectively denying a priori a right of self-determination to groups that in many instances passionately assert it as a basis for their demands, this limited conception may serve to inflame tensions. Moreover, as will be argued, an effectively state-centered conception of self-determination is anachronistic in a world in which state boundaries mean less and less and are by no means coextensive with all relevant spheres of community.

Proponents of a third variant accept the premise of a world divided into mutually exclusive territorial communities. This view, however, does not define the "peoples" entitled to self-determination by the status quo of recognized statehood or colonial territorial boundaries but rather by an alternative political geography defined by perceived spheres of ethnographic cohesion and historically exercised territorial sovereignty; "peoples" are those units that either once were sovereign states or, by virtue of a postulate of ethnonationalist theory, are entitled to be states.[30] This view, frequently invoked by self-determination claimants, partially explains the redivision of Europe at the end of World War I along ethnographic lines.[31] However, the view is problematic in that it misstates the value accorded ethnicity and historical community within the international system outside the highly charged political context of post–World War I Europe. Rights of self-determination affirmed in the decolonization context did not attach to groups by virtue of ethnic makeup or historical sovereignty.[32] And the international community has not in recent times generally responded favorably to self-determination claims solely on the strength of ethnonationalist assertions or accounts of historical sovereignty.[33]

More fundamentally, the foregoing variants of the narrow conception of the term *peoples* are flawed in their limited underlying vision of a world divided into mutually exclusive "sovereign" territorial communities.[34] This vision corresponds with the traditional Western theoretical perspective that limits humanity to two perceptual categories—the individual and the state—and which views states according to the post-Westphalian model of mutually exclusive spheres of territory, community, and centralized authority.[35] The limited conception of "peoples," accordingly, largely ignores the multiple, overlapping spheres of community, authority, and interdependency that actually exist in the human experience. Humanity effectively is reduced to units of organization defined by a perceptual grip of statehood categories; the human rights character of self-determination is thereby obscured as is the relevance of self-determination values in a world that is less and less state centered.

The term *peoples* as it relates to a contemporary understanding of self-determination must attend to the broad range of associational and cultural patterns actually found in the human experience.[36] At the same time local communities have gained greater autonomy and new states have emerged, communities at all levels have sought greater integration. Virtually at the same time the Baltic republics gained independence from the former Soviet Union, for example, they became part of the United Nations and its expanding web of authority and cooperation, and Baltic leaders initiated steps to enter into trade alliances with Nordic countries[37] and to gain membership in the European Union.[38] As indigenous

peoples of Nicaragua have achieved greater political autonomy, they simultaneously have secured greater representation in the institutions of the Nicaraguan
state[39]; they have attempted to secure greater recognition of authority at the village level[40] while opening their isolated region to more commerce and seeking political linkages with the outside world.[41] And in the years following the
death of its longtime dictator Francisco Franco, Spain devolved substantial authority to autonomous, culturally distinctive communities,[42] while moving toward greater integration with Europe and the rest of the world.[43]

In an informative article addressing patterns of identity among indigenous
Americans, Professor Duane Champagne discusses the traditional forms of political organization of the Iroquois Confederacy and the Creek Indians of North
America.[44] Professor Champagne points out that these groups, typically of Native American tribes, do not represent singular political or national identities for
the people they encompass.[45] He observes that both the Iroquois and the Creek
people traditionally had—and to great extent continue to have—segmentary
political structures defined by kinship, geography, and function.[46]

The political philosophy for the Iroquois Confederacy, or the Haudenosaunee,
is expressed in the Great Law of Peace, which describes a great tree with roots
extending in the four cardinal directions to all peoples of the earth; all are invited to follow the roots to the tree and join in peaceful coexistence and cooperation under its great long leaves.[47] The Great Law of Peace promotes unity
among individuals, families, clans, and nations while upholding the integrity of
diverse identities and spheres of autonomy.[48] Similar ideals have been expressed
by leaders of other indigenous groups in contemporary appeals to international
bodies.[49] Such conceptions outside the mold of classical Western liberalism would
appear to provide a more appropriate foundation for understanding humanity,
its aspirations, and its political development than the model of a world divided
into exclusive, monolithic communities, and hence a more appropriate backdrop
for understanding the subject matter of self-determination.

To understand self-determination as concerned only with narrowly defined,
mutually exclusive "peoples" is to diminish the relevance of self-determination
values in a world that is in fact evolving differently. Although the history of
the world is of both integration and disintegration, the overriding trend appears
now to be one of enhanced interconnectedness. This observation does not
diminish the value of diverse cultures or local authority but, rather, supports the
fact of increasing linkages, commonalities, and interdependencies among people,
economies, and spheres of power. Group challenges to the political structures
that engulf them appear to be not so much claims of absolute political autonomy
as they are efforts to secure the integrity of the group while rearranging the
terms of integration or rerouting its path. Even where secession and independent statehood are achieved, they are but steps in an ongoing process of global
interconnectedness.

Any conception of self-determination that does not take into account the multiple patterns of human association and interdependency is at best incomplete and more likely distorted. The values of freedom and equality implicit in the concept of self-determination have meaning for the multiple and overlapping spheres of human association and political ordering that characterize humanity. Properly understood, the principle of self-determination, commensurate with the values it incorporates, benefits groups—that is, "peoples" in the ordinary sense of the term—throughout the spectrum of humanity's complex web of interrelationships and loyalties, and not just peoples defined by existing or perceived sovereign boundaries. And in a world of increasingly overlapping and integrated political spheres, self-determination concerns the constitution and functioning of all levels and forms of government under which people live. The term *peoples* in this context, a context that joins consideration of human rights with political ordering, should be understood to refer to all those spheres of community, marked by elements of identity and collective consciousness, within which people's lives unfold—independently of considerations of historical or postulated sovereignty.[50] These include not just the aggregate populations of states and colonial territories but other spheres of community that define human existence and place in the world, including indigenous peoples as well as other groups.[51] Ordinarily, terms in international legal instruments are to be interpreted according to their plain meaning and context.[52] There should be no exception for the term *peoples*.

The Content of Self-Determination

At bottom, the resistance toward acknowledging self-determination as implying rights for literally all peoples is founded on the misconception that self-determination in its fullest sense means a right to independent statehood, even if the right is not to be exercised right away or is to be exercised to achieve some alternative status. This misconception is often reinforced by reference to decolonization, which has involved the transformation of colonial territories into new states under the normative aegis of self-determination.[53] Inextricably wedding self-determination to entitlements or attributes of statehood is misguided for reasons already discussed, and such a linkage does not necessarily follow from decolonization.

Given its prominence in the international practice of self-determination, decolonization indeed provides a point of reference for understanding the scope and content of self-determination. As already indicated, however, it is a mistake to equate self-determination with the decolonization regime, which has entailed a limited category of subjects, prescriptions, and procedures.[54] Decolonization prescriptions do not themselves embody the *substance* of the principle of self-determination; rather, they correspond with measures to *remedy* a sui generis deviation from the principle existing in the prior condition of colonialism in its classical form.

Self-determination precepts comprise a world-order standard with which colonialism was at odds and with which other institutions of government also may conflict. The substantive content of the principle of self-determination, therefore, inheres in the precepts by which the international community has held colonialism illegitimate and which apply universally to benefit all human beings individually and collectively. The *substance* of the norm—the precepts that define the standard—must be distinguished from the *remedial* prescriptions that may follow a violation of the norm, such as those developed to undo colonization. In the decolonization context, procedures that resulted in independent statehood were means of discarding alien rule that had been contrary to the enjoyment of self-determination. Remedial prescriptions in other contexts will vary according to the relevant circumstances and need not inevitably result in the formation of new states.

Accordingly, while the substantive elements of self-determination apply broadly to benefit all segments of humanity, that is, all peoples, self-determination applies more narrowly in its remedial aspect. Remedial prescriptions and mechanisms developed by the international community necessarily only benefit groups that have suffered violations of substantive self-determination. Indigenous peoples characteristically are within the more narrow category of self-determination beneficiaries, which includes groups entitled to remedial measures; but the remedial regime developing in the context of indigenous peoples is not one that favors the formation of new states.[55] Before the application and development of the principle of self-determination in the particular context of indigenous peoples is more specifically discussed, a description of the general contours of the principle's substantive and remedial aspects is in order.

Substantive Aspects

As discussed previously, self-determination entails a universe of human rights precepts extending from core values of freedom and equality and applying in favor of human beings in relation to the institutions of government under which they live. In essence, self-determination comprises a standard of governmental legitimacy within the modern human rights frame. Despite divergence in models of governmental legitimacy, relevant international actors at any given point in time after the creation of the United Nations Charter have shared a nexus of opinion and behavior about the minimum conditions for the constitution and functioning of legitimate government. The substance of the principle of self-determination, which presumptively benefits all segments of humanity, is in that more or less identifiable nexus. In brief, substantive self-determination consists of two normative strains: First, in what may be called its *constitutive* aspect, self-determination requires that the governing institutional order be substantially the creation of processes guided by the will of the people, or peoples, governed. Second, in what may be called its *ongoing* aspect, self-determination requires that the governing institutional order, independently of the processes leading to its creation or alteration, be one under which people may live and develop freely on a continuous basis.

The framework articulated here differs from the dichotomy of "internal" versus "external" self-determination that has appeared in much of the scholarly literature on the subject.[56] The internal/external dichotomy views self-determination as having two discrete domains: one having to do with matters entirely internal to a people (such as rights of political participation) and the other having to do exclusively with a people's status or dealings vis-à-vis other peoples (such as freedom from alien rule). The internal/external dichotomy effectively is premised on the conception, rejected earlier, of a limited universe of "peoples" comprising mutually exclusive spheres of community (i.e., states). Given the reality of multiple human associational patterns in today's world, including but not exclusively those organized around the state, it is distorting to attempt to organize self-determination precepts into discrete internal versus external spheres defined by reference to presumptively mutually exclusive peoples. The alternative framework presented here of constitutive and ongoing self-determination instead identifies two phenomenological aspects of self-determination that apply throughout the spectrum of multiple and overlapping spheres of human association, and that both have implications for the inward- and outward-looking dimensions of units of human organization.

In its constitutive aspect, self-determination comprises a standard that enjoins the occasional or episodic procedures leading to the creation of or change in institutions of government within any given sphere of community. When institutions are born or merged with others, when their constitutions are altered, or when they endeavor to extend the scope of their authority, these phenomena are the domain of constitutive self-determination. Constitutive self-determination does not itself dictate the outcome of such procedures; but where they occur it imposes requirements of participation and consent such that the end result in the political order can be said to reflect the collective will of the people, or peoples, concerned. This aspect of self-determination corresponds with the provision common to the international human rights covenants and other instruments that state that peoples "freely determine their political status" by virtue of the right of self-determination.[57] It is not possible to identify precisely the bounds of international consensus concerning the required levels and means of individual or group participation in all contexts of institutional birth or change. Certain minimum standards, however, are evident.

Colonization was rendered illegitimate in part by reference to the processes leading to colonial rule, processes that today clearly represent impermissible territorial expansion of governmental authority.[58] The world community now holds in contempt the imposition of government structures upon people, regardless of their social or political makeup.[59] The world community now appears generally to accept President Woodrow Wilson's admonition, made as he was elaborating his view of self-determination in the midst of the European turmoil of World War I, that "no right anywhere exists to hand peoples about from sovereignty to sovereignty as if they were property."[60] Today, procedures toward the creation, alteration, or territorial extension of governmental authority normally are regulated by self-determination precepts requiring minimum levels of participation on the part of all affected peoples commensurate with their respective interests.[61]

Apart from self-determination's constitutive aspect, which applies to discrete episodes of institutional birth or change, *ongoing* self-determination continuously enjoins the form and functioning of the governing institutional order. In essence, ongoing self-determination requires a governing order under which individuals and groups are able to make meaningful choices in matters touching upon all spheres of life on a continuous basis. In the words of the self-determination provision common to the international human rights covenants and other instruments, peoples are to "freely pursue their economic, social, and cultural development."[62]

In this respect as well, the international community's condemnation of colonial administration represents a minimum standard. The world community has come to regard classical colonialism as an oppressive form of governance, independently of its origins. Despite the divergence of political theory at the height of the decolonization movement in the 1950s and 1960s, a divergence that fueled the polarization of geopolitical forces for decades, there was a certain consensus on precepts of freedom and equality upon which the international community viewed colonial governance as oppressive.[63] Accordingly, at least since the middle part of the last century, colonial structures have been widely deplored for depriving the indigenous inhabitants of equal status vis-à-vis the colonizers in the administration of their affairs.[64] In more recent years, notions of democracy and cultural pluralism increasingly have informed the expectations of the international community in regard to the ongoing functioning of government at all levels of authority.[65] Hence, for a culturally differentiated group, ongoing self-determination requires a democratic political order in which the group is able to continue its distinct character and "to have this character reflected in the institutions of government under which it lives."[66]

Remedial Aspects

The international concern over conditions that deviate from the substantive elements of self-determination has given rise to remedial prescriptions and mechanisms, most prominently those of the decolonization regime. As already noted, decolonization manifests the remedial aspect of the principle of self-determination, rather than its substantive elements. The prescriptions promoted through the international system to undo colonization, while not themselves equal to the principle of self-determination, were contextually specific *remedial* prescriptions arising from colonialism's deviation from the generally applicable norm. As we have seen, colonialism violated both the constitutive and ongoing aspects of self-determination. Although the violation of constitutive self-determination in the context of colonial territories was mostly a historical one, it was linked to a contemporary condition of oppression including the denial of ongoing self-determination.

Decolonization demonstrates that self-determination's remedial aspect may trump or alter otherwise applicable legal doctrine. In particular, the doctrine of effectiveness ordinarily confirms *de jure* sovereignty over territory once it is exercised *de facto*, independently of the legitimacy of events leading to the effective control. Further, under the doctrine of intertemporality, events ordinarily are to be judged in accordance with the contemporaneous law. Historical patterns of colonization appear to be consistent with or confirmed by international law prior to the modern era of human rights. Around the turn of the century international law doctrine upheld imperial spheres of influence asserted by Western powers and deferred to their effective exercise of authority over lands inhabited by "backward," "uncivilized," or "semi-civilized" people.[67]

The modern international law of self-determination, however, forges exceptions to or alters the doctrines of effectiveness and intertemporal law. Pursuant to the principle of self-determination, the international community has deemed illegitimate historical patterns giving rise to colonial rule and has promoted corresponding remedial measures, irrespective of the effective control exercised by the colonial power and notwithstanding the law contemporaneous with the historical colonial patterns. Decolonization demonstrates that constitutional processes may be judged retroactively in light of self-determination values—notwithstanding effective control or contemporaneous legal doctrine—where such processes remain relevant to the legitimacy of governmental authority or otherwise manifest themselves in contemporary inequities.

By the same token, remedies to redress historical violations of self-determination do not necessarily entail a reversion to the status quo ante but, rather, are to be developed in accordance with the present-day aspirations of the aggrieved groups, whose character may be substantially altered with the passage of time. Liberation movements in Africa promoted decolonization through the establishment of new political orders organized on the basis of the territorial boundaries imposed by the colonial powers, despite the arbitrary character of most such boundaries in relation to precolonial political and social organization. This model of decolonization ultimately was adopted by the United Nations and confirmed by the Organization of African Unity (now the African Union).[68] On-going self-determination—a governing institutional order in which people may live and develop freely—was deemed implemented for a colonial territory through "(a) [e]mergence as a sovereign independent State; (b) [f]ree association with an independent State; or (c) [i]ntegration with an independent State" on the basis of equality.[69] And because the decolonization remedy itself involved change in the governing institutional order, constitutive self-determination dictated deference to the aspirations of the people concerned for the purposes of arriving at the appropriate institutional arrangement. In most instances, independent statehood was the presumed or express preference.

In its focus on the colonial territorial unit, this model of decolonization bypassed spheres of community—that is, tribal and ethnic groupings—that existed prior to colonialism; but it also largely ignored the ethnic and tribal identities that *continued* to exist and hold meaning in the lives of people. Hence, as to some enclave groups or groups divided by colonial frontiers, decolonization procedures alone may not have allowed for a sufficient range of choice or otherwise may not have constituted a complete remedy.[70] In any event, as far as they went toward the objective of purging colonial territories of alien rule, decolonization procedures adhered to the preferences of living human beings—if only the preferences of the majority voice in the colonial territories.

In the *Western Sahara* case,[71] the International Court of Justice affirmed that self-determination gives precedence to the present-day aspirations of aggrieved peoples over historical institutions. In an advisory opinion, the Court held that the Western Sahara was not *terra nullius* at the time it was acquired by Spain in the late nineteenth century, because of an immediately prior course of dealings between Europeans and indigenous political leaders demonstrating contemporaneous recognition of organized communities.[72] The Court refused to give weight to legal theory of that period treating all lands not under a Western sovereign as *terra nullius*. The Court then found legally relevant "historical ties" between the people of the Western Sahara and the political communities corresponding with the modern (newly independent) states of Morocco and Mauritania.[73] In the end, however, the Court held that these historical ties of political community and allegiance were subordinate to the wishes of the present-day people of the Western Sahara in the decolonization of the territory.[74] The Court stressed that self-determination, the overriding principle in the decolonization of the Western Sahara, required regard for the freely expressed wishes of the people of the territory, notwithstanding their character or political status immediately prior to colonization.[75]

To the extent the international community is generally concerned with promoting self-determination precepts, and as it develops and expands its common understanding about those precepts, it may identify contextual deviations from self-determination beyond classical colonialism and promote appropriate rem-

edies in accordance with the aspirations of the groups concerned. With appropriate attentiveness to the particular character of deviant conditions or events,
and with an understanding of the interconnected character of virtually all forms
of modern human association, these remedies need not entail the formation of
new states.[76] Secession, however, may be an appropriate remedial option in
limited contexts (as opposed to a generally available "right") where substantive self-determination for a particular group cannot otherwise be assured or
where there is a net gain in the overall welfare of all concerned.[77] In most cases
in the postcolonial world, however, secession would most likely be a cure worse
than the disease from the standpoint of all concerned.

Considerations of state sovereignty form a backdrop for the elaboration of
self-determination remedies and influence the degree to which remedies may
be subject to international scrutiny. The limitations of the international doctrine
of sovereignty in its modern formulation are essentially twofold. First, sovereignty upholds a substantive preference for the status quo of political ordering
through its corollaries protective of state territorial integrity and political unity.[78]
Second, the doctrine limits the capacity of the international system to regulate
matters within the spheres of authority asserted by states recognized by the international community. This limitation upon international competency is reflected
in the United Nations Charter's admonition against intervention "in matters which
are essentially within the domestic jurisdiction of any state."[79]

Under contemporary international law, however, the doctrine of sovereignty
and its Charter affirmations are conditioned by the human rights values also
expressed in the Charter and embraced by the international community.[80] In a
global community that remains organized substantially by state jurisdictional
boundaries, sovereignty principles continue, in some measure, to advance human
values of stability and ordered liberty, and they guard the people within a state
against disruptive forces coming from outside the state's domestic domain. But
since the atrocities and suffering of the two world wars, international law does
not much uphold sovereignty principles when they would serve as an accom-
plice to the subjugation of human rights or act as a shield against international
concern that coalesces to promote human rights. This of course is the lesson of
decolonization and the modern human rights movement within the international
system. Vattel's conception of sovereignty principles as arising fundamentally
from human interests carries weight today.[81]

Thus, ideally, self-determination and sovereignty principles will work in tan-
dem to promote a peaceful, stable, and humane world. But, where there is a violation of self-determination and human rights, presumptions in favor of territorial
integrity or political unity of existing states may be offset to the extent required
by an appropriate remedy.[82] Furthermore, heightened international scrutiny and
even intervention is justified in the degree to which violations of human rights

are prone to lingering unchecked by decision makers within the domestic realm. Such heightened international scrutiny, along with a limited suspension of state sovereignty presumptions, has been forged in the context of indigenous peoples.

Self-Determination and Contemporary International Practice Concerning Indigenous Peoples

The contemporary international concern for indigenous peoples already discussed at length in chapter 2 is based effectively on the identification of a long-standing *sui generis* deviation from the self-determination standard, one that is in addition to the *sui generis* deviation represented by twentieth-century classical colonialism. Indeed, the rubric of indigenous peoples or populations is generally understood to refer to culturally cohesive groups that suffer inequities within the states in which they live in connection with historical patterns of empire and conquest.[83] Indigenous peoples of today typically share much the same history of colonialism suffered by those still living in the last century under formal colonial structures and targeted for decolonization procedures. But despite the contemporary absence of colonial structures in the classical form, indigenous peoples have continued to suffer impediments or threats to their ability to live and develop freely as distinct groups in their original homelands. The historical violations of indigenous peoples' self-determination, together with contemporary inequities against them, still cast a dark shadow on the legitimacy of state authority, regardless of effective control or the law contemporaneous with historical events. Accordingly, the developing constellation of indigenous rights norms identified in chapter 2 in large measure comprises a remedial regime, although the constellation also contains prescriptions that detail the substantive elements of self-determination in the specific context of indigenous peoples.[84]

The Draft United Nations Declaration on the Rights of Indigenous Peoples which was developed by the U.N. Working Group on Indigenous Populations and approved by its parent body, the Sub-Commission on Prevention of Discrimination and Protection of Minorities (now the Sub-Commission on Promotion and Protection of Human Rights), contains specific recognition of the right of indigenous peoples to self-determination. The draft declaration, borrowing from the self-determination language of the international human rights covenants, states: "Indigenous peoples have the right of self-determination. By virtue of that right they freely determine their political status and freely pursue their economic, social and cultural development."[85]

Such an express affirmation of indigenous self-determination has been slow to command a broad consensus among governments participating in the standard-setting work of either the United Nations or the Organization of American States, mostly as a result of the misguided tendency to equate the word *self-*

determination with decolonization procedures or with an absolute right to form an independent state.[86] It is noteworthy that the Proposed American Declaration on the Rights of Indigenous Peoples, which was drafted by the OAS Inter-American Commission on Human Rights, does not contain an explicit affirmation of indigenous self-determination.[87]

More and more governments, however, have moved away from an opposition to the term *self-determination* and have demonstrated a disposition toward its express usage in association with an articulation of indigenous peoples' rights. The Australian government signaled this trend in a statement to the 1991 session of the U.N. Working Group on Indigenous Populations, expressing "hope" that it would be possible to find an acceptable way to refer to self-determination in the U.N. declaration:

> Events in all parts of the world show us that the concept of self-determination must be considered broadly, that is, not only as the attainment of national independence. Peoples are seeking to assert their identities, to preserve their languages, cultures, and traditions and to achieve greater self-management and autonomy, free from undue interference from central governments.[88]

Along these same lines, the government of Canada, in a statement before the working group established by the U.N. Commission on Human Rights to study the draft declaration on indigenous rights, said that it

> accepts a right of self-determination for indigenous peoples which respects the political, constitutional and territorial integrity of democratic states. In that context, exercise of the right involves negotiations between states and the various indigenous peoples within those states to determine the political status of the indigenous peoples involved, and the means of pursuing their economic, social and cultural development. These negotiations must reflect the jurisdictions and competence of governments and must take account of the different needs, circumstances and aspirations of the indigenous peoples involved.[89]

Although in more qualified terms, the United States also adopted, in 2001, a position in favor of understanding the right of self-determination to apply to indigenous peoples. Accepting the problematic internal versus external dichotomy of self-determination, the U.S. administration established the policy of supporting

> use of the term "internal self-determination" in both the UN and OAS declarations on indigenous rights, defined as follows: 'Indigenous peoples have a right of internal self-determination. By virtue of that right, they may negotiate their political status within the framework of the existing nation-state and are free to pursue their economic, social, and cultural development. Indigenous peoples, in exercising their right of internal self-determination have the internal right of autonomy or self-government in matters relating to their local affairs, including determination of membership, culture, language, religion, education, informa-

tion, media, health, housing, employment, social welfare, economic activities, lands and resources management, environment and entry by non-members, as well as ways and means for financing these autonomous functions.[90]

The U.S. position in this regard had already been suggested in earlier statements made to the U.N. Working Group on Indigenous Populations[91] and by its initial report to the U.N. Human Rights Committee, submitted in 1994, pursuant to its reporting obligations under the International Covenant on Civil and Political Rights. As part of its effort to establish compliance with the right of self-determination affirmed in article 1 of the covenant, the United States gave an extensive account of its law and policy concerning Native Americans, particularly in regards to rights of self-government.[92]

Several other states have indicated support for explicitly recognizing self-determination as a norm that in some measure extends to indigenous peoples, in the course of the discussions aimed at promulgating U.N. and OAS declarations on indigenous rights. These states include (but are not limited to) Brazil, Chile, Cuba, Denmark, Ecuador, Finland, France, Guatemala, Mexico, Norway, New Zealand, Pakistan, Russia, Spain, Switzerland, and Venezuela.[93] At the 2002 session of the U.N. Commission on Human Rights working group on the draft declaration, Mexico went so far as to endorse complete acceptance of the sub-commission draft of the U.N. declaration, which includes the far-reaching language quoted earlier affirming the right of indigenous peoples to self-determination.[94] Summarizing the discussion on self-determination among the numerous states participating in the 1999 session of the Commission on Human Rights working group, the delegate from Guatemala observed approvingly that no state had expressly rejected inclusion of the right to self-determination for indigenous peoples in the declaration.[95] The chair of the working group at the same session concluded from the discussion that the "participants in general agreed that the right to self-determination was the cornerstone of the draft declaration."[96] He further identified "broad agreement" that "the right to self-determination could not be exercised to the detriment of the independence and territorial integrity of States," and he observed that states expressing support for recognizing indigenous peoples' right of self-determination did so with the understanding that this right does not imply a right of secession.[97] This understanding has been reaffirmed in subsequent sessions of the Commission on Human Rights working group, even while a consensus on the precise formulation of indigenous self-determination has remained elusive.[98]

It is in any case proper to conclude that, as a matter of already existing international law, the principle or right of self-determination applies in one way or another to indigenous peoples. This conclusion has been advanced by the U.N. Human Rights Committee in relation to the self-determination provision in article 1 of the International Covenant on Civil and Political Rights. The U.N.

Human Rights Committee, which is charged with monitoring compliance with the covenant, has interpreted article 1 to apply to indigenous peoples in a manner consistent with the prevailing themes in the discussions on the self-determination provision of the Draft U.N. Declaration on the Rights of Indigenous Peoples. In commenting upon Canada's fourth periodic report under the Covenant, the committee stated that the right of self-determination affirmed in article 1 protects indigenous peoples, *inter alia*, in their enjoyment of rights over traditional lands and resources, and it recommended that, in relation to the aboriginal people of Canada, "the practice of extinguishing inherent aboriginal rights be abandoned as incompatible with article 1 of the Covenant."[99] The committee also has invoked the right of self-determination in examining reports from Australia, Norway, and Mexico as they relate to indigenous peoples.[100] Thus far the Human Rights Committee has tended to address indigenous issues within the framework of the right of self-determination of article 1 only in relation to those states that have already conceded its applicability in this context. Nonetheless, in order that it may be deemed to be conforming with basic precepts of coherence and uniformity that are required of all human rights instruments, the committee must be assumed to be applying what it considers to be the scope and meaning of article 1 for all state parties.

Even though rhetorical sensitivities continue among states toward usage of the term *self-determination*, those sensitivities generally do not entail an aversion to applying self-determination's underlying normative precepts to indigenous peoples, if those precepts are understood not to require a state for every "people." Government statements to relevant U.N. and other international bodies are consistent with understanding self-determination to mean that indigenous groups and their members are entitled to be full and equal participants in the creation of the institutions of government under which they live and, further, to live within a governing institutional order in which they are perpetually in control of their own destinies.[101]

Insofar as indigenous peoples have been denied self-determination thus understood, the international indigenous rights regime prescribes remedial measures that may involve change in the political order and hence, in keeping with constitutive self-determination, are to be developed in accordance with the aspirations of indigenous peoples themselves. Thus, ILO Convention No. 169 on Indigenous and Tribal Peoples requires the development of "special measures" to safeguard indigenous "persons, institutions, property, labour, cultures and environment"[102] and specifies that the measures be consistent with "the freely-expressed wishes of the peoples concerned."[103] Also, the convention requires that consultations with indigenous peoples "be undertaken, in good faith . . . with the objective of achieving agreement or consent."[104]

Professor Erica-Irene Daes, the long time chair of the U.N. Working Group on Indigenous Populations, describes self-determination in this context as entailing a form of "belated state-building" through negotiation or other appropriate peaceful procedures involving meaningful participation by indigenous groups.[105] According to Professor Daes, self-determination entails a process

> through which indigenous peoples are able to join with all the other peoples that make up the State on mutually-agreed upon and just terms, after many years of isolation and exclusion. This process does not require the assimilation of individuals, as citizens like all others, but the recognition and incorporation of distinct peoples in the fabric of the State, on agreed terms.[106]

In an illustrative case, the Inter-American Commission on Human Rights promoted such belated state building as a means of remedying the effective denial of self-determination suffered by the Miskito and other Indians of the Atlantic Coast region of Nicaragua. The Atlantic Coast region was incorporated within the Nicaraguan state by a series of nineteenth-century events that were devoid of adequate procedures of consultation with the indigenous population.[107] In the aftermath of the imposed incorporation, the indigenous Miskito, Mayangna (Sumo), and Rama Indians of the Atlantic Coast have lived at the margins of Nicaraguan society in terms of basic social welfare conditions.[108] Moreover, having retained their distinct indigenous identities, the Indians have suffered the imposition of government structures that have inhibited their capacity to exist and develop freely as distinct cultural communities.[109] Hence it can be said that the Indians of the Atlantic Coast have been deprived of self-determination in both its constitutive and ongoing aspects, especially if ongoing self-determination is understood to include precepts of cultural pluralism.

Not long after the revolutionary Sandinista government took power in 1979, it faced demands for political autonomy on the part of the Atlantic Coast indigenous communities. Early resistance to the demands led to a period of turmoil, exacerbated by the civil war that gripped the country during the 1980s. The Indians took their case to the Inter-American Commission on Human Rights, asserting violations of their human rights, including the right to self-determination.[110] Effectively equating self-determination with decolonization procedures, the commission found that the Indians were not self-determination beneficiaries.[111] However, defying its own limited articulation of self-determination, the commission acknowledged the inequitable condition of the Indians dating from their forced incorporation into the Nicaraguan state and found that their ability to develop freely in cultural and economic spheres was suppressed by the existing political order.[112] The commission thus suggested the elaboration of a new political order for the Indians[113]—in effect, a remedy to implement an ongoing condition of self-determination where it had been denied. And in accordance with precepts of constitutive self-determination, which also had been denied, the commission further held that such a remedy "can only effectively carry out its assigned purposes to the extent it is designed in the context of broad consultation, and carried out with the direct participation of the ethnic minorities of Nicaragua, through their freely chosen representatives."[114]

Following the commission's decision, the Nicaraguan government entered into negotiations with Indian leaders and eventually developed a constitutional and legislative regime of political and administrative autonomy for the Indian-populated Atlantic Coast region of the country.[115] Although the autonomy regime is widely acknowledged to be faulty, and its implementation has been exceedingly slow and difficult,[116] it nonetheless is by most accounts a step in the right direction. More significantly for the present purposes, it represents the kind of context-specific effort at belated state building now promoted by the international community to remedy the long-standing denial of indigenous peoples' self-determination.

Notes

1. U.N. Charter art. 1, para. 2.

2. *See infra* notes 13–16.

3. See Ian Brownlie, *Principles of Public International Law* 489 (6th ed. 2003); Héctor Gross Espiell, "Self-Determination and Jus Cogens," in *U.N. Law/Fundamental Rights: Two Topics in International Law* 167 (Antonio Cassese ed., 1979); Hurst Hannum, *Autonomy, Sovereignty and Self-Determination* 45 (1990); Patrick Thornberry, *International Law and the Rights of Minorities* 14 (1991); Malcolm Shaw, *Title to Territory in Africa: International Legal Issues* 89 (1988); *The Right to Self-Determination: Implementation of the United Nations Resolutions Relating to the Right of Peoples under Colonial and Alien Domination to Self-Determination*, para. 74, U.N. Doc. E/CN.4/Sub.2/405/Rev.1, U.N. Sales No. E.79.XIV.5 (1980) (Héctor Gross Espeill, special rapporteur).

4. *See* Louis René Beres, "Self-Determination, International Law and Survival on Planet Earth," 11 *Ariz. J. Int'l & Comp. L.* 1 (1994) (pointing out problems arising from use of self-determination to justify militaristic ethnonationalism); Asbjorn Eide, "In Search of Constructive Alternatives to Secession," in *Modern Law of Self Determination* 139 (Christian Tomuschat ed., 1993) (arguing that the "alleged right to self-determination all too frequently serves to justify" peace-threatening ethnonationalism); Ethan A. Klingsberg, "International Human Rights Intervention on Behalf of Minorities in Post–World War I Eastern Europe and Today: Placebo, Poison, or Panacea?" 1993 *U. Chi. L. Sch. Roundtable* 1, 10–21 (identifying a "self-determination syndrome" in connection with tactics of collective aggression among ethnic groups). *See generally* Daniel Patrick Moynihan, *Pandaemonium: Ethnicity in International Politics* (1993) (assessing nationalist movements in the aftermath of the cold war and their linkage to the principle of self-determination).

5. *See, e.g.,* opposition to express recognition of indigenous peoples' right to self-determination in the context of negotiating the text of ILO Convention No. 169, discussed in chapter 2, *supra*, notes 66–69 and accompanying text.

6. The conception of self-determination articulated here and its implications beyond the context of indigenous peoples are discussed more fully in S. James Anaya, "A

Contemporary Definition of the International Norm of Self-Determination," 3 *Transnat'l L. & Contemp. Probs.* 131 (1993). This interpretation of the international law of self-determination differs from that of such works as Antonio Cassese, *Self-Determination of Peoples: A Legal Reappraisal* (1995), which tend to emphasize what is already clearly reflected in the actual behavior of states and international actors, or what has already been decided in formal texts, judgments, and resolutions, rather than engage in an interpretation of the meaning of self-determination from the standpoint of relevant core values and with attention to ongoing dynamic processes and the aspirations of self-determination claimants. For a study of the right to self-determination in relation to indigenous peoples in particular with conclusions somewhat similar to those reached here, but through a different route of analysis which argues for application to indigenous peoples of the post-World War II decolonization regime, *see* Maivan C. Lâm, *At the Edge of the State: Indigenous Peoples and Self-Determination* (2000).

7. *See* Edward M. Morgan, "The Imagery and Meaning of Self-Determination," 20 *N.Y.U. J. Int'l L. & Pol.* 355, 357–58 (1988).

8. *See, e.g.*, Umozurike O. Umozurike, *Self-Determination in International Law* 6–11 (1972); Dov Ronen, *The Quest for Self-Determination* ix (1979).

9. Legal Consequences for States of the Continued Presence of South Africa in Namibia (South West Africa) notwithstanding Security Council Resolution 276 (1970), Advisory Opinion, 1971 I.C.J. 16, 77–78. *Cf.* Karen Knop, *Diversity and Self-Determination in International Law* (2002) (evaluating the diverse cultural perspectives that are brought to bear in the positing of self-determination claims and identifying the problems raised by excluding many groups and women from the process of interpreting what self-determination means).

10. *See* Umozurike, *supra* note 8, at 11–12.

11. *Id.* at 13–14.

12. *See* Vladimir I. Lenin, "*The Right of Nations to Self-Determination*," in 20 *Collected Works* (English ed. 1947); Joseph Stalin, *Marxism and the National-Colonial Question* (1975). *See generally* Walker Connor, *The National Question in Marxist-Leninist Theory and Strategy* (1984).

13. U.N. Charter art. 1, para. 2.

14. International Covenant on Economic, Social and Cultural Rights, Dec. 16, 1966, G.A. Res. 2200(XXI), art. 1(1), 993 U.N.T.S. 3 (entered into force Jan. 3, 1976); International Covenant on Civil and Political Rights, Dec. 16, 1966, G.A. Res. 2200(XXI), art. 1(1), 999 U.N.T.S. 171 (entered into force Mar. 23, 1976). The self-determination provision common to the international human rights covenants reads: "All peoples have the right of self-determination. By virtue of that right they freely determine their political status and freely pursue their economic, social and cultural development." Self-determination is affirmed by substantially the same language in other U.N.-sponsored international instruments, e.g., Declaration on Principles of International Law Concerning Friendly Relations and Co-operation among States in Accordance with the Charter of the United Nations, G.A. Res. 2625, Oct. 24, 1970, U.N. GAOR, 25th Sess., Supp. No. 28, at 121, U.N. Doc. A/8028 (1971) [hereinafter U.N. Friendly Relations Declaration]; Declaration on the Granting of Independence to Colonial Countries and Peoples, G.A. Res. 1514 (XV), Dec. 14, 1960, U.N. GAOR, 15th Sess., Supp. No. 16, at 66, para. 2, U.N. Doc. A/4684 (1961).

15. African Charter on Human and Peoples' Rights, June 27, 1981, Organization of African Unity, art. 20, 21 *I.L.M.* 58 (1982) (entered into force Oct. 21, 1986).

16. Final Act of the Conference on Security and Cooperation in Europe (Helsinki), Aug. 1, 1975, principle 8, 14 *I.L.M.* 1292 (1975).

17. *See supra* chapter 1, notes 47–52, 99–106, and accompanying text. See also Tom J. Farer, "The United Nations and Human Rights: More Than a Whimper, Less Than a Roar" 9 *Hum. Rts. Q.* 550 (1987) ("Until the Second World War . . . international law did not impede the natural right of each equal sovereign to be monstrous to his or her subjects.").

18. *See supra* chapter 2, notes 20–24 and accompanying text.

19. *See The Right to Self-Determination: Historical and Current Developments on the Basis of United Nations Instruments*, U.N. Doc. E/CN.4/Sub.2/404/Rev.1, at 31, para. 220, U.N. Sales No. E.80.XIV.3 (1981) (Aureliu Cristescu, special rapporteur) (hereinafter U.N. Study on Self-Determination) ("The principles of equal rights and self-determination of peoples is [*sic*] part of the group of human rights and fundamental freedoms."); Yoram Dinstein, "Self-Determination and the Middle East Conflict," in *Self-Determination: National, Regional and Global Dimensions* 243 (Yonah Alexander & Robert A. Friedlander eds., 1980) ("Self-determination must be perceived as an international human right."); Hurst Hannum, "Self-Determination as a Human Right," in *Human Rights in the World Community: Issues and Action* 125 (Richard P. Claude & Burns H. Weston eds., 2d ed. 1992).

20. Burns H. Weston, "Human Rights," in *Human Rights in the World Community, supra* note 19, at 14, 17 ("If a right is determined to be a human right it is quintessentially general or universal in character, in some sense equally possessed by all human beings everywhere, including in certain instances even the unborn.").

21. *See* Umozurike, *supra* note 8, at 11–12.

22. *See id.* at 59–95.

23. *See* G. A. Res. 2775, U.N. GAOR, 26th Sess., Supp. No. 29, at 41, U.N. Doc. A/8429 (1971); G.A. Res. 3411, U.N. GAOR, 30th Sess., Supp. No. 34, at 36, U.N. Doc. A/10034 (1975). *See also* S.C. Res. 392, U.N. SCOR, 31st Sess., at 11, U.N. Doc. S/Res/392 (1976); International Convention on the Suppression and Punishment of the Crime of "Apartheid," Nov. 30, 1973, G.A. Res. 3068(XXVIII), U.N. GAOR, 28th Sess., Supp. No. 30 , at 75, U.N. Doc. A/9030 (1974).

24. *See supra* notes 13–16 and accompanying text.

25. *See Webster's Collegiate Dictionary* 860 (10th ed. 1993) (defining "peoples" as "a body of persons that are united by a common culture, tradition, or sense of kinship, that typically have common language, institutions, and beliefs, and that often constitute a politically organized group").

26. This view was implicit, for example, in India's reservation to article 1 of the International Covenant on Civil and Political Rights, *supra* note 14, made at the time of its ratification of the covenant:

With reference to article 1 . . . , the Government of the Republic of India declares that the words "the right of self-determination" appearing in this article apply only to the peoples under foreign domination and that these words do not apply to sovereign independent States or to a section of a people or nation—which is the essence of national integrity.

U.N. Centre for Human Rights, *Human Rights: Status of International Instruments* 9 (1987), U.N. Sales No. E.87.XIV.2. In a subsequent statement to the U.N. Human Rights Committee, India reiterated its position that "the right to self-determination in the international context [applies] only to dependent Territories and peoples." Statement by the Representative of India to the Human Rights Committee, U.N. Doc. CCPR/C/SR.498, at 3 (1984).

27. *See infra* notes 53–67 and accompanying text (explaining the relationship between decolonization and self-determination).

28. *See, e.g.*, Rosalyn Higgins, *Problems & Process: International Law and How We Use It* 12–25 (1994); David J. Harris, *Cases and Materials in International Law* 91–93 (1979). Typical of this approach, many embrace the notion that self-determination includes *internal* and *external* aspects whose relative spheres are defined by reference to the state unit. *See infra* note 56 and accompanying text.

29. *See* Rosalyn Higgins, "Post-Modern Tribalism and the Right to Secession, Comments," in *Peoples and Minorities in International Law* 29, 32 (Catherine Brölmann et al. eds., 1993) (holding that substate groups generally are not entitled to self-determination under international law). Higgins argues that, while "minorities *as such* do not have a right of self-determination," their members, as individuals, are beneficiaries of the self-determination right held by the people of the territory as a whole. Higgins, *Problems & Process*, *supra* note 28, at 124 (emphasis in original).

30. This view has roots in the ethnonationalist thought of the early part of this century, *see* W. Ofuatey-Kodjoe, *The Principle of Self-Determination in International Law* 30–31 (1977), and is reflected in much of the political rhetoric of many contemporary self-determination demands and in much of the literature advocating self-determination for indigenous communities. *See, e.g.*, Rachel S. Kronowitz et al., Comment, "Toward Consent and Cooperation; Reconsidering the Political Status of Indian Nations," 22 *Harv. C.R.–C.L. L. Rev.* 507, 597–600 (1987); John H. Clinebell & Jim Thomson, "Sovereignty and Self-Determination: The Rights of Native Americans under International Law," 27 *Buff. L. Rev.* 669, 707, 710–14 (1978).

31. *See generally* Ofuatey-Kodjoe, *supra* note 30, at 80–84 (discussing the application of Allied policy at the close of World War I).

32. *See* Christopher C. Mojekwu, "Self-Determination: The African Perspective, in *Self-Determination: National, Regional and Global Dimensions, supra* note 19, at 221, 228–29 (explaining that U.N. policy was to pursue the independence of the colonial territories without regard to precolonial political units based primarily on ethnic affinity or tribal affiliation).

33. *See* Knop, *supra* note 9, at 167–90 (analyzing the EC Arbitration Commission Opinion No. 2 on Yugoslavia, in which the commission "held the post-Cold War international law did not underwrite the Romantic ideal of the ethnic nation-state"). *See generally* Morton H. Halperin et al., *Self Determination in the New World Order* 27–44 (1992) (discussing international responses to self-determination claims in the post-cold war era).

34. For an insightful exposition about the flaws in the concept of "sovereignty" from an indigenous perspective, see Taiaiake Alfred, *Peace, Power, Righteousness: An Indigenous Manifesto* 55–65 (1999).

35. *See supra* chapter 1, notes 62–64 and accompanying text.

36. *Cf.* John Borrows, "'Landed' Citizenship: Narratives of Aboriginal Political Participation," in *Citizenship in Diverse Societies* 326 (Will Kymlicka & Wayne Norman eds., 2000) (arguing for a conception of citizenship and connection to land that, more in line with human experience, does not rely on "artificial lines" to separate aboriginal from non-aboriginal peoples or places).

37. *See* "EFTA Signs Cooperation Accords," *Wall St. J.*, Dec. 11, 1991, at A13; (reporting that the European Free Trade Association signed cooperative agreements with Bulgaria, Romania, and the Baltic states to speed their integration into the European economy); R. C. Longworth, "New Europe Restructures Blocs of Past," *Haw. Trib.-Herald*, Sept. 14, 1990, at 23 (describing a proposal for revival of the Hanseatic League, a historic trade alliance linking Russia, the Baltic states, Scandinavia, Poland, Germany, and the Netherlands).

38. "New Europe Begins Taking Shape in Giant Common Market," *Agence France Presse*, Oct. 22, 1991, available in LEXIS, Nexis Library, AFP file.

39. In 1987 the Nicaraguan government adopted its Statute of Autonomy for the Atlantic Coast Regions of Nicaragua, Law No. 28 of September 7, 1987 [hereinafter Nicaraguan Statute of Autonomy], which established semiautonomous regional governing bodies and guaranteed representation in the national legislative assembly. In 1990, the people of the autonomous regions elected for the first time delegates to the regional governing bodies as well as to the national legislature. *See* Mario Rizo Zeledón, "Identidad étnica y elecciones; El Caso de la RAAN," 8 *WANI*, July/Dec. 1990, at 28 (*WANI* is published by the Centro de Investigaciones y Documentación de la Costa Atlántica and the Universidad de Centro América) (analyzing the 1990 elections in the autonomous regions).

40. Pursuant to the Nicaraguan Statute of Autonomy, *supra* note 39, art. 23, there have been initiatives to demarcate local municipal boundaries and to formalize local authority and indigenous traditional decision-making structures. *See, e.g.*, Ley de Municipios, Ley No. 40 (La Gaceta, Diario Oficial, No. 155, Aug. 17, 1998), as amended by Ley No. 261 (La Gaceta, Diario Oficial, No. 162, Aug. 20, 1997), arts. 67–69. Along with these initiatives, the regime of local communal autonomy has been formalized in the new land demarcation law approved by the Nicaraguan National Assembly on the basis of a proposal agreed upon with regional actors and approved by the regional councils. *See* Ley del Régimen de Propiedad Comunal de los Pueblos Indígenas y Comunidades Étnicas de las Regiones Autónomas de Nicaragua y de los Ríos Bocay, Coco, Indio y Maíz, Law No. 445, 22 Jan. 2003 (La Gaceta, Diario Oficial, No. 16, Jan. 23, 2003), arts. 4–10.

41. Interview with Brooklyn Rivera, director of the Instituto Nicaragüense para el Desarollo de las Regiones Autónomas (Apr. 1992).

42. *See* Hannum, *supra* note 3, at 263–79 (discussing the system of regional autonomous governments in Spain, particularly as regards the Basque country and Catalonia).

43. *See* Elizabeth Pond, "Spain Lays Political and Economic Groundwork for EC Membership," *Christian Sci. Monitor*, Nov. 24, 1980, at 10.

44. Duane Champagne, "Beyond Assimilation as a Strategy for National Integration: The Persistence of American Indian Political Identities," 3 *Transnat'l L. & Contemp. Probs.* 109, 112 (1993).

45. *Id.* at 112–13.

46. *Id.* at 112–14.

47. *See* Paul Wallace, *The Iroquois Book of Life: White Roots of Peace* 25–30 (1994); Oren R. Lyons, "The American Indian in the Past," in *Exiled in the Land of the Free* 13, 14, 37–39 (Oren R. Lyons & John C. Mohawk eds., 1992).

48. *Id.*

49. *See, e.g.*, "Living History: Inauguration of the International Year of the World's Indigenous People," 3 *Transnat'l L. & Contemp. Probs.* 165 (1993) (statements by indigenous leaders).

50. Will Kymlicka has provided a compelling account of how individual freedom, and hence basic human rights, are intimately tied up with membership in "societal cultures" at least insofar as the practices of those cultures do not themselves suppress individual freedom. *See* Will Kymlicka, *Multicultural Citizenship* 75–106 (1995).

51. Kymlicka is correct that this characterization of "peoples" also extends the right to self-determination to national minorities, such as the Catalans, the Scots and the Quebecois, groups that would not necessarily be considered "indigenous peoples." *See* Will Kymlicka, *Politics in the Vernacular* 120, 126 (2001). In his review of the first edition of this work, Kymlicka disputes this characterization of international law as it concerns self-determination on the grounds that he can find no evidence in existing legal texts to support it. *Id.* at 127. However, that assessment of international law is based on a narrow, positivistic jurisprudential perspective that is rejected throughout this work and by increasingly influential schools of thought in international law; it ignores the role of interpretation in discerning the meaning of international law, especially in the nebulous and often highly dynamic realm between the *is* and the *ought*, a role commonly taken up scholars and decision-makers in international legal processes to go beyond what is already explicit in existing legal texts. *See, e.g.*, Felipe Gómez Isa, "El derecho de autodeterminación en el derecho internacional contemporáneo," in *Derecho de autodeterminación y la realidad vasca* 267 (2002) (an international legal analysis assessing the applicability of the principle of self-determination to the Basques). *See generally* Knop, *supra* note 9, at 109–90 (surveying scholarly opinion and decisions about the subjects and meaning of self-determination in international law)

52. The Vienna Convention on the Law of Treaties, which is considered to represent customary international law in this respect, states: "A treaty shall be interpreted in good faith in accordance with the ordinary meaning to be given to the terms of the treaty in their context and in the light of its object and purpose." Vienna Convention on the Law of Treaties, opened for signature May 23, 1969, art. 31, para. 1, 1155 U.N.T.S. 331. *See also* Competence of the General Assembly for the Admission of a State to the United Nations, Advisory Opinion, 1950 I.C.J. 4, 8 ("If the relevant words in their natural and ordinary meaning make sense in their context, that is an end of the matter.").

53. The decolonization regime is discussed *supra* chapter 2, notes 26–29 and accompanying text.

54. This point is emphasized in Efrén Rivera-Ramos, "Self-Determination and Decolonization in the Society of the Modern Colonial Welfare State," in *Issues of Self-Determination* 115, 127 (William Twining ed., 1991).

55. *See infra* notes 83–115 and accompanying text.

56. *E.g.*, Rosalyn Higgins, "Post-Modern Tribalism and the Right to Secession, Comments," *supra* note 29, at 31; Allan Rosas, "Internal Self-Determination" in *Modern Law of Self-Determination* 225 (Christian Tomuschat ed., 1993). *But see* Gudmundur Alfredsson, "The Right of Self-Determination and Indigenous Peoples," in *Modern Law of Self-Determination, id.* at 21, 50–54 (questioning the usefulness of the term "internal self-determination").

57. International Covenant on Economic, Social and Cultural Rights, *supra* note 14, art. 1(1); International Covenant on Civil and Political Rights, *supra* note 14, art. 1(1). The full text of art. 1(1) of the covenants is quoted *supra*, at note 14. *See also* United Nations Friendly Relations Declaration, *supra* note 14.

58. For a description of procedures for acquiring territorial title adopted by European states in the colonization of Africa, *see* Shaw, *supra* note 3, at 31–58. *See also supra* chapter 1 (discussing theoretical justifications historically advanced for such processes).

59. *See* Paul G. Lauren, *Power and Prejudice: The Politics and Diplomacy of Racial Discrimination* 150–65 (1988) (discussing government statements at the San Francisco conference which gave rise to the United Nations Charter); Declaration on the Granting of Independence to Colonial Countries and Peoples, *supra* note 14, at para. 1 (declaring, inter alia, that "[t]he subjection of peoples to alien subjugation, domination and exploitation constitutes a denial of fundamental human rights"); *Report of the United Nations Seminar on the Effects of Racism and Racial Discrimination on the Social and Economic Relations between Indigenous Peoples and States*, U.N. Doc. E/CN.4/1989/22, HR/PUB/89/5, at 8 (1989) (Ted Moses, special rapporteur) [hereinafter *Report of Seminar on Racism*] ("The concepts of *"terra nullius,"* "conquest" and "discovery" as modes of territorial acquisition are repugnant, have no legal standing, and are entirely without merit or justification.").

60. President Woodrow Wilson, Address to Congress of May 1917 (quoted in Umozurike, *supra* note 8, at 14).

61. This is evident, for example, in the steps of institution building of the European Community and the expansion of its territorial jurisdiction, *see generally* P. S. R. F. Mathijsen, *A Guide to European Community Law* 1–14 (5th ed. 1990) (background on the development of the European Community, now the European Union); in efforts at domestic constitutional reform, e.g., Canada's effort in the early 1990s in which representatives of aboriginal peoples and Quebec participated in reform negotiations, *see* Mary Ellen Turpel, "Indigenous Peoples' Rights of Political Participation and Self-Determination: Recent International Legal Developments and the Continuing Struggle for Recognition," 25 *Cornell Int'l L. J.* 579, 593–94 (1992); and in the dissolution of existing states, e.g., the peaceful break-up of Czechoslovakia, which followed supporting votes by the elected parliamentary delegates of both Czech and Slovak legislative bodies; *but see* Adrian Bridge, "Few Cheers as Two New States are Born," *The Independent* (London), Dec. 31, 1992, at 14 (criticizing the procedures leading to the dissolution of the Czechoslovakian federation).

62. Covenant on Economic, Social and Cultural Rights, note 14, art. 1(1); Covenant on Civil and Political Rights, *supra* note 14, art. 1(1). The full text of article 1(1) of the covenants is in note 14, *supra*. *See also* U.N. Friendly Relations Declaration, *supra* note 14, principle V.

63. Compare, for example, Stalin's anticolonial statements in Stalin, *supra* note 12, at 314–22, with the policy prescriptions of U.S. leaders as summarized in W. Ofuatey-Kodjoe, *supra* note 30, at 99–100.

64. *See* Robert H. Jackson, *Quasi-States: Sovereignty, International Relations and the Third World* 85 (1990) (discussing the preponderant view of the 1950s that colonialism is "an absolute wrong: an injury to the dignity and autonomy of those peoples and of course a vehicle for their economic exploitation and political oppression"). *See also supra* chapter 2, notes 26–29 and accompanying text.

65. Thus, for example, the "common position on the process of recognition" adopted by the European Community (which is now the European Union) reads in part:

> The Community and its Member States confirm their attachment to the principles of the Helsinki Final Act and the Charter of Paris, in particular the principle of self-determination. They affirm their readiness to recognize, subject to the normal standards of international practice and the political realities in each case, those new States which, following the historic changes in the region, *have constituted themselves on a democratic basis.*

Guidelines on the Recognition of New States in Eastern Europe and in the Soviet Union, adopted by the Council of the European Community, Dec. 16, 1991, EC Bulletin 12-1992, p. 119; U.N. Doc. S/23293 (1991), Annex 2, 31 *I.L.M.* 1486 (1992) (emphasis added). Extensive minority rights were also among the EC's conditions for the recognition of new states emerging in Eastern Europe. *See* Knop, *supra* note 9, at 173. The scholarly literature increasingly has linked rights of political participation, notions of democracy, and cultural pluralism to the principle of self-determination. *E.g.*, Yves Beigbeder, *International Monitoring of Plebiscites, Referenda and National Elections: Self-Determination and Transition to Democracy* (1994); Jordan J. Paust, "Self-Determination: A Definitional Focus," in *Self-Determination: National, Regional, and Global Dimensions, supra* note 19, at 3; Patrick Thornberry, "The Democratic or Internal Aspect of Self-Determination with Some Remarks on Federalism," in *Modern Law of Self-Determination, supra* note 56, at 101. *See also infra* chapter 4, notes 173–76 and accompanying text (discussing developments toward a "democratic entitlement" under international law). A discussion on international law's enhanced attention to values of cultural pluralism is in chapter 4, *infra*, notes 18–30 and accompanying text.

66. Ian Brownlie, "The Rights of Peoples in Modern International Law," in *The Rights of Peoples* 1, 5 (James Crawford ed., 1988).

67. *See supra* chapter 1, notes 101–22 and accompanying text. *See generally* Gerrit W. Gong, *The Standard of "Civilization" in International Society* (1984).

68. *See* Mojekwu, *supra* note 32, at 230–332; Radha K. Ramphul, "The Role of International and Regional Organizations in the Peaceful Settlement of Internal Disputes (with Special Emphasis on the Organization of African Unity)," 13 *Ga. J. Int'l & Comp. L.* 371, 377–78 (1983).

69. G.A. Res. 1541(XV), Dec. 15, 1960, principle 6, U.N. GAOR, 15th Sess., Supp. No. 16, at 29, U.N. Doc. A/4684 (1961). *See supra* chapter 2, notes 26–29 and accompanying text (discussing U.N. and related practice concerning decolonization).

70. *See supra* chapter 2, notes 30–32 and accompanying text (discussing the limitations of the decolonization regime in respect of enclave tribal or ethnic groups).

71. Western Sahara, Advisory Opinion, 1975 I.C.J. 12.

72. *Id.* at 38–40.

73. *Id.* at 68.

74. *Id.*

75. *See id.* at 33, 68.

76. In *Reference re Secession of Quebec*, [1998] 2 S.C.R. 217, the Supreme Court of Canada affirmed in general terms that:

> Peoples are expected to achieve self-determination within the framework of their existing state. A state whose government represents the whole of the people or peoples resident within its territory, on a basis of equality and without discrimination, and respects the principles of self-determination in its internal arrangements, is entitled to maintain its territorial integrity under international law and to have that territorial integrity recognized by other states

Id. at para. 154.

77. *See* Lee C. Buchheit, *Secession: The Legitimacy of Self-Determination* 222 (1978) (arguing that international law provides for remedial secession in extreme cases of oppression); Ved Nanda, "Self-Determination outside the Colonial Context: The Birth of Bangladesh in Retrospect," in *Self Determination: National, Regional, and Global Dimensions, supra* note 19, at 193, 204 (stating that secession may properly follow a persistent pattern of human rights abuses against a group); *see also* Allen E. Buchanan, *Secession: The Morality of Political Divorce from Fort Sumter to Lithuania & Quebec* 38–45 (1991) (synthesizing arguments for secession, all of which relate to rectifying some form of injustice). While secession may in limited contexts comprise an appropriate remedy, it is doubtful that the world community will support—for any denomination of groups—a unilaterally exercisable right to secede in the absence of a remedial justification. *See* Thomas M. Franck, "Postmodern Tribalism and the Right to Secession," in *Peoples and Minorities in International Law, supra* note 29, at 3, 19 (surveying international practice and concluding that "[t]he international system does not recognize a general right of secession but may assist the government of a state which is a member in good standing to find constructive alternatives to a secessionist claim"); Halperin et al., *supra* note 33, at 27–44 (discussing international responses to recent secessionist efforts). At the very least, however, substantive self-determination implies that individuals and groups, even without a strong remedial justification, are entitled to petition for and work toward fundamental change, including secession, through peaceful means. *Cf. In re Secession of Quebec*, [1998] 2 S.C.R. 217 (holding that Canada would have to negotiate the terms of Quebec's separation if a substantial majority of the population of the province opted for secession). And to the extent such initiatives engender real movement toward change, self-determination requires minimum levels of participation and consent

on the part of all concerned, commensurate with their interests, in the decision-making procedures that will determine the outcome. Thus, while popular support for a secessionist movement may not be sufficient for the world community to act in favor of the movement, it is at least a necessary condition for secession in both remedial and nonremedial contexts. International recognition of states emerging from the dissolution of the former Soviet Union and states in Eastern Europe followed referenda or other expressions of popular support by the constituents of the nascent independent states. *See generally* Marc Weller, Current Developments Note, "The International Response to the Dissolution of the Socialist Federal Republic of Yugoslavia," 86 *Am. J. Int'l L.* 569 (1992). Halperin et al., *supra* note 33, at 27–38 (discussing international responses to the break-ups of the former Soviet Union and Yugoslavia).

78. *See* U.N. Charter art. 2(4).

79. U.N. Charter art. 2(7).

80. *See* Hannum, *supra* note 3, at 19–20 (discussing the "limits of sovereignty"). *See also Report of the Secretary General: An Agenda for Peace; Preventive Diplomacy, Peacemaking and Peacekeeping,* U.N. GAOR, 47th Sess., Agenda Item 10, U.N. Doc. A/47/277 (1992) (discussing the balancing of state sovereignty and humanitarian concerns at times of crisis).

81. *See supra* chapter 1, notes 57–61 and accompanying text (discussing Vattel and state sovereignty doctrine).

82. This is reflected in the U.N. Friendly Relations Declaration, *supra* note 14, principle V, which states: "Nothing in the foregoing paragraphs shall be construed as authorizing or encouraging any action which would dismember or impair, totally or in part, the territorial integrity or political unity of sovereign and independent States *conducting themselves in compliance with the principle of equal rights and self-determination of peoples*" (emphasis added).

83. The *U.N. Study of the Problem of Discrimination against Indigenous Populations* contains the following definition:

> Indigenous communities, peoples and nations are those which, having a historical continuity with pre-invasion and pre-colonial societies that developed on their territories, consider themselves distinct from other sectors of the societies now prevailing in those territories, or parts of them. They form at present non-dominant sectors of society and are determined to preserve, develop and transmit to future generations their ancestral territories, and their ethnic identity, as the basis of their continued existence as peoples, in accordance with their own cultural patterns, social institutions and legal systems.

U.N. Doc. E/CN.4/Sub.2/1986/7/Add.4, at 29, para. 379 (1986).

84. Contrary to what Kymlicka surmises in his critique of this theory of self-determination, *see* Kymlicka, *Politics in the Vernacular, supra* note 51, at 128, the position advanced here is *not* that the contemporary indigenous rights regime is *purely* remedial or that the remedies prescribed are *solely* for historical wrongs. As stated here, and as demonstrated in the following chapter, the regime contains remedial prescriptions along with elaborations on the substantive elements of self-determination in the specific context of indigenous peoples. But indeed the indigenous rights regime is sub-

stantially remedial, and this is precisely what justifies its existence, because the remedial prescriptions and heightened international concern that are part of the regime are aimed at a particular set of problems that are characteristic of groups identified as indigenous as opposed to other types of groups. Also as demonstrated in the following chapter, the remedial prescriptions—that is, the prescriptions that mandate change in the existing governing institutional order—are not just to correct historical wrongs, but also to protect against current and potential future wrongs in light of the particular set of vulnerabilities that characterize indigenous peoples. These vulnerabilities are understood in terms of disparities in economic and political power rooted in history, and not just in terms of radical cultural difference as suggested by Kymlicka. It may be that the remedial components of the indigenous rights regime may loose saliency as indigenous peoples gain economic and political power and become secure in their cultural survival—and that will be a welcome development. But it will more likely be that a regime to address the particular set of problems associated with the rubric of indigenous rights will always have some relevancy. In any case, under the view advanced here, indigenous peoples will continue to enjoy the substantive right to live and develop freely, just as will all other "peoples," including those that today are already powerful and secure in their self-determination.

85. Draft United Nations Declaration on the Rights of Indigenous Peoples, adopted by the Subcommission on Prevention of Discrimination and Protection of Minorities by its res. 1994/45, Aug. 26, 1994, art. 3, U.N. Doc. E/CN.4/1995/2, E/CN.4/Sub.2/1994/56, at 105 (1994), reprinted in the appendix, *infra*. The development of the draft declaration and its status are discussed in *supra* chapter 2, notes 89–93 and accompanying text.

86. For an analytical discussion of the resistance that existed toward express usage of the term *self-determination* in association with indigenous peoples' rights during the earlier years of the U.N. Working Group on Indigenous Populations, *see* Catherine J. Iorns, "Indigenous Peoples and Self-Determination: Challenging State Sovereignty," 24 *Case W. Res. J. Int'l L.* 199 (1992).

87. Rather, it tends to avoid the issue with a provision, similar to that in ILO Convention (No. 169) on Indigenous and Tribal Peoples, which states: "The use of the term 'peoples' in this Instrument shall not be construed as having any implication with respect to any other rights that might be attached to the term in international law." Proposed American Declaration on the Rights of Indigenous Peoples, approved by the Inter-American Commission on Human Rights on Feb. 26, 1997, at its 1333rd sess., 95th regular sess., art. 1(3), published in the *Annual Report of the Inter-American Human Rights Commission*, 1997, O.A.S. Doc. OEA/Ser.L/V/II.95, Doc. 7 Rev. (March 14, 1997), reprinted in the appendix, *infra*.

88. Australian Government Delegation, Speaking Notes on Self-Determination, at 2 (July 24, 1991).

89. Canadian Statement to the UN Commission on Human Rights Working Group on the Draft Declaration on the Rights of Indigenous Peoples, Oct. 31, 1996.

90. Cable attached to Memorandum of Jan. 18, 2001, by Robert A. Bratke, Executive Secretary, National Security Council, to Kristie Kenny, Executive Secretary, Department of State; Julie Falkner, Director of Executive Secretariat, Department of the Interior; Frances Townsend, Counsel for Intelligence Policy, Department of Justice; Chris Klein, Staff Assistant to the Representative of the United States to the United Nations

(Jan. 18, 2001). This policy was adopted by the administration of former President Bill Clinton literally on its last day of power; however, as of this writing, it has not been repudiated by the subsequent administration of President George W. Bush.

91. For example, the U.S. government delegation to the 1994 session of the working group expressed U.S. support for the "basic goals of the draft declaration" and added that "[s]ince the 1970's, the U.S. Government has supported the concept of self-determination for Indian tribes and Alaska Natives within the United States." Observer Delegation of the United States of America, Statement to the Working Group on Indigenous Populations, Geneva, at 1 (July 26, 1994).

92. U.S. Department of State, *Civil and Political Rights in the United States: Initial Report of the United States of America to the U.N. Human Rights Committee under the International Covenant on Civil and Political Rights,* July 1994, at 36–46, Dept. State Pub. 10200 (1994). The reporting obligations under the covenant are discussed *infra* in chapter 6, notes 60–69 and accompanying text.

93. *See Report of the working group established in accordance with Commission on Human Rights resolution 1995/32,* U.N. Doc. E/CN.4/2000/84, paras. 43–85 (Dec. 6, 1999) (summarizing statements by representatives of states and of indigenous peoples on self-determination) [hereinafter *"Report of the 1999 session of the Commission working group on the draft declaration"*]; *Report of the working group established in accordance with Human Rights Commission resolution 1995/32,* U.N. Doc. E/CN.4/2001/95, paras. 62–109 (6 Feb. 2001) (report on session held Nov. 20–Dec. 1, 2000) [hereinafter *"Report of the 2000 session of the Commission working group on the indigenous declaration"*]; Special Meeting of the Working Group to Prepare the Draft American Declaration on the Rights of Indigenous Peoples, Comments by the Delegation of the Bolivarian Republic of Venezuela, O.A.S. Doc. OEA/Ser.K/XVI, GT/DADIN-76/02 (March 27, 2002); Supplemental Statement by the Government of New Zealand to the Working Group (July 1990) (seeking to "put the record straight" to rebut any inference that New Zealand is not willing to recognize the "right to self-determination" of indigenous peoples); Statement of the Representative of Chile, Pedro Oyarce, Working Group on Indigenous Populations, 11th Sess., at 2–3 (July 23, 1993) (stating that Chile favors affirmation of the right to self-determination in the indigenous rights declaration).

94. Gobierno de México, Documento de posición ante el Grupo de Trabajo encargado de elaborar una Declaración de los Derechos de los Pueblos Indígenas, Grupo de Trabajo de la Comisión de Derechos Humanos sobre el Proyecto de Declaración de los Derechos de los Pueblos Indígenas, 90 periodo de sesiones (Jan. 28–Feb. 8, 2002).

95. *Report of the 1999 session of the Commission and the Working Group on the draft declaration, supra* note 93, para. 73.

96. *Id.* para. 82.

97. *Id.* para. 82.

98. *See Report of the 2000 session of the Commission working group on the indigenous declaration, supra* note 93, paras. 62–109; *Report of the working group established in accordance with Commission on Human Rights resolution 1995/32,* U.N. Doc. E/CN.4/2001/85 (Feb. 6, 2001), paras. 56–115; *Report of the working group established in accordance with Commission on Human Rights resolution 1995/32,* U.N. Doc. E/CN.4/2002/98 (March 6, 2002), paras. 56–115.

99. *Concluding Observations and Recommendations of the Human Rights Committee: Canada* (April 7, 1999), U.N. Doc. CCPR/C/79/Add.105., para. 8.

100. *See Concluding Observations of the Human Rights Committee: Australia*, U.N. Doc. A/55/40, paras. 506–08 (July 24, 2002) (admonishing Australia that, in connection with art. 1, para. 2 of the covenant, it should "take the necessary steps in order to secure for the indigenous inhabitants a stronger role in decision-making over their traditional lands and natural resources"); *Concluding Observations of the Human Rights Committee: Norway*, U.N. Doc. CCPR/C/79/Add.112 17 (Nov. 1, 1999), para. 17 (expressing its expectation that Norway "report on the Sami people's right to self-determination under article 1 of the Covenant, including paragraph 2 of that article"). *See also Concluding Observations of the Human Rights Committee: Mexico*, U.N. Doc. CCPR/C/79/Add.109, para. 19 (July 27, 1999) (urging "appropriate measures . . . to increase [indigenous] participation in the country's institutions and the exercise of the right to self-determination"). *See generally* Human Rights Committee, General Comment No. 12—The Right of Self-Determination (art. 1), twenty-first session, 1984, in *Compilation of General Comments and Recommendation Adopted by the Human Rights Treaty-Bodies*, U.N. Doc. HRI/GEN/1/Rev.5 (Apr. 26, 2001), at 121–22.

101. Government attitudes in favor of the *concept* of self-determination in association with indigenous peoples (as opposed to their reservations about express use of the term in this context) is especially evident in government statements on domestic policies and initiatives. *See generally Report of the Working Group on Indigenous Populations on Its Eleventh Session*, U.N. Doc. E/CN.4/Sub.2/1993/29, at 22–23 (Aug. 23, 1993) (synthesizing government statements on developments under the heading "Right of Self-Determination and Political Participation").

102. Convention (No. 169) Concerning Indigenous and Tribal Peoples in Independent Countries, June 27, 1989, art. 4(1), International Labour Conference (entered into force Sept. 5, 1990), reproduced in the appendix, *infra*.

103. *Id*. art. 4(2).

104. *Id*. art. 6(2).

105. Erica-Irene A. Daes, "Some Considerations on the Right of Indigenous Peoples to Self-Determination," 3 *Transn'l L. & Contemp. Probs.* 1, 9 (1993).

106. *Id*.

107. The history of the Atlantic Coast region is summarized in Jorge Jenkins Molieri, *El Desafío indígena en Nicaragua: El Caso de los Miskitos* 33–114 (1986); and in Theodore Macdonald, "The Moral Economy of the Miskito Indians: Local Roots of a Geopolitical Conflict," in *Ethnicities and Nations: Processes of Interethnic Relations in Latin America, Southeast Asia, and the Pacific* 107, 114–22 (Remo Guidieri et al. eds., 1988).

108. *See* Jenkins Molieri, *supra* note 107, at 175–229 (discussing the social and economic conditions in the Atlantic Coast region at the time of the 1979 revolution in Nicaragua).

109. *See* John N. Burnstein, Student Note, "Ethnic Minorities and the Sandinist Government," 36 *J. Int'l Aff.* 155, 155–59 (1982) (discussing the imposition of government structures both before and after the 1979 revolution).

110. *See* Inter-American Commission on Human Rights, *Report on the Situation of Human Rights of a Segment of the Nicaraguan Population of Miskito Origin and Reso-*

lution on the Friendly Settlement Procedure Regarding the Human Rights Situation of a Segment of the Nicaraguan Population of Miskito Origin, O.A.S. Doc. OEA/Ser.L/V/II.62, doc. 10, rev. 3 (1983), OEA/Ser.L/V/II.62, doc. 26 (1984) (Case No. 7964 (Nicaragua)) [hereinafter *Miskito Report and Resolution*].

111. *Miskito Report and Resolution* at 78–81.

112. *Id*. at 1–7, 81.

113. *Id*. at 81–82.

114. *Id*. at 82. For further discussion of the case, particularly in regards to its procedural aspects, see *infra* chapter 7, notes 92–96, 104–07, and accompanying text.

115. *See* Macdonald, *supra* note 107, at 138–47.

116. *See infra* chapter 4, at notes 124–36, and chapter 7, at notes 128–57 (discussing the *Awas Tingni* case, which resulted from the continued failure of the Nicaraguan government to implement the land rights protections of the autonomy regime).

4

Norms Elaborating the Elements of Self-Determination

As indicated in the foregoing discussion, the principle of self-determination and related human rights precepts undergird more particularized norms concerning indigenous peoples. Newly developing norms contain substantive and remedial prescriptions and, in conjunction with already established human rights standards of general applicability, form the benchmarks for ensuring indigenous peoples of ongoing self-determination. This body of international norms indicates the minimum range of choices to which indigenous peoples are entitled in remedial-constitutive procedures (i.e., in belated state-building procedures that aim to secure redress for historical and continuing wrongs). The international norms concerning indigenous peoples, which thus elaborate upon the requirements of self-determination, generally fall within the following categories: nondiscrimination, cultural integrity, lands and resources, social welfare and development, and self-government. The general contours of these norms are identified and discussed in the following synthesis of relevant conventional and customary law, including new and emergent law.

Nondiscrimination

A minimum condition for the exercise of self-determination, particularly in its ongoing aspect, is the absence of official policies or practices that invidiously discriminate against individuals or groups. In its statement of guiding principles, the United Nations Charter admonishes "respect for human rights and for fundamental freedoms for all without distinction as to race, sex, language, or religion."[1] This norm of nondiscrimination is emphasized and elaborated upon in numerous existing international and regional human rights instruments, including the U.N.-sponsored Convention on the Elimination of All Forms of Racial Discrimination,[2] the American Convention on Human Rights,[3] the African

Charter on Human and Peoples' Rights,[4] the Declaration on the Elimination of All Forms of Discrimination Based on Religion or Belief,[5] the American Declaration of the Rights and Duties of Man,[6] and the Universal Declaration of Human Rights.[7] It is generally accepted, moreover, that states are enjoined by customary international law not to promote or condone systemic racial discrimination.[8]

The nondiscrimination norm is acknowledged to have special implications for indigenous groups which, practically as a matter of definition, have been treated adversely on the basis of their immutable or cultural differences. A seminar of experts convened by the United Nations to discuss the effects of racial discrimination on indigenous-state relations concluded that "[i]ndigenous peoples have been, and still are, the victims of racism and racial discrimination."[9] The report on the seminar elaborates:

> Racial discrimination against indigenous peoples is the outcome of a long historical process of conquest, penetration and marginalization, accompanied by attitudes of superiority and by a projection of what is indigenous as "primitive" and "inferior." The discrimination is of a dual nature: on the one hand, gradual destruction of the material and spiritual conditions [needed] for the maintenance of their [way of life], on the other hand, attitudes and behaviour signifying exclusion or negative discrimination when indigenous peoples seek to participate in the dominant society.[10]

In the same vein, the U.N. Committee on the Elimination of Racial Discrimination (CERD) has emphasized

> that in many regions of the world indigenous peoples have been, and are still being, discriminated against and deprived of their human rights and fundamental freedoms and in particular that they have lost their land and resources to colonists, commercial companies and State enterprises. Consequently, the preservation of their culture and their historical identity has been and still is jeopardized.[11]

The "problem of discrimination against indigenous populations"[12] was in fact the point of departure for the surge of U.N. activity concerning indigenous peoples over the last few decades. International Labour Organization Convention No. 169 on Indigenous and Tribal Peoples and the draft indigenous rights declarations being considered by the United Nations and the Organization of American States (OAS) reiterate the norm against discrimination with specific reference to indigenous peoples.[13] Clearly, it is no longer acceptable for states to incorporate institutions or tolerate practices that perpetuate an inferior status or condition for indigenous individuals, groups, or their cultural attributes. It is for this reason that CERD has paid special attention to indigenous peoples in its efforts to achieve compliance with the U.N. Convention on the Elimination of All Forms of Racial Discrimination, a convention that has been widely ratified.[14]

Convention No. 169 and the draft U.N. and OAS declarations, furthermore, prescribe that governments take affirmative steps to eliminate the incidents and legacies of discrimination against indigenous individuals and aspects of indigenous group identity.[15] The requirement of such affirmative action is today generally accepted, although the precise nature of the measures needed to eliminate discrimination against indigenous peoples will vary in practice according to circumstances.[16]

Cultural Integrity

The nondiscrimination norm, viewed in light of broader self-determination values, goes beyond ensuring for indigenous *individuals* either the same civil and political freedoms accorded others within an existing state structure or the same access to the state's social welfare programs. It also upholds the right of indigenous *groups* to maintain and freely develop their cultural identities in coexistence with other sectors of humanity. Hence, in connection with the U.N. Convention against Racial Discrimination, CERD has called upon states to

> (a) Recognize and respect indigenous distinct culture, history, language and way of life as an enrichment of the State's cultural identity and to promote its preservation;
> (b) Ensure that members of indigenous peoples are free and equal in dignity and rights and free from any discrimination, in particular that based on indigenous origin or identity;
> (c) Provide indigenous peoples with conditions allowing for a sustainable economic and social development compatible with their cultural characteristics;
> (d) Ensure that members of indigenous peoples have equal rights in respect of effective participation in public life and that no decisions directly relating to their rights and interests are taken without their informed consent;
> (e) Ensure that indigenous communities can exercise their rights to practise and revitalize their cultural traditions and customs and to preserve and to practise their languages.[17]

This statement by CERD extends to indigenous peoples the same general notion of respect for cultural integrity that has developed within international law in other contexts since some time ago. The notion of respect for cultural integrity was a feature of treaties among European powers, negotiated at the close of World War I.[18] In its advisory opinion on *Minority Schools in Albania*,[19] the Permanent Court of International Justice explained the minority rights provisions of the European treaties as deriving from equality precepts:

> The idea underlying the treaties for the protection of minorities is to secure for certain elements incorporated in a State, the population of which differs from

them in race, language or religion, the possibility of living peaceably along-side that population and co-operating amicably with it, while at the same time preserving the characteristics which distinguish them from the majority, and satisfying the ensuing special needs.

In order to attain this object, two things were regarded as particularly nec-essary, and have formed the subject of provisions in these treaties.

The first is to ensure that nationals belonging to racial, religious or lin-guistic minorities shall be placed in every respect on a footing of perfect equality with the other nationals of the State.

The second is to ensure for the minority elements suitable means for the preservation of their racial peculiarities, their traditions and their national characteristics.

These two requirements are indeed closely interlocked, for there would be no true equality between a majority and a minority if the latter were de-prived of its own institutions, and were consequently compelled to renounce that which constitutes the very essence of its being as a minority.[20]

Accordingly, the states participating in the Conference on Security and Coop-eration in Europe (subsequently the Organization for Security and Cooperation in Europe— OSCE) have declared the right of national minorities to "maintain and develop their culture in all its aspects, free of any attempts at assimilation against their will,"[21] and the Council of Europe has promulgated a Framework Convention on the Rights of National Minorities[22] which embraces and devel-ops this theme. Extending beyond the OSCE and European contexts, the Con-vention Against Genocide, the first U.N.-sponsored human rights treaty, upholds that *all* cultural groupings have a right to exist.[23]

Respect for cultures in addition to those of European derivation is promoted further by article 27 of the International Covenant on Civil and Political Rights.[24] Article 27 affirms in universalist terms the right of persons belonging to "ethnic, linguistic or religious minorities . . . , in community with other members of their group, to enjoy their own culture, to profess and practise their own religion [and] to use their own language."[25] Such rights are reaffirmed and elaborated upon in the 1992 U.N. Declaration on the Rights of Persons Belonging to National, Eth-nic, Religious and Linguistic Minorities.[26]

Affirmation of the world's diverse cultures was the central concern of a reso-lution by the Fourteenth General Conference of the United Nations Educational, Scientific and Cultural Organization. The 1966 UNESCO Declaration of the Principles of International Cultural Cooperation proclaims in its first article:

1. Each culture has dignity and value which must be respected and preserved.
2. Every people has the right and duty to develop its culture.
3. In their rich variety and diversity, and in the reciprocal influence they exert on one another, all cultures form part of the common heritage belonging to all mankind.[27]

More recently, UNESCO adopted a Universal Declaration on Cultural Diversity, in which it proclaimed:

> The defence of cultural diversity is an ethical imperative, inseparable from respect for human dignity. It implies a commitment to human rights and fundamental freedoms, in particular the rights of persons belonging to minorities and those of indigenous peoples.[28]

Article 27 of the covenant, the U.N. and European minority rights instruments, and the UNESCO declarations are each framed by preambular language establishing their derivation from the human rights principles of the United Nations Charter.[29] A number of other human rights instruments also have provisions upholding rights of cultural integrity.[30]

The affirmation of the cultural integrity norm within the framework of human rights establishes a strong foundation for the norm within international law. However, it also necessarily means that the exercise of culture is limited by that very framework, such that certain cultural practices may not be protected. Concerns are often raised about cultural practices that discriminate against or inflict harm on women.[31] The latter UNESCO declaration just cited adds to its endorsement of culture, "No one may invoke cultural diversity to infringe upon human rights guaranteed by international law, nor to limit their scope."[32] While this principal can hardly be challenged if the human rights framework is accepted, the question remains: By what process of decision making may it be legitimately determined that a particular cultural practice is illegitimate? Whatever the ultimate answer to this question, the internal decision-making dynamics that are themselves part of cultural group identity should count as starting points, In any assessment of whether a particular cultural practice is prohibited rather than protected, the cultural group concerned should be accorded a certain margin of deference for its own interpretive and decision-making processes for the application of universal human rights norms, just as states are accorded such deference. It may be paradoxical to think of universal human rights as having to accommodate to diverse cultural traditions, but that is a paradox embraced by the international human rights regime by including rights of cultural intergrity among the universally applicable human rights, precisely in an effort to promote common standards of human dignity in a world in which diverse cultures flourish.[33]

While rights of cultural integrity outside the specific context of indigenous peoples have been associated with "minority rights,"[34] indigenous rights advocates have frequently rejected calling indigenous groups minorities in their attempts to establish indigenous peoples within a separate regime with greater legal entitlements. For example, in a communication to the U.N. Human Rights Committee concerning the Mikmaq of Canada,[35] the author of the communication asserted that the "Mikmaq tribal society" was not a "minority" but rather a "people" within the meaning of article 1 of the Covenant on Civil and Political

Rights, which holds that "[a]ll peoples have the right to self-determination." International practice has not endorsed such a formalistic dichotomy but rather has tended to treat indigenous peoples and minorities as comprising distinct but overlapping categories subject to common normative considerations. The specific focus on indigenous peoples through international organizations indicates that groups within this rubric are acknowledged to have distinguishing concerns and characteristics that warrant treating them apart from, say, minority populations of Western Europe. At the same time, indigenous and minority rights issues intersect substantially in related concerns of nondiscrimination and cultural integrity.[36]

The cultural integrity norm, particularly as embodied in article 27 of the covenant, has been the basis of decisions favorable to indigenous peoples by the U.N. Human Rights Committee and the Inter-American Commission on Human Rights of the OAS. Both bodies have held the norm to cover all aspects of an indigenous group's survival as a distinct culture, understanding culture to include economic or political institutions and land use patterns, as well as language and religious practices. In the case concerning the Indians of Nicaragua, discussed in chapter 3, the Inter-American Commission on Human Rights cited Nicaragua's obligations under article 27 and found that the "special legal protections" accorded the Indians for the preservation of their cultural identity should extend to "the aspects linked to productive organization, which includes, among other things, the issue of ancestral and communal lands."[37]

In its 1985 decision concerning the Yanomami of Brazil, the commission again invoked article 27 and held that "international law in its present state . . . recognizes the right of ethnic groups to special protection on their use of their own language, for the practice of their own religion, and, in general, for all those characteristics necessary for the preservation of their cultural identity."[38] The commission viewed a series of incursions into Yanomami ancestral lands as a threat not only to the Yanomami's physical well-being but also to their culture and traditions.[39] Significantly, the commission cited article 27 to support its characterization of international law even though Brazil was not a party to the International Covenant on Civil and Political Rights, thus indicating the norm's character as general or customary international law. This same interpretation of the content and reach of the cultural integrity norm and article 27 in relation to indigenous peoples was reiterated by the commission in its 1997 human rights report on Ecuador, a report that included an analysis of the situation of indigenous peoples in the Amazon region who had experienced environmental damage because of oil development.[40]

A similarly extensive view of the cultural integrity norm as applied to indigenous peoples has been taken by the U.N. Human Rights Committee, although clearly in the context of applying treaty obligations assumed under the covenant. In *Ominayak v. Canada*[41] the committee construed the cultural rights guarantees of article 27 to extend to "economic and social activities" upon which the Lubicon Lake Band of Cree Indians relied as a group.[42] Thus the committee found that Canada, a party to the covenant and its Optional Protocol, had violated its obligation under article 27 by allowing the provincial government of Alberta to grant leases for oil and gas exploration and for timber development within the aboriginal territory of the Band. The committee acknowledged that the Band's survival as a distinct cultural community was bound up with the sustenance that it derived from the land.[43]

After its decision in the *Ominayak* case, the committee incorporated its broad and contextual interpretation of article 27 into its General Comment No. 23(50), which states that

> culture manifests itself in many forms, including a particular way of life asso-
> ciated with the use of land resources, especially in the case of indigenous
> peoples. That right may include such traditional activities as fishing or hunt-
> ing and the right to live in reserves protected by law. The enjoyment of those
> rights may require positive legal measures of protection and measures to en-
> sure the effective participation of members of minority communities in deci-
> sions which affect them.[44]

Article 27 articulates "rights of *persons* belonging to" cultural groups,[45] as opposed to specifying rights held by the groups themselves. It is apparent, however, that in its practical application article 27 protects group as well as individual interests in cultural integrity. As the cases just discussed indicate, the enjoyment of rights connected with culture are mostly meaningful in a group context. It would be impossible or lacking in meaning, for example, for an indigenous individual to *alone* partake of a traditional indigenous system of dispute resolution, or to alone speak an indigenous language or engage in a communal religious ceremony.[46] This understanding is implicit in article 27 itself, which upholds rights of persons to enjoy their culture "*in community* with other members of their group."[47] Culture, ordinarily, is an outgrowth of a collectivity, and, to that extent, affirmation of a cultural practice is an affirmation of the associated group.

Conversely, and as more clearly expressed by article 27, the individual human being is in his or her own right an important beneficiary of cultural integrity. The relationship of the individual to the group entitlement of cultural integrity was signaled by the U.N. Human Rights Committee in the case of Sandra Lovelace.[48] Lovelace, a woman who had been born into an Indian band residing on the Tobique Reserve in Canada, challenged section 12(1)(b) of Canada's Indian Act, which denied Indian status and benefits to any Indian woman who married a non-Indian. The act did not operate similarly with respect to Indian men. Because she had married a non-Indian, section 12(1)(b) denied Lovelace residency on the Tobique Reserve. She alleged violations of various provisions of the covenant, including articles proscribing sex discrimination, but the committee considered article 27 as "most directly applicable" to her situation. In ruling in her favor, the committee held that "the right of Sandra Lovelace to access to her native culture and language 'in community with the other members' of her group, has in fact been, and continues to be interfered with, because there is no place outside the Tobique Reserve where such a community exists."[49]

While the *Lovelace* case emphasizes the rights of the individual, the Human Rights Committee's decision in *Kitok v. Sweden*[50] demonstrates that the group interest in cultural survival may take priority. Ivan Kitok challenged the Swedish Reindeer Husbandry Act, which reserved reindeer herding rights exclusively for members of Saami villages. Although ethnically a Saami, he had lost his membership in his ancestral village, and the village had denied him readmission. The Human Rights Committee acknowledged that reindeer husbandry, although an economic activity, is an essential element of the Saami culture. The committee found that, while the Swedish legislation restricted Kitok's participation in Saami cultural life, his rights under article 27 of the covenant had not been violated. The committee concluded that the legislation was justified as a means of ensuring the viability and welfare of the Saami as a whole. In these and other cases the Human Rights Committee has emphasized that article 27 of the covenant broadly protects indigenous cultural integrity in a manner attentive to the particularities of diverse indigenous cultures and the interests of groups as well individuals.

At the same time, the Human Rights Committee has also instructed that rights of cultural integrity are not absolute when confronted with the interests of society as a whole. In another case concerning the Saami, *Lansmänn and others v. Finland*,[51] the committee considered the effects of state-authorized stone quarrying in the Mount Riutusvaara area in northern Finland where Saami groups herd reindeer. The committee reiterated that reindeer herding forms part of Saami culture, despite the use of modern technologies to carry out this activity and its economic aspects, and that hence it is protected under article 27 of the covenant.[52] The cultural integrity norm applied in this case even though Saami claims to property rights over the area in question remained unresolved.[53] Nonetheless, the committee decided, with the following analysis, that the circumstances of the case did not constitute a violation of article 27.

> A State may understandably wish to encourage development or allow economic activity by enterprises. . . . [M]easures that have a certain limited impact on the way of life of persons belonging to a minority will not necessarily amount to a denial of the right under article 27.
>
> The question that therefore arises in this case is whether the impact of the quarrying on Mount Riutusvaara is so substantial that it does effectively deny to the [Saami] authors the right to enjoy their cultural rights in that region.
>
> [T]he Committee concludes that quarrying on the slopes of Mt. Riutusvaara, in the amount that has already taken place, does not constitute a denial of the au-

thors' right, under article 27, to enjoy their own culture. It notes in particular that the interests of the Muotkatunturi [Saami] Herdsmens' Committee and of the authors [of the complaint against the state] were considered during the proceedings leading to the delivery of the quarrying permit, that the authors were consulted during the proceedings, and that reindeer herding in the area does not appear to have been adversely affected by such quarrying as has occurred.[54]

But while declining to finding a violation of article 27 under the circumstances, the committee was careful to warn that an increase in the stone-quarrying activity in the area used by Saami reindeer herders could in the future give rise to a violation of article 27.[55] It should also be noted that the committee arrived at its conclusion of no existing violation without any consideration of the dispute over ownership of the area, effectively accepting the state as the owner of the lands claimed by the Saami.[56]

The Human Rights Committee has reinforced the norm of cultural integrity by requiring recognition of the particularities of indigenous cultures in the application of articles of the covenant other than article 27. In the case of *Hopu & Bessert v. France*,[57] the committee considered allegations of human rights violations stemming from the planned construction of a hotel complex in a beach area in Tahiti in which were located the burial remains of Polynesians who lived hundreds of years ago. The contemporary indigenous people who complained of the construction could not establish direct ancestral links to the people whose remains were buried. Nonetheless the committee found violations of the rights to family and privacy, which are protected by articles 17 and 23 of the covenant. The committee deemed it necessary to apply the particular concept of "family" alive in the culture of the contemporary indigenous people concerned. In doing so the committee found that for these people the "family" included historical ancestors, regardless of direct kinship ties, and that, within such a contextual understanding of family, the burial grounds implicated family and privacy interests. Thus the committee agreed that the planned construction of the hotel complex, without sufficient accommodation for those interests, violated articles 17 and 23.[58]

International practice related to articulating standards into texts specifically concerning indigenous peoples is in accord with the foregoing interpretations of the norm of cultural integrity, and the practice manifests a convergence of opinion and expectations that can be understood as constituting customary international law. Ambassador España-Smith of Bolivia, chair of the International Labour Organization committee that drafted ILO Convention No. 169 on Indigenous and Tribal Peoples, summarized the consensus of the committee:

> The proposed Convention takes as its basic premise respect for the specific characteristics and the differences among indigenous and tribal peoples in the cultural, social and economic spheres. It consecrates respect for the integrity of the values, practices and institutions of these peoples in the general framework of guarantees enabling them to maintain their own different identities

and ensuring self-identification, totally exempt from pressures which might lead to forced assimilation, but without ruling out the possibility of their integration with other societies and life-styles as long as this is freely and voluntarily chosen.[59]

The same cultural integrity theme is at the core of the Draft United Nations Declaration on the Rights of Indigenous Peoples and previous drafts that were produced by the chair of the U.N. Working Group on Indigenous Populations pursuant to that body's standard-setting mandate. States have joined indigenous rights advocates in expressing widespread agreement with that essential thrust even while diverging in their views on particular aspects of the drafts.[60] In 1990, the chair of this working group of the Sub-Commission on Prevention of Discrimination and Protection of Minorities (now the Sub-Commission on the Promotion and Protection of Human Rights) concluded, on the basis of comments by governments and nongovernmental organizations, that a consensus supported all but three of the preambular paragraphs of the chair's first revised draft declaration.[61] Representative of the preambular paragraphs for which the working group chair reported widespread support is the following: "*Endorsing* calls for the consolidation and strengthening of indigenous societies and their cultures and traditions through development based on their own needs and value systems and comprehensive participation in and consultation about all other relevant development efforts. . . ."[62]

The sub-commission working group chair also reported general agreement among governments and NGOs with regard to the following operative provisions of the first revised draft:

3. the [collective] right to exist *as distinct peoples* and to be protected against genocide. . . .
4. the [collective] right to maintain and develop their ethnic and cultural characteristics and distinct identity, including the right of peoples and individuals to call themselves by their proper names.[63]

In addition, support for such precepts is a thread running throughout government comments solicited by the OAS Inter-American Commission on Human Rights as part of its preliminary work toward developing an OAS instrument on indigenous peoples' rights.[64]

While in principle the cultural integrity norm can be understood to apply to all segments of humanity, the norm has developed remedial aspects particular to indigenous peoples in light of their historical and continuing vulnerability. Until relatively recently in the history of societies in the Western Hemisphere, the Pacific, and elsewhere that have developed from patterns of settlement and colonization, those societies did not value indigenous cultures and instead promoted their demise through programs of assimilation.[65] Even as such policies have been abandoned or reversed, indigenous cultures remain threatened as a result of the lingering effects of those historical policies and because, typically, indigenous communities hold a nondominant position in the larger societies within which they live.[66]

As the international community has come to consider indigenous cultures equal in value to all others, the cultural integrity norm has developed to entitle indigenous groups to affirmative measures to remedy the past undermining of their cultural survival and to guard against continuing threats in this regard, as manifested by the resolution of the U.N. Committee on the Elimination of Racial Discrimination cited earlier.[67] It is not sufficient, therefore, that states simply refrain from coercing assimilation of indigenous peoples or abandonment of their cultural practices. ILO Convention No. 169 provides: "Governments shall have the responsibility for developing, with the participation of the peoples concerned, coordinated and systematic action to protect the rights of these peoples and to guarantee respect for their integrity."[68] The draft U.N. declaration echoes the requirement of "effective measures" to secure indigenous culture in its many manifestations.[69] Comments by governments to the sub-commission working group and other international bodies, as well as trends in government initiatives domestically, indicate broad acceptance of the requirement of affirmative action to secure indigenous cultural survival.

States have manifested their assent to a requirement of affirmative action with particular regard to language, although with some divergence of views. The trend, nonetheless, is in favor of greater efforts to promote the revitalization of indigenous languages and accomodate their use.[70] Indigenous peoples' representatives have advocated that their peoples be permitted to use their mother tongues in legal proceedings, and that position has found support among some states.[71] Other states, while demonstrating support for the use of indigenous languages in legal proceedings and other official contexts, have appeared reluctant to accede to a strict requirement to that effect.[72] But normative expectations converge at least to the extent that states feel an obligation to provide *some* affirmative support for the use of indigenous languages and to ensure that indigenous people do not suffer discrimination for failure to speak the dominant language of the state in which they live.

As for religion, states have conceded that the preservation of sacred sites and guarantees of access to them are among the affirmative measures that may be required in particular circumstances. Thus the government of Australia reported to the U.N. sub-commission working group that it had halted the construction of a dam that would have submerged a number of sacred sites near Alice Springs.[73] The Australian government also reported that it had stopped a mining project that would have damaged an area of significant cultural and religious import to the aboriginal Jawoyn people.[74] Similarly, the government of New Zealand reported to the same U.N. working group on newly established protections for sites of special religious significance to the indigenous Maori of that country.[75] Rights of access to sacred sites, however, are generally not held to be absolute. Canada, for example, has agreed with rights of access to sacred sites and burial grounds, but while stressing the need to balance such rights with competing claims and interests of nonindigenous groups and the state itself.[76] It is clear in any case that states are held, and often hold themselves, to certain minimum standards to ensure indigenous peoples the free exercise of their religious traditions.[77]

Related issues of indigenous cultural integrity requiring special attention have to do with indigenous peoples' works of art, scientific knowledge (especially with regard to the natural world), songs, stories, human remains, funerary objects, and other such tangible and intangible aspects of indigenous cultural heritage. These issues have been the subject of a study by Professor Erica-Irene Daes, under the sponsorship of the U.N. Sub-Commission on Promotion and Protection on Human Rights. The 1993 *Study on the Protection of the Cultural and Intellectual Property of Indigenous Peoples*[78] identifies widespread historical and continuing practices that have unjustly deprived indigenous peoples of the enjoyment of the tangible and intangible objects that comprise their cultural heritage.[79] The study identifies legislative and policy initiatives in a number of countries to correct these practices and proposes additional such initiatives as well as measures for greater international cooperation in this regard.[80]

At the request of the sub-commission, Professor Daes followed her study with a draft statement of principles on indigenous cultural heritage,[81] and this draft was the subject of a seminar convened by the Office of the High Commissioner for Human Rights.[82] These principles build upon indigenous peoples' articulated demands[83] and the consensus reflected in international instruments already adopted by states, including resolutions of the 1992 U.N. Conference on Environment and Development. The Rio Declaration on Environment and Development recognizes the "vital" role indigenous peoples may play in sustainable development "because of their knowledge and traditional practices."[84] In addition, the conference resolution adopted as "Agenda 21" calls upon states, in "full partnership with indigenous people and their communities," to adopt or strengthen appropriate policies and legal mechanisms to empower indigenous peoples in the enjoyment of and control over the knowledge, resources and practices that comprise their cultural heritage.[85] The Convention on Biological Diversity, another outcome of the 1992 conference, establishes that each state party shall, "[s]ubject to its national legislation, respect, preserve and maintain knowledge, innovations and practices of indigenous and local communities embodying traditional lifestyles relevant for the conservation and sustainable use of biological diversity."[86] Consensus on these and related precepts have engendered a discussion within the World Intellectual Property Organization to reevaluate the international intellectual property regime as it relates to indigenous peoples.[87]

International practice thus indicates affirmative duties protective of culture to be commensurate with the broad interpretation of the cultural integrity norm that has been advanced by the Inter-American Commission on Human Rights and the U.N. Human Rights Committee. In statements to international human rights bodies, governments have reported a broad array of domestic initiatives concerning indigenous peoples, including constitutional and legislative reforms, and have characterized those initiatives as generally intended to safeguard the integrity and life of indigenous cultures.[88] The reported reforms, which vary in scope and content, owe that variance at least in part to the diversity of circumstances and characteristics of the indigenous groups concerned. The indigenous peoples of the United States, for example, who to one degree or another have developed pervasive linkages with the global economy, are properly regarded as having requirements different from those of the isolated forest-dwelling tribes of Brazil. Government representatives have been quick to point out the diversity among indigenous groups in the context of efforts to articulate prescriptions protective of indigenous rights.[89] That diversity, however, does not undermine the strength of the cultural integrity norm as much as it leads to an understanding that the norm requires diverse applications in diverse settings. In all cases, the operative premise is that of securing the survival and flourishing of indigenous cultures through mechanisms devised in accordance with the preferences of the indigenous peoples concerned.

Lands and Natural Resources

The Inter-American Commission on Human Rights and the U.N. Human Rights Committee in the cases previously mentioned acknowledged the importance of lands and resources to the survival of indigenous cultures and, by implication, to indigenous self-determination. That understanding is a widely accepted tenet of contemporary international concern over indigenous peoples.[90] It follows from indigenous peoples' articulated ideas of communal stewardship over land and a deeply felt spiritual and emotional nexus with the earth and its fruits.[91] Indigenous peoples, furthermore, typically have looked to a secure land and natural resource base to ensure the economic viability and development of their communities.

Relevant to indigenous land claims is the self-determination provision, common to both the international human rights covenants, which affirms: "In no case may a people be deprived of its own means of subsistence."[92] This prescription intersects with the idea of property, a long established feature common to societies throughout the world. The concept of property includes the notion that human beings have rights to lands and chattels that they, by some measure of legitimacy, have reduced to their own control.[93] Legal systems have varied in prescribing the rules by which the rights are acquired and in defining the rights. The most commonly noted dichotomy has been between the system of private property rights in Western societies and the now rare classical Marxist systems in which the state retains formal ownership of most or all real estate and natural resources while granting rights of use.[94] The common feature, however, is that people *do* acquire and retain rights of a proprietary nature in relation to other people, and respect for those rights is valued.

Property has been affirmed as an international human right. The Universal Declaration of Human Rights states that "[e]veryone has the right to own property alone as well as in association with others," and that "[n]o one shall be arbitrarily deprived of his property."[95] Similar prescriptions are repeated in the American Convention on Human Rights,[96] the American Declaration on the Rights and Duties of Man,[97] and the European Convention on Human Rights.[98]

Inasmuch as property is a human right, the fundamental norm of nondiscrimination requires recognition of the forms of property that arise from the traditional or customary land tenure of indigenous peoples, in addition to the property regimes created by the dominant society. Several U.N. and OAS studies and declarations have highlighted that among the most troublesome manifestations of historical discrimination against indigenous peoples has been the lack of recognition of indigenous modalities of property.[99] A study commissioned by the Sub-Commission on the Promotion and Protection of Human Rights, *Indigenous Peoples and their Relationship to Land*, identifies the still persistent effects of this historical discrimination and calls for reforms in domestic legal systems to abolish the doctrines and practices that hinder recognition of indigenous land and resource tenure systems.[100]

Early international jurisprudence invoked property precepts to affirm that indigenous peoples in the Americas and elsewhere had original rights to the lands they used and occupied prior to contact with the encroaching white societies.[101] That jurisprudence made its way into the legal and political doctrine of some of the countries that were born of colonial patterns, most notably the United States.[102] That doctrine, however, developed without valuing indigenous cultures or recognizing the significance of their ongoing relationship with the land. Thus, under U.S. law, indigenous peoples have long enjoyed rights to lands on the basis of historical use and occupancy; but the government may unilaterally "extinguish" those rights, and any claims arising from such extinguishment historically have been satisfied, in the best of cases, by a simple money transfer. Within the Western liberal frame adopted into the political and juridical culture of the United States, indigenous peoples' lands have been treated as fungible with cash.[103]

In contemporary international law, by contrast, modern notions of cultural integrity, nondiscrimination, and self-determination join property precepts in the affirmation of sui generis indigenous land and resource rights, as evident in ILO Convention No. 169 on Indigenous and Tribal Peoples. The land rights provisions of Convention No. 169 are framed by article 13(1), which states:

> In applying the provisions of this Part of the Convention governments shall respect the special importance for the cultures and spiritual values of the peoples concerned of their relationship with the lands or territories, or both as applicable, which they occupy or otherwise use, and in particular the collective aspects of this relationship.

The concept of indigenous territories embraced by the convention is deemed to cover "the total environment of the areas which the peoples concerned occupy or otherwise use."[104] Indigenous land and resource—or territorial—rights are of a collective character,[105] and they include a combination of possessory, use, and management rights. In its article 14(1), Convention No. 169 affirms:

> The rights of ownership and possession of [indigenous peoples] over the lands which they traditionally occupy shall be recognised. In addition, measures shall be taken in appropriate cases to safeguard the right of the peoples concerned to use lands not exclusively occupied by them, but to which they have traditionally had access for their subsistence and traditional activities.

Article 15, furthermore, requires states to safeguard indigenous peoples' rights to the natural resources throughout their territories, including their right "to participate in the use, management and conservation" of the resources. The convention falls short of upholding rights to mineral or subsurface resources in cases in which the state generally retains ownership of those resources.[106] Pursuant to the norm of nondiscrimination, however, indigenous peoples must not be denied subsurface and mineral rights where such rights are otherwise accorded landowners. In any case, the convention mandates that indigenous peoples are to have a say in any resource exploration or extraction on their lands and to benefit from those activities.[107] In applying the convention, relevant ILO institutions have emphasized that, when natural resource development activities may affect indigenous communities, a process of consultation with the communities, prior to commencement of the development activities, is at minimum required.[108] Prior consultation and appropriate mitigation measures are required in respect to any natural resource extraction from indigenous ancestral or traditional lands, regardless of formal ownership of the lands or the exclusivity of indigenous occupation, when the extraction may in some way affect the lives of the indigenous people concerned.[109]

The convention adds that indigenous peoples "shall not be removed from the lands which they occupy" unless under prescribed conditions and where necessary as an "exceptional measure."[110] When the grounds for relocation no longer exist, they "shall have the right to return to their traditional lands" and when return is not possible "these peoples shall be provided in all possible cases with lands of quality and legal status at least equal to that of the lands previously occupied by them."[111] The convention also provides for recognition of indigenous land tenure systems,[112] which typically are based on long-standing custom.

These systems regulate community members' relative interests in collective land-holdings, and they also have bearing on the character of collective landholdings vis-à-vis the state and others.

Thus Convention No. 169 affirms the notion, promoted by various international institutions, that indigenous peoples as groups are entitled to a *continuing* relationship with lands and natural resources according to traditional patterns of use or occupancy. Use of the words *traditionally occupy* in article 14(1), as opposed to use of the past tense of the verb, suggests that the occupancy must be connected with the present in order for it to give rise to possessory rights. In light of the article 13 requirement of respect for cultural values related to land, however, a sufficient present connection with lost lands may be established by a continuing cultural attachment to them, particularly if dispossession occurred recently.

Also relevant in this regard is article 14(3), which requires "[a]dequate procedures . . . within the national legal system to resolve land claims by" indigenous peoples. This provision is without any temporal limitation and thus empowers claims originating well in the past. Article 14(3) is a response to the historical processes that have afflicted indigenous peoples, processes that have trampled on their cultural attachment to ancestral lands, disregarded or minimized their legitimate property interests, and left them without adequate means of subsistence. In light of the acknowledged centrality of lands and resources to indigenous cultures and economies, the requirement to provide meaningful redress for indigenous land claims implies an obligation on the part of states to provide remedies that include for indigenous peoples the option of regaining lands and access to natural resources.[113]

The essential aspects of Convention No. 169's land rights provisions are strongly rooted in an expanding nexus of international opinion and practice. In responding to a questionnaire circulated by the International Labour Office in preparation for the drafting of the convention, governments overwhelmingly favored strengthening the land rights provisions from the older ILO Convention No. 107 of 1957, including governments not parties to that convention.[114] Although Convention No. 107 is generally regarded as flawed, it contains a recognition of indigenous land rights that has operated in favor of indigenous peoples' demands through the ILO's supervisory machinery.[115] The discussion on the new convention proceeded on the premise that indigenous peoples were to be accorded greater recognition of land rights than they were in Convention No. 107.[116] The land rights provisions of Convention No. 169 were finalized by a special working party of the Labour Conference committee that developed the text of the convention, and the committee approved the provisions by consensus.[117]

Government statements to the U.N. Working Group on Indigenous Populations and other international bodies confirm general acceptance of at least the core aspects of the land rights norms expressed in Convention No. 169. The statements tell of worldwide initiatives to secure indigenous possessory and use rights over land and to redress historical claims.[118] And discussions over language for the U.N. indigenous rights declaration have included efforts—albeit sometimes contentious efforts—to build upon the already recognized rights.[119] The acceptance of indigenous land rights is further evident in the preparatory work for the proposed OAS juridical instrument on indigenous peoples' rights,[120] Chapter 26 of Agenda 21 adopted by U.N. Conference on Environment and Development,[121] and the World Bank's Operational Directive 4.20 for bank-funded projects affecting indigenous peoples,[122] among other sources.

The growing international acceptance of indigenous rights to land reflected in ILO Convention No. 169 and related developments coincides with the jurisprudence, discussed above, of the U.N. Human Rights Committee and the Inter-American Commission on Human Rights regarding the implications of the cultural integrity norm.[123] It also coincides with the interpretations of the general human right to property that has been promoted by the inter-American commission and adopted by the Inter-American Court of Human Rights.

In *Case of the Mayagna (Sumo) Awas Tingni Community v. Nicaragua*,[124] the Inter-American Court of Human Rights accepted the commission's conclusion that Nicaragua had violated the property rights of the indigenous Mayangna community of Awas Tingni by granting to a foreign company a concession to log within the community's traditional lands and by failing to otherwise provide adequate recognition and protection of the community's traditional land tenure. The Court held that the concept of property articulated in the American Convention on Human Rights[125] includes the communal property of indigenous peoples, even if that property is not held under a deed of title or is not otherwise specifically recognized by the state. Awas Tingni, like most of the indigenous communities of the Atlantic Coast, was without specific government recognition of its traditional lands in the form of a land title or other official document, despite provisions in Nicaragua's constitution and laws affirming in general terms the rights of indigenous peoples to the lands they traditionally occupy.[126] In the absence of such specific government recognition, Nicaraguan authorities had treated the untitled traditional indigenous lands—or substantial parts of them— as state lands, as they had done in granting concessions for logging in the Awas Tingni area.[127] The Court concluded, especially in light of articles 1 and 2 of the convention, which require affirmative state measures to protect rights recognized by the convention and domestic law, that such negligence on the part of the state violated the right to property of article 21 of the American Convention.[128]

Although the Court stressed that Nicaragua's domestic law itself affirms indigenous communal property, the Court also emphasized that the rights articulated in international human rights instruments have "autonomous meaning for which reason they cannot be made equivalent to the meaning given to them in domestic law."[129] The Inter-American Commission on Human Rights had pressed this point in prosecuting the case before the Court, invoking in its written submissions the jurisprudence of the European Court of Human Rights regarding the analogous property rights provision of the European Convention on Human Rights, and referencing developments elsewhere in international law and institutions specifically concerning indigenous peoples' rights over lands and natural resources.[130] The inter-American Court accepted the commission's view that, in its meaning autonomous from domestic law, the international human right of property embraces the communal property regimes of indigenous peoples as defined by their own customs and traditions, such that "possession of the land should suffice for indigenous communities lacking real title to property of the land to obtain official recognition of that property."[131] Accordingly, the Court determined that indigenous peoples not only have property rights to their traditional lands protected by the American Convention on Human Rights but that they also are entitled under the convention to have the state demarcate and title those lands in their favor in circumstances where those rights are not otherwise secure. The Court found that Awas Tingni in particular has the "right that the State . . . carry out the delimitation, demarcation, and titling of the territory belonging to the Community."[132] This holding is commensurate with article 14(2) of ILO Convention No. 169, which provides: "Governments shall take steps as necessary to identify the lands which the peoples concerned traditionally occupy, and to guarantee effective protection of their rights of ownership and possession."[133]

In arriving at its conclusions in the *Awas Tingni* case, the Court applied what it termed an "evolutionary" method of interpretation, taking into account modern developments in conceptions about property as related to indigenous peoples and their lands.[134] In his concurring opinion, Judge Garcia Ramírez expounded upon this interpretive methodology, making specific references to the relevant provisions of ILO Convention No. 169, even though Nicaragua is not a party to that convention, as well as to parts of the draft U.N. and OAS declarations on the rights of indigenous peoples.[135] Judge Cançado Trindade, the president of the court, joined judges Pacheco Gómez and Abreu Burelli in another concurring opinion, reiterating the cultural and spiritual underpinnings of indigenous peoples' relations to lands.[136]

The Inter-American Commission on Human Rights followed the precedent and interpretive methodology of the *Awas Tingni* case in addressing a dispute concerning the land rights of the Western Shoshone people. In the case of *Mary and Carrie Dann v. United States*,[137] the commission extended the interpretation of the right to property of the American Convention on Human Rights advanced in the *Awas Tingni* case to the similar property rights provision of the American Declaration on the Rights and Duties of Man,[138] emphasizing the due process and equal protection prescriptions that are to attach to indigenous property interests in lands and natural resources. The case arose from the refusal of Western Shoshone sisters Mary and Carrie Dann to submit to the permit system imposed by the United States for grazing on large parts of Western Shoshone traditional lands.[139] Faced with efforts by the U.S. government to forcibly stop them from grazing cattle without a permit and to impose substantial fines on them for doing so, the Danns argued that the permit system contravened Western Shoshone land rights. The United States conceded that the land in question was Western Shoshone ancestral land but contended that Western Shoshone rights in the land had been "extinguished" through a series of administrative and judicial determinations. The commission examined the proceedings by which the United States contended that Western Shoshone land rights had been lost and determined that those proceedings did not afford the Danns and other Western Shoshone groups adequate opportunity to be heard and that the proceedings otherwise denied these groups the same procedural and substantive protections generally available to property holders under U.S. law.[140] The commission noted the inadequacy of the historical rationale for the presumed taking of Western Shoshone land—the need to encourage settlement and agricultural developments in the western United States— and also cited the United States' failure to apply to the Western Shoshone the same just compensation standard ordinarily applied for the taking of property interests under U.S. law.[141] Thus the commission found that the United States had "failed to ensure the Danns' right to property under conditions of equality contrary to Articles II [right to equal protection, XVIII [right to fair trial] and XXIII [right to property] of the American Declaration in connection with their claims to property rights in the Western Shoshone ancestral lands."[142]

In applying and interpreting the cited provisions of the American declaration in the *Dann* case, the commission was explicit in its reliance on developments and trends in the international legal system regarding the rights of indigenous peoples.[143] Significantly the commission declared that the "basic principles reflected in many of the provisions" of the Proposed American Declaration on the Rights of Indigenous Peoples, "including aspects of [its] article XVIII, reflect general international legal principles developing out of and applicable inside and outside of the Inter-American system and to this extent are properly considered in interpreting and applying the provisions of the American Declaration in the context of indigenous peoples."[144] Article XVIII of that cited proposed declaration[145] provides for the protection of traditional forms of land tenure in terms similar to those found in ILO Convention No. 169, which the commission also highlighted in its analysis.[146] Thus the commission further signaled the development of a sui generis regime of international norms and jurisprudence concerning indigenous peoples and the benchmark represented by ILO Convention No. 169 in that development, even in regard to states, like the United States, that are not parties to the convention.

In the *Awas Tingni* case, the commission had maintained that, given the gradual emergence of an international consensus on the rights of indigenous peoples to their traditional lands, such rights are now a matter of customary international law.[147] Continuing this line of thought in the *Dann* case, the commission summarized what it considers the pertinent "general international legal principles" that are *now* aplicable both within and outside the Inter-American system:

—the right of indigenous peoples to legal recognition of their varied and specific forms and modalities of their control, ownership, use and enjoyment of territories and property;

—the recognition of their property and ownership rights with respect to lands, territories and resources they have historically occupied; and

—where property and user rights of indigenous peoples arise from rights existing prior to the creation of a state, recognition by that state of the permanent and inalienable title of indigenous peoples relative thereto and to have such title changed only by mutual consent between the state and respective indigenous peoples when they have full knowledge and appreciation of the nature or attributes of such property. This also implies the right to fair compensation in the event that such property and user rights are irrevocably lost.[148]

It is thus evident that certain minimum standards concerning indigenous land rights, rooted in otherwise accepted precepts of property, cultural integrity, non-discrimination, and self-determination, have made their way not just into conventional law but also into general or customary international law.[149]

Social Welfare and Development

As just indicated, indigenous peoples' interests in a secure land base are both cultural and economic. Related to these interests are entitlements of social welfare and development, entitlements also grounded in the United Nations Charter and adjoined to the principle of self-determination. Chapter IX of the Charter, under the heading "International Economic and Social Co-Operation," states in part:

Article 55

With a view to the creation of conditions of stability and well-being which are necessary for peaceful and friendly relations among nations based on respect for the principle of equal rights and self-determination of peoples, the United Nations shall promote:

a. higher standards of living, full employment, and conditions of economic and social progress and development;

b. solutions of international economic, social, health, and related problems; and international cultural and educational co-operation. . . .

Article 56

All members pledge themselves to take joint and separate action in co-operation with the Organization for the achievement of the purposes set forth in Article 55.

Building upon the Charter provisions, the International Covenant on Economic, Social, and Cultural Rights[150] affirms an array of social welfare rights and corresponding state obligations that are to benefit "everyone."[151] Emphasized in the covenant are rights to health, education, and an adequate standard of living. The U.N. Educational, Scientific and Cultural Organization, the Food and Agricultural Organization of the United Nations, the World Health Organization, and the International Labour Organization have been sources of a number of additional instruments or programs establishing generally applicable standards and policies within the realm of social welfare concerns.

Linked with those rights of social welfare that generally are articulated as benefiting the individual is the right to development, which has been deemed to extend also to "peoples."[152] In December 1986 the U.N. General Assembly adopted by an overwhelming majority the Declaration on the Right to Development.[153] The declaration defines the right to development as "an inalienable human right by virtue of which every human person and all peoples are entitled to participate in, contribute to, and enjoy economic, social, cultural and political development, in which all human rights and fundamental freedoms can be fully realized."[154] The greater part of the declaration is occupied with articulating a series of duties on the part of states to promote and ensure the realization of the right to development through international cooperation and domestic programs.[155] The right to development increasingly has been considered alongside the global environmental agenda, such that development that is environmentally sustainable has become the overriding goal, as evidenced by the concluding documents of the 2002 World Summit on Sustainable Development.[156]

Within the framework of the foregoing precepts, a special rubric of entitlements and corresponding duties has developed with regard to indigenous peoples. These norms are aimed at remedying two distinct but related historical phenomena that place most indigenous communities in economically disadvantaged conditions. The first phenomenon is the progressive plundering of indigenous peoples' lands and resources over time, processes that have impaired or devastated indigenous economies and subsistence life, and left indigenous people among the poorest of the poor.[157] The second is the discrimination that has tended to exclude members of indigenous communities from enjoying the social welfare benefits generally available in the states within which they live.[158]

In response to these historical phenomena, ILO Convention No. 169 establishes as "a matter of priority" the "improvement of the conditions of life and work and levels of health and education of [indigenous] peoples," and it mandates "[s]pecial projects . . . to promote such improvement."[159] The convention, furthermore, specifies duties on the part of states to ensure the absence of discriminatory practices and effects in areas of employment, vocational training, social security and health, education, and means of communication.[160] The convention emphasizes, in accordance with core precepts of self-determination, that the special programs devised to ensure the social welfare and development of indigenous peoples are to be established in cooperation with the indigenous peoples concerned[161] and in accordance with their own collectively formulated priorities.[162] The Draft U.N. Declaration on the Rights of Indigenous Peoples follows in the same vein, stating that indigenous peoples are entitled "to have access to adequate financial and technical assistance, from States and through international cooperation, to pursue freely their political economic, social, cultural and spiritual development."[163] In addition, the Proposed American Declaration on the Rights of Indigenous Peoples affirms, "Indigenous Peoples shall be entitled to obtain, on a non-discriminatory basis, appropriate means for their own development according to their preferences and values."[164]

The provisions of Convention No. 169 and the draft declarations just noted represent a consensus that extends well beyond states that have ratified Convention No. 169 or the authorized experts that developed the drafts. Although there is controversy about the outer bounds of state obligation to promote indigenous social welfare and development, a core consensus exists that states are in some measure obligated to that end. In reports on domestic initiatives to the U.N. Working Group on Indigenous Populations and other international bodies, states frequently have indicated their assent to duties to take steps and commit resources to advance the social welfare and development of indigenous individuals and communities.[165] State obligations to promote indigenous development are related to a strong policy of international cooperation in this regard, as evidenced by initiatives specifically for the benefit of indigenous peoples within the World Bank,[166] the Inter-American Development Bank,[167] and the U.N. Development Programme (UNDP);[168] and by the creation of the Indigenous Peoples' Fund in the Americas.[169]

Self-Government: Autonomy and Participation

Self-government is the overarching political dimension of ongoing self-determination. Along with variance in political theory, conceptions about the normative elements of self-government vary. It is possible, however, to identify a core of widely held convictions about the self-government concept. That core consists of the idea that government is to function according to the will of the people governed. Self-government stands in opposition to institutions that disproportionately or unjustly concentrate power in the reins of government, whether the concentration is centered *within* the relevant community—as in cases of despotic or racially discriminatory rule—or *outside* the community—as in cases of foreign domination. The international community recognized classical colonial institutions of government as contrary to self-government because they subjected people to "alien subjugation, domination and exploitation."[170] Hence, the term *non-self-governing territories* designated the beneficiaries of decolonization,[171] and the beneficiary territories were deemed self-governing upon "(a) emergence as an independent state; (b) [f]ree association with an independent State; or (c) [i]ntegration with an independent state" on the basis of equality.[172]

Two significant developments in dominant conceptions about the requirements of governmental legitimacy have emerged since the height of the decolonization movement, developments which bear upon contemporary understanding of the functional elements of self-government. One is the dramatic decline of Soviet-style Marxist and other authoritarian systems in many parts of the world, accompanied by a worldwide movement that espouses faith in nonauthoritarian democratic institutions. Especially since the demise of the Soviet Union, an embrace of democratic precepts has been reflected in developments worldwide[173] and has been promoted through the United Nations and other international institutions,[174] although in many parts of the planet transition to democracy wanes or simply doesn't take hold. Accordingly, there is now a body of scholarly literature articulating rights of "political participation" and a nascent "democratic entitlement" under international law,[175] which challenges the still entrenched despots of the world. Closely linked with modern precepts of democracy is the notion of subsidiarity, the idea that, consistent with values promoted by patterns of political integration, decisions should be made at the most local level possible,[176] an idea reflected not only in Western societies but also in indigenous communities that traditionally have maintained decentralized systems of governance.[177]

A second major development is the ever greater embrace of notions of cultural pluralism identified earlier. Over the last several years, the international community increasingly has come to value and promote the integrity of diverse cultures within existing state units, including non-European indigenous cultures.[178] Within the contemporary processes by which modern democracies are evolving or being constructed, the classical ideal of the culturally or ethnically homogenous "nation-state" is giving way to the model of a plurinational or pluricultural state.[179] This multicultural move is encouraged by an increasingly important strain of political philosophy, led by authors such as Will Kymlicka.[180]

In the particular context of indigenous peoples, notions of democracy (including decentralized government) and of cultural integrity join to create a *sui generis* self-government norm. The norm includes two distinct but interrelated strains. One upholds spheres of governmental or administrative autonomy for indigenous communities; the other seeks to ensure the effective participation of those communities in all decisions affecting them that are left to the larger institutions of decision making.

Autonomy

Many indigenous communities have retained *de facto* their own institutions of autonomous governance, which are at least partly rooted in historical patterns of social and political interaction and control. These systems often include customary or written laws as well as dispute resolution and adjudicative mechanisms developed over centuries.[181] For some indigenous groups, such as Indian tribes within the United States, such autonomous institutions have also existed *de jure* within legal systems of the states within which they live.[182] Pursuant to precepts of constitutive self-determination, any diminishment in the authority or altering of *de facto* or *de jure* indigenous institutions of autonomous governance should not occur unless pursuant to the wishes of the affected groups. To the contrary, states are enjoined to uphold the existence and free development of indigenous institutions. Hence, ILO Convention No. 169 upholds the right of indigenous peoples to "retain their own customs and institutions"[183] and requires that "the methods customarily practised by the peoples concerned for dealing with offences committed by their members shall be respected."[184] Similarly, the draft U.N. declaration states: "Indigenous peoples have the right to promote, develop and maintain their institutional structures and their distinctive juridical customs, traditions, procedures and practices, in accordance with internationally recognized human rights standards."[185]

Independently of the extent to which indigenous peoples have retained *de facto* or *de jure* autonomous institutions from previous eras, they generally are entitled to develop autonomous governance appropriate to their circumstances on grounds instrumental to securing ongoing self-determination. In general, autonomous governance for indigenous communities is considered instrumental to their capacities to control the development of their distinctive cultures, including their use of land and resources. In the context of indigenous Hawaiians, for example, Michael Dudley and Keoni Agard echo the demand for "nationhood" and "sovereignty"—that is, some form of autonomous political status for Native Hawaiians—as a means of securing space for the education of children in Hawaiian language, for reclaiming Native Hawaiian spiritual heritage and connection with the natural world, and, in general, for the natural evolution of Hawaiian culture cushioned from the onslaught of outside influences that have thus far had devastating effects.[186]

Autonomous governance, furthermore, is understood as a means of enhancing democracy. Because of their nondominant positions within the states in which they live, indigenous communities and their members typically have been denied full and equal participation in the political processes that have sought to govern over them.[187] Even as indigenous individuals have been granted full rights of citizenship and overtly racially discriminatory policies have diminished, indigenous groups still typically constitute economically disadvantaged numerical minorities within the states in which they live.[188] This condition is one of political vulnerability. To devolve governmental authority onto indigenous communities is to diminish their vulnerability in the face of powerful majority or elite interests and to enhance the responsiveness of government to the unique interests of indigenous communities and their members.

Hence, the draft U.N. declaration states:

> Indigenous peoples, as a specific form of exercising their right to self-determination, have the right to autonomy or self-government in matters relating to their internal and local affairs, including culture, religion, education, information, media, health, housing, employment, social welfare, economic activities, land and resources management, environment and entry by non-members, as well as ways and means for financing these autonomous functions.[189]

The Proposed American Declaration on the Rights of Indigenous Peoples recognizes "the right to autonomy or self-government" in similar terms.[190] Although differing in their willingness to accept such a formulation of a "right to autonomy," states increasingly have expressed agreement that indigenous peoples are entitled to maintain and develop their traditional institutions and to otherwise enjoy autonomous spheres of governmental or administrative authority appropriate to their circumstances.[191]

Following the 1983 decision of the Inter-American Commission on Human Rights in favor of a new political order for the Indians of the Atlantic Coast region of Nicaragua, the Nicaraguan government entered into negotiations with Indian leaders and eventually developed a constitutional and legislative regime of political and administrative autonomy for the Indian-populated region.[192] Emphasizing the ideal represented by the autonomy regime, rather than focusing on the problems in its implementation, the Nicaraguan government held out the autonomy arrangement as advancing the self-determination of the Atlantic Coast indigenous peoples. Several other states have reported to international bodies the use of constitutional, legislative, and other official measures to reorder governing institutional matrices in response to indigenous peoples' demands for autonomous governance and recognition of their culturally specific institutions of social and political control.[193] Even though in most instances these initiatives are not fully or adequately implemented, they represent a growing consensus of global opinion and expectation in this regard.

Participation/Consultation

While the norm of indigenous self-government upholds the development of autonomous institutions for indigenous peoples, it also upholds their effective participation in the larger political order. The draft U.N. declaration affirms the overwhelmingly accepted view that "[i]ndigenous peoples have the right to participate fully, if they so choose, at all levels of decision-making which may affect their rights,"[194] a view affirmed in similar terms in the proposed American declaration.[195] Likewise, ILO Convention No. 169 requires effective means by which indigenous peoples "can freely participate . . . at all levels of decision-making" affecting them.[196] It is evident that this requirement applies not only to decision making within the framework of domestic or municipal processes but also to decision making within the international realm. U.N. bodies and other international institutions increasingly have allowed for, and even solicited, the participation of indigenous peoples' representatives in their policy-making and standard-setting work in areas of concern to indigenous groups.[197] The U.N. Permanent Forum on Indigenous Issues, which was established to give indigenous peoples a greater voice within the U.N. system, and which is composed in part of indigenous persons, is now perhaps the principal manifestation of a general acceptance of indigenous participation within relevant international spheres.[198]

In the context of indigenous-state relations, the concept of participation has given rise to requirements of consultation that are to be applied whenever the state makes decisions that may affect indigenous peoples. ILO Convention No. 169 in its article 6 affirms the duty of governments to "[c]onsult the peoples concerned, through appropriate procedures and in particular through their representative institutions, whenever consideration is being given to legislative or administrative measures which may affect them directly."[199] Article 15 of the Convention makes clear that among the many situations in which this consultation requirement applies are those in which natural resource or other development projects are proposed for areas that are within traditional indigenous territories, even when the resources at stake are not, under state law, owned by the indigenous peoples concerned.[200] ILO authorities have interpreted the convention to not require that the consultations lead to agreement with indigenous peoples in all instances.[201] Nonetheless the convention stipulates that the consultations "shall be undertaken, in good faith and in a form appropriate to the circumstances, *with the objective of achieving agreement or consent* to the proposed measures."[202]

This requirement that agreement should at least be an objective of the consultations means that the consultations cannot simply be a matter of informing indigenous communities about the measures that will affect them. Consultation processes must be crafted to allow indigenous peoples the opportunity to genuinely influence the decisions that affect their interest. This requires governments to fully engage indigenous peoples in the discussions about what the outcomes of those decisions should be before they are taken. It also requires procedural safeguards to account for indigenous peoples' own decision-making mechanisms, including relevant customs and organizational structures, and ensuring that indigenous peoples have access to all needed information and relevant expertise.[203] Further, as pointed out by ILO supervisory bodies, the objective of consultations should also be understood in connection with the convention's other provisions and its general mandate that governments develop, "with the participation of the peoples' concerned, co-ordinated and systematic action to protect their rights and to guarantee respect for their integrity."[204] Thus, in addition to the procedural safeguards that apply, and whether or not agreement is to be achieved, the consultations should lead to decisions that are consistent with indigenous peoples' substantive rights. This puts a burden on a government to justify, in terms consistent with the full range of applicable international norms concerning indigenous peoples, any decision that is contrary to the expressed preferences of the affected indigenous group.

As established previously, the requirements of consultation and participation incorporated in Convention No. 169 are grounded in general principles of self-government and self-determination, principles that are considered fundamental within contemporary international law. These requirements are also related to norms of nondiscrimination and cultural integrity, as has been manifested by CERD and the Human Rights Committee. In connection with the Convention on the Elimination of All Forms of Racial Discrimination, CERD has called upon states to ensure that "indigenous peoples have equal rights in respect of effective participation in public life and no decisions directly relating to their rights and interests are taken without their informed consent."[205] In the same vein, the U.N. Human Rights Committee has understood the norm of cultural integrity, as incorporated into the International Covenant on Civil and Political Rights through its article 27, to require the "effective participation" of indigenous peoples in any decision that may affect their cultural attributes, including decisions concerning cultural ties with lands and natural resources.[206]

With their strong normative foundations, the basic elements of the consultation provisions of Convention No. 169 have been generally accepted within various spheres of international and domestic practice, independently of specific treaty obligations imposed by this or other international conventions. For example, the World Bank, which itself is a subject of international law within is realm of competency,[207] includes "informed participation" by indigenous peoples and "direct consultation" with them as among the "central activities" that are specified by its Operational Directive 4.20 to be undertaken in connection with any bank-funded project that may affect the interests of these peoples.[208] Going beyond the context of international development assistance, the draft U.N. and OAS declarations include provisions that clearly incorporate minimum requirements of consultation that approximate or exceed the mandates of Convention No. 169.[209] It is evident that there exists a broad acceptance of minimum requirements of consultation among states and others participating in the discussions on these drafts, even while certain disagreement persists about the particular wording that should make its way into the final declarations.[210] It can also be observed that, in their communications to international institutions about relevant developments, states usually make references to consultations undertaken with the indigenous peoples affected by the developments,[211] which further manifests an ever greater acceptance of the principles of prior consultation included in Convention No. 169. Even if it may not yet be said that a norm of indigenous self-government in all its aspects has achieved sufficient definition and acceptance to qualify as customary international law, it can be affirmed that customary international law has crystallized around that component of self-government that requires consultation with indigenous peoples and their effective participation in all matters affecting them.

The dual thrust of the normative regime concerning indigenous peoples' self-government—on the one hand autonomy and on the other participatory engagement—reflects the view, apparently held by indigenous peoples themselves, that they are not to be considered a priori unconnected from larger social and political structures. Rather, indigenous groups—whether characterized as communities, peoples, nations, or other—are appropriately viewed as simultaneously distinct from yet parts of larger units of social and political interaction, units that may include indigenous federations, the states within which they live, and the global community itself. This view challenges traditional Western conceptions that envisage mutually exclusive states as the primary factor for locating power and community, and the view promotes a political order that is less state centered and more centered on people in a world of distinct yet increasingly integrated and overlapping spheres of community and authority.

Self-government for indigenous peoples, therefore, typically is established in the consensual development of a nuanced political order that accommodates both inward- and outward-looking associational patterns. International law does not require or allow for any one particular form of structural accommodation for all indigenous peoples—indeed, the very fact of the diversity of indigenous cultures and their surrounding circumstances belies a singular formula. The underlying objective of the self-government norm, however, is that of allowing indigenous peoples to achieve meaningful self-determination through political institutions and consultative arrangements that reflect their specific cultural patterns and that permit them to be genuinely associated with all decisions affecting them on an ongoing basis. Constitutive self-determination, furthermore, requires that such institutions and arrangements in no case be imposed upon indigenous peoples but rather be the outcome of procedures that defer to their preferences among justifiable options.

Notes

1. U.N. Charter art. 1(3).

2. International Convention on the Elimination of All Forms of Racial Discrimination, Dec. 21, 1965, G.A. Res. 2106 A(XX), 660 U.N.T.S. 195 (entered into force Jan. 4, 1969).

3. American Convention on Human Rights, Nov. 22, 1969, OAS Treaty Ser. No. 36, 1144 U.N.T.S. 123 (entered into force July 18, 1978) (affirming, *inter alia*, in article 24 that "all persons are equal before the law").

4. African Charter on Human and Peoples' Rights, June 27, 1981, Organization of African Unity, art. 20, 21 *I.L.M.* 58 (1982) (entered into force Oct. 21, 1986) (affirm-

ing, in article 3 the equality of every individual and, in article 19 that "[a]ll peoples shall be equal").

5. Declaration on the Elimination of All Forms of Intolerance and of Discrimination Based on Religion or Belief, G.A. Res. 36/55, Nov. 25, 1981, U.N. GAOR, 36th Sess., Supp. No. 51, at 171, U.N. Doc A/36/684 (1981).

6. American Declaration on the Rights and Duties of Man, adopted by the Ninth International Conference of American States (Mar. 30–May 2, 1948), O.A.S. Res. 30, O.A.S. Doc. OEA/Ser.L/V/I.4, rev. (1965) (affirming, *inter alia*, in article II that "[a]ll persons are equal before the law . . . without distinction as to race, sex, language, creed or any other factor").

7. Universal Declaration of Human Rights, G.A. Res. 217 A(III), Dec. 10, 1948 (affirming, *inter alia*, in arts. 1 and 2 that "[a]ll persons are born free and equal in dignity and rights" and entitled to the enjoyment of human rights "without distinction of any kind"), reprinted in *Human Rights: A Compilation of International Instruments*, U.N. Doc. ST/HR/1/rev.4 (vol. 1, pt. 1), at 1, Sales No. E.93.XIV.1 (1993) [hereinafter *U.N. Compilation of Instruments*].

8. *Restatement of the Law (Third): The Foreign Relations Law of the United States*, sec. 702 (1987); Richard Lillich, "Civil Rights," in *Human Rights in International Law* 115, 133, 151 (Theodor Meron ed., 1984). *See also* Barcelona Traction (Belg. v. Spain), 1970 I.C.J. 3, 32.

9. *Report of the United Nations Seminar on the Effects of Racism and Racial Discrimination on the Social and Economic Relations between Indigenous Peoples and States*, U.N. Doc. E/CN.4/1989/22, HR/PUB/89/5 at 5 (1989).

10. *Id*. at 5.

11. CERD, *General Recommendation XXIII: Indigenous Peoples*, U.N. Doc. CERD/C/51/misc 13/Rev 4 (1997), para. 3. [hereinafter *CERD General Recommendation on Indigenous Peoples*].

12. E.S.C. Res. 1589(L), May 21, 1971, U.N. ESCOR, 50th Sess., Supp. No. 1, at 16, U.N. Doc. E/5044 (1971) (Economic and Social Council resolution authorizing the U.N. Sub-Commission on Prevention of Discrimination and Protection of Minorities to conduct a "[c]omplete and comprehensive study of the problem of discrimination against indigenous populations").

13. *See* Convention (No. 169) Concerning Indigenous and Tribal Peoples in Independent Countries, June 27, 1989, art. 3(1), International Labour Conference (entered into force Sept. 5, 1990), reprinted in the appendix, *infra* [hereinafter ILO Convention No. 169] ("Indigenous and tribal peoples shall enjoy the full measure of human rights and fundamental freedoms without hindrance or discrimination."); Draft United Nations Declaration on the Rights of Indigenous Peoples, adopted by the Sub-Commission on Prevention of Discrimination and Protection of Minorities by its res. 1994/45, Aug. 26, 1994, art. 2, U.N. Doc. E/CN.4/1995/2, E/CN.4/Sub.2/1994/56, at 105 (1994), reprinted in the appendix, *infra* [hereinafter Draft United Nations Declaration] ("Indigenous individuals and peoples are free and equal to all other individuals and peoples in dignity and rights, and have the right to be free from any kind of adverse discrimination."); Proposed American Declaration on the Rights of Indigenous Peoples, art. VI, approved by the Inter-American Commission on Human Rights on February 26, 1997, at its 1333rd

session, 95th Regular Session, art. VI.1 published in the *Annual Report of the Inter-American Commission on Human Rights 1996*, O.A.S. Doc. OEA/Ser.L/V/II.95, Doc. 7 Rev. (March 14, 1997), reprinted in the Appendix, *infra* ("Indigenous peoples have the right to special guarantees against discrimination that may have to be instituted to enjoy internationally and nationally-recognized human rights"). The development of the U.N. and OAS draft declarations and their status are discussed *supra* chapter 2, notes 89–92, 100–07, and accompanying text.

14. *See, e.g., CERD General Recommendation on Indigenous Peoples*, *supra* note 11, and examination by CERD of issues concerning indigenous peoples in particular countries, identified in chapter 6 *infra* at notes 73-87.

15. *E.g.*, ILO Convention No. 169, *supra* note 13, art. 2(2) ("Such action shall include measures for . . . ensuring that members of these peoples benefit on an equal footing from the rights and opportunities which national laws and regulations grant to other members of the population.").

16. The consensus on the need for affirmative measures is reflected, for example, in a summary of government and indigenous peoples' comments on the proposed Organization of American States instrument on indigenous rights, in the part of the summary under the heading "Equality before the law and equal protection under the law." Inter-American Commission on Human Rights, *Report on the First Round of Consultations Concerning the Future Inter-American Legal Instrument on the Rights of Indigenous Populations*, reprinted in *Annual Report of the Inter-American Commission on Human Rights, 1992–1993*, O.A.S. Doc. OEA/Ser.L/V/II.83, at 263, 283–84 (1993) [hereinafter *Report on First Round of Consultations on Inter-American Instrument*], reproduced in Inter-American Commission on Human Rights, *The Human Rights Situation of Indigenous Peoples in the Americas*, O.A.S. Doc. OEA/Ser.L/V/II.108, Doc. 62 (Oct. 20, 2000), Chapter II.

The Convention on the Elimination of All Forms of Racial Discrimination, *supra* note 2, requires states to pursue the eradication of racial discrimination by "all appropriate means," *id.* art. 2(1), but considers "[s]pecial measures" aimed at particular groups to be transitory and "not to lead to the maintenance of separate rights for different racial groups," *id.* art. 1(4). It is apparent that this caveat was drafted without consideration of the particular circumstances of indigenous groups whose goal is not complete assimilation and who thus may require more than transitory measures to be maintained in a position of equality vis-à-vis other segments of the population of the states in which they live. In its application, article 1(4) of the convention has not been a barrier to such measures; to the contrary, the Committee on the Elimination of Racial Discrimination, charged with overseeing compliance with the convention, has promoted measures to secure the survival of indigenous peoples as distinct groups. *See infra* chapter 6, notes 73–87 and accompanying text (discussing the committee's review of government reports under the convention).

17. *CERD General Recommendation on Indigenous Peoples, supra* note 11, para. 4.

18. *See* Natan Lerner, *Group Rights and Discrimination in International Law* 7 (1991) (listing European treaties with provisions protecting the rights of religious and ethnic minorities).

19. Minority Schools in Albania, Advisory Opinion, 1935 P.C.I.J. (Ser. A/B) No. 64.

20. *Id.* at 17. *See also* European Convention for the Protection of Human Rights and Fundamental Freedoms, Nov. 4, 1950, art. 14, Europ. T.S. No. 5, 213 U.N.T.S. 221 (entered into force Sept. 3, 1953) (prohibiting discrimination on grounds, *inter alia*, of "language, religion, . . . [and] association with a national minority").

21. Document of the Copenhagen Meeting of the Conference on the Human Dimension of the CSCE, June 29, 1990, art. 32. *See also id.* arts. 32.1–32.6 (detailing this right). Similarly, the states participating in the CSCE affirmed in the Charter of Paris for a New Europe, CSCE, Nov. 21, 1991, 30 *I.L.M.* 193 (1991) "that the ethnic, cultural, linguistic and religious identity of national minorities will be protected and that persons belonging to national minorities have the right freely to express, preserve and develop that identity without any discrimination and in full equality before the law." The CSCE is now called the Organization for Security and Cooperation in Europe. At the Budapest Summit in 1994, the CSCE became a permanent organization, the Organization for Security and Cooperation in Europe.

22. Framework Convention for the Protection of National Minorities, Nov. 10, 1995, 34 I.L.M. 351 (1995) (entered into force Feb. 1, 1998)

23. Convention on the Prevention and Punishment of the Crime of Genocide, Dec. 9, 1948, G.A. Res. 260 A(III), 78 U.N.T.S. 277 (entered into force Sept. 3, 1953) (defining, at art. 2, genocide as "acts committed with intent to destroy, in whole or in part, a national, ethnical, racial or religious group as such").

24. International Covenant on Civil and Political Rights, Dec. 16, 1966, G.A. Res. 2200(XXI), art. 27, 999 U.N.T.S. 171 (entered into force Mar. 23, 1976).

25. *Id.*

26. Declaration on the Rights of Persons Belonging to National, Ethnic, Religious and Linguistic Minorities, G.A. Res. 47/135, Dec. 18, 1992 [hereinafter Minority Rights Declaration], reprinted in *U.N. Compilation of Instruments, supra* note 7, vol. 1, pt. 1 at 140.

27. Declaration of the Principles of International Cultural Cooperation, proclaimed by the general conference of the United Nations Educational, Scientific and Cultural Organization at its 14th session, Nov. 4, 1966, art. 1, reprinted in *Human Rights: A Compilation of International Instruments, supra* note 7, vol. 1, pt. 2 at 591.

28. Universal Declaration on Cultural Diversity, proclaimed by the General Conference of the UNESCO at its 31st session, Nov. 2, 2001, art. 4.

29. *See* International Covenant on Civil and Political Rights, *supra* note 24, preambular para. 4 ("*Considering* the obligation of States under the Charter of the United Nations to promote universal respect for, and observance of, human rights and freedoms"); Minority Rights Declaration, *supra* note 26, preambular para. 3 ("*Desiring* to promote the realization of principles contained in the Charter of the United Nations"); UNESCO Declaration of the Principles of International Cultural Cooperation, *supra* note 27, preambular para. 9 (proclaiming the declaration "to the end that governments, authorities, [etc.] . . . may constantly be guided by these principles; and for the purpose . . . of advancing . . . the objectives of peace and welfare that are defined in the Charter of the United Nations").

30. *E.g.*, Convention against Discrimination in Education (UNESCO), Dec. 14, 1960, art. 5, 429 U.N.T.S. 93 (entered into force May 22, 1962) (recognizing "the right

of all members of national minorities to carry out educational activities of their own, among them that of establishing and maintaining schools, and according to the policy of each state on education, to use their own language").

31. *See, e.g.*, Ayalet Shachar, *Multicultural Jurisdictions: Cultural Differences and Women's Rights* 45–62 (2001) (discussing subordination of women through cultural norms concerning family relations).

32. Universal Declaration on Cultural Diversity, *supra* note 28, art. 4.

33. Ayalet Shachar provides an excellent effort to unravel this paradox and promote practical institutional arrangements that accommodate distinctive cultural groups while protecting individual interests in liberty and equality. *See* Shachar, *supra* note 31.

34. An extensive survey of the topic is in U.N. Sub-Commission on Prevention of Discrimination and Protection of Minorities, *Study on the Rights of Persons Belonging to Ethnic, Religious and Linguistic Minorities*, U.N. Doc. E/CN.4/Sub.2/38/Rev.1 (1979), Sales No. E.78.XIV.1 (Francesco Capotorti, special rapporteur). *See also* Patrick Thornberry, *International Law and the Rights of Minorities* (1991); Fernando Mariño *et al.*, *La Protección Internacional de las Minorías* (2001).

35. *See* Mikmaq Tribal Society v. Canada, Communication No. 78/1980, *Report of the Human Rights Committee*, U.N. GAOR, 39th Sess., Supp. No. 40, at 200, 202, U.N. Doc. A/39/40, Annex 16 (1984) (decision on admissibility adopted July 29, 1984).

36. *See* Ian Brownlie, "The Rights of Peoples in Modern International Law," in *The Rights of Peoples* 1, 5 (James Crawford ed., 1988) ("[H]eterogeneous terminology which has been used over the years—references to 'nationalities,' 'peoples,' 'minorities,' and 'indigenous populations'—involves essentially the same idea.").

37. Inter-American Commission on Human Rights, *Report on the Situation of Human Rights of a Segment of the Nicaraguan Population of Miskito Origin and Resolution on the Friendly Settlement Procedure Regarding the Human Rights Situation of a Segment of the Nicaraguan Population of Miskito Origin*, O.A.S. Doc. OEA/Ser.L/V/II.62, doc. 10 rev. 3 (1983), O.A.S. Doc. OEA/Ser.L/V/II.62, doc. 26 (1984) (Case No. 7964 (Nicaragua), at 81 [hereinafter *Miskito Report and Resolution*]. The commission noted that the requirement of special measures to protect indigenous culture is

> based on the principle of equality: for example, if a child is educated in a language which is not his native language, this can mean that the child is treated on an equal basis with other children who are educated in their native language. The protection of minorities, therefore, requires affirmative action to safeguard the rights of minorities whenever the people in question . . . wish to maintain their distinction of language and culture.

Id. at 77 (quoting U.N. Secretary-General: *The Main Types and Causes of Discrimination*, U.N. Publ. 49.XIV.3, paras. 6–7).

38. Case No. 7615 (Brazil), Inter-Am. Commission Res. No. 12/85 (March 5, 1985), *Annual Report of the Inter-American Commission on Human Rights, 1984–1985*, O.A.S. Doc. OEA/Ser.L/V/II.66, doc. 10, rev. 1, at 24, 31 (1985).

39. *Id.* at 29–31.

40. *See* Inter-American Commission on Human Rights, *Report on the Situation of*

Human Rights in Ecuador, O.A.S. Doc. OEA/Ser.L/V/II.96, doc 10, rev. 1, Chapter IX (April 24, 1997).

41. Ominayak, Chief of the Lubicon Lake Band v. Canada, Communication No. 267/1984, *Report of the Human Rights Committee*, U.N. GOAR, 45th Sess., Supp. No. 40, Vol. 2, at 1, U.N. Doc. A/45/40, Annex 9 (A) (1990) (views adopted Mar. 26, 1990). The case is discussed and analyzed in Dominic McGoldrick, "Canadian Indians, Cultural Rights and the Human Rights Committee," 40 *Int'l & Comp. L.Q.* 658 (1991).

42. Ominayak v. Canada, *supra* note 41, at 27. *See also* Human Rights Committee, General Comment Adopted by the Human Rights Committee under Article 40, Paragraph 4, of the International Covenant on Civil and Political Rights: General Comment No. 23(50) (art. 27), U.N. Doc. CCPR/C/21/Rev. 1./Add. 5 (1994) ("Culture manifests itself in many forms, including a particular way of life associated with the use of land resources, specially in the case of indigenous peoples").

43. The *Lubicon Lake Band* case is discussed further *infra* chapter 7, notes 39–48, 56–58 and accompanying text. Compare the *Ominayak* case with Diergaardt et al. v. Namibia, Communication No. 760/1997, U.N. Doc. CCPR/C/69/D/60/1997 (views adopted Sept. 6, 2000), in which the committee considered a claim by the Rehoboth Baster Community, a community descended from Africaans settlers and indigenous Khoï, that their rights under article 27 were violated due to impediments to their use and enjoyment of certain lands. The committee declined to find a violation of article 27, having determined that there were insufficient cultural connections between the land claimed, on which community members grazed cattle and engaged in other activities, and a distinctive way of life. *Id.* para. 10.6.

44. Human Rights Committee, *General Comment Adopted by the Human Rights Committee under Article 40, Paragraph 4, of the International Covenant on Civil and Political Rights: General Comment No. 23(50) (art. 27)*, U.N. Doc. CCPR/C/21/Rev.1/Add.5 (1994), para. 7 (footnote omitted).

45. Covenant on Civil and Political Rights, *supra* note 24, art. 27 (emphasis added).

46. This point is made and elaborated upon in Douglas Sanders, "Collective Rights," 13 *Hum. Rts. Q.* 368 (1991).

47. Covenant on Civil and Political Rights, *supra* note 24, art. 27 (emphasis added).

48. Lovelace v. Canada, Communication No. 24/1977, *Report of the Human Rights Committee*, U.N. GOAR, 36th Sess., Supp. No. 40, at 166, U.N. Doc. A/36/40, Annex 18 (1977) (views adopted July 30, 1981).

49. *Id.* at 173 (quoting article 27).

50. Communication No. 197/1985, *Report of the Human Rights Committee*, U.N. GOAR, 43rd Sess., Supp. No. 40, at 207, U.N. Doc. A/43/40, Annex 7(G) (1988) (views adopted July 27, 1988).

51. Länsman et al v. Finland, Communication No. 511/1992, Human Rights Committee, U.N. Doc. CCPR/C/52/D/511/1992 (views adopted Oct. 26, 1994).

52. The committee emphasized that article 27 "does not only protect traditional means of livelihood of national minorities" and that reindeer herding formed a protected part of the Saami culture despite the fact that the Saami "may have adapted their methods of reindeer herding over the years and practice it with the help of modern technology." *Id.* para. 9.3 (emphasis in the original).

53. *See id.* para. 9.5.

54. *Id.* paras. 9.4–9.6.

55. *Id.* para. 9.7. The committee also applied this analytical framework in a subsequent case in which the same Saami group from Finland challenged state logging plans in their reindeer herding area, Länsman et al. v. Finland, Communication No. 671/1995, Human Rights Committee, U.N. Doc. CCPR/C/58/D/671/1995 (views adopted Oct. 30, 1996). Similar to the previous *Länsman* case, the committee in *Länsman II* ruled that the planned lumber exploitation did not amount to a violation of article 27, but warned about future plans and the aggregate effect of these with plans for quarrying within the same area, *id.* paras. 10.6, 10.7. *See also* Sara et al. v. Finland, Communication No. 431/1990, Human Rights Committee, U.N. Doc. CCPR/C/50/D/431/1990 (Revised Decision on Admissibility, Mar. 23, 1994) (reiterating that Saami reindeer herding is a protected cultural activity under article 27 of the covenant, but declaring the case inadmissible for failure to exhaust internal remedies). In another case the committee recognized the cultural significance for the Maori of access to their traditional fishing grounds, and that Maori commercial and noncommercial fishery enjoyed protection under article 27. Mahuika et al. v. New Zealand, Communication No. 547/1993, Human Rights Committee, U.N. Doc. CCPR/C/70/D/547/1993 (views adopted Nov. 15, 2000), para. 9.3. However the committee ruled that the circumstances presented, in which the State of New Zealand limited Maori fishing according to an agreement negotiated with Maori leaders, did not constitute a violation of the Covenant. *Id.* paras. 9.4–9.8.

56. A different conclusion about the legality of the impugned acts could result from the application of international norms upholding property rights of indigenous peoples over their traditional lands. *See infra* notes 92–149 and corresponding text.

57. Hopu & Bessert v. France, Communication No. 549/1993, Human Rights Committee, U.N. Doc. CCPR/C/60/D/549/1993 /Rev.1. (views adopted July 29, 1997).

58. *Id.* para. 10.3. The committee declined to apply article 27 of the covenant to this case, because upon acceding to the covenant, France had made a declaration that article 27 was inapplicable to it. In a joint dissenting opinion, committee members David Kretzmer, Thomas Buergenthal, Nisuke Ando, and Lord Colville saw the case as not establishing violations of articles 17 and 23 but rather as only raising claims under article 27 which could not be invoked because of France's reservation. By contrast, in their separate concurring opinion, committee members Elizabeth Evatt, Cecilia Medina Quiroga, Fausto Pocar, Martin Scheinin, and Maxwell Yalden viewed France's reservation as having no effect in respect to its overseas territories and considered the case to raise important issues under article 27. This case is discussed further *infra* chapter 7, notes 50, 63–64 and corresponding text.

59. International Labour Conference, Provisional Record 31, 76th Sess., at 31/4–5 (1989) [hereinafter 1989 ILO Provisional Record 31]. *See also* government statements in International Labour Conference, Provisional Record 32, 76th Sess., at 32/11–32/13 (1988) [hereinafter 1988 ILO Provisional Record 32].

60. This is evident, *inter alia*, in the documents produced by the working group chair synthesizing or summarizing government and other statements commenting on the drafts: *Analytical Commentary on the Draft Principles Contained in the First Revised Text of the Draft Declaration on the Rights of Indigenous Peoples*, U.N. Doc E/CN.4/

Sub.2/AC.4/1990/39 (1990) [hereinafter *1990 Analytical Commentary*]; *Analytical Compilation of Observations and Comments Received Pursuant to Sub-Commission Resolution 1988/18*, U.N. Doc. E/CN.4/Sub.2/1989/33/Adds.1–3 (1989) [hereinafter *1989 Compilation of Observations*]; *Draft Declaration on the Rights of Indigenous Peoples: Revised Working Paper submitted by the Chairperson/Rapporteur, Ms. Erica-Irene Daes, Pursuant to Sub-Commission on Prevention of Discrimination and Protection of Minorities Resolution 1990/26*, U.N. Doc. E/CN.4/Sub.2/1991/36 (1991) [hereinafter *1991 Revised Working Paper*].

61. *See 1990 Analytical Commentary, supra* note 60, at 3.

62. First Revised Text of the Draft Universal Declaration on Rights of Indigenous Peoples, preambular para. 7, U.N. Doc. E/CN.4/Sub.2/1989/33 (1989).

63. *Id.* operative paras. 3, 4.

64. This thread of support for indigenous cultural integrity is especially evident in the comments summarized under the headings "Right to have differences accepted," "Right to preserve and develop their traditional economic structures, institutions and lifestyles," and "Rights relative to their own cultural development." *Report on First Round of Consultations on Inter-American Instrument, supra* note 16, at 293, 295–98.

65. *See supra* chapter 1 (discussing such patterns of colonization and the underlying premise of indigenous inferiority).

66. Rodolfo Stavenhagen observes that many elites in the Americas still regard "Indian cultures [as] backward, traditional, and not conducive to progress and modernity." Rodolfo Stavenhagen, *The Ethnic Question: Conflicts, Development, and Human Rights* 49, U.N. Sales No. E.90.III.A.9 (1990).

67. *See supra* note 13, 21, and accompanying text.

68. ILO Convention No. 169, *supra* note 13, art. 2(1).

69. *See* Draft United Nations Declaration, *supra* note 13, art. 13 (with particular regard to religion), art. 14 (historiography, language, philosophy, and literature), art. 15 (education), art. 12 (restitution of cultural and intellectual property).

70. *See, e.g.,* 1989 Statement by the Government of Brazil to the U.N. Working Group on Indigenous Populations under Item 5, at 2 (reporting on the new provisions of the Brazilian Constitution affirming indigenous language rights); 1991 Statement of the Government of Colombia to the U.N. Working Group on Indigenous Populations (reporting on the provisions of the new Colombian Constitution giving the languages of indigenous groups official character and establishing bilingual education); *Information Submitted to the Working Group by the Government of Finland*, U.N. Doc. E/CN.4/Sub.2/AC.4/1991/1, at 3 (1991) (reporting on recent legislation that will allow the use of the Saami language in courts of law and that will require official documents relevant to Saami interests be published in the Saami language); 1989 Statement of the Government of New Zealand to the U.N. Working Group on Indigenous Populations Under Item 5, at 5 (reporting on the Maori Language Act of 1987, which "declares Maori to be an official language and establishes a commission to promote the Maori language as an ordinary means of communication"). *See also* statements of Colombia, Egypt, Finland, Mexico, New Zealand, Norway, Sweden, the United States, and Australia in *Partial Revision of the Indigenous and Tribal Populations Convention, 1957 (No. 107)*, Report 4(2A), International Labour Conference, 76th Sess., at 29 (1989); and in *Partial Revision of the*

Indigenous and Tribal Populations Convention, 1957 (No. 107), Report 6(2), International Labour Conference, 75th Sess., at 86–88 (1988).

71. During the drafting of Convention No. 169, for example, the government delegate from Ecuador posed an amendment to allow indigenous peoples to use their languages in legal proceedings. The delegate from Argentina responded that, although the amendment was laudable, it was impractical. The amendment was withdrawn. *Report of the Committee on Convention No. 107*, International Labour Conference, Provisional Record 25, 76th Sess., at 25/16 (1989) [hereinafter 1989 ILO Provisional Record 25].

72. Canada, for example, has reported to the U.N. sub-commission working group that it "encourages and financially supports its aboriginal citizens in maintaining, using and promoting their own languages and cultures in their own communities, in educating their children, in legal proceedings, etc. However, . . . it would be administratively and financially difficult, if not impossible, to provide for the use of over 50 aboriginal languages for administrative or other official purposes." *Information Submitted by the Government of Canada*, U.N. Doc. E/CN.4/Sub.2/AC.4/1990, at 3 (1990). Similarly, the government of New Zealand stated to the working group that it can "fully support" the concept of the right of indigenous peoples to use their language in judicial administrative proceedings but suggested that the principle be couched in terms of being an objective for states to work toward "in a determined and thorough-going manner." Text of New Zealand Statement to the U.N. Working Group on Indigenous Populations, Agenda Item 4: Standard Setting Activities: Evolution of Standards Concerning the Rights of Indigenous Populations, at 3–4 (July 22, 1991).

ILO Convention 169 provides that "[m]easures shall be taken to ensure that members of [indigenous peoples] can understand and be understood in legal proceedings, where necessary through the provision of interpretation or by other effective means." ILO Convention No. 169, *supra* note 13, art. 12. In this vein, Argentina suggested the following for inclusion in the proposed Universal Declaration on Indigenous Rights: "The right to develop and promote their own languages, including an own [*sic*] literary language, and to use them for cultural and other purposes. In legal and administrative proceedings, when the indigenous person does not know the national language, the State shall obligatorily provide and/or make available the services of interpreters" U.N. Doc. E/CN.4/Sub.2/1991/36, at 57 (1991). Similar suggestions have been made by Mexico, Guatemala, and Colombia in commenting on the proposed inter-American instrument on indigenous rights. See *Report on First Round of Consultations on Inter-American Instrument*, *supra* note 16, at 283, 309.

73. 1991 Statement of the Government of Australia to the U.N. Working Group on Indigenous Populations at 8.

74. *Id.*

75. 1989 New Zealand Statement to the U.N. Working Group at 5 ("All Crown agencies responsible for the management and disposal of Crown land must follow a procedure [prior to disposal of any land] in order that wahi tapu [sacred sites] be protected.").

76. *1989 Compilation of Observations*, *supra* note 60, at 20.

77. *See* comments by Chile, Canada, Peru, Guatemala, and Colombia summarized in *Report on the First Round of Consultations on Inter-American Instrument*, *supra* note 16, at 300–01.

78. Sub-Commission on Prevention of Discrimination and Protection of Minorities, *Study on the Protection of the Cultural and Intellectual Property of Indigenous Peoples*, U.N. Doc. E/CN.4/Sub.2/1993/28 (1993) (Erica-Irene Daes, special rapporteur) [hereinafter *U.N. Study on the Protection of Cultural Property*].

79. The study identifies these practices in association with historical patterns of European exploration and settlement, and as an element of continuing industrial and commercial forces of both European and non-European societies:

> 18. As industrialization continued, European States turned to the acquisition of tribal art and the study of exotic cultures. Indigenous peoples were, in succession, despoiled of their lands, sciences, ideas, arts and cultures.
>
> 19. This process is being repeated today, in all parts of the world. . . . Ironically, publicity about the victimization of indigenous peoples in these newly-exploited areas has also renewed Europeans' interest in acquiring indigenous peoples' arts, cultures and sciences. Tourism in indigenous areas is growing, along with the commercialization of indigenous arts and the spoiling of archaeological sites and shrines.
>
> 20. At the same time, the "Green Revolution," biotechnology, and demand for new medicines to combat cancer and AIDS are resulting in a renewed and intensified interest in collecting medical, botanical and ecological knowledge of indigenous peoples. . . . There is an urgent need, then, for measures to enable indigenous peoples to retain control over their remaining cultural and intellectual, as well as natural, wealth, so that they have the possibility of survival and self-development.

Id. at 7. Similar observations were included in U.N. Secretary-General, *Intellectual Property of Indigenous Peoples: Concise Report of the Secretary-General*, U.N. Doc. E/CN.4/Sub.2/1992/30 (1992). *See also Information Concerning the Report of the Special Rapporteur on the Study of the Cultural and Intellectual Property of Indigenous Peoples: Information Submitted by the Movement "Tupay Katari,"* U.N. Doc. E/CN.4/Sub.2/AC.4/1993 (1993).

80. As examples of initiatives already taken, the study cites, *inter alia*, the Native American Graves Protection and Repatriation Act of 1990 (United States), and the Aboriginal Affairs and Torres Strait Islander Heritage Act of 1984 (Australia). *U.N. Study on the Protection of Cultural Property*, *supra* note 78, at 10. The study also surveys existing international legal instruments and mechanisms regulating the transfer and control over intellectual and cultural property (e.g., the UNESCO Convention on the Means of Prohibiting and Preventing the Illicit Import, Export and Transfer of Ownership of Cultural Property (1970)) and points out the inadequacies of these existing mechanisms for the purposes of securing indigenous peoples' enjoyment and control over their cultural heritage. *Id.* at 30–35.

81. *See Principles and Guidelines for the Protection of the Heritage of Indigenous Peoples, Preliminary Report of the Special Rapporteur, Mrs. Erica-Irene Daes, Submitted in Conformity with Sub-Commission Resolution 1993/44 and Decision 1994/105 of the Commission on Human Rights*, U.N. Doc. E/CN.4/Sub.2/1994/31, Annex (1994). After considering comments by governments, international institutions, indigenous

peoples, and NGOs, the working group chair revised the set of principles and guidelines. *See Protection of the Heritage of Indigenous People: Final Report of the Special Rapporteur, Mrs. Erica-Irene Daes, in Conformity with Sub-commission Resolution 1993/94 and Decision 1994/105 of the Commission on Human Rights,* U.N. Doc. E/CN.4/Sub.2/1995/26 (1995). The revised "Principles and Guidelines for the Protection of the Heritage of Indigenous People" appears in *id.,* at 9. Ms. Daes recommended that her text be the basis for a declaration by the U.N. General Assembly in 1996. *Id.* at 8.

82. *See Human Rights of Indigenous Peoples: Report of the seminar on the draft principles and guidelines for the protection of the heritage of indigenous peoples (Geneva, 28 February-1 March, 2000),* U.N. Doc. E/CN.4/Sub.2/2000/26 (2000). The forty-five participants of the seminar included "representatives of Governments, United Nations bodies and organizations, specialized agencies, organizations of indigenous peoples and competent indigenous persons." *Id.* paras. 1, 3.

83. *See The Mataatua Declaration on Cultural and Intellectual Property Rights of Indigenous Peoples,* adopted by the First International Conference on the Cultural & Intellectual Property Rights of Indigenous Peoples, June 1993, U.N. Doc. E/CN.4/Sub.2/AC.4/1993/CRP.5 (a conference of over 150 indigenous representatives from several countries in the Pacific and the Americas).

84. Rio Declaration on Environment and Development, U.N. Conference on Environment and Development, Rio de Janeiro, June 13, 1992, principle 22, U.N. Doc. A/CONF.151/26 (vol. 1), Annex 1 (1992).

85. Agenda 21, U.N. Conference on Environment and Development, Rio de Janeiro, June 13, 1992, paras. 26.3, 26.4(b), U.N. Doc. A/CONF.151/26 (vol. 3), Annex 2 (1992), reprinted in the appendix, *infra.*

86. Convention on Biological Diversity, June 5, 1992, UNCED, art. 8(j), 1992, U.N. Doc. UNEP/Bio.Div./N7INC.5/4 (1992). This and related provisions of the Convention on Biodiversity are the subject of ongoing discussions within the framework of periodic meetings of the "Conference of the Parties" to the convention. *See supra* chapter 2, note 137.

87. See *Roundtable on Intellectual Property and Traditional Knowledge* (Geneva, Nov. 1–2, 1999): *Report,* WIPO/IPTK/RT/99/7 (May 4, 2000); *Intergovernmental Committee on Intellectual Property and Genetic Resources, Traditional Knowledge and Folklore* (Geneva, April 30 to May 3, 2001): *Report,* WIPO/GRTKF/IC/1/13 (2001); *Intergovernmental Committee on Intellectual Property and Genetic Resources, Traditional Knowledge and Folklore* (Geneva, June 13 to 21, 2002): *Report,* WIPO/GRTKF/IC/3/17 (June 21, 2002). For critical assessments of the international intellectual property regime as it relates to indigenous peoples knowledge and works of art, see Michael Brown, *Who Owns Native Culture?* (2003); Darrell Posey & Graham Dutfield, *Beyond Intellectual Property: Toward Traditional Resource Rights for Indigenous Peoples* (1996).

88. Representatives of the following governments reported on such domestic initiatives to the committee of the International Labour Conference that drafted Convention No. 169: New Zealand, Brazil, Soviet Union, United States, Mexico, and Honduras. These reports are summarized in 1989 ILO Provisional Record 25, *supra* note 71, at 25/2–25/4 (paras. 9–14). The following additional governments reported on similar initiatives to the plenary of the 1989 International Labour Conference upon submission of

the revised convention for a record vote: Bangladesh, India, Argentina, and Peru. International Labour Conference, Provisional Record 32, 76th Sess. at 32/11–32/12 (1989).

Additional domestic initiatives reflective of the norm of cultural survival and flourishment have been reported to the U.N. sub-commission working group and other U.N. bodies. *E.g.*, Pekka Aikio, president of the Finnish Saami Parliament, Statement by the Observer Delegation of the Government of Finland to the U.N. Working Group on Indigenous Populations: Review of Developments (July 1993) (describing initiatives to amend the Finnish Constitution to enhance guarantees for maintenance and development of Saami culture); Intervention of the Mexican Delegation to the 50th Session of the U.N. Commission on Human Rights (Feb. 1994) at 3 (describing provisions of the Mexican Constitution to provide recognition of and protection for indigenous peoples and their cultures); Declaración de Colombia en Nombre del Grupo Latinoamericano y del Caribe en la Conmemoración del Año International de Poblaciones Indígenas, Conferencia Mundial de Derechos Humanos, Vienna (June 18, 1993) (statement of Colombia on behalf of Latin American and Caribbean Group reporting developments in Latin America).

89. *See, e.g., Information Submitted by the Government of Canada in Regard to the Revised Draft Declaration on Indigenous Rights*, U.N. Doc. E/CN.4/Sub.2/AC.4/1990/1/Add.3, at 1–2 (1990); 1991 Statement of the Government of New Zealand to the U.N. Working Group under Agenda Item 4, at 2.

90. *See* U.N. Sub-Commission on Prevention of Discrimination and Protection of Minorities, *Study of the Problem of Discrimination against Indigenous Populations*, U.N. Doc. E/CN.4/Sub.2/1986/7, Add. 4, at 39 (1986) (Jose R. Martínez Cobo, special rapporteur) [hereinafter *U.N. Indigenous Study*] ("It must be understood that, for indigenous populations, land does not represent simply a possession or means of production. . . . It is also essential to understand the special and profoundly spiritual relationship of indigenous peoples with Mother Earth as basic to their existence and to all their beliefs, customs, traditions and culture."). A more recent study of the sub-commision, which was entirely focused on the issue of indigenous peoples and land, reinforces these principles, arguing the need to take effective actions to guarantee indigenous peoples' rights over land and natural resources based on their traditions and customs. *See* Sub-Commission on the Promotion and Protection of Human Rights, *Indigenous Peoples and their relationship to land—Final working paper prepared by the Special Rapporteur Mrs. Erica-Irene A. Daes*, E/CN.4/Sub.2/2001/21 (2001) (hereinafter *Study on indigenous peoples and land*).

91. For a compilation of indigenous people's statements about the land and its meaning, see *Touch the Earth: A Self Portrait of Indian Existence* (T. C. McLuhan ed., 1971); Thomas R. Berger, *Village Journey: The Report of the Alaska Native Review Commission* (1985) (documenting the testimony of Alaska Natives concerning their feelings about the lands and resources that traditionally have sustained them); Julian Burger, *Report from the Frontier: The State of the World's Indigenous Peoples* 13–16 (1987) (on indigenous "land and philosophy").

92. Covenant on Civil and Political Rights, *supra* note 24, art. 1(2); International Covenant on Economic, Social, and Cultural Rights, Dec. 16, 1966, G.A. Res. 2200(XXI), art. 1(2), 993 U.N.T.S. 3 (entered into force Jan. 3, 1976). In its concluding observations

on the fourth periodic report by Canada regarding the International Covenant on Civil and Political Rights, the UN Human Rights Committee "emphasized" article 1(2) of the covenant in recommending that Canada reform its laws and internal policies, to guarantee the indigenous peoples of that country the full enjoyment of their rights over lands and natural resources. *See Concluding observations of the Human Rights Committee: Canada,* U.N. Doc. CCPR/C/79/Add.105 (Apr. 7, 1999), para. 8.

93. *See generally* Rene David & John E. C. Brierly, *Major Legal Systems in the World Today* 290–95 (3d ed. 1985) (comparative discussion of "ownership").

94. The following literature reflects many of the dimensions of this dichotomy: Edward J. Epstein, "The Theoretical System of Property Rights in China's General Principles of Civil Law: Theoretical Controversy in the Drafting Process and Beyond," 52 *L. & Contemp. Probs.* 177 (1989); Randy Bergman & Dorothy C. Lawrence, "New Developments in Soviet Property Law," 28 *Colum. J. Transnat'l L.* 189 (1990); Symposium, "Property: The Founding, the Welfare State, and Beyond," the Eighth Annual National Federalist Society Symposium on Law and Public Policy—1989, 13 *Harv. J. L. & Pub. Policy* 1–165 (1990).

95. *See* Universal Declaration of Human Rights, *supra* note 7, art. 17.

96. *See* American Convention on Human Rights, *supra* note 3, art. 21.

97. *See* American Declaration of the Rights and Duties of Man, *supra* note 6, art. XXIII.

98. *See* Protocol (No. 1) to the European Convention for the Protection of Human Rights and Fundamental Freedoms, art. 1, March 20, 1952, Europ.T.S. No. 9 (entered into force May 18, 1954).

99. *See U.N. Indigenous Study, supra* note 90, pp. 10–12; *The Human Rights Situation of Indigenous Peoples in the Americas, supra* note 16, preamble; *Resolution on Special Protection for Indigenous Populations,* Inter-American Commission on Human Rights, Dec. 28, 1972, O.A.S. Doc. OEA/Ser.P, AG/doc.305/73 rev. 1 (1973); CERD *General Recommendation on Indigenous Peoples,* supra note 11, para. 3 ("indigenous peoples have been, and are still being, discriminated against and . . . they have lost their land and resources to colonists, commercial companies and State enterprises").

100. *See Study on indigenous peoples and land, supra* note 90, paras. 40–48, 144.

101. A common theme of the classical theorists of international law (1500s through early 1700s) was that non-European aboriginal peoples had territorial and autonomy rights which the Europeans were bound to respect. *See supra* chapter 1, notes 17–71 and accompanying text.

102. *See* Worcester v. Georgia, 31 U.S. (6 Pet.) 515, 554, 559 (1832) (drawing upon the "law of nations" to affirm the "original natural rights" of Indians to their lands); United States *ex. rel.* Hualpai Indians v. Santa Fe Pac. R.R., 314 U.S. 339 (1942) (affirming that "aboriginal title" exists until Congress by clear and unambiguous action authorizes its extinguishment); *see generally* Felix S. Cohen, "Original Indian Title," 32 *Minn. L. Rev.* 28 (1947).

103. *See* S. James Anaya, "Native Land Claims in the United States: The Unatoned for Spirit of Place," in *The Cambridge Lectures* (Frank McArdle ed., 1993) (criticizing the scheme, under the Indian Claims Commission Act of 1946, to settle Indian land claims by cash payments).

104. ILO Convention No. 169, *supra* note 13, art. 13(2).

105. *See Report of the Committee set up to examine the representation alleging non-observation by Peru of the Convention on Indigenous and Tribal Peoples, 1989 (No. 169), made under Article 24 of the ILO Constitution by the General Confederation of Workers of Peru (CGTP)*, ILO Doc. GB.273/14/4 (Nov. 1998), para. 32(b) (emphasizing the "collective aspects" of the relationship of indigenous peoples with land, and that "when communally owned indigenous lands are divided and assigned to individuals or third parties [as permitted by Peruvian law] this often weakens the exercise of their rights by the community or the indigenous peoples and in general they may end up losing all or most of the land, resulting in a general reduction of the resources that are available to indigenous peoples when they own their lands communally.")

106. *See* ILO Convention No. 169, *supra* note 13, art. 15(1).

107. *Id.* art. 15(2).

108. For an analysis of the requirement of consultation established by the Convention and the application of this requirement through ILO supervisory mechanisms, see *infra* notes 196–204 and accompanying text.

109. *See Third Supplementary Report of the Committee established to examine the representation alleging non-observance by Colombia of the Indigenous and Tribal Peoples Convention, 1989 (No. 169), made under article 24 of the ILO Constitution by the Single Confederation of Workers of Colombia (CUT)*, ILO Docs. GB. 276/17/1, GB 282/14/3 (Nov. 14, 2001), para. 86 (specifying that Colombia was required to adequately apply the convention's consultation provisions prior to authorizing oil development in an area outside the U'wa reserve, and rejecting the government's position that the provisions applied only in regard to areas regularly and permanently occupied by indigenous communities).

110. ILO Convention No. 169, *supra* note 13, art. 16.

111. *Id.* art. 16(3).

112. *Id.* art. 17(1).

113. For a concurring analysis of the land rights provisions of Convention No. 169 by the legal officer of the International Labour Organization primarily involved in the drafting of the Convention, see Lee Swepston, "A New Step in the International Law on Indigenous and Tribal Peoples," 15 *Okla. City U. L. Rev.* 677, 696–710 (1990).

114. Responses to the land rights part of the questionnaire are summarized and analyzed in *Partial Revision of Indigenous and Tribal Populations Convention, 1957 (No. 107)*, Report 4(2), International Labour Conference, 75th Sess. at 45–64 (1988).

115. For example, the ILO Committee of Experts on the Application of Conventions and Recommendations and the Conference Committee on the Application of Standards have been active in attempts at resolving problems concerning the land and territorial rights of tribal peoples in the Chittagong Hill Tracts of Bangladesh and in addressing land rights, as well as basic human rights, concerns of the Yanomami of Brazil. *See Note by the International Labour Office*, U.N. Doc E/CN.4/Sub.2/AC.4/1991/6, at 2 (1991); *Report of the Committee of Experts on the Application of Conventions and Recommendations*, Report 3(4A), International Labour Conference, 78th Sess. at 349–51, 353–54 (1991). The ILO's supervisory machinery is discussed *infra* chapter 6, notes 47–57; chapter 7, notes 1–26 and accompanying text.

116. Although the drafting of the land rights provisions of Convention No. 169 was controversial, the controversy was a result of resistance to efforts by indigenous peoples' representatives, worker delegates, and some governments to attain specification of greater land and resource rights than that ultimately included in the convention. *See* Swepston, *supra* note 113, at 696–98.

117. 1989 ILO Provisional Record 25, *supra* note 71, at 25/21.

118. *See, e.g.,* Statement of the Hon. Mr. Robert Tickner, M.P. federal minister for Aboriginal and Torres Strait Island affairs, speaking on behalf of the government of Australia, U.N. Working Group on Indigenous Populations, 12th Sess. (July 27, 1994) (discussing recently adopted Native Title Act of 1994 to confirm indigenous possessory rights and to provide compensation for the dispossessed); Statement by the Observer Delegation of Brazil, U.N. Working Group on Indigenous Populations, 12th Sess. (July 1994) (discussing legislative initiative to implement constitutional provisions regarding indigenous land rights and to revise nonconforming laws); Review of Developments Pertaining to the Promotion and Protection of Human Rights and Fundamental Freedoms of Indigenous Populations, Statement by the Observer Delegation of Canada—Delivered by Gerald E. Shanon, ambassador and permanent representative, U.N. Working Group on Indigenous Populations, 11th Sess. (July 29, 1993) (discussing land claim settlement procedures involving indigenous groups throughout Canada); *Information Received from Governments*, U.N. Doc. E/CN.4/Sub.2/AC.4/1991/4 (June 5, 1991) (information from Colombia regarding government measures to secure indigenous territorial rights); *Information Received from Governments*, U.N. Doc. E/CN.4/Sub.2/AC.4/1989/2, at 7–8 (1989) (information from Brazil reporting constitutional guarantees and efforts to demarcate indigenous lands).

119. *See 1990 Analytical Commentary, supra* note 60, at 10–15 (discussing commentary by government and indigenous observers on the land rights provisions of the first revised text of the U.N. draft declaration on indigenous rights). *See also Report of the working group established in accordance with Commission on Human Rights resolution 1995/32*, E/CN.4/2001/85 (Feb. 6, 2001), paras. 105–15; *Report of the working group established in accordance with Commission on Human Rights resolution 1995/32*, E/CN.4/2002/98 (March 6, 2002), paras. 38–44 (discussions on the land rights provisions of the U.N. draft declaration involving state and indigenous representatives).

120. *See Report on First Round of Consultations on Inter-American Instrument, supra* note 16, at 306–7 (summarizing government and indigenous organizations' comments on "territorial rights"); *Report of the Chair, Special meeting of the Working Group to prepare the Draft American Declaration on the Rights of Indigenous Peoples held in Washington D.C., April 2–6, 2001*, O.A.S. Doc. OEA/Ser.K/XVI, GT/DADIN/doc.23/01 rev. 1 (July 26, 2001), pp. 68–71; *Report of the Rapporteur, Special session of the Working Group to prepare the Draft American Declaration on the Rights of Indigenous Peoples held in Washington D.C., February 24–28, 2003*, O.A.S. Doc. OEA/Ser.K/XVI, GT/DADIN/doc.138/03 (May 5, 2003) pp. 4–8.

121. Chapter 26 recognizes indigenous peoples' "historical relationship with *their* lands," Agenda 21, *supra* note 85, para. 26.1 (emphasis added), and prescribes a number of measures to protect and strengthen that relationship, *id.* paras. 26.1, 26.3, 26.4.

122. *World Bank Operational Manual*, Operational Directive 4.20: "Indigenous Peoples," para. 15(c) (1991) (establishing recognition of customary or traditional indige-

nous land tenure systems as a premise of bank-assisted projects). This Operational Directive is currently in the process of review. The World Bank policy on indigenous peoples is addressed *infra* note 208 and *supra* chapter 2, notes 124–26. This Operational Directive is currently in the process of review. The World Bank policy on indigenous peoples is addressed *infra* note 208 and *supra* chapter 2, notes 124–26.

123. *See supra* notes 37–58 and accompanying text.

124. The Case of the Mayagna (Sumo) Awas Tingni Community v. Nicaragua, Inter-Am. Ct. H.R. (Ser. C) No. 79 (Judgment on merits and reparations of August 31, 2001), published in abridged version in 19 *Ariz. J. Int'l & Comp. L.* 395 (2002) [hereinafter *Awas Tingni* case]. The procedural aspects of this case are discussed in chapter 7, *infra*, notes 128–57 and accompanying text.

125. By virtue of article 21 of the American Convention on Human Rights, *supra* note 3, "Everyone has the right to the use and enjoyment of his property. The law may subordinate such use and enjoyment to the interest of society. . . . No one shall be deprived of his property except upon payment of just compensation, for reasons of public utility or social interest, and in the cases and according to the forms established by law." The Court declared that "Article 21 of the American Convention recognizes the right to private property. . . . 'Property' can be defined as those material things which can be possessed, as well as any right which may be part of a person's patrimony; that concept includes all movables and immovables, corporeal and incorporeal elements and any other intangible object capable of having value." *Awas Tingni* case, *supra* note 124, at paras. 143–44.

126. Political Constitution of Nicaragua (1987), amended by Law No. 92 (1995), arts. 5, 89, and 180; Statute of Autonomy for the Autonomous Regions of Nicaragua's Atlantic Coast, Law No. 28 , Oct. 30, 1987 (La Gaceta, No. 238), art. 36.

127. For relevant background, *see* Jorge Jenkins Molieri, *El Desafío indígena en Nicaragua: El Caso de los Miskitos* 33–114 (1986) (a history on the Atlantic Coast region); Theodore Macdonald, "The Moral Economy of the Miskito Indians: Local Roots of a Geopolitical Conflict," in *Ethnicities and Nations: Processes of Interethnic Relations in Latin America, Southeast Asia, and the Pacific* 114–22 (Remo Guidieri et al., eds. 1988); S. James Anaya, "The Awas Tingni Petition to the Inter-American Commission on Human Rights: Indigenous Lands, Loggers, and Government Neglect in Nicaragua," 9 *St. Thomas L. Rev.* 157 (1996); S. James Anaya and Claudio Grossman, *"The Case of Awas Tingni v. Nicaragua:* A New Step in the International Law of Indigenous Peoples," 19 *Ariz. J. Int'l & Comp. L.* 1 (2002).

128. *Awas Tingni* case, *supra* note 124, at paras. 142–55.

129. *Id.* at para. 146.

130. *See Final Written Arguments of the Inter-American Commission on Human Rights before the Inter-American Court of Human Rights in the Case of the Mayagna (Sumo) Indigenous Community of Awas Tingni Against the Republic of Nicaragua,* Aug. 10, 2001, published in 19 *Ariz. J. Int'l & Comp. L.* 367 (2002), at paras. 62–66 [hereinafter *Final Arguments of the Inter-American Commission in the Awas Tingni Case*].

131. *Awas Tingni* case, *supra* 124, at para. 151. In the *Maya* case, the commission reaffirmed that the international human right to property upholds indigenous land rights

such that, as a matter of international law, indigenous land rights do not depend on prior recognition within the applicable domestic legal system. *See* Maya Indigenous Communities, Case No. 12.053 (Belize), Inter-Am. C.H.R. Report No. 96/03 (preliminary version, Oct. 24, 2003), paras. 116–18. Compare the decision of the European Commission of Human Rights in *Könkmämä and 38 other Saami Villages v. Sweden*, Application No. 27033/95, Hudoc REF00003222 (admissibility decision of Nov. 25, 1996), in which the applicant Saami villages claimed exclusive hunting and fishing rights on the basis of immemorial custom and asserted that state regulations infringed on those rights in violation of the "right to peaceful enjoyment of . . . possessions" articulated in Protocol 1, article 1, of the European Convention on Human Rights. Having observed that, along with reindeer herding, hunting and fishing "are fundamental elements of Saami culture," the commission considered that the rights claimed "can be regarded as possessions within the meaning" of the Protocol. However, the commission noted that the existence of the claimed rights remained disputed and declared the case inadmissible for failure to pursue the claim through domestic courts.

132. *Awas Tingni* case, *supra* note 124, para. 153.

133. *Cf. Report of the Committee set up to examine the representation alleging non-observance by Denmark of the Indigenous and Tribal Peoples Convention, 1989 (No. 169), made under article 24 of the ILO Constitution by the National Confederation of Trade Unions of Greenland (Sulinermik Inuussutissarsiuteqartut Kattuffiat-SIK)* I.L.O. Doc. GB.280/18/5 (Nov. 2000) (concluding that, because the Greenland Home Rule Act recognizes the entire territory of Greenland as belonging to the Inuit of Greenland as a whole, Denmark is under no obligation under the convention to demarcate the particular lands within Greenland that correspond to a particular Inuit community).

134. *Awas Tingni* case, *supra* note 124, at paras. 146–49.

135. *See Awas Tingni* case, *supra* note 124 (separate opinion of Judge Sergio García Ramírez, at paras. 7–9).

136. *See id.* (separate opinion of Judges A. A. Cançado Trindade, M. Pacheco Gómez, and Abreu Burelli).

137. Mary and Carrie Dann, Case 11.140 (United States), Inter-Am. C.H.R. Report No. 75/02 (merits decision of Dec. 27, 2002) [hereinafter *Dann* case]. This case is discussed further in chapter 7, *infra*, notes 98–101 and corresponding text.

138. *See* American Declaration of the Rights and Duties of Man, *supra* note 6, art. XXII: "Every person has a right to own such private property as meets the essential needs of decent living and helps to maintain the dignity of the individual and of the home." As noted by the commission, its examination of state conduct in relation to the declaration is to promote observance of the general human rights obligations of OAS member states that derive from the OAS Charter. *See Dann* case, *supra* note 137, para. 95, n. 55. The Inter-American Court of Human Rights has held that the provisions of the American Declaration on the Rights and Duties of Man are expressive of the human rights obligations of states under the OAS Charter. *See* Inter-Am. Ct. H.R., *Interpretation of the American Declaration of the Rights and Duties of Man Within the Framework of Article 64 of the American Convention on Human Rights*, Advisory Opinion OC-10/89, July 14, 1989, Ser. A No. 10 (1989), paras. 42–45.

139. For background on this case and the domestic proceedings before United States' courts, see John D. O'Connell, "Constructive Conquest in the Courts: A Legal History of the Western Shoshone Lands Struggle—1864 to 1991," 42 *Nat. Resources J.* 765 (2003); Thomas E. Luebben & Cathy Nelson, "The Indian Wars: Efforts to Resolve Western Shoshone Land and Treaty Issues and to Distribute the Indian Claims Commission Judgment Fund," 42 *Nat. Resources J.* 835 (2003).

140. *See Dann* case, *supra* note 137, para. 133–44.

141. *See id.* paras. 144–45.

142. *Id.* para. 172. In effect, the commission found that many aspects of United States law relating to indigenous peoples are incompatible with international human rights law. These aspects include the doctrine by which the United States is deemed capable of unilaterally "extinguishing" indigenous rights, including land rights and treaty rights, *see* Lonewolf v. Hitchcock, 187 US 553 (1903), and by which indigenous land rights arising from prior occupation (*aboriginal title*) can be extinguished without the United States incurring an obligation of just compensation, *see* Tee-Hit-Ton v. United States, 348 US 272 (1955). For a critical analysis of this and other related doctrines of United States law, *see* Robert Williams, Jr., "The Algebra of Federal Indian Law: The Hard Trail of Decolonizing and Americanizing the White Man's Indian Jurisprudence," *Wis. L. Rev.*, No. 1986, 219 (1986).

143. *See Dann* case, *supra* note 137, paras. 124–28. The commission noted that "a review of pertinent treaties, legislation and jurisprudence reveals the development over more than 80 years of particular human rights norms and principles applicable to the circumstances and treatment of indigenous peoples." *Id.* para. 125.

144. *Id.* at para. 129.

145. Article XVIII of the Proposed American Declaration on the Rights of Indigenous Peoples, *supra* note 13, establishes, *inter alia*, "Indigenous peoples have the right to legal recognition of their varied and specific forms and modes of possession, control and enjoyment of their territories and property [and] are entitled to recognition of their property and ownership rights with respect to lands, territories and resources they have historically occupied and to the use of those to which they have also had access for their traditional activities and livelihood."

146. *See Dann* case, *supra* note 137, at paras. 127–28.

147. *See Final Arguments of the Inter-American Commission in the Awas Tingni Case*, *supra* note 130, at para. 64.

148. *Dann* case, *supra* note 137, at para. 130 (footnotes omitted). The inter-American commission reiterated and applied these principles in its subsequent decision in the *Maya* case, holding that Belize violated the international property rights of Maya communities by not effectively recognizing and protecting their traditional land tenure and by granting concessions for logging and oil development on Maya traditional lands. *See Maya* case, *supra* note 131, paras. 121–52.

149. The distinction between *customary* international law and *general principles* of international law is ambiguous in modern doctrine. Essentially, norms of customary international law are those deriving from state and other authoritative practice that extends into the international plane, *see supra* chapter 2, at notes 74–79; whereas general principles of international law are variously identified as those that can be seen reflected

on a widespread basis in such practice, those articulated or discernible from numerous international treaties and other standard-setting documents, or those widely shared among domestic legal systems, *see generally* Ian Brownlie, *Principles of Public International Law* 18–19 (6th ed., 2003). Especially where human rights are concerned, as developments in the field of indigenous peoples' human rights demonstrate, there can be considerable overlap between what might be understood to constitute general and customary international law. In any event, both categories establish legal obligations even for states that have not ratified or acceded to the treaties in which the norms or principles may be found.

150. Covenant on Economic, Social, and Cultural Rights, *supra* note 92.

151. *E.g., id.* art. 6(1) (regarding the "right to work, which includes the right of everyone to the opportunity to gain his living by work which he freely chooses or accepts").

152. *See generally* Roland Rich, "The Right to Development: A Right of Peoples?" in *The Rights of Peoples* 39 (James Crawford ed., 1988) (providing justification for the right to development and defending it against skeptics).

153. Declaration on the Right to Development, G.A. Res. 41/128, Dec. 4, 1986, reprinted in *U.N. Compilation of Instruments, supra* note 7, vol. 1, pt. 2 at 544 (adopted by a vote of 146 in favor, 1 against, and 8 abstentions). Although the United States (alone) voted against the declaration, its express reason was not concerned with the essential normative thrust of the declaration; rather, it alleged "imprecise and confusing" language, the declaration's linkage of disarmament and development, and disagreement with a perceived emphasis on transfers of resources from the developed to the developing world as the primary means of achieving development. Rich, *supra* note 152, at 52. A precursor to the 1986 declaration was the Declaration on Social Progress and Development, G.A. Res. 2542(XXIV), Dec. 11, 1969, reprinted in *U.N. Compilation of Instruments, supra* note 7, vol. 1, pt. 1 at 497.

154. Declaration on the Right to Development, *supra* note 153, art. 1(1).

155. *Id.* arts. 2–8, 10.

156. *See Plan of Implementation*, World Summit on Sustainable Development, Johannesburg, South Africa (Aug. 26–Sept. 4, 2002), found at http://www.un.org/esa/sustdev/documents/docs.htm (including references to the interests of indigenous communities in numerous parts of the plan, including paras. 7(e), 7(h), 37(f), 38(i), 40(d), 40(h), 40(r), 42(e), 4(b), 44(h), 44(j), 44(k), 44(l), 45(h), 46(b), 53, 54(h), 59(b), 63, 64(d), 70(c), 109(a). The final political declaration of the conference, the *Johannesburg Declaration on Sustainable Development* (Sept. 4, 2002), found at http://www.un.org/esa/sustdev/documents/WSSD_POI_PD/English/POI_PD.htm, at para. 25, includes a specific reference to indigenous peoples in the following terms: "We reaffirm the vital role of the indigenous peoples in sustainable development."

157. *See generally* Burger, *supra* note 91, at 17–33 (describing "life at the bottom" for the world's indigenous peoples).

158. *See generally U.N. Indigenous Study, supra* note 90, Add. 4, paras. 54–119, 163–90, (describing discriminatory rendering of government services in areas of health, housing, education, and employment).

159. ILO Convention No. 169, *supra* note 13, art. 7(2).

160. *Id.* arts. 20–31.

161. *E.g.*, *id.* art. 20(1) ("[S]pecial measures" regarding conditions of employment are to be adopted "in co-operation with the peoples concerned.").

162. *See id.* art. 7(1) ("The peoples concerned shall have the right to decide their own priorities for the process of development as it affects their lives, beliefs, institutions.").

163. Draft United Nations Declaration, *supra* note 13, art. 38.

164. Proposed American Declaration on the Rights of Indigenous Peoples, *supra* note 13, art. XXI(1).

165. *See*, *e.g.*, Statement by Mr. Robert Tickner, minister for aboriginal and Torres Strait Islander Affairs, on behalf of the government of Australia, U.N. Working Group on Indigenous Populations, 10th Sess. at 2, 10–13 (July 28, 1992) (reporting measures to implement and "[f]oster a commitment from [Australian] governments at all levels to cooperate to address progressively aboriginal disadvantage and aspirations in relation to land, housing, law and justice, cultural heritage, education, employment, health, infrastructure, economic development and other relevant matters"); 1994 Statement of Brazil to the U.N. Working Group, *supra* note 118, at 3 (discussing recent executive decree establishing an interagency commission to address environmental and health concerns of indigenous communities); New Zealand Statement on Recent Developments (delivered by Miriama Evans to the U.N. Working Group on Indigenous Populations, 11th Sess. (July 27, 1993)) (discussing health care reforms and initiatives to benefit the indigenous Maori; also reporting government support for Maori educational programs).

166. For example, the World Bank in 2003 established a "Grants Facility for Indigenous Peoples," which is to provide small grants directly to indigenous peoples' organizations to support implementation of sustainable development projects and programs based on their cultural preferences. *See* "World Bank Grants Facility for Indigenous Peoples Announcement," *World Bank Indigenous Peoples Policy Update*, May 15, 2003; Haider Rizvi, " 'Pay for destruction,' Indigenous people tell corporations," *World News* No. 227 (2003) (providing feedback from indigenous peoples on the Bank initiative). Additionally, the World Bank has launched regional initiatives to promote indigenous development interests such as the "Pilot Program to Protect the Brazilian Rain Forest" in Latin America (focusing on demarcation and protection of the Brazilian Amazon) and the "Coastal Wetlands Protection and Development Project" in East Asia (providing socio-economic services to Khmer indigenous communities in Vietnam). *See* "The World Bank and Indigenous Peoples Policy and Program Initiatives," World Bank Report (1999); *Information Received from the United Nations System—The World Bank and Indigenous Peoples*, U.N. Doc. E/CN.19/Sub.2/2002/Add.12 (2002), paras. 15–22. In its effort to contribute to data collection on indigenous issues, the Bank is developing national profiles for indigenous peoples in Latin American and East Asia, completing forestry sector reviews in Mexico, Papua New Guinea, and Russia; and conducting poverty assessments of indigenous peoples in Panama and Peru. *See* "The World Bank and Indigenous Peoples Policy and Program Initiatives," *supra*, at 3–4; *Information Received from the United Nations System—The World Bank and Indigenous Peoples*, *supra*, paras. 26–30.

167. Since the development of its Indigenous Peoples and Community Development Unit in 1994, the Inter-American Development Bank has assisted in the demarcation of indigenous lands, health programs for indigenous peoples, and other economic and social development initives to benefit indigenous communities. *See Indigenous Issues*

and the Inter-American Development Bank: A Summary Report, U.N. Doc. E/C.19/2003/ CRP.4 (2003) (summarizing the history of the IDB's activities relating to indigenous peoples). For a discussion on the effectiveness of these initiatives see Roger Plant & Soren Hvalkof, *Land Titling and Indigenous Peoples*, IDB Doc. IND-109 (2001) (review of IDB land titling and regularization policies in Latin America); Jonathan Renshaw, *Social Investment Funds and Indigenous Peoples*, IDB Doc. IND-108 (2001) (analysis of the IDB social investment funds for indigenous people); William Savedoff & Carlos César Perafán, *Indigenous Peoples Health: Issues for Discussion and Debate*, IDB Working Paper (2001) (exploring areas of need for IDB involvement in indigenous health). In response to internal reports and feedback received from the United Nations Permanent Forum on Indigenous Issues, the IDB is in the process of creating a "Profile of the Strategic Framework for Indigenous Development." *See Indigenous Issues and the Inter-American Development Bank: A Summary Report, supra*, at 4; "IND Unit Work Plan," I.D.B. Report (2003).

168. The UNDP sets forth its policy on indigenous peoples in a 2001 framework document, *see UNDP and Indigenous Peoples: A Policy of Engagement* (2001). Within that framework, the UNDP has set forth initiatives in the areas of poverty reduction, human rights, democratic governance, globalization and indigenous knowledge. *Information received from the United Nations System, United Nations Development Programme*, U.N. Doc. E/C.19/2003/19 (2003). The UNDP sponsors the Indigenous Knowledge Programme (supporting conservation and promotion of indigenous knowledge) and the Global Environment Facility, Small Grants Program (funding over 300 projects related to indigenous issues as of 2001). *See* UNDP, *UNDP Draft Report: An Assessment of UNDP Activities Involving Indigenous Peoples* (1999).

169. The Indigenous Peoples Fund ("Fondo Indígena") was established in 1992 at the Second Summit Meeting of Ibero-American Heads of State. *See* Convenio Constitutivo del Fondo para el Desarrollo de los Pueblos Indígenas de América y el Caribe, Madrid, 24 Jul. 1992. Currently operating with the support of an inter-agency network of international organizations, the Indigenous Peoples Development Network, the Fund focuses on resources for sustainable development, indigenous human rights, institutional strengthening and training, and culture and identity of indigenous peoples. *See Indigenous Issues and the Inter-American Development Bank: A Summary Report, supra* note 167, at 4; meeting minutes and annual reports of the Indigenous Fund are available in Spanish on the Fondo Indígena website at: http://www.fondoindigena.org. For critical discussions of international development initiatives and indigenous peoples, see generally Fergus MacKay, "Universal Rights Or A Universe Unto Itself? Indigenous Peoples' Human Rights and the World Bank's Draft Operational Policy 4.10 on Indigenous Peoples," 17 *Am. U. Int'l Rev.* 527 (2002); and Tom Griffiths, *A Failure of Accountability: Indigenous Peoples, Human Rights and Development Agency Standards* (2003) (report from the Forest Peoples Programme comparing policies and operational procedures of development agencies and their effect on indigenous peoples rights).

170. Declaration on the Granting of Independence to Colonial Countries and Peoples, G.A. Res. 1514(XV), Dec. 14, 1960, para. 1, U.N. GAOR, 15th Sess., Supp. No. 16, U.N. Doc. A/4684 (1961).

171. Chapter XII of the U.N. Charter concerns the obligations of member states with regard to "Non-Self-Governing Territories," which were generally understood at the time of the Charter's adoption to include those of a classic, colonial type. *See* W. Ofuatey-Kodjoe, *The Principle of Self-Determination in International Law* 104–13 (1977). The criteria for identifying non-self-governing territories subject to U.N.-promoted decolonization procedures were set forth in the General Assembly resolution, Principles Which Should Guide Members in Determining Whether or Not an Obligation Exists to Transmit the Information Called for in Article 73(e) of the Charter of the United Nations (Declaration on Non-Self-Governing Territories), G.A. Res. 1541(XV), Dec. 15, 1960, U.N. GAOR, 15th Sess., Supp. No. 16, at 29, U.N. Doc. A/4684 (1961), discussed *supra* chapter 2, notes 28–29 and accompanying text.

172. G.A. Res. 1541, *supra* note 171, principle 6.

173. *See* Mark Falcoff, "The Democratic Prospect in Latin America," 13 *Wash. Q.*, Spring 1990, at 183; Elie Abel, *The Shattered Bloc: Behind the Upheaval in Eastern Europe* (1990); Carol Lancaster, "Democracy in Africa," *Foreign Pol'y*, Winter 1991–92, at 148; Samuel P. Huntington, *The Third Wave: Democratization in the Late Twentieth Century* (1991).

174. *See* David Stoelting, "The Challenge of UN-Monitored Elections in Independent Nations," 28 *Stan. J. Int'l L.* 371, 375 (1992) (discussing the "United Nations' emerging role in monitoring independent states' elections" in the context of "an emerging right to political participation under international law"); Morton Halperin et al., *Self Determination in the New World Order* 63 (1992) (discussing Organization of American States resolutions deploring authoritarian coups against elected officials in Haiti and Peru).

175. *E.g.*, Halperin et al., *supra* note 174, at 420–24 ("Toward a Democratic Entitlement"); Gregory H. Fox, "The Right to Political Participation in International Law," 17 *Yale J. Int'l L.* 539 (1992); Thomas M. Franck, "The Emerging Right to Democratic Governance," 86 *Am. J. Int'l L.* 46 (1992); Harold Koh, "The Right to Democracy," in U.S. Dept. of State, *Country Reports on Human Rights Practices for 1998*, vol. 1, xv (1999).

176. *See generally* Paolo G. Carozza, "Subsidiarity as a Structural Principle of International Human Rights Law," 97 *Am. J. Int'l L.* 38 (2003). Emphasis within Western democratic theory on the importance of local government within a larger political framework is long-standing. *See* Mark Tushnet, *Red, White and Blue: A Critical Analysis of Constitutional Law* 4–17 (1988) (discussing the dominant strands of political theory adopted by the framers of the U.S. Constitution).

177. *See supra* chapter 3, notes 44–49 and accompanying text.

178. *See supra* notes 17–30 and accompanying text.

179. The multicultural model is explicitly incorporated in the amended constitutions of several countries in the Americas and elsewhere. *See, e.g.*, Political Constitution of Colombia, 1991, art. 7 (affirming that "[t]he State affirms and protects the ethnic and cultural diversity of the Colombian Nation"); Political Constitution of Bolivia, 1967 (as amended in 1995), art. 1 (defining Bolivia as "free, independent, sovereign, multiethnic and pluricultural"); Political Constitution of Nicaragua, 1987 (as amended in 1995), art. 8 (stating that "[t]he people of Nicaragua is of a multiethnic nature"); Political Constitu-

tion of the United States of Mexico, 1917 (as amended in 2001), art. 2 (stating that "[t]he Nation has a pluricultural composition originally founded in the indigenous peoples"); Political Constitution of Ecuador, 1998, art. 1 (defining Ecuador as "a social state of law, sovereign, unitary, independent, democratic, pluricultural and multiethnic") (translations from Spanish by author).

180. *See* Will Kymlicka, *Multicultural Citizenship* (1995); Will Kymlicka, *Politics in the Vernacular* (2001); Will Kymlicka, ed., *Citizenship in Diverse Societies* (2000). For analysis of the multicultural model and how it might be operationalized through institutional arrangements that accommodate both individual and group interests, see Ayalet Shachar, *supra* note 31. *But see* Giovanni Sartori, *La Sociedad Multiétnica: Pluralismo, multiculturalismo y extranjeros* (2001) (a critique of multiculturalism).

181. *See* Instituto Indigenista Interamericano and Instituto Interamericano de Derechos Humanos, *Entre ley y la costumbre: El Derecho consuetudinario indígena en América Latina* (1990) (a compilation of studies on indigenous customary laws and institutions in Latin America).

182. *See generally* David H. Getches et al., *Federal Indian Law: Cases and Materials* 373–682 (4th ed. 1998) (materials on institutions of tribal self-government, including tribal courts, and the scope of their jurisdiction within the U.S. legal framework).

183. ILO Convention No. 169, *supra* note 13, art. 8(2).

184. *Id.*, art. 9.

185. Draft United Nations Declaration, *supra* note 13, art. 33.

186. Michael Kioni Dudley & Keoni Kealoha Agard, *A Hawaiian Nation*, vol. 2, *A Call for Hawaiian Sovereignty* 89–99 (1990).

187. The *U.N. Indigenous Study, supra* note 90, observes that "[v]arious factors, economic and social ones for the most part, everywhere influence the effectiveness of political rights," *id.* Add. 4, para. 255, and concludes that political "representation of indigenous peoples remains inadequate and is sometimes purely symbolic" *id.* Add. 4, para. 261.

188. *See* Julian Burger, *supra* note 91, at 17–33 (describing "life at the bottom" for the world's indigenous peoples); *see also U.N. Indigenous Study, supra* note 90, Add. 4, paras. 54–190) (describing social and economic conditions of indigenous peoples).

189. Draft United Nations Declaration, *supra* note 13, art. 33.

190. *See* Proposed American Declaration on the Rights of Indigenous Peoples, *supra* note 13, art. XV(1).

191. *See, e.g., 1991 Revised Working Paper, supra* note 60, at 89 (proposed language by Argentina for U.N. declaration on indigenous rights); *Information received from Governments*, U.N. Doc. E/CN.4/Sub.2/AC.4/1991/1(1991) (comments from Mexico on first revised text of indigenous rights declaration); *Report on First Round of Consultations on Inter-American Instrument, supra* note 16, at 293–98 (comments by Costa Rica, Mexico, Peru, Colombia, Canada, Chile, and Guatemala); *Report of the Chair, Special meeting of the Working Group to prepare the Draft American Declaration on the Rights of Indigenous Peoples held in Washington D.C., April 2–6, supra* note 120, at 66 (proposal submitted by the United States stating that "States should recognize . . . a broad range of autonomy for indigenous peoples in managing their local and internal affairs); *Report of Rapporteur, Special meeting of the Working Group to prepare the*

Draft American Declaration on the Rights of Indigenous Peoples held in Washington D.C., March 11–15, 2002, supra note 120, at 11–12 (comments from states linking the self-government provisions of the proposed American declaration to the principle of "internal" self-determination).

192. *See supra* chapter 3, notes 113–16 and accompanying text.

193. *See, e.g.,* Statement by the Delegation of the Observer Government of Brazil on Item 5 of the Agenda: Review of Developments, U.N. Working Group on Indigenous Populations, 11th Sess. at 3–4 (July 29, 1993) (recounting efforts of the government of Brazil to implement "special policies" to ensure indigenous people the enjoyment of their traditions and autonomous organization of their communities"); *Information Received from Governments,* U.N. Doc. E/CN.4/Sub.2/AC.4/1991/4, at 4–5 (June 5, 1991) (information received from the government of Colombia) (outlining steps to afford indigenous groups in Colombia "the necessary conditions to organize themselves in accordance with their own usages and customs and to strengthen indigenous participation in decision making on policies and programs affecting them"); Canadian Statement to United Nations Working Group on Indigenous Populations on the Review of Developments, at 4–5 (July 29, 1991) (government program by which the country's "first nations . . . can negotiate self-government through new legislative arrangements that reflect more closely their particular circumstances" and "open discussions [involving indigenous representatives] leading toward the constitutional entrenchment of aboriginal self-government"); Intervention of the Delegation of Canada to the Main Committee of the World Conference on Human Rights on the Subject of Indigenous Peoples, Delivered by Denis Marantz, Canadian Delegation, Vienna, at 1 (June 22, 1993) (describing efforts at constitutional recognition of aboriginal self-government and legislation for self-government negotiations across Canada, initiatives aimed at "transfer[ring] to the aboriginal peoples of Canada . . . increased responsibility for planning and managing their own affairs"); 1994 Statement by the Hon. Robert Tickner, M.P. federal minister on behalf of Australia, *supra* note 118, at 12–13 (describing the establishment of the Torres Strait Regional Authority—an elected body of Torres Strait Islanders—in which is vested certain powers of decision making); 1989 Statement by the Philippine Government to the U.N. Working Group, at 2–3 (constitutional and legislative measures for the creation of autonomous regions in the Muslin Mindanao and the Cordilleras, characterized as "the granting of autonomy to indigenous populations"); Statement by the Observer Delegation of Norway to the Seventh Session of the U.N. Working Group at 2 (1987 legislation concerning the establishment of a "Sami assembly" which will "comprise all matters affecting the Sami people in Norway, and will be elected by direct elections"); Nordic Contributions to the International Year for the World's Indigenous People, Statement by Jens Brosted, Nordic Council of Ministers, representing Denmark, Finland, Iceland, Norway, Sweden, and the three self-governing territories of the Faroe Islands, Greenland, and Åland, U.N. Working Group on Indigenous Populations, 11th Sess. at 2 (July 1993) (describing decision of Nordic Counsel of Ministries "to provide major support for a joint meeting among the Sami Parliaments in Norway, Sweden, and Finland").

After a campaign of criticism against the government of Bangladesh concerning its treatment of the tribal peoples in the Chittagong Hill Tracts, the government of Bangladesh reported on legislation in that regard. *Information Received from Governments*, U.N. Doc. E/CN.4/Sub.2/AC.4/1989/2/Add.1, at 2–5 (1989) (information received from Bangladesh government reporting that the legislation sets up three "local elected and autonomous government councils . . . with adequate power for the tribal power to run their own affairs and preserve their socio-cultural heritage and separate identity").

See also 1989 Provisional Record 25, *supra* note 59, at 25/2. The government of the Soviet Union informed the ILO about "associations of indigenous peoples [that] would be set up to improve the legal status of autonomous groups." *Id.* "The government member of Honduras drew the [ILO] Committee's attention to a new law precluding state interference in matters within the competence of indigenous peoples, which was drafter [*sic*] following extensive consultations with their representatives." *Id.*

194. Draft United Nations Declaration, *supra* note 13, art. 19.

195. Proposed American Declaration on the Rights of Indigenous Peoples, *supra* note 13, art XV(2). Several states and indigenous peoples' organizations have stressed the importance of this right in commenting on the proposal for an inter-American instrument on indigenous rights. *See Report on First Round of Consultations on Inter-American Instrument, supra* note 16, at 282–83.

196. ILO Convention No. 169, *supra* note 13, art. 6.1(b).

197. Thus, indigenous peoples and their organizations have been permitted to participate actively in discussions within the United Nations concerning the development of an indigenous rights declaration and related topics. *See* Robert A. Williams, Jr., "Encounters on the Frontiers of International Human Rights Law: Redefining the Terms of Indigenous Peoples' Survival in the World," 1990 *Duke L.J.* 660, 676–85 (1990). The U.N. sub-commission's Working Group on Indigenous Populations solicited written commentary from indigenous peoples in the course of developing the draft U.N. declaration, and the group allowed any indigenous representative attending its meetings to participate in the discussion of the declaration. The Commission on Human Rights, which is now considering the draft declaration, established a special procedure for indigenous representatives to participate in its drafting working group, *see supra* chapter 2, note 92, a procedure designed to provide for greater participation by nonstate entities than that ordinarily allowed in the commission's proceedings. Similarly, the International Labour Organization relaxed its rules of procedure in order to allow indigenous groups limited direct participation in the development of ILO Convention No. 169 of 1989. *See* Swepston, *supra* note 113, at 686–87. From the start indigenous peoples have participated in the deliberations of the OAS working group established to discuss the Proposed American Declaration on the Rights of Indigenous Peoples. *See Report on the First Round of Consulatations Concerning the Future Inter-American Legal Instrument on the Rights of Indigenous Populations, supra* note 16; *Propuestas Presentadas por los Estados y los Representantes de los Pueblos Indígenas sobre los Artículos Considerados en las Sesiones Especiales del Grupo de Trabajo para Preparar el Proyecto de Declaración Americana de Derechos de los Indígenas, 11–15 de marzo de 2002*, O.A.S. Doc. EA/Ser.K/XVI, GT/DADIN/doc.71 /02 (Apr. 11, 2002).

198. For a discussion of the Permanent Forum, see *infra* chapter 6, at notes 11–18. Another example of indigenous participation in at the international level is the Arctic Council. The council is a high level intergovernmental forum, instituted September 19,

1996 in Ottawa, Canada, to consider the common concerns and challenges of the governments and peoples of the Arctic. Members of the Council are Canada, Denmark, the Russian Federation, Finland, Iceland, Norway, Sweden and the United States of America. The following indigenous organizations have status as "permanent participants," with the right to participate and be consulted within the Arctic Council: the Inuit Circumpolar Conference; the Saami Counsel; the Aleutian International Association; the Arctic Athabaskan Council, and the Gwich'in Council International. Similarly, other organizations with an interest in indigenous issues, such as the International Working Group on Indigenous Affairs (IWGIA) and the Association of World Reindeer Herders, can attend the Council's activities as observers.

199. ILO Convention No. 169, *supra* note 13, art. 6(1)(a). Also relevant in this regard is article 7(1) of the convention, which recognizes "the right [of indigenous peoples] to decide their own priorities for the process of development as it affects their lives, beliefs, institutions and spiritual well-being and the lands they occupy or otherwise use, and to exercise control, to the extent possible, over their own economic, social and cultural development."

200. *See id.* art. 15. The Governing Body of the ILO, through tripartite *ad hoc* committees created to analyze complaints of violations of the convention, has warned against a lack of adequate consultative processes in various cases in which states have endeavored to develop natural resources on traditional indigenous territories. *See Report of the Committee set up to examine the representation alleging non-observance by Bolivia of the Indigenous and Tribal Peoples Convention, 1989 (No. 169), made under article 24 of the ILO Constitution by the Bolivian Central of Workers (COB)*, ILO Doc. GB.274/16/7 (Mar. 1999) (signaling need to correct lack of consultation prior to granting of concessions for logging on traditional indigenous lands in Bolivian Amazon region); *Third Supplementary Report of the Committee established to examine the representation alleging non-observance by Colombia of the Indigenous and Tribal Peoples Convention, 1989 (No. 169), made under article 24 of the ILO Constitution by the Single Confederation of Workers of Colombia (CUT)*, GB. 276/17/1, ILO Docs. GB 282/14/3 (Nov. 2001), para. 86 (specifying that Colombia was required to adequately apply the convention's consultation provisions prior to authorizing oil development in an area outside the U'wa reserve, and rejecting the government's position that the provisions applied only in regard to areas regularly and permanently occupied by indigenous communities); *Report of the Committee set up to examine the representation alleging non-observance by Ecuador of the Indigenous and Tribal Peoples Convention, 1989 (No. 169), made under article 24 of the ILO Constitution by the Confederación Ecuatoriana de Organizaciones Sindicales Libres (CEOSL)* ILO Doc. GB.282/14/2 (Nov. 2001) (lack of consultation prior to oil exploitation within Shuar territory in Amazon region).

201. *See id. at* para. 39; Statement of the International Labour Office, summarized in *Report of the Committee on Convention No. 107*, International Labour Conference, Provisional Record 25, 76th Sess. at 25/12, para. 74 (1989).

202. ILO Convention No. 169, *supra* note 13, art. 6(2) (emphasis added). The International Labour Organization has affirmed that "consultations with indigenous and tribal peoples are compulsory: prior to any exploration or exploitation of mineral and/or

other natural resources within their lands; when it might be necessary to remove indigenous or tribal communities from their traditional lands and resettle them somewhere else, and prior to the design and launching of vocational training programmes for them." Manuela Tomei & Lee Swepston, *Indigenous and Tribal Peoples: A Guide to ILO Convention No. 169*, 8 (1996).

203. Such is the interpretation of the consultation provisions of ILO Convention No. 169 provided by the competent ILO officials, as manifested in *Manuela Tomei & Lee Sweston, supra* note 202, at sec. 1, an ILO publication whose authors are the organization's principal officials in charge of applying the convention. This interpretation is also advanced by the *ad hoc* ILO committees charged with examining complaints. For example, in finding Ecuador in violation of article 6 for its failure adequately consult the Shuar people with regard to oil development that would affect 70% of the Shaur territory, the relevant ILO committee stated,

> the concept of consulting the indigenous communities that could be affected by the exploration or exploitation of natural resources includes establishing a genuine dialogue between both parties characterized by communication and understanding, mutual respect, good faith and the sincere wish to reach a common accord. A simple information meeting cannot be considered as complying with the provisions of the Convention. In addition, Article 6 requires that the consultation should occur beforehand, which implies that the communities affected should participate as early as possible in the process, including in the preparation of environmental impact studies. . . . [I]f an appropriate consultation process is not developed with the indigenous and tribal institutions or organizations that are truly representative of the communities affected, the resulting consultations will not comply with the requirements of the Convention

Report of the Committee set up to examine the representation alleging non-observance by Ecuador, made by CEOSL, supra note 200, paras. 38, 44. *Accord, Report of the Committee set up to examine the representation alleging non-observance by Bolivia, made by COB, supra* note 200, para. 40; *Report of the Committee set up to examine the representation alleging on-observance by Colombia of the Indigenous and Tribal Peoples Convention, 1989 (No. 169) made under article 24 of the ILO Constitution by the Central Unitary Workers' Union (CUT) and the Colombian Medical Trade Union Association (ADESMAS),* I.L.O. Doc. GB.282/14/4 (Nov. 2001), para. 61.

204. ILO Convention No. 169, *supra* note 13, art. 2(1), cited in *Report of the Committee set up to examine the representation alleging non-observance by Colombia, made by CUT and ADESMAS supra* note 203, para. 58 (in which the committee found that the government had not adequately consulted some Embera-Katio and Zenu communities affected by the construction of a hydroelectric dam, which involved the diversion of a river and affected the economic and cultural sustainability of those communities). *See also Third Report of the Committee set up to examine the representation alleging non-observance by Colombia, made by CUT, supra* note 200, at para. 77 (affirming that "the requirement for prior consultation must be viewed in the light of one of the fundamental principles of the Convention", that is, the right of indigenous peoples to decide their own priorities with respect to development projects [art. 7.1]

and the corresponding obligation of governments to evaluate the sociocultural impact of these projects [art. 7.3]).

205. *See CERD General Recommendation on Indigenous Peoples, supra* note 11, para 4 (d).

206. *See General Comment 23 (50) to Article 27, supra* note 44, at para 7.

207. *See* Daniel Bradlow, "The World Bank, the IMF and Human Rights," *Transnat'l L. & Contemp. Prob.*, No. 6, 1996, p. 63 (arguing that the World Back is a subject of international law because it has rights and obligations that are determined by international law).

208. *See* World Bank, Operational Directive O.D. 4.20. Indigenous Peoples (Sept. 2001), para. 8 (currently under review, *see* chapter 2 *supra*, note 126). The emphasis on the requirement of participation and consent by indigenous peoples and other particularly vulnerable social groups is especially obvious in the World Bank's recent policy pronouncements. The new Operational Policy of the Bank regarding natural habitats requires consultation with "affected groups" including especially indigenous peoples, before and after the conducting of environmental impact studies. World Bank, *Operational Policy 4.04. Natural Habitats* (June 2001), paras. 15, 17. In regard to the construction of dams, the official position of the Bank is to require "free and significant consultation with indigenous groups directly affected." "World Bank Position with respect to the World Commission on Dams" (Dec. 2001), in World Bank, *Summary of Consultations with External Stakeholders regarding the World Bank Draft Indigenous Peoples Policy (Draft OP/BP 4.10)"* (Apr. 18, 2002), Annex C, at 12. A similar policy has been adopted with respect to involuntary resettlement resulting from the Bank's development projects, which pays special attention to the participation of indigenous peoples and accords priority to their preferences in resettlement strategies. World Bank, *Operational Policy O.P. 4.12. Involuntary resettlement* (Dec. 2001), paras. 7–11.

In practice, however, the bank's actions have not always been faithful to these principles. A study by the bank itself carried out in 1992 made clear that more than a third of the bank's projects affecting indigenous communities had not taken into account Operational Directive 4.10 on indigenous peoples, including that part of the directive mandating consultation with affected communities. *See* John Swartz & Jorge Uquillas, *Aplicación de la Política del Banco sobre Poblaciones Indígenas (OD 4.20) en América Latina (1992–1997)*, Washington, DC, World Bank, Regional Office for Latin America and the Caribbean, 1999, p. 2. A later, independent study, based on an evaluation of seven specific Bank projects, concluded that the affected indigenous communities perceived the consultation as "often" superficial and "normally limited to brief visits to the field" that were ineffective because they "contradicted the gradual and consensual collective decision-making processes common in indigenous cultures." Thomas Griffiths & Marcus Colchester, "Report of a Workshop on Indigenous Peoples, Forests and the World Bank: Policies and Practice (Washington, May 9–10, 2002)," Program for Forest Peoples, Centre for Information on Multilateral Development Banks, 2000, p. 32. But despite these significant shortcomings, the study also noted that the existence of the World Bank directive "has been important to promote changes in the practice of some countries and to mitigate the adverse effects of development plans on indigenous peoples." *Id.* at 3.

209. Among the relevant provisions of the draft United Nations declaration, *supra* note 13, are the following: arts. 19, 20, 30, 37. The Proposed American Declaration, *supra* note 13, includes the following relevant provisions, among others: arts. XIII, XV, XVII, XXI. These provisions and the full texts of both documents are reproduced in the appendix, *infra*.

210. *See, e.g.*, Comments by the Delegation of Canada on Articles VII through XVIII and on the issue of self determination in the Proposed American Declaration on Indigenous Rights (Mar. 14, 2002), O.A.S. Doc. OEA/Ser.K/XVI, GT/DADIN/doc.69/02 ("Canada supports the principle that indigenous individuals have the right to participate in the general political processes of the state in which they live, without discrimination, consistent with international standards"); Comments of the Delegation of Guyana (Mar. 15, 2002), O.A.S. Doc. OEA/Ser.K/XVI, GT/DADIN-73/02 (Mar. 26, 2002) ("I wish to reiterate Guyana's support for, and commitment to both informing and consulting with indigenous communities on environmental and all other issues related to the affairs of Guyana"); Proposal of the Delegation of the United States (Mar. 13, 2002), O.A.S. Doc. OEA/Ser.K/ XVI GT/DADIN/doc.66/02 rev. 1 ("Where a national policy, regulation, decision, legislative comments or legislation will have substantial or direct effects for indigenous peoples, States should consult with indigenous peoples prior to the taking of such actions, where practicable and permitted by law"). *See also Report of the working group established in accordance with Commission on Human Rights resolution 1995/32*, U.N. Doc. E/CN.4/ 1997/102 (Dec. 10, 1996) (summarizing government comments on the draft United Nations declaration): comments by delegation of Mexico, *id.* para. 44 (stating that indigenous peoples "have the right to participate in economic, cultural, social and political development"); comments by delegation of Canada, *id* at para. 199 (referencing articles 18 and 19 of the draft United Nations declaration and supporting indigenous peoples' "participation in State decisions which directly affected certain areas of particular concern to indigenous peoples"); comments by the delegation of Argentina, *id.*, para. 205 (supporting the participation of indigenous peoples in decision-making processes, and citing to the relevant provisions of the Argentine constitution); proposal of the delegation of Brazil on article 20 of the draft declaration, *id.* para 214 ("States shall consult the peoples concerned, whose informed opinion shall be expressed freely, before implementing and adopting those measures"); comments by the U.S. delegation, *id.* para. 221 (supporting the right of indigenous peoples to participate effectively at the local and national levels "particularly with respect to decisions directly affecting them").

211. *See, e.g, Report of the Working Group on Indigenous Populations on its 19th Session*, U.N. Doc. E/CN.4/Sub.2/2001/17 (Aug. 9, 2001), paras. 35–37 (interventions of Canada, Chile and New Zealand regarding the participation of indigenous peoples in the design and implementation of policies that affect them.); *Report of the Working Group on Indigenous Populations on its 20th Session*. U.N. Doc. E/CN.4/Sub.2/2002/ 24 (Aug. 8, 2002), paras. 51–52. (informing of positive measures taken by the governments of Canada and Finland toward guaranteeing the participation of indigenous peoples in government programs affecting them).

5

The Duty of States to Implement International Norms

The principle of self-determination and the development of related norms discussed in the preceding chapters represent significant elements in indigenous peoples' centuries-long quest for survival. International norms today provide legal grounds, however limited, for indigenous peoples to roll back the lingering scourge of colonial patterns and to exist as distinct communities in pursuit of their own destinies under conditions of equality. The United Nations Charter and other widely ratified international treaties affirm the principle of self-determination of peoples or include related human rights norms. Particularly relevant to indigenous peoples is International Labour Organization Convention No. 169 on Indigenous and Tribal Peoples, which has been ratified by a number of countries. States, moreover, are subject to norms concerning indigenous peoples insofar as those norms are part of general or customary international law. Customary norms are binding upon the constituent units of the world community regardless of any formal act of assent to those norms.

It is one thing, however, for international law to incorporate norms concerning indigenous peoples; it is quite another thing for the norms to take effect in the actual lives of people. Hence, the corpus of international law aimed at securing the survival and flourishment of indigenous peoples includes a requirement that states take the needed action toward that end, action through domestic channels of decision making that involve indigenous peoples themselves.

In general, an integral part of international human rights law is the duty of states to secure enjoyment of human rights and to provide remedies where the rights are violated. This duty relates to the substantial corpus of international law on the responsibility of states in regard to unlawful acts and omissions.[1] It is implicit, if not express, in human rights treaties and is similarly implicit in discernible customary human rights law.[2] In the *Awas Tingni* case, the Inter-American Court of Human Rights invoked this duty, as expressed in general terms in articles 1 and 2 of the American Convention on Human Rights, to find that Nicaragua was under an affirmative obligation to take the steps necessary to recognize and protect the land rights of indigenous communities and to effectively respond to their claims.[3] The Draft United Nations Declaration on the Rights of Indigenous Peoples, in its following provision, articulates a norm that is applicable beyond particular treaty obligations: "Indigenous peoples have the right to have access to and prompt decision through mutually acceptable and fair procedures for the resolution of conflicts and disputes with States, as well as to effective remedies for all infringements of their individual and collective rights."[4]

In the context of indigenous peoples, the duty of states to secure enjoyment of human rights is heightened, and it is shared with the international community at large. With increased intensity over the last several years, the international community has maintained indigenous peoples as special subjects of concern and sought cooperatively to secure their rights and well-being. The United Nations, the Organization of American States (OAS), the International Labour Organization (ILO), and other international institutions have acknowledged the need for special programs for indigenous peoples at both the state and global levels. The Inter-American Commission on Human Rights, for example, recognized some time ago that "special protection for indigenous populations constitutes a sacred commitment of the States."[5] In his statement to the United Nations General Assembly at the inauguration of the International Year of the World's Indigenous People, Secretary-General Boutros Boutros-Ghali emphasized that "[t]he commitment of the United Nations' system to the cause of indigenous people is long-standing. It goes back to a time before the creation of the United Nations itself."[6]

Indigenous peoples are thus subjects of a special duty of care on the part of individual states and the international community, akin to the "sacred trust" articulated in the United Nations Charter with regard to the peoples of non-self-governing territories.[7] Notions of trusteeship toward indigenous peoples have in varying degrees existed in Western jurisprudence and state practice for centuries.[8] The terms *trust* or *trusteeship*, however, are not commonly used in contemporary international discourse to describe obligations toward indigenous peoples. Today, the principle of a special duty of care on the part of states and the international community is largely devoid of the paternalism and negative regard for non-European cultures previously linked to the rhetoric and practice of trusteeship. Instead, the principle rests on widespread acknowledgment, in light of contemporary values, of the relatively disadvantaged condition of indigenous peoples, a result of centuries of systemic oppression. Moreover, the duty to secure for indigenous peoples the enjoyment of their rights does not today entail efforts to assimilate or "civilize" them; rather, it requires the implementation of contemporary treaty and customary norms grounded in the principle of self-determination.

Toward Negotiated Agreement and
Respect for Historical Treaties

The implementation of contemporary norms concerning indigenous peoples may involve, as demonstrated in chapters 3 and 4, remedial or affirmative measures to provide redress for historical land claims, the development of social welfare programs, and change in the governing institutional order to secure cultural integrity and self-government. Such measures correspond with what the former chair of the U.N. Working Group on Indigenous Populations, Erica-Irene Daes, has called belated state building.[9] In keeping with self-determination, belated state-building measures should be developed in accordance with the aspirations of the indigenous groups concerned.[10] When state officials endowed with the requisite authority negotiate with truly representative leaders of indigenous peoples, and appropriate ratification procedures follow, indigenous communities have a framework within which they can be heard and their preferences be realized.

A process of negotiation that involves good faith dialogue toward achieving agreement helps to build mutual understanding and trust in what might otherwise be contentious and even volatile situations. Good faith dialogue makes it possible to accord to historically aggrieved groups the dignity they need and to identify shared interests and objectives. Negotiation itself may thus help to diffuse conflicts and discourage extreme positions. Moreover, an agreement resulting from good faith dialogue and mutual understanding, and ultimately approved by the relevant constituencies through democratic procedures, is likely to be invested with a substantial sense of legitimacy on the part of all concerned.[11]

Negotiation makes possible nuanced solutions to potentially complex issues of redistribution of power and resources in diverse circumstances. In most instances, self-determination for indigenous peoples cannot be achieved simply by allowing them to choose from among limited predetermined options. In the decolonization of overseas colonial territories, self-determination was considered to advance when the people of those territories could choose independent statehood, free association with an independent state, or full integration with an independent state.[12] Even if practicable, such a choice in the context of the vast majority of indigenous groups today living within the exterior boundaries of independent states would be at best a minimal, partial step toward the realization of self-determination and related human rights norms. Indigenous peoples typically seek neither independent statehood nor full integration, and what most of them do seek can hardly be said to fit a single formula somewhere in between. The realization of self-determination for indigenous peoples— including the enjoyment of nondiscrimination, cultural integrity, land rights, social welfare and development, and self-government—is context-specific, given the vast diversity of circumstances of indigenous peoples throughout the world. Negotiation procedures allow for exploring and choosing from an indeterminate number of context-specific mechanisms to secure indigenous peoples' rights.

Indigenous peoples, particularly in North America, have long relied upon negotiated agreement as a framework for securing rights related to their survival as distinct communities. Early contacts between Europeans and North American Indians led to treaties that defined the terms of coexistence between or among the peoples concerned. The United States and Canada continued the practice of treaty making with Indian nations until the latter part of the nineteenth century.[13] These historical treaties typically were negotiated in the context of superior bargaining power on the part of the non-Indian parties, and the treaties' aggregate effect was to facilitate non-Indian settlement. Nonetheless, in exchange for vast areas of land and other concessions, Indian treaty signatories often received express or implied guarantees including, in many instances, the right to remain on ancestral lands not ceded. North American Indian peoples have continued to look to their treaties as at least partial acts of constitutive self-determination and hence as critical points of reference for determining their specific ongoing rights and place vis-à-vis the larger world. Similarly, the Maori of New Zealand regard the Treaty of Waitangi entered into with Great Britain in 1840 as a constitutional instrument of sacred proportions.[14] In many instances, therefore, securing indigenous peoples' self-determination and related rights may substantially be a function of giving effect to historically negotiated treaties or renegotiating their terms in light of modern conditions.

Agreements, although not typically called treaties, have been negotiated in more recent years between indigenous peoples and states (or their political subdivisions) to secure indigenous peoples' rights. Several of Canada's indigenous groups have negotiated or are in the process of negotiating with the federal or provincial governments on self-government, joint management, or land settlement agreements.[15] Although the route of negotiation typically has been contentious, it has resulted in agreement on a number of occasions.[16] In perhaps the most far-reaching such agreement to date, Inuit people in the far northern part of Canada negotiated a substantial land settlement package and the creation of a new political subdivision known as Nunavut (an Inuit term meaning "our land"), which rivals in size the largest of Canada's existing provinces.[17] The agreement was put into practice beginning in 1999.[18]

In the United States a number of Indian tribes have negotiated agreements pursuant to the federal government's Tribal Self-Governance Demonstration Project, which was initiated in 1988.[19] Under the agreements, tribes have taken over local administration of programs previously under the charge of the federal Bureau of Indian Affairs, which historically has exercised pervasive authority over Indian people.[20] Additionally, many land and resource claims in the United States have been dealt with in recent decades through negotiation.[21] Taos Pueblo negotiated the return of ancestral lands in the vicinity of the sacred Blue Lake which had been under the administration of the U.S. Forest Service. In another case, the Passamaquoddy and Penobscot tribes of Maine reached an agreement with the state and federal governments settling claims to an extensive area of land.[22] More recently, the Timbisha Shoshone Tribe entered into an agreememt with the U.S. government to secure access and use rights within ancestral lands that are part of a national park.[23]

The international juridical character of historical and contemporary agreements with indigenous peoples remains a subject of controversy. There has been considerable argument that historical treaties concluded with indigenous groups in North America and elsewhere prior to the last century have full international status, in part on the grounds that they were considered to have such status at the time they were concluded.[24] On the other hand, the preponderance of scholarly opinion and practice in the early part of the twentieth century refused to accord international legal status to the historical treaties with indigenous non-European peoples,[25] and since then such treaties have not actively been regarded by states and international institutions as having the same character as treaties between recognized independent states.

In any case, the status historically accorded treaties with indigenous peoples—whether favorable or unfavorable—is not necessarily controlling today. And whether or not treaties or agreements with indigenous peoples have the same juridical status as interstate treaties is not *in itself* an issue of much practical importance. What matters is the respect accorded such agreements and the availability of mechanisms to ensure their effectiveness. Even if not of the same character as interstate treaties, agreements with indigenous peoples increasingly are acknowledged to be matters of international concern and hence, in their own right, can be said to have an international character. This is evident particularly in the 1989 U.N. Economic and Social Council resolution mandating a study on "treaties, agreements and other constructive arrangements between States and indigenous populations."[26] The special rapporteur who was charged with the study, Miguel Alfonso Martínez, issued a report with an extensive evaluation of the role of treaties and agreements in the history and contemporary lives of indigenous peoples, pointing out numerous problems of noncompliance and recommending a series of domestic and international measures to address these problems.[27] In addition, in its resolution "on Action Required Internationally to Provide Effective Protection for Indigenous Peoples," the European Parliament called upon states "in the strongest possible to terms" to honor treaties signed with indigenous peoples and expressed support for the U.N. treaty study.[28] Accordingly, agreements between indigenous peoples and states, both historical and contemporary ones, have been recurrent subjects of discussion in the meetings of international institutions in which indigenous issues are addressed.[29]

State Institutional Mechanisms

International law, including applicable conventional or customary norms concerning indigenous peoples, theoretically binds the state as a corporate whole. That is, on the international plane, a state is judged as a unitary actor, notwithstanding a division of powers that may exist among branches of a state's government or as a result of confederation. Yet in meeting or failing to meet its international obligations, the state acts or fails to act through its functional institutions, notwithstanding whether the state's system is characterized as *monist* or *dualist*.[30] In the *Awas Tingni* case, Nicaragua incurred international responsibility because of the particular acts and omissions of legislative, executive, and judicial agencies that, in the aggregate, resulted in a failure to protect indigenous land rights. The Inter-American Court of Human Rights in that case found responsibility by virtue of an inadequate legislative and administrative framework to address land titling petitions by indigenous communities, executive action permitting logging on indigenous lands, and judicial procedures that were flawed in their treatment of indigenous complaints against the logging.[31]

In virtually all modern states, discrete branches of government function within separate yet interrelated spheres of competency. The following discussion identifies mechanisms of state action within these distinct spheres and establishes their bearing upon the obligation to secure agreement with indigenous peoples or to otherwise implement relevant international norms.

Executive Action

A key institutional actor both internationally and domestically in all modern states is the executive arm of government. While the scope of executive power depends upon the applicable legislative and constitutional framework, typically the executive has broad authority to act in areas of concern to indigenous peoples. In other words, in most cases, the power of the executive to garner an effective response to the demands of indigenous peoples is substantial. Correspondingly, the duty of the state to implement international norms concerning indigenous peoples translates in significant measure into a responsibility of the executive.

The negotiated agreements mentioned previously have in large part entailed the exercise of executive authority. Officials of the U.S. Department of Interior, sometimes acting in close coordination with aides to the president and always subject to his authority, have been the ones on the part of the United States to negotiate the transfer of programs to tribal governments pursuant to the Tribal Self-Governance and Demonstration Project. Self-government and land settlement negotiations have been undertaken by officials within the Canadian Department of Indian Affairs and Northern Development, a cabinet-level executive agency, although usually with the involvement of relevant provincial officials.

In negotiating recent agreements for greater indigenous autonomy, officials in the United States have acted pursuant to enabling legislation. The Tribal Self-Governance Demonstration Project in the United States was established by an act of Congress in 1988. However, in the United States as well as in other countries, the executive has certain powers of initiative upon which to proceed to negotiate indigenous peoples' claims in the absence of specific authorizing legislation. At various times in the history of the United States, the country's president, acting through field agents, has negotiated treaties or agreements with Indian tribes on his own initiative, although subject to ratification by the U.S. Senate or, in the case of agreements subsequent to 1871, approval by the full Congress.[32] At least since constitutional amendments in 1982, the Canadian executive similarly has proceeded on the basis of constitutionally derived powers of initiative in negotiating over land rights and self-government with aboriginal peoples. Another example of the exercise of executive initiative is the agreement of the Bolivian president to secure land rights guarantees for lowland Indians in response to demands punctuated by a thirty-four-day protest march in 1990.[33]

Depending upon the nature of measures taken by the executive in response to indigenous peoples' demands and the applicable legislative and constitutional framework, either the executive alone may give the measures legal effect and see to their implementation or legislative action may be required. In the Bolivian example, the agreement with Indian leaders took the form of executive decrees establishing indigenous territories and regulating competing land and resource use.[34] The decrees were followed by legislation giving greater permanency to the measures taken.[35] Whether or not legislation is required in conjunction with an executive decision, the executive—acting through its competent ministries or departments—will almost invariably play a major role in securing the decision's implementation, if only by virtue of the character of the executive's function within the larger scheme of government.

The executive responsibility to secure indigenous peoples' rights extends beyond adopting or implementing measures specifically aimed at these peoples' concerns. In carrying out its myriad administrative functions, the executive characteristically enjoys a broad measure of discretion. Executive discretion over lands and natural resources can have especially broad implications for indigenous peoples, who in many cases have claims to or depend upon lands and resources under state control. It has become all too commonplace for senior or low-level executive officials in many countries to administer lands under state control in violation of international norms—for example, by granting concessions for logging on indigenous traditional lands without adequate consultation or mitigation measures, as Nicaraguan officials did in the *Awas Tingni* case.[36] It is incumbent upon the executive in exercising discretionary authority to act, instead, in conformity with applicable international norms in order to avoid casting the state as an international outlaw. In a statement to Indian leaders gathered at the White House, then U.S. President Bill Clinton said:

> This then is our first principle: respecting your values, your religions, your identity, and your sovereignty. This brings us to the second principle that should guide our relationship: We must dramatically improve the Federal Government's relationships with the tribes and become full partners with the tribal nations.
>
> I don't want there to be any mistake about our commitment to a stronger partnership between our people. Therefore, in a moment, I will also sign an historic Government directive that requires every executive department and agency of Government to take two simple steps: first, to remove all barriers that prevent them from working directly with tribal governments and, second, to make certain that if they take action affecting tribal trust resources, they consult with tribal governments prior to that decision.[37]

President Clinton's statement implicitly recognizes precepts of indigenous self-determination now incorporated into international human rights law. Although former President Clinton made no mention of the *international* character of the norms invoked to guide executive action, his directive exemplifies the kind of approach that could help bring a state into conformity with international law as it concerns indigenous peoples.

Legislative Action and Constitutional Reform

As already indicated, executive authority normally operates within the framework of a state's constitution and, at least to some extent, its legislative enactments; and that framework bears upon the scope of executive authority to respond to indigenous peoples' claims or to otherwise implement relevant international norms. Constitutional norms and legislative acts themselves usually bear directly upon the effective enjoyment of human rights, including indigenous peoples' rights, if only by omission. Accordingly, legislative institutions and mechanisms of constitutional reform are potential, and often necessary, conduits for the implementation of international norms concerning indigenous peoples.

In many countries, domestic law enacted in earlier periods has come into conflict with international norms concerning indigenous peoples as the international norms have developed into their contemporary form. For example, Colombia's Law 89 of 1890, which establishes a system of indigenous *resguardos*, or reserves, refers to the Indians as "savages" and endorses a policy of leading them to "civilized life" under the guidance of the Catholic Church.[38] These particular elements of Law 89 have been nullified by a new constitutional and legislative order that incorporates international standards of respect for indigenous peoples' own religious practices and cultural traditions.[39] Indeed, the system of reserves authorized by the 1890 statute has been revitalized to support the territorial aspirations of indigenous communities in Colombia. Until recently, the constitution of Argentina characterized the power of the national legislature in respect of Indian peoples in the following terms: "to maintain peaceful relations with the Indians, and to promote their conversion to Catholicism."[40] The adoption of a reformed constitution in 1994 voided this provision of nineteenth-century origins.[41] The Brazilian Congress has been considering a new "Statute on Indian Societies," which would replace the parts of Brazil's 1916 Civil Code establishing a regime of government tutelage over those Indians still regarded as "savages."[42] Recognizing anachronistic elements of the Canadian Indian Act[43] in light of current standards, the Canadian Parliament has enacted certain amendments granting more powers to Indian "bands" over membership and taxation and has supplanted the act for specific Indian groups through legislation based upon agreements with those groups.[44]

Legislative enactment or constitutional revision beyond purging domestic law of anachronistic elements is typically required or useful in states with significant indigenous populations. In such states, including those with federal structures, the constitutional power of the central legislative body to legislate in areas of concern to indigenous peoples tends to be broad. Duly enacted legislation may provide an impetus and framework for the executive to negotiate indigenous peoples' demands, as, for example, the U.S. legislation supporting initiatives toward greater Indian self-government. Legislation may also be a necessary or preferred means of ultimately adopting specific measures for the benefit of particular indigenous groups, as it has been in the case of Canadian parliamentary approval of various self-government and land settlement agreements with diverse groups.[45] In a number of other countries, framework legislation has been enacted to demarcate indigenous lands and territories or to otherwise establish programs for the benefit of indigenous groups,[46] as in the case of the Nicaraguan land demarcation and titling law, enacted in the aftermath of the inter-American Court's judgment in *Awas Tingni*.[47] Legislation ordinarily will be required to implement measures securing the rights of indigenous peoples, where the measures are not easily reconcilable with the existing land tenure regime or where they involve substantial reallocation of resources or governmental authority. In some cases a reallocation of government resources or authority may require or be aided by constitutional amendment.[48]

Legislative programs may focus on particular issues of common concern to indigenous peoples. An example of such issue-specific legislation is the U.S. Native American Graves Protection and Repatriation Act of 1990,[49] a regime of rules and procedures to secure Native American interests in ancestral remains, burial grounds, and funerary objects. The act, devised in close consultation with Indian leaders and advocacy organizations, advances the implementation of international norms concerning indigenous cultural integrity.[50]

The implementation of international norms may more generally be promoted by constitutional or statutory provisions. Several American states have amended their constitutions or passed legislation in recent years to broadly affirm indigenous peoples' rights in a way consistent with the developing international norms.[51] Constitutional or statutory provisions that give domestic legal expression to international norms, even if only in modest form, may substantially motivate the implementation of the norms in concrete settings. Norms that have constitutional status typically are accorded the highest level of respect within the domestic realm of both public and private decision making, and the institutions of government usually place the highest priority on securing compliance with constitutional norms. Statutory prescriptions may give more detailed expression to typically broad constitutional prescriptions, further clarifying and specifying the bounds of decision making within public and private sectors.

The constitutions of many countries include provisions that give domestic legal status to international conventional or customary law in general.[52] Under these constitutions, relevant international legal standards concerning indigenous peoples, even if not specifically mentioned in domestic law, theoretically have at least the same status as domestically enacted law via the incorporation provision. Even so, the specific content of international norms incorporated by general reference may be subject to the vagaries of interpretation, especially where customary norms are concerned. Thus, it is desirable in any event that domestic constitutional or statutory law expressly include prescriptions reflecting contemporary international norms concerning indigenous peoples.

Judicial Procedures

In modern states the judicial branch of government plays an important, if not ultimately definitive, role in the application and development of legal prescriptions. Accordingly, international law, as manifested in several multilateral treaties, obligates states to provide adequate and effective judicial procedures to address claims of human rights violations. Access to adequate and effective judicial process is itself treated as a human right.[53] Charged with the even administration of justice and usually more insulated from the politics of power and economic interest than the other branches of government,[54] the judiciary is, at least potentially, an important conduit for implementing international norms concerning indigenous peoples. Ideally, the judiciary should function to complement, give effect to, or correct the actions or inactions of the other branches of government that bear upon these norms.

Domestic constitutional or statutory prescriptions that reflect or otherwise give effect to international norms may be invoked in judicial proceedings within ordinary constraints on jurisdiction and justiciability.[55] In addition, in some countries domestic tribunals may directly apply as rules of decision international customary norms or provisions in treaties that have been ratified in accordance with relevant constitutional procedures.[56] At the very least, domestic courts usually are capable of *indirectly* implementing international norms by using them to guide judicial interpretation of domestic rules. Thus, provisions of ILO Convention No. 169 on Indigenous and Tribal Peoples[57] have been invoked and applied, directly or indirectly, in judicial proceedings in countries that have ratified the convention.[58] Likewise, domestic courts have applied article 27 of the International Covenant on Civil and Political Rights[59] in cases involving indigenous group claims.[60]

International law was a factor in the early U.S. Supreme Court cases concerning the status of Indian peoples, emblematic cases that continue to influence judicial decision making in common law jurisdictions. The Supreme Court decision in *Worcester v. Georgia*,[61] particularly, can be cited as an example of the application of international law by the domestic judiciary. In its 1832 decision in *Worcester*, the Court invoked international legal doctrine of the period to conclude that the Cherokee people had "original natural rights," that the Cherokee's legal status was that of a political community under the protection of the United States akin to the "tributary or feudatory" states of Europe, and that as a consequence Georgia could not extend its criminal jurisdiction over Cherokee territory.[62] *Worcester* was decided on the premise, emphasized by the Supreme Court decades later in *The Paquete Habana*,[63] that "[i]nternational law is part of our law, and must be ascertained and administered by the courts of justice of appropriate jurisdiction, and as often as questions of right depending upon it are duly presented for their determination."[64] International law, including its formulation in the context of indigenous peoples, has undergone significant evolutionary changes since *Worcester* was decided.[65] Nonetheless, as it evolves it continues to be applicable by United States courts as well as by courts in other countries whose constitutional framework automatically incorporates binding treaty or customary law into domestic law.[66]

The import of *Worcester* as an example of domestic judicial application of international law, however, can only be correctly understood by reference to the constraints that present themselves in this regard. Even in countries whose courts are empowered to directly apply international law without any implementing legislation, judicial application of express treaty provisions may be limited by the requirement of self-execution—an amorphous doctrine that limits the class of treaty norms that are judicially enforceable.[67] Courts in the United States have held the human rights provisions of the United Nations Charter to be non-self-executing and hence not capable of establishing grounds for a cause of action or otherwise providing judicially enforceable rules of decision.[68] The requirement of self-execution does not apply to customary norms,[69] but it may still be questioned whether a customary norm gives rise to a cause of action as opposed to merely providing a rule of decision in cases otherwise before the courts.[70] In *Worcester*,[71] international law did not function to provide a cause of action but rather was invoked in favor of the defense in a criminal proceeding.[72] Other constraints related to jurisdiction or justiciability may arise in particular contexts. Such constraints may be statutory, constitutional, or based on long-standing, judicially created doctrine; or they may be primarily the result of a court's more context-specific concerns over the bounds of its institutional competency.[73]

A common factor limiting judicial enforcement of international law is the political question doctrine, under which courts have refrained from adjudicating issues deemed fundamentally political or constitutionally committed to the discretion of one of the political branches of government.[74] *Worcester v. Georgia* was authored by Chief Justice John Marshall who, in light of political question considerations, had been more circumspect about the applicability of international law in rendering the U.S. Supreme Court's earlier decision in *Johnson v. M'Intosh*.[75] In that case Marshall declined to question the assertion of U.S. title to Indian lands, even while suggesting that the assertion might be contrary to international law if based upon European discovery alone. In *Johnson*, Marshall was somewhat ambiguous in his view of the legal status of Indian nations,[76] but he nonetheless seemed to perceive the applicable international law as potentially bringing into question U.S. territorial sovereignty and the system of property rights it upheld. Yet unlike the later case of *Worcester v. Georgia*, in which international law would be invoked against the state of Georgia, a political subdivision of the United States, international law in *Johnson* cast a shadow on foundational constitutive elements of the United States itself. Marshall held:

> However extravagant the pretension of converting the discovery of an inhabited country into conquest may appear; if the principle has been asserted in the first instance, and afterwards sustained; if a country has been acquired and held under it; if the property of the great mass of the community originates in it, it becomes the law of the land, and cannot be questioned. So, too, with respect to the concomitant principle, that the Indian inhabitants are to be considered merely as occupants, to be protected, indeed, while in peace, in the possession of their lands, but to be deemed incapable of transferring the absolute title to others. However this restriction may be opposed to natural right, and to the usages of civilized nations, yet, if it be indispensable to that system under which the country has been settled, and be adapted to the actual condition of the two people, it may, perhaps, be supported by reason, and certainly cannot be rejected by Courts of justice.[77]

Marshall's position in *Johnson* presaged a pattern of judicial deference to the political branches of the federal government, particularly Congress, in the field of Indian affairs.[78] And outside this field, the political question doctrine reflected in *Johnson*—or some variant of the doctrine—has functioned repeatedly to thwart judicial review of congressional and high-level executive action bearing upon obligations arising out of international customary or treaty law.[79]

Judicial scrutiny of lower-level executive action with minimal foreign policy implications, however, is less vulnerable to political question considerations. A notable example in the context of Indian rights is *United States v. Abeyta*,[80] in which a U.S. federal district court dismissed a criminal proceeding against a Pueblo Indian who had killed an eagle for religious purposes without a federal permit. Although the court cited the religious free exercise provision of the U.S. Constitution, it based its decision primarily upon the 1848 Treaty of Guadalupe-Hidalgo between the United States and Mexico.[81] The court held that the federal regulatory scheme for obtaining a permit to take an eagle, as applied to Indian religious practitioners, violated the provision of the treaty, which guaranteed religious freedom to the inhabitants of the U.S. territory that had been part of Mexico prior to 1848.[82] The court did not dispute that it would be bound by congressional action overriding the treaty guarantee but held that Congress had not unambiguously intended such action by the eagle protection legislation under which the restrictive federal regulations were issued.

Notwithstanding constitutional or other limitations that may constrain direct judicial application of international treaty or customary law, domestic courts should at least indirectly give effect to international norms concerning indigenous peoples by using them to guide the interpretation and application of relevant domestic rules in cases properly before the courts.[83] This principle holds especially for courts in common law jurisdictions—such as Australia, Canada, New Zealand, and the United States—in which the judiciary has been active not only in interpreting statutory or constitutional law concerning indigenous peoples but also in developing supplemental (if not the foundational) legal doctrine in the common law tradition.[84] Insofar as courts in fact engage in developing and applying the domestic law as it concerns indigenous peoples, they should endeavor to conform the law and its application to international standards. To do otherwise is to risk placing the state at odds with its international obligations.[85] Courts may appropriately use international standards as interpretive tools even if the standards appear in unratified treaties or are otherwise considered nonbinding.[86]

The use of international standards to guide the judicial interpretation and application of domestic rules in the context of indigenous peoples is exemplified in the 1992 decision of the High Court of Australia in *Mabo v. Queensland*.[87] That case involved an effort by aboriginal people to assert rights in lands designated as government, or Crown, lands. The Queensland state government argued that Crown ownership of lands precluded aboriginal rights over the same lands, on the theory that the common law derived from England established "universal and absolute beneficial" ownership in the Crown.[88] In separate opinions the High Court rejected this theory, emphasizing that previous judicial renderings of the common law doctrine in this respect had been based on the premise that the lands were *terra nullius*—that is, legally uninhabited—prior to European settlement, despite the presence of indigenous people. In what is considered the principal opinion in the case, Justice Brennan held that "unjust and discriminatory doctrine of that kind can no longer be accepted."[89] Instead, Brennan reasoned, the common law in its present formulation should be interpreted in conformity with contemporary values embraced by Australian society and also in light of contemporary international law:

> If it were permissible in past centuries to keep the common law in step with international law, it is imperative in today's world that the common law should neither be nor be seen to be frozen in an age of racial discrimination.
>
> The fiction by which the rights and interests of indigenous inhabitants in land were treated as non-existent was justified by a policy which has no place in the contemporary law of this country. . . . The expectations of the international community accord in this respect with the contemporary values of the Australian people. The opening up of international remedies to individuals pursuant to Australia's accession to the Optional Protocol to the International Covenant on Civil and Political Rights . . . brings to bear on the common law the powerful influence of the Covenant and the international standards it imports. The common law does not necessarily conform with international law, but international law is a legitimate and important influence on the development of the common law, especially when international law declares the existence of universal human rights.[90]

Justice Brennan also cited the advisory opinion of the International Court of Justice in the *Western Sahara* case, which critically examined and brought into question the theory of *terra nullius* as a device for the acquisition of sovereignty over non-European peoples.[91]

Bowing to political question considerations akin to those prevalent in *Johnson v. M'Intosh*, Brennan held that the High Court could not question the sovereignty of Australia over the lands in question, nor could it interpret the common law to recognize retroactively indigenous land rights "if the recognition were to fracture a skeletal principle of our legal system."[92] Brennan stressed that the Court's own competency rested on the sovereignty of the Australian state, and that colonial-era common law doctrine was foundational to the Australian system of property rights. However, guided by the "important influence" of international law, the Court found a middle ground. The High Court divorced the issue of sovereignty from that of property and reinterpreted the common law property regime by discarding the previously relied-upon theory of *terra nullius*. The result was a reinterpretation of common law doctrine to recognize "native title": rights of beneficial ownership on the basis of historical use and occupancy, rights alienable only to the state and subject to extinguishment by the state through conveyances or other official acts.[93]

Because they are deemed subject to extinguishment by the state, the domestic common law land rights recognized in *Mabo* have fallen short of the aspirations of many indigenous people in Australia. And indeed the Court in *Mabo* may be faulted for not invoking contemporary international norms that have developed specifically with regard to indigenous land rights in order to inform its assessment of the incidents of native title. Recourse to contemporary international standards, which require attention to the cultural and spiritual significance that indigenous peoples typically attach to lands and to a larger territorial environment,[94] may well have strengthened the character of the land rights recognized in *Mabo*.

The *Mabo* decision nonetheless represents a meaningful use of international law to shape domestic norms in furtherance of indigenous peoples' claims within the framework of institutional constraints faced by a court. However limited, the recognition of native title, achieved in part by reference to the international law of nondiscrimination, undoubtedly advances indigenous peoples' efforts to effectively enjoy rights over ancestral lands.[95] The High Court decision in *Mabo* motivated the political branches of the Australian government to step up efforts to resolve long-standing indigenous land claims. Following the decision, the executive arm of government entered into extensive negotiations with aboriginal leaders.[96] These negotiations led to the Native Title Act, adopted by the Australian Parliament in December 1993, which creates a framework by which indigenous peoples may secure possessory rights in lands and compensation for lands lost.[97] The act appeared to have gone beyond *Mabo* in recognizing the importance of indigenous peoples' continuous use and possession of lands, and in limiting the conditions under which native land rights may be extinguished.[98] But amendments to the act in 1998 diminished the procedural protections for native title and enhanced the possibilities for its extinguishment in favor of nonindigenous economic interests,[99] drawing criticism not only from a broad spectrum of indigenous Australians but also from the U.N. Committee on the Elimination of Racial Discrimination.[100] Hence, these amendments can be counted as a counterexample of the domestic implementation of international norms on the part of a state's legislative body, in tension with earlier advances. The decision of the High Court in *Mabo*, nonetheless, stands as a watershed in the development and domestic implementation of protections for the rights of indigenous peoples.[101]

As these developments illustrate, the judiciary may play an important role in the implementation of international norms, even within the bounds of limited judicial competency to directly invoke the norms or enforce them against the political branches of government. And independently of the extent to which they may be free from domestic legal constraints or judicial scrutiny, the political branches themselves must be attentive to applicable international norms and should serve as conduits for the norms' implementation. Ultimately, the state as a whole is bound to indigenous rights standards embodied in or derivative of treaties to which the state is a party as well as to those standards now part of customary international law. A special, affirmative duty under international law enjoins states to adopt the measures necessary, through their various competent institutions, to give practical meaning to indigenous peoples' rights.

Notes

1. For a discussion of state responsibility to effectively remedy violations of human rights under conventional and customary international law, *see* Theodor Meron, *Human Rights and Humanitarian Norms as Customary Law* 136–245 (1989); B. G. Ramcharan, "State Responsibility for Violations of Human Rights Treaties," in *Contemporary Problems of International Law: Essays in Honour of Georg Schwarzenberger on his Eightieth Birthday* 242–61 (Bin Cheng & Edward D. Brown eds., 1988); Menno T. Kamminga, *Inter-State Accountability for Violations of Human Rights* 127–90 (1992). For a discussion on the law of state responsibility generally, *see* Ian Brownlie, *Principles of Public International Law* 419–56 (6th ed. 1998).

2. *See* Meron, *supra* note 1, at 139, 155.

3. *See* The Case of the Mayagna (Sumo) Awas Tingni Community v. Nicaragua, Inter-Am. Ct. H.R. (Ser. C) No. 79 (Judgment on merits and reparations of Aug. 31, 2001), published in abridged version in 19 *Ariz. J. Int'l & Comp. L.* 395 (2002) [hereinafter *Awas Tingni* case].

4. Draft United Nations Declaration on the Rights of Indigenous Peoples, adopted by the Sub-Commission on Prevention of Discrimination and Protection of Minorities by its res. 1994/45, Aug. 26, 1994, art. 39, U.N. Doc. E/CN.4/1995/2, E/CN.4/Sub.2/1994/56, at 105 (1994), reprinted in the appendix, *infra* [hereinafter Draft United Nations Declaration]. The development of the draft declaration and its status are discussed *supra* chapter 2, notes 89–92 and accompanying text.

5. Resolution on Special Protection for Indigenous Populations, Inter-American Commission on Human Rights, Dec. 28, 1972, O.A.S. Doc. OEA/Ser.P, AG/doc. 305/73 rev. 1, at 90–91 (1973).

6. Boutros Boutros-Ghali, Statement to the United Nations General Assembly, at the Inauguration of the International Year of the World's Indigenous People, Dec. 10, 1992, U.N. Doc. A/47/pv.82, at 12 (1992).

7. U.N. Charter art. 73.

8. *See supra* chapter 1, notes 24–25 and accompanying text (discussing trusteeship notions advanced by Vitoria in the sixteenth century); *id.* notes 136–54 and accompanying text (discussing nineteenth- and early-twentieth-century trusteeship theory and practice).

9. *See supra* chapter 3, notes 105–06 and accompanying text.

10. *See supra* chapter 3, notes 56–61 and accompanying text (discussing the *constitutive* aspect of self-determination, by which the governing institutional order is to be determined according to the will of the people, or peoples, governed); *id.* notes 85–98 and accompanying text (discussing related prescriptions developed in the specific context of indigenous peoples).

11. Such reasoning was invoked by the government of Australia in proposing to develop a compact or agreement with aboriginal people to settle historical grievances. *See*

"Foundations for the Future," Statement by Gerry Hand, Minister for Aboriginal Affairs (Dec. 1987), reprinted in part in Heather McRae et al., *Aboriginal Legal Issues: Commentary and Materials* 29, 31 (1991). *See also* Harvey Feit, "Negotiating Recognition of Aboriginal Land Rights: History, Strategies and Reactions to the James Bay and Northern Quebec Agreement," in *Aborigines, Land and Land Rights* 416, 421–22 (Nicholas Peterson & Marcia Langton eds., 1983) (discussing the advantages of negotiated settlement over judicial determination for the handling of indigenous land claims in Canada).

12. *See supra* chapter 2, notes 26–29; chapter 3, notes 68–69 and accompanying text (discussing the decolonization regime promoted through the United Nations).

13. For references to scholarly works describing the early treaty making with North American Indian nations, see *supra* chapter 1, note 41.

14. *See generally Waitangi: Maori and Pakeha Perspectives of the Treaty of Waitangi* (I. H. Kawharu ed., 1989).

15. *See generally* Bryan Keon-Cohen & Bradford W. Morse, "Indigenous Land Rights in Australia and Canada," in *Aborigines and the Law* 74, 93–95 (Peter Hanks & Bryan Keon-Cohen eds., 1984) (describing framework and procedures of land claims negotiations in Canada); Royal Commission on Aboriginal Peoples, *Partners in Confederation: Aboriginal Peoples, Self-Government, and the Constitution* (1993) (explaining the domestic legal and policy basis for aboriginal self-government); Christopher McKee, *Treaty Talks in British Columbia* (2d ed. 2000) (analyzing the treaty-making process and related issues in the aftermath of the Nisga'a treaty); Committee on Aboriginal Rights in Canada, Canada Bar Association, *Aboriginal Rights in Canada: An Agenda for Action* (1988) (appraising the state of self-government negotiations and implementation of Canadian-indigenous treaties); Departmental Audit Branch, Department of Indian Affairs and Northern Development, *Audit of Community-Based Self-Government Program: Audit Report*, Project 91/101 (Feb. 1993) (describing and assessing initiatives for indigenous self-government started in October 1983). *See also* John U. Bayly, "Entering the Canadian Confederation: The Dene Experiment," in *Indigenous Law and the State* 223 (Bradford W. Morse & Gordon R. Woodman eds., 1988) (describing the Dene Nation attempt to negotiate a separate system of government based on the Dene structures of government for all residents of the MacKenzie area, regardless of race).

16. Aboriginal leaders and their advocates have resisted the Canadian government's usual insistence that traditional, or aboriginal, title to land be forever ceded as a condition for settlement packages that would include recognized land rights. *See* Keon-Cohen & Morse, *supra* note 15, at 95. Aboriginal leaders also have criticized the government's program for negotiating community-based indigenous self-government, a program developed at the ministerial level in the 1980s, because it is premised on a devolution of presumed Canadian *federal power* over Indians as opposed to a recognition of *inherent sovereignty* on the part of indigenous peoples. Controversy over the government's framework of negotiation, however, has not always impeded agreement, nor has it thwarted a trend toward achieving practical solutions that can be seen as guided by contemporary international standards.

17. Under the agreement, the Inuit receive a substantial cash settlement and title to over 350,000 square kilometers within the territory that is under the jurisdiction of Nunavut, a public administrative unit which itself encompasses around 2.2 million square

kilometers. Inuits comprise around 80 percent of the population of the territory and hence are assured a political majority in Nunavut, which has substantial autonomous powers especially over mineral and surface resource development. *See* John Merritt & Terry Fenge, "The Nunavut Land Claims Settlement: Emerging Issues in Law and Public Administration," 15 *Queens L.J.* 255 (1990) (discussing the scope of the powers to be exercised by Nunavut over government and resource management).

18. *See generally* Nunavut Implementation Panel, *Annual Report 1999-2000: The Implementation of the Nunavut Land Claims Agreement* (2000) (available at www.ainc inac.gc.ca/pr/agr/nunavut/ntar00_e.pdf); Charles J. Marecic, "Nunavut Territory: Aboriginal Governing in the Canadian Regime of Governance," 24 *Am. Indian L. Rev.* 275 (2000) (background on the peoples and territory of Nunavut and analysis of the *Nunavut Land Claims Agreement* and relevant legislation).

Another important agreement negotiated in Canada is the Nisga'a treaty, signed in Aug. 1998. This agreement confirms land rights over 2,000 square kilometers within the traditional Nisga'a territory and provides a mechanism for indigenous self-government within the framework of the Canadian constitution. *See* Douglas Sanders, "We Intend to Live Here Forever': A primer on the Nisga'a Treaty," 33 *Univ. British Columbia L. Rev.* 103 (1999). Althought the Nisga'a treaty may be an important step in indigenous-state relations and an important precedent for the realization of indigenous rights through negotiated agreement, it has been the subject of criticism by both indigenous and nonindigenous groups. While some indigenous people express disappointement with some of the concessions made in the treaty, certain nonindigenous groups have expressed disagreement with what they see as illegitimate discrimination on the basis of ethnic characteristics contrary to the Canadian constitution. *See id.* at 105. These criticisms demonstrate the important challenges that indigenous peoples confront in the contemporary practice of treaty making.

19. *See* Indian Self-Determination and Education Assistance Act Amendments of 1988, sec. 209, Pub. L. No. 100–472, 102 Stat. 2296 (1988).

20. For a description of the Tribal Self-Governance Demonstration Project by three of the beneficiary tribes, see Jamestown Band of Klallam, Lummi Indian Tribe, & Quinalt Indian Nation, *Tribal Self-Governance: Shaping Our Own Future—A Red Paper* (June 1, 1989). *See also* Rennard Strickland, "Trying a New Way: An Independent Assessment Report on the Self-Governance Demonstration Project," section 2, p. 1 of *The World of the People*, Sovereignty Symposium VI (June 8–10, 1993, Tulsa, Okla.); Rudolph C. Ryser, "Between Indigenous Nations and the State: Self Determination in the Balance," 7 *Tulsa J. Comp. & Int'l L.* 129 (1999) (analyzing the history and legal and political dynamics that lead to the Tribal Self-governance Project, and describing the agreements within the framework of the project).

21. *See generally* Thomas R. McGuire, "Getting to Yes in the New West," in *State and Reservation: New Perspectives on Federal Indian Policy* 224 (George P. Castille & Robert L. Bee eds., 1992) (discussing the development of U.S. policy in negotiating water rights with Native American groups).

22. *See* R. C. Gordon-McCutchan, *The Taos Indians and the Battle for Blue Lake* (1991). The Passamaquoddy-Penobscot settlement, which came after a complex process of negotiation that engaged the White House, involved a congressionally approved trans-

fer of $54.5 million to purchase land for the tribes and an additional $27 million to be divided evenly between the Passamaquoddies and Penobscots. *See* Jack Campisi, "The Trade and Intercourse Acts: Land Claims on the Eastern Seaboard," in *Irredeemable America: The Indians' Estate and Land Claims* 337, 342–47 (Imre Sutton ed., 1985).

23. The agreement resulted in the Timbisha Shoshone Homeland Act, Pub. L. No. 106-423 (Jan. 24, 2000), S. 2102-3, 106th Cong., which restored parts of the Death Valley National Park to tribal control.

24. This argument is made in Howard R. Berman, "Perspectives on American Indian Sovereignty and International Law, 1600–1776," in *Exiled in the Land of the Free: Democracy, Indian Nations, and the U.S. Constitution* 125 (Oren Lyons & John Mohawk eds., 1992); Siegfried Wiessner, "American Indian Treaties and Modern International Law," 7 *St. Thomas L. Rev.* 576 (1995). It is advanced with particular regard to the Treaty of Waitangi in Jennifer S. McGinty, Student Note, "New Zealand's Forgotten Promises: The Treaty of Waitangi," 25 *Vand. J. Transnat'l L.* 681 (1992).

25. *See supra* chapter 1, notes 120–22, 130–32, and accompanying text.

26. ECOSOC Res. 1989/77 (May 24, 1989).

27. *See Study on Treaties, Agreements and Other Constructive Arrangements between States and Indigenous Populations: Final Report Submitted by the Special Rapporteur, Mr. Miguel Alfonso Martínez*, U.N. Doc. E/CN.4/Sub.2/1999/20 (1999). In particular, the special rapporteur recomended that states establish special domestic institutions to adjudicate indigenous claims, especially treaty-based claims, and that the United Nations convene a seminar to further study establishing an internacional mechanism to address such claims in cases in which they are not resolved domestically. *Id.* paras. 30–17. The rapporteur also identified the contradictory arguments that have been posited concerning the juridical status of historical treaties, and he posited that the relevant questions in this regard are fundamentally ethical ones that cannot be adequately addressed soley through legal reasoning. *See id.* paras. 110–21, 254. Nonetheless, in the final part of his report, the rapporteur concluded, on the basis of a legal analysis, that the historical treaties with indigenous peoples were and continue have international legal status. *See id.* paras. 265–72. The final treaty study was preceded by the following progress reports: *Study on Treaties, Agreements and Other Constructive Arrangements between States and Indigenous Populations: First Progress Report submitted by Mr. Miguel Alfonso Martínez, Special Rapporteur,* U.N. Doc. E/CN.4/Sub.2/1992/32 (1992); *Study on Treaties, Agreements and Other Constructive Arrangements between States and Indigenous Populations: Second Progress Report submitted by the Special Rapporteur, Mr. Miguel Alfonso Martínez* U.N. Doc. E/CN.4/Sub.2/1995/27 (1995).

28. Resolution on Action Required Internationally to Provide Effective Protection for Indigenous Peoples, Feb. 9, 1994, Eur. Parl. Doc. PV 58(II), para. 10, at 4 (1994), reprinted in the appendix, *infra*.

29. *See, e.g.,* Statement by Robert Tickner, M.P., minister for aboriginal affairs, to the Working Group on Indigenous Populations, 9th Sess. at 4 (July 31, 1991) (discussing a process of "reconciliation" with aboriginal people toward some form of agreement); Review of Developments Pertaining to the Promotion and Protection of Human Rights and Fundamental Freedoms of Indigenous Populations, Statement by the Observer Delegation of Canada, delivered by Gerald E. Shannon, ambassador and permanent

representative, to the U.N. Working Group on Indigenous Populations, 8th Sess. at 2 (July 1990) (discussing ongoing self-government negotiations with indigenous communities); Review of Developments Pertaining to the Promotion and Protection of Human Rights and Fundamental Freedoms of Indigenous Populations, Statement by the Observer Delegation of Canada, delivered by Gerald E. Shannon, ambassador and permanent representative, to the U.N. Working Group on Indigenous Populations, 11th Sess. at 3 (July 29, 1993) (describing British Columbia Treaty Commission and related treaty negotiation process); Statement on Recent Developments by Miranda Evans, representative of the Observer Delegation of New Zealand, to the Working Group on Indigenous Populations, 11th Sess. (July 27, 1993) (describing the Maori Fisheries Settlement of Sept. 1992 resulting from claims under the 1840 Treaty of Waitangi); *Report of the Working Group on Indigenous Populations on Its Twelfth Session*, U.N. Doc. E/CN.4/Sub.2/1994/30, at 23 (1994) (comment to the working group by the Australian representative that the U.N. treaty study would be of help in developing an instrument of reconciliation between the Australian government and indigenous peoples of that country).

30. Much of the discussion about the binding character of international law in regard to actions of state institutions has been framed in terms of whether the state adheres to a *monist* or *dualist* legal system. A monist system is one in which international law is deemed to exist as part of the domestic law without any specific act of incorporation, whereas dualist systems require acts of incorporation. As Professor Brownlie notes, however, legal systems "rarely adhere to any very pure form of incorporation." Ian Brownlie, *supra* note 1, at 47. Further, the monist/dualist dichotomy tends to lure analysis away from the more pertinent underlying question of the relative competencies of the institutions of government as they bear on a state's international obligations. *See id.* at 49–50. For these reasons, the discussion that follows avoids the traditional monist/dualist frame of analysis in favor of an approach that focuses on the functions of state institutions as they may be invoked to secure effective implementation of international norms. *Cf.* Legal Division, Commonwealth Secretariat, "The Application of International Human Rights Standards in Domestic Law," 22 *Victoria U. Wellington L. Rev.* (Monograph 4) 1 (1992) (discussing the Commonwealth initiative of 1988, involving a series of conferences and studies, on ways to incorporate international human rights standards into domestic law).

31. *See Awas Tingni* case, *supra* note 3, paras. 152–53.

32. *See generally* Felix Cohen, *Handbook of Federal Indian Law* 48–66 (1942; Univ. of New Mexico Press ed. 1971) (outlining the history of treaty negotiations between the federal government and various tribes from the close of the Revolutionary War to 1871, when Congress ended treaty making with Indian tribes). Some treaty negotiations proceeded pursuant to congressional directive or express statement of support. *See, e.g.,* Omer Stewart, "The Shoshone Claims Cases," in *Irredeemable America* 187 (Imre Sutton ed., 1985) (discussing background of treaties with Shoshone).

33. *See* Carlos Navia Ribera, "Reconocimiento, demarcación y control de territorios indígenas: Situación y experiencias en Bolivia," in *Reconocimiento y demarcación de territorios indígenas en la Amazonía* 145, 146 (Martha Cárdenas & Hernán Darío Correa eds., 1993).

34. Presidencia de la República de Bolivia, Decreto Supremo No. 22609 (1990); Presidencia de la República de Bolivia, Decreto Supremo No. 22610 (1990); Presidencia

de la República de Bolivia, Decreto Supremo No. 22611 (1990). These executive decrees are reprinted and discussed in Carlos Navia Ribera, *supra* note 33, at 174–81.

35. *See* Ley de Servicio Nacional de Reforma Agraria (Bolivia), Ley 1715 de 18 de octubre de 1996, segunda disposición transitoria (mandating the issuance of titles by the Servicio Nacional de Reforma Agraria for the territories recognized by the presidential decrees).

36. *See Awas Tingni* case, *supra* note 3, para. 103.

37. William J. Clinton, "Remarks to American Indian and Alaska Native Tribal Leaders," Apr. 29, 1994, 30 *Weekly Compilation of Presidential Documents*, No. 18, 941, 942 (May 9, 1994). A memorandum by the U.S. Department of Justice states that former President Clinton's position "builds on the firmly established federal policy of self-determination for Indian tribes" that has been supported by previous U.S. presidents, including former Presidents Bush and Reagan. U.S. Department of Justice, Office of the Attorney General, *Department of Justice Policy on Indian Sovereignty and Government-to-Government Relations with Indian Tribes*, June 1, 1995, at 2.

38. Law 89 of 1890, arts. 1, 2. An annotated version of the law is in Roque Roldán Ortega et al., eds., *Fuero Indígena Colombiano* 65 (3d ed. 1994).

39. *See id.* at 65, n. 10 (identifying the modifications promoted by the Political Constitution of Colombia of 1991). By its Law 21 of March 4, 1991, Colombia ratified ILO Convention No. 169 on Indigenous and Tribal Peoples, which is discussed in chapter 2 *supra* at notes 55–73 and accompanying text. The effect of Law 21 within the Colombian constitutional order was to give domestic legal status to the norms of indigenous rights articulated in that convention. Referring to ILO Convention No. 169, the Colombian Constitutional Court declared invalid the articles of Law 89 of 1890 that referred to "savages" and that established the charge of "civilizing" them. *See* Const, Ct. Judgment No. C-139/96 (Apr. 9, 1996). For references to additional relevant Colombian judicial decisions, see *infra* notes 55, 58.

40. Constitution of Argentina art. 67, para. 15 (1853, as amended 1860, 1866, 1898, 1957) (Pan-American Union trans., 1968).

41. *See* Constitution of Argentina (sanctioned by the National Constitutional Convention convened by Law 24.309, 1994). The new constitution directs the Congress of Argentina, *inter alia*, to guarantee respect for the cultural identity of indigenous peoples, to recognize the juridical personality of indigenous communities, and to secure their ancestral land rights. *Id.* art. 75(17).

42. *See* Núcleo de Direitos Indígenas, *Cámara aprova estatuto das sociedades indígenas* (undated press release) (reporting passage on June 28, 1994, of proposed Indian statute by a special commission of the lower house of the Brazilian Congress); Instituto Socioambiental, "Por qué Estatuto das "Sociedades Indígenas?" *Notícias Socioambientais*, Feb. 5 2000.

43. Indian Act. R.S. 1970, c.I-6, s. 1. The act originated within a policy framework of directing the acculturation of Indians into the dominant Canadian society. It defines who qualifies as an Indian and who can live on an Indian reserve, and it determines the terms by which Indian lands and resources are to be managed. For a discussion of the Indian Act and its nineteenth-century origins, see J. Rick Ponting & Roger Gibbons, *Out of Irrelevance: A Socio-Political Introduction to Indian Affairs in Canada* 3–14 (1980).

44. *See* Richard H. Bartlett, *The Indian Act of Canada* 32–36 (2d ed. 1988) (discussing such legislative developments, including legislation to establish aboriginal self-government or self-management, while arguing that they do not go far enough). In addition, following the decision of the United Nations Human Rights Committee in the case of Sandra Lovelace, discussed *supra* chapter 4, notes 48–49 and accompanying text, Canada amended the Indian Act to do away with the provision that denied Indian status to any Indian female who married a non-Indian. An Act to Amend the Indian Act, S.C. 1985, c.27. The Human Rights Committee had held that the provision denied Lovelace, who had married a non-Indian, her right to enjoy the culture of the indigenous group into which she was born.

45. *E.g.*, Nunavut Land Claims Agreement Act, S.C. 1993, c.29; The Sechelt Indian Band Self-Government Act, S.C. 1986, c.27.

46. *E.g.*, Native Title Act 1993 (Commonwealth), No. 110 of 1993 (Australia); Indigenous Law (Number 19, 253 D. of 5/10/93) (1993) (Chile); Statute of Indigenous Communities, Law No. 904 of 1981 (Paraguay); Statute of Autonomy for the Atlantic Coast Regions of Nicaragua, Law No. 28 of 1987. *See Reconocimiento y demarcación de territorios indígenas en la Amazonía, supra* note 33 (discussing developments in South American countries of the Amazon region). Roque Roldán observes that, while there have been advancements generally in South American government policies regarding recognition of indigenous territories, Brazil, Colombia, and Paraguay have taken particularly noteworthy measures, backed by legislation, elevating indigenous territorial rights. Roque Roldán Ortega, "Adjudicación de tierras indígenas en la Amazonía: La Experiencia de los paises," in *id.* at 241, 243–44.

47. *See* Ley de Régimen de Propiedad Comunal de los Pueblos Indígenas y Comunidades Étnicas de las Regiones Autónomas de la Costa Atlántica de Nicaragua, y de los Ríos Bocay, Coco, Indió y Maíz (No. 445) (La Gaceta Diario Oficial No. 16, de 23 de enero de 2003).

48. *See, e.g.*, Political Constitution of Colombia arts. 63, 286, 287, 329, 330 (establishing the foundations for indigenous territorial rights and administrative autonomy); Constitution of the Federated Republic of Brazil art. 231 (foundations for indigenous land rights regime); Political Constitution of Nicaragua art. 181 (as amended 1995) (authorizing a regime of political and administrative autonomy for the indigenous peoples of the Atlantic Coast region of the country).

49. Native American Graves Protection and Repatriation Act, 25 U.S.C.A. secs. 3001–13 (Supp. 1991).

50. *See supra* chapter 4, notes 78–83 and accompanying text (discussing norms related to objects of indigenous cultural heritage).

51. *E.g.*, Constitution of Argentina art. 75(17) (1994) (recognizing indigenous peoples, their distinctive cultural identities, and their ancestral land rights, and authorizing congress to act accordingly); Constitution of Nicaragua art. 5 (as amended 1995) (affirming that the country's indigenous peoples have the right to live and develop according to the forms of social organization that correspond to their historical and cultural traditions); Constitution of the Federated Republic of Brazil art. 231 (1988) (recognizing rights of Indians to their own forms of social organization, customs, language, beliefs and traditions, and original rights over the lands they traditionally occupy); Political Constitution

of Mexico art. 4 (as amended 1992 and 2001) (declaring Mexico a pluriethnic nation and affirming indigenous communities' rights to cultural expression and their distinctive forms of organization); Constitution of Guatemala art. 66 (1985) (pledging to respect and promote the cultural rights of indigenous Mayan groups); Political Constitution of Colombia arts. 286, 287, 329, 330 (1991) (affirming indigenous territories and establishing the foundations for a regime of indigenous autonomy within the administrative framework of the state).

Many of the processes of constitutional reform that have taken place in Latin America are connected to the adoption of ILO Convention No. 169, or otherwise incorporate standards similar to those set forth in that instrument. See Donna Lee Van Cott, *The Friendly Liquidation of the Past: The Politics of Diversity in Latin America*, 262–265, 271–273 (2000) (a discussion on the role of Convention No. 169 in the articulation of a "multicultural constitutionalism" in Latin America).

52. *E.g.*, Constitution of Argentina art. 31 (1994) (establishing treaties as part of the supreme law of the nation); U.S. Constitution art. VI (same); Constitution of Honduras arts. 16, 17 (1982) (establishing international treaties as part of the domestic law and with supremacy over conflicting domestic law). The Russian Constitution expressly accords constitutional status to international law as it concerns indigenous peoples: "The Russian Federation shall guarantee the rights of indigenous ethnic minorities in accordance with universally acknowledged principles and rules of international law and the international treaties of the Russian Federation." Constitution of the Russian Federation art. 69 (1993) (Vladimir V. Belyakov & Walter J. Raymond trans., 1993).

53. *See, e.g.*, American Convention on Human Rights, Nov. 22, 1969, OAS Treaty Ser. No. 36, 1144 U.N.T.S. 123 (entered into force July 18, 1978), art. 8. (establishing the right to a fair trial by a competent, independent, and impartial tribunal in the determination of criminal charges), art. 25 (establishing the right to effective judicial protection by a competent court or tribunal); International Covenant on Civil and Political Rights, Dec. 16, 1966, G.A. Res. 2200(XXI), 999. U.N.T.S. 171 (entered into force Mar. 23, 1976), art. 2(3) (ensuring the right to an effective remedy as determined by competent judicial, administrative or legislative authorities), art. 14(1) (establishing the right to a fair and public hearing by a competent and impartial tribunal in the determination of criminal charges).

54. *Cf.* Alexander M. Bickel, *The Least Dangerous Branch: The Supreme Court at the Bar of Politics* (1962) (a characterization of the U.S. judiciary and rationale for its power of review over the coordinate branches of government).

55. For example, the provisions of Colombia's constitution regarding indigenous territorial and autonomy rights can be seen as roughly corresponding with contemporary international standards, Political Constitution of Colombia arts. 286, 287, 329, 330 (1991). These provisions have been the bases of judgments by the Constitutional Court of Colombia that have been favorable to indigenous groups. *E.g.*, Const. Ct. Judgment No. T-257 (1993) (Case of Asociación Evangélica Nuevas Tribus) (affirming indigenous territorial rights as the basis for denying missionary group access to indigenous lands); Const. Ct. Judgment No. T-188 (1993) (Case of Crispín Laoza) (holding government officials in violation of indigenous property rights for not acting on petition to demarcate indigenous lands). *But see* Const. Ct. Judgment T-405 (1993) (Case of Comunidad

Indígena de Monochoa) (upholding installation of antinarcotics trafficking radar on indigenous lands, reasoning that indigenous peoples' constitutionally–protected territorial and cultural interests may be outweighed by the interests of the nation as a whole). Similarly, the Canadian constitutional affirmation of "existing aboriginal and Treaty rights," Constitution Act, 1982, s.35, has been the source of litigation and judicial decisions responsive to the demands of indigenous peoples in Canada. In Sparrow v. R., [1990] 1 S.C.R. 1075, the Supreme Court of Canada held that s.35(1) of the Constitution Act affirms aboriginal fishing rights and that such rights were not extinguished by the Canadian Fisheries Act. *See also*, Delgamuukw v. British Columbia [1997] 3 S.C.R. 1010 (validating claim to constitutionally-protected aboriginal title on the basis of oral evidence); Regina v. McPherson, (1994) 111 D.L.R. 278 (holding that provincial laws must be deemed inapplicable to aboriginal persons when conflicting with aboriginal treaty rights). *See also* Supreme Court (Nicaragua) Judgment No. 23 (Caso Comunidad Indígena Rama Kay) (June 13, 2000) (applying indigenous land rights provisions of constitution and statute of autonomy to invalidate permits issued by government agencies to third parties); State of Roraima Federal Court (Brazil), Process No. 92, 0001615-4 (July 16, 2001) (applying provisions of the Constution of Brazil to upold government demarcatation of Yanomami lands on the basis of traditional occupancy and ruling against the asserted claims of third party over a part of the same land).

56. The extent to which a domestic court will give effect to international law is a function of the court's jurisdiction and the status accorded international law vis-à-vis domestic law within the applicable constitutional scheme. The U.S. Constitution and interpretive practice, for example, places U.S.–adopted treaties and customary law among the federal law, which comprises "the supreme law of the land," U.S. Const. art. VI. *See Restatement of the Law (Third): The Foreign Relations Law of the United States*, secs. 102, 111–15 (1987). Thus U.S. courts, within the boundaries of their jurisdiction to enforce federal law, may sometimes directly invoke international treaty and customary norms as rules of decision. Argentina, Brazil, Colombia, Mexico, and other American states also entail systems by which treaties ratified in accordance with the constitution are directly enforceable through courts of competent jurisdiction. *See* Kaye Hollowaye, *Modern Trends in Treaty Law: Constitutional Law, Reservations and the Three Modes of Legislation* 311–13 (1967); Brownlie, *supra* note 1, at 47–48; Guido F. S. Soares, "The Treaty-Making Process under the 1988 Federal Constitution of Brazil," 67 *Chi.-Kent L. Rev.* 495, 507–08 (1991). By contrast, in Australia, Canada, New Zealand, and other British Commonwealth countries in which the executive may enter treaties without legislative approval, treaties are not part of the body of law ordinarily binding upon the courts; treaty norms thus can only become rules of decision for courts through specific legislative acts of incorporation. *See* Günther Doeker, *The Treaty-Making Power in the Commonwealth of Australia* (1966); Allen E. Gotleib, *Canadian Treaty-Making* 4–6 (1968); Philip A. Joseph, *Constitutional and Administrative Law in New Zealand* 431 (1993) (citing cases from New Zealand and other Commonwealth jurisdictions); Brownlie, *supra* note 1, at 45–46 (citing cases from Canada and the United Kingdom); Andrée Lawrey, "Contemporary Efforts to Guarantee Indigenous Rights under International Law," 23 *Vand. J. Transnat'l L.* 703, 735–38 (1990) (discussing incorporation of treaties by legislation in New Zealand and Canada). On the other hand, courts in many

of these same Commonwealth countries may be found to invoke *customary* international norms, at least in the absence of a controlling domestic rule, *see* Brownlie, *supra* note 1, at 41–44, or to invoke treaty or customary norms in the course of developing the domestic common law, *see infra* notes 83–91 and accompanying text. As can be seen, the treatment of international law by domestic tribunals is extremely variable and often involves complex constitutional and jurisdictional issues beyond the scope of this discussion. The point here is that at least limited possibilities exist in a number of states for direct judicial application of international treaty or customary norms. *See generally* Anne Bayefsky & Joan Fitzpatrick, "International Human Rights Law in United States Courts: A Comparative Perspective," 14 *Mich. J. Int'l L* 1 (1992); Richard B. Lillich, "The Role of Domestic Courts in Enforcing International Human Rights Law," in *Guide to International Human Rights Practice* 228 (Hurst Hannum ed., 1992).

57. Convention (No. 169) Concerning Indigenous and Tribal Peoples in Independent Countries, June 27, 1989, International Labour Conference (entered into force Sept. 5, 1990), reprinted in the appendix, *infra* [hereinafter ILO Convention 169].

58. *See, e.g.*, the following decisions of the Colombian Constitucional Court applying provisions of ILO Convention 169: Const. Ct. Judgment No. T-254/94 (1994) (backing the decision of an indigenous authority to expel a member of the community, relying on articles 8 and 9 of Convention No. 169 which concern indigenous customary law and penal matters); Const. Ct. Judgment No. C-139/96 (1996) (declaring invalid various articles of the Ley de Resguardos Indígenas of 1890 on the basis of Convention No. 169); Const. Ct. Judgment No. SU-039/97 (1997) (ruling a against a government permit for oil exploration that affected the U'wa people, on the grounds that the permit was granted without consultation in accordance with ILO Convention No. 169); Const. Ct. Judgment No. SU-510/97 (1998) (upholding the decision of an indigenous community to refuse entry by evangelical clergy, on the basis, *inter alia*, of the regime of territorial autonomy promoted by Convention No. 169); Const. Ct. Judgment No. T-652 (1998) (providing relief to an Embera-Katio community against a hydroelectric Project, citing the consultation requirements of ILO Convention No. 169). Similarly invoking ILO Convention No. 169 are the following decisions of the Costa Rican Supreme Court of Justice: S. Ct. Decision 2253/96 (1996) (declaring unconstitutional parts of the law creating a national commission on indigenous issues because those parts were deemed to undermine rights of indigenous participation recognized in Convention No. 169); S. Ct. Decision 3515-97 (1997) (granting relief to various indigenous organizations against cuts in the budget for the national commission on indigenous issues, on the grounds that the budget cuts were contrary to the state's obligation under article 2 of Convention No. 169 to effectively implement indigenous peoples' rights). Compare S. Ct. Decision 3197-95 (1995) (ruling against a challenge to a government decree, finding that the affected indigenous people were adequately consulted in accordance with Convention No. 169).

59. *See* International Covenant on Civil and Political Rights, *supra* note 53, art. 27.

60. *See, e.g.*, Kayano et al. v. Hokkaido Expropriation Comm. (The Nibutani Dam Decision) [March 27, 1997] (Sapporo District Ct., Japan), 38 I.L.M. 394 (1999) (applying article 27 to find illegal the building of a dam that adversely affected the interests of the Ainu people, which the court found to qualify as indigenous, but denying relief on

public interest grounds because the dam was near completion); Supreme Court of Finland, No. 117 (June 22, 1995) (recognizing Saami reindeer herding as protected under art. 27, but finding that plans for logging operations did not violate the article); Supreme Administrative Court of Finland, Nos. 692 and 693 (Mar. 31, 1999) (government authorized mineral exploration ruled in violation of Saami cultural rights protected under article 27 and the Finnish constitution because of its potential effects on Saami reindeer herding).

61. 31 U.S. (6 Pet.) 515 (1832).

62. *Id.* at 559–61. *Worcester* and its international legal foundations are discussed more fully *supra* in chapter 1, notes 84–94 and accompanying text.

63. 175 U.S. 677 (1900).

64. *Id.* at 700.

65. *See supra* chapter 1 (discussing the evolution of international law from the colonial period through the early twentieth century, particularly in regard to indigenous peoples).

66. *See supra* note 56.

67. *See, e.g.*, Dreyfus v. von Finck, 534 F.2d 24, 30 (2d Cir.), *cert. denied*, 429 U.S. 835 (1976) ("It is only when a treaty is self-executing, when it prescribes rules by which private rights may be determined, that it may be relied upon for the enforcement of such rights"). Argentina and Mexico also apply a self-execution doctrine. *See* Virginia A. Leary, *International Labour Conventions and National Law* 70–71, 82–88, 101–12 (1982) (discussion of the requirement of self-execution in Argentina and Mexico as applied to ILO conventions). Professor Lillich has observed that "while there is general agreement about the effects of a self-executing treaty, there is considerable confusion about the criteria to be used in determining whether a treaty is self-executing in the first place." Lillich, *supra* note 56, at 229. For additional discussion of the requirement of self-execution as developed in United States courts, see Jordan J. Paust, "Self-Executing Treaties," 82 *Am. J. Int'l L.* 760, 769 (1988); Bayefsky & Fitzpatrick, *supra* note 56, at 45–46.

68. *E.g.*, Manybeads v. United States, 730 F. Supp. 1515, 1521 (D. Ariz. 1989); Frovolo v. U.S.S.R., 761 F.2d 370, 374 (7th Cir. 1985); Sei Fujii v. California, 38 Cal. 2d 718, 722–24, 242 P.2d 617, 619–22 (1952). In Manybeads v. United States, 730 F. Supp. at 1520–21, a U.S. federal district court rejected arguments that the relocation of Navajo Indians pursuant to the Navajo-Hopi Land Settlement Act violated the U.N. Charter. In addition to stating that the U.N. Charter is not self-executing, the court concluded that the relocation scheme devised by Congress would in any event not violate the United States' international obligations. *Id.* Cf. *In re* Alien Children Education Litigation, 501 F.Supp. 544, 589–90 (S.D. Tex. 1978), *aff'd* (5th Cir. 1981), *aff'd sub nom*, Plyler v. Doe, 437 U.S. 202 (1982) (holding that the provision affirming a right to education in the Charter of the Organization of American States, as amended by the 1967 Protocol of Buenos Aires, is non-self-executing).

Another international treaty relevant to indigenous peoples in the United States is the International Covenant on Civil and Political Rights, adopted by the United States in 1992. In ratifying the covenant, however, the U.S. Senate did so subject to a declaration of non-self-execution. Such declarations have become the standard for other human rights treaties adopted by the United States or proposed for U.S. adoption. *But see* Jordan Paust, "Avoiding 'Fraudulent' Executive Policy: Analysis of Non-Self-Execution of the Covenant on Civil and Political Rights," 42 *DePaul L. Rev.* 1257 (1993) (advancing several arguments for considering the non-self-execution declaration attached to the covenant to be invalid).

69. *See* Lillich, *supra* note 56, at 235–37; Bayefsky & Fitzpatrick, *supra* note 56, at 47.

70. In Filartiga v. Peña-Irala, 630 F.2d 876 (2d Cir. 1980), the U.S. Court of Appeals for the Second Circuit upheld an action for violation of the customary human rights norm against torture in a suit brought under the Alien Tort Claims Act, 28 U.S.C. sec. 1350. The act provides federal court jurisdiction over suits by aliens involving torts in violation of international law. The extent to which other human rights norms can be grounds for a cause of action without specific domestic legislation in addition to the Alien Tort Claims Act has been a matter of some controversy. Representing one extreme in the debate is Judge Bork's concurrence in Tel-Oren et al. v. Libyan Arab Republic, 726 F.2d 774, 819 (D.C. Cir. 1984), *cert. denied*, 470 U.S. 1003 (1985), in which he said that "[c]urrent international human rights law, in whatever sense it may be called 'law,' . . . does not today generally provide a private right of action." *See generally* Jordan J. Paust et al., *International Law and Litigation in the U.S.* (2000).

71. 31 U.S. (6 Pet.) 515 (1832).

72. *Worcester* involved a criminal prosecution by the state of Georgia for alleged criminal violations in Cherokee territory. *See supra* chapter 1, note 84.

73. For a comprehensive discussion and compilation of materials on this subject in the U.S. context, see David Weissbrodt et al., *International Human Rights: Law, Policy and Process* 569–81 (3d ed. 2001). *See also* Bayefsky & Fitzpatrick, *supra* note 56, at 82–89 (discussing the "countermajoritarian specter" which limits the propensity of courts to give force to international norms that have not arisen through normal domestic democratic processes, especially where to do so would result in a decision against another public institution).

74. *See generally* Geoffrey Lindell, "The Justiciability of Political Questions: Recent Developments," in *Australian Constitutional Perspectives* 191–218 (H. P. Lee & George Winterton eds., 1992) (a comparative discussion of the political question doctrine as developed in the United States, Australia, and Canada).

75. 21 U.S. (Wheat.) 543 (1823).

76. *See supra* chapter 1, notes 75–76, 91–95, and accompanying text (describing Marshall's characterization of Indian peoples in terms that deemphasized their character as political communities with rights as such, terms unlike those later used in *Worcester* to ascribe the status of "nation" to the Cherokee people).

77. 21 U.S. at 591–92.

78. Through this pattern, the political question doctrine has developed a particular strain in the context of Indian rights; the U.S. Congress is deemed to have "plenary" authority over Indian affairs, subject only to a minimal rationality standard of judicial review. *See, e.g,* United States v. Kagama, 118 U.S. 375 (1886); Lone Wolf v. Hitchcock, 187 U.S. 553 (1903); Morton v. Mancari, 417 U.S. 535 (1974); Delaware Tribal Business Comm. v. Weeks, 430 U.S. 371 (1980). Under this doctrine, the courts have deferred to

congressional enactments even when directly opposed to prior treaties entered into with Indian tribes and acknowledged to be part of United States law. *E.g.*, *Lone Wolf*, 187 U.S. at 564; Seneca Nation of Indians v. Brucker, 262 F.2d 27 (D.C. Cir. 1958), *cert. denied*, 360 U.S. 909 (1959). *See generally* Nell Jessup Newton, "Federal Power Over Indians: Its Sources, Scope, and Limitations," 132 *U. Pa. L. Rev.* 195 (1984).

79. U.S. courts have been especially reluctant to enforce international law against executive decisions involving foreign relations or wartime activities. *E.g.*, Committee of U.S. Citizens Living in Nicaragua v. Reagan, 859 F.2d 929 (D.C. Cir. 1988); Sanchez-Espinoza v. Reagan, 568 F. Supp. 596 (D.D.C. 1983), *aff'd on other grounds*, 770 F.2d 202 (D.C. Cir. 1985); Industrial Panificadora, S.A. v. United States, 763 F. Supp. 1154 (D.D.C. 1991). *See also* Garcia-Mir v. Meese, 788 F.2d 1446 (11th Cir. 1986) (rejecting Cuban aliens' efforts to secure release from detention on international human rights grounds, where such detention was pursuant to attorney general's decision). In the case of congressional legislative action conflicting with previously adopted treaties, judicial deference to the later legislative action is supported by the "last in time" rule. Reid v. Covert, 354 U.S. 1, 18 (1957). Courts generally will not apply customary law in the face of a conflicting act of Congress, regardless of which came last. Weissbrodt et al., *supra* note 73, at 707. Some commentators have argued, however, that the later-in-time rule should apply between a customary norm and an executive decision. *E.g.*, Frederic L. Kirgis, "Federal Statutes, Executive Orders and Self-Executing Custom," 81 *Am J. Int'l L.* 371 (1987).

80. 632 F. Supp. 1301, 1301 (D.N.M. 1986).

81. The principal function of the Treaty of Guadalupe-Hidalgo, 9 Stat. 992 (1848), was to end the war between Mexico and the United States. The treaty ceded vast territories to the United States and secured guarantees for the people of those territories including the Pueblos Indians. The court in *Abeyta* characterized the treaty thusly:

> Because the Treaty of Guadalupe Hidalgo afforded protection to the pueblos, however, it is in this dimension more than a settlement between then-hostile nations: it is a living Indian treaty. It memorializes a pledge to the Mexican nation that the United States would honor the rights of Indians living in the ceded territory at the time the Treaty was executed.

632 F. Supp. at 1305.

82. *Id.* at 1307. *Abeyta* contrasts with the Supreme Court's decision in United States v. Dion, 476 U.S. 734 (1986), a case involving the killing of eagles by Indians, but not for religious purposes. In *Dion* the Court held that the federal Eagle Protection Act abrogated the right of Indians to hunt eagles under the treaty of 1958 between the United States and the Yankton Sioux. The Court added, however, that it was not passing on the religious freedom dimensions of the right affirmed in *Abeyta*.

83. *See, e.g.*, S. Ct. (Venezula) Judgment No. 392-1998 (1998) (declaring a municipal ordinance unconstitutional on the grounds that it undermined indigenous land rights, citing standards articulated Convention No. 169 even though at the time Venezuela was not a party to the convention); S. Ct. (Venezuela) Judgment No. 2019-2000 (2000) (declaring a concesion for natural resource exploitation to be void because of a lack of adequate consultation with the affected indigenous groups, citing the requirements of Convention No. 169).

84. The development of judicial doctrine on indigenous rights in the United States is detailed in: Robert N. Clinton et al., *American Indian Law: Native Nations and the Federal System* (4th ed. 2003); David Getches et al., *Federal Indian Law: Cases and Materials* (4th ed. 1998). Both of these casebooks also include comparative law sections addressing the development of relevant judicial doctrine in Canada, New Zealand, and Australia. Clinton et al., *supra* at 1447–1606; Getches et al., *supra* at 976–1026.

85. As Chief Justice Marshall of the U.S. Supreme Court stated in Murray v. The Schooner Charming Betsy, 6 U.S. (2 Cranch) 64, 118 (1804), "an act of congress ought never to be construed to violate the law of nations, if any other possible construction remains." In this same vein, Chief Justice Dickason of the Canadian Supreme Court, in speaking for the majority in Slaight Communications Inc. v. Davidson, [1989] 1 S.C.R. 1038, 1056–57 (Can.), said, "Canada's international human rights obligations should inform not only the interpretation of the content of the rights guaranteed by the [Canadian] Charter [of Rights and Freedoms] but also the interpretation of what can constitute pressing and substantial [Charter] objectives which may justify restrictions upon those rights."

86. Instructive is the plurality opinion of the U.S. Supreme Court in Trop v. Dulles, 356 U.S. 86, 101–02 (1957), in which the Court held that the constitutional prohibition of cruel and unusual punishment should "draw its meaning from the evolving standards that mark the progress of a maturing society" and accordingly referred to the evident consensus of the international community in this regard. More recently, the U.S. Supreme Court invoked international standards in Lawrence v. Texas, 532 U.S. 558 (2003).

87. (1992) 175 C.L.R. 1.

88. *Id.* at 25 (per Brennan, J.).

89. *Id.* at 42 (per Brennan, J.). Chief Justice Mason and Justice McHugh expressly agreed with the conclusions and reasoning of Justice Brennan's opinion. Justices Deane and Gaudron jointly authored an opinion, and Justice Toohey wrote an additional one, each in most respects concurring with Brennan's. Justice Dawson was the sole dissenter.

90. *Id.* at 41–42 (per Brennan, J.).

91. *Id.* at 40–41 (per Brennan, J.) (citing Western Sahara, 1975 I.C.J. 12). *See also* 175 C.L.R. at 181–82 (per Toohey, J.). The *Western Sahara* case, and its treatment of the theory of *terra nullius* is discussed *supra* chapter 3, notes 71–75 and accompanying text.

92. 175 C.L.R. at 29, 32–33, 43 (per Brennan, J.).

93. *Id.* at 58–60 (per Brennan, J.), 110–13 (per Deane and Gaudron, JJ.), 182–83 (per Toohey, J.). In recognizing and defining "native title," the Australian High Court in *Mabo* invoked common law precedents in the United States and Canada that established similarly circumscribed indigenous land rights. *Id.* at 60 (per Brennan, J.), 89 (per Deane and Gaudron, JJ.), 183–89 (per Toohey, J.). For a discussion of the principles emerging from the *Mabo* decision, see Michael Hunt, "Mineral Development and Indigenous People—The Implications of the *Mabo* Case," 11 *J. Energy & Nat. Resources L.* 155 (1993).

94. *See supra* chapter 4, notes 90–149 and accompanying text.

95. *See generally Mabo: A Judicial Revolution* (M. A. Stephenson & Suri Ratnapala eds., 1993) (an anthology on the High Court decision and its impact on Australian law).

96. This negotiation process is summarized in International Work Group for Indigenous Affairs, *The Indigenous World: 1993–94*, at 82–83 (1994).

97. Native Title Act 1993 (Commonwealth), No. 110 of 1993. For descriptions of the features of the act and its ramifications, see Peter Butt et al., "'Mabo' Revisited—Native Title Act," 9 *J. Int'l Banking L.* 75 (1994); Rick Ladbury & Jenny Chin, "Legislative Responses to the Mabo Decisions: Implications for the Australian Resources Industry," 12 *J. Energy & Nat. Resources L.* 207 (1994).

98. The act, for example, requires a process of negotiation or mediation involving native titleholders before the government takes certain future acts that may limit or extinguish native title. Native Title Act, *supra* note 97, secs. 26–44. If negotiations fail, the National Native Title Tribunal established by the act may decide the conditions under which the proposed action should go forward, or whether it should go forward at all, taking into account its impact on the life, culture, and tradition of the native title parties. *Id.*, secs. 35, 38, 39. *See generally* Butt et al., *supra* note 97, at 79–80 (describing the negotiation, mediation, and decision-making features of the act).

99. *See* Native Title Amendment Act 1998 (Commonwealth) (Mar. 18, 1999). The 1998 amendments, *inter alia*, limit the category of government acts affecting native title that give rise to the right to negotiate on the part of native title claimants, and it provides for "validation" of government land use grants to non-indigenous interests with the corresponding effect of extinguishing native title. *See* Gary D. Meyers & Sally Raine, "Australian Aboriginal Land Rights in Transition (Part II): The Legislative Response to the High Court's Native Title Decisions in *Mabo v. Queensland* and *Wik v. Queensland*," 9 *Tulsa J. Comp. & Int'l L.* 15–59 (2001). The authors conclude that the amendments constitute an "an effort to severely limit the reach and scope of native title rights in Australia and subject those rights to the interests of traditional economic interests." *Id.* at 167.

100. See *infra* chapter 6, at notes 83–84, discussing the committee's decision under its "urgent action/early warning" procedure and expressing concern about the amendment's compatibility with International Convention on the Elimination of All Forms of Racial Discrimination and calling up on Australia to suspend implementation of the amendments. *See also* United Nations High Commissioner for Human Rights, *Committee on Elimination of Racial Discrimination Urges Australia to Suspend Implementation of Amended Act on Aboriginal Land Rights*, U.N. Doc. HR/CERD/99/29, paras. 1–2 (Mar. 18, 1999).

101. Since the *Mabo* decision and adoption of the original Native Title Act, Australian courts have struggled with defining the nature and attributes of native title in the face of sharply contending political and economic forces. In Wik v. Queensland (1996) 141 A.L.R. 129, the High Court held that government grants of pastoral leases did not have the effect of extinguishing native title, thus casting a shadow on the interests of non-indigenous lease holders, many of them mining companies and other influential industrial actors that derived their interests from such leaseholds. The 1998 amendments to the Native Title Act were in large part motivated by the *Wik* decision. Subsequent to the amendments, the High Court revisited the issue of Native title in Western Australia v. Ward [2002] HCA 28 (Aust.), and Wilson v. Anderson & Ors [2002] HCA 29 (Aust.), and in doing so elaborated upon the hurdles for finding native title rights as well as upon the variable conditions by which such rights may be found extinguished under the amended Native Title Act regime.

III

NORM IMPLEMENTATION AND INTERNATIONAL PROCEDURES

6

International Monitoring Procedures

Previous chapters have discussed the development of international norms concerning indigenous peoples and the duty of states to effectively implement these norms. While arising from dynamics that involve multiple actors extending their influence into the international arena, this regime of international law is to be operationalized through procedures that engage the institutional mechanisms of states at the domestic level. Even so, when the international system functions to generate norms within the ambit of human rights, as it has in this context, it typically also and sometimes simultaneously functions to oversee the norms' implementation by responsible actors. Hence, to encourage the domestic implementation of international norms concerning indigenous peoples are procedures involving international institutions, the subject of the final part of this book.

The relationship between the domestic and international procedural matrices is regulated by the principle of noninterference in matters essentially within the domestic jurisdiction of states, a corollary to the doctrine of state sovereignty, which is reflected in article 2(7) of the United Nations Charter. This principle stems from a policy of favoring decision making at more local levels where possible, including decision making on the implementation of international human rights standards, and it reflects the realities of a world system that is still largely state-centered.

The principle of noninterference in domestic affairs, however, is not absolute, nor does it constitute the impenetrable barrier to international concern into the domestic realm that existed in earlier periods in the development of international law.[1] Today, the principle only conditionally shields states from international scrutiny or intervention in human rights matters arising within their respective spheres of authority. International procedures exist to scrutinize state behavior with regard to human rights, and the intrusiveness of such procedures into the domestic realm is only partly a function of state consent to the procedures. Offending states—regardless of their consent—may find themselves subject to a level of international scrutiny depending upon the gravity of noncompliance with applicable norms or the degree to which violations of human rights linger unchecked by domestic institutions and decision makers.[2]

As noted throughout this book, indigenous peoples in particular have been victims of widespread patterns of officially sanctioned oppressive action or neglect, which has led the international community at large to establish indigenous peoples as special subjects of concern. Indigenous peoples remain vulnerable even in states that have taken concrete steps toward compliance with contemporary international standards concerning their rights. In the United States, for example, despite a resolution of Congress acknowledging and apologizing for historical wrongs against Native Hawaiians, executive officials have attempted to minimize federal responsibility for remedying those wrongs; and Native Hawaiian access to ancestral lands and resources remains threatened by economic forces driven by the tourism industry.[3] In Canada, a government policy of negotiating land rights and self-government agreements with aboriginal peoples did not abate an armed confrontation with the Mohawk people, who saw their sacred ancestral lands being converted into a golf course.[4] In Bolivia, measures to implement and give greater permanency to presidential decrees recognizing indigenous territories have been slow in coming.[5] In parts of Brazil, despite constitutional and legislative land rights guarantees, indigenous peoples continue to see their lands invaded by outsiders, and local politicians advocate the reversal of government policies in the name of economic development.[6] In Mexico, the San Andrés accords agreed to by the government and indigenous leaders to bring an end to the conflicts in Chiapas and to establish an emblematic framework for recognition and protection of indigenous rights were not put into practice because of a lack of sufficient backing by the country's dominant political forces.[7]

These cases exemplify the political and economic forces, even if only forces of inertia, that typically confront indigenous peoples and stand in the way of the full realization of their rights, notwithstanding official state policies affirming those rights. The international system does not today replace mechanisms needed at the state level to secure indigenous peoples' rights. But a level of international competency to promote the implementation of norms upholding indigenous rights and to scrutinize state behavior in this regard is important, and justified, insofar as it may help blunt the countervailing political and economic forces that capture or influence decision making at the more local levels.

Even if not entirely adequate, a number of distinct international procedures exist and function in ways that are in some measure useful to promoting the implementation of norms concerning indigenous peoples. Relevant international procedures include the ongoing monitoring of state policies and practices as they relate to compliance with human rights norms. These procedures may involve periodic reporting by states to international bodies concerned with promoting human rights in general or in particular fields of concern. Continuous or periodic international oversight of official behavior encourages states to secure, within their respective spheres of asserted authority, the implementation of human rights norms. Governments usually want to appear to the world as being in compliance with their international obligations, in order to avoid public condemnation or more serious consequences for violating those obligations. Motivated *to appear* in compliance with their international obligations when under the scrutiny of international bodies, states are more likely *to actually be* in compliance. The monitoring process, furthermore, provides an information base and engenders a dialogue useful to the cooperative promotion of human rights.[8] In addition to reporting or other general monitoring procedures, there are international procedures to adjudicate and provide some form of response to complaints of specific violations of human rights, although these complaint procedures are more limited in their scope of application.

Some of the existing monitoring and complaint procedures within international institutions are part of treaty regimes that define substantive norms; treaty-based procedures usually apply only to the state parties to the governing treaty and with regard to the norms articulated in the treaty. Other procedures are not treaty-based and apply more generally. The remainder of this chapter surveys a number of existing monitoring procedures, both treaty- and non-treaty-based, that have been useful to indigenous peoples' efforts to be secure in the enjoyment of their rights. An examination of procedures that provide for structured adjudication of complaints is found in the next chapter. The following discussion is not exhaustive of all such relevant existing international procedures and their intricacies.[9] Rather, by examining a range of international norm implementation mechanisms as they relate to indigenous peoples and by identifying their essential characteristics, this and the following chapter are intended to inform a general understanding of relevant current institutional capacities and behavior.

The Creation of the Permanent Forum on Indigenous Issues

Heeding the call for such action by the 1993 World Conference on Human Rights, and after a period of evaluation, the U.N. Economic and Social Council established as one of its subsidiary bodies the Permanent Forum on Indigenous Issues,[10] which met for the first time in 2002.[11] The initiative for a permanent U.N. institution for indigenous peoples was premised on the widespread sentiment that existing international institutions and procedures were inadequate to address fully the concerns of indigenous peoples.[12] The relatively weak informal procedures developing in the U.N. Working Group on Indigenous Populations, discussed later, were the only existing procedures that functioned on an ongoing basis specifically for the benefit of indigenous peoples. The other procedures that existed prior to the creation of the Permanent Forum were not created in anticipation of the special genre of problems faced by indigenous peoples as a result of long-standing systemic wrongs against them, and many such other procedures allow limited or no access to indigenous peoples as such.

The Permanent Forum, by contrast, was created with a mandate to advise and make recommendations to the Economic and Social Council specifically on "indigenous issues" and to promote awareness and coordination of the activities concerning these issues within the U.N. system.[13] In addition, eight of the sixteen members who constitute the Permanent Forum as independent experts are named by the president of the Council in consultation with indigenous organizations, and the eight individuals originally named by the Council's president for these positions are themselves leaders of indigenous organizations or peoples.[14] Borrowing from the work method of the Working Group on Indigenous Populations, the Permanent Forum opens its meetings to representatives of indigenous peoples and support groups from throughout the world, in addition to a wide range of government and international agency representatives, providing them the opportunity to raise their concerns and make recommendations in the forum's public sessions.[15]

The definition of the Permanent Forums' particular functions within the framework of its general mandate is still in its early stages of development, such that the forum's role in the monitoring and implementation of international norms concerning indigenous peoples has been limited thus far. The Permanent Forum's work, in accordance with its specific mandate, has centered principally on the review and coordination of the programs of various U.N. agencies that concern indigenous peoples, programs dealing with such areas as economic and social development, health, the environment, culture, and education.[16] This review and coordination of international agency activity, at a time when that activity has an ever greater impact on the lives of indigenous people, entails a process of normative assessment that itself plays an important role in the development and application of relevant international standards that are to guide or bind the behavior of international institutions as well as states.[17] The forum's broad mandate in connection with the concerns and rights of indigenous peoples, and its prominent place within the hierarchy of U.N. organization and within the indigenous movement, will undoubtedly lead to the creation of specialized procedures that will enhance indigenous peoples' access to the international system and further promote the implementation of relevant international standards. But for the Permanent Forum to fully realize its potential to became a major international actor in the monitoring of indigenous peoples' rights, greater expertise and institutional resources will have to be developed within the forum or made available to it, and it will have to develop a method of coordinating its monitoring activities with those of already existing procedures.[18]

Review of Developments by the U.N. Working Group on Indigenous Populations

Despite concerns that the establishment of the Permanent Forum might mean the end of the U.N. Working Group on Indigenous Populations because of perceived or actual redundancies, this working group has continued thus far as a viable institution of the U.N. Commission on Human Right's Sub-Commission on the Promotion and Protection of Human Rights.[19] The informal oversight mechanism that has developed in the practice of the sub-commission working group can be counted as a nontreaty procedure of particular relevance and some utility to indigenous people, and this mechanism can be seen as complementing the work of the Permanent Forum. Under its mandate from the U.N. Economic and Social Council to review developments concerning indigenous peoples, the five-member working group receives written and oral reports from governments, intergovernmental institutions, indigenous peoples' representatives, and nongovernmental organizations (NGOs).[20] The working group has included in its annual sessions, in addition to examination of developments in general, discussions focused around particular themes of interest to indigenous peoples, such as cultural heritage, education, language, land rights, development, and self-determination. Government reports typically focus on progress being made toward securing indigenous peoples' rights, while the reports from indigenous peoples and NGOs typically stress the continuing deficiencies in government action.

No state or institution is formally required to report to the working group, but virtually all states of the Western Hemisphere, Australia, New Zealand, and other states with significant indigenous populations have presented reports at the group's annual sessions, and several have done so with regularity. Since the mid 1990s, indigenous participation in the working group's annual sessions has increased such that the interventions of indigenous representatives have come to dominate the discussion about developments, while participation by state representatives has diminished. Nonetheless, the large volume of written and oral reports by indigenous representatives from around the world, along with the review and summary publication of these reports by the working group, provides for an important measure of scrutiny over state conduct in relation to indigenous peoples in many parts of the world. Several states continue to report periodically to the working group, understanding that if they do not submit reports, the public record compiled by the working group is likely to be dominated by statements focusing on the shortcomings of state conduct or inaction.[21]

The working group allows virtually anyone to speak at its annual public sessions and to submit written material for its consideration. This practice is aimed at allowing indigenous peoples broad access to its deliberations, regardless of official consultative or other status at the United Nations. In the course of the working group's review of developments at its public meetings, indigenous peoples' representatives and NGOs repeatedly have called attention to particular instances of government abuse or neglect. In the early years of the working group, these statements were often interrupted by the working group's chair, who would admonish against making specific complaints. But in more recent years, such interventions usually have been permitted if they communicate mostly facts in an objective manner as opposed to conclusory allegations of rights violations.

Indigenous representatives often look to the working group to take some action in response to their communications. The working group, however, is not equipped to investigate or otherwise respond to the numerous statements it hears alleging violations of indigenous peoples' rights, and hence whatever effect these communications may have is usually limited to the value of their utterance in an official public forum of the United Nations. This value, however, should not be underestimated. Credible statements by clearly authorized representatives of indigenous peoples or respected NGOs may themselves threaten a government with embarrassment. Such statements to the working group often elicit public responses by the governments concerned. In limited instances in which problems have been shown to be particularly grave or have an urgency about them, the working group or its members have provided an ad hoc response. Notably, in the early 1990s the working group took an active interest in the situation of the Yanomami people of Brazil when it became apparent that the Yanomami's physical and cultural survival was being threatened by the invasion of gold miners on their lands, an invasion that the Brazilian government had been slow to abate. Working group members publicly expressed concern for the situation. With the approval of the U.N. secretary-general, the working group chair established direct contacts with the Brazilian government, and she traveled to Brazil to promote a solution to the problems.

The *de facto* monitoring procedure of the working group is simultaneously part of the development of customary international norms and part of their implementation. As discussed in chapter 2, government reports to international bodies on domestic initiatives concerning indigenous peoples made outside the purview of any specific treaty obligation, as in the working group context, provide strong indication of the existence and content of emergent customary norms.[22] While government reports reveal general acceptance of certain standards of conduct in respect to indigenous peoples, the compulsion toward reporting and the accompanying international oversight encourages behavior that can be characterized as in compliance with the accepted standards.

Monitoring by the U.N. Commission on Human Rights, Its Sub-Commission, and Its Special Rapporteur

Related nontreaty monitoring procedures involve the working group's parent bodies within the United Nations, especially the Commission on Human Rights and its Sub-Commission on Promotion and Protection of Human Rights (previously the Sub-Commission on Prevention of Discrimination and Protection of Minorities).[23] Although more generally concerned with human rights matters, both these bodies have come to include agenda items in their annual sessions to consider developments and problems concerning indigenous peoples.[24] Other agenda items of the annual sessions of the commission and sub-commission, such as items on racial discrimination, are also relevant to indigenous peoples. Under these agenda items, states and NGOs in consultative status with the United Nations have submitted statements similar to those communicated to the sub-commission working group, although the reports to the sub-commission itself and the commission have been fewer and less encompassing because of the more limited attention of these bodies to indigenous peoples' special concerns.[25] Unlike the sub-commission and its Working Group on Indigenous Populations, which consist of experts acting in their individual capacities, the Human Rights Commission is composed of government representatives. Hence, political factors play more prominently in its deliberations. On the other hand, because the commission is more elevated in the hierarchy of U.N. organization, the commission may bring to bear greater scrutiny upon the promotion of indigenous peoples' rights.

In addition to providing a forum for discussing indigenous issues at its annual sessions, the Commission on Human Rights authorized in 2001 the appointment, for an initial term of three years, of a "special rapporteur on the situation of human rights and fundamental freedoms of indigenous people."[26] The establishment of this position added to the commission's system of extraconventional, thematic mechanisms which includes special rapporteurs and working groups on matters such as torture, religious intolerance, and forced disappearances.[27] The commission provided the special rapporteur on indigenous peoples with authority to "gather, request, receive and exchange information and communications from all relevant sources" concerning human rights violations against "indigenous people themselves and their communities and organizations," as well as to "formulate recommendations and proposals . . . to prevent and remedy" such violations.[28] The position of the special rapporteur began to function with the appointment of the respected anthropologist Rodolfo Stavenhagen, who presented his first report to the commission in February 2002. In that first report the special rapporteur highlighted in general terms the existence of persistent patterns of human rights violations against indigenous peoples "everywhere," and expressed concern over the "the problem of a 'protection gap' between existing human rights legislation and specific situations facing indigenous people."[29] Furthermore, the special rapporteur's first report indicated that future work would examine a series of issues that are of special importance to indigenous peoples, such as the impacts of development projects on indigenous communities, the implementation of recently enacted domestic laws to protect indigenous rights, the relationship between formal state law and customary indigenous law, indigenous cultural rights, indigenous children, indigenous participation in policy- and decision-making processes, and various forms of discrimination against indigenous individuals.[30]

Following his first report the special rapporteur began examining information on specific situations in which indigenous peoples are experiencing or claiming violations of their human rights. Within the framework of his initiative to examine the impact of large-scale development projects, the special rapporteur conducted an on-site visit to the Philippines, to which the Philippine government reluctantly acquiesced. He reported problems concerning the definition of indigenous land rights in that country, as well as serious human rights violations resulting from development projects, such as the construction of dams, large-scale logging concessions, commercial plantations, and mining, and he provided recommendations on action to address those problems.[31] In addition, the special rapporteur's second report included an annex summarizing numerous communications alleging violations of indigenous peoples rights in several other countries.[32] As revealed in that report, when he receives such a communication the practice of the special rapporteur has been simply to forward it to the governments concerned, to request the government to provide pertinent information, and to include in his report a summary of the government response, if any, along with the summary of the communication. With time it can be expected that the special rapporteur will more fully develop his mandate to examine violations and formulate proposals to remedy them, much like other thematic mechanisms of the Commission on Human Rights have done.[33]

The authority of the special rapporteur on indigenous people is linked to the more general capacities of the Commission on Human Rights and its Sub-Commission on the Promotion and Protection of Human Rights to hear and act in response to allegations of human rights violations. Economic and Social Council (ECOSOC) Resolution 1235(XLII) of 1967 authorizes the commission and the sub-commission to "examine information relevant to gross violations of human rights and fundamental freedoms," and to "make a thorough study of situations which reveal a consistent pattern of violations of human rights."[34] Information of human rights abuses may come from virtually any source. Individuals and groups often communicate such information to the U.N. Secretariat, which in turn functions as an information resource for the commission and its various agencies.[35] NGOs with official consultative status at the United Nations may communicate directly with the commission and sub-commission through oral or written statements.[36] There is no assurance, however, of any response to communications alleging violations of human rights, and in the vast majority of cases no responsive action is forthcoming. Responsive action is entirely discretionary, and the resources available to the commission and sub-commission to address the numerous communications they receive are limited, especially in the case of the sub-commission.[37] In 2001 the Commission on Human Rights decided that the sub-commission should refrain from issuing resolutions that point out human rights problems in specific situations and countries, thereby substantially limiting the capacity of the sub-commission alone to respond to allegations of violations of human rights.[38]

Nonetheless, the authorization provided by ECOSOC Resolution 1235 has been used on several occasions by the Commission on Human Rights, and previously by its sub-commission, to adopt resolutions addressing situations in which specific countries are identified as experiencing human rights problems on broad or systemic scales. Through much of the 1980s and early 1990s, Guatemala, whose majority indigenous population was plagued by grave human rights abuses during that period, was under scrutiny by both the commission and sub-commission. In one of several resolutions on Guatemala, the commission expressed concern for the "grave situation faced since time immemorial by the indigenous populations" and urged "the Government of Guatemala to strengthen the policies and programs relating to [their] situation . . . taking into account their proposals and aspirations."[39]

Acting over a range of situations, including and beyond those clearly falling within the category of "gross violations" contemplated by Resolution 1235, the commission and sub-commission also have responded to allegations of human rights violations through operational fact-finding activities and advisory services.[40] Upon the initiative of NGOs, the sub-commission turned its attention to the dispute surrounding the relocation of Navajo and Hopi families from northern Arizona. The sub-commission authorized two of its members, including the expert from the United States, to investigate the situation, and it adopted relatively mild statements against involuntary resettlement and urging constructive resolution of the dispute.[41] In another case, in response to appeals by Mexican NGOs, the chairman of the sub-commission appointed Erica Daes, then the chairperson of the Working Group on Indigenous Populations, to investigate the situation of indigenous peoples in that country. The investigation resulted in a detailed report in which Daes identified and made a series of recommendations concerning problems of land, self-government, and socioeconomic conditions in connection with the conflicts in Chiapas and in other parts of the country.[42]

A more structured procedure within the Human Rights Commission and its sub-commission is pursuant to ECOSOC Resolution 1503(XLVIII) of 1970. This and related resolutions establish a complex machinery for considering "communications" from individuals and nongovernmental organizations relating to "situations which appear to reveal a consistent pattern of gross and reliably attested violations of human rights."[43] This machinery operates in closed sessions of the commission and a sub-commission working group, and any resulting action is usually through communication with the state concerned without public disclosure.[44] In 1980 the Indian Law Resource Center, a U.S.-based NGO, submitted a petition under the Resolution 1503 procedure on behalf of several Indian nations and communities in the United States.[45] The petition alleged that the effect of U.S. policies and laws concerning indigenous land rights was to deny the petitioners and other Indian peoples their legitimate property interests on a racially discriminatory basis. Despite the confidentiality of the ensuing proceedings, it later became known that the United States was called upon to answer the petition, and hence it joined the ranks of select states subjected to some level of scrutiny under the Resolution 1503 procedure.

Professor Alston has observed that the Resolution 1503 procedure is best characterized as a "petition-information" system, as opposed to a "petition-redress" system, such as the complaint procedures discussed later in chapter 7. This is "because its objective is to use complaints as . . . evidence [which] might, if accompanied by a sufficient number of related cases, spur the United Nations into action of some kind,"[46] rather than to provide an assessment and resolution of each complaint. The same can be said of the other, less structured procedures within the Commission on Human Rights and its subsidiary bodies.

ILO Convention Compliance Monitoring

While non-treaty-based reporting and oversight procedures are neither formally binding upon states nor very structured, treaty-based procedures typically are both binding and structured, at least in certain respects. States that have ratified International Labour Organization Convention No. 169 on Indigenous and Tribal Peoples,[47] or its predecessor ILO Convention No. 107,[48] are subject to the reporting requirements and supervisory mechanisms attached to ILO conventions generally under the ILO Constitution.[49] Required periodic government reports on the implementation of ratified conventions are reviewed by the ILO Committee of Experts on the Application of Conventions and Recommendations. The committee may solicit additional information from reporting governments and often does so, especially if implementation problems are identified. The committee compiles its observations on noteworthy aspects of government reports, highlighting shortcomings in government conduct, and publishes them in its annual report. On occasion, the Committee of Experts may commission an on-site visit to engage in fact-finding or provide advisory assistance. On the basis of the Committee of Experts' report, a committee of the annual Labour Conference designated as the Conference Committee on the Application of Conventions and Recommendations selects a number of problem cases and requests the governments concerned to appear before it to explain the reasons for the identified problems.

Especially noteworthy are the proceedings surrounding reports submitted by Mexico, one of the first countries to ratify Convention No. 169. Parallel to Mexico's reports in the 1990s were several communications by a number of important labor and indigenous organizations alleging Mexico's noncompliance with various aspects of the convention. These parallel communications prompted the Committee of Experts to engage in a close examination of that country's conduct in relation to the convention. The Committee of Experts paid particular attention to the process of dialogue and constitutional reform that followed developments in Chiapas beginning in 1994, reiterating its call for consultations with the relevant indigenous peoples[50] and expressing concern for the "lack of real dialogue between the Government and the indigenous communities to discuss their situation and to find answers to their problems."[51] The committee referred to the initiatives that led to the controversial Mexican constitutional reform of 2001, which was strongly opposed by the Mexican indigenous movement, and it asked the government for details about the reform initiatives and their results.[52] The Committee of Expert's observations on Mexico were on several occasions the subject of discussions within the Conference Committee on the Application of Conventions and Recommendations, in which labor and other government representatives called upon Mexico to adopt effective measures to resolve the problems highlighted by the Committee of Experts.[53]

In addition to the reporting and oversight activity that is proceeding under Convention No. 169, such activity has continued under the older Convention No. 107 of 1957, which remains in effect for those states that ratified the older convention until they ratify Convention No. 169. Although Convention No. 107 includes assimilationist and paternalistic elements at odds with contemporary norms,[54] those elements are now absent from the supervisory activity attached to the convention. The Committee of Experts' published observations on government reports over the last several years indicate that it reviews the reports submitted under Convention No. 107 in light of standards that do not incorporate the now discredited elements of that convention. Exemplary of the committee's practice are its series of observations concerning the obligations of Brazil and Bangladesh as parties to Convention No. 107. Brazil is now a party to Convention 169, while Bangladesh remains a party to Convention No. 107. When both countries were under Convention No. 107, they were subject to particular scrutiny by the ILO's supervisory machinery with regard to the treatment of vulnerable indigenous groups within their borders, especially the Yanomami of the northern Amazon region of Brazil and tribal peoples of the Chittagong Hill Tracts of Bangladesh. In its published observations concerning these countries, the committee has reiterated its interest in reforms in government policy and practice that would secure land rights, self-sufficiency, and cultural integrity for indigenous peoples.[55] The Conference Committee on Application of Conventions and Recommendations also repeatedly examined, within the framework of promoting compliance with Convention No. 107, the situation of indigenous peoples in Brazil and Bangladesh, and it exhibited a similar posture in favor of reforms in those countries.[56]

Thus, the ILO supervisory mechanisms may serve to promote the implementation of contemporary norms concerning indigenous peoples in relation to states that are parties to either Convention No. 169 or Convention No. 107. The ILO supervisory bodies have effectively interpreted government obligations under Convention No. 107, not principally on the basis of that convention's express provisions, but instead according to general normative precepts consistent with the newer Convention No. 169.[57] The use of Convention No. 107 to advance the objectives of the newer convention is entirely appropriate. The central commitment of signatories to Convention No. 107 is to advance the human rights and legitimate interests of indigenous peoples within the convention's scope of concern. It would be anomalous to apply the convention without regard to contemporary standards regarding those rights and interests. A government would be ill advised to report technical compliance with Convention No. 107 by reference, for example, to a long-standing program of indigenous assimilation, where such "compliance" would run afoul of the core precepts of indigenous self-determination and cultural integrity present in Convention No. 169.

Monitoring/Reporting Procedures of the U.N. Human Rights Committee and CERD

Treaty-based reporting and oversight mechanisms within the United Nations include those attached to seven principal U.N. human rights treaties: the International Covenant on Civil and Political Rights; the International Covenant on Economic, Social and Cultural Rights; the Convention on the Elimination on All Forms of Racial Discrimination; the Convention on the Elimination of All Forms of Discrimination against Women; the Convention against Torture and Other Cruel, Inhuman or Degrading Treatment or Punishment; the Convention on the Rights of the Child; and the Convention on the Protection of the Rights of All Migrant Workers and Members of their Families.[58] Each of these treaties and their respective monitoring mechanisms is relevant, within its sphere of concern, to indigenous individuals and, to some extent, to the collective interests of indigenous groups.[59]

The U.N. treaty mechanisms that in practice have been most relevant to indigenous peoples are those based on the International Covenant on Civil and Political Rights and the Convention on the Elimination of All Forms of Racial Discrimination. These two treaties, in addition to articulating substantive norms, respectively create the Human Rights Committee and the Committee on the Elimination of Racial Discrimination (CERD), both of which consist of individuals noted for their expertise in fields of human rights. In line with the other U.N. treaty regimes, each of the treaties requires state parties to submit periodic reports on implementation of treaty norms for review and comment by the corresponding committee.[60] Both committees meet with the reporting governments

to discuss their reports and to inquire about problems. The committees' deliberations and commentary on the reports are summarized and published annually.[61]

The Human Rights Committee established by the Covenant on Civil and
Political Rights has been active in examining government reports bearing upon
the rights of indigenous peoples and in encouraging official policies and behavior in line with contemporary norms, mostly in connection with the minority rights
provision of article 27 of the covenant. As already discussed in chapter 4, the
Human Rights Committee has interpreted article 27 broadly to secure the cultural integrity of indigenous groups, including cultural attributes linked to land
use, economic activity and political organization.[62] This broad interpretation can
be seen to guide the committee in its deliberations and commentary on government reports. Illustrative is the following excerpt from the committee's 2001
summary of its consideration of reported developments in Guatemala:

> Even though the Committee recognizes that the State party has made efforts to
> improve the situation of members of indigenous communities, it regrets that it
> has not been possible to adopt legislation designed to guarantee the full enjoy-
> ment of all their rights under the Covenant, including the restitution of com-
> munal lands, the elimination of discrimination in employment and education
> and participation in other areas of the life of society. The State party should
> continue its efforts to guarantee members of indigenous communities the en-
> joyment of all the rights recognized by article 27 of the Covenant and adopt
> comprehensive legislation for this purpose. It should also ensure that the imple-
> mentation of this legislation improves the situation of members of indigenous
> communities in practice and not only on paper.[63]

A basis for government reporting and committee oversight concerning indigenous peoples, one that is broader than the minority rights provision of the
covenant, is the right of self-determination affirmed in article 1 of the covenant.[64]
Governments have tended to avoid reference to the self-determination provision
of the covenant as a result of confusion and sensitivity over its implications.[65]
The Human Rights Committee, however, increasingly has considered government
reports concerning political participation and group cultural and autonomy rights
as falling under the purview of article 1.[66] In its 1992 summary commentary on
the Colombian government's third periodic report, the committee expressed its
satisfaction at that government's reported progress toward implementing self-
determination through efforts at securing democratic freedoms and the full equality of minority groups.[67] The Colombian government had reported, referring to
its obligations under article 1, constitutional and other reform measures including those intended to "enabl[e] the least advantaged groups to have an influence
in the political life of the nation."[68] The U.S. government went a step further in
its 1994 report to the committee, by extensively addressing the rights and status
of Native Americans under the rubric of article 1 self-determination.[69] The United
States mentioned, among other things, rights pertaining to the self-governing

capacities of Indian tribes and control over economic and cultural development. While both the Colombian and U.S. reports may be criticized for glossing over existing controversies, they nonetheless manifest the scope of coverage accorded article 1.

In reviewing Canada's fourth periodic report under the covenant, the Human Rights Committee took note of "the concept of self-determination as applied by Canada to the aboriginal peoples," while lamenting that Canada had not included an adequate explanation of the application of this concept in its report.[70] Furthermore, the committee urged upon Canada that "the practice of extinguishing inherent aboriginal rights be abandoned as incompatible with article 1 of the Covenant."[71] In the same vein, the committee expressed concerns about state laws and policies in Australia and Norway relating to indigenous lands, making reference to obligations deriving from article 1.[72] In connection with the situation of indigenous peoples in Mexico, the committee called upon the government of that country to take "[a]ppropriate measures . . . to increase their participation in the country's institutions and the exercise of the right to self-determination."[73]

CERD also has regularly considered government reports bearing on indigenous peoples' rights. CERD has considered issues of indigenous peoples within the general framework of the nondiscrimination norm running throughout the Convention on Elimination of All Forms of Racial Discrimination, and not usually in connection with any particular article of the convention which governs the committee's deliberations. Its consideration of government reports in connection with indigenous issues is now guided by the committee's General Recommendation on Indigenous Peoples, a statement of CERD's understanding of the nondiscrimination norm in this context.[74] Within this general framework, CERD has acted much like the Human Rights Committee and effectively promoted the integrity and survival of indigenous groups in line with current developments in normative assumptions.[75] As set forth in its published summaries of country reports and observations, CERD has considered and evaluated a broad range of issues corresponding with indigenous group demands.[76] Its queries of reporting governments from countries in which indigenous peoples live demonstrate that the committee expects such governments to address fairly comprehensively their efforts to secure indigenous peoples' rights.

Upon reviewing the United States' first periodic report under the convention, for example, the committee expressed concern about aspects of U.S. law by which the government purports to "abrogate unilaterally" treaties entered into with Indian tribes and regards the tribes as "domestic dependent nations" subject to its plenary power and guardianship, indicating that such aspects are contrary to applicable international norms.[77] The committee went beyond expressions of concern about indigenous peoples generally in the United States, singling out the specific situation of the Western Shoshone people. It pointedly criticized the application of the cited domestic legal doctrines to the Western Shoshone people, whose traditional lands the United States now regards as it own and targets for military use and resource extraction.[78] Signaling the coherence in its approach in relation to the broader international indigenous rights regime, the committee included in its recommendations to the United States that it look to ILO Convention No. 169 for guidance in its treatment of indigenous peoples,[79] even though the United States is not a party to that convention.[80]

As part of its general human rights monitoring authority, CERD has developed on its own initiative a procedure to examine and pronounce on specific problem situations that come to its attention through whatever means, and it has used this procedure to address indigenous group claims in at least one instance. At its forty-fourth session in 1993, CERD decided to adopt in appropriate circumstances "early-warning measures" or "urgent procedures" to address or prevent the escalation of specific situations of conflict stemming from racial discrimination.[81] Within this framework of preventive measures, CERD may examine a situation without any periodic report from the state party concerned or a complaint under article 14 of the convention.[82] The procedure is initiated by CERD itself or one of its members, although anyone may approach CERD or its members to urge invocation of the procedure.

It was at the urging of a coalition of aboriginal groups of Australia that CERD examined within the early-warning/urgent-action procedure a series of issues concerning land rights and government administration. After requesting and receiving from the Australian government written and oral information responding to the issues raised by the aboriginal groups, CERD adopted a "decision" in which it found amendments to the Native Title Act to be racially discriminatory and expressed its concern about the abolition of the position of the Aboriginal and Torres Strait Islander Social Justice Commissioner.[83] CERD called upon Australia to address these concerns "as a matter of utmost urgency" and urged the government "to suspend implementation of the 1998 amendments and re-open discussions with the representatives of the Aboriginal and Torres Strait Islander peoples with a view to finding solutions acceptable to the indigenous peoples and which would comply with Australia's obligations under the Convention."[84]

Although the norm of nondiscrimination forms the principal basis of CERD's monitoring work, the committee has indicated a disposition toward expressly invoking the principle of self-determination in its deliberations concerning indigenous peoples. For example, in considering Canada's report in 1992, and within the context of examining a range of human rights issues including the dispute between Mohawk Indians and the Quebec provincial government, the committee asked whether Canada had adopted any legislative or constitutional provision concerning the exercise of the right to self-determination.[85] The Canadian government responded that self-determination issues were outside the competency of the committee; however, in that same response it proceeded to provide information about government programs, including initiatives for the benefit of indigenous peoples.[86] Even though the convention against discrimination, which defines CERD's jurisdiction, does not include an explicit reference to the principal or right of self-determination, the committee confirmed that it is competent to examine self-determination issues when it issued its General Recommendation on Self-Determination, which provides an interpretation of the principle and its relationship to the committee's scope of concern.[87]

Country Reports by the Inter-American Commission on Human Rights

An important regional body with oversight functions relevant to the promotion of indigenous peoples' rights is the Inter-American Commission on Human Rights of the Organization of American States. The development of its authority to advance indigenous rights throughout the Americas signals the kind of activities that may be engaged in by other regional human rights bodies, in particular the African Commission on Human Rights which in 2003 established a new working group to focus special attention on and promote the rights of peoples identifying as indigenous in the African region.[88]

Initially established by a simple resolution of foreign ministers meeting in Chile in 1959, the Inter-American Commission on Human Rights became a permanent organ of the OAS by an amendment to the OAS Charter in 1967[89] and its terms of reference were further specified in the American Convention on Human Rights[90] and in the commission's statute.[91] Pursuant to its mandate of promoting human rights among all OAS member states (whether or not parties to the convention),[92] the commission has developed a practice of issuing special reports on human rights situations in particular countries. This practice does not involve mandatory periodic reporting by governments but rather is largely driven by the commission's own initiative, subject ordinarily to the cooperation of the governments concerned.[93] The commission generally gathers information from various sources to compile its reports, and not just from the governments concerned, and it sends a delegation to the country to conduct an on-site investigation.[94] This process of investigation itself places the state under a significant level of international scrutiny, and this scrutiny increases with the publication of a final report, which may be voluminous.

The commission started to show interest in the human rights of indigenous peoples in particular when, in 1972, it resolved that "for historical reasons and because of moral and humanitarian principles, special protection for indigenous populations constitutes a sacred commitment of the States."[95] Subsequent to that resolution the commission began to engage indigenous issues in the context of proceedings initiated by complaints of specific abuses, as discussed in chapter 7.[96] But it was not until more than twenty years later, with its 1993 reports on Guatemala and Colombia, that the commission began a consistent pattern of including in its country reports specific consideration of the situation of indigenous peoples as such.[97] This pattern got under way roughly around the time that the commission became fully engaged in developing what became its Proposed American Declaration on the Rights of Indigenous Peoples, following a mandate by the OAS General Assembly to draft an instrument on indigenous rights.[98] The commission's current reporting practice is reflected by the inclusion of entire chapters on indigenous peoples in the several country reports it has issued since the mid-1990s.[99]

In evaluating the conditions faced by indigenous peoples and making relevant recommendations, the commission's practice has been to favor a progressive interpretation and application of the norms included in the American Convention on Human Rights and the American Declaration on the Rights and Duties of Man. In addition, demonstrating that its mandate is not limited to promoting human rights as they are articulated in the American convention and declaration,[100] the commission takes into account other instruments that are relevant to indigenous peoples, such as ILO Convention No. 169, the International Covenant on Civil and Political Rights, and even the draft declarations on indigenous rights under consideration within the United Nations and OAS.

A noteworthy example of the commission's examination of indigenous issues is in its *Report on the Situation of Human Rights in Ecuador*, in which the commission focused especially on the conditions of indigenous peoples who are affected by the government-authorized oil development in the Amazon region.[101] The commission conducted an on-site visit in which it heard from numerous governmental and nongovernmental sources, including representatives of indigenous organizations and communities. The commission's report concluded, among other things, that the widespread environmental degradation caused by the exploitation of surface and subsurface resources constituted a grave threat to the enjoyment of the right to life of several Amazonian indigenous communities, the right to life being protected in general terms in both the American convention and declaration. According to the commission, "the right to life, and to physical security and integrity is necessarily related to and in some ways dependent upon one's physical environment."[102] In order to arrive at this interpretation, the commission linked the right to life of the American convention and declaration with other international instruments concerning human rights and the natural environment that have been ratified or supported by Ecuador. The commission saw these instruments, read together, as establishing the "critical connection between the sustenance of human life and the environment."[103] Thus the commission in its report concluded that the right to life guaranteed by the American convention and declaration, and associated norms, "in the appropriate case give rise to an obligation on the part of a state to take reasonable measures to prevent such risk [to the environment], or the necessary measures to respond when persons have suffered injury,"[104] and it recommended that Ecuador take specific steps, in consultation with the indigenous peoples concerned, to mitigate the negative effects for them of the development projects in the Amazon region.[105]

The commission's report on Ecuador, like many of its other reports, shed important light on problems that had gone without adequate attention by state authorities, raised those problems to a higher place in the hierarchy of governmental priorities, and provided guidance on how the problems should be addressed in accordance with contemporary norms. It is hard to gauge exactly what the practical impact is of such intervention by the commission. But it can at least be said that, as with other such interventions by international monitoring agencies, it is on the positive side of efforts to hold states to their duty to effectively implement international norms concerning indigenous peoples.

Notes

1. *See supra* chapter 2, notes 4–22 and accompanying text.

2. This is apparent, for example, in the procedures of the U.N. Commission on Human Rights and its subsidiary bodies, discussed *infra* notes 23–46 and accompanying text.

3. The congressional resolution acknowledging illegal acts against Native Hawaiians, S.J. Res. 19, 103d Cong., 1st Sess., 107 Stat. 5110 (1993), was adopted on the occasion of the hundredth anniversary of the overthrow of the Hawaiian monarchy. Around the same time the resolution was adopted, however, the U.S. Department of Justice was engaged in litigation in which it took the position that the United States has no legal responsibility to secure redress for wrongs against Native Hawaiians. An account of the conditions of Native Hawaiians in the face of contemporary political and economic forces is in Davianna Pomaika McGregor, "Ho'omauke Ea O Ka Lahui Hawai'i: The Perpetuation of the Hawaiian People," in *Ethnicity and Nation Building in the Pacific* 74, 85–91 (1989). *See also* Elizabeth Buck, *Paradise Remade: The Politics of Culture and History in Hawai'i* 183–91 (1993) (discussing the impact of the tourism industry on Hawaiian culture and way of life).

4. *See* Rick Hornung, *One Nation under the Gun* 181–91 (1991); Bruce E. Johansen, *Life and Death in Mohawk Country* 133–58 (1993).

5. *See* Arnaldo Lijerón Casanovas, "Bolivia: The Indigenous Territories of Amazonia," *Indigenous Affairs* (No. 4), Oct.–Dec. 1994, at 16, 17; International Work Group for Indigenous Affairs, *The Indigenous World: 1993–94*, at 61–63 (1994); Judith Marinissen, *Legislación Boliviana y Pueblos Indígenas* 124–50 (2d ed. 1998); José Aylwin, *Ponencia para la Sesión del Grupo de Trabajo sobre la Sesión Quinta del Proyecto de Declaración con especial énfasis en las "Formas Tradicionales de propiedad y supervivencia cultural. Derechos a tierras y territorios*," O.A.S. Doc. OEA/

Ser.K/KVI, GT/DADIN/doc. 96/02 (2002) at 7–9; *Atlas: Territorios Indígenas de Bolivia*, 12 (José Martínez ed., 2002).

6. *See* International Work Group for Indigenous Affairs, *supra* note 5, at 63–65. Aylwin, *supra* note 5, at 9–11; Sergio Leitão, *Ponencia para la Reunión del Grupo de Trabajo sobre la Sesión Quinta del Proyecto de Declaración con especial atención en las "Formas tradicionales de propiedad y de supervivencia cultural: Derechos a la tierra a los territorios*," O.A.S. Doc. OEA/Ser.K/XVI, GT/DADIN/doc.100/02 (2002).

7. *See* Francisco López Bárcenas et al., *Los Derechos Indígenas y la Reforma Constitucional en Mexico* (2001). *Cf. Comentarios a la Reforma Constitucional en Materia Indígena* (Miguel Carbonell & Karla Portilla Pérez eds., 2002).

8. *See generally* Philip Alston, "The Purposes of Reporting," in United Nations Centre for Human Rights & United Nations Institute for Training and Research, *Manual on Human Rights Reporting*, U.N. Doc. HR/PUB/91/1, Sales No. E.91.XIV.l, at 13 (1991) (describing the various functions of reporting procedures pursuant to U.N.-sponsored treaty regimes).

9. A number of fine works exist detailing the myriad international procedures for the implementation of human rights norms. *E.g.*, Henry Steiner & Philip Alston, *International Human Rights in Context: Law, Politics, Morals* (2d ed. 2000). *The United Nations and Human Rights* (Philip Alston ed., 1992); Dominic McGoldrick, *The Human Rights Committee: Its Role in the Development of the International Covenant on Civil and Political Rights* (1991); *Guide to International Human Rights Practice* (Hurst Hannum ed., 3d ed. 1999); David Weissbrodt et al., *International Human Rights: Law, Policy and Process* (3d ed. 2001); Nicolas Valticos, *International Labour Law* (1979). For detailed descriptions of different international procedures and their application to indigenous peoples, *see* Fergus Mackay, *Los Derechos de los Pueblos Indígenas en el Sistema International: Un fuente instrumental par alas organizaciones indígenea* (1999); Patrick Thornberry, *The Human Rights of Indigenous Peoples* (2002).

10. *See* ECOSOC Res. E/RES/2000/22 (July 28, 2000). The forum's creation was proposed in the Vienna Declaration and Programme of Action, World Conference on Human Rights, June 14–25, 1993, pt. 2, para. 32, U.N. Doc. A/CONF.157/23 (1993). The U.N. General Assembly responded by asking the Commission on Human Rights and its subsidiary organs to give "priority consideration" to the idea of a permanent forum. General Assembly Res. 48/163 (Dec. 21, 1993) (declaring the "International Decade of the World's Indigenous People"). The commission later assigned the task of considering the proposal to the Working Group on Indigenous Populations in consultation with interested parties. Human Rights Commission Res. 1994/28 (Mar. 4, 1994).

11. *See Permanent Forum on Indigenous Issues: Report on the First Session* (New York, May 13–24, 2002), U.N. Doc. E/2002/43 rev. 1 (Part I), E/CN.19/2002/3, rev. 1 Annex II (Part II) (2002) [hereinafter *Permanent Forum Report, 2002*].

12. *See* Working Group on Indigenous Populations, *Consideration of a Permanent Forum for Indigenous People: Information Received from Governments and Indigenous Organizations*, U.N. Doc. E/CN.4/Sub.2/AC.4/1994/11/Add.l (1994); *A Permanent Forum in the United Nations for Indigenous Peoples: Information Received from Governments*, U.N. Doc. E/CN.4/Sub.2/AC.4/1994/CRP.3 (1994). *Consideration of a Permanent Forum for Indigenous People: Report of the Workshop Held in Accordance with*

Commission Resolution 1995/30, U.N. Doc. E/CN.4/Sub.2/AC.4/1995/7 (1995); *Consideration of a Permanent Forum for Indigenous People: Information Received from Governments*, U.N. Doc. E/CN.4/Sub.2/AC.4/1995/Add.1 (1995); *Consideration of a Permanent Forum for Indigenous People: Working Paper Prepared by Mrs. Erica-Irene A. Daes, Expert and Chairperson-Rapporteur of the Working Group on Indigenous Populations*, U.N. Doc. E/CN.4/Sub.2/AC.4/1995/7/Add.2 (1995); *Consideration of a Permanent Forum for Indigenous People: Information Received from Indigenous Peoples' Organizations*, U.N. Doc. E/CN.4/Sub.2/AC.4/1995/7/Add.3 (1995).

13. *See* ECOSOC Res. E/RES/2000/22, *supra* note 10, para. 2.

14. *See id.* para. 1; The original members of the Permanent Forum were as follows. Experts named in consultation with indigenous organizations: Antonio Jacanamijoy (Colombia); Ayitegan Kouevi (Togo); Wilton Littlechild (Canada); Ole Henrik Magga (Norway); Zinaida Strogalschikova (Russian Federation); Parshuram Tamang (Nepal); Mililani Trask (United States); Fortunato Turpo Choquehuanca (Peru). Experts named in consultation with governments: Yuri Boychenko (Russian Federation); Njuma Ekundanayo (Democratic Republic of Congo); Yuji Iwasawa (Japan); Wayne Lord (Canada); Otilia Lux de Coti (Guatemala); Marcos Matías Alonso (México); Ida Nicolaisen (Denmark). *See Permanent Forum Report 2002*, *supra* note 11, Annex II.

15. *See id.* para. 87; "Historic Permanent Forum on Indigenous Issues Breaks New Ground for World's Indigenous Peoples," U.N. Press Release (reporting that over 900 representatives of indigenous peoples attended the first session of the Forum in 1991).

16. The Economic and Social Council Resolution established as the forum's specific areas of competence social and economic development, education, health, culture and human rights. *See* ECOSOC Res. E/RES/2000/22, *supra* note 10, para. 2. According to the forum's methodology adopted in its initial sessions, these issues constitute the "mandate spheres," which receive individualized treatment apart from the specific theme of the session. *See Permanent Forum on Indigenous Issues, Second Session: Provisional Agenda*, U.N. Doc. E/C.19/2003/1 (2003). Independent of whether human rights constitute a distinct focus of the forum's work, clearly all the issues covered by the forum's mandate have direct implications for the indigenous rights regime. *See supra* chapters 3 and 4 (discussing the scope of various interrelated human rights norms in relation to indigenous peoples).

17. On the need to include respect for human rights standards in the work of international agencies, *see* Andrew Clapham, "Mainstreaming Human Rights at the United Nations: The Challenges for the First High Commissioner for Human Rights," in *Collected Courses of the Academy of European Law*, vol VII, book 2, 159–234 (Academy of European Law ed., 1996). The forum's coordination efforts have led to the creation of the "Inter-Agency Support Group for the Forum," which brings together the different UN specialized agencies, and an "interdepartmental task force," made up of ECOSOC's different departmental units. *See Outcomes achieved in response to the first session of the Forum, Note by the secretariat of the Forum*, U.N. Doc. E/C.19/2003/3, paras. 12–16 (Mar. 17, 2003).

18. *See Mandated Areas: Human Rights, Chairperson's Summary of Discussion*, U.N. Doc. E/C.19/2003/L.2/Add.2, paras. 2, 4, 11 (May 21, 2003) (summarizing forum participants' and members' statements emphasizing the need for the forum to coordinate with existing UN procedures, especially those of the Working Group on Indigenous

Populations). *See also Report of the Working Group on Indigenous Populations on its twentieth session*, U.N. Doc. E/CN.4/Sub.2/2002/24, paras. 34–40 (2002) (discussing coordination among the Permanent Forum, the sub-commission Working Group on Indigenous Populations, and the special rapporteur on indigenous peoples' human rights).

19. *See generally* Human Rights Commission Res. 2003/55 (Apr. 24, 2003) (noting that the mandates of the working group, the Permanent Forum and the special rapporteur on indigenous peoples' human rights are "complementary and do not give rise to duplication"); Sub-Commission on Human Rights Res. 2002/21 (Aug. 14, 2002), para. 9 (requesting a working paper on the future collaboration between the working group and the Permanent Forum), para. 11 (establishing the future themes of the working group sessions through the year 2006). *See also Report of the Working Group on Indigenous Populations on its twentieth session, supra* note 18, paras. 17–24 (2002) (summarizing discussion among indigenous participants on "future vision" for working group); Sub-Commission on Human Rights Res. 2002/9 (Aug. 14, 2002), para. 8 (noting indigenous peoples' expressions of support for the continuation of the working group and affirming that the working group will continue to carry out its "ample, flexible mandate").

20. *See supra* chapter 2, notes 86–88 and accompanying text (discussing the working group and its mandate).

21. Written reports submitted by governments, intergovernmental institutions, and NGOs with official consultative status with the United Nations are published verbatim and circulated as U.N. documents. Reports delivered orally at the working group's annual sessions are summarized in the working group's annual reports. *See supra* chapter 2, notes 93, 105, 157 and accompanying text.

22. *See supra* chapter 2, notes 154–60 and accompanying text.

23. *See generally* Philip Alston, "The Commission on Human Rights," in *The United Nations and Human Rights, supra* note 9, at 126.

24. *See, e.g.,* Provisional Agenda, U.N. Doc. E/CN.4/Sub.2/1993/1, at 2 (1993) (provisional agenda for the 45th session of the sub-commission, including "[d]iscrimination against indigenous peoples"); Annotations to Provisional Agenda, U.N. Doc. E/CN.4/1991/Add.2 (1991) (annotations to provisional agenda for the 47th session of the commission including references to item concerning the International Year of the World's Indigenous People).

25. *See, e.g.,* discussion of issues concerning indigenous peoples summarized in *Report of the Sub-Commission on Prevention of Discrimination and Protection of Minorities on Its Forty-Fifth Session*, U.N. Doc. E/CN.4/1995/2, E/CN.4/Sub.2/1994/56, at 177–81 (1994); *Report of the Sub-Commission on Prevention of Discrimination and Protection of Minorities on Its Forty-Fifth Session*, U.N. Doc. E/CN.4/1994/2, E/CN.4/Sub.2/1993/45, at 154–55 (1993); *Commission on Human Rights: Report on the Forty-Ninth Session*, U.N. ESCOR, 1993, Supp. No. 3, U.N. Doc. E/1993/23, E/CN.4/1993/122, at 424 (1993); *Report of the Sub-Commission on Prevention of Discrimination and Protection of Minorities on Its Forty-Fourth Session*, U.N. Doc. E/CN.4/1993/2, E/CN.4/Sub.2/1992/58, at 146–49 (1992).

26. Human Rights Commission Res. 2001/57, U.N. Doc. E/CN.4/DEC/2001/571 (Apr. 24, 2001).

27. For descriptions and analyses of the Commission on Human Rights thematic mechanisms, see Steiner & Alston, *supra* note 9, at 641–48; Weissbrodt et al., *supra* note 9, at 246–81. *See also Seventeen Frequently Asked Questions about United Nations Special Rapporteurs,* Fact Sheet No. 27 (2001) [hereinafter *Fact Sheet No. 27*]; *Report of the United Nations High Commissioner for Human Rights and Follow-Up to the World Conference on Human Rights—Effective Functioning of Human Rights Mechanisms, Annex: Report of the Meeting of Special Rapporteurs/Representatives, experts and Chairpersons of Working Groups of the Special Procedures of the Commission on Human Rights and of the Advisory Services Programme.* U.N. Doc. E/CN.4/2000/5 (1999) (discussing the co-operative efforts among the special rapporteurs and other U.N. agencies).

28. Human Rights Commission Res. 2001/57, *supra* note 26, paras. 1(a), 1(b).

29. *Report of the Special Rapporteur on the situation of human rights and fundamental freedoms of indigenous people, Mr. Rodolfo Stavenhagen, submitted pursuant to Commission resolution 2001/57,* U.N. Doc. E/CN.4/2002/97, paras. 102, 109 (2002),

30. *Id.* para. 103.

31. *See Report of the Special Rapporteur on the situation of human rights and fundamental freedoms of indigenous people, Mr. Rodolfo Stavenhagen, submitted in accordance with Commission on Human Rights Resolution 2002/65, Addendum: Mission to the Philippines,* U.N. Doc. E/CN.4/2003/90/Add.3, paras. 29–56, 67 (2003). *See also Report of the Special Rapporteur on the situation of human rights and fundamental freedoms of indigenous people, Mr. Rodolfo Stavenhagen, submitted in accordance with Commision on Human Rights Resolution 2001/57, Addendum: Mission to Guatemala,* U.N. Doc. E/CN.4/2003/90/Add.2 (2003).

32. *See Report of the Special Rapporteur on the situation of human rights and fundamental freedoms of indigenous people, Rodolfo Stavenhagen, submitted in accordance with Commission Resolution 2002/65, Addendum: Communications Received by the Special Rapporteur,* U.N.Doc. E/CN.4/2003/90/Add.1, paras. 5–29 (2003) (summary of communications and observations about them from the governments of Argentina, Chile, Colombia, United States, India, México, and Peru).

33. Some of the other thematic mechanisms of the Commission on Human Rights have developed urgent-action procedures. *See Fact Sheet No. 27, supra* note 27, at 9, and some have developed quasi complaint procedures. Some special rapporteurs, for example, have developed systems for submitting information and for following up on the submissions. *See* Weissbrodt et al., *supra* note 9, at 253. In addition, the Working Group on Enforced or Involuntary Disappearances issues "opinions" about cases that it examines. *See* Alston & Steiner, *supra* note 9, at 642. Some thematic mechanisms have even developed their own rules to govern such procedures, as have the Working Group on Involuntary Detention and the Representative of the Secretary General for Internally Displaced Persons. *See Fact Sheet No. 27, supra* note 27, at 14.

34. For a discussion of procedures under ECOSOC Res. 1235 (XLII) (June 6, 1967), *see* Nigel S. Rodley, "United Nations Non-Treaty Procedures for Dealing with Human Rights Violations," in *Guide to International Human Rights Practice, supra* note 9, at 62–65.

35. Specific authorization for the secretariat to collect and circulate communications of human rights abuses was provided initially in ECOSOC Res. 728F(XXVIII)(1959).

See generally Frederic L. Kirgis, *International Organizations in Their Legal Setting* 969–70 (2d ed. 1993). This authorization became an element in the more structured procedure set forth in ECOSOC Res. 1503(XLVIII)(1970), discussed *infra*.

36. *See generally* David Weissbrodt, "The Contribution of International Nongovernmental Organizations to the Protection of Human Rights," in *Human Rights in International Law: Legal and Policy Issues* 403 (Theodor Meron ed., 1984); Ton Zuijdwijk, *Petitioning in the United Nations* 46–50 (1982).

37. The legal and practical aspects of the commission and sub-commission's capacities to consider complaints are analyzed in Alston, *supra* note 23, at 138–73.

38. *See* Human Rights Commission Res. 2001/60 (Apr. 24, 2001). In its resolution, the commission determined the sub-commission "should not adopt country-specific resolutions and, in negotiating and adopting thematic resolutions, should refrain from including references to specific countries." *Id.*, para. 4(a). Nevertheless, the resolution permits the sub-commission to debate specific situations that are not being examined by the commission, and other "urgent matters involving serious violations of human rights." *Id.*, para. 4(b).

39. Human Rights Commission Res. 1991/51 (Mar. 5, 1991). *See also, e.g.*, Sub-Commission on Prevention of Discrimination and Protection of Minorities Res. 1992/18 (calling upon the "Government of Guatemala . . . to respond to the requests and proposals of the indigenous peoples through the adoption of practical measures to improve their economic, social and cultural conditions"); Sub-Commission on Prevention of Discrimination and Protection of Minorities Res. 1994/23 (requesting the Guatemalan government to "strengthen in particular policies and programmes concerning the indigenous population").

40. The commission and sub-commission resolutions cited in the preceding note followed separate reports by an independent expert, Christian Tomuschat, operating under commission mandate to examine the human rights situations in Guatemala and to supervise the provision of advisory services. These reports are in U.N. Doc. E/CN.4/1991/5 & Add.1 (1991); U.N. Doc. E/CN.4/1992/5 (1992). An earlier report on fact-finding and advisory services in Guatemala pursuant to commission mandate was by Héctor Gros Espiell, U.N. Doc. E/CN.4/1989/39 (1989).

41. The two sub-commission members, Erica-Irene Daes (expert from Greece and chair of the Working Group on Indigenous Populations) and John Carey (alternate expert from the United States), issued separate reports on the Navajo-Hopi situation. Mr. Carey's report, which urged the sub-commission not to take a position on the dispute, is in U.N. Doc. E/CN.4/Sub.2/1989/35 (pt. 2). Ms. Daes's report, which urged a moratorium on further resettlement and advised that U.N. advisory services be offered for resolution of the dispute, is in U.N. Doc. E/CN.4/Sub.2/1989/35 (pt. I). Relevant sub-commission resolutions include Sub-Commission Res. 1989/37; Sub-Commission Res. 1990/34; Sub-Commission Res. 1992/36; Sub-Commission Res. 1994/44.

42. *See Report submitted by Mrs. Erica-Irene A. Daes, Chairperson-Rapporteur of the Working Group on Indigenous Populations, on her visit to Mexico (January 28–February 14, 2000)*, U.N. Doc. E/CN.4/Sub.2/2000/CRP.1 (2000).

43. ECOSOC Res. 1503(XLVIII)(May 27, 1970). The admissibility requirements for communications under the 1503 procedure are in Sub-Commission Res. 1(XXIV) (Aug. 13, 1971).

44. Confidentiality is mandated by ECOSOC Res. 1503(XLVIII), para. 8. For a description of the 1503 procedure and the machinery attached to it, *see* Rodley, *supra* note 34, at 64–70. The 1503 procedure was reformed by Economic and Social Council in 2000, based on suggestions proposed by the Human Rights Commissions' *ad hoc* working group on improving its mechanisms' effectiveness. *See* ECOSOC Res. 2000/3 (June 16, 2000); Human Rights Commission Res. 2000/109 (Apr. 26, 2000) (adopting the conclusions and recommendations of the working group without a vote); *Report of the Open-Ended Inter-Sessional Working Group on Enhancing the Effectiveness of the Mechanisms of the Commission on Human Rights*, U.N. Doc. E/CN.4/2000/112 (2000).

45. The petition, dated March 11, 1980, is reprinted in *Rethinking Indian Law* 141 (National Lawyers Guild, Committee on Native American Struggles ed., 1982). The petition was on behalf of the traditional Seminoles, the Houdenousaunee, the Hopi, the Western Shoshone, and the Lakota Nation.

46. Alston, *supra* note 23, at 146.

47. Convention (No. 169) Concerning Indigenous and Tribal Peoples in Independent Countries, June 27, 1989, International Labour Conference (entered into force Sept. 5. 1991), reprinted in the appendix, *infra* [hereinafter ILO Convention No. 169].

48. Convention (No. 107) Concerning the Protection and Integration of Indigenous and other Tribal and Semi-Tribal Populations in Independent Countries, June 26, 1957, International Labour Conference, 328 U.N.T.S. 247 (entered into force June 2, 1959) [hereinafter ILO Convention No. 107].

49. The reporting procedure is grounded in articles 22 and 23 of the Constitution of the International Labour Organization, Oct. 9, 1946, 15 U.N.T.S. 35. *See generally* Valticos, *supra* note 9, at 233–34. A compilation of materials and documents further explaining the ILO reporting procedures is in Kirgis, *supra* note 35, at 524–29.

50. *See* Committee of Experts on the Application of Conventions and Recommendations (CEACR), *Individual Observation concerning Convention No. 169, Indigenous and Tribal Peoples, 1989 Mexico* (ratification: 1990), Publication: 1997, para. 3, in ILOLEX, database of the International Labour Organization, available on the web at http://www.ilo.org/ilolex/spanish/index.htm [hereinafter ILOLEX] ("The Committee asks the Government to keep it informed of the practical effects of the consultations and the number of proposals taken into account in the planned reforms"); CEACR, *Individual Observation concerning Convention No. 169, Indigenous and Tribal Peoples, 1989 Mexico*, Publication: 1999, ILOLEX, *supra*, para. 2 ("Bearing in mind that the Convention was used as a reference document in these negotiations [at San Andrés], the Committee requests the Government to continue to provide information on any developments in the situation with regard to the practical implementation of the agreements reached during the negotiations").

51. CEACR, *Individual Observation concerning Convention No. 169, Indigenous and Tribal Peoples, 1989 Mexico*, Publication: 2000, ILOLEX, *supra* note 50, para. 3.

52. *See* CEACR, *Individual Observation concerning Convention No. 169, Indigenous and Tribal Peoples, 1989 Mexico*, Publication: 1999, ILOLEX, *supra* note 50, para. 2 ("The Committee also requests the Government to continue to provide information on the nature of the constitutional initiatives that have been submitted and on the stage which they have reached in the Federal Congress"); CEACR, *Individual Ob-*

servation concerning Convention No. 169, Indigenous and Tribal Peoples, 1989 Mexico, Publication: 2002, ILOLEX, *supra* note 50, para. 4 ("[T]he Committee is aware that these reforms have generated a great deal of controversy and that some sections of Mexican society, including indigenous and workers' organizations, have expressed concern that these reforms will have a negative impact on the social, economic and legal situation of the indigenous peoples of Mexico"). The committee examined in great detail the constitutional reform in a (confidential) request sent directly to the Mexican government. *See id.*, para. 5.

53. *See* International Labour Conference Committee Report (ILCCR), *Examination of individual case concerning Convention No. 169, Indigenous and Tribal Peoples, 1989 Mexico*, Publication: 1995, ILOLEX, *supra* note 50, (analyzing recent events in Chiapas and suggesting the Mexican government request technical assistance from the International Labour Office); CEACR, *Individual Observation concerning Convention No. 169, Indigenous and Tribal Peoples, 1989 Mexico*, Publication: 2000, ILOLEX, *supra* note 50, (analyzing complaints filed by labor unions on behalf of indigenous groups).

54. *See supra* chapter 2, notes 33–41 and accompanying text.

55. *See, e.g., Report of the Committee of Experts on the Application of Conventions and Recommendations: General Report and Observations Concerning Particular Countries*, Report 3 (pt. 4A), International Labour Conference, 81st Sess. at 348–52 (1994); *Report of the Committee of Experts on the Application of Conventions and Recommendations: General Report and Observations Concerning Particular Countries*, Report 3 (pt. 4A), International Labour Conference, 78th Sess. at 349–51, 353–54 (1991); *Report of the Committee of Experts on the Application of Conventions and Recommendations: General Report and Observations Concerning Particular Countries*, Report 2 (pt. 4A), International Labour Conference, 78th Sess. at 355–68 (1989).

56. *See, e.g., Report of the Committee on the Application of Standards*, International Labour Conference, 80th Sess., Provisional Record 25, at 25/51–25/52 (1993); *Report of Committee on the Application of Standards*, International Labour Conference, 76th Sess., Provisional Record 26, at 26/80–26/84 (1989).

57. The essential normative elements of ILO Convention No. 169 are discussed in *supra* chapter 2, notes 59–72 and accompanying text.

58. International Covenant on Civil and Political Rights, Dec. 16, 1966, G.A. Res. 2200(XXI), art. 40, 999 U.N.T.S. 171 (entered into force Mar. 23, 1976); International Covenant on Economic, Social and Cultural Rights, G.A. res. 2200A (XXI), 21 U.N. GAOR Supp. (No. 16) at 49, U.N. Doc. A/6316 (1966), 993 U.N.T.S. 3 (entered into force Jan. 3, 1976); International Convention on the Elimination of All Forms of Racial Discrimination, Dec. 21,1965, G.A. Res. 2106A(XX), 660 U.N.T.S. 195 (entered into force Jan. 4, 1969); Convention on the Elimination of All Forms of Discrimination against Women, G.A res. 34/180, 34 U.N. GAOR Supp. (No. 46) at 193, U.N.Doc. A/34/46 (entered into force Sept. 3, 1981); Convention against Torture and Other Cruel, Inhuman or Degrading Treatment or Punishment, G.A. res. 39/46, annex, 39 U.N. GAOR Supp. (No. 51) at 197, U.N. Doc. A/39/51 (1984) (entered into force June 26, 1987); Convention on the Rights of the Child, G.A res. 44/25, annex, 44 U.N. GAOR Supp. (No. 49) at 167, U.N. Doc A/44/49 (1989) (entered into force Sept. 2, 1990); Convention on the Protection of the Rights of All Migrant Workers and Members of their Families,

G.A. res. 47/110, 47 U.N. GAOR Supp. (No. 49A), at 262, U.N. Doc. A/47/49 (1990) (entered into force July 1, 2003).

59. For overviews of the U.N. treaty-monitorings system, see *Manual on Human Rights Reporting, supra* note 8; Weissbrodt et al., *supra* note 9, at 153–210.

60. *See* International Covenant on Civil and Political Rights, *supra* note 58, art. 40; International Convention on the Elimination of All Forms of Racial Discrimination, *supra* note 58, art. 9. *See generally Manual on Human Rights Reporting, supra* note 8, at 79–151 (detailing reporting under the covenant and convention). Parallel reporting requirements involving similar committee structures within the United Nations exist in connection with the other U.N.-sponsored human rights treaties, *see generally id.*

61. The annual reports issued by each of the committees include a summary of the government reports and a description of the ensuing deliberations and dialogue with government representatives. The government reports themselves are published separately as U.N. documents. At its meeting on March 24, 1992, the Human Rights Committee decided that it would adopt and publish comments reflecting the views of the committee as a whole at the end of consideration of each state party report. *Report of the Human Rights Committee*, U.N. GAOR, 47th Sess., Supp. No. 40, U.N. Doc. A/47/40, at 18 (1992). The Committee for the Elimination of Racial Discrimination also has the practice of adopting and publishing "final observations" on state reports. Documents produced and published by these U.N. committees include—in addition to conclusions and recommendations regarding state reports—summaries of discussions between the committees and government representatives. Similarly, the government reports are published separately as U.N. documents. These documents are in the database of the Office of the United Nations High Commissioner for Human Rights, available at www.unhchr.ch/.

62. *See supra* chapter 4, at notes 41–56 and accompanying text.

63. *Concluding Observations of the Human Rights Committee: Guatemala,* U.N.Doc. CCPR/CO/72/GTM, para. 29 (2001). Other examples of the committee's discussion of country reports with specific reference to indigenous peoples are in *Report of the Human Rights Committee*, U.N. GAOR, 49th Sess., Supp. No. 40, U.N. Doc. A/49/40, vol. 1, at 22 (1994) (commending Norway's devolution of authority to the indigenous Saami Assembly); *id.* at 36 (recommending that Mexico attend to the aspirations of indigenous groups in connection with agrarian reform and facilitate their participation in matters that concern them); *Report of the Human Rights Committee*, U.N. GAOR, 48th Sess., Supp. No. 40, U.N. Doc. A/48/40, pt. 1, at 66–67 (1993) (questioning aspects of Venezuela's constitution and laws with regard to indigenous group cultural survival and land rights); *Report of the Human Rights Committee (1992), supra* note 61, 58–67 (1992) (discussing social organization and land rights issues concerning the indigenous peoples of the Ecuadoran Amazon); *id.*, at 84–85 (discussion of political participation, land rights, and autonomous organization of indigenous communities in Peru); *Report of the Human Rights Committee*, U.N. GAOR, Supp. No. 40, U.N. Doc. A/46/40, at 22–25 (1991) (inquiring about various developments concerning indigenous peoples in Canada, including self-government negotiations with Indian communities, land claims settlements, treaty rights, revision of the Canadian Indian Act, parliamentary representation, and the resolution of conflicts involving the Mohawk people).

64. *See* International Covenant on Civil and Political Rights, *supra* note 58, art. 1, para. 1 ("All peoples have the right to self-determination.").

65. *See supra* chapter 3, notes 86–87 and accompanying text (discussing a prior tendency to avoid express usage of the term self-determination, despite widespread agreement over underlying normative precepts).

66. *See, e.g., Report of the Human Rights Committee (1992), supra* note 61, at 52 (noting that "the right of self-determination applied not only to colonial situations but to other situations as well and that the people of a given territory should be allowed to determine their political and economic destiny" and requesting of Iraq "clarification of the position of the autonomy of Iraqi Kurdistan"); *Report of the Human Rights Committee (1991), supra* note 63, at 105 (discussing "self-determination in its domestic dimensions" in Panama, particularly in regard to elections and parliamentary rule); *id.* at 131 (discussing "ethnic and community structure" and electoral reform in Madagascar); *Report of the Human Rights Committee*, U.N. GAOR, 45th Sess., Supp. No. 40, U.N. Doc. A/45/40, vol. 1, at 122 (1990) (discussing policy of Zaire toward apartheid regime in South Africa). *Cf. Report of the Human Rights Committee (1994), supra* note 63, at 51 (affirming, contrary to the position taken by Azerbaijan, that article 1 of the covenant "applies to all peoples and not just colonized peoples"). *See also* Human Rights Committee, *General Comment 12(21)*, reprinted in *Manual on Human Rights Reporting, supra* note 8, at 82–83 (commenting on the breadth of coverage of article 1).

67. *See Report of the Human Rights Committee (1992), supra* note 63, at 101.

68. *Third Periodic Reports of States Parties Due in 1990: Colombia*, U.N. Doc. CCPR/C/64/Add.3, at 9 (1991).

69. U.S. Department of State, *Civil and Political Rights in the United States: Initial Report of the United States of America to the U.N. Human Rights Committee under the International Covenant on Civil and Political Rights*, July 1994, at 36–46, Dept. of State Pub. 10200 (1994).

70. *Concluding Observations of the Human Rights Committee: Canada*, U.N. Doc. CCPR/C/79/Add.105, para. 7 (1999).

71. *Id.* para. 8.

72. *See Concluding Observations of the Human Rights Committee: Norway*, U.N. Doc. CCPR/C/79/Add.112, paras. 16, 17 (1999); *Concluding Observations of the Human Rights: Australia*, U.N. Doc. A/55/40, paras. 509–10 (2000).

73. *Concluding Observations of the Human Rights Committee: México*, U.N. Doc. CCPR/C/79/Add.109, para. 19 (1999).

74. *See* CERD, General Recommendation XXIII Concerning Indigenous Peoples, U.N. Doc. CERD/C/51/misc.13/Rev. 4 (1997), reprinted in the appendix, *infra*.

75. The relationship between nondiscrimination and indigenous group rights is discussed in *supra* chapter 4, notes 9–20 and accompanying text.

76. *See, e.g., Report of the Committee on the Elimination of Racial Discrimination*, U.N. GAOR, 49th Sess., Supp. No. 18, U.N. Doc. A/49/18, at 30 (1994) (considering the legal regime applicable to Saami land and hunting rights in Sweden) [hereinafter *CERD Report (1994)*]; *id.* at 88, 92 (evaluating developments in Australia concerning indigenous land rights); *Report of the Committee on the Elimination of Racial Discrimination*, U.N. GAOR, 48th Sess., Supp. No. 18, U.N. Doc. A/48/18, at 40–43 (1993)

(evaluating government programs in Ecuador concerning indigenous languages, lands, benefits from natural resource exploitation, and participation in government decision making) [hereinafter *CERD Report (1993)*]; *Report of the Committee on the Elimination of Racial Discrimination*, U.N. GAOR, 47th Sess., Supp. No. 18, U.N. Doc. A/47/18, at 38–44, 47–52, 59–62 (1992) (discussing a broad range of issues concerning indigenous peoples in connection with reports by Costa Rica, Bangladesh, Colombia, and Chile) [hereinafter *CERD Report (1992)*]; *Report of the Committee on the Elimination of Racial Discrimination*, U.N. GAOR, 46th Sess., Supp. No. 18, U.N. Doc. A/46/18, at 28–32, 50–56, 62–69, 90–94 (1991) (similar discussion in connection with reports by Argentina, Canada, Sweden, Australia, and Mexico) [hereinafter *CERD Report (1991)*].

77. *Concluding Observations of the Committee on the Elimination of Racial Discrimination : United States of America*. U.N. Doc. CERD/C/59/Misc.17/Rev.3., para. 21 (Aug. 14, 2001).

78. *See id.*

79. *See id.*

80. *See also CERD Report (1994), supra* note 76, at 30 (asking the Swedish government for additional information regarding Saami rights); *CERD Report (1993), supra* note 76, at 40–41 (criticizing Ecuadoran report on natural resource development programs on grounds that "such programs did not appear to be of direct benefit to the [indigenous] populations whose lands were being used and no mention of their views had been included in the report"); *id.* at 42 (asking Ecuadoran government to state what demands had been made by indigenous populations in 1990, particularly with regard to land); *CERD Report (1991), supra* note 76, at 62–65 (expressing surprise that Swedish government had not included more information about the indigenous Saami in its report).

81. Under this mechanism, "efforts to prevent serious violations of the [convention against racial discrimination] would include . . . Early-warning measures to address existing structural problems from escalating into conflicts . . . [and] Urgent procedures to respond to problems requiring immediate attention to prevent or limit the scale or number of serious violations of the Convention." *Prevention of Racial Discrimination, Including Early Warning and Urgent Action Procedures: Working Paper Adopted by the Committee on the Elimination of Racial Discrimination*, U.N. GOAR, 48th Sess., Supp. No. 18, U.N. Doc. A/48/18, Annex III, para. 8 (1993). Early-warning or urgent measures might include a range of action on the part of CERD, from the issuance of written recommendations to the state concerned to more active measures such as on site visits and active engagement with state authorities through advisory services. *See id.*, para. 10.

82. The article 14 complaint procedure is discussed in *infra* chapter 7, at notes 31–36.

83. *See* Decision (2)54 on Australia, U.N. Doc. CERD/C/54/Misc.40/Rev.2, paras. 6–10 (Mar. 18, 1999). CERD found the Native Title Act amendments to be discriminatory in that together they "extinguish or impair the exercise of indigenous title rights . . . the amended Act appears to create legal certainty for governments and third parties at the expense of indigenous title." *Id.* para. 6.

84. *Id.* para. 11. Faced with the obstinate position of the Australian government toward CERD's intervention, CERD reiterated its decision 2(54) in its decision 2(55),

U.N. Doc. A/54/18, para. 23(2) (Aug. 16, 1999), and, subsequently, upon commenting upon Australia's next periodic report, CERD criticized the government for its failure to implement those decisions. *See Concluding Observations by the Committee on the Elimination of Racial Discrimination : Australia*, U.N. Doc. CERD/C/304/Add.101, paras. 8–11 (2001).

85. See *CERD Report (1992)*, *supra* note 76, at 45.

86. *See id.* at 47.

87. *See* CERD, *General Recommendation XXI: Right to Self-Determination*, U.N. Doc. CERD/48/Misc.7/Rev.3 (1996).

88. *See supra* chapter 2, notes 116–19 and accompanying text.

89. The charter amendment is known as the Protocol of Buenos Aires, Feb. 27, 1967, O.A.S. Doc. OEA/Ser.G/CP/Doc.499/76, rev., corr. 1 (1977), reprinted in 6 *I.L.M.* 310 (1967). *See generally The Inter-American System of Human Rights* (David Harris & Stephen Livingstone eds., 1998); Hector Faundez Ledesma, *El Sistema Interamericano de Proteccion de los Derechos Humanos* (1996); David Padilla, "The Inter-American System for the Promotion and Protection of Human Rights," 20 *Ga. J. Int'l & Comp. L.* 395 (1990).

90. American Convention on Human Rights, Nov. 22, 1969, OAS Treaty Ser. No. 36, 1144 U.N.T.S. 123 (entered into force July 18, 1978) [hereinafter American Convention].

91. Statute of the Inter-American Commission on Human Rights, as approved by Res. 447, taken at the 9th Regular Session of the General Assembly of the OAS, La Paz, Bolivia, in October 1979, as amended by Res. 508 at the 10th Session in November 1980, reprinted in *Human Rights in the Inter-American System*, pt. 1: Basic Documents, booklet 9.1 (Thomas Buergenthal & Robert E. Norris eds., 1993) [hereinafter IACHR Statute].

92. Charter of the Organization of American States, Apr. 30, 1948, art. 112, OAS Treaty Series No. 66, 721 U.N.T.S. 324; American Convention, *supra* note 90, art. 41; IACHR Statute, *supra* note 91, art. 18.

93. Parties to the American Convention are required to submit requested information to the commission in regard to compliance with the convention's substantive terms. American Convention, *supra* note 90, art. 43. OAS member states that are not parties to the convention are also, but less specifically, bound to cooperate with the commission by implication of the O.A.S. Charter, art. 41, and the commission's statute, art. 18.

94. The commission conducts an on-site visit only after an "invitation" from the country concerned. *See generally* IACHR Statute, *supra* note 91, art 18(g) (authorizing the commission to "conduct on-site observations in a state, with the consent or at the invitation of the government in question"). Such invitations are usually more accurately characterized as manifestations of government consent, since they typically are solicited by the commission, the OAS General Assembly or another member state. *See* Padilla, *supra* note 89, at 398–99.

95. Resolution on Special Protection for Indigenous Populations, Inter-American Commission on Human Rights, Dec. 28, 1972, O.A.S. Doc. OEA/Ser.P, AG/doc.305/73, rev. 1, at 90–91 (1973).

96. *See infra* chapter 7, notes 80–121 and accompanying text.

97. *See* Inter-American Commission on Human Rights, *Fourth Report on the Situation of Human Rights in Guatemala*, O.A.S. Doc. OEA/L/V/II.83, Doc. 16, rev. (1993);

Inter-American Commission on Human Rights, *Second Report on the Situation of Human Rights in Colombia*, O.A.S. Doc. OEA/Ser.L/V/II.84, Doc. 39, rev. (1993).

Prior to the 1990s, and despite its relative autonomy of initiative, the commission had not generally included discussion of specific problems of indigenous peoples in its country reports, which contrasted with the practice of the U.N. Human Rights Committees discussed *supra*. In a 1987 report on Paraguay, the commission did not mention the situation of Paraguayan indigenous groups, *see* Inter-American Commission on Human Rights, *Report on the Situation of Human Rights in Paraguay*, O.A.S. Doc. OEA/Ser.L/ V/II.71, Doc. 19, rev. 1 (1987), despite the fact that, as discussed *infra*, the commission had previously denounced violations of the rights of the Aché people of that country, in the context of responding to a complaint before it. *See* chapter 7, *infra* notes 83 and accompanying text. In its report on Paraguay in 1978, the commission referred to the Aché situation only briefly, in a footnote. *See* Inter-American Commission on Human Rights; *Report on the Situation of Human Rights in Paraguay*, O.A.S. Doc. OEA/Ser.L/ V/II.43, at 9–10, n.8 (1978). This tendency could also be seen in the early 1990s. In its summary reports on Peru and Nicaragua, both countries with significant indigenous problems, virtually no mention was made of developments or problems concerning indigenous peoples per se. *See Annual Report on the Inter-American Commission on Human Rights 1993*, O.A.S. Doc. OEA/Ser.L/V/II.85, Doc. 9, rev., at 442, 478 (1994).

98. *See supra* chapter 2, notes 110–11 and accompanying text.

99. *See, e.g., Report on the Situation of Human Rights in Ecuador*, O.A.S. Doc. OEA/Ser.L/V/II.96, Doc.10, rev. 1 (1997) (including a general chapter on "Human Rights Issues of Special Relevance to the Indigenous Inhabitants of the Country," and another specifically dealing with "The Human Rights Situation of the Inhabitants of the Interior of Ecuador Affected by Development," which studied the consequences of subsurface resource extraction projects on indigenous communities in the Amazon); *Report on the Situation of Human Rights in Brazil*, O.A.S. Doc. OEA/Ser.L/V/II.97, Doc. 29, rev. 1 (1997) (including a chapter on "Human Rights of the Indigenous Peoples in Brazil" with special emphasis on the legal regime for indigenous lands in the country, and a specific analysis of the situation of the Macuxi and Yanomami peoples); *Report on the Situation of Human Rights in Mexico*, O.A.S. Doc. OEA/Ser.L/V/II.100, Doc. 7, rev. 1 (1998) (including a chapter on "The Situation of Indigenous Peoples and Their Rights," with special attention to the militarization of indigenous regions in Chiapas, Guerrero, and Oaxaca); *Third Report on the Situation of Human Rights in Colombia*, O.A.S. Doc. OEA/ Ser.L/V/II.102, Doc. 9, rev. 1 (1999) (including a part on "The Rights of Indigenous Peoples," analyzing relevant constitutional and legislative reforms and the consequences of political violence and drug trafficking on indigenous peoples); *Second Report on the Situation of Human Rights in Peru*, O.A.S. Doc. OEA/Ser.L/V/II.106, Doc. 59, rev. (2000) (with a chapter on "The Rights of Indigenous Communities," which analyzes, *inter alia*, issues of indigenous landholding and discrimination against indigenous individuals); *Third Report of the Situation of Human Rights in Paraguay*, O.A.S. Doc. OEA/ Ser./L/VII.110, Doc. 52 (2001) (including a chapter titled "The Rights of Indigenous Peoples") (translated into the Aché language under the title: "Marandu Mbohapyha Derecho Humano Kuéra Rehegua Paraguápie"); *Fifth Report on the Situation of Human Rights in Guatemala*, O.A.S. Doc. OEA/Ser.L/V/II.111, Doc. 21 rev. (2001) (including

a chapter on "The Rights of Indigenous Peoples," which analyzes the implementation of the Peace Accords and the situation resulting from the failed constitutional reform of 1999). *See also Special Report on the Human Rights Situation in the so-called "Communities of People in Resistance" in Guatemala*, O.A.S. Doc. OEA/Ser.L/V/II.86, Doc. 5 rev. 1 (1994) (report on the situation of indigenous communities that fled to the rainforest and mountains during the armed conflict in Guatemala and openly returned in 1991, calling themselves "communities of people in resistance").

100. *See* OAS Charter art. 112 (stating that the commission's "principal function shall be to promote the observance and protection of human rights"); American Convention, *supra* note 90, art. 41(a)–(d) (stating that "the Commission shall . . . promote respect for and defense of human rights"). The statute of the commission specifies that the human rights referred to in the statute include the convention and the American Declaration of the Rights and Duties of Man. IACHR Statute, *supra* note 91, art. 2; American Declaration of the Rights and Duties of Man, adopted by the Ninth International Conference of American States (Mar. 30–May 2, 1948), O.A.S. Res. 30, O.A.S. Doc. OEA/Ser.L/V/I.4, rev. (1965). However, that specification, read in light of the relevant provisions of the OAS Charter and the overall context, is not exclusionary and hence does not preclude the commission from looking beyond the American Convention and Declaration of Rights.

101. *See Report on the Situation of Human Rights in Ecuador*, *supra* note 99, chap. VIII (analyzing the "The human rights situation of the inhabitants of the Ecuadoran interior affected by development activities").

102. *Id.* at 93.

103. *Id.* at 92 (citing the Additional Protocol to the American Convention in the Area of Economic, Social and Cultural Rights; the International Covenants on Economic, Social and Cultural Rights (ICESCR) and on Civil and Political Rights (ICCPR); the Stockholm Declaration; the Treaty for Amazonian Cooperation; the Amazon Declaration; the World Charter for Nature; the Convention on Nature Protection and Wildlife Preservation in the Western Hemisphere; the Rio Declaration on Environment and Development; the Convention on Biological Diversity).

104. *Id.* at 94.

105. *See id.* at 100–01.

7

International Complaint Procedures

The procedures described in the previous chapter provide varying levels of on-going international scrutiny that encourages state action to implement international norms concerning indigenous peoples. In addition to those procedures are international mechanisms, in some cases involving the same international institutions, that are specifically designed to examine complaints of human rights abuses and, as a matter of course, to lead to decisions or recommendations in response to the complaints. International complaint procedures, which may generate heightened scrutiny on problem situations, are important adjuncts to the compliance-monitoring procedures ordinarily functioning in less contentious contexts.

A decision by an authoritative body of the United Nations or other international organization declaring a government in violation of human rights can be an embarrassment for the government with ripple effects in its international relations. Even a statement couched in terms of a recommendation that brings to light unacceptable government behavior can coalesce the mobilization of shame damaging to a country's prestige. Governments, including the most powerful among them, would rather avoid being seen as violators of human rights in the eyes of the world community. In addition, institutions with the capacity to hear grievances may provide guidance or act as conduits of dialogue useful to arriving at appropriate remedies where violations are found to exist.

The following is a discussion of the international complaint procedures that have been most active in examining the group claims of indigenous peoples. These procedures are limited in their scope of application in accordance with the treaty regimes to which they are attached. And, as will be shown, the effectiveness of these procedures remains constrained by the inherent weaknesses of the international human rights system due to configurations of authority that favor state discretion especially in relation to matters deemed within the primary jurisdiction of states. But despite these weaknesses, international complaint procedures are, at least potentially, significant tools to help alter the course of state action or inaction when needed to bring about the implementation of international norms.

Complaint Procedures Connected to ILO Conventions

Two distinct complaint procedures attach to all International Labour Organization conventions; because of the existing ILO conventions on indigenous peoples,[1] these procedures are available to address specifically indigenous peoples' concerns. The complaint procedures themselves are designed in accordance with the ILO's central focus on labor issues and its commensurate concern with facilitating communication among labor unions, employers organizations, and governments. Thus, neither complaint procedure can be invoked directly by an indigenous people or community. Nonetheless, the ILO complaint procedures, in conjunction with the relevant ILO conventions, offer some possibilities for securing redress for the violation of indigenous peoples' rights.

Under article 24 of the ILO Constitution, an association of workers or employers may make a "representation" to the ILO that a country "has failed to secure in any respect the effective observance within its jurisdiction of any [ILO] Convention to which it is a party."[2] Representations are reviewed by a committee of three members of the ILO Governing Body. In accordance with the tripartite structure of the Governing Body and other ILO forums,[3] the committee consists of a government member, an employer member, and a worker member. Under the Governing Body's "Standing Orders" (rules of procedure),[4] the committee considers the allegations, solicits comments from the accused government, and on the basis of its investigation reports back to the Governing Body. If the Governing Body decides that a government's explanations are unsatisfactory, it may publish the representation and the government's response, along with the committee's commentary on the case.[5] The committee's published commentary may well amount to a finding of a violation, which may prod an offending government into remedial action.[6]

Article 26 of the ILO Constitution establishes a second, more elaborate procedure for complaints alleging that a state is not complying with an ILO convention that it has ratified.[7] Such a complaint under article 26 may be filed by any ILO member state that has ratified the same convention or by a delegate to the annual International Labour Conference. Conference delegates include employers and workers as well as government representatives. Also, the ILO Governing Body may initiate the procedure on its own motion.[8] After soliciting comments from the government charged with a complaint, the Governing Body usually appoints a "Commission of Inquiry" to act upon the complaint, as specifically authorized under article 26. Commissions of inquiry have functioned through quasi-judicial proceedings involving formal hearings and written submissions, and on occasion commission members have made on-site visits to gather evidence.[9] A commission arrives at conclusions and may make recommendations for corrective measures if a state is found to have problems complying with its obligations under an ILO convention.[10] The conclusions and recommendations are communicated to the Governing Body and the governments concerned, and then published.[11] A commission decision is appealable to the International Court of Justice, and the decision of the ICJ in an appealed case is deemed "final" under the ILO Constitution.[12]

The two ILO complaint procedures have been used relatively sparingly,[13] indicating a preference within the ILO for less contentious or less formal means of securing compliance with ILO conventions. As of this writing the complaint procedure under article 26 has not been invoked in connection with one of the ILO conventions on indigenous peoples. However, there have been a number of cases involving application of Convention No. 169 on Indigenous and Tribal Peoples under the less elaborate article 24 procedure, a procedure with regard to which labor interests appear to have greater power of initiative. In fact, Convention No. 169 has been one of the most invoked instruments in relation to the article 24 procedure.

Even though indigenous peoples themselves cannot directly file complaints to the ILO, others may do so on their behalf. The cases relating to ILO Convention No. 169 under the article 24 procedure have been initiated through complaints filed by labor unions, which generally are likely surrogates for indigenous peoples, given the demographic overlap and political alliances between indigenous and labor sectors.[14] The tripartite committee that considered a representation regarding indigenous communities in Ecuador confirmed there is no requirement that a party initiating a complaint under article 24 of the ILO Constitution, or the party's constituency, be directly affected by the alleged infraction.[15] In addition, the ILO Governing Body itself is authorized to initiate article 26 complaints and could do so upon information provided by indigenous groups or by nongovernmental organizations concerned with indigenous peoples' rights.

It is noteworthy that neither of the ILO complaint procedures described here, unlike most international human rights complaint procedures, requires the exhaustion of domestic remedies.[16] However, as a practical matter, the strength of a claim to establish state responsibility for a violation of an ILO convention may be diminished in cases in which domestic remedies have not been exhausted, as indicated in the first case brought under the article 24 procedure in relation to ILO Convention No. 169. In that case, which concerned the Wixárrika (Huichol) of Mexico, a committee was formed to evaluate the complaint, even though the subject of the complaint was still pending before a Mexican agrarian tribunal;[17] but the committee declined to engage in a rigorous evaluation of the relevant facts or to find a violation of the convention, because of those same still pending domestic procedures.[18] The committee considered that "there are procedures in place to resolve land disputes . . . accessible to indigenous communities."[19]

The tripartite committees that have been formed to consider cases brought under article 24 in connection with Convention No. 169 generally have focused on the convention's requirements of indigenous consultation and participation.

In cases subsequent to that of the Wixárrika of Mexico, tripartite committees of the Governing Body have more closely examined the relevant facts and in several of those cases have declared violations of Convention No. 169 upon finding deficiencies in consultation processes with indigenous peoples or that states have failed to provide adequate procedures to address their claims. In addressing the complaint brought by Central Unificada del Trabajo (CUT) against Colombia regarding the situation of various indigenous peoples in that country, for example, a tripartite committee of the Governing Body concluded that the enactment of Decree No. 1320 of 1998—itself governing consultation with black and indigenous communities—without consulting with the peoples' directly affected by the decree "was not compatible with the Convention,"[20] and that "the process of prior consultation" defined in that decree "[was] not consistent" with the procedural requirements of prior consultation of the Convention.[21] In addressing another complaint, in which the Governing Body committee found inadequate consultation in relation to the construction and operation of a hydroelectric dam that affected particular indigenous communities, the committee urged the government of Colombia "to amend Decree No. 1320 of 1998 to bring it into line with the spirit of the Convention, in consultation with and with the active participation of the representatives of the indigenous peoples . . . in accordance with the provisions of the Convention."[22]

In a number of other cases, the Governing Body's tripartite committees have found violations of the requirement of prior consultation in relation to natural resource exploitation projects in indigenous territories. In a case concerning the U'wa people of Colombia, a tripartite committee determined that the consultation process regarding exploitation of natural resources in the U'wa traditional territory was deficient, noting that "meetings or consultations conducted *after* an environmental license has been granted do not meet the requirements of Articles 6 and 15(2) of the Convention."[23] In a similar case brought against Ecuador over the signing of a petroleum exploration agreement in the territory of the Shuar people, the tripartite committee stated that "[a] simple information meeting cannot be considered as complying with the provisions of the Convention."[24] The committee emphasized that consultations must involve "indigenous and tribal institutions or organizations that are truly representative of the communities affected," concluding that exclusion of the main Shuar organization from the signing of the agreement was a violation of the convention.[25]

While the article 24 complaint mechanism can be seen to apply close scrutiny under Convention No. 169's procedural requirements of due consultation, it has not similarly provided for exacting scrutiny of state behavior under the convention's substantive standards. Revealing in this respect is the report of the tripartite committee established to examine a representation based upon the land claims by an Inuit group in Greenland, which is a territory of Denmark governed under a special statutory home-rule regime. The Inuit claimant group, a subgroup of the larger majority Inuit population in Greenland, claimed violations of its land rights under the convention as the result of a series of events and conditions stemming from the Danish government's removal of the group from their traditional lands in 1953 in order to make way for a U.S. air base. Alleged were violations of the convention's article 14, which provides substantive protection for indigenous peoples' ownership and other interests in traditional lands. The committee convened to examine that case focused mainly on the Danish procedures and decisions relevant to the Inuit group's claims and found that the home-rule regime and the Danish judicial system provided an adequate basis for resolving those claims. Reiterating the view expressed in other cases, the committee emphasized that the ILO's supervisory mechanisms are to ensure that states have adequate procedures to resolve indigenous peoples' claims and that the principles of the Convention are duly followed, not to provide alternative means to resolve those claims.[26] The committee thus decided that the situation in which the Inuit group found itself did not constitute violations of any of the relevant provisions of the conventions.[27]

This and other cases suggest that even when a tripartite committee established to examine an article 24 representation examines state action in relation to an indigenous claim, it will accord substantial deference to domestic mechanisms to resolve the claim. Such deference will apply as long as the state domestic mechanisms are found to comport with the consultation requirements of Convention No. 169 and to include due consideration of the convention's substantive principles, unlike the domestic mechanisms in the cases in which violations of the Convention were declared.

The reluctance to go beyond questions of procedural fairness and closely scrutinize state decisions in relation to substantive standards is partly a function of the predisposition toward noninterference in domestic affairs that still permeates the international system even if with diminished effects. But because states in fact consent to intervention through the ILO complaint procedures upon ratifying ILO conventions, the reluctance is perhaps best explained as emanating from the ILO's institutional policy of favoring technical advisory services and ongoing dialogue to resolve disputes, as well as perhaps from a relative lack of expertise on indigenous issues within an organization established to focus on labor concerns. But as the ILO develops greater expertise on indigenous issues in the application of ILO Convention No. 169, and hence greater understanding about the depth of the problems indigenous peoples frequently face at the hands of overpowering political forces that capture state behavior, the ILO bodies established to evaluate complaints may see the need to more aggressively judge state acts and omissions and make relevant recommendations on the basis of the substantive norms of the convention, and not just on the basis of a somewhat minimalist requirement of procedural adequacy on the part of domestic agencies.

The U.N. Human Rights Committee and Individual Communications under the Optional Protocol to the ICCPR

Although not connected to a legal instrument specifically concerning indigenous peoples, an additional relevant procedure is that involving the U.N. Human Rights Committee pursuant to the Optional Protocol to the International Covenant on Civil and Political Rights. The Human Rights Committee and certain other U.N. treaty bodies among those identified in chapter 6, in addition to having more general monitoring authority, are competent to review and decide on specific allegations of violations of the human rights articulated in the treaties to which these bodies respectively are attached. Like the ILO complaint mechanisms, these procedures are structured to include elements of due process, and when invoked in particular cases they may lead to published decisions on procedural, factual, or legal issues. Worth mentioning among the U.N. treaty bodies, other than the Human Rights Committee, is the Committee on the Elimination of Racial Discrimination (CERD), because of CERD's demonstrated interest in indigenous issues alongside that of the Human Rights Committee's.[28] Both the Human Rights Committee and CERD are empowered to receive and consider complaints by states against other states for breaches of corresponding treaty norms.[29] In general, states have been slow to point the finger at each other with regard to human rights issues unless they also have ulterior political motives.[30] This has been especially true in respect to problems, such as those commonly associated with indigenous peoples, that are endemic to a large number of states and that in many cases call for reforms of a constitutional nature. Thus, neither the interstate complaint procedure of CERD nor that of the Human Rights Committee may reliably or consistently function to address the fundamental concerns of indigenous peoples, even though both bodies have viewed these concerns as falling within their respective fields of competency.

Both the Human Rights Committee and CERD, however, have additional capacities by which they may hear directly from victims of human rights abuse. Article 14 of the Convention on the Elimination of all Forms of Racial Discrimination authorizes CERD to receive complaints, or "communications," from "individuals or groups of individuals" claiming to be victims of violations of rights specified in the convention.[31] CERD may only consider article 14 petitions if the state party concerned has issued a formal declaration recognizing CERD's competence to do so.[32] The Human Rights Committee's competence to hear complaints by actors other than states is governed by the Optional Protocol to the Covenant on Civil and Political Rights.[33] State parties to the Optional Protocol assent to the competence of the committee to hear "communications" from "individuals" subject to their jurisdiction who claim to be victims of violations of rights included in the covenant.[34] Both procedures are subject to similar admissibility requirements (i.e., requirements of form and context that are preconditions to consideration of the merits),[35] with the notable exception that, unlike CERD, the Human Rights Committee is enjoined against hearing complaints regarding matters already being considered by another international institution.[36]

Thus far, relatively few states have made declarations under article 14 of the antidiscrimination convention, while a majority of the state parties to the Covenant on Civil and Political Rights are also parties to its Optional Protocol; a number of those in both categories have indigenous peoples within their borders.[37] As of this writing, the private complaint procedure involving CERD has been little utilized, and no indigenous people or group as such has sought to advance its demands through the procedure. This could be expected to change, given CERD's practice outside its complaint procedures to consider indigenous peoples' rights as falling substantially under the protection of the nondiscrimination norm that runs throughout the corresponding convention.[38]

In contrast to CERD, the Human Rights Committee has a record of adjudicating complaints concerning indigenous peoples pursuant to the Optional Protocol. The committee has interpreted its authorization under the Optional Protocol to hear complaints from "individuals" not to extend to complaints based on the right of self-determination, which is affirmed in article 1 of the Covenant on Civil and Political Rights as a right of "peoples." This interpretation, however, has constituted mostly a limitation of form for admissibility purposes and has not kept the committee from adjudicating what amount to issues of self-determination and groups rights common to indigenous peoples. The committee revealed its posture in this regard in the case of *Ominayak, Chief of the Lubicon Lake Band v. Canada*,[39] which resulted in the committee finding against Canada in a dispute over natural resource development on the ancestral lands of the Lubicon Lake Band of Cree Indians. Chief Ominayak, acting on behalf of the Lubicon Cree, alleged that Canada violated the right of self-determination of article 1 of the covenant by allowing the provincial government of Alberta to expropriate lands of the Lubicon Lake Band for the benefit of private corporate interests. Canada challenged the admissibility of the communication on the ground that the Lubicon Lake Band did not constitute a "people" for the purposes of article 1. In ruling in favor of admissibility, the committee avoided the issue raised by Canada by *sua sponte* reformulating the complaint under other articles of the covenant—in particular, article 27, which upholds the rights of "persons belonging to minorities." In its final decision in the case, the committee recounted its interim decision on admissibility:

> [T]he Committee observed that the author [of the communication, Chief Ominayak], as an individual, could not claim under the Optional Protocol to be a victim of a violation of the right of self-determination enshrined in article 1 of the Covenant, which deals with rights conferred upon peoples, as such.
>
> 13.4 The Committee noted, however, that the facts as submitted might raise issues under other articles of the Covenant, including article 27. Thus, in so far as the author and other members of the Lubicon Lake Band were

affected by the events which the author has described, these issues should be examined on the merits, in order to determine whether they reveal violations of article 27 or other articles of the Covenant.[40]

Affirming its interim decision on admissibility, the committee added:

> The Optional Protocol provides a procedure under which individuals can claim that their individual rights have been violated. These rights are set out in part III of the Covenant, articles 6 to 27 inclusive. There is, however, no objection to a group of individuals, who claim to be similarly affected, collectively to submit a communication about alleged breaches of their rights.[41]

On the merits of the case the committee comprehensively addressed the problems raised by the Lubicon Lake Band's original factual allegations, from the standpoint of prevailing normative assumptions favoring the integrity and survival of indigenous peoples and their cultures. In the end, the committee held: "Historical inequities . . . and certain more recent developments threaten the way of life and culture of the Lubicon Lake Band, and constitute a violation of article 27."[42]

It can thus be surmised that, in order to be admissible, a communication to the committee under the Optional Protocol must be *by an individual* (or group of individuals) alleging a violation of a right articulated as an *individual right* in the covenant. An indigenous group, nonetheless, may effectively bring a complaint through a representative individual and petition for implementation of a meaningful range of covenant norms, including article 27 which—although articulated as a right of "persons"—has been interpreted broadly in favor of indigenous cultural integrity and group survival.[43] In addition, in more recent decisions the committee has clarified that although article 1 cannot be a basis of a complaint under the Optional Protocol, article 1 can be used to interpret the meaning and application of other articles that are properly invoked, such as article 27.[44]

The committee's deliberations in *Ominayak v. Canada* also are instructive on the requirement that domestic remedies be exhausted, another condition of admissibility, but one with a clearer textual basis in the Optional Protocol.[45] The exhaustion requirement, which is common to the individual complaint procedures involving CERD and other international bodies, is a corollary to state sovereignty principles that impose deference to local decision making where possible. Canada had attempted to preclude consideration of the merits of the Lubicon Lake Band's petition in *Ominayak* on the alternative ground that domestic remedies, in particular through judicial proceedings initiated years earlier, had not diligently been pursued to completion.[46] In upholding its earlier decision of admissibility, however, the committee remained unpersuaded that continuing "the road of litigation would have represented an effective method of saving or restoring the traditional or cultural livelihood of the Lubicon Lake Band which, at the material time, was allegedly on the brink of collapse."[47] The committee thus emphasized that the exhaustion of domestic remedies requirement applies only to the extent domestic avenues of recourse are real and not ineffective or inadequate. On the other hand, the Committee has readily declined to admit cases involving indigenous group claims in which it perceives the existence of adequate domestic judicial procedures that have not been invoked or exhausted.[48]

The committee's decisions in *Ominayak v. Canada* signify its willingness to scrutinize state action or inaction under substantive standards and take a stand against persistent action or inaction that is squarely against the values implicit in the covenant. It was evident to the committee that, under the totality of the circumstances, including the lack of an effective domestic remedy, the cultural survival of the Lubicon Lake Band was truly threatened. The committee' disposition is further revealed in *Lovelace v. Canada*,[49] in which it concluded that the Canadian Indian Act violated the covenant because of provisions that excluded certain classes of indigenous women from membership in Indian "bands" recognized by the government; and in *Hopu & Bessert v. France*,[50] in which the committee determined that France violated the covenant by authorizing the building of a hotel complex on the historical burial grounds of indigenous Tahitians.

However, not unlike the ILO committees, the Human Rights Committee has been deferential to state action or programs affecting indigenous peoples when it effectively sees such action or programs as good faith efforts to address indigenous concerns. This has been so even in cases the committee admits and subjects to examination on the merits. For example, the committee examined but ultimately rejected a claim on behalf of the Mikmaq Tribal Society that its rights (or its members' rights) to political participation under the covenant were violated by Canada's refusal to allow a representative of the Society direct participation in discussions over reform of Canada's constitution.[51] The committee found that "in the specific circumstances of the present case," the right of the Mikmaq to take part in public affairs was not infringed.[52] The committee observed that a number of national aboriginal peoples' associations were invited to participate in various phases of the constitutional reform process. As a whole, these associations and leaders were presumed to represent the interests of all aboriginal peoples of Canada, a point stressed to the committee by the Canadian government. The committee did not suggest that the scheme for aboriginal participation in constitutional talks was optimal, given the legitimate particularized interests of the Mikmaq and other discrete aboriginal groups. However, the committee clearly saw any deficiencies in the arrangement as a matter of fine-tuning in the democratic process, best worked out by Canadian and aboriginal authorities at the more local level.

The committee likewise declined to find a violation of the covenant in aspects of a complex agreement that New Zealand had negotiated with Maori leaders to settle a long-standing claim over fisheries based on the Treaty of Waitangi.[53] In a complaint to the committee, a group of Maori opposed to the agreement alleged violations of the covenant because of the quota system for Maori fishing it established and because of the discontinuance of related domestic judicial proceedings that was also part of the agreement. Although emphasizing that the challenged aspects of the agreement raised issues under article 27 (cultural integrity) and article 14 (right to judicial protection) of the covenant, the committee found no violation, stressing that the challenged aspects of the agreement were part of a comprehensive settlement arrived at through a process of broad consultation with Maori leaders and communities.[54] The committee did not unquestionably endorse the agreement, but rather it applied a substantial measure of deference to what it apparently saw as a good faith measure by New Zealand within its domestic jurisdiction to address an indigenous claim under complicated circumstances.[55]

A different scenario is when the committee assumes a deferential posture toward domestic decision making even in cases where, unlike those of the Mikmaq and Maori, the committee has identified violations of covenant-protected rights. Typical of its practice, the committee's finding of a violation of the covenant in *Ominayak v. Canada* was accompanied by an indication of its views on an appropriate remedy. It is here that the committee may be faulted for not taking a more active stance. At the conclusion of its views on the merits of the case, the committee stated obliquely, "The State party proposes to rectify the situation by a remedy that the Committee deems appropriate."[56] What this proposed remedy consisted of is not specified or otherwise clear from the committee's published decision. But subsequent to the decision, the Canadian government attempted to force a settlement on terms roundly rejected by the Lubicon Cree,[57] and matters were left at an impasse with no further apparent involvement by the committee. In an editorial opinion, the *Edmonton Journal* called the Canadian government's method of attempting to reach a settlement of the Lubicon Cree's land claim "manipulative" and "deceitful," and urged the government to abandon its "take it or leave it" stance.[58]

The committee's finding of a violation in the *Lubicon* case made clear that the Canadian government had to do *something* to remedy the situation, and indeed the Canadian government effectively acknowledged it had to do something. But, given the nature of that case, the committee's weight did not much come to bear on what that something might be. The *Lubicon* case involved an indigenous land claim in which controversy raged about how the claim should be resolved, even assuming its validity. The committee's finding that the status quo constituted a violation of the rights of the Lubicon Cree could not itself clarify the issue of remedy. And by not providing more guidance on the remedy issue, the committee left it subject to continuing controversy within Canada's internal processes in which the Canadian government had the upper hand. Thus, however pathbreaking the committee's decision in the *Lubicon* case is in other respects, its effectiveness in that very case was undermined.

Similarly, the committee refrained from providing specific guidance for the remedy to be enacted to replace the discriminatory aspects of the membership requirements of the Canadian Indian Act that were found in violation of the covenant in *Lovelace v. Canada*.[59] After the committee's finding of a violation, Canada reformed the act to prevent the discriminatory effect against women identified in it.[60] However, the reforms, which created a complex system of membership in indigenous "bands," itself became the subject of an important dispute because in some cases it expands band membership and in others contracts membership in ways that do not fit with relevant social or cultural patterns;[61] and this dispute continued with apparently little attention by the committee.[62] In the case of *Hopu & Bessert v. France*, the committee's finding of a violation of the covenant likewise was not accompanied by specific guidance on a remedy nor by the committee's active engagement with the dispute in the aftermath of its finding of a violation.[63] Tourists now play on the grounds of the luxury hotel complex that, in its planning stages, was the basis of the committee's finding of a violation because of its likely effect on ancestral indigenous burial grounds.[64]

As with the ILO procedures, the deferential stance of the Human Rights Committee can be explained on the basis of the principle—or, more accurately, the presumption—of noninterference, which favors decision making at the domestic level to the extent consistent with overarching values. At least in the *Lubicon* case, however, the committee struck the wrong balance between the presumption of noninterference and the variable need for international involvement in matters ordinarily within the realm of more local decision making. While in other contexts the committee may be able to effectively promote the implementation of human rights norms by authoritatively declaring a violation, situations like that of the Lubicon Cree and other indigenous peoples facing entrenched historical inequities require more active involvement. The committee has a useful role to play not only in identifying the violation of indigenous peoples' rights but also in identifying or working to ensure the enactment of appropriate remedies, especially in light of the international communities' special concern for promoting redress for long-standing wrongs against indigenous peoples. The committee could fulfill this role, not only by requesting follow-up information from governments as it now normally does[65] but also by offering good offices to promote or mediate dialogue toward agreement on remedies. The committee has taken certain initiatives in this direction, which may eventually lead it to function as an important conduit for practical solutions to the problems it identifies.[66]

Complaint Procedures within the Inter-American System

At the regional level, the inter-American system for the protection of human rights, which functions as part of the Organization of American States, includes complaint procedures that increasingly have been used to address the concerns of indigenous peoples. Two institutions are the conduits for the inter-American complaint procedures. One is the Inter-American Commission on Human Rights, which was discussed in chapter 6 in regard to its general monitoring function. In addition to issuing general reports on country situations, the commission may investigate and make recommendations in response to specific complaints against any OAS member state. The other inter-American institution is the Inter-American Court of Human Rights. It has a more limited jurisdiction to adjudicate complaints, but within that jurisdiction its decisions are legally binding.

Petitions to the Inter-American Commission on Human Rights

Under its statute and rules of procedure, the Inter-American Commission on Human Rights may hear and act on complaints, or "petitions," concerning human rights violations involving any of the countries that are members of the Organization of American States.[67] When confronted with a complaint concerning a state that is a party to the American Convention on Human Rights, the commission's terms of reference include the substantive rights and procedures specified in that convention.[68] Some provisions of the other treaties in the inter-American human rights system also may form the basis for a complaint before the commission with respect to state parties to those treaties.[69] OAS member states that are not parties to the American Convention or other applicable inter-American treaties may have complaints lodged against them by reference to the human rights norms articulated in the American Declaration of the Rights and Duties of Man; the competence of the commission in this respect is derived from the theory that the declaration defines the human rights obligations that all OAS member states assume as parties to the organization's Charter.[70]

In most respects the procedures for complaints to the commission are the same regardless of the instrument that is alleged to be violated, including criteria for admissibility, fact-finding, and decision making.[71] "Any person or group of persons or nongovernmental entity legally recognized" in an OAS member state may submit a complaint to the commission.[72] Unlike individual petitions to the U.N. Human Rights Committee, complaints to this commission may be filed by parties, including groups and organizations, other than the victims, and with or without the victims' knowledge or consent. Otherwise, admissibility requirements for commission complaints, including the requirement of exhaustion of domestic remedies, are much like the admissibility criteria for individual or group petitions to the U.N. Human Rights Committee.[73]

The commission engages in fact-finding by reviewing the parties' initial written submissions and usually by soliciting additional written information.[74] The commission may also convene hearings or conduct on-site investigations.[75] This fact-finding and exchange of information itself often facilitates dialogue conducive to reaching solutions to problems upon which complaints are founded. In addition, the commission may formally assume the role of mediator at the request of the parties or upon its own initiative under its so called "friendly settle-ment" procedure.[76] At any stage of its consideration of a case, the commission can request that the state in question adopt precautionary measures "[i]n serious and urgent cases," with a view "to prevent irreparable harm to persons."[77] If a case is formally admitted and is not resolved during the investigation or friendly settlement stages, the commission drafts a report with conclusions and recom-mendations on the merits of the petition. If human rights violations are estab-lished, the commission communicates the report first to the impugned state, without providing a copy to the petitioner and without publication. If the commission's recommendations are not implemented or a satisfactory settlement is not otherwise achieved within a prescribed deadline, the commission may decide to publish its conclusions[78] or, in appropriate cases, to bring the case before the Inter-American Court of Human Rights, whose judgments are binding.[79] The conditional withholding of publication adds to the incentive for states to resolve human rights problems brought to the commission's attention.

Since the early 1970s, the commission has considered a number of peti-tions alleging human rights violations against particular indigenous groups.[80] Two important early cases involved the Guahibo of Colombia and the Aché of Paraguay, both groups faced with patterns of violence and social ills that caught the attention of international nongovernmental organizations.[81] In the *Guahibo* case, the commission's main concern was with establishing its competence to investigate the allegations presented and to require an initially uncooperative Colombian government to supply relevant information. Upon reaching a level of satisfaction with the information eventually provided by the government, the commission effectively suspended proceedings on the case "without prejudice to reopening examination thereof in the event that new evidence so requires."[82] In the later *Aché* case, the commission went further and made a decision on the merits of the complaint after reaching an impasse with the Paraguayan govern-ment. In a published resolution the commission denounced violations of rights affirmed in the American Declaration of Rights—including violations of the right to life and personal security, the right to a family, and the right to health and well-being—and called upon the Paraguayan government to take "vigorous measures" to correct the violations committed against the Aché.[83]

Shelton Davis faults the commission for not going far enough in either of these cases to address the core problems faced by the indigenous groups con-cerned. He mentions in particular critical land tenure situations that had led to societal tensions and mounting human rights abuses.[84] Davis attributes the commission's inattention to these issues in part to a general lack of expertise in indigenous peoples and their rights.[85] The commission's actions in these cases can also be explained by the express scope of its jurisdiction in respect to com-plaints. The commission is empowered to receive and act upon petitions that allege facts constituting violations of the substantive norms included in the

American Declaration of Rights or, in cases involving state parties to the American Convention, norms in that convention.[86] These human rights instruments articulate traditional, broadly applicable individual and social rights and do not include specific reference to indigenous peoples.

In later cases involving indigenous peoples, however, the commission clearly has considered and advanced norms regarding indigenous land and other group rights. In 1980 a number of concerned NGOs submitted a petition on behalf of the Brazilian Yanomami, whose ancestral lands were being invaded by gold prospectors and other outsiders. The abrupt and uncontrolled contact with outsiders led to widespread disease and death among the previously isolated forest-dwelling Yanomami, and to the uprooting of entire Yanomami villages.[87] After closely monitoring events and soliciting information from the government of Brazil, the commission adopted a resolution finding violations of rights specifically articulated in the American Declaration, including the rights to life, residence, and health.[88] In addition, the commission looked beyond the American Declaration and observed that, "international law in its present state . . . recognizes the right of ethnic groups to special protection . . . for all those characteristics necessary for the preservation of their cultural identity."[89] The only specific authority cited by the commission to support this statement of law was article 27 of the International Covenant on Civil and Political Rights, even though Brazil was not a party to the covenant. Hence it can be surmised that the commission considered the principle to be one of customary or general international law.[90] Viewing land tenure as an important part of Yanomami culture, the commission included in its recommendations that Brazil proceed with plans to demarcate Yanomami lands and secure them from encroachment by outsiders.[91]

The commission took a similar approach in acting on a complaint brought on behalf of the Miskito and other indigenous people of the Atlantic Coast region of Nicaragua. As discussed in chapter 3, that case was initiated in the midst of the violent conflicts that engulfed Nicaragua in the 1980s. The Miskito, Mayangna (Sumo), and Rama Indians of the Atlantic Coast region of that country were especially affected by the conflicts; Indian leaders were imprisoned, villages were forcibly relocated, countless noncombatant Indians killed, and demands for land and autonomy rights were suffocated.[92] The commission published an extensive report on the case,[93] examining recent events in light of rights affirmed in the American Convention, to which Nicaragua is a party. Noting that the American Convention is not to be interpreted as restricting the enjoyment of rights otherwise recognized, the commission also considered Nicaragua's international obligations under other instruments, particularly its obligations as a party to the International Covenant on Civil and Political Rights.[94]

The commission found certain instances of illegal conduct by the Nicaraguan government[95] but mostly recounted facts and signaled problems that needed continued attention, stressing the complexities of the situation. Significantly, the commission went beyond examining the immediate conflicts; it identified long-standing problems facing the indigenous peoples of the Atlantic Coast and addressed demands for political autonomy articulated by indigenous leaders. Relying especially on the cultural rights guarantees of article 27 of the International Covenant on Civil and Political Rights, the commission recommended measures to secure indigenous land rights and to develop a new institutional order that would better accommodate to the distinctive cultural attributes and traditional forms of organization of the indigenous groups.[96]

The Yanomami and Miskito cases demonstrate that the complaint procedure involving the Inter-American Commission may be a conduit for implementing norms concerning indigenous peoples beyond those norms specifically articulated in the American Declaration of Rights and the American Convention. The commission's willingness to apply sources of international human rights law other than the relevant inter-American instruments in these and subsequent cases is consistent with its approach in its parallel procedure of generally reporting on the human rights situations of indigenous peoples, as exemplified in its 1997 report on the human rights situation in Ecuador.[97] For admissibility purposes, a complaint must allege facts constituting a violation of the declaration or the convention. But once the commission proceeds to consider the merits of a case, international norms that are otherwise applicable may be invoked. In considering the merits of cases involving indigenous peoples, and particularly when proceeding in such cases to propose solutions to identified problems, the commission may more completely fulfill its general mandate to promote human rights by applying the relevant conventional or customary norms as they have developed in the context of indigenous peoples.

Thus, in the aftermath of its decisions in the *Yanomami* and *Miskito* cases the commission is developing and applying a jurisprudence of indigenous rights that considers the inter-American instruments to be, in relevant respects, integrated within the larger body of international law that concerns indigenous peoples. As exemplified in the commission's more recent decision in the case of *Carrie and Mary Dann v. United States*,[98] norms articulated in the inter-American instruments are seen as both supportive of and informed by the broad universe of international developments that increasingly affirm the rights of indigenous peoples. In that case the commission found the United States to be in violation of the rights to equality, judicial protection, and property of the American Declaration on the Rights and Duties of Man, because of the various problems it saw in the U.S. treatment of the land claims advanced by the Dann sisters and others who constitute the Western Shoshone people.[99] The commission interpreted the invoked rights of the American Declaration in light of multiple relevant developments and instruments concerning indigenous peoples—including provisions of the commission's own Proposed American Declaration on the Rights of Indigenous Peoples.[100] For the commission, the American Declaration on the Rights and Duties of Man and other inter-American instruments are linked with, and hence are to be interpreted in reference to, a contemporary body of "international legal principles developing out of and applicable inside and outside of the Inter-American system."[101]

In addition to revealing the commission's normative frame of reference, the *Yanomami, Miskito,* and *Dann* cases also are instructive as to the manner and extent to which the commission's intervention through its petition procedure may actually advance solutions to disputes in accordance with relevant international norms. In the *Yanomami* case, the commission made successive requests for information from the Brazilian government over a period of years, each time building on information already provided by the government or obtained by interested NGOs.[102] This process of interaction with the Brazilian government and concerned NGOs itself pressured the government to take note of specific problems, despite the government's initial resistance to the commission's intervention. The commission's published recommendations of remedial measures, based upon findings that Brazil had committed violations of human rights, sharpened this pressure and the commission's role of helping to steer authorities toward appropriate corrective measures.[103]

In the *Miskito* case, the commission engaged in an effort to mediate a settlement of the dispute, after conducting an investigation of the case and submitting to the Nicaraguan government an unpublished report of its findings and recommendations.[104] Within this effort at friendly settlement, the commission communicated extensively with interested parties and labored to develop a framework for constructive dialogue between the government and Indian leaders.[105] The commission suspended its efforts at friendly settlement and published its report, mostly because the Nicaraguan government persisted in its refusal to negotiate with certain exiled Indian leaders. But in publishing its report and bringing to light the problems faced by the indigenous peoples of Nicaragua's Atlantic Coast, the commission appears to have promoted further, and ultimately more successfully, dialogue toward corrective measures. A few months after the report was published in 1984, the Nicaraguan government entered direct talks with a group of the same exiled Indian leaders it had earlier sought to avoid.[106] These negotiations were the catalyst for a larger process of ensuing consultations resulting in major restructuring of Nicaragua's policy and legal regime concerning indigenous peoples.[107]

In the *Dann* case the commission similarly rested its attempt at influencing state behavior on its publication of a report finding human rights violations, subsequent to an unsuccessful attempt at friendly settlement. After the commission issued its decision that the case was admissible,[108] the United States ignored for over a year the commission's requests for additional information and rebuffed the commission's proposal for a process of friendly settlement. While the commission suspended its adjudication of the case to await a response from the United States on is proposal for a friendly settlement process, the United States continued and even stepped up efforts to deny the Danns and other Western Shoshone people access to the lands that were the subject of the case.[109] It was not until the commission eventually communicated to the United States a confidential report finding it in violation of the American Declaration on the Rights and Duties of Man in regard to Western Shoshone claims over traditional lands that the United States engaged the commission on the merits of the dispute, if only to reject the commission's findings. In its written response to the commission's report, the United States implicitly acknowledged that it is subject to certain international human rights standards, but it disagreed with the commission's interpretation and application of those standards.[110] The commission subsequently published its final report on the case, reiterating its conclusions and recommendations and refuting the U.S. points of disagreement.[111] The United States will likely continue a formal position of rejecting the commission's report, in a stark manifestation of the limitations of the commission's influence over a powerful actor.[112] But discussion and decision making has continued about the Western Shoshone claim within domestic and international spheres in the aftermath of the commission's report; and within that discussion the United States has been made to contend with the commission's findings of human rights violations and its recommendations of remedial action by government agencies.[113] To the extent the commission might make a difference in this case, it is through publication of its report setting out the facts credibly and providing a well-reasoned statement and application of the relevant international human rights law, as it did, and not by an effort to mediate a solution to the dispute.

The commission did manage to oversee a successful process of friendly settlement in the case of the Lamenxay and Riachito indigenous communities of Paraguay,[114] a case initiated by a petition alleging violations of the American Convention on Human Rights in relation to the land rights of the indigenous communities. The parties agreed to the commission's proposal for a friendly settlement conference in the Paraguayan capital, at which a settlement of the dispute was promptly reached. The Paraguayan government agreed to purchase from third parties the lands claimed by the Lamenxay and Riachito communities, to title the lands in favor of the communities, and to assist them in resettling those lands.[115] Although the commission undoubtedly played an important role in the case, that role appears to be one of mostly encouraging and providing oversight to a settlement that was already contemplated by the state. The Lemanxay and Riachito land claims already had been validated by the Paraguayan judiciary,[116] within the framework of a relatively new constitutional order that explicitly recognizes that "Indian peoples have the right, as communities, to a shared ownership of a piece of land, which will be sufficient both in terms of size and quality for them to preserve and to develop their own lifestyles."[117]

Paraguayan authorities acknowledged the validity of the claim and fairly readily agreed to the measures to resolve it.[118]

Despite the outcome in the *Lamenxay and Riachito* case, the commission has not yet demonstrated itself capable of actively and effectively mediating a solution to an indigenous group claim in which the state concerned, unlike Paraguay in that case, resists or is passive toward the claim. As illustrated by the *Dann* case, the friendly settlement process may act more frequently as a mechanism for the state to delay a determination of its responsibility than as a means of genuine conciliation.

The limitations of the commission's friendly settlement mechanism are especially exposed by the case of the Maya communities of Belize, a case initiated with a petition by the Toledo Maya Cultural Council in August 1998 in an attempt to stop logging and oil development on Maya traditional lands and to secure legal recognition of Maya communal rights over those lands.[119] Shortly after the petition was filed, Maya leaders and the government of Belize agreed to engage in negotiations over the issues raised in the petition, within the framework of the commission's friendly settlement procedure. Several rounds of negotiation were attempted with little active participation by the commission and with no results other than agreements to define the terms of or reinitiate talks that had failed in earlier rounds.[120] In October 2000, after more than two years of failed efforts toward a friendly settlement, the commission declared the case admissible and it issued precautionary measures calling upon Belize to halt the logging and oil development while the commission proceeded to investigate the case.[121] The government of Belize ignored the precautionary measures, as trees continued to fall on Maya lands. A delegation of the commission subsequently conducted an on-site visit to Belize, during which it urged further negotiations and assisted in the development of yet another document to set the terms of the talks. But the settlement talks that followed, just as the previous rounds, were not accompanied by sustained intervention or mediation by the commission, and they ended with the Maya parties urging the commission to proceed quickly to issue a report finding Belize responsible for human rights violations and making appropriate recommendations. The commission eventually acceded to this request and in October 2003 issued to the government a preliminary report, in which the commission found violations of the American Declaration on the Rights and Duties of Man in relation to Maya land rights.[122]

The commission's friendly settlement procedure is a potentially important and useful mechanism for the development of remedial measures in particular cases in which indigenous people experience the violation of their rights. But as the Maya and other cases reveal, the procedure has not yet lived up to its potential. Typical of many indigenous group claims, the Maya claims over traditional lands and resources call for significant reforms in domestic institutional and legal regimes and for a level of sensitivity among government actors toward indigenous peoples that has been absent in the past. In such cases the commission may contribute greatly to mobilizing government resources around indigenous peoples' concerns, to educating government actors about relevant norms, and to devising practical solutions. But in order to consistently and reliably contribute in this way, the commission must increase its mediation capacities through the deployment of more resources and expertise. The commission should also be sensitive to the likely situations in which government resistance makes friendly settlement difficult or impossible, especially in the absence of any finding or admission of state responsibility. In such situations, a commission report authoritatively establishing the facts, setting forth the relevant normative framework, finding violations, and making appropriate recommendations will likely do much more toward advancing solutions and inducing the state toward meaningful dialogue than the commission's good offices alone.

The Adjudication of Complaints by the Inter-American Court of Human Rights: The *Awas Tingni* Case

The inter-American commission may also advance the rights of indigenous peoples in certain cases by invoking the authority of the Inter-American Court of Human Rights. As noted earlier, the commission itself may receive and adjudicate claims against any OAS member state, including those that are not parties to the American Convention on Human Rights. But for those procedures subject to the American Convention, there exists the additional possibility of intervention by the inter-American Court, a judicial body created by the American Convention with the authority to issue legally binding decisions. The Court may exercise jurisdiction over a case if the state concerned is a party to the convention and also has accepted the optional jurisdiction of the Court.[123] But only the commission or the state concerned may refer a case to the Court after proceedings in the commission have been completed.[124] The commission amended its Rules of Procedure in 2000 to establish a presumption in favor of submitting to the Court those cases in which the commission's recommendations have not been followed.[125] The 2000 amendments also specify that the party that submitted the petition initiating the case with the commission will be consulted about whether or not to submit the case to the Court.[126]

Of the hundreds of cases that have been adjudicated by the commission, relatively few have reached the Court, and very few of those have been cases involving indigenous peoples.[127] The *Case of the Mayagna Community of Awas Tingni v. Nicaragua* is a case in which the Court considered and ruled in favor of the collective land rights of an indigenous community of Nicaragua's Atlantic Coast, after the Nicaraguan state had granted a concession for logging on the community's traditional lands and had ignored the community's objections to the concession and its request for demarcation and titling of its lands.[128] At the time of this writing, the *Awas Tingni* case is the only case to have been decided by the Court centering on the asserted collective rights of an indigenous people or community.[129] Other cases that have reached a judgment by the Court have dealt with claims stemming primarily from acts of physical violence against individuals who were members of indigenous communities, such as the case of *Aleoboetoe v. Suriname*. In that case, which related to a massacre perpetrated by a group of soldiers against a Saramaca village suspected of collaborating with a guerrilla group, the Court did not have to determine the merits of the case, because Suriname had admitted the responsibility of its agents for the impugned acts.[130] Although the case involved straightforward violations of classic individual rights to life and physical integrity, the Court considered Saramaca customary law on family relations and succession when determining the compensation due as reparation and the beneficiaries of that compensation.[131] The *Aleoboetoe* and *Awas Tingni* cases both provide bases upon which the Court may build its capacity to address the concerns of indigenous peoples, in situations in which states have resisted cooperating with the inter-American commission or have ignored its recommendations regarding those concerns.

In the *Awas Tingni* case especially, the inter-American Court followed the commission's lead in advancing a progressive application of the inter-American instruments, one that takes into account contextual factors and a range of normative developments concerning indigenous peoples. When Awas Tingni, a Mayangna indigenous community, petitioned the inter-American commission in 1995,[132] it brought to the fore the problems that continued to persist for the Mayangna, Miskito, and other indigenous peoples in the Atlantic Coast region of Nicaragua, even in the aftermath of the institutional and legal reforms that followed the commission's earlier examination of the Atlantic Coast.[133] Despite formal recognition of traditional indigenous land tenure in the Nicaraguan Constitution and laws,[134] Awas Tingni and most other indigenous communities continued without a deed of title or any other form of specific government recognition of rights to their traditional lands. And in the absence of such specific government recognition, government agencies continued to regard the untitled indigenous lands as state-owned lands, which was the premise of government authorization for logging by foreign companies on lands claimed by the Awas Tingni community.[135] The government of Nicaragua readily agreed to the inter-American commission's suggestion of a process of friendly settlement, as did the community. But more than two years passed without any resolution of the community's land claim—yet another example of the limitations of the friendly settlement procedure. The commission finally made a determination of state responsibility and submitted a confidential report to the government with recommendations of measures for the government to take to secure Awas Tingni's traditional lands.[136] After the government failed to indicate its willingness to fully and promptly implement the commission's recommendations, the commission submitted the case to the inter-American Court.[137]

A highly contentious process of litigation followed, lasting more than an additional three years, during which the Court disposed of Nicaragua's effort to have the case dismissed based on preliminary objections,[138] received written arguments by the parties on the legal and factual issues, evaluated hundreds of pages of documentary evidence, and convened a hearing to receive the testimony of several witnesses.[139] The hearing, a remarkable two-and-a-half-day event at the Court's seat in San José, Costa Rica, was itself a form of relief for members and leaders of the Awas Tingni community, an opportunity to directly confront Nicaraguan government representatives and see them have to answer the community's grievances before a neutral decision maker in a public and highly visible forum.[140] From the testimony of Awas Tingni leaders at the hearing unfolded a story of people and land, and of a struggle to maintain the connection between the two. The social science and legal professionals who also testified gave context for this story, providing insights into its broader implications and validating the perspective of territory advanced by the indigenous leaders.[141] The government official who testified, and the government lawyers who cross-examined the commission's witnesses, persisted in advancing a perspective of state dominance over territory and resistance to understanding the meaning of the indigenous presence.[142]

In the end, the inter-American Court accepted Awas Tingni's account of its relationship to territory and ruled that Awas Tingni does possess rights to lands and natural resources that the government must account for and respect. As discussed in chapter 4, the Court in its judgment found a violation of the right to property of article 21 of the American Convention on Human Rights, interpreting property to include the communal land tenure of indigenous peoples in accordance with evolving international standards of indigenous rights.[143] The Court also found violations of article 25 of the Convention, which affirms the right to judicial protection, in connection with articles 1 and 2 of the Convention, which obligate state parties to adopt the measures necessary to secure the enjoyment of fundamental rights. In this regard the Court noted the failure of the Nicaraguan judiciary and administrative agencies to respond adequately to demands by Awas Tingni and to make effective those rights regarding indigenous lands that are affirmed in Nicaragua's own constitution and laws.[144] The Court thus established that the faithful implementation of both international and domestic legal protections for the rights of indigenous peoples is an affirmative obligation under the American Convention on Human Rights and that states may incur international responsibility if they fail to make those rights effective. Exercising its authority under article 63(1) of the American Convention to order reparations in which violations are found, the Court ordered Nicaragua to develop an adequate procedure for the demarcation and titling of the traditional lands of indigenous communities "in accordance with their customary laws, values, customs, and mores,"[145] to proceed to demarcate and title Awas Tingni's traditional lands in particular within fifteen months, and, until such the titling is complete, to refrain from allowing or tolerating any act that would affect the Awas Tingni community's use and enjoyment of its rights over those lands.[146]

While marking a path in the doctrine of international law to embrace indigenous peoples' rights over lands and natural resources, the Court was notably timid and less careful in its assessments of monetary reparations and the recoverable costs incurred by Awas Tingni in the domestic and international proceedings. Under article 63(1) of the American Convention, the Court is able to order monetary relief as well as nonmonetary remedial measures. Thus the Court in numerous other cases has ordered monetary relief to compensate for material and moral harm to the victims, and furthermore has ordered payment to compensate for the legal and other costs incurred by the victims in seeking vindication of their rights in the relevant domestic and international proceedings.[147] In prior cases the Court had conducted extensive proceedings, sometimes over a period of months, subsequent to finding a violation of the convention in order to determine reparations.[148] In the *Awas Tingni* case, however, the Court avoided a reparations phase, following what has become its preferred practice of merging consideration of the merits and reparations, but it did so without making its intention to do so known at the outset of the proceedings.[149] Without confronting the community's or the commission's arguments for much larger sums, and without considering specific evidence on damages and costs,[150] the Court ordered that, "in accordance with equity," Nicaragua invest the total sum of US $50,000 "in works or services of collective interest for the benefit of the Awas Tingni Community" and that it pay the community US$30,000 for its expenses and costs.[151]

Another matter is the actual implementation of the Court's order of reparations, however faulty its monetary component. It was several months before Nicaragua made a public statement of commitment to adhere to the Court's judgment, owing in part to presidential elections and a change in government in the period immediately following the judgment. The Nicaraguan ambassador to the OAS announced that commitment in a meeting at the commission's headquarters and at that same meeting handed over a check for US$30,000 for the costs ordered by the Court.[152] A process of negotiation ensued between the community and the government to establish agreement on the US$50,000 in works and services that the government was to provide, to attempt to facilitate the process of demarcation and titling of the community, and to extract specific provisional commitments and action by the government to secure the community's lands.[153] The government eventually completed work on a boardinghouse for students from the community, to fulfill its agreement with the community for the expenditure of US$50,000 in works and services. In addition, the Nicaraguan legislative assembly passed, and the president signed, a law establishing a specific procedure for the demarcation and titling of indigenous lands.[154]

Nonetheless, real land tenure security for Awas Tingni—the principal objective of the Awas Tingni appeal to the inter-American system—remained elusive. Failure on the part of the government to take provisional steps to secure Awas Tingni lands from ongoing incursions by unauthorized loggers and others prompted the community to return to the Court with a request for provisional measures, to which the Court acceded. In its provisional measures resolution of September 6, 2002, the Court ordered Nicaragua to "adopt, withoug delay, the measures necessary to protect the Mayagna Community of Awas Tingni's use and enjoyment of their lands and the natural resources therein, specifically measures to prevent immediate and irreparable harm arising from activities by third parties who have settled in the community's territory or have exploited its natural resources."[155] But to the disappointment of Awas Tingni, little changed in the immediate aftermath of that order.[156] Furthermore, the part of the Court's judgment that Nicaragua specifically demarcate and title the lands of Awas Tingni remained unfulfilled, with the fifteen-month deadline set by the Court for doing so having passed in December 2002.[157] Government officials continued to express resolve to fully implement the inter-American Court's judgment; it would just take time.

Despite the problematic outcome of the Court's judgment in regard to monetary reparations and Nicaragua's sluggishness in implementing the Court's judgment in its most important respects, the Court's intervention in this case is on balance a positive factor for Awas Tingni and other indigenous communities of Nicaragua. The Court's intervention has prompted Nicaragua to accept the need to take specific measures to secure indigenous peoples' land rights in accordance with contemporary norms, and it has fostered greater awareness and the deployment of greater government institutional energies toward meeting that need. Even though the level of government attention to the issues raised by the *Awas Tingni* case remains deficient, Awas Tingni and other indigenous communities are farther along the path toward land tenure security than before the Court's intervention.

The role of the inter-American Court in the *Awas Tingni* case, along with that of the inter-American commission, thus reflects existing capacities within the international system in relation to the implementation of indigenous peoples' rights. Even when states agree to submit themselves to heightened levels of international scrutiny through formal complaint procedures, existing international capacities are limited in their ability to intervene in problem situations and bring about change. While authorized international institutions with increasing frequency examine the problems faced by indigenous peoples and make relevant recommendations, a formally binding international judicial decision to counter state behavior in violation of international norms is a rare occurrence. And even the rare legally binding international decision may yield compliance only with great difficulty. Still, on the other hand, international procedures are in some measure capable of promoting the realization of indigenous peoples' rights in accordance with contemporary norms. They shed light on problem situations that might otherwise go unnoticed by all but the indigenous peoples concerned; they provide conduits for indigenous peoples to confront state authorities with their grievances where inadequate channels exist at the domestic level; and they provide the possibility of changing the terms of dialogue so that it is grounded in the language of human rights, rather than being constrained by the existing and often oppressive parameters of legality at the domestic level.

Notes

1. Convention (No. 169) Concerning Indigenous and Tribal Peoples in Independent Countries, June 27, 1989, International Labour Conference (entered into force Sept. 5. 1991), reprinted in the appendix, *infra* [hereinafter ILO Convention No. 169]; Convention (No. 107) Concerning the Protection and Integration of Indigenous and other Tribal and Semi-Tribal Populations in Independent Countries, June 26, 1957, International Labour Conference, 328 U.N.T.S. 247 (entered into force June 2, 1959) [hereinafter ILO Convention No. 107].

2. Constitution of the International Labour Organization, Oct. 9, 1946, 15 U.N.T.S. 35, art. 24. The procedure for article 24 representations is discussed in Frederic L. Kirgis, Jr., *International Organizations in Their Legal Setting* 408–09 (2d ed. 1993); Lee Swepston, "Human Rights Complaint Procedures of the International Labour Organization," in *Guide to International Human Rights Practice* 85, 90–92 (Hurst Hannum ed., 3d ed. 1999).

3. For a description of the structure of governance in the ILO, see Kirgis, *supra* note 2, at 104–05.

4. *See Standing orders concerning the procedure for the examination of representations under articles 24 and 25 of the Constitution of the International Labour Organization*, 64 ILO Official Bulletin, ser. A., no. 1, at 63–65 (1981).

5. Publication of the representation and government's reply is authorized by the ILO Constitution in the case that "no statement is received within a reasonable time from the government in question, or if the statement when received is not deemed to be satisfactory by the Governing Body," ILO Const., art. 25.

6. *See, e.g., Report of the Committee Set Up Under Article 24 to Consider the Representation Alleging Non-Observance of the Discrimination Convention by Czechoslovakia*, 61 ILO Official Bulletin, ser. A, no. 3, at 1 (1978).

7. ILO Const., *supra* note 2, art. 26(1); *see generally* Kirgis, *supra* note 2, at 389–408; Swepston, *supra* note 2, at 92–95.

8. Accordingly, the Governing Body's Standing Orders concerning article 24 representations provide that it may make a representation into an article 26 complaint at any time. *See* Swepston, *supra* note 2, at 93.

9. A description of early proceedings involving ILO commissions of inquiry is in C. W. Jenks, *Social Justice* in *the Law of Nations* 48–54 (1970). The quasi-judicial char-

acter of commission of inquiry proceedings can be discerned from commission reports. *E.g., Report of the Commission Instituted under Article 26 to Examine the Complaint on the Observance by Poland of the Freedom of Association and Right to Organize Conventions,* 67 ILO Official Bulletin, ser. B, special supp. (1984).

10. *See* ILO Const., *supra* note 2, art. 28.

11. *See id.* art. 29.

12. *Id.* arts. 30–31.

13. As of the year 2000 only six commisions of inquiry under the article 26 procedure had been constituted. *See* Kimberly Ann Elliott, "The I.L.O. and Enforcement of Core Labor Standards," *International Economics Policy Brief,* No. 00-6 (2000), p. 5. Three of these commissions were constituted in the 1990s, all relating to covenants considered fundamental to the organization. *See Report of the Commission of Inquiry set up to examine the complaint concerning the observance by Romania of the Discrimination (employment and occupation) Convention, 1958 (No.111),* I.L.O. Doc. GB.250/ 5/4, ILO Official Bulletin, Vol. 74 (1991), ser. B, supp. 3; *Report of the Commission of Inquiry appointed under article 26 of the Constitution of the International Labour Organization to examine the complaint concerning the observance by Nicaragua of conventions on Freedom of Association and Protection of the Right to Organize, 1948 (No. 87), the Right to Organise and Collective Bargaining, 1949 (No. 98), and Tripartite Consultation, 1976 (No. 144),* ILO Doc. GB.249/5/6 ILO Official Bulletin, Vol. 74 (1991), ser. B, supp. 2 (Nov. 23, 1990); *Report of the Commission of Inquiry appointed under article 26 of the Constitution of the International Labour Organization to examine the observance by Myanmar of the Forced Labour Convention, 1930 (No. 49),* GB.269/15/1 (July 2, 1998).

With respect to the article 24 procedure, the pace of complaints grew since the beginning of the 1980s, reaching ten cases a year. Lee Swepston, "Supervision of ILO Standards," 13(4) *Int'l J. Comp. Labour L. & Indus. Relations* 327 (1997). This pace remained constant throughout the 1990s.

14. Thus, for example, worker representatives to the 1988 and 1989 sessions of the International Labour Conference advocated positions put forward by indigenous peoples' representatives in the development of ILO Convention (No. 169) on Indigenous and Tribal Peoples. *See* Lee Swepston, "A New Step in the International Law on Indigenous and Tribal Peoples: ILO Convention No. 169 of 1989," 15 *Okla. City U. L. Rev.* 677, 686 (1990).

15. *See Report of the Committee set up to examine the representation alleging nonobservance by Ecuador of the Indigenous and Tribal Peoples Convention, 1989 (No. 169), made under article 24 of the ILO Constitution by the Confederación Ecuatoriana de Organizaciones Sindicales Libres (CEOSL),* ILO Doc. GB.282/14/2, para. 29 (Nov. 2001) (finding that the " Standing Orders concerning the procedure for the examination of representations . . . do not require the complainant organization to have a direct connection with the events that constitute the basis of the complaint").

16. Both procedures begin with a complaint alleging the state in question "has failed to secure in any respect the effective observance" of a convention it has ratified, without any requirement that the complaint must first be brought before domestic administrative or judicial authorities. *See* ILO Const., *supra* note 2, art. 24.

17. *See Report of the Committee set up to examine the representation alleging non-observance by Mexico of the Indigenous and Tribal Peoples Convention, 1989 (No. 169), made under article 24 of the ILO Constitution by the Trade Union Delegation, D-III-57, section XI of the National Trade Union of Education Workers (SNTE), Radio Education,* ILO Doc. GB.272/7/2, para. 13 (June 1998).

18. *See id.* para. 41.

19. *Id.*

20. *Report of the Committee set up to examine the representation alleging non-observance by Colombia of the Indigenous and Tribal Peoples Convention, 1989 (No. 169), made under article 24 of the ILO Constitution by the Central Unitary Workers' Union (CUT),* ILO Doc.GB.282/14/3, para. 74 (Nov. 2001).

21. *Id.* para. 79

22. *Report of the Committee set up to examine the representation alleging non-observance by Colombia of the Indigenous and Tribal Peoples Convention, 1989 (No. 169), made under article 24 of the ILO Constitution by the Central Unitary Workers' Union (CUT) and the Colombian Medical Trade Union Association (ASMEDAS),* ILO Doc. GB.282/14/4, para. 68 (a) (Nov. 2001).

23. *Report of the Committee set up to examine the representation alleging non-observance by Colombia, made by CUT, supra* note 20, paras. 79, 90 (emphasis added). This case was addressed by the same tripartite committee and in the same report that addressed the petition, also brought by CUT, in relation to Decree No. 1320 of 1998.

24. *Report of the committee set up to examine the representation alleging non-observance by Ecuador, made by the Confederación Ecuatoriana de Organizaciones Sindicales Libres (CEOSL) supra* note 15, para. 38.

25. *Id.* para. 44.

26. The committee stated that it "considers that its essential task in such cases is not to offer an alternative venue for parties dissatisfied with the outcome of a claim for compensation before the national administrative or judicial bodies, but rather to ensure that the appropriate procedures for resolving land disputes have been applied and that the principles of the Convention have been taken into account in dealing with the issues affecting indigenous and tribal peoples." *Report of the Committee set up to examine the representation alleging non-observance by Denmark of the Indigenous and Tribal Peoples Convention, 1989 (No. 169), made under article 24 of the ILO Constitution by the National Confederation of Trade Unions of Greenland (Sulinermik Inuussutissarsiuteqartut Kattuffiat-SIK) (SIK),* ILO Doc. GB.280/18/5, para. 34 (Nov. 2001).

27. *See id.* para. 43.

28. *See supra* chapter 6, notes 60–87 and accompanying text (discussing the Human Rights Committee's and CERD's examinations of indigenous issues in considering government reports)

29. The interstate complaint procedures involving CERD apply automatically to all parties to the International Convention on the Elimination of All Forms of Racial Discrimination, Dec. 21, 1965, G.A. Res. 2106A(XX), 660 U.N.T.S. 195 (entered into force Jan. 4, 1969), pursuant to its article 11. By contrast, the interstate complaint procedure involving the Human Rights Committee under the Covenant on Civil and Political Rights functions only among states that have issued declarations recognizing the

relevant competence of that committee. International Covenant on Civil and Political Rights, Dec. 16, 1966, G.A. Res. 2200(XXI), art. 41, para. 1, 999 U.N.T.S. 171 (entered into force Mar. 23, 1976).

30. Hence the skepticism that has been expressed about the utility of the interstate complaint procedure involving the Human Rights Committee. Torkal Opsahl, "The Human Rights Committee," in *The United Nations and Human Rights* 420 (Philip Alston ed., 1992). Opsahl points out that "[a]lthough this skepticism may be exaggerated, other interstate complaints systems seem to confirm that this measure will be resorted to only very sparingly." *Id.*

31. Convention on the Elimination of All Forms of Racial Discrimination, *supra* note 29, art. 14. *See generally* Siân Lewis-Anthony, "Treaty-Based Procedures for Making Human Rights Complaints within the U.N. System," in *Guide to Human Rights Practice, supra* note 2, at 41, 50–53; Karl Josef Partsch, "The Committee on the Elimination of Racial Discrimination," in *The United Nations and Human Rights, supra* note 30, at 339, 363.

32. Convention on the Elimination of All Forms of Racial Discrimination, *supra* note 29, art. 14, para. 1.

33. Optional Protocol to the International Covenant on Civil and Political Rights, Dec. 16, 1966, 999 U.N.T.S. 302.

34. *Id.* art. 1. *See generally* Lewis-Anthony, *supra* note 31, at 41–50; Dominic McGoldrick, *The Human Rights Committee: Its Role in the Development of the International Covenant on Civil and Political Rights* 120–246 (1991); Opsahl, *supra* note 30, at 420–23 (outlining the committee's procedures and method of work in considering individual complaints). Pursuant to article 5 of the Optional Protocol the committee meets in closed session to consider the written information submitted to it in connection with a complaint under the Optional Protocol, including responsive statements by the state concerned. However, the committee publishes its final decisions, called "views," and includes them in its annual reports. The publication of views is not specifically authorized by the protocol, but follows from a decision of the committee itself. Decision at the 7th Session, summarized in *Selected Decisions Under the Optional Protocol*, U.N. Doc. CCPR/C/OP/1 (1985).

35. In general, a complaint is admissible under the Optional Protocol if

> it is compatible with the Covenant, i.e., concerns one of the rights and freedoms recognized in the Covenant, does not represent an abuse, and is not anonymous. Moreover, it must be submitted by or on behalf of the alleged victim. All domestic remedies must have been exhausted, and the same matter must not at the same time be under examination by another international procedure.

Opsahl, *supra* note 30, at 423. Compare discussion of admissibility requirements for individual complaints involving CERD in Partsch, *supra* note 31, at 363; and in Lewis-Anthony, *supra* note 31, at 49–51.

36. Optional Protocol, *supra* note 33, art. 5, para. 2(b).

37. As of November 2, 2003, forty-two of the 165 state parties to the Convention on the Elimination of All Forms of Discrimination had made declarations under article 14 recognizing the jurisdiction of CERD to receive complaints, while 104 states were parties to the Optional Protocol. Office of the United Nations High Commissioner

for Human Rights, *Status of Ratifications of the Principal Human Rights Treaties, as of November 2, 2003*.

38. *See supra* chapter 6, notes 74–87 and accompanying text (discussing CERD's practice in reviewing government reports).

39. Bernard Ominayak, Chief of the Lubicon Lake Band v. Canada, Communication No. 167/1984, *Report of the Human Rights Committee*, U.N. GAOR, 45th Sess., Supp. No. 40, vol. 2, at 1, U.N. Doc. A/45/40, Annex 9(A) (1990) (views adopted Mar. 26, 1990). This and other significant cases decided by the committee, including cases involving indigenous peoples, are analyzed in *Leading Cases of the Human Rights Committee* (Raija Hanski & Martin Scheinin eds., 2003).

40. *Id.* at 9–10.

41. *Id.* at 27.

42. *Id.*

43. *Cf.* Mikmaq Tribal Society v. Canada, Communication No. 78/1980, *Report of the Human Rights Committee*, U.N. GAOR, 39th Sess., Supp. No. 40, at 200, U.N. Doc. A/39/40, Annex 16 (1984) (decision on admissibility adopted July 29,1984) (holding the communication inadmissible on the ground that its author had failed to show that he was authorized to act on behalf of the Mikmaq Tribal Society).

44. *See* Apirana Mahauika et al. v. New Zealand, Communication No. 547/1993, U.N. Doc. CCPR/C/70/D/547/1993, para. 9.2 (views adopted Nov. 15, 2000) (regarding a claim by Maori petitioners, discussed *infra*, notes 153–54 and accompanying text); Diergaardt et al. v. Namibia, Communication No. 760/199, U.N. Doc. CCPR/C/69/D/60/1977, para. 10.3 (views adopted Sept. 6, 2000) (interpreting article 27 in light of article 1 in relation to a land claim by the Rehoboth Baster Community, but finding no violation of article 27 due to the lack of a sufficient nexus between the claimed land and a distinct culture); Gillot et al. v. France, Communication No. 932/2000, U.N. Doc. CCPR/C/75/D/932/2000 (views adopted July 15, 2002) (interpreting the right to political participation of article 25 in light of article 1 to reject a challenge to special electoral residency requirements for referendums to implement self-determination accords for New Caledonia).

45. *See* Optional Protocol, *supra* note 33, art. 5, para 2(b).

46. Judicial proceedings concerning the Lubicon Cree had meandered and become mired in a labyrinth of contention, which the Lubicon Cree faulted for not producing any results, while Canada argued that delays in the litigation were the fault of the Lubicon Cree themselves. *See Ominayak, supra* note 39, at 4–5, 11–13, 16, 18.

47. *Id.* at 26.

48. *See, e.g.,* Sara et al. v. Finland, Communication No. 431/1990, U.N. Doc. CCPR/C/50/D/431/1990, paras. 8(4) (admissibility decision of Mar. 23, 1994) (in which it was alleged that Finland had violated article 27 of the covenant in authorizing logging activities and construction of a road in a nature reserve and adjacent lands, both within traditional Saami territory; the committee declared the complaint inadmissible for failure to exhaust domestic administrative and judicial remedies, particularly considering that Finnish courts had previously considered claims based on article 27); R.L. et al. v. Canada, Communication No. 358/1989, U.N. Doc. CCPR/C/43/D/358/1989, para. 6(40 (admissibility decision of Nov. 6, 1991) (complaint alleging violation of the covenant

by Canada's approval of Bill C-31 to amend the Indian Act in the aftermath of the
Lovelace case; the committee declared the case inadmissible because the complainants
had not made the required "reasonable efforts" to exhaust domestic remedies, including
bringing the case before the Supreme Court of Canada).

49. Sandra Lovelace v. Canada, Communication No.. 24/1977, U.N. Doc. CCPR/
C/13/D/24/1977, paras. 17, 19 (views adopted July 30, 1981). This case is discussed
further *supra* chapter 4, notes 48–49.

50. Francis Hopu y Tepoaitu Bessert v. France, Communication No. 549/1993, U.N.
Doc. CCPR/C/60/D/549/1993/Rev.1 (views adopted July 29, 1997). This case is discussed *supra* chapter 4, notes 57–58.

51. Mikmaq People v. Canada, Communication No. 205/1986, *Report of the Human
Rights Committee*, U.N. GAOR, 47th Sess., Supp. No. 40, at 213, U.N. Doc. A/47/40,
Annex 9(A) (1992) (views adopted Nov. 4, 1991). The Mikmaq communication originally claimed a violation of the right of self-determination of article 1 of the covenant,
but later was revised to allege also a violation of article 25(a), which provides that every
citizen has the right "[t]o take part in the conduct of public affairs, directly or through
freely chosen representatives." The committee ruled the communication admissible only
as to the claim under article 25(a). *See id.* at 215.

52. *See id.* at 217.

53. *See Mahauika, supra* note 44, para. 9(8).

54. *See id.* para. 9(10).

55. *Cf.* cases discussed *supra* chapter 4, at notes 50–56 and accompanying text, in
which the committee also failed to find violations of the covenant in state legislative or
administrative regimes affecting indigenous peoples: Ivan Kitok v. Sweden, Communication No. 197/1985, U.N. Doc. CCPR/C/33/D/197/1985, para. 9(8) (views adopted July
27, 1988); Ilmari Länsman et al. v. Finland, Communication No. 511/1992, U.N. Doc.
CCPR/C/52/D/511/1992, para. 9.8 (views adopted Oct. 26, 1994); Jouni E. Länsman
et al. v. Finland, Communication No. 671/1995, U.N. Doc. CCPR/C/58/D/671/1995,
paras. 10(7),11 (views adopted Oct. 30, 1996).

56. *Omniyak, supra* note 39, para. 33. The Human Rights Committee in this case
did not include in its views its now typical request for follow-up information to be provided by the state indicating the actions taken to remedy the violation and to ensure that
similar violations do not occur in the future. *See, e.g.,* Edgar A. Cañón García v. Ecuador,
Communication No. 319/1988, *Report of the Human Rights Committee*, U.N. GAOR, 47th
Sess., Supp. No. 40, at 298, paras. 6 & 7, U.N. Doc. A/47/40 (1992) (requesting information from the state party on measures taken to investigate and remedy the situation to be
submitted within 90 days). In 1990 the committee formally adopted a policy of requesting
follow-up information from governments in order to monitor compliance with its decisions, and the committee decided to appoint a special rapporteur to seek and evaluate information on measures taken by states in respect of the committee's views. *See Measures
to Monitor Compliance With the Committee's Views under the First Optional Protocol*,
U.N. GAOR, 45th Sess., Supp. No. 40, U.N. Doc. A/45/40, Annex 11 (1990).

57. Canada's offer included placing lands in reserve status and a money settlement,
but in amounts considered by the Lubicon Cree as inadequate. Responding to the settlement proposal, Chief Ominayak stated:

It is frankly very hard not to conclude that the Federal Government is not sincere about negotiating a settlement of Lubicon land rights and is only seeking to maintain the pretense of sincere negotiations in order to deflect criticism and buy time until the Lubicon society deteriorates to the point where the Lubicon people can no longer fight for our rights.

Letter from Chief Ominayak, Lubicon Lake Band, to Tom Siddon, minister of Indian affairs and northern development (Aug. 19, 1992), at 2.

58. "Opinion: The Lubicons Still Waiting," *Edmonton Journal*, Nov. 11, 1991.

59. In its decision on the merits, the committee limited itself to the determination that "the facts of the present case, which establish that Sandra Lovelace has been denied the legal right to reside on the Tobique Reserve, disclose a breach by Canada of article 27 of the Covenant." *Lovelace, supra* note 49, para. 19 .

60. *See* An Act to Amend the Indian Act, S.C. 1985, c.27. The eventual amendment of the Indian Act following the Lovelace decision is discussed in Wendy Moss, "Indigenous Self-Government in Canada and Sexual Equality under the *Indian Act:* Resolving Conflicts between Collective and Individual Rights,"15 *Queens L.J.* 279 (1990).

61. For a critical analysis of the relevant legislation, Bill C-31, see Pamela D. Palmater, "Forum on R. v. Marshall: An Empty Shell of a Treaty Promise: R. v. Marshall and the Rights of Non-Status Indians," 23 *Dalhousie L.J.* 102, 116–17 (2000) (explaining the differences between the determination of band membership and the determination of Indian status under the reformed Indian Act and how it has contributed to the "disappearing Indian" phenomenon in Canada).

62. The reforms to the Indian Act resulting from the *Lovelace* case were the subject of a new complaint against Canada under the covenant, which the committee found inadmissible for failure to exhaust internal remedies. *See* R.L. et al. v. Canada, *supra* note 48. The committee did raise concern about the matter in commenting on Canada's fourth periodic report under the covenant. *See Concluding Observations of the Human Rights Committee: Canada*, U.N. Doc. CCPR/C/79./Add.105 (Apr. 7, 1999), para 19 (recommending that the Indian Act be further amended to protect the status of subsequent generations of Indians that may be denied membership under the law as it stands).

63. After concluding that France had violated the covenant, the committee limited itself to declaring that "[t]he State Party has the obligation to protect the authors' rights effectively and ensure that violations are not repeated in the future." *Hopu y Bessert v. France, supra* note 50, para. 12. The committee requested that France provide information regarding measures taken to comply with the decision, within ninety days, but there is no indication that that request lead to any meaningful follow up.

64. The hotel complex was already under construction when the committee rendered its decision, and it appears that under the circumstances the committee itself had little expectation that the hotel construction project would be reversed.

65. *See supra* note 56.

66. *See* Opsahl, *supra* note 30, at 427. In 1990 the committee established the mandate of a special rapporteur to communicate with victims and states to obtain information relative to state compliance with committee decisions. *See supra* note 56.

Subsequently, in 1994, the committee authorized the special rapporteur to conduct on-site fact-finding visits. *See* David Weissbrodt et al., *International Human Rights: Law, Policy, and Process* 195 (3d ed. 2001). However, the follow-up regime still does not appear to be operating effectively or with consistent results.

67. *See* Statute of the Inter-American Commission on Human Rights, as approved by Res. 447, taken at the 9th Regular Session of the General Assembly of the OAS, La Paz, Bolivia, in October 1979, as amended by Res. 508 at the 10th Session in 1980, arts. 19, 20, O.A.S. Doc. OEA/Ser.L/V/I.4, Rev. 9 (Jan. 31, 2003) [hereinafter IACHR Statute]; Rules of Procedure of the Inter-American Commission on Human Rights (Apr. 1980, as modified Oct. 2002), art. 27, O.A.S. Doc. OEA/Ser.L/V/I.4, Rev. 9 (Jan. 31, 2003) [hereinafter IACHR Rules of Procedure].

68. *See* American Convention on Human Rights Nov. 22, 1969, OAS Treaty Ser. No. 36, 1144 U.N.T.S. 123 (entered into force July 18, 1978), arts. 41(f), 44–51 [hereinafter American Convention]; IACHR Rules of Procedure, *supra* note 67, arts. 23, 26-48.

69. The following instruments explicitly contemplate that some of their respective provisions may be invoked as the basis for a petition before the commission: Additional Protocol to the American Convention on Human Rights in the Area of Economic, Social and Cultural Rights, "Protocol of San Salvador," adopted in San Salvador, El Salvador on Nov. 17, 1988, OAS Treaty Series, No. 69, art. 6 (entered into force Nov. 16, 1999); Inter-American Convention on Forced Disappearance of Persons, adopted in Belém do Pará, Brazil on June 9, 1994, OAS Treaty Series, No. 68, art. XIII (entered into force Mar. 28, 1996); Inter-American Convention on the Prevention, Punishment, and Eradication of Violence Against Women, adopted in Belém do Pará, Brazil on June 9, 1994, OAS Treaty Series, No. 68, art. 12 (entered into force Mar. 5, 1995).

70. According to the Inter-American Court of Human Rights, the Declaration "is the text that defines the human rights referred to in the Charter [of the OAS]." *Interpretation of the American Declaration of the Rights and Duties of Man Within the Framework of Article 64 of the American Convention on Human Rights*, Advisory Opinion OC-10/89, July 14, 1989, Inter-Am. Ct. H.R. (Ser. A) No. 10, para. 45 (1989).

71. *See* American Convention, *supra* note 68, arts. 44–51; IACHR Rules of Procedure, *supra* note 67, arts. 28–34, 49–50. For summaries and syntheses of the complaint procedures involving the commission, see Héctor Faúndez Ledesma, *El sistema interamericano de protección de los derechos humanos: Aspectos institucionales y procesales* 173–285 (1996); Dinah L. Shelton, "The Inter-American Human Rights System," in *Guide to International Human Rights Practice, supra* note 2, at 121, 124–31.

72. American Convention, *supra* note 68, art. 44; IACHR Rules of Procedure, *supra* note 67, art. 28.

73. In general, in order for a petition to the commission to be admissible, there must be a showing that (1) domestic remedies have been exhausted; (2) no more than six months have passed since such exhaustion of domestic remedies; (3) the subject of the petition is not pending in another international proceeding; and (3) the petition alleges facts that constitute a violation of rights included in the American Convention (in a case involving a state party to the Convention) or the American Declaration (in a case involving any other OAS member state). *See* American Convention, *supra* note

68, art. 46(1); IACHR Rules of Procedure, *supra* note 67, arts. 27–28 and 31–34. Compare admissibility requirements for individual complaints to the U.N. Human Rights Committee, *supra* note 35.

74. Government silence or lack of cooperation may lead to the presumption that facts alleged in a complaint are true, and the commission is authorized to render a decision accordingly. IACHR Rules of Procedure, *supra* note 67, art. 39.

75. *See* American Convention, *supra* note 68, art. 48(1); IACHR Rules of Procedure, *supra* note 67, arts. 38(3),40; IACHR Statute, *supra* note 67, art. 18(g).

76. The American Convention, *supra* note 68, arts. 48(1)(f), 49, specifically authorizes a "friendly settlement" procedure as to complaints under the convention. The commission's rules of procedure have been amended to provide for the "friendly settlement" procedure also with regard to complaints against states that are not parties to the convention. *See* IACHR Rules of Procedure, *supra* note 67, arts. 41, 50.

77. *Id.*, art. 25.

78. *See* American Convention, *supra* note 68, arts. 50, 51; IACHR Rules of Procedure, *supra* note 67, arts. 43, 45.

79. *See infra* notes 123–57 and accompanying text (analyzing the complaint procedure before the Inter-American Human Rights Court).

80. The commission's reports on cases examined prior to 2000 relating to indigenous peoples are reproduced in *The Human Rights Situation of the Indigenous People in the Americas*, O.A.S. Doc. OEA/Ser.L/VII.108, Doc. 62, chapter III, Annexes (Oct. 20, 2000).

81. For an excellent summary and background on these cases, see Shelton H. Davis, *Land Rights and Indigenous Peoples: The Role of the Inter-American Commission on Human Rights* 10–12, 17–40 (1988).

82. Case No. 1690 (Colombia), *Report on the Work Accomplished by the Inter-American Commission on Human Rights During Its Thirtieth Session*, O.A.S. Doc. OEA/Ser.L/V /II.30, doc. 45, rev. 1, at 21, 23 (1973).

83. Case No. 1802 (Paraguay), *Annual Report of the Inter-American Commission on Human Rights, 1977*, O.A.S. Doc. OEA/Ser.L/V/II.43, doc. 21, at 37 (1978).

84. *See* Davis, *supra* note 81, at 23, 34.

85. *See id.* at 14–15.

86. *See* supra notes 68–70 and accompanying text.

87. For background on the situation leading to the petition to the commission on behalf of the Yanomami, and for a summary of the relevant information submitted to the commission by concerned NGOs, *see* Davis, *supra* note 81, at 41–52.

88. Case No. 7615 (Brazil), Inter-Am. C.H.R. Res. No. 12/85 (Mar. 5, 1985), *Annual Report of the Inter-American Commission on Human Rights, 1984–1985*, O.A.S. Doc. OEA/Ser.L/V/II.66, doc. 10, rev. 1, at 24, 33 (1985).

89. *Id.* at 31.

90. A discussion of article 27 of the Covenant on Civil and Political Rights and its linkage to customary international law upholding indigenous cultural integrity is in chapter 4, *supra*, notes 25–77 and accompanying text.

91. Case No. 7615 (Brazil), *supra* note 88, at 33. The plans for demarcation of a "Yanomami Park" had been developed by the government Indian affairs ministry, FUNAI,

and an interministerial working group, and had been advocated by a group of Brazilian and foreign NGOs. *See* Davis, *supra* note 81, at 43–56.

92. *See supra* chapter 3, notes 107–13 and accompanying text.

93. Inter-American Commission on Human Rights, *Report on the Situation of Human Rights of a Segment of the Nicaraguan Population of Miskito Origin and Resolution on the Friendly Settlement Procedure Regarding the Human Rights Situation of a Segment of the Nicaraguan Population of Miskito Origin*, O.A.S. Doc. OEA/Ser.L/V/II.62, doc. 10, rev. 3 (1983), OEA/Ser.L/V/II.62, doc. 26 (1984) (Case No. 7964 (Nicaragua)) [hereinafter *Miskito Report and Resolution*].

94. *Id.* at 76.

95. For example, the commission held that "the Government of Nicaragua illegally killed a considerable number of Miskitos in [the village of] Leimus . . . in violation of Article 4 of the American Convention on Human Rights." *Id.* at 129.

96. *Id.* at 76–77, 81–82. The commission stressed the interrelationship between the freedoms recognized in the American Convention—such as freedom of thought, expression, and association—and the ability of groups to preserve and develop their cultural values. *Id.* at 81. On the other hand, the commission took a restrictive view of the right of self-determination, holding that the "current status of international law" rendered the right inapplicable to the indigenous peoples of Nicaragua's Atlantic Coast. *Id.* at 78–81, 129. This assessment, made in 1983, was before developments that make such a view now much less tenable and, furthermore, was based on formalistic, misguided premises about the character and scope of self-determination as a principle of international law. As argued in chapter 3, the commission's decision in this case—which called for a restructuring of the Nicaraguan state to better allow for the integrity and free development of indigenous groups—can itself be identified as part of the development of the principle or right of self-determination as applied in the context of indigenous peoples. *See supra* chapter 3, notes 110–14 and accompanying text. *See also supra* chapter 4 (discussing the relationship between the norm of indigenous cultural integrity and other aspects of indigenous peoples' rights, including rights of self-determination).

97. *See Report on the Situation of Human Rights in Ecuador*, O.A.S. Doc. OEA/Ser.L/V/II.96, Doc.10 rev. 1 (1997). This report is discussed *supra* chapter 6, notes 101–5.

98. Mary and Carrie Dann, Case No. 11.140 (United States), Inter-Am. C. H.R. Report No. 75/02 (merits decision of Dec. 27, 2002) [hereinafter *Dann* case].

99. *Id.* paras. 142, 145, 172. The *Dann* case is discussed *supra* chapter 4, notes 137–48 and accompanying text.

100. *See id.* paras. 129–30 (citing the Proposed American Declaration on the Rights of Indigenous Peoples), para. 168 (refuting the United States' objection that the provisions of the proponed declaration were irrelevant to the case).

101. *Id.* para. 129.

102. *See* Davis, *supra* note 81, at 48–56.

103. In its initial response to the complaint, the Brazilian government downplayed any problems associated with the invasion of Yanomami lands and attempted to defend its existing policy and legal regime as it concerned the Yanomami and other indigenous peoples. *Id.* at 49–50. Later, the government consolidated and stepped up plans to secure Yanomami land rights, *id.* at 52–56, and the commission expressed its approval of

these initiatives in its 1985 resolution on the case, *see supra* notes 88–91 and accompanying text. In 1989, when the Brazilian government adopted a "Plan for the Defense of the Yanomami Indigenous Areas and of the National Forest," it later communicated this and related developments to the commission. *See* Note of Ambassador Bernardo Pericas Neto, ambassador and permanent representative of Brazil to the OAS, to Edith Márquez Rodríguez, executive secretary of the Inter-American Commission on Human Rights (Washington, D.C., Sept. 26, 1990). However, even after this and subsequent measures to secure the Yanomami territory, the Yanomami continued to suffer encroachments— and often violent ones—onto their lands. Concerned NGOs accused the government of foot-dragging and of a lack of political will in carrying out its own plans. *See, e.g., Written Statement Submitted by the Indian Law Resource Center to the U.N. Commission on Human Rights*, 47th Sess., Agenda Item 12 (Feb. 1992).

104. The commission formally assumed the role of mediator in response to a proposal of the Nicaraguan government to attempt to reach a friendly settlement in accordance with article 48(1)(f) of the American Convention. *See Miskito Report and Resolution, supra* note 93, at 35–36. The government made its proposal after it received the commission's initial unpublished report finding a series of problems and making recommendations to rectify the problems. *See id.* at 28–35.

105. *See id.* at 46–74.

106. In September 1984, Nicaraguan president Daniel Ortega invited Brooklyn Rivera, the exiled leader of the Nicaraguan indigenous organization, MISURASATA, to return to Nicaragua to commence a process of reconciliation. Rivera traveled to Nicaragua in October of the same year with an entourage of other leaders and accompanied by a group of international observers. Initial meetings with Ortega and other government officials led to a series of talks, at sites both inside and outside of Nicaragua, which proceeded in fits and starts over the next few years.

107. This process is described in Hurst Hannum, *Autonomy, Sovereignty, and Self-Determination: The Accommodation of Conflicting Rights* 210–17 (1990).

108. *See* Mary and Carrie Dann, Case No. 11.140 (United States), Inter-Am. C.H.R. Report No. 99/99 (admissibility decision of Sept. 27, 1999), *Annual Report of the Inter-American Commission on Human Rights 1999*, O.A.S. Doc. OEA/Ser.L/V/II.106, doc. 26 (2000).

109. The U.S. Bureau for Land Management, for example, continued to sanction the Danns for unauthorized grazing on "public lands" *See* Indian Law Resource Center, "BLM continues harassment of Western Shoshone—Inter-American Commission on Human Rights Issues Precautionary Measures," 6 *Indian Rights-Human Rights*, No. 2 (Summer 1999).

110. *See Dann* case, *supra* note 98, paras. 150–62.

111. *See id.* paras. 162–69.

112. Harassment by government authorities continued despite publication of the commission's final report. The government's strategies of intimidation have reportedly included nighttime raids and helicopter surveillance. In July 2001, the federal government also confiscated and auctioned off more than 200 head of cattle belonging to the Dann sisters, for "illegal entry on public lands." "BLM surveys Western Shoshone Livestock in Nevada," *Reno Gazette Journal* (Mar. 9, 2003). Since January 2003, the

government has attempted to make available the Dann sisters' "ownerless" horses for "adoption." *See* Indian Law Resource Center, "980 Horses in Nevada in Need of Help" (Jan. 10, 2003).

113. *See, e.g.*, Oral Intervention by Carrie Dann, Western Shoshone (United States) at the Special Meeting of the Working Group to prepare the Draft American Declaration on the Rights of Indigenous Peoples (Feb. 24, 2003). Since the release of the commission's decision on the *Dann* case, advocates have publicized the lack of response by the U.S. government with the help of international human rights organizations. *See, e.g.*, Public Citizen, *Bechtel: Profiting from Destruction* (June 9, 2003), at 17,19, (a joint publication by international non-governmental organizations, Public Citizen, Global Exchange and CorpWatch, acknowledging the *Dann* case and condemning the ongoing invasion of Western Shoshone land on the part of the United States and the Bechtel Corporation); Amnesty International, *Indigenous Rights are Human Rights: Four Cases of Rights Violations in the Americas* (May 2003), at 30–34 (affirming the decision by the Inter-American Commission and denouncing the lack of response by the U.S. government as an ongoing violation of international law).

114. *See* Enxet-Lamenxay and Kayleyphapopyet (Riachito) Indigenous Communities, Case No. 11.713 (Paraguay), Inter-Am. C.H.R. Report No. 90/99 (friendly settlement) (1999), *Annual Report of the Inter-American Commission on Human Rights 1999*, O.A.S. Doc. OEA/Ser.L/V/II.106, doc. 6, rev., para. 2 (2000).

115. *See id.* paras. 10–21.

116. *See id.* para. 6.

117. Paraguay National Const., promulgated June 20, 1992, art. 64(1) (Anja Schoeller-Schletter, trans.).

118. However, in a similar case also related to an indigenous community in the Paraguayan Chaco, the friendly settlement procedure failed to result in an agreement between the parties. *See* Yakye Axa Indigenous Community of the Enxet-Lengua People, Report No. 2/02 Case 12.313 (Paraguay) (27 Feb. 2002), *Annual Report of the Inter-American Comisión on Human Rights 2002*, OAS Doc. OEA/Ser.L/V/II.117, Doc. 1 rev. 1 (2003) [hereinafter *Yakye Axa* case], at paras. 15–18. At the time of this writing, the case is before the Inter-American Court of Human Rights.

119. *See* Indian Law Resource Center-Toledo Maya Cultural Council, "Maya File Petition with the Inter-American Commission on Human Rights," Press Release (Aug. 10, 2000)· An edited version of the Maya petition and a background note are in S. James Anaya, "The Maya Petition to the Inter-American Commission on Human Rights: Indigenous Land and Resource Rights and the Conflict over Logging and Oil in Southern Belize," in *Giving Meaning to Economic Social and Cultural Rights* 180 (Isfahan Merali & Valerie Oosterveld eds., 2001). *See also* S. James Anaya, "Maya Aboriginal Land and Resource Rights and the Conflict Over Logging in Southern Belize," 1 *Yale Hum. Rts. & Dev. L. J.* 17, 17–51 (1998). For a general description of the situation of Maya lands in the Toledo District, *see generally* Toledo Maya Cultural Council & Toledo Alcaldes Association, *Maya Atlas: The Struggle to Preserve Maya Land in Southern Belize* (1997). The author was one of the attorneys for the Maya petitioners in this case.

120. *See* Maya Indigenous Communities and their Members, Case No. 12.053 (Belize), Inter-Am. C.H.R. Report No. 78/00 (admissibility decision of Oct. 5, 2000),

Annual Report of the Inter-American Commission on Human Rights 1999, O.A.S. Doc. OEA/Ser./L/V/II.111, doc. 6, paras. 16–25 (Apr. 16, 2001).

121. *See id.* para. 26. Precautionary measures were granted by the commission on October 20, 2000. In its decision, the commission requested that Belize "take the necessary steps to suspend all permits, licenses, and concessions allowing for the drilling of oil and any other tapping of natural resources on lands used and occupied by the Maya Communities in the District of Toledo, in order to investigate the allegations in this case." *Annual Report of the Inter-American Commission on Human Rights 2000*, O.A.S. Doc. OEA/Ser./L/V/II.111, doc. 20 rev., chap. 3(c), para. 11 (Apr. 16, 2001).

122. *See* Maya Indigenous Communities, Case No. 12.053, (Belize), Inter-Am. C.H.R. Report No. 96/03 (merits, preliminary version, Oct. 24, 2003). Despite the confidential nature of the preliminary report in accordance with the commission's rules of procedure, the government of Belize publicly released the report with the consent of the commission.

123. *See* American Convention, *supra* note 68, arts. 52–60 (establishing the Inter-American Court of Human Rights), arts. 61–65 (jurisdiction and functions). *See generally* Antonio Augusto Cançado Trindade, "The Operation of the Inter-American Court of Human Rights," in *The Inter-American System of Human Rights* (D. J. Harris & Stephen Livingstone eds., 1998); Cecilia Medina, "The Inter-American Commission on Human Rights and the Inter-American Court of Human Rights: Reflections on a Joint Venture," 12 *Human Rights Q.* 439 (1990). Together with its jurisdiction over cases, the Court has the power to issue consultative opinions regarding "treaties concerning the protection of human rights in the American states," at the request of an OAS member state or the an OAS Charter organ, including the commission itself. *See* American Convention, *supra* note 68, art. 64. *See generally*, Faúndez Ledesma, *supra* note 71, at 424–50; Medina, *supra*, at 451–53.

124. *See* American Convention, *supra* note 68, art. 61(1).

125. *See* IACHR Rules of Procedure, *supra* note 67, art. 44(1).

126. *See id.* art. 44(2)(a).

127. For summaries of the Court's recent activity, see *Annual Report of the Inter-American Court on Human Rights 2001*, O.A.S. Doc. OEA/Ser.G/CP/doc.3555/02 (Mar. 15, 2002); *Annual Report of the Inter-American Commission on Human Rights 2001*, O.A.S. Doc. OEA/Ser./L/V/II.114, doc. 5 rev. paras. 103–62 (Apr. 16, 2001); Richard J. Wilson & Jan Perlin, "The Inter-American Human Rights System: Activities from Late 2000 throughout October 2002," in ACLU International Human Rights Task Force, *ACLU International Civil Liberties Report* 72–1000 (2002 ed.). For a perspective of the Court from some of its members, see Lynda Frost, "The Evolution of the Inter-American Court of Human Rights: Reflections of Present and Former Judges," 14 *Human Rights Q.* 171 (1992).

128. *See* The Case of the Mayagna (Sumo) Awas Tingni Community v. Nicaragua, Inter-Am. Ct. H.R., (Ser. C) No. 79, (Judgment on merits and reparations of Aug. 31, 2001) published in abridged version in 19 *Ariz. J. Int'l & Comp. L.* 395 (2002) [hereinafter *Awas Tingni* case].

129. At the time of this writing, the Inter-American Court on Human Rights is considering a second case pertaining to indigenous land rights. The case involves the Yakye Axa community's claim of ownership over its ancestral lands, which are currently occupied by non-indigenous individuals. The case went through an unsuccessful friendly

settlement procedure under the auspices of the inter-American commission. *See Yakye Axa* case, *supra* nota 118, at para. 18. Upon the completion of the friendly settlement effort, the commission prepared its report on the merits of the case in October 2002. Responding to Paraguay's lack of implementation of the recommendations set forth in the report, the commission filled a complaint before the Court in July 2003.

130. Aloeboetoe et al. Case, Inter-Am. Ct. H.R., (Ser. C) No. 11, paras. 22–23 (Judgment of Dec. 4, 1991).

131. Aloeboetoe et al. Case, Inter-Am. Ct. H.R., (Ser. C) No. 15, paras. 55-63 (Reparations, Sept. 10, 1993). According to the Inter-American Court, to calculate the compensation it had to "take Saramaka custom into account. That custom will be the basis for the interpretation of those terms, to the degree that it does not contradict the American Convention." *Id.* para. 62.

132. Awas Tingni's petition to the Inter-American Commission, along with a background note, is published in S. James Anaya, "The Awas Tingni Petition to the Inter-American Commission on Human Rights: Indigenous Lands, Loggers, and Government Neglect in Nicaragua," 9 *St. Thomas L. Rev.* 157 (1996). The author was lead counsel to the Awas Tingni community in the proceedings before the commission and the inter-American Court in the case, and he also assisted the commission in its prosecution of the case before the Court.

133. *See supra* notes 92–96 and accompanying text.

134. *See* Constitution of the Republic of Nicaragua (as amended Jan. 9, 1987, Feb. 1, 1995 and Jan. 18, 2000), arts. 5, 89, 180; Statute of Autonomy for the Regions of the Atlantic Coast of Nicaragua, Law No. 28, September 2, 1987 (La Gaceta, Diario oficial No. 238).

135. *See* Julia Preston, "It's Indians vs. Loggers in Nicaragua," *New York Times*, June 25, 1996, at A5 (quoting government official saying, in relation to Awas Tingni land claim, "Until somebody shows me a title, that land is government land").

136. The proceedings before the commission and its confidential report in the case are summarized in the final judgment of the inter-American Court, *Awas Tingni* case, *supra* note 128, paras. 6–28.

137. The main submissions of the parties and the complete transcript of the hearing on the merits are published in 19(1) *Ariz. J. Int'l & Comp. L* (2002) (a special edition of the journal on "The Case of the Mayagna (Sumo) Indigenous Community of Awas Tingni against the Republic of Nicaragua"). For additional background on the case and a more detailed description of the proceedings before the commission and the Court, *see* S. James Anaya & Claudio Grossman, "*The Case of Awas Tingni v. Nicaragua*: A New Step in the International Law of Indigenous Peoples," *id.* at 1.

138. Nicaragua attempted to have the case dismissed on the grounds that Awas Tingni had failed to exhaust all available domestic remedies. On February 1, 2000, the Inter-American Court unanimously ruled against Nicaragua's preliminary objections and held the case admissible, stating that Nicaragua had waived any objection based on failure to exhaust domestic remedies by not properly raising it in a timely manner in the earlier proceedings before the commission. *See* The Case of the Mayagna (Sumo) Awas Tingni Community v. Nicaragua, Inter-Am. Ct. H.R., February 1, 2000, (Ser. C.) No. 66, paras. 52–58, 60(2) (Preliminary Objections, Feb. 1, 2000).

139. For a list of the documentary evidence filed by the parties, see *Awas Tingni* case, *supra* note 128, paras. 75, 82.

140. For an assessment of the significance of such proceedings, understood in terms of their therapeutic value for aggrieved parties, see David Wexler, "Therapeutic Jurisprudence and Changing Conceptions of Legal Scholarship," 11 *Behav. Sci. & L.* 17 (1993); *Law in a Therapeutic Key* (David Wexler & Bruce Durham Winick eds., 1996).

141. The commission presented twelve witnesses who included Awas Tingni and other indigenous leaders from the Atlantic Coast, the anthropologist who had assisted the community with an ethnographic study and map of its traditional lands, and several other individuals—some of them qualified by the Court as expert witnesses—with relevant knowledge on conditions among indigenous peoples in the Atlantic Coast and more generally on indigenous-state relations in the Hemisphere. *See* "Transcript of the Public Hearings on the Merits," 19 *Ariz. J. Int'l & Comp. L.* 129–306 (2002).

142. The government failed to provide a witness list to the Court within the allotted time, and hence was not permitted to present witnesses of its own. However, the Court itself called one of the government officials that Nicaragua had proposed as a witness, and this person in effect served as a government witness. *See Awas Tingni* case, *supra* note 128, para. 55; "Transcript of the Public Hearings on the Merits," *supra* note 141, at 265–86.

143. *Awas Tingni* case, *supra* note 128 at para. 148. This part of the Court's judgment is discussed in chapter 4, *supra* notes 124–33 and accompanying text.

144. *See Awas Tingni* case, *supra* note 128 paras 128–39. As the Court recounted in its judgment, the Awas Tingni community had filed two unsuccessful lawsuits to stop the logging concession that threatened its lands. *See id.* para. 129. A third lawsuit, filed by two members of the Regional Council of the North Atlantic Autonomous Region, did result in a decision by the Nicaraguan Supreme Court that the concession was invalid; but that decision was on grounds of a defect found in the procedure by which the concession was granted and not by a finding of a violation of Awas Tingni land rights. *See id.* para. 130; Anaya & Grossman, *supra* note 137, at 7–8. The Court also noted the community's various unsuccessful attempts to appeal to government agencies for assistance and the lack of an adequate administrative procedure for the titling of indigenous lands. *See Awas Tingni* case, *supra* note 128, paras. 123–27.

145. *Id.* paras. 138, 164, 173(3).

146. *See id.* paras. 153, 164, 173(4).

147. *See generally*, Dinah Shelton, "Reparations in the Inter-American System," *in The Inter-American System of Human Rights* (David Harris & Stephen Livingston eds., 1998).

148. *See* "Petition and Preliminary Declaration of the Mayagna Community of Awas Tingni on Reparations and Costs," in 19 *Ariz. J. Int'l & Comp. L.* 381 (2002) (citing Inter-Am Ct. H.R., Caballero Delgado and Santana Case (Reparations), Jan. 29, 1997, (Ser. C) No. 31 (1997); Garrido and Biagorria Case (Reparations), Aug. 27, 1998 (Ser. C) No. 39 (1998); Aloeboetoe et al. Case (Reparations), Sept. 1993 (Ser. C) No. 15 (1993); Suárez Roser Case (Reparations), Jan. 20, 1999, (Ser. C) No. 44 (1999); Velásquez Rodríguez Case (Compensatory Damages), July 21, 1989, (Ser. C) No. 7 (1989); El

Amparo Case (Reparations), Sept. 14, 1996, (Ser. C) No. 28 (1996); Neira Alegría et al. Case (Reparations), Sept. 29, 1996, (Ser. C) No. 29 (1996)).

149. The Court's rules of procedure that were in effect when the *Awas Tingni* case was initiated reflected the Court's previous practice of having a separate phase of proceeding on reparations subsequent to the merits phase. *See* Rules of Procedure of the Inter-American Court of Human Rights, approved by the Court at its XXXIV Regular Session held Sept. 9–20, 1996, art. 23, *Basic Documents Pertaining to Human Rights in the Inter-American System* (1997) OEA/Ser.L/V/1.4 Rev.7 (repealed 2001) (stating that "[at] the reparations stage, the representatives of the victims or of their next of kin may independently submit their own arguments and evidence"). Relying on Court's prior practice and its rules of procedure then in effect, the commission had initially foregone presenting specific evidence and arguments on compensable damages and costs, and instead had explicitly reserved the right to present such evidence and arguments at a subsequent reparations phase. *See* "Complaint of the Inter-American Commission on Human Rights Submitted to the Inter-American Court of Human Rights," in 19 *Ariz. J. Int'l & Comp.* L 85 (2002). Some two years after the commission filed its complaint to the Court in the case, and while the case was still pending, the Court amended its rules of procedure to remove the above reference to a separate reparations phrase. *See* Rules of Procedure of the Inter-American Court of Human Rights, approved by the court at its forty-ninth regular session, held from November 16–25, 2000, *Basic Documents Pertaining to Human Rights in the Inter-Americans System*, O.A.S. Doc. OEA/Ser.L/V/I.4, Rev. 9 (Jan. 31, 2003).

150. Prior to issuing its decision on the merits of the case, the Court requested the inter-American commission and Nicaragua to provide written arguments and documentary evidence on damages and costs, and it set a deadline allowing them a mere ten days to do so. *See Awas Tingni* case, *supra* note 128, para. 159. Because of an internal administrative error, the commission did not notify the community's legal representatives of the Court's request or otherwise act on it until after the deadline had passed. A few days after being notified by the commission of the Court's request, and acting autonomously through its own legal counsel, the community submitted a brief on damages and costs, requesting that the Court order a total of US$1,500,000 for moral and material damages plus a total of US$360,000 for costs. *See* "Petition and Preliminary Declaration of the Mayagna Community of Awas Tingni on Reparations and Cost," in 19 *Ariz. J. Int'l & Comp.* L 386–92 (2002). The Court, however, ignored that brief in its judgment. It referred only to the commission's own submission on reparations, which incorporated by reference the community's arguments, and ruled that submission inadmissible for being untimely. See *Awas Tingni* case, *supra* note 128, at 433–34, para. 159.

151. *See id.* paras. 167 and 173(7). The community's postjudgment request to the Court that it reconsider its reparations decision and provide for a full reparations proceeding was summarily rejected in a terse note written by the Court's secretary. The note admonished that neither the community nor its attorneys had standing to make submissions on reparations to the Court independently of the commission, even though the Court's rules of procedure had been amended to allow the victims or their representatives to act autonomously at all phases of the proceedings, *see* Rules of Procedure of the Inter-American Court of Human Rights, *supra* note 149, art. 23(1) (as amended). The

secretary noted that, under the Court's older rules of procedure in effect at the time the case began, the victims were permitted to participate autonomously only in a reparations phase and that, since in this case there was no reparations phase, there was no opportunity for the victim's attorneys to make submissions independently of the commission. *See* Note from Manuel E. Ventura Robles, Secretary, Inter-American Court of Human Rights, to Professor S. James Anaya, Legal Representative of the Awas Tingni Community (Dec. 4, 2001).

152. *See* "Government of Nicaragua reiterated its commitment to enforcing the Judgment of the Inter-American Court in the case of the Awas Tingni Community." *Inter-American Commission on Human Rights, Press Release No. 8/02, Washington D.C.* (Feb. 22, 2002).

153. At the first meeting between the Nicaraguan government and Awas Tingni regarding implementation of the Court's judgment, attended also by special delegates from the inter-american commission, two joint commissions made up of government and community representatives were agreed upon to negotiate the terms of implementation. *See* Comunicado de prensa conjunto del Gobierno de la República de Nicaragua y la Comunidad Mayagna (Sumo) Awas Tingni, Apr. 16, 2002; *Acta de la Reunión sobre la Implementación de la Sentencia de la Corte Interamericana de Derechos Humanos* (Managua, Apr. 16, 2002).

154. *See* Ley del Régimen de Propiedad Comunal de los Pueblos Indígenas y Comunidades Étnicas de las Regiones Autónomas de la Costa Atlántica de Nicaragua y de los Ríos Bocay, Coco, Indio y Maíz (Law Regarding the Property Regime of the Indigenous Peoples and Ethnic Communities of the Atlantic Coast, Bocay, Coco and Indio Maiz Rivers), No. 445, Jan. 22, 2003 (La Gaceta Diario Oficial No. 16, Jan. 23, 2003).

155. The Case of the Mayagna (Sumo) Awas Tingni Community v. Nicaragua, Inter-Am Ct. H.R., (Ser. E) (Provisional Measures of Sept. 6, 2002).

156. *See* Indian Law Resource Center, "The Awas Tingni Case—Fifteen Months Later: The Challenge to the Implementation of the Decision of the Inter-American Court of Human Rights," Press Release (Jan. 16, 2003).

157. *See id.* At the end of the time period allowed by the Court for demarcation and titling of Awas Tingni lands, the community filed an *amparo* action before the Nicaraguan courts, arguing that the failure to comply with both the judgment and the provisional measures ordered by the court established new violations of the community's rights, and in particular, their property rights over their land and natural resources and the right to effective legal protections, including the right to compliance with judgments of the courts. *See* Recurso de Amparo interpuesto ante el Honorable Tribunal de Apelaciones de Bilwi (Puerto Cabezas) por la Comunidad Mayangna (Sumo) Awas Tingni, por medio de su apoderada y representante legal, la Dra. Lottie Cunningham Wren (Jan. 16, 2003).

Conclusion

Contact and interaction among the diverse peoples of the world are inevitable. Even the most isolated communities require some level of contact with other segments of humanity if only to secure their continued isolation. A look back in history reveals patterns of encounter that are, however, no longer acceptable: patterns associated with empire building, conquest, or colonization. Indigenous peoples were at the raw end of such encounters and have continued to suffer inequities as a result. Historically, international law developed to facilitate empire building and colonization, but today it promotes a very different model of human encounter and provides grounds for remedying the contemporary manifestations of the oppressive past.

Over the last several years, the development of international law has been influenced by indigenous peoples' efforts to secure a future in which they may retain their unique characteristics and develop freely in coexistence with all of humankind. Through the international human rights program, they and their supporters have been successful in moving states and other relevant actors to an ever closer accommodation of their demands. The traditional doctrine of state sovereignty and related, lingering strains of legal thought that originated in European or Western perspectives have tended to limit the capacity of the international legal order to affirm the integrity and survival of indigenous peoples as distinct units of human interaction. Nonetheless, the movement toward ever greater international affirmation of indigenous peoples' rights—fueled by the world community's espoused commitment to human rights in general and its move away from Eurocentric biases—is apparent. Moreover, while the movement can be expected to continue as indigenous peoples continue to press their cause, international law already has developed in substantial measure to support their survival and flourishment.

International law today includes a body of conventional and customary norms concerning indigenous peoples, grounded in the principle of self-determination. Self-determination is an extraordinary regulatory vehicle in the contemporary international system, broadly establishing rights for the benefit of all peoples, including indigenous peoples. It enjoins the incidents and legacies of human encounter and interaction to conform with the essential idea that all are equally entitled to control their own destinies. Self-determination especially opposes, both prospectively and retroactively, patterns of empire and conquest. To the extent indigenous peoples have been denied self-determination by virtue of historical and continuing wrongs, they are entitled to remedial measures. These measures must, at a minimum, implement contemporary norms as they have developed with particular regard to indigenous peoples, including prescriptions of nondiscrimination, cultural integrity, control of lands and resources, social welfare and development, and self-government.

Remedial measures, furthermore, should be the outcome of procedures that themselves accord with precepts of self-determination; hence, such procedures should entail meaningful participation on the part of the indigenous peoples concerned and defer to their choices from among justifiable options. Negotiation is a preferred procedure for the development of remedial measures and the implementation of corresponding norms. It provides a potential framework for dialogue and agreement, both of which are conducive to practical solutions and conciliation.

States have a duty under contemporary international law to remedy the violation of indigenous peoples' rights and to implement relevant international norms through negotiated agreement or other appropriate means. Diverse state institutions operating within their respective spheres of competency—including executive, legislative and judicial institutions—may function to fulfill this duty in diverse ways depending on governing constitutional parameters. But whatever the division of powers within the state apparatus, the state as a corporate whole is bound to implement relevant conventional and customary norms concerning indigenous peoples.

An array of procedures involving international institutions exists encouraging states to comply with their obligations under international human rights law and bringing pressure to bear on them when they fail. For the most part, these procedures are not devised specifically to address the historically rooted grievances of indigenous peoples, nor are they clearly jurisdictionally equipped to promote the full range of conventional and customary norms that are most relevant to remedying those grievances. Furthermore, the functioning of international procedures remains tied to state consent, although not entirely so, and many states have resisted acquiescing to heightened levels of international scrutiny over matters traditionally deemed within their respective spheres of domestic concern. Nonetheless, existing international procedures do provide certain limited means of coalescing international concern for the benefit of many of the world's indigenous peoples, and these procedures have functioned in numerous instances to promote remedies for the violation of indigenous peoples' rights in accordance with contemporary norms. New international procedures are on the horizon, including those associated with the newly established U.N. Permanent Forum on Indigenous Issues. These new procedures, justified by the particular vulnerabilities of indigenous peoples in the face of long-standing inequities, are likely to enhance the capacities of the international system to promote the effective implementation of relevant international norms.

In short, international law today includes a certain universe of norms and procedures that benefit indigenous peoples. Through history, indigenous peoples have been assaulted physically and suffered discrimination; they have seen their cultures undermined, their lands stolen, and their economies plundered; moreover, their very existence as distinct communities has been threatened. International law has evolved, however modestly, to challenge the legacy of this history and the forces that would see it continue.

Appendix: Selected Documents

DRAFT DECLARATION OF PRINCIPLES
FOR THE DEFENSE OF THE INDIGENOUS NATIONS
AND PEOPLES OF THE WESTERN HEMISPHERE

Developed and circulated by indigenous participants at the Non-Governmental Organization Conference on Discrimination Against Indigenous Populations, Geneva, 1977.
Reprinted in U.N. Doc. E/CN.4/Sub.2/476/Add.5, Annex 4 (1981).

Preamble

Having considered the problems relating to the activities of the United Nations for the
promotion and encouragement of respect for human rights and fundamental freedoms,

Noting that the Universal Declaration of Human Rights and related international
covenants have the individual as their primary concern, and

Recognizing that individuals are the foundation of cultures, societies, and nations, and

Whereas, it is a fundamental right of any individual to practise and perpetuate the
cultures, societies and nations into which they are born, and

Recognizing that conditions are imposed upon peoples that suppress, deny, or
destroy the cultures, societies, or nations in which they believe or of which they are
members,

Be it affirmed, that,

1. Recognition of Indigenous Nations

Indigenous peoples shall be accorded recognition as nations, and proper subjects of international law, provided the people concerned desire to be recognized as a nation and meet
the fundamental requirements of nationhood, namely:

(a) Having a permanent population
(b) Having a defined territory
(c) Having a government
(d) Having the ability to enter into relations with other States.

2. Subjects of International Law

Indigenous groups not meeting the requirements of nationhood are hereby declared to be subjects of international law and are entitled to the protection of this Declaration, provided they are identifiable groups having bonds of language, heritage, tradition, or other common identity.

3. Guarantee of Rights

No indigenous nation or group shall be deemed to have fewer rights, or lesser status for the sole reason that the nation or group has not entered into recorded treaties or agreements with any State.

4. Accordance of Independence

Indigenous nations or groups shall be accorded such degree of independence as they may desire in accordance with international law.

5. Treaties and Agreements

Treaties and other agreements entered into by indigenous nations or groups with other States, whether denominated as treaties or otherwise, shall be recognized and applied in the same manner and according to the same international laws and principles as the treaties and agreements entered into by other States.

6. Abrogation of Treaties and Other Rights

Treaties and agreements made with indigenous nations or groups shall not be subject to unilateral abrogation. In no event may the municipal law of any State serve as a defence to the failure to adhere to and perform the terms of treaties and agreements made with indigenous nations or groups. Nor shall any State refuse to recognize and adhere to treaties or other agreements due to changed circumstances where the change in circumstances has been substantially caused by the State asserting that such change has occurred.

7. Jurisdiction

No States shall assert or claim or exercise any right of jurisdiction over any indigenous nation or group or territory of such indigenous nation or group unless pursuant to a valid treaty or other agreement freely made with the lawful representatives of the indigenous nation or group concerned. All actions on the part of any State which derogate from the indigenous nations' or groups' right to exercise self-determination shall be the proper concern of existing international bodies.

8. Claims to Territory

No State shall claim or retain, by right of discovery or otherwise, the territories of an indigenous nation or group, except such lands as may have been lawfully acquired by valid treaty or other cession freely made.

9. Settlement of Disputes

All States in the Western Hemisphere shall establish through negotiation or other appropriate means a procedure for the binding settlement of disputes, claims, or other matters relating to indigenous nations or groups. Such procedures shall be mutually acceptable to the parties, fundamentally fair, and consistent with international law. All procedures presently in existence which do not have the endorsement of the indigenous nations or groups concerned, shall be ended, and new procedures shall be instituted consistent with this Declaration.

10. National and Cultural Integrity

It shall be unlawful for any State to take or permit any action or course of conduct with respect to an indigenous nation or group which will directly or indirectly result in the destruction or disintegration of such indigenous nation or group or otherwise threaten the national or cultural integrity of such nation or group, including, but not limited to, the imposition and support of illegitimate governments and the introduction of non-indigenous religions to indigenous peoples by non-indigenous missionaries.

11. Environmental Protection

It shall be unlawful for any State to make or permit any action or course of conduct with respect to the territories of an indigenous nation or group which will directly or indirectly result in the destruction or deterioration of an indigenous nation or group through the effects of pollution of earth, air, water, or which in any way depletes, displaces or destroys any natural resource or other resources under the dominion of, or vital to the livelihood of an indigenous nation or group.

12. Indigenous Membership

No State, through legislation, regulation, or other means, shall take actions that interfere with the sovereign power of an indigenous nation or group to determine its own membership.

13. Conclusion

All of the rights and obligations declared herein shall be in addition to all rights and obligations existing under international law.

DECLARATION OF PRINCIPLES OF INDIGENOUS RIGHTS

Adopted by the Fourth General Assembly of the World Council of Indigenous Peoples, Panama, Sept. 1984. Reprinted in U.N. Doc. E/CN.4/1985/22, Annex 2 (1985).

Principle 1

All indigenous peoples have the right of self-determination. By virtue of this right they may freely determine their political status and freely pursue their economic, social, religious and cultural development.

Principle 2

All states within which an indigenous people lives shall recognize the population, territory and institutions of the indigenous people.

Principle 3

The cultures of the indigenous peoples are part of the cultural heritage of mankind.

Principle 4

The tradition and customs of indigenous people must be respected by the states, and recognized as a fundamental source of law.

Principle 5

All indigenous peoples have the right to determine the person or groups of persons who are included within its population.

Principle 6

Each indigenous people has the right to determine the form, structure and authority of its institutions.

Principle 7

The institutions of indigenous peoples and their decisions, like those of states, must be in conformity with internationally accepted human rights both collective and individual.

Principle 8

Indigenous peoples and their members are entitled to participate in the political life of the state.

Principle 9

Indigenous people shall have exclusive rights to their traditional lands and its resources: Where the lands and resources of the indigenous peoples have been taken away without their free and informed consent such lands and resources shall be returned.

Principle 10

The land rights of an indigenous people include surface and subsurface rights, full rights and interior and coastal waters and rights to adequate and exclusive coastal economic zones within the limits of international law.

Principle 11

All indigenous peoples may, for their own needs, freely use their natural wealth and resources in accordance with Principles 9 and 10.

Principle 12

No action or course of conduct may be undertaken which, directly or indirectly, may result in the destruction of land, air, water, sea ice, wildlife, habitat or natural resources without the free and informed consent of the indigenous peoples affected.

Principle 13

The original rights to their material culture, including archaeological sites, artifacts, designs, technology and works of art lie with the indigenous people.

Principle 14

The indigenous peoples have the right to receive education in their own language or to establish their own educational institutions. The languages of the indigenous peoples are to be respected by the states in all dealings between the indigenous people and the state on the basis of equality and non-discrimination.

Principle 15

The indigenous peoples and their authorities have the right to be previously consulted and to authorize the realization of all technological and scientific investigations to be conducted within their territories and to be informed and have full access to the results of the investigation.

Principle 16

Indigenous peoples have the right, in accordance with their traditions, to move freely and conduct traditional activities and maintain kinship relationships across international boundaries.

Principle 17

Treaties between indigenous nations or peoples and representatives of states freely entered into, shall be given full effect under national and international law.

These principles constitute minimum standards which States shall respect and implement.

DECLARATION OF PRINCIPLES ON THE RIGHTS OF INDIGENOUS PEOPLES

Adopted by representatives of indigenous peoples and organizations meeting in Geneva, July 1985, in preparation for the fourth session of the United Nations Working Group on Indigenous Populations; as reaffirmed and amended by representatives of indigenous peoples and organizations meeting in Geneva, July 1987, in preparation for the working group's fifth session. Reprinted in U.N. Doc. E/CN.4/Sub.2/1987/22, Annex 5 (1987).

1. Indigenous nations and peoples have, in common with all humanity, the right to life, and to freedom from oppression, discrimination, and aggression.

2. All indigenous nations and peoples have the right to self-determination, by virtue of which they have the right to whatever degree of autonomy or self-government they choose. This includes the right to freely determine their political status, freely pursue

their own economic, social, religious and cultural development, and determine their own membership and/or citizenship, without external interference.

3. No State shall assert any jurisdiction over an indigenous nation and people, or its territory, except in accordance with the freely expressed wishes of the nation and people concerned.

4. Indigenous nations and peoples are entitled to the permanent control and enjoyment of their aboriginal ancestral-historical territories. This includes air space, surface and subsurface rights, inland and coastal waters, sea ice, renewable and non-renewable resources, and the economies based on these resources.

5. Rights to share and use land, subject to the underlying and inalienable title of the indigenous nation or people, may be granted by their free and informed consent, as evidenced in a valid treaty or agreement.

6. Discovery, conquest, settlement on a theory of *terra nullius* and unilateral legislation are never legitimate bases for States to claim or retain the territories of indigenous nations or peoples.

7. In cases where lands taken in violation of these principles have already been settled, the indigenous nation or people concerned is entitled to immediate restitution, including compensation for the loss of use, without extinction of original title. Indigenous peoples' right to regain possession and control of sacred sites must always be respected.

8. No State shall participate financially or militarily in the involuntary displacement of indigenous populations, or in the subsequent economic exploitation or military use of their territory.

9. The laws and customs of indigenous nations and peoples must be recognized by States' legislative, administrative and judicial institutions and, in case of conflicts with State laws, shall take precedence.

10. No State shall deny an indigenous nation, community, or people residing within its borders the right to participate in the life of the State in whatever manner and to whatever degree they may choose. This includes the right to participate in other forms of collective action and expression.

11. Indigenous nations and peoples continue to own and control their material culture, including archaeological, historical and sacred sites, artefacts, designs, knowledge, and works of art. They have the right to regain items of major cultural significance and, in all cases, to the return of the human remains of their ancestors for burial according with their traditions.

12. Indigenous nations and peoples have the right to education, and the control of education, and to conduct business with States in their own languages, and to establish their own educational institutions.

13. No technical, scientific or social investigations, including archaeological excavations, shall take place in relation to indigenous nations or peoples, or their lands, without their prior authorization, and their continuing ownership and control.

14. The religious practices of indigenous nations and peoples shall be fully respected and protected by the laws of States and by international law. Indigenous nations and peoples shall always enjoy unrestricted access to, and enjoyment of sacred sites in accordance with their own laws and customs, including the right of privacy.

15. Indigenous nations and peoples are subjects of international law.

16. Treaties and other agreements freely made with indigenous nations or peoples shall be recognized and applied in the same manner and according to the same international laws and principles as treaties and agreements entered into with other States.

17. Disputes regarding the jurisdiction, territories and institutions of an indigenous nation or people are a proper concern of international law, and must be resolved by mutual agreement or valid treaty.

18. Indigenous nations and peoples may engage in self-defence against State actions in conflict with their right to self-determination.

19. Indigenous nations and peoples have the right freely to travel, and to maintain economic, social, cultural and religious relations with each other across State borders.

20. In addition to these rights, indigenous nations and peoples are entitled to the enjoyment of all the human rights and fundamental freedoms enumerated in the International Bill of Human Rights and other United Nations instruments. In no circumstances shall they be subjected to adverse discrimination.

21. All indigenous nations and peoples have the right to their own traditional medicine, including the right to the protection of vital medicinal plants, animals and minerals. Indigenous nations and peoples also have the right to benefit from modern medical techniques and services on a basis equal to that of the general population of the States within which they are located. Furthermore, all indigenous nations and peoples have the right to determine, plan, implement, and control the resources respecting health, housing, and other social services affecting them.

22. According to the right of self-determination, all indigenous nations and peoples shall not be obligated to participate in State military services, including armies, paramilitary or "civil" organizations with military structures, within the country or in international conflicts.

DECLARATION OF SAN JOSÉ

Adopted by the UNESCO Meeting of Experts on Ethno-Development and Ethnocide in Latin America, San José, Dec. 11, 1981. UNESCO Doc. FS 82/WF.32 (1982).

For the past few years, increasing concern has been expressed at various international forums over the problems of the loss of cultural identity among the Indian populations of Latin America. This complex process, which has historical, social, political and economic roots, has been termed *ethnocide*.

Ethnocide means that an ethnic group is denied the right to enjoy, develop and transmit its own culture and its own language, whether collectively or individually. This involves an extreme form of massive violation of human rights and, in particular, the right of ethnic groups to respect for their cultural identity, as established by numerous declarations, covenants and agreements of the United Nations and its Specialized Agencies, as well as various regional intergovernmental bodies and numerous non-government organizations.

In response to this demand, UNESCO organized an international meeting on ethnocide and ethno-development in Latin America, in collaboration with FLACSO, which was held in December 1981 in San José, Costa Rica.

The participants in the meeting, Indian and other experts, made the following Declaration:

1. We declare that ethnocide, that is, cultural genocide, is a violation of international law equivalent to genocide, which was condemned by the United Nations Convention on the Prevention and Punishment of the Crime of Genocide of 1948.

2. We affirm that ethno-development is an inalienable right of Indian groups.

3. By ethno-development we mean the extension and consideration of the elements of its own culture, through strengthening the independent decision-making capacity of a culturally distinct society to direct its own development and exercise self-determination, at whatever level, which implies an equitable and independent share of power. This means that the ethnic group is a political and administrative unit, with authority over its own territory and decision-making powers within the confines of its development project, in a process of increasing autonomy and self-management.

4. Since the European invasion, the Indian peoples of America have seen their history denied or distorted, despite their great contributions to the progress of mankind, which has led to the negation of their very existence. We reject this unacceptable misrepresentation.

5. As creators, bearers and propagators of a civilizing dimension of their own, as unique and specific facets of the heritage of mankind, the Indian peoples, nations and ethnic groups of America are entitled, collectively and individually, to all civil, political, economic, social and cultural rights now threatened. We, the participants in this meeting, demand universal recognition of all these rights.

6. For the Indian peoples, the land is not only an object of possession and production. It forms the basis of their existence, both physical and spiritual, as an independent entity. Territorial space is the foundation and source of their relationship with the universe and the mainstay of their view of the world.

7. The Indian peoples have a natural and inalienable right to the territories they possess as well as the right to recover the land taken away from them. This implies the right to the natural and cultural heritage that this territory contains and the right to determine freely how it will be used and exploited.

8. An essential part of the cultural heritage of these peoples is their philosophy of life and their experience, knowledge and achievements accumulated throughout history in the cultural, social, political, legal, scientific and technological sphere. They therefore have a right to access to and use, dissemination and transmission of this entire heritage.

9. Respect for the forms of autonomy required by the Indian peoples is an essential condition for guaranteeing and implementing these rights.

10. Furthermore, the Indian peoples' own forms of internal organization are part of their cultural and legal heritage which has contributed to their cohesion and to maintaining their socio-cultural traditions.

11. Disregard for these principles constitutes a gross violation of the right of all individuals and peoples to be different, to consider themselves as different and to be regarded as such, a right recognized in the Declaration on Race and Racial Prejudice adopted by the UNESCO General Conference in 1978, and should therefore be condemned, especially when it creates a risk of ethnocide.

12. In addition. disregard for these principles creates disequilibrium and lack of harmony within society and may incite the Indian peoples to the ultimate resort of rebellion against tyranny and oppression, thereby endangering world peace. It therefore contravenes the United Nations Charter and the Constitution of UNESCO.

As a result of their reflections, the participants appeal to the United Nations, UNESCO, the ILO, WHO, and FAO, as well as to the Organizations of American States and the Inter-American Indian Institute, to take the necessary steps to apply these principles in full.

The participants address their appeal to Member States of the United Nations and the above-mentioned Specialized Agencies, requesting them to give special attention to the application of these principles, and also to collaborate with international, intergovernmental and non-governmental organizations, both universal and regional including, in particular, Indian organizations, in order to ensure observance of the fundamental rights of the Indian peoples of America.

This appeal is also addressed to officials in the legislative, executive, administrative and legal branches, and to all public servants concerned in the countries of America, with the request that in the course of their daily duties they will always act in conformity with the above principles.

The participants appeal to the conscience of the scientific community, and the individuals comprising it, who have the moral responsibility for ensuring that their research, studies and practices, as well as the conclusions they draw, cannot be used as a pretext for misrepresentation or interpretations which could harm Indian nations, peoples and ethnic groups.

Finally, the participants draw attention to the need to provide for due participation by genuine representatives of Indian nations, peoples and ethnic groups in any activity that might affect their future.

CONVENTION (No. 169) CONCERNING INDIGENOUS AND TRIBAL PEOPLES IN INDEPENDENT COUNTRIES

Adopted by the General Conference of the International Labour Organization, Geneva, June 27, 1989. Entered into force Sept. 5, 1991.

The General Conference of the International Labour Organization,

Having been convened at Geneva by the Governing Body of the International Labour Office, and having met in its 76th Session on 7 June 1989, and

Noting the international standards contained in the Indigenous and Tribal Populations Convention and Recommendation, 1957, and

Recalling the terms of the Universal Declaration of Human Rights, the International Covenant on Economic, Social and Cultural Rights, the International Covenant on Civil and Political Rights, and the many international instruments on the prevention of discrimination, and

Considering that the developments which have taken place in international law since 1957, as well as developments in the situation of indigenous and tribal peoples in all regions of the world, have made it appropriate to adopt new international standards on the subject with a view to removing the assimilationist orientation of the earlier standards, and

Recognising the aspirations of these peoples to exercise control over their own institutions, ways of life and economic development and to maintain and develop their identities, languages and religions, within the framework of the States in which they live, and

Noting that in many parts of the world these peoples are unable to enjoy their fundamental human rights to the same degree as the rest of the population of the States within which they live, and that their laws, values, customs and perspectives have often been eroded, and

Calling attention to the distinctive contributions of indigenous and tribal peoples to the cultural diversity and social and ecological harmony of humankind and to international co-operation and understanding, and

Noting that the following provisions have been framed with the co-operation of the United Nations, the Food and Agriculture Organisation of the United Nations, the United Nations Educational, Scientific and Cultural Organisation and the World Health Organisation, as well as of the Inter-American Indian Institute, at appropriate levels and in their respective fields, and that it is proposed to continue this co-operation in promoting and securing the application of these provisions, and

Having decided upon the adoption of certain proposals with regard to the partial revision of the Indigenous and Tribal Populations Convention, 1957 (No. 107), which is the fourth item on the agenda of the session, and

Having determined that these proposals shall take the form of an international Convention revising the Indigenous and Tribal Populations Convention, 1957;

adopts this twenty-seventh day of June of the year one thousand nine hundred and eighty-nine the following Convention, which may be cited as the Indigenous and Tribal Peoples Convention, 1989:

Part I. General Policy

Article 1

1. This Convention applies to:

(a) tribal peoples in independent countries whose social, cultural and economic conditions distinguish them from other sections of the national community, and whose status is regulated wholly or partially by their own customs or traditions or by special laws or regulations;

(b) peoples in independent countries who are regarded as indigenous on account of their descent from the populations which inhabited the country, or a geographical region to which the country belongs, at the time of conquest or colonisation or the establishment of present state boundaries and who, irrespective of their legal status, retain some or all of their own social, economic, cultural and political institutions.

2. Self-identification as indigenous or tribal shall be regarded as a fundamental criterion for determining the groups to which the provisions of this Convention apply.

3. The use of the term "peoples" in this Convention shall not be construed as having any implications as regards the rights which may attach to the term under international law.

Article 2

1. Governments shall have the responsibility for developing, with the participation of the peoples concerned, co-ordinated and systematic action to protect the rights of these peoples and to guarantee respect for their integrity.

2. Such action shall include measures for:

   (a) ensuring that members of these peoples benefit on an equal footing from the rights and opportunities which national laws and regulations grant to other members of the population;

   (b) promoting the full realisation of the social, economic and cultural rights of these peoples with respect for their social and cultural identity, their customs and traditions and their institutions;

   (c) assisting the members of the peoples concerned to eliminate socio-economic gaps that may exist between indigenous and other members of the national community, in a manner compatible with their aspirations and ways of life.

Article 3

1. Indigenous and tribal peoples shall enjoy the full measure of human rights and fundamental freedoms without hindrance or discrimination. The provisions of the Convention shall be applied without discrimination to male and female members of these peoples.

2. No form of force or coercion shall be used in violation of the human rights and fundamental freedoms of the peoples concerned, including the rights contained in this Convention.

Article 4

1. Special measures shall be adopted as appropriate for safeguarding the persons, institutions, property, labour, cultures and environment of the peoples concerned.

2. Such special measures shall not be contrary to the freely-expressed wishes of the peoples concerned.

3. Enjoyment of the general rights of citizenship, without discrimination, shall not be prejudiced in any way by such special measures.

Article 5

In applying the provisions of this Convention:

   (a) the social, cultural, religious and spiritual values and practices of these peoples shall be recognised and protected, and due account shall be taken of the nature of the problems which face them both as groups and as individuals;

(b) the integrity of the values, practices and institutions of these peoples shall be respected;

(c) policies aimed at mitigating the difficulties experienced by these peoples in facing new conditions of life and work shall be adopted, with the participation and co-operation of the peoples affected.

Article 6

1. In applying the provisions of this Convention, governments shall:

(a) consult the peoples concerned, through appropriate procedures and in particular through their representative institutions, whenever consideration is being given to legislative or administrative measures which may affect them directly;

(b) establish means by which these peoples can freely participate, to at least the same extent as other sectors of the population, at all levels of decision-making in elective institutions and administrative and other bodies responsible for policies and programmes which concern them;

(c) establish means for the full development of these peoples' own institutions and initiatives, and in appropriate cases provide the resources necessary for this purpose.

2. The consultations carried out in application of this Convention shall be undertaken, in good faith and in a form appropriate to the circumstances, with the objective of achieving agreement or consent to the proposed measures.

Article 7

1. The peoples concerned shall have the right to decide their own priorities for the process of development as it affects their lives, beliefs, institutions and spiritual well-being and the lands they occupy or otherwise use, and to exercise control, to the extent possible, over their own economic, social and cultural development. In addition, they shall participate in the formulation, implementation and evaluation of plans and programmes for national and regional development which may affect them directly.

2. The improvement of the conditions of life and work and levels of health and education of the peoples concerned, with their participation and co-operation, shall be a matter of priority in plans for the overall economic development of areas they inhabit. Special projects for development of the areas in question shall also be so designed as to promote such improvement.

3. Governments shall ensure that, whenever appropriate, studies are carried out, in co-operation with the peoples concerned, to assess the social, spiritual, cultural and environmental impact on them of planned development activities. The results of these studies shall be considered as fundamental criteria for the implementation of these activities.

4. Governments shall take measures, in co-operation with the peoples concerned, to protect and preserve the environment of the territories they inhabit.

Article 8

1. In applying national laws and regulations to the peoples concerned, due regard shall be had to their customs or customary laws.

2. These peoples shall have the right to retain their own customs and institutions, where these are not incompatible with fundamental rights defined by the national legal system and with internationally recognised human rights. Procedures shall be established, whenever necessary, to resolve conflicts which may arise in the application of this principle.

3. The application of paragraphs 1 and 2 of this Article shall not prevent members of these peoples from exercising the rights granted to all citizens and from assuming the corresponding duties.

Article 9

1. To the extent compatible with the national legal system and internationally recognised human rights, the methods customarily practised by the peoples concerned for dealing with offences committed by their members shall be respected.

2. The customs of these peoples in regard to penal matters shall be taken into consideration by the authorities and courts dealing with such cases.

Article 10

1. In imposing penalties laid down by general law on members of these peoples account shall be taken of their economic, social and cultural characteristics.

2. Preference shall be given to methods of punishment other than confinement in prison.

Article 11

The exaction from members of the peoples concerned of compulsory personal services in any form, whether paid or unpaid, shall be prohibited and punishable by law, except in cases prescribed by law for all citizens.

Article 12

The peoples concerned shall be safeguarded against the abuse of their rights and shall be able to take legal proceedings, either individually or through their representative bodies, for the effective protection of these rights. Measures shall be taken to ensure that members of these peoples can understand and be understood in legal proceedings, where necessary through the provision of interpretation or by other effective means.

Part II. Land

Article 13

1. In applying the provisions of this Part of the Convention governments shall respect the special importance for the cultures and spiritual values of the peoples concerned

of their relationship with the lands or territories, or both as applicable, which they occupy or otherwise use, and in particular the collective aspects of this relationship.

2. The use of the term "lands" in Articles 15 and 16 shall include the concept of territories, which covers the total environment of the areas which the peoples concerned occupy or otherwise use.

Article 14

1. The rights of ownership and possession of the peoples concerned over the lands which they traditionally occupy shall be recognised. In addition, measures shall be taken in appropriate cases to safeguard the right of the peoples concerned to use lands not exclusively occupied by them, but to which they have traditionally had access for their subsistence and traditional activities. Particular attention shall be paid to the situation of nomadic peoples and shifting cultivators in this respect.

2. Governments shall take steps as necessary to identify the lands which the peoples concerned traditionally occupy, and to guarantee effective protection of their rights of ownership and possession.

3. Adequate procedures shall be established within the national legal system to resolve land claims by the peoples concerned.

Article 15

1. The rights of the peoples concerned to the natural resources pertaining to their lands shall be specially safeguarded. These rights include the right of these peoples to participate in the use, management and conservation of these resources.

2. In cases in which the State retains the ownership of mineral or sub-surface resources or rights to other resources pertaining to lands, governments shall establish or maintain procedures through which they shall consult these peoples, with a view to ascertaining whether and to what degree their interests would be prejudiced, before undertaking or permitting any programmes for the exploration or exploitation of such resources pertaining to their lands. The peoples concerned shall wherever possible participate in the benefits of such activities, and shall receive fair compensation for any damages which they may sustain as a result of such activities.

Article 16

1. Subject to the following paragraphs of this Article, the peoples concerned shall not be removed from the lands which they occupy.

2. Where the relocation of these peoples is considered necessary as an exceptional measure, such relocation shall take place only with their free and informed consent. Where their consent cannot be obtained, such relocation shall take place only following appropriate procedures established by national laws and regulations, including public inquiries where appropriate, which provide the opportunity for effective representation of the peoples concerned.

3. Whenever possible, these peoples shall have the right to return to their traditional lands, as soon as the grounds for relocation cease to exist.

4. When such return is not possible, as determined by agreement or, in the absence of such agreement, through appropriate procedures, these peoples shall be provided in all possible cases with lands of quality and legal status at least equal to that of the lands previously occupied by them, suitable to provide for their present needs and future development. Where the peoples concerned express a preference for compensation in money or in kind, they shall be so compensated under appropriate guarantees.

5. Persons thus relocated shall be fully compensated for any resulting loss or injury.

Article 17

1. Procedures established by the peoples concerned for the transmission of land rights among members of these peoples shall be respected.

2. The peoples concerned shall be consulted whenever consideration is being given to their capacity to alienate their lands or otherwise transmit their rights outside their own community.

3. Persons not belonging to these peoples shall be prevented from taking advantage of their customs or of lack of understanding of the laws on the part of their members to secure the ownership, possession or use of land belonging to them.

Article 18

Adequate penalties shall be established by law for unauthorised intrusion upon, or use of, the lands of the peoples concerned, and governments shall take measures to prevent such offences.

Article 19

National agrarian programmes shall secure to the peoples concerned treatment equivalent to that accorded to other sectors of the population with regard to:

(a) the provision of more land for these peoples when they have not the area necessary for providing the essentials of a normal existence, or for any possible increase in their numbers;

(b) the provision of the means required to promote the development of the lands which these peoples already possess.

Part III. Recruitment and Conditions of Employment

Article 20

1. Governments shall, within the framework of national laws and regulations, and in co-operation with the peoples concerned, adopt special measures to ensure the effective protection with regard to recruitment and conditions of employment of workers be-

longing to these peoples, to the extent that they are not effectively protected by laws applicable to workers in general.

2. Governments shall do everything possible to prevent any discrimination between workers belonging to the peoples concerned and other workers, in particular as regards:

(a) admission to employment, including skilled employment, as well as measures for promotion and advancement;

(b) equal remuneration for work of equal value;

(c) medical and social assistance, occupational safety and health, all social security benefits and any other occupationally related benefits, and housing;

(d) the right of association and freedom for all lawful trade union activities, and the right to conclude collective agreements with employers or employers' organisations.

3. The measures taken shall include measures to ensure:

(a) that workers belonging to the peoples concerned, including seasonal, casual and migrant workers in agricultural and other employment, as well as those employed by labour contractors, enjoy the protection afforded by national law and practice to other such workers in the same sectors, and that they are fully informed of their rights under labour legislation and of the means of redress available to them;

(b) that workers belonging to these peoples are not subjected to working conditions hazardous to their health, in particular through exposure to pesticides or other toxic substances;

(c) that workers belonging to these peoples are not subjected to coercive recruitment systems, including bonded labour and other forms of debt servitude;

(d) that workers belonging to these peoples enjoy equal opportunities and equal treatment in employment for men and women, and protection from sexual harassment.

4. Particular attention shall be paid to the establishment of adequate labour inspection services in areas where workers belonging to the peoples concerned undertake wage employment, in order to ensure compliance with the provisions of this Part of this Convention.

Part IV. Vocational Training, Handicrafts and Rural Industries

Article 21

Members of the peoples concerned shall enjoy opportunities at least equal to those of other citizens in respect of vocational training measures.

Article 22

1. Measures shall be taken to promote the voluntary participation of members of the peoples concerned in vocational training programmes of general application.

2. Whenever existing programmes of vocational training of general application do not meet the special needs of the peoples concerned, governments shall, with the participation of these peoples, ensure the provision of special training programmes and facilities.

3. Any special training programmes shall be based on the economic environment, social and cultural conditions and practical needs of the peoples concerned. Any studies made in this connection shall be carried out in co-operation with these peoples, who shall be consulted on the organisation and operation of such programmes. Where feasible, these peoples shall progressively assume responsibility for the organisation and operation of such special training programmes, if they so decide.

Article 23

1. Handicrafts, rural and community-based industries, and subsistence economy and traditional activities of the peoples concerned, such as hunting, fishing, trapping and gathering, shall be recognised as important factors in the maintenance of their cultures and in their economic self-reliance and development. Governments shall, with the participation of these people and whenever appropriate, ensure that these activities are strengthened and promoted.

2. Upon the request of the peoples concerned, appropriate technical and financial assistance shall be provided wherever possible, taking into account the traditional technologies and cultural characteristics of these peoples, as well as the importance of sustainable and equitable development.

Part V. Social Security and Health

Article 24

Social security schemes shall be extended progressively to cover the peoples concerned, and applied without discrimination against them.

Article 25

1. Governments shall ensure that adequate health services are made available to the peoples concerned, or shall provide them with resources to allow them to design and deliver such services under their own responsibility and control, so that they may enjoy the highest attainable standard of physical and mental health.

2. Health services shall, to the extent possible, be community-based. These services shall be planned and administered in co-operation with the peoples concerned and take into account their economic, geographic, social and cultural conditions as well as their traditional preventive care, healing practices and medicines.

3. The health care system shall give preference to the training and employment of local community health workers, and focus on primary health care while maintaining strong links with other levels of health care services.

4. The provision of such health services shall be co-ordinated with other social, economic, and cultural measures in the country.

Part VI. Education and Means of Communication

Article 26

Measures shall be taken to ensure that members of the peoples concerned have the opportunity to acquire education at all levels on at least an equal footing with the rest of the national community.

Article 27

1. Education programmes and services for the peoples concerned shall be developed and implemented in co-operation with them to address their special needs, and shall incorporate their histories, their knowledge and technologies, their value systems and their further social, economic and cultural aspirations.

2. The competent authority shall ensure the training of members of these peoples and their involvement in the formulation and implementation of education programmes, with a view to the progressive transfer of responsibility for the conduct of these programmes to these peoples as appropriate.

3. In addition, governments shall recognise the right of these peoples to establish their own educational institutions and facilities, provided that such institutions meet minimum standards established by the competent authority in consultation with these peoples. Appropriate resources shall be provided for this purpose.

Article 28

1. Children belonging to the peoples concerned shall, wherever practicable, be taught to read and write in their own indigenous language or in the language most commonly used by the group to which they belong. When this is not practicable, the competent authorities shall undertake consultations with these peoples with a view to the adoption of measures to achieve this objective.

2. Adequate measures shall be taken to ensure that these peoples have the opportunity to attain fluency in the national language or in one of the official languages of the country.

3. Measures shall be taken to preserve and promote the development and practice of the indigenous languages of the peoples concerned.

Article 29

The imparting of general knowledge and skills that will help children belonging to the peoples concerned to participate fully and on an equal footing in their own community and in the national community shall be an aim of education for these peoples.

Article 30

1. Governments shall adopt measures appropriate to the traditions and cultures of the peoples concerned, to make known to them their rights and duties, especially in re-

gard to labour, economic opportunities, education and health matters, social welfare and their rights deriving from this Convention.

2. If necessary, this shall be done by means of written translations and through the use of mass communications in the languages of these peoples.

Article 31

Educational measures shall be taken among all sections of the national community, and particularly among those that are in most direct contact with the peoples concerned, with the object of eliminating prejudices that they may harbour in respect of these peoples. To this end, efforts shall be made to ensure that history textbooks and other educational materials provide a fair, accurate and informative portrayal of the societies and cultures of these peoples.

Part VII. Contacts and Co-operation Across Borders

Article 32

Governments shall take appropriate measures, including by means of international agreements, to facilitate contacts and co-operation between indigenous and tribal peoples across borders, including activities in the economic, social, cultural, spiritual and environmental fields.

Part VIII. Administration

Article 33

1. The governmental authority responsible for the matters covered in this Convention shall ensure that agencies or other appropriate mechanisms exist to administer the programmes affecting the peoples concerned, and shall ensure that they have the means necessary for the proper fulfillment of the functions assigned to them.

2. These programmes shall include:

(a) the planning, co-ordination, execution and evaluation, in co-operation with the peoples concerned, of the measures provided for in this Convention;

(b) the proposing of legislative and other measures to the competent authorities and supervision of the application of the measures taken, in co-operation with the peoples concerned.

Part IX. General Provisions

Article 34

The nature and scope of the measures to be taken to give effect to this Convention shall be determined in a flexible manner, having regard to the conditions characteristic of each country.

Article 35

The application of the provisions of this Convention shall not adversely affect rights and benefits of the peoples concerned pursuant to other Conventions and Recommendations, international instruments, treaties, or national laws, awards, custom or agreements.

Part X. Final Provisions

Article 36

This Convention revises the Indigenous and Tribal Populations Convention, 1957.

Article 37

The formal ratifications of this Convention shall be communicated to the Director-General of the International Labour Office for registration.

Article 38

1. This Convention shall be binding only upon those Members of the International Labour Organization whose ratifications have been registered with the Director-General.

2. It shall come into force twelve months after the date on which the ratifications of two Members have been registered with the Director-General.

3. Thereafter, this Convention shall come into force for any Member twelve months after the date on which its ratification has been registered.

Article 39

1. A Member which has ratified this Convention may denounce it after the expiration of ten years from the date on which the Convention first comes into force, by an act communicated to the Director-General of the International Labour Office for registration. Such denunciation shall not take effect until one year after the date on which it is registered.

2. Each Member which has ratified this Convention and which does not, within the year following the expiration of the period of ten years mentioned in the preceding paragraph, exercise the right of denunciation provided for in this Article, will be bound for another period of ten years and, thereafter, may denounce this Convention at the expiration of each period of ten years under the terms provided for in this Article.

Article 40

1. The Director-General of the International Labour Office shall notify all Members of the International Labour Organization of the registration of all ratifications and denunciations communicated to him by the Members of the Organization.

2. When notifying the Members of the Organisation of the registration of the second ratification communicated to him, the Director-General shall draw the attention of the Members of the Organization to the date upon which the Convention will come into force.

Article 41

The Director-General of the International Labour Office shall communicate to the Secretary-General of the United Nations for registration in accordance with Article 102 of the Charter of the United Nations full particulars of all ratifications and acts of denunciation registered by him in accordance with the provisions of the preceding Articles.

Article 42

At such times as it may consider necessary the Governing Body of the International Labour Office shall present to the General Conference a report on the working of this Convention, and shall examine the desirability of placing on the agenda of the Conference the question of its revision in whole or in part.

Article 43

1. Should the Conference adopt a new Convention revising this Convention in whole or in part, then, unless the new Convention otherwise provides—

   (a) the ratification by a Member of the new revising Convention shall *ipso jure* involve the immediate denunciation of this Convention, notwithstanding the provisions of Article 39 above, if and when the new revising Convention shall have come into force;
   (b) as from the date when the new revising Convention comes into force this Convention shall cease to be open to ratification by the Members.

2. This Convention shall in any case remain in force in its actual form and content for those Members which have ratified it but have not ratified the revising Convention.

Article 44

The English and French versions of the text of this Convention are equally authoritative.

AGENDA 21: CHAPTER 26

Adopted by the U.N. Conference on Environment and Development, Rio de Janeiro, June 13, 1992. U.N. Doc. A/CONF.151/26 (vol. 3), at 16, Annex 2 (1992).

Chapter 26
Recognizing and Strengthening the Role of Indigenous People and Their Communities

Programme Area

Basis for action

26.1. Indigenous people and their communities have an historical relationship with their lands and are generally descendants of the original inhabitants of such lands. In the context of this chapter the term "lands" is understood to include the environment of the areas which the people concerned traditionally occupy. Indigenous people and their communities represent a significant percentage of the global population. They have developed over many generations a holistic traditional scientific knowledge of their lands, natural resources and environment. Indigenous people and their communities shall enjoy the full measure of human rights and fundamental freedoms without hindrance or discrimination. Their ability to participate fully in sustainable development practices on their lands has tended to be limited as a result of factors of an economic, social and historical nature. In view of the interrelationship between the natural environment and its sustainable development and the cultural, social, economic and physical well-being of indigenous people, national and international efforts to implement environmentally sound and sustainable development should recognize, accommodate, promote and strengthen the role of indigenous people and their communities.

26.2. Some of the goals inherent in the objectives and activities of this programme area are already contained in such international legal instruments as the ILO Indigenous and Tribal Peoples Convention (No. 169) and are being incorporated into the draft universal declaration on indigenous rights, being prepared by the United Nations working group on indigenous populations. The International Year for the World's Indigenous People (1993), proclaimed by the General Assembly in its resolution 45/164 of 18 December 1990, presents a timely opportunity to mobilize further international technical and financial cooperation.

Objectives

26.3. In full partnership with indigenous people and their communities, Governments and, where appropriate, intergovernmental organizations should aim at fulfilling the following objectives:

(a) Establishment of a process to empower indigenous people and their communities through measures that include:

  (i) Adoption or strengthening of appropriate policies and/or legal instruments at the national level;

  (ii) Recognition that the lands of indigenous people and their communities should be protected from activities that are environmentally unsound or that the indigenous people concerned consider to be socially and culturally inappropriate;

    (iii) Recognition of their values, traditional knowledge and resource management practices with a view to promoting environmentally sound and sustainable development;

    (iv) Recognition that traditional and direct dependence on renewable resources and ecosystems, including sustainable harvesting, continues to be essential to the cultural, economic and physical well-being of indigenous people and their communities;

    (v) Development and strengthening of national dispute-resolution arrangements in relation to settlement of land and resource-management concerns;

    (vi) Support for alternative environmentally sound means of production to ensure a range of choices on how to improve their quality of life so that they effectively participate in sustainable development;

    (vii) Enhancement of capacity-building for indigenous communities, based on the adaptation and exchange of traditional experience, knowledge and resource-management practices, to ensure their sustainable development;

(b) Establishment, where appropriate, of arrangements to strengthen the active participation of indigenous people and their communities in the national formulation of policies, laws and programmes relating to resource management and other development processes that may affect them, and their initiation of proposals for such policies and programmes;

(c) Involvement of indigenous people and their communities at the national and local levels in resource management and conservation strategies and other relevant programmes established to support and review sustainable development strategies, such as those suggested in other programme areas of Agenda 21.

Activities

26.4. Some indigenous people and their communities may require, in accordance with national legislation, greater control over their lands, self-management of their resources, participation in development decisions affecting them, including, where appropriate, participation in the establishment or management of protected areas. The following are some of the specific measures which Governments could take:

(a) Consider the ratification and application of existing international conventions relevant to indigenous people and their communities (where not yet done) and provide support for the adoption by the General Assembly of a declaration on indigenous rights;

(b) Adopt or strengthen appropriate policies and/or legal instruments that will protect indigenous intellectual and cultural property and the right to preserve customary and administrative systems and practices.

26.5. United Nations organizations and other international development and finance organizations and Governments should, drawing on the active participation of indigenous people and their communities, as appropriate, take the following measures, *inter alia*, to incorporate their values, views and knowledge, including the unique contribution of indigenous women, in resource management and other policies and programmes that may affect them:

(a) Appoint a special focal point within each international organization, and organize annual interorganizational coordination meetings in consultation with Governments and indigenous organizations, as appropriate, and develop a procedure within and between operational agencies for assisting Governments in ensuring the coherent and coordinated incorporation of the views of indigenous people in the design and implementation of policies and programmes. Under this procedure, indigenous people and their communities should be informed and consulted and allowed to participate in national decision-making, in particular regarding regional and international cooperative efforts. In addition, these policies and programmes should take fully into account strategies based on local indigenous initiatives;

(b) Provide technical and financial assistance for capacity-building programmes to support the sustainable self-development of indigenous people and their communities;

(c) Strengthen research and education programmes aimed at:

(i) Achieving a better understanding of indigenous people's knowledge and management experience related to the environment, and applying this to contemporary development challenges;

(ii) Increasing the efficiency of indigenous people's resource management systems, for example, by promoting the adaptation and dissemination of suitable technological innovations;

(d) Contribute to the endeavours of indigenous people and their communities in resource management and conservation strategies (such as those that may be developed under appropriate projects funded through the Global Environmental Facility and Tropical Forestry Action Plan) and other programme areas of Agenda 21, including programmes to collect, analyse and use data and other information in support of sustainable development projects.

26.6. Governments, in full partnership with indigenous people and their communities should, where appropriate:

(a) Develop or strengthen national arrangements to consult with indigenous people and their communities with a view to reflecting their needs and incorporating their values and traditional and other knowledge and practices in national policies and programmes in the field of natural resource management and conservation and other development programmes affecting them;

(b) Cooperate at the regional level, where appropriate, to address common indigenous issues with a view to recognizing and strengthening their participation in sustainable development.

Means of implementation

(a) Financing and cost evaluation

26.7. The Conference secretariat has estimated the average total annual cost (1993–2000) of implementing the activities of this programme to be about $3 million on grant or concessional terms. These are indicative and order-of-magnitude estimates only and have not been reviewed by Governments. Actual costs and financial terms, including any that are non-concessional, will depend upon, *inter alia*, the specific strategies and programmes Governments decide upon for implementation.

(b) Legal and administrative frameworks

26.8. Governments should incorporate, in collaboration with the indigenous people affected, the rights and responsibilities of indigenous people and their communities in the legislation of each country, suitable to the country's specific situation. Developing countries may require technical assistance to implement these activities.

(c) Human resource development

26.9. International development agencies and Governments should commit financial and other resources to education and training for indigenous people and their communities to develop their capacities to achieve their sustainable self-development, and to contribute to and participate in sustainable and equitable development at the national level. Particular attention should be given to strengthening the role of indigenous women.

DRAFT UNITED NATIONS DECLARATION ON THE RIGHTS OF INDIGENOUS PEOPLES

As agreed upon by the members of the U.N. Working Group on Indigenous Populations at its eleventh session, Geneva, July 1993. Adopted by the U.N. Subcommission on Prevention of Discrimination and Protection of Minorities by its resolution 1994/45, August 26, 1994. U.N. Doc. E/CN.4/1995/2, E/CN.4/Sub.2/1994/56, at 105 (1994).

Affirming that indigenous peoples are equal in dignity and rights to all other peoples, while recognizing the right of all peoples to be different, to consider themselves different, and to be respected as such,

Affirming also that all peoples contribute to the diversity and richness of civilizations and cultures, which constitute the common heritage of humankind,

Affirming further that all doctrines, policies and practices based on or advocating superiority of peoples or individuals on the basis of national origin, racial, religious, ethnic or cultural differences are racist, scientifically false, legally invalid, morally condemnable, and socially unjust,

Reaffirming also that indigenous peoples, in the exercise of their rights, should be free from discrimination of any kind,

Concerned that indigenous peoples have been deprived of their human rights and fundamental freedoms, resulting, *inter alia*, in their colonization and dispossession of their lands, territories and resources, thus preventing them from exercising, in particular, their right to development in accordance with their own needs and interests,

Recognizing the urgent need to respect and promote the inherent rights and characteristics of indigenous peoples, especially their rights to their lands, territories and resources, which derive from their political, economic and social structures and from their cultures, spiritual traditions, histories and philosophies,

Welcoming the fact that indigenous peoples are organizing themselves for political, economic, social and cultural enhancement and in order to bring an end to all forms of discrimination and oppression wherever they occur,

Convinced that control by indigenous peoples over developments affecting them and their lands, territories and resources will enable them to maintain and strengthen their institutions, cultures and traditions, and to promote their development in accordance with their aspirations and needs,

Recognizing also that respect for indigenous knowledge, cultures and traditional practices contributes to sustainable and equitable development and proper management of the environment,

Emphasizing the need for demilitarization of the lands and territories of indigenous peoples, which will contribute to peace, economic and social progress and development, understanding and friendly relations among nations and peoples of the world,

Recognizing in particular the right of indigenous families and communities to retain shared responsibility for the upbringing, training, education and well-being of their children,

Recognizing also, that indigenous peoples have the right freely to determine their relationships with States in a spirit of coexistence, mutual benefit and full respect,

Considering that treaties, agreements and other arrangements between States and indigenous peoples are properly matters of international concern and responsibility,

Acknowledging that the Charter of the United Nations, the International Covenant on Economic, Social and Cultural Rights and the International Covenant on Civil and Political Rights affirm the fundamental importance of the right of self-determination of all peoples, by virtue of which they freely determine their political status and freely pursue their economic, social and cultural development,

Bearing in mind that nothing in this Declaration may be used to deny any peoples their right of self-determination,

Encouraging States to comply with and effectively implement all international instruments, in particular those related to human rights, as they apply to indigenous peoples, in consultation and cooperation with the peoples concerned,

Emphasizing that the United Nations has an important and continuing role to play in promoting and protecting the rights of indigenous peoples,

Believing that this Declaration is a further important step forward for the recognition, promotion and protection of the rights and freedoms of indigenous peoples and in the development of relevant activities of the United Nations system in this field,

Solemnly proclaims the following United Nations Declaration on the Rights of Indigenous Peoples:

Part I

Article 1

Indigenous peoples have the right to the full and effective enjoyment of all human rights and fundamental freedoms recognized in the Charter of the United Nations, the Universal Declaration of Human Rights and international human rights law.

Article 2

Indigenous individuals and peoples are free and equal to all other individuals and peoples in dignity and rights, and have the right to be free from any kind of adverse discrimination, in particular that based on their indigenous origin or identity.

Article 3

Indigenous peoples have the right of self-determination. By virtue of that right they freely determine their political status and freely pursue their economic, social and cultural development.

Article 4

Indigenous peoples have the right to maintain and strengthen their distinct political, economic, social and cultural characteristics, as well as their legal systems, while retaining their rights to participate fully, if they so choose, in the political, economic, social and cultural life of the State.

Article 5

Every indigenous individual has the right to a nationality.

Part II

Article 6

Indigenous peoples have the collective right to live in freedom, peace and security as distinct peoples and to full guarantees against genocide or any other act of violence, including the removal of indigenous children from their families and communities under any pretext.

In addition, they have the individual rights to life, physical and mental integrity, liberty, and security of person.

Article 7

Indigenous peoples have the collective and individual right not to be subjected to ethnocide and cultural genocide, including prevention of and redress for:

(a) Any action which has the aim or effect of depriving them of their integrity as distinct peoples, or of their cultural values or ethnic identities;

(b) Any action which has the aim or effect of dispossessing them of their lands, territories or resources;

(c) Any form of population transfer which has the aim or effect of violating or undermining any of their rights;

(d) Any form of assimilation or integration by other cultures or ways of life imposed on them by legislative, administrative or other measures;

(e) Any form of propaganda directed against them.

Article 8

Indigenous peoples have the collective and individual right to maintain and develop their distinct identities and characteristics, including the right to identify themselves as indigenous and to be recognized as such.

Article 9

Indigenous peoples and individuals have the right to belong to an indigenous community or nation, in accordance with the traditions and customs of the community or nation concerned. No disadvantage of any kind may arise from the exercise of such a right.

Article 10

Indigenous peoples shall not be forcibly removed from their lands or territories. No relocation shall take place without the free and informed consent of the indigenous peoples concerned and after agreement on just and fair compensation and, where possible, with the option of return.

Article 11

Indigenous peoples have the right to special protection and security in periods of armed conflict.

States shall observe international standards, in particular the Fourth Geneva Convention of 1949, for the protection of civilian populations in circumstances of emergency and armed conflict, and shall not:

(a) Recruit indigenous individuals against their will into the armed forces and, in particular, for use against other indigenous peoples;

(b) Recruit indigenous children into the armed forces under any circumstances;

(c) Force indigenous individuals to abandon their lands, territories or means of subsistence, or relocate them in special centres for military purposes;

(d) Force indigenous individuals to work for military purposes under any discriminatory conditions.

Part III

Article 12

Indigenous peoples have the right to practise and revitalize their cultural traditions and customs. This includes the right to maintain, protect and develop the past, present and future manifestations of their cultures, such as archaeological and historical sites, artifacts, designs, ceremonies, technologies and visual and performing arts and literature, as well as the right to restitution of cultural, intellectual, religious and spiritual property taken without their free and informed consent or in violation of their laws, traditions and customs.

Article 13

Indigenous peoples have the right to manifest, practise, develop and teach their spiritual and religious traditions, customs and ceremonies; the right to maintain, protect, and have access in privacy to their religious and cultural sites; the right to the use and control of ceremonial objects; and the right to the repatriation of human remains.

States shall take effective measures, in conjunction with the indigenous peoples concerned, to ensure that indigenous sacred places, including burial sites, be preserved, respected and protected.

Article 14

Indigenous peoples have the right to revitalize, use, develop and transmit to future generations their histories, languages, oral traditions, philosophies, writing systems and literatures, and to designate and retain their own names for communities, places and persons.

States shall take effective measures, whenever any right of indigenous peoples may be threatened, to ensure this right is protected and also to ensure that they can understand and be understood in political, legal and administrative proceedings, where necessary through the provision of interpretation or by other appropriate means.

Part IV

Article 15

Indigenous children have the right to all levels and forms of education of the State. All indigenous peoples also have this right and the right to establish and control their educational systems and institutions providing education in their own languages, in a manner appropriate to their cultural methods of teaching and learning.

Indigenous children living outside their communities have the right to be provided access to education in their own culture and language.

States shall take effective measures to provide appropriate resources for these purposes.

Article 16

Indigenous peoples have the right to have the dignity and diversity of their cultures, traditions, histories and aspirations appropriately reflected in all forms of education and public information.

States shall take effective measures, in consultation with the indigenous peoples concerned, to eliminate prejudice and discrimination and to promote tolerance, understanding and good relations among indigenous peoples and all segments of society.

Article 17

Indigenous peoples have the right to establish their own media in their own languages. They also have the right to equal access to all forms of non-indigenous media.

States shall take effective measures to ensure that State-owned media duly reflect indigenous cultural diversity.

Article 18

Indigenous peoples have the right to enjoy fully all rights established under international labour law and national labour legislation.

Indigenous individuals have the right not to be subjected to any discriminatory conditions of labour, employment or salary.

Part V

Article 19

Indigenous peoples have the right to participate fully, if they so choose, at all levels of decision-making in matters which may affect their rights, lives and destinies through representatives chosen by themselves in accordance with their own procedures, as well as to maintain and develop their own indigenous decision-making institutions.

Article 20

Indigenous peoples have the right to participate fully, if they so choose, through procedures determined by them, in devising legislative or administrative measures that may affect them.

States shall obtain the free and informed consent of the peoples concerned before adopting and implementing such measures.

Article 21

Indigenous peoples have the right to maintain and develop their political, economic and social systems, to be secure in the enjoyment of their own means of subsistence and development, and to engage freely in all their traditional and other economic activities. Indigenous peoples who have been deprived of their means of subsistence and development are entitled to just and fair compensation.

Article 22

Indigenous peoples have the right to special measures for the immediate, effective and continuing improvement of their economic and social conditions, including in the areas of employment, vocational training and retraining, housing, sanitation, health and social security.

Particular attention shall be paid to the rights and special needs of indigenous elders, women, youth, children and disabled persons.

Article 23

Indigenous peoples have the right to determine and develop priorities and strategies for exercising their right to development. In particular, indigenous peoples have the right to determine and develop all health, housing and other economic and social programmes affecting them and, as far as possible, to administer such programmes through their own institutions.

Article 24

Indigenous peoples have the right to their traditional medicines and health practices, including the right to the protection of vital medicinal plants, animals and minerals.

They also have the right to access, without any discrimination, to all medical institutions, health services and medical care.

Part VI

Article 25

Indigenous peoples have the right to maintain and strengthen their distinctive spiritual and material relationship with the lands, territories, waters and coastal seas and other resources which they have traditionally owned or otherwise occupied or used, and to uphold their responsibilities to future generations in this regard.

Article 26

Indigenous peoples have the right to own, develop, control and use the lands and territories, including the total environment of the lands, air, waters, coastal seas, sea-ice, flora and fauna and other resources which they have traditionally owned or otherwise occupied or used. This includes the right to the full recognition of their laws, traditions and customs, land-tenure systems and institutions for the development and management of resources, and the right to effective measures by States to prevent any interference with, alienation of or encroachment upon these rights.

Article 27

Indigenous peoples have the right to the restitution of the lands, territories and resources which they have traditionally owned or otherwise occupied or used, and which have been confiscated, occupied, used or damaged without their free and informed consent. Where this is not possible, they have the right to just and fair compensation. Unless otherwise freely agreed upon by the peoples concerned, compensation shall take the form of lands, territories and resources equal in quality, size and legal status.

Article 28

Indigenous peoples have the right to the conservation, restoration and protection of the total environment and the productive capacity of their lands, territories and resources, as well as to assistance for this purpose from States and through international cooperation. Military activities shall not take place in the lands and territories of indigenous peoples, unless otherwise freely agreed upon by the peoples concerned.

States shall take effective measures to ensure that no storage or disposal of hazardous materials shall take place in the lands and territories of indigenous peoples.

States shall also take effective measures to ensure, as needed, that programmes for monitoring, maintaining and restoring the health of indigenous peoples, as developed and implemented by the peoples affected by such materials, are duly implemented.

Article 29

Indigenous peoples are entitled to the recognition of the full ownership, control and protection of their cultural and intellectual property.

They have the right to special measures to control, develop and protect their sciences, technologies and cultural manifestations, including human and other genetic resources, seeds, medicines, knowledge of the properties of fauna and flora, oral traditions, literatures, designs and visual and performing arts.

Article 30

Indigenous peoples have the right to determine and develop priorities and strategies for the development or use of their lands, territories and other resources, including the right to require that States obtain their free and informed consent prior to the approval of any project affecting their lands, territories and other resources, particularly in connection with the development, utilization or exploitation of mineral, water or other resources. Pursuant to agreement with the indigenous peoples concerned, just and fair compensation shall be provided for any such activities and measures taken to mitigate adverse environmental, economic, social, cultural or spiritual impact.

Part VII

Article 31

Indigenous peoples, as a specific form of exercising their right to self-determination, have the right to autonomy or self-government in matters relating to their internal and local affairs, including culture, religion, education, information, media, health, housing, employment, social welfare, economic activities, land and resources management, environment and entry by non-members, as well as ways and means for financing these autonomous functions.

Article 32

Indigenous peoples have the collective right to determine their own citizenship in accordance with their customs and traditions. Indigenous citizenship does not impair the right of indigenous individuals to obtain citizenship of the States in which they live.

Indigenous peoples have the right to determine the structures and to select the membership of their institutions in accordance with their own procedures.

Article 33

Indigenous peoples have the right to promote, develop and maintain their institutional structures and their distinctive juridical customs, traditions, procedures and practices, in accordance with internationally recognized human rights standards.

Article 34

Indigenous peoples have the collective right to determine the responsibilities of individuals to their communities.

Article 35

Indigenous peoples, in particular those divided by international borders, have the right to maintain and develop contacts, relations and cooperation, including activities for spiritual, cultural, political, economic and social purposes, with other peoples across borders.

States shall take effective measures to ensure the exercise and implementation of this right.

Article 36

Indigenous peoples have the right to the recognition, observance and enforcement of treaties, agreements and other constructive arrangements concluded with States or their successors, according to their original spirit and intent, and to have States honour and respect such treaties, agreements and other constructive arrangements. Conflicts and disputes which cannot otherwise be settled should be submitted to competent international bodies agreed to by all parties concerned.

Part VIII

Article 37

States shall take effective and appropriate measures, in consultation with the indigenous peoples concerned, to give full effect to the provisions of this Declaration. The rights recognized herein shall be adopted and included in national legislation in such a manner that indigenous peoples can avail themselves of such rights in practice.

Article 38

Indigenous peoples have the right to have access to adequate financial and technical assistance, from States and through international cooperation, to pursue freely their political, economic, social, cultural and spiritual development and for the enjoyment of the rights and freedoms recognized in this Declaration.

Article 39

Indigenous peoples have the right to have access to and prompt decision through mutually acceptable and fair procedures for the resolution of conflicts and disputes with States, as well as to effective remedies for all infringements of their individual and collective rights. Such a decision shall take into consideration the customs, traditions, rules and legal systems of the indigenous peoples concerned.

Article 40

The organs and specialized agencies of the United Nations system and other intergovernmental organizations shall contribute to the full realization of the provisions of this Declaration through the mobilization, *inter alia*, of financial cooperation and technical assistance. Ways and means of ensuring participation of indigenous peoples on issues affecting them shall be established.

Article 41

The United Nations shall take the necessary steps to ensure the implementation of this Declaration including the creation of a body at the highest level with special competence in this field and with the direct participation of indigenous peoples. All United Nations bodies shall promote respect for and full application of the provisions of this Declaration.

Part IX

Article 42

The rights recognized herein constitute the minimum standards for the survival, dignity and well-being of the indigenous peoples of the world.

Article 43

All the rights and freedoms recognized herein are equally guaranteed to male and female indigenous individuals.

Article 44

Nothing in this Declaration may be construed as diminishing or extinguishing existing or future rights indigenous peoples may have or acquire.

Article 45

Nothing in this Declaration may be interpreted as implying for any State, group or person any right to engage in any activity or to perform any act contrary to the Charter of the United Nations.

RESOLUTION ON ACTION REQUIRED INTERNATIONALLY TO PROVIDE EFFECTIVE PROTECTION FOR INDIGENOUS PEOPLES

Adopted by the European Parliament in its plenary session, Strasbourg, Feb. 9, 1994. Eur. Parl. Doc. PV 58(II) (1994).

The European Parliament,

having regard to the motion for a resolution by Mr. Christiansen and others on the implementation of effective international legislation on the environment and the rights of indigenous peoples in the world in order to protect our planet and all its inhabitants (B3–1519/91),

having regard to its numerous resolutions on the protection of human rights,

having regard to its resolution of 12 March 1992 on 1992, indigenous peoples and the quincentenary,[1]

having regard to Rule 45 of its Rules of Procedure,

having regard to the report of the Committee on Foreign Affairs and Security and the opinion of the Committee on Development and Cooperation (A3–0059/94),

A. whereas the most commonly used definition of indigenous peoples is that given in ILO Convention No. 169; whereas, according to UN estimates, such communities represent 300 million individuals spread over almost 4000 peoples,

B. convinced that all peoples contribute to the diversity and richness of the civilizations and cultures which constitute mankind's common heritage,

C. whereas many international texts, in particular the UN Charter, the Universal Declaration of Human Rights and ILO Convention No. 169, set out in detail the inalienable basic rights of all human beings, including that of determining their political status by freely choosing their way of economic, cultural and social development,

D. whereas the United Nations Organization, despite its name, represents only states and not peoples, and solutions to many problems concerning peoples, particularly indigenous peoples, are therefore difficult to find within it,

E. regretting that, in general, international treaties quite simply neglect the rights of indigenous peoples, even if it is they who must bear the direct or indirect consequences thereof,

F. noting that certain states have concluded treaties with indigenous peoples in the past and that some of those treaties have been shamelessly violated; whereas in this connection, in the context of increasing impoverishment, indigenous peoples are often the first to be dispossessed of rights, land and resources,

G. dismayed by the violence of every kind to which indigenous peoples have been subjected in the past, and still are; whereas, in this connection, the UN has recognized the right to intervene when fundamental human rights are under serious threat,

1. Adopts the definition of indigenous peoples given by the ILO in its Convention No. 169 and believes that this convention together with the Kari Oca Declaration (Rio,

1. OJ C 94, 13.5.1992, p. 268.

June 1992) and the declaration of the UN conference in Vienna on the rights of indigenous peoples (June 1993) are the benchmark texts in this regard;

2. Declares that pursuant to UN provisions, and in the context of a non-violent and fully democratic procedure with due regard for the rights of other citizens, indigenous peoples have the right to determine their own destiny by choosing their institutions, their political status and that of their territory;

3. Takes the view that the UN must take advantage of its 50th anniversary to make its bodies more democratic and more effective by enabling peoples without a state, in particular indigenous peoples, to be better represented, especially by involving them in the work of the General Assembly;

4. Solemnly reaffirms that those belonging to indigenous peoples have, just as any other human being has, the right to life, to respect, the right to freedom of thought and action, to physical security, to health, to justice and to equality concerning the right to work, to housing, to education and to culture; this right to a separate culture must involve the right to use and disseminate their mother tongue and to have the tangible and intangible features of their culture protected and disseminated and to have their religious rights and their sacred land respected;

5. Calls for censuses to be taken of indigenous peoples in the states in which they are established;

6. Calls for indigenous peoples to be given help in marketing the craft products made by indigenous peoples, with verification of origin;

7. Declares that indigenous peoples have the right to the common ownership of their traditional land sufficient in terms of area and quality for the preservation and development of their particular ways of life, such land to be placed at their disposal free of charge; it will therefore be indivisible, non-transferable, imprescriptible and cannot be rented;

8. Takes the view that, with regard to legal matters, those belonging to indigenous peoples have the right to a qualified defence lawyer and to full information about their rights, with the assistance of an interpreter if necessary, and that, as far as is compatible with the Universal Declaration of Human Rights, preference should be given to the use of customary law to judge their offences;

9. Declares that indigenous peoples who have been robbed of their rights must be able to obtain fair compensation; if deprivation involves the loss of land, this will be made good, first and foremost, by returning the land in question or, alternatively, by providing land at least equal in terms of quality and size to that which has been lost;

10. Calls in the strongest possible terms on states which in the past have signed treaties with indigenous peoples to honour their undertakings, which remain imprescriptible, and in this connection gives its firm backing to the UN special rapporteur responsible for studying and resolving this problem;

11. Reaffirms the positive contribution of indigenous peoples' civilizations to mankind's common heritage and the essential role which they have played and which they must continue to play in the conservation of their natural environment;

12. Considers that the European Union, but also the United Nations, should take all possible steps to ensure that international treaties, policies and the activities of commercial undertakings do not, either directly or indirectly, adversely affect the rights

of indigenous peoples; calls in this connection for the Council and the Commission to make a precise political statement on indigenous peoples;

13. Calls on the Commission and the Council to make a tangible contribution to the International Year of Indigenous Peoples and to this end calls for:

criteria to be drawn up for the financing of Community projects in the light of the rights of indigenous peoples,

indigenous peoples to be directly involved, as part of development and cooperation policy, in projects concerning them,

European officials to be given special training and assigned for following-up questions concerning indigenous peoples,

the technical and legal information intended for indigenous peoples' representatives to be enhanced,

appropriate budget lines to be clearly allocated for the defence of the rights of these peoples;

14. Undertakes to set up, at the beginning of the next parliamentary term, an inter-parliamentary delegation composed of Members of this Parliament and representatives of indigenous peoples and instructs its Subcommittee on Human Rights to monitor questions concerning their rights very closely;

15. Calls on the Member States of the European Union to show their determination to provide tangible protection for indigenous peoples by acceding to ILO Convention No. 169 and by calling on other states to do the same;

16. Instructs its President to forward this resolution to the Council, the Commission, the Secretary-General of the UN, the Secretary of the UN Subcommittee on Sustainable Development and the Secretary of the UN Commission on Human Rights.

PROPOSED AMERICAN DECLARATION ON THE RIGHTS OF INDIGENOUS PEOPLES

Approved by the Inter-American Commission on Human Rights on February 26, 1997, at its 1333rd session, 95th regular session. O.A.S. Doc. OEA/Ser.L/V/II.95, Doc. 7, rev. (1996).

Preamble

1. Indigenous Institutions and the Strengthening of Nations

The Member States of the OAS (hereafter the States),

Recalling that the indigenous peoples of the Americas constitute an organized, distinctive and integral segment of their population and are entitled to be part of the national identities of the countries of the Americas, and have a special role to play in strengthening the institutions of the state and in establishing national unity based on democratic principles; and,

Further recalling that some of the democratic institutions and concepts embodied in the constitutions of American states originate from institutions of the indigenous peoples, and that in many instances their present participatory systems for decision-making and for authority contribute to improving democracies in the Americas.

Recalling the need to develop their national juridical systems to consolidate the pluricultural nature of our societies.

2. Eradication of Poverty and the Right to Development

Concerned about the frequent deprivation afflicting indigenous peoples of their human rights and fundamental freedoms; within and outside their communities, as well as the dispossession of their lands, territories and resources, thus preventing them from exercing, in particular, their right to development in accordance with their own traditions, needs and interests.

Recognizing the severe impoverishment afflicting indigenous peoples in several regions of the Hemisphere and that their living conditions are generally deplorable.

And recalling that in the Declaration of Principles issued by the Summit of the Americas in December 1994, the heads of state and governments declared that in observance of the International Decade of the World's Indigenous People, they will focus their energies on improving the exercise of democratic rights and the access to social services by indigenous peoples and their communities.

3. Indigenous Culture and Ecology

Recognizing the respect for the environment accorded by the cultures of indigenous peoples of the Americas, and considering the special relationship between the indigenous peoples and the environment, lands, resources and territories on which they live and their natural resources.

4. Harmonious Relations, Respect and the Absence of Discrimination

Reaffirming the responsibility of all states and peoples of the Americas to end racism and racial discrimination, with a view to establishing harmonious relations and respect among all peoples.

5. Territories and Indigenous Survival

Recognizing that in many indigenous cultures, traditional collective systems for control and use of land, territory and resources, including bodies of water and coastal areas, are a necessary condition for their survival, social organization, development and their individual and collective well-being; and that the form of such control and ownership is varied and distinctive and does not necessarily coincide with the systems protected by the domestic laws of the states in which they live.

6. Security and Indigenous Areas

Reaffirming that the armed forces in indigenous areas shall restrict themselves to the performance of their functions and shall not be the cause of abuses or violations of the rights of indigenous peoples.

7. Human Rights Instruments and Other Advances in International Law

Recognizing the paramouncy and applicability to the states and peoples of the Americas of the American Declaration of the Rights and Duties of Man, the American Convention on Human Rights and other human rights instruments of inter-American and international law; and

Recognizing that indigenous peoples are a subject of international law, and mindful of the progress achieved by the states and indigenous organizations, especially in the sphere of the United Nations and the International Labor Organizations, in several international instruments, particularly in the ILO Convention 169.

Affirming the principle of the universality and indivisibility of human rights, and the application of international human rights to all individuals.

8. Enjoyment of Collective Rights

Recalling the international recognition of rights that can only be enjoyed when exercised collectively.

9. Advances in the Provisions of National Instruments

Noting the constitutional, legislative and jurisprudential advances achieved in the Americas in guaranteeing the rights and institutions of indigenous peoples.

Declare:

Section One. Indigenous Peoples

Art. 1. Scope and Definitions

1. This Declaration applies to indigenous peoples as well as peoples whose social, cultural and economic conditions distinguish them from other sections of the national community, and whose status is regulated wholly or partially by their own customs or traditions or by special laws or regulations.

2. Self identification as indigenous shall be regarded as a fundamental criterion for determining the peoples to which the provisions of this Declaration apply.

3. The use of the term "peoples" in this Instrument shall not be construed as having any implication with respect to any other rights that might be attached to that term in international law.

Section Two. Human Rights

Article II. Full Observance of Human Rights

1. Indigenous peoples have the right to the full and effective enjoyment of the human rights and fundamental freedoms recognized in the Charter of the OAS, the American Declaration of the Rights and Duties of Man, the American Convention on Human Rights,

and other international human rights law; and nothing in this Declaration shall be construed as in any way limiting or denying those rights or authorizing any action not in accordance with the instruments of international law including human rights law.

2. Indigenous peoples have the collective rights that are indispensable to the enjoyment of the individual human rights of their members. Accordingly the states recognize inter alia the right of the indigenous peoples to collective action, to their cultures, to profess and practice their spiritual beliefs, and to use their languages.

3. The states shall ensure for indigenous peoples the full exercise of all rights, and shall adopt in accordance with their constitutional processes such legislative or other measures as may be necessary to give effect to the rights recognized in this Declaration.

Article III. Right to Belong to Indigenous Peoples

Indigenous peoples and communities have the right to belong to indigenous peoples, in accordance with the traditions and customs of the peoples or nation concerned.

Article IV. Legal Status of Communities

Indigenous peoples have the right to have their legal personality fully recognized by the states within their systems.

Article V. No Forced Assimilation

1. Indigenous peoples have the right to freely preserve, express and develop their cultural identity in all its aspects, free of any attempt at assimilation.

2. The states shall not undertake, support or favour any policy of artificial or enforced assimilation of indigenous peoples, destruction of a culture or the possibility of the extermination of any indigenous peoples.

Article VI. Special Guarantees against Discrimination

1. Indigenous peoples have the right to special guarantees against discrimination that may have to be instituted to fully enjoy internationally and nationally-recognized human rights; as well as measures necessary to enable indigenous women, men and children to exercise, without any discrimination, civil, political, economic, social, cultural and spiritual rights. The states recognize that violence exerted against persons because of their gender and age prevents and nullifies the exercise of those rights.

2. Indigenous peoples have the right to fully participate in the prescription of such guarantees.

Section Three. Cultural Development

Article VII. Right to Cultural Integrity

1. Indigenous peoples have the right to their cultural integrity, and their historical and archeological heritage, which are important both for their survival as well as for the identity of their members.

2. Indigenous peoples are entitled to restitution in respect of the property of which they have been dispossessed, and where that is not possible, compensation on a basis not less favorable than the standard of international law.

3. The states shall recognize and respect indigenous ways of life, customs, traditions, forms of social, economic and political organization, institutions, practices, beliefs and values, use of dress, and languages.

Article VIII. Philosophy, Outlook and Language

1. Indigenous peoples have the right to indigenous languages, philosophy and outlook as a component of national and universal culture, and as such, shall respect them and facilitate their dissemination.

2. The states shall take measures and ensure that broadcast radio and television programs are broadcast in the indigenous languages in the regions where there is a strong indigenous presence, and to support the creation of indigenous radio stations and other media.

3. The states shall take effective measures to enable indigenous peoples to understand administrative, legal and political rules and procedures, and to be understood in relation to these matters. In areas where indigenous languages are predominant, states shall endeavor to establish the pertinent languages as official, languages and to give them the same status that is given to non-indigenous official languages.

4. Indigenous peoples have the right to use their indigenous names, and to have the states recognize them as such.

Article IX. Education

1. Indigenous peoples shall be entitled: a) to establish and set in motion their own educational programs, institutions and facilities; b) to prepare and implement their own educational plans, programs, curricula and materials; c) to train, educate and accredit their teachers and administrators. The states shall endeavor to ensure that such systems guarantee equal educational and teaching opportunities for the entire population and complementarity with national educational systems.

2. When indigenous peoples so decide, educational systems shall be conducted in the indigenous languages and incorporate indigenous content, and they shall also be provided with the necessary training and means for complete mastery of the official language or languages.

3. The states shall ensure that those educational systems are equal in quality, efficiency, accessibility and in all other ways to that provided to the general population.

4. The states shall take measures to guarantee to the members of indigenous peoples the possibility to obtain education at all levels, at least of equal quality with the general population.

5. The states shall include in their general educational systems, content reflecting the pluricultural nature of their societies.

6. The states shall provide financial and any other type of assistance needed for the implementation of the provisions of this article.

Article X. Spiritual and Religious Freedom

1. Indigenous peoples have the right to freedom of conscience, freedom of religion and spiritual practice, and to exercise them both publicly and privately.

2. The states shall take necessary measures to prohibit attempts to forcibly convert indigenous peoples or to impose on them beliefs against their will.

3. In collaboration with the indigenous peoples concerned, the states shall adopt effective measures to ensure that their sacred sites, including burial sites, are preserved, respected and protected. When sacred graves and relics have been appropriated by state institutions, they shall be returned.

4. The states shall encourage respect by all people for the integrity of indigenous spiritual symbols, practices, sacred ceremonies, expressions and protocols.

Article XI. Family Relations and Family Ties

1. The family is the natural and basic unit of societies and must be respected and protected by the state. Consequently the state shall recognize and respect the various forms of indigenous family, marriage, family name and filiation.

2. In determining the child's best interest in matters relating to the protection and adoption of children of members of indigenous peoples, and in matters of breaking of ties and other similar circumstances, consideration shall be given by courts and other relevant institutions to the views of the peoples, including individual, family and community views.

Article XII. Health and Well-Being

1. Indigenous peoples have the right to legal recognition and practice of their traditional medicine, treatment, pharmacology, health practices and promotion, including preventive and rehabilitative practices.

2. Indigenous peoples have the right to the protection of vital medicinal plants, animal and mineral in their traditional territories.

3. Indigenous peoples shall be entitled to use, maintain, develop and manage their own health services, and they shall also have access, on an equal basis, to all health institutions and services and medical care accessible to the general population.

4. The states shall provide the necessary means to enable the indigenous peoples to eliminate such health conditions in their communities which fall below international accepted standards for the general population.

Article XIII. Right to Environmental Protection

1. Indigenous peoples have the right to a safe and healthy environment, which is an essential condition for the enjoyment of the right to life and collective well-being.

2. Indigenous peoples have the right to be informed of measures which will affect their environment, including information that ensures their effective participation in actions and policies that might affect it.

3. Indigenous peoples shall have the right to conserve, restore and protect their environment, and the productive capacity of their lands, territories and resources.

4. Indigenous peoples have the right to participate fully in formulating, planning, managing and applying governmental programmes of conservation of their lands, territories and resources.

5. Indigenous peoples have the right to assistance from their states for purposes of environmental protection, and may receive assistance from international organizations.

6. The states shall prohibit and punish, and shall impede jointly with the indigenous peoples, the introduction, abandonment, or deposit of radioactive materials or residues, toxic substances and garbage in contravention of legal provisions; as well as the production, introduction, transportation, possession or use of chemical, biological and nuclear weapons in indigenous areas.

7. When a State declares an indigenous territory as protected area, any lands, territories and resources under potential or actual claim by indigenous peoples, conservation areas shall not be subject to any natural resource development without the informed consent and participation of the peoples concerned.

Section Four. Organizational and Political Rights

Article XIV. Rights of Association, Assembly, Freedom of Expression and Freedom of Thought

1. Indigenous peoples have the right of association, assembly and expression in accordance with their values, usages, customs, ancestral traditions, beliefs and religions.

2. Indigenous peoples have the right of assembly and to the use of their sacred and ceremonial areas, as well as the right to full contact and common activities with their members living in the territory of neighboring states.

Article XV. Right to Self Government

1. Indigenous peoples have the right to freely determine their political status and freely pursue their economic, social, spiritual and cultural development, and accordingly, they have the right to autonomy or self-government with regard to inter alia culture, religion, education, information, media, health, housing, employment, social welfare, economic activities, land and resource management, the environment and entry by nonmembers; and to determine ways and means for financing these autonomous functions.

2. Indigenous peoples have the right to participate without discrimination, if they so decide, in all decision-making, at all levels, with regard to matters that might affect their rights, lives and destiny. They may do so directly or through representatives chosen by them in accordance with their own procedures. They shall also have the right to maintain and develop their own indigenous decision-making institutions, as well as equal opportunities to access and participate in all state institutions and fora.

Article XVI. Indigenous Law

1. Indigenous law shall be recognized as a part of the states' legal system and of the framework in which the social and economic development of the states takes place.

2. Indigenous peoples have the right to maintain and reinforce their indigenous legal systems and also to apply them to matters within their communities, including systems related to such matters as conflict resolution, crime prevention and maintenance of peace and harmony.

3. In the jurisdiction of any state, procedures concerning indigenous peoples or their interests shall be conducted in such a way as to ensure the right of indigenous peoples to full representation with dignity and equality before the law. This shall include observance of indigenous law and custom and, where necessary, use of their language.

Article XVII. National Incorporation of Indigenous Legal and Organizational Systems

1. The states shall facilitate the inclusion in their organizational structures, the institutions and traditional practices of indigenous peoples, and in consultation and with consent of the peoples concerned.

2. State institutions relevant to and serving indigenous peoples shall be designed in consultation and with the participation of the peoples concerned so as to reinforce and promote the identity, cultures, traditions, organization and values of those peoples.

Section Five. Social, Economic, and Property Rights

Article XVIII. Traditional Forms of Ownership and Cultural Survival. Rights to Land, Territories and Resources

1. Indigenous peoples have the right to the legal recognition of their varied and specific forms and modalities of their control, ownership, use and enjoyment of territories and property.

2. Indigenous peoples have the right to the recognition of their property and ownership rights with respect to lands, territories and resources they have historically occupied, as well as to the use of those to which they have historically had access for their traditional activities and livelihood.

3.

i) Subject to 3. ii.) where property and user rights of indigenous peoples arise from rights existing prior to the creation of those states, the states shall recognize the titles of indigenous peoples relative thereto as permanent, exclusive, inalienable, imprescriptible and indefeasible.

ii) Such titles may only be changed by mutual consent between the state and respective indigenous peoples when they have full knowledge and appreciation of the nature or attributes of such property.

iii) Nothing in 3.i.) shall be construed as limiting the right of indigenous peoples to attribute ownership within the community in accordance with their customs, traditions, uses and traditional practices, nor shall it affect any collective community rights over them.

4. Indigenous peoples have the right to an effective legal framework for the protection of their rights with respect to the natural resources on their lands, including the ability to use, manage, and conserve such resources; and with respect to traditional uses of their lands, interests in lands, and resources, such as subsistence.

5. In the event that ownership of the minerals or resources of the subsoil pertains to the state or that the state has rights over other resources on the lands, the governments must establish or maintain procedures for the participation of the peoples concerned in determining whether the interests of these people would be adversely affected and to what extent, before undertaking or authorizing any program for planning, prospecting or exploiting existing resources on their lands. The peoples concerned shall participate in the benefits of such activities, and shall receive compensation, on a basis not less favorable than the standard of international law for any loss which they may sustain as a result of such activities.

6. Unless exceptional and justified circumstances so warrant in the public interest, the states shall not transfer or relocate indigenous peoples without the free, genuine, public and informed consent of those peoples, but in all cases with prior compensation and prompt replacement of lands taken, which must be of similar or better quality and which must have the same legal status; and with guarantee of the right to return if the causes that gave rise to the displacement cease to exist.

7. Indigenous peoples have the right to the restitution of the lands, territories and resources which they have traditionally owned or otherwise occupied or used, and which have been confiscated, occupied, used or damaged, or when restitution is not possible, the right to compensation on a basis not less favorable than the standard of international law.

8. The states shall take all measures, including the use of law enforcement mechanisms, to avert, prevent and punish, if applicable, any intrusion or use of those lands by unauthorized persons to take possession or make use of them. The states shall give maximum priority to the demarcation and recognition of properties and areas of indigenous use.

Article XIX. Workers Rights

1. Indigenous peoples shall have the right to full enjoyment of the rights and guarantees recognized under international labor law and domestic labor law; they shall also have the right to special measures to correct, redress and prevent the discrimination to which they have historically been subject.

2. To the extent that they are not effectively protected by laws applicable to workers in general, the states shall take such special measures as may be necessary to:

a. effectively protect the workers and employees who are members of indigenous communities in respect of fair and equal hiring and terms of employment;

b. to improve the labor inspection and enforcement service in regions, companies or paid activities involving indigenous workers or employees;

c. ensure that indigenous workers:

    i)   enjoy equal opportunity and treatment as regards all conditions of employment, job promotion and advancement; and other conditions as stipulated under international law;

    ii)   enjoy the right to association and freedom for all lawful trade union activities, and the right to conclude collective agreements with employers or employers' organizations;

    iii) are not subjected to racial, sexual or other forms of harassment;

    iv) are not subjected to coercive hiring practices, including servitude for debts or any other form of servitude, even if they have their origin in law, custom or a personal or collective arrangement, which shall be deemed absolutely null and void in each instance;

    v)   are not subjected to working conditions that endanger their health and safety;

    vi) receive special protection when they serve as seasonal, casual or migrant workers and also when they are hired by labor contractors in order that they benefit from national legislation and practice which must itself be in accordance with established international human rights standards in respect of this type of workers, and,

    vii) as well as their employers are made fully aware of the rights of indigenous workers, under such national legislation and international standards, and of the recourses available to them in order to protect those rights.

Article XX. Intellectual Property Rights

1. Indigenous peoples have the right to the recognition and the full ownership, control and protection of their cultural, artistic, spiritual, technological and scientific heritage, and legal protection for their intellectual property through trademarks, patents, copyright and other such procedures as established under domestic law; as well as to special measures to ensure them legal status and institutional capacity to develop, use, share, market and bequeath that heritage to future generations.

2. Indigenous peoples have the right to control, develop and protect their sciences and technologies, including their human and genetic resources in general, seed, medicine, knowledge of plant and animal life, original designs and procedure.

3. The states shall take appropriate measures to ensure participation of the indigenous peoples in the determination of the conditions for the utilization, both public and private, of the rights listed in the previous paragraphs 1. and 2.

Article XXI. Right to Development

1. The states recognize the right of indigenous peoples to decide democratically what values, objectives, priorities and strategies will govern and steer their development course, even where they are different from those adopted by the national government or by other segments of society. Indigenous peoples shall be entitled to obtain on a non-discriminatory basis appropriate means for their own development according to their

preferences and values, and to contribute by their own means, as distinct societies, to national development and international cooperation.

2. Unless exceptional circumstances so warrant in the public interest, the states shall take necessary measures to ensure that decisions regarding any plan, program or proposal affecting the rights or living conditions of indigenous peoples are not made without the free and informed consent and participation of those peoples, that their preferences are recognized and that no such plan, program or proposal that could have harmful effects on those peoples is adopted.

3. Indigenous peoples have the right to restitution or compensation no less favorable than the standards of international law, for any loss which, despite the foregoing precautions, the execution of those plans or proposals may have caused them; and measures taken to mitigate adverse environmental, economic, social, cultural or spiritual impact.

Section Six. General Provisions

Article XXII. Treaties, Acts, Agreements and Constructive Arrangements

Indigenous peoples have the right to the recognition, observance and enforcement of treaties, agreements and constructive arrangements, that may have been concluded with states or their successors, as well as historical Acts in that respect, according to their spirit and intent, and to have states honor and respect such treaties, agreements and constructive arrangements as well as the rights emanating from those historical instruments. Conflicts and disputes which cannot otherwise be settled should be submitted to competent bodies.

Article XXIII.

Nothing in this instrument shall be construed as diminishing or extinguishing existing or future rights indigenous peoples may have or acquire.

Article XXIV.

The rights recognized herein constitute the minimum standards for the survival, dignity and well-being of the indigenous peoples of the Americas.

Article XXV.

Nothing in this instrument shall be construed as granting any rights to ignore boundaries between states.

Article XXVI.

Nothing in this Declaration may be construed as permitting any activity contrary to the purposes and principles of the OAS, including sovereign equality, territorial integrity and political independence of states.

Article XXVII. Implementation

The Organization of American States and its organs, organisms and entities, in particular the Inter-American Indian Institute, the Inter-American Commission of Human Rights shall promote respect for and full application of the provisions in this Declaration.

COMMITTEE ON THE ELIMINATION OF RACIAL DISCRIMINATION (CERD), GENERAL RECOMMENDATION (XXIII) CONCERNING INDIGENOUS PEOPLES

Adopted by the U.N. Committee on the Elimination of Racial Discrimination at its 1235th meeting, on 18 August 1997. U.N. Doc. CERD/C/51/misc. 13/Rev. 4 (1997).

1. In the practice of the Committee on the Elimination of Racial Discrimination, in particular in the examination of reports of States parties under article 9 of the International Convention on the Elimination of All Forms of Racial Discrimination, the situation of indigenous peoples has always been a matter of close attention and concern. In this respect the Committee has consistently affirmed that discrimination against indigenous peoples falls under the scope of the Convention and that all appropriate means must be taken to combat and eliminate such discrimination.

2. The Committee, noting that the General Assembly proclaimed the International Decade of the World's Indigenous People commencing on 10 December 1994, reaffirms the provisions of the International Convention on the Elimination of All Forms of Racial Discrimination apply to indigenous peoples.

3. The Committee is conscious of the fact that in many regions of the world indigenous peoples have been, and are still being, discriminated against, deprived of their human rights and fundamental freedoms and in particular that they have lost their land and resources to colonists, commercial companies and State enterprises. Consequently the preservation of their culture and their historical identity has been and still is jeopardized.

4. The Committee calls in particular upon States parties to:

   a. recognize and respect indigenous distinct culture, history, language and way of life as an enrichment of the State's cultural identity and to promote its preservation;

   b. ensure that members of indigenous peoples are free and equal in dignity and rights and free from any discrimination, in particular that based on indigenous origin or identity;

   c. provide indigenous peoples with conditions allowing for a sustainable economic and social development compatible with their cultural characteristics;

   d. ensure that members of indigenous peoples have equal rights in respect of effective participation in public life, and that no decisions directly relating to their rights and interests are taken without their informed consent;

   e. ensure that indigenous communities can exercise their rights to practice and revitalize their cultural traditions and customs, to preserve and to practice their languages.

5. The Committee especially calls upon States parties to recognise and protect the rights of indigenous peoples to own, develop, control and use their communal lands, territories and resources and, where they have been deprived of their lands and territories traditionally owned or otherwise inhabited or used without their free and informed consent, to take steps to return these lands and territories. Only when this is for factual reasons not possible, the right to restitution should be substituted by the right to just, fair and prompt compensation. Such compensation should as far as possible take the form of lands and territories.

6. The Committee further calls upon States parties with indigenous peoples in their territories to include in their periodic reports full information on the situation of such peoples, taking into account all relevant provisions of the Convention.

Bibliography

This bibliography includes the books, book chapters, and scholarly articles that were consulted in preparing this work. Also listed are a number of other references, including studies by U.N. agencies and other international institutions, that are substantial publications devoted especially to issues concerning indigenous peoples. Additional references may be found in the table of principal documents, the table of cases, and the notes to the chapters in this book.

Abel, Elie. *The Shattered Bloc: Behind the Upheaval in Eastern Europe.* Boston: Houghton Mifflin, 1990.

Akehurst, Michael. "Custom as a Source of International Law." *British Yearbook of International Law* 47 (1974–75): 1–53.

Akwesasne Mohawk Counselor Organization [Ray Fadden]. *Deskaheh: Iroquois Statesman and Patriot.* Rooseveltown, N.Y.: Akwesasne Notes, Mohawk Nation, 1984.

Alexander, Yonah, and Robert A. Friedlander, eds. *Self-Determination: National, Regional and Global Dimensions.* Boulder, Colo.: Westview Press, 1980.

Alexandrowicz, C. H. *An Introduction to the History of the Law of Nations in the East Indies.* Oxford: Clarendon Press, 1967.

Alfred, Taiaiake. *Peace, Power, Righteousness: An Indigenous Manifesto.* Ontario: Oxford University Press, 1999.

Alfredsson, Gudmundur. "International Law, International Organizations, and Indigenous Peoples." *Journal of International Affairs* 36 (1982): 113–24.

———. "The Right of Self-Determination and Indigenous Peoples." In *Modern Law of Self-Determination*, pp. 41–54. Edited by Christian Tomuschat. Dordrecht and Boston: M. Nijhoff Publishers, 1993.

Alston, Philip. "The Commission on Human Rights." In *The United Nations and Human Rights: A Critical Appraisal*, pp. 126–220. Edited by Philip Alston. Oxford: Clarendon Press, 1992.

———. "The Purposes of Reporting." In *Manual on Human Rights Reporting.* Edited by U.N. Centre for Human Rights & U.N. Institute for Training and Research. U.N. Sales No. E.91.XIV.1. New York: United Nations, 1991.

———, ed. *The United Nations and Human Rights: A Critical Appraisal.* Oxford: Clarendon Press, 1992.

Altman, Jon C., and John Nieuwenhuysen. *The Economic Status of Australian Aborigines.* Cambridge and New York: Cambridge University Press, 1979.

American Law Institute. *Restatement of the Law (Third): The Foreign Relations Law of the United States.* St. Paul, Minn.: American Law Institute, 1987.

Anaya, S. James. "The Awas Tingni Petition to the Inter-American Commission on Human Rights: Indigenous Lands, Loggers, and Government Neglect in Nicaragua." *St. Thomas Law Review* 9 (1996): 157–207.

———. "A Contemporary Definition of the International Norm of Self-Determination." *Transnational Law and Contemporary Problems* 3 (1993): 131–64.

———. "Maya Aboriginal Land and Resource Rights and the Conflict Over Logging in Southern Belize." *Yale Human Rights and Development Law Journal* 1 (1998): 17–51.

———. "The Maya Petition to the Inter-American Commission on Human Rights: Indigenous Land and Resource Rights and the Conflict over Logging and Oil in Southern Belize." In *Giving Meaning to Economic Social and Cultural Rights*, p. 180. Edited by Isfahan Merali and Valerie Oosterveld. Philadelphia: University of Pennsylvania Press, 2001.

———. "Native Land Claims in the United States: The Unatoned for Spirit of Place." In *The Cambridge Lectures, 1991*, pp. 25–36. Edited by Frank McArdle. Cowansville, Quebec: Les Editions Yvon Blais, 1993.

———. "The Rights of Indigenous Peoples and International Law in Historical and Contemporary Perspective." In *1989 Harvard Indian Law Symposium*, pp. 191–226. Cambridge, Mass: Harvard Law School Publication Center, 1990.

Anaya, S. James, and Claudio Grossman. "The Case of Awas Tingni v. Nicaragua: A New Step in the International Law of Indigenous Peoples." *Arizona Journal of International and Comparative Law* 19 (2002): 1–15.

Anderson, William L. *Cherokee Removal: Before and After.* Athens: University of Georgia Press, 1991.

Asch, Michael, ed. *Aboriginal and Treaty Rights in Canada: Essays on Law, Equity, and Respect for Difference*, Vancouver, University of British Columbia Press, 1997.

Assis, Willem, Gemma van der Haar, and André Hoekema, eds. *The Challenge of Diversity—Indigenous Peoples and Reform of the State in Latin America.* Amsterdam: Thela Thesis, 2000.

Bachman, Ronet. *Death and Violence on the Reservation: Homicide, Family Violence, and Suicide in American Indian Populations.* New York: Auburn House, 1992.

Barsh, Russel Lawrence. "An Advocates' Guide to the Convention on Indigenous and Tribal Peoples." *Oklahoma City University Law Review* 15 (1990): 209–36.

———. "Indigenous Peoples in the 1990s: From Object to Subject of International Law?" *Harvard Human Rights Journal* 7 (1994): 33–86.

Barsh, Russel Lawrence, and James Youngblood Henderson. *The Road: Indian Tribes and Political Liberty.* Berkeley: University of California Press, 1980.

Bartlett, Richard H. *The Indian Act of Canada.* 2d ed. Saskatoon: University of Saskatchewan, Native Law Centre, 1988.

Bastone, David. *From Conquest to Struggle: Jesus of Nazareth in Latin America.* Albany: State University of New York Press, 1991.

Bayefsky, Anne, and Joan Fitzpatrick. "International Human Rights Law in United States Courts: A Comparative Perspective." *Michigan Journal of International Law* 14 (1992): 1–89.

Bayly, John U. "Entering Canadian Confederation: The Dene Experiment." In *Indigenous Law and the State*, pp. 223–28. Edited by Bradford W. Morse and Gordon R. Woodman. Dordrecht and Providence: Foris Publications, 1988.

Beetham, David. "The Future of the Nation State." In *The Idea of the Modern State*, pp. 208–22. Edited by Gregor McLennan et al. Milton Keynes (U.K.) and Philadelphia: Open University Press, 1984.

Beigbeder, Yves. *International Monitoring of Plebiscites, Referenda and National Elections: Self-Determination and Transition to Democracy.* Dordrecht and Boston: M. Nijhoff Publishers, 1994.

Bennett, Gordon. *Aboriginal Rights in International Law.* London: Royal Anthropological Institute of Great Britain and Ireland, 1978.

Beres, Louis René. "Self-Determination, International Law and Survival on Planet Earth," *Arizona Journal of International and Comparative Law* 11 (1994): 1–26.

Berger, Thomas R. *Village Journey: The Report of the Alaska Native Review Commission.* New York: Hill and Wang, 1985.

Bergman, Randy, and Dorothy C. Lawrence. "New Developments in Soviet Property Law." *Columbia Journal of Transnational Law* 28 (1990): 189–206.

Berman, Howard. "The Concept of Aboriginal Rights in the Early Legal History of the United States." *Buffalo Law Review* 27 (1979): 637–67.

———. "Perspectives on American Indian Sovereignty and International Law, 1600–1776." In *Exiled in the Land of the Free: Democracy, Indian Nations, and the U.S. Constitution*, pp. 125–88. Edited by Oren Lyons and John Mohawk. Santa Fe, N.M.: Clear Light Publishers, 1992.

Betancourt, Fernando. *Derecho Romano Clásico.* Sevilla: University of Sevilla, 1995.

Bickel, Alexander M. *The Least Dangerous Branch: The Supreme Court at the Bar of Politics.* Indianapolis: Bobbs-Merrill, 1962.

Bobbio, Norberto. *Thomas Hobbes and the Natural Law Tradition.* Translated by Daniela Gobetti. Chicago: University of Chicago Press, 1993.

Borrows, John. "Landed Citizenship: Narratives of Aboriginal Political Participation." In *Citizenship in Diverse Societies*, pp. 326–42. Edited by Will Kymlicka and Wayne Norman. Oxford: Oxford University Press, 2000.

Bowett, David W. *The Law of International Institutions.* 4th ed. London: Stevens, 1982.

Bradlow, Daniel. "The World Bank, the IMF, and Human Rights." *Transnational Law and Contemporary Problems* 6 (1996): 47–90.

Bridge, Adrian. "Few Cheers as Two New States Are Born." *The Independent* (London), December 31, 1992, p. 14.

Brierly, J. L. *The Law of Nations : An Introduction to the International Law of Peace.* 6th ed. Oxford: Clarendon Press, 1963.

Brown, Michael F. *Who Owns Native Culture?* Boston, Mass.: Harvard University Press, 2003.

Brownlie, Ian. *Principles of Public International Law.* 6th ed. Oxford: Clarendon Press, 2003.

———. "The Rights of Peoples in Modern International Law." In *The Rights of Peoples*, pp. 1–16. Edited by James Crawford. Oxford: Clarendon Press, 1988.

Brölmann, Catherine, et al., eds. *Peoples and Minorities in International Law*. Dordrecht and Boston: M. Nijhoff Publishers, 1993.

Brysk, Alison. *From Tribal Village to Global Village: Indian Rights and International Relations in Latin America*. Stanford, Cal.: Stanford University Press, 2000.

Buchanan, Allen E. *Secession: The Morality of Political Divorce From Fort Sumter to Lithuania and Quebec*. Boulder, Colo.: Westview Press, 1991.

Buchheit, Lee C. *Secession: The Legitimacy of Self-Determination*. New Haven: Yale University Press, 1978.

Buck, Elizabeth. *Paradise Remade: The Politics of Culture and History in Hawai'i*. Philadelphia: Temple University Press, 1993.

Buergenthal, Thomas, and Robert E. Norris, eds. *Human Rights in the Inter-American System*. Dobbs Ferry, N.Y.: Oceana Publications, 1993.

Burger, Julian. *Report from the Frontier: The State of the World's Indigenous Peoples*. London: Zed Books, 1987.

Burnstein, John N. Student Note. "Ethnic Minorities and the Sandinist Government." *Journal of International Affairs* 36 (1982): 155–61.

Butt, Peter, et al. "'Mabo' Revisited—Native Title Act." *Journal of International Banking Law* 9 (1994): 75–84.

Campisi, Jack. "The Trade and Intercourse Acts: Land Claims on the Eastern Seaboard." In *Irredeemable America: The Indians' Estate and Land Claims*, pp. 337–62. Edited by Imre Sutton. Albuquerque: University of New Mexico Press, 1985.

Cançado Trindade, Antonio Augusto. "The Operation of the Inter-American Court of Human Rights." In *The Inter-American System of Human Rights*. Edited by D. J. Harris and Stephen Livingstone. Oxford: Clarendon Press; Oxford and New York: Oxford University Press, 1998.

Carbonell, Miguel, and Karla Portilla Pérez, cords. *Comentarios a la Reforma Constitucional en Materia Indígena*. Mexico D.F.: Instituto de Investigaciones Jurídicas—UNAM, 2002.

Carroza, Paolo G. "Subsidiary as a Structural Principle of International Human Rights Law." *American Journal of International Law* 97 (2003): 38–79.

Casanovas, Arnaldo Lijerón. "Bolivia: The Indigenous Territories of Amazonia." *Indigenous Affairs* 4 (1994).

Casas, Bartolomé de las. *History of the Indies: Selections*. Translated and edited by Andrée Collard. New York: Harper and Row, 1971.

Cassese, Antonio. *Self-Determination of Peoples: A Legal Reappraisal*. Cambridge: Cambridge University Press, 1995.

Castañeda, Jorge. *Legal Effects of United Nations Resolutions*. Translated by Alba Amoia. New York: Columbia University Press, 1969.

Cernea, Michael. "Sociologist in a Development Agency: Experiences from the World Bank." New York: The World Bank Environment Department, May 1993.

Champagne, Duane. "Beyond Assimilation as a Strategy for National Integration: The Persistence of American Indian Political Identities." *Transnational Law and Contemporary Problems* 3 (1993): 109–29.

——. *Social Order and Political Change: Constitutional Governments among the Cherokee, the Choctaw, the Chickasaw, and the Creek.* Stanford, Cal.: Stanford University Press, 1992.

Charney, Jonathan I. "Transnational Corporations and Developing Public International Law." *Duke Law Journal* (1983): 748–88.

Cheng, Bin. "United Nations Resolutions on Outer Space: Instant International Customary Law?" *Indian Journal of International Law* 5 (1965): 23–48.

Chiang, Pei-heng. *Non-Governmental Organizations at the United Nations: Identity, Role, and Function.* New York: Praeger, 1981.

Churchill, Ward. "The Earth Is Our Mother: Struggles for American Indian Land and Liberation in the Contemporary United States." In *The State of Native America: Genocide, Colonization, and Resistance.* Edited by Annette Jaimes. Boston: South End Press, 1992.

Clapham, Andrew. "Mainstreaming Human Rights at the United Nations: The Challenges for the First High Commissioner for Human Rights." In *Collected Courses of the Academy of European Law*, vol. VII, book 2, 159–234. Edited by Academy of European Law. The Hague: Kluwer Law International. 1996.

Claude, Richard P., and Burns H. Weston, eds. *Human Rights in the World Community: Issues and Action.* 2d ed. Philadelphia: University of Pennsylvania Press, 1992.

Clavero, Bartolomé. *Derecho indigena y cultura constitutional en América.* Mexico City: Siglo Veintiuno, 1994.

——. *La destrucción de las indias, ayer y hoy.* Madrid: Marcial Pons, 2002.

Clinebell, John H., and Jim Thomson. "Sovereignty and Self-Determination: The Rights of Native Americans under International Law." *Buffalo Law Review* 27 (1978): 669–714.

Clinton, Robert N. "The Proclamation of 1763: Colonial Prelude to Two Centuries of Federal-State Conflict over the Management of Indian Affairs." *Boston University Law Review* 69 (1989): 329–85.

Clinton, Robert N., Carol E. Goldberg, and Rebecca Tsosie. *American Indian Law: Native Nations and the Federal System.* Newark, N.J.: Matthew Bender, 2003.

Clinton, William J. "Remarks to American Indian and Alaska Native Tribal Leaders." *Weekly Compilation of Presidential Documents* 30, no. 18 (May 9, 1994): 941–1005.

Cohen, Felix S. *Handbook of Federal Indian Law.* Edited by Rennard Strickland et al. 2d ed. Charlottesville, Va.: Michie/Bobbs-Merrill, 1989.

——. *Handbook of Federal Indian Law.* Reprint of 1942 edition. Albuquerque: University of New Mexico Press, 1971.

——. "Original Indian Title." *Minnesota Law Review* 32 (1947): 28–59.

——. "The Spanish Origin of Indian Rights in the Law of the United States." *Georgetown Law Journal* 31 (1942): 1–21.

Coleman, Michael C. *Presbyterian Missionary Attitudes toward American Indians, 1837–1893.* Jackson: University Press of Mississippi, 1985.

Committee on Aboriginal Rights in Canada, Canadian Bar Association. *Aboriginal Rights in Canada: An Agenda for Action.* Ottawa: Canadian Bar Association, 1988.

Conn, Stephen. "Inside Brazilian Indian Law: A Comparative Perspective." In *Indigenous Law and the State*, pp. 269–93. Edited by Bradford W. Morse and Gordon R. Woodman. Dordrecht and Providence: Foris Publications, 1988.

Connor, Walker. *The National Question in Marxist-Leninist Theory and Strategy.* Princeton: Princeton University Press, 1984.

Crawford, James, ed. *The Rights of Peoples.* Oxford: Clarendon Press, 1988.

Curtin, Philip D., ed. *Imperialism.* New York: Harper and Row, 1971.

Daes, Erica-Irene A. "Some Consideration on the Right of Indigenous Peoples to Self-Determination." *Transnational Law and Contemporary Problems* 3 (1993): 1–11.

———. *Status of the Individual and Contemporary International Law: Promotion, Protection, and Restoration of Human Rights at the National, Regional and International Levels.* U.N. Sales No. E.91.XIV.3. New York: United Nations, 1992.

D'Amato, Anthony. "The Concept of Human Rights in International Law." *Columbia Law Review* 82 (1982): 1110–59.

Damerow, Harold. "A Critical Analysis of the Foundations of International Law." Ph.D. dissertation, Rutgers University, 1978.

Davenport, Frances G., ed. *European Treaties Bearing on the History of the United States and Its Dependencies to 1648.* Carnegie Institution of Washington Publication No. 254. Gloucester, Mass.: Peter Smith, 1967.

David, Rene, and John E. C. Brierley. *Major Legal Systems in the World Today: An Introduction to the Comparative Study of Law.* 3d ed. London: Stevens, 1985.

Davis, Shelton H. *Land Rights and Indigenous Peoples: The Role of the Inter-American Commission on Human Rights.* Cambridge, Mass.: Cultural Survival, 1988.

Davis, Shelton, and William Partridge. "Promoting the Development of Indigenous People in Latin America." *Finance and Development,* March 1994, pp. 38–40.

Deloria, Vine, Jr. *Custer Died for Your Sins.* New York: McMillan, 1969.

D'Estéfano, Miguel A. *Esquemas de derecho internacional público.* Playa, Ciudad de la Habana: Editorial Pueblo y Educación, 1986.

Dinstein, Yoram. "Self-Determination and the Middle East Conflict." In *Self-Determination: National, Regional and Global Dimensions,* pp. 243–47. Edited by Yonah Alexander and Robert A. Friedlander. Boulder, Colo.: Westview Press, 1980.

Doeker, Günther. *The Treaty-Making Power in the Commonwealth of Australia.* The Hague: M. Nijhoff Publishers, 1966.

Dudley, Michael Kioni, and Keoni Kealoha Agard. *A Hawaiian Nation.* Vol. 2, *A Call for Hawaiian Sovereignty.* Honolulu: Na Kane O Ka Malo Press, 1990.

Durán, Carlos Villán: *Curso de derecho internacional de los derechos humanos,* Madrid: Editorial Trotta, 2002.

Dworkin, Ronald: *Law's Empire,* Cambridge, Mass.: Belknap Press, 1986.

Eide, Asbjorn. "In Search of Constructive Alternatives to Secession." In *Modern Law of Self Determination,* pp. 139–76. Edited by Christian Tomuschat. Dordrecht and Boston: M. Nijhoff Publishers, 1993.

Epstein, Edward J. "The Theoretical System of Property Rights in China's General Principles of Civil Law: Theoretical Controversy in the Drafting Process and Beyond." *Law and Contemporary Problems* 52 (1989): 177–216.

Falcoff, Mark. "The Democratic Prospect in Latin America." *Washington Quarterly* 13 (Spring 1990): 183–92.

Falk, Richard. "The Theoretical Foundations of Human Rights." In *Human Rights in the World Community: Issues and Actions*, pp. 31–41. Edited by Richard P. Claude and Burns H. Weston. 2d ed. Philadelphia: University of Pennsylvania Press, 1992.

Farer, Tom J. "The United Nations and Human Rights: More Than a Whimper, Less Than a Roar." *Human Rights Quarterly* 9 (1987): 550–86.

Faulkner, Robert K. *The Jurisprudence of John Marshall*. Princeton: Princeton University Press, 1968.

Faúndez Ledesma, Héctor. *El Sistema Intermaericano de Protección de los Derechos Humanos: Aspectos institucionales y procesales*. San Jose, Costa Rica: Instituto Intermaericano de Derechos Humanos, 1996.

Feit, Harvey. "Negotiating Recognition of Aboriginal Land Rights: History, Strategies and Reactions to the James Bay and Northern Quebec Agreement." In *Aborigines, Land and Land Rights*, pp. 416–38. Edited by Nicholas Peterson and Marcia Langton. Canberra: Australian Institute of Aboriginal Studies; distributed in North and South America by Humanities Press, 1983.

Feld, W. *Nongovernmental Forces and World Politics: A Study of Business, Labor and Political Groups*. New York: Praeger, 1972.

Fox, Gregory H. "The Right to Political Participation in International Law." *Yale Journal of International Law* 17 (1992): 539–607.

Franck, Thomas M. "The Emerging Right to Democratic Governance." *American Journal of International Law* 86 (1992): 46–91.

———. "Legitimacy in the International System." *American Journal of International Law* 82 (1988): 705–59.

———. "Postmodern Tribalism and the Right to Secession." In *Peoples and Minorities in International Law*, pp. 3–27. Edited by Catherine Brölmann et al. Dordrecht and Boston: M. Nijhoff Publishers, 1993.

Friedmann, Wolfgang. *The Changing Structure of International Law*. New York: Columbia University Press, 1964.

Frost, Lynda. "The Evolution of the Inter-American Court of Human Rights: Reflections of Present and Former Judges." *Human Rights Quarterly* 14 (1992): 171–205.

Fuller, Lon L. *The Morality of Law*. Rev. ed. New Haven: Yale University Press, 1977.

Gavin, R. J., and J. A. Betley, comp., ed., and trans. *The Scramble for Africa: Documents on the Berlin West African Conference and Related Subjects, 1884–1885*. Ibadan, Nigeria: Ibadan University Press, 1973.

Getches, David, Charles Wilkinson, and Robert Williams, Jr. *Federal Indian Law: Cases and Materials*. 4th ed. St. Paul, Minn.: West Publishing, 1998.

Gómez, Magdalena, ed. *Derecho Indígena*. Mexico: Instituto Nacional Indigenista, Asociación Mexicana para las Naciones Unidas, 1997.

Gómez Isa, Felipe. "El derecho de autodeterminación en el derecho internacional contemporáneo." In *Derecho de autodeterminación y la realidad vasca*, pp. 267–324. Vitoria-Gasteiz: Servicio Central de Publicaciones del Gobierno Vasco, 2002.

Gordon-McCutchan, R. C. *The Taos Indians and the Battle for Blue Lake.* Santa Fe, N.M.: Red Crane Books, 1991.

Gong, Gerrit, W. *The Standard of "Civilization" in International Society.* Oxford: Clarendon Press, 1984.

Gotleib, Allan E. *Canadian Treaty-Making.* Toronto: Butterworth Publishers, 1968.

Green, Leslie C., and Olive P. Dickason. *The Law of Nations and the New World.* Edmonton: University of Alberta Press, 1989.

Griffiths, Thomas, and Marcus Colchester. "Report of a Workshop on 'Indigenous Peoples, Forests and the World Bank: Policies and Practice' (Washington, May 9–10, 2000)." Moreton-in-Marsh, England: Forest Peoples Program, 2000.

Gross, Leo, et al., eds. *International Law in the Twentieth Century.* New York: Appleton-Century-Crofts, 1969.

Gross Espiell, Héctor. "Self-Determination and Jus Cogens." In *U.N. Law/Fundamental Rights: Two Topics in International Law*, pp. 167–73. Edited by Antonio Cassese. Alphen aan den Rijn: Sijthoff and Noordhoff, 1979.

Grotius, Hugo. *The Freedom of the Seas.* Translation of 1633 edition by Ralph van Deman Magoffin. Carnegie Endowment for International Peace edition. New York: Oxford University Press, 1916.

———. *The Law of War and Peace.* Translation of 1646 edition by Francis W. Kelsey. Classics of International Law series. Oxford: Clarendon Press, 1925.

Guidieri, Remo, et al., eds. *Ethnicities and Nations: Processes of Interethnic Relations in Latin America, Southeast Asia, and the Pacific.* Austin: University of Texas Press, 1988.

Guilmartin, John F., Jr. "The Cutting Edge: An Analysis of the Spanish Invasion and Overthrow of the Inca Empire." In *Transatlantic Encounters: Europeans and Andeans in the Sixteenth Century*, pp. 40–69. Edited by Kenneth J. Andrien and Rolena Adorno. Berkeley and Oxford: University of California Press, 1991.

Hall, Stuart. "The State in Question." In *The Idea of the Modern State.* Edited by Gregor McLennan et al. Milton Keynes (U.K.) and Philadelphia: Open University Press, 1984.

Hall, William E. *A Treatise on International Law.* Edited by Alexander Pearce Higgins. 8th ed. Oxford: Clarendon Press, 1924.

Halperin, Morton H., et al. *Self-Determination in the New World Order.* Washington, D.C.: Carnegie Endowment for International Peace, 1992.

Hanke, Lewis. *The Spanish Struggle for Justice in the Conquest of America.* 3d printing. Boston: Little, Brown, 1965.

Hanks, Peter, and Bryan Keon-Cohen, eds. *Aborigines and the Law.* Sydney and Boston: George Allen and Unwin, Australia, 1984.

Hannum, Hurst. *Autonomy, Sovereignty, and Self-Determination: The Accommodation of Conflicting Rights.* Philadelphia: University of Pennsylvania Press, 1990.

———, ed. *Guide to International Human Rights Practice.* 3d ed. Ardsley, N.Y.: Transnational Publishers, 1999.

———. "New Developments in Indigenous Rights." *Virginia Journal of International Law* 28 (1988): 649–78.

————. "Self-Determination as a Human Right." In *Human Rights in the World Community: Issues and Action*, pp. 175–84. Edited by Richard P. Claude and Burns H. Weston, 2d ed. Philadelphia: University of Pennsylvania Press, 1992.

Hanski, Raija, and Martin Scheinin, eds. *Leading Cases of the Human Rights Committee.* Åbo: Finland: Akademi University, Institute for Human Rights, 2003.

Harris, David J. *Cases and Materials in International Law.* London: Sweet and Maxwell, 1979.

Harris, David J., and Stephen Livingstone, eds. *The Inter-American System of Human Rights.* Oxford: Clarendon Press, 1998.

Harvard Journal of Law and Public Policy. Symposium. "Property: The Founding, the Welfare State, and Beyond." The Eighth Annual National Federalist Society Symposium on Law and Public Policy—1989. *Harvard Journal of Law and Public Policy* 13 (1990): 1–165.

Higgins, Rosalyn. "Post-Modern Tribalism and the Right to Secession, Comments." In *Peoples and Minorities in International Law*, pp. 29–35. Edited by Catherine Brölmann et al. Dordrecht and Boston: M. Nijhoff Publishers, 1993.

————. *Problems and Process: International Law and How We Use It.* Oxford: Clarendon Press, 1994.

————. "The Role of Resolutions of International Organizations in the Process of Creating Norms in the International System." In *International Law and the International System*, pp. 21–44. Edited by W. Butler. Dordrecht and Boston: M. Nijhoff Publishers, 1987.

Hobbes, Thomas. *Leviathan.* Edited by Richard Tuck. Cambridge and New York: Cambridge University Press, 1991.

Hollowaye, Kaye. *Modern Trends in Treaty Law: Constitutional Law, Reservations and the Three Modes of Legislation.* London: Stevens & Sons, 1967.

Hornung, Rick. *One Nation under the Gun.* New York: Pantheon Books, 1991.

Hu-DeHart, Evelyn. *Missionaries, Miners, and Indians: Spanish Contact with the Yacqui Nation of Northwestern New Spain.* Tuscon: University of Arizona Press, 1981.

Hunt, Michael. "Mineral Development and Indigenous People—The Implications of the *Mabo* Case." *Journal of Energy and Natural Resources Law* 11 (1993): 155–78.

Huntington, Samuel P. *The Third Wave: Democratization in the Late Twentieth Century.* Norman: University of Oklahoma Press, 1991.

Hyde, Charles C. *International Law Chiefly as Interpreted and Applied by the United States.* Boston: Little, Brown, 1922.

Iglesias, Juan. *Derecho Romano.* 12th ed. Madrid: Ariel Derecho, 1999.

Indian Law Resource Center. *Indian Rights, Human Rights: Handbook for Indians on International Human Rights Complaint Procedures.* Washington D.C.: Indian Law Resource Center, 1984.

Institut de Droit International. *Annuaire (1888–1889).* Vol 10. Bruxelles: Librairie Européenne C. Muquardt, 1889.

Instituto Indigenista Interamericano and Instituto Interamericano de Derechos Humanos. *Entre ley y la costumbre: El Derecho consuetudinario indígena en América Latina.* Mexico City: Instituto Indigenista Interamericano, 1990.

Inter-American Commission on Human Rights. *The Human Rights Situation of Indigenous Peoples in the Americas*, O.A.S. Doc. OEA/Ser.L/V/II.108, Doc. 62 (2000).

————. *Fifth Report on the Situation of Human Rights in Guatemala*, O.A.S. Doc. OEA/
Ser.L/V/II.111, Doc. 21, rev. (2001).

————. *Fourth Report on the Situation of Human Rights in Guatemala*, O.A.S. Doc.
OEA/L/V/II.83, Doc. 16, rev. (1993).

————. *Report on the First Round of Consultations Concerning the Future Inter-Ameri-
can Legal Instrument on the Rights of Indigenous Populations*. Reprinted in
Annual Report of the Inter-American Commission on Human Rights. O.A.S. Doc.
OEA/Ser.L/V/II.83 (1993), pp. 263–312.

————. *Report on the Situation of Human Rights in Brazil*, O.A.S. Doc. OEA/Ser.L/V/
II.97, Doc. 29, rev. 1 (1997).

————. *Report on the Situation of Human Rights in Ecuador*, O.A.S. Doc. OEA/Ser.L/
V/II.96, Doc. 10, rev. 1 (1997).

————. *Report on the Situation of Human Rights in Mexico*, O.A.S. Doc. OEA/Ser.L/
V/II.100, Doc. 7, rev. 1 (1998).

————. *Report on the Situation of Human Rights in Paraguay*, O.A.S. Doc. OEA/Ser.L/
V/II.43, at 9–10, n.8 (1978).

————. *Report on the Situation of Human Rights of a Segment of the Nicaraguan Population of Miskito Origin and Resolution on the Friendly Settlement Procedure
Regarding the Human Rights Situation of a Segment of the Nicaraguan Population of Miskito Origin*. O.A.S. Doc OEA/Ser.L/V/II.62, Doc. 10, rev. 3 (1983),
O.A.S. Doc OEA/Ser.L/V/II.62, Doc. 26 (1984).

————. *Second Report on the Situation of Human Rights in Colombia*, O.A.S. Doc. OEA/
Ser.L/V/I.84, Doc. 39, rev. (1993).

————. *Second Report on the Situation of Human Rights in Paraguay*, O.A.S. Doc. OEA/
Ser.L/V/II.71, Doc. 19, rev. 1 (1987).

————. *Second Report on the Situation of Human Rights in Peru*, O.A.S. Doc. OEA/
Ser.L/V/II.106, Doc. 59, rev. (2000).

————. *Special Report on the Human Rights Situation in the so-called "Communities
of People in Resistance" in Guatemala*, O.A.S. Doc. OEA/Ser.L/V/II.86, Doc. 5,
rev. 1 (1994).

————. *Third Report on the Situation of Human Rights in Colombia*, O.A.S. Doc. OEA/
Ser.L/V/II.102, Doc. 9, rev. 1 (1999).

————. *Third Report on the Situation of Human Rights in Paraguay*, O.A.S. Doc. OEA/
Ser.L/V/II.110, Doc. 52 (1997).

International Labour Organization. *Partial Revision of the Indigenous and Tribal Populations Convention, 1957 (No. 107)*. Report VI(1), International Labour Conference, Geneva, 75th Sess. (1988).

————. *Partial Revision of Indigenous and Tribal Populations Convention, 1957, (No.
107)*. Report VI(2), International Labour Conference, Geneva, 75th Sess. (1988).

————. *Partial Revision of the Indigenous and Tribal Populations Convention, 1957 (No.
107)*. Report IV(2A), International Labour Conference, Geneva, 76th Sess. (1989).

International Work Group for Indigenous Affairs. *The Indigenous World: 1993–94*.
Copenhagen: International Work Group for Indigenous Affairs, 1994.

Iorns, Catherine J. "Indigenous Peoples and Self-Determination: Challenging State Sovereignty." *Case Western Reserve Journal of International Law* 24 (1992): 199–348.

Jackson, Robert H. *Quasi-States: Sovereignty, International Relations and the Third World*. Cambridge and New York: Cambridge University Press, 1990.

Jaimes, Annette, ed. *The State of Native America: Genocide, Colonization, and Resistance*. Boston: South End Press, 1992.

Jamestown Band of Klallam, Lummi Indian Tribe, and Quinalt Indian Nation. *Tribal Self-Governance: Shaping Our Own Future—A Red Paper*. June 1, 1989.

Janis, Mark W. *An Introduction to International Law*. 4th ed. Boston: Little, Brown, 2003.

Jenkins Molieri, Jorge. *El Desafío indígena en Nicaragua: El Caso de los Miskitos*. Mexico City: Editorial Katun, 1986.

Jenks, C. W. *Social Justice in the Law of Nations*. London and New York: Oxford University Press, 1970.

Jennings, Francis. *The Founders of America: How Indians Discovered the Land, Pioneered in It, and Created Great Classical Civilizations; How They Were Plunged into a Dark Age by Invasions and Conquest; and How They Are Reviving*. New York: W. W. Norton, 1993.

Johansen, Bruce E., *Life and Death in Mohawk Country*. Golden, Colo.: North American Press, 1993.

Joseph, Philip A. *Constitutional and Administrative Law in New Zealand*. Sydney: Law Book Company, 1993.

Kamminga, Menno T. *Inter-State Accountability for Violations of Human Rights*. Philadelphia: University of Pennsylvania Press, 1992.

Kawharu, I. H., ed. *Waitangi: Maori and Pakeha Perspectives of the Treaty of Waitangi*. Auckland, New York, and Oxford: Oxford University Press, 1989.

Kent, James. *Commentaries on American Law*. New York: O. Halsted, 1826–30; 14th ed., edited by John M. Gould. Boston: Little, Brown, 1896.

Keon-Cohen, Bryan, and Bradford Morse. "Indigenous Land Rights in Australia and Canada." In *Aborigines and the Law*, pp. 74–102. Edited by Peter Hanks and Bryan Keon-Cohen. Sydney and Boston: Allen & Unwin, 1984.

Kingbury, Benedict, "'Indigenous Peoples' in International Law: A Constructivist Approach to the Asian Controversy." *American Journal of International Law* 92 (1998): 414–57.

Kirgis, Frederic L. "Federal Statutes, Executive Orders and 'Self-Executing Custom.'" *American Journal of International Law* 81 (1987): 371–75.

———. *International Organizations in Their Legal Setting*. 2d ed. St. Paul, Minn.: West Publishing, 1993.

Klingsberg, Ethan A. "International Human Rights Intervention on Behalf of Minorities in Post–World War I Eastern Europe and Today: Placebo, Poison, or Panacea?" *University of Chicago Law School Roundtable* 1 (1993): 1–21.

Knop, Karen. *Diversity and Self-Determination in International Law*. Cambridge: Cambridge University Press, 2002.

Koh, Harold Hongju. "The Right to Democracy." In *Country Reports on Human Rights Practices for 1998 (vol. 1)*, pp. xv–xxxiv. U.S. Dept. of State. Washington, D.C.: U.S. Government Printing Office, 1999.

Kronowitz, Rachel S., et al. Comment. "Toward Consent and Cooperation: Reconsidering the Political Status of Indian Nations." *Harvard Civil Rights–Civil Liberties Law Review* 22 (1987): 507–622.

Kymlicka, Will. *Multicultural Citizenship.* Oxford: Clarendon Press, 1995.

———. *Politics in the Vernacular: Nationalism, Multiculturalism and Citizenship.* Oxford: Oxford University Press, 2002.

Kymlicka, Will, and Wayne Norman, eds. *Citizenship in Diverse Societies.* Oxford: Oxford University Press, 2000.

Ladbury, Rick, and Jenny Chin. "Legislative Responses to the Mabo Decisions: Implications for the Australian Resources Industry." *Journal of Energy and Natural Resources Law* 12 (1994): 207–25.

Lâm, Maivan C. *At the Edge of the State: Indigenous Peoples and Self-Determination.* Ardsley, N.Y.: Transnational Publishers, 2000.

Lancaster, Carol. "Democracy in Africa." *Foreign Policy* 85 (Winter 1991–92): 148–65.

Lauren, Paul G. *Power and Prejudice: The Politics and Diplomacy of Racial Discrimination.* Boulder, Colo.: Westview Press, 1988.

Lauterpacht, Hersch. "The Grotian Tradition in International Law." *British Year Book of International Law* 23 (1946): 1–53.

Lawrey, Andrée. "Contemporary Efforts to Guarantee Indigenous Rights under International Law." *Vanderbilt Journal of Transnational Law* 23 (1990): 703–77.

Leary, Virginia A. *International Labour Conventions and National Law.* The Hague: M. Nijhoff Publishers, 1982.

Legal Division, Commonwealth Secretariat. "The Application of International Human Rights Standards in Domestic Law." Monograph 4, *Victoria University of Wellington Law Review* 22 (1992): 1–20.

Legarreta, Josu. *Derechos de los pueblos indígenas.* Vitoria-Gasteiz: Servicio Central de Publicaciones del Gobierno Vasco, 1998.

Lenin, Vladimir Ilich. "The Right of Nations to Self-Determination." In *Collected Works* (Vol. 20). 45 vols. English edition. Moscow: Progress Publishers, 1947.

Lerner, Natan. *Group Rights and Discrimination in International Law.* Dordrecht and Boston: M. Nijhoff Publishers, 1991.

Lewis-Anthony, Siân. "Treaty-Based Procedures for Making Human Rights Complaints within the United Nation System." In *Guide to Human Rights Practice*, pp. 41–59. Edited by Hurst Hannum. 3d ed. Ardsley, N.Y.: Transnational Publishers, 1999.

Lijerón Casanovas, Arnaldo. "Bolivia: The Indigenous Territories of Amazonia." *Indigenous Affairs*, No. 4 (Oct.–Dec. 1994): 16–18.

Lillich, Richard B. "Civil Rights." In *Human Rights in International Law*, pp. 115–70. Edited by Theodore Meron. Oxford: Clarendon Press, 1984.

———. "The Role of Domestic Courts in Enforcing International Human Rights Law." In *Guide to International Human Rights Practice*, pp. 228–46. Edited by Hurst Hannum. 2d ed. Philadelphia: University of Pennsylvania Press, 1992.

Lindell, Geoffrey. "The Justiciability of Political Questions: Recent Developments." In *Australian Constitutional Perspectives*, pp. 180–250. Edited by H. P. Lee and George Winterton. Sydney: Law Book Company, 1992.

Lindley, Mark F. *The Acquisition and Government of Backward Territory in International Law.* London and New York: Longmans, Green, 1926.

Locke, John. *Two Treatises of Government.* Edited by Peter Laslett. 2d ed. London: Cambridge University Press, 1970.

López Bárcenas, Francisco, et al., *Los Derechos Indígenas y la Reforma Constitucional en Mexico.* Mexico, D.F.: Centro de Orientación y Asesoría a Pueblos Indígenas, A.C., 2001.

Luebben, Thomas E., and Cathy Nelson, "The Indian Wars: Efforts to Resolve Western Shoshone Land and Treaty Issues and to Distribute the Indian Claims Commission Judgment Fund," *Natural Resources Journal* 42 (2003): 835.

Lutz, Ellen, Hurst Hannum, and Kathryn Burk, eds. *New Directions in Human Rights.* Philadelphia: University of Pennsylvania Press, 1989.

Lyons, Oren R. "The American Indian in the Past." In *Exiled in the Land of the Free*, pp. 13–42. Edited by Oren R. Lyons and John C. Mohawk. Santa Fe, N.M.: Clear Light Publishers, 1992.

Macdonald, Theodore. "The Moral Economy of Miskito Indians: Local Roots of a Geopolitical Conflict." *Ethnicities and Nations: Processes of Interethnic Relations in Latin America, Southeast Asia, and the Pacific*, pp. 107–53. Edited by Remo Guidieri et al. Houston: Rothko Chapel; distributed in U.S. by University of Texas Press, 1988.

Mackay, Fergus. *Los Derechos de los Pueblos Indígenas en el Sistema Internacional: Un fuente instrumental par alas organizaciones indígenea.* Lima: Asociación Pro Derechos Humanos y Federación Internacional de Derechos Humanos, 1999.

———. "Universal Rights or a Universe unto Itself? Indigenous Peoples' Human Rights and the Work Bank's Draft Operation Policy 4.10 on Indigenous Peoples." *American University Law Review.* 17 (2002): 527–624.

McCutchan, Gordon. *The Taos Indians and the Battle for Blue Lake.* Santa Fe, New Mexico: Red Crane Books, 1991.

McDougal, Myres S., Harold Laswell, and Lung-chu Chen. *Human Rights and World Public Order: The Basic Policies of an International Law of Human Dignity.* New Haven: Yale University Press, 1980.

McDougal, Myres S., Harold Laswell, and W. Michael Reisman. "Theories about International Law: A Prologue to a Configurative Jurisprudence." *Virginia Journal of International Law* 8 (1968): 188–299.

McGinty, Jennifer S. Student Note: "New Zealand's Forgotten Promises: The Treaty of Waitangi." *Vanderbilt Journal of Transnational Law* 25 (1992): 681–722.

McGoldrick, Dominic. "Canadian Indians, Cultural Rights, and the Human Rights Committee." *International and Comparative Law Quarterly* 40 (1991): 658–69.

———. *The Human Rights Committee: Its Role in the Development of the International Covenant on Civil and Political Rights.* Oxford: Clarendon Press, 1991.

McGregor, Davianna Pomaika. "Ho'omauke Ea O Ka Lahui Hawai'i: The Perpetuation of the Hawaiian People." In *Ethnicity and Nation Building in the Pacific*, pp. 74–97. Edited by Michael C. Howard. Tokyo: United Nations University, 1989.

McGuire, Thomas R. "Getting to Yes in the New West." In *State and Reservation: New Perspectives on Federal Indian Policy*, pp. 224–46. Edited by George Pierre Castille and Robert L. Bee. Tucson: University of Arizona Press, 1992.

McKee, Christopher. *Treaty Talks in British Columbia.* 2d ed. Vancouver: University of British Columbia Press, 2000.

McLennan, Gregor, et al., eds. *The Idea of the Modern State.* Milton Keynes (U.K.) and Philadelphia: Open University Press, 1984.

McLoughlin, William G. *Cherokees and Missionaries, 1789–1839.* New Haven: Yale University Press, 1984.

———. *Cherokee Renascence in the New Republic.* Princeton, N.J.: Princeton University Press, 1986.

McLuhan, T. C., ed. *Touch the Earth: A Self-Portrait of Indian Existence.* New York: Outerbridge and Dienstfrey; distributed in U.S. by E. P. Dutton, 1971.

McRae, Heather, et al. *Aboriginal Legal Issues: Commentary and Materials.* Sydney: Law Book Company, 1991.

Maiguashca, Bice. "The Role of Ideas in a Changing World Order: The Case of the International Indigenous Movement." Paper presented at conference, Changing World Order and the United Nations System, sponsored by the United Nations University, Yokohama, Japan, March 24–27, 1992.

Mangus Martín, Araceli, ed. *La escuela de Salamanca y el Derecho Internacional en América.* Salamanca: Consejo Social de la Universidad de Salamanca, 1993.

Marecic, Charles J. "Nunavut Territory: Aboriginal Governing in the Canadian Regime of Governance." *American Indian Law Review* 24 (2000): 275–95.

Marinissen, Judith. *Legislación boliviana y pueblos indígenas: Inventario y análisis en la perspectiva de las demandas indígenas.* 2d ed. Santa Cruz: Centro de Estudios Jurídicos e Investigación Social, 1998.

Mariño Menéndez, Fernando, et al., *La Protección Internacional de las Minorías.* Madrid: La. Ministerio de Trabajo y Asuntos Sociales, 2001.

Marks, Greg C. "Indigenous Peoples in International Law: The Significance of Francisco de Vitoria and Bartolome de las Casas." *Australian Yearbook of International Law* 13 (1992): 1–51.

Martínez, José, ed. *Atlas: Territorios Indígenas de Bolivia.* Santa Cruz: Confederación de Pueblos Indígenas de Bolivia, 2002.

Mathijsen, P. S. R. F. *A Guide to European Community Law.* 5th ed. London: Sweet and Maxwell, 1990.

Medina, Cecilia. "The Inter-American Commission on Human Rights and the Inter-American Court of Human Rights: Reflections on a Joint Venture." *Human Rights Quarterly* 12 (1990): 439–64.

———. *The Legal Status of Indians in Brazil.* Washington, D.C.: Institute for the Development of Indian Law, 1977.

Meron, Theodor. *Human Rights and Humanitarian Norms as Customary Law.* Oxford: Clarendon Press, 1989.

Merritt, John, and Terry Fenge. "The Nunavut Land Claims Settlement: Emerging Issues in Law and Public Administration." *Queens Law Journal* 15 (1990): 255–77.

Meyers, Gary D., and Sally Raine. "Australian Aboriginal Land Rights in Transition (Part II): The Legislative Response to the High Court's Native Title Decisions in Mabor v. Queensland and Wik v. Queensland." *Tulsa Journal of Comparative and International Law* 9 (2001): 15–59.

Mojekwu, Christopher C. "Self-Determination: The African Perspective." In *Self-Determination: National, Regional, and Global Dimensions*, pp. 221–39. Edited by Yonah Alexander and Robert A. Friedlander. Boulder, Colo: Westview Press, 1980.

Morgan, Edward M. "The Imagery and Meaning of Self-Determination." *New York University Journal of International Law and Politics* 20 (1988): 355–403.

Morris, Glenn T. "In Support of the Right of Self-Determination for Indigenous Peoples under International Law." *German Yearbook of International Law* 29 (1986): 277–316.

Morse, Bradford W. "Aboriginal Peoples and the Law." In *Aboriginal Peoples and the Law: Indian, Metis and Inuit Rights in Canada*, pp. 1–15. Edited by Bradford W. Morse. Ottawa: Carleton University Press Inc., 1989.

Morse, Bradford W., and Gordon R. Woodman, eds. *Indigenous Law and the State*. Dordrecht: Foris Publications, 1988.

Moss, Wendy. "Indigenous Self-Government in Canada and Sexual Equality under the *Indian Act*: Resolving Conflicts between Collective and Individual Rights." *Queens Law Journal* 15 (1990): 279–305.

Moynihan, Daniel Patrick. *Pandaemonium: Ethnicity in International Politics.* Oxford and New York: Oxford University Press, 1993.

Nanda, Ved. "Self-Determination outside the Colonial Context: The Birth of Bangladesh in Retrospect." In *Self-Determination: National, Regional and Global Dimensions*, pp. 193–220. Edited by Yonah Alexander and Robert Friedlander. Boulder, Colo.: Westview Press, 1980.

National Lawyers Guild, Committee on Native American Struggles, ed. *Rethinking Indian Law*. New Haven: The Advocate Press, 1982.

Navia Ribera, Carlos. "Reconocimiento, demarcación y control de territorios indígenas: Situación y experiencias en Bolivia." In *Reconocimiento y demarcación de territorios indígenas en la Amazonía*, pp. 145–73. Serie Amerindia, no. 4. Edited by Martha Cárdenas and Hernán Darío Correa, Bogota: CEREC, 1993.

Newton, Nell Jessup. "Federal Power Over Indians: Its Sources, Scope, and Limitations." *University of Pennsylvania Law Review* 132 (1984): 195–288.

Niezen, Ronald. *The Origins of Indigenism: Human Rights and the Policy of Indigenism.* Berkeley: University of California Press, 2003.

Nino, Carlos Santiago. *The Ethics of Human Rights.* Oxford: Clarendon Press, 1991.

Nock, David A. A Victorian Missionary and Canadian Indian Policy: Cultural Synthesis vs. Cultural Replacement. Waterloo, Ontario: Wilfred University Press, 1988.

Nussbaum, Arthur. *A Concise History of the Law of Nations.* Rev. ed. New York: Macmillan, 1954.

O'Connell, John D. "Constructive Conquest in the Courts: A Legal History of the Western Shoshone Lands Struggle—1864 to 1991." *Natural. Resources Journal* 42 (2003): 765.

Ofuatey-Kodjoe, W. *The Principle of Self-Determination in International Law.* 2d ed. New York: Nellen Publishing, 1977.

Oppenheim, Lassa F. L. *International Law.* Edited by Ronald F. Roxburgh. 3d ed. London and New York: Longmans, 1920.

Opsahl, Torkal. "The Human Rights Committee." In *The United Nations and Human Rights: A Critical Appraisal*, pp. 369–443. Edited by Philip Alston. Oxford: Clarendon Press, 1992.

Padilla, David. "The Inter-American System for the Promotion and Protection of Human Rights." *Georgia Journal of International and Comparative Law* 20 (1990): 395–405.

Palmater, Pamela D., "Forum on R.V. Marshall: An Empty Shell of a Treaty Promise: R. V. Marshall and the Rights of Non-Status Indians," *Dalhousie Law Journal* 23 (2000): 102–48.

Partsch, Karl Josef. "The Committee on the Elimination of Racial Discrimination." In *The United Nations and Human Rights*, pp. 339–68. Edited by Philip Alston. Oxford: Clarendon Press; New York: Oxford University Press, 1992.

Paton, George W. *A Text-book of Jurisprudence*. Edited by David P. Derham. 3d ed. Oxford: Clarendon Press, 1964.

Paust, Jordan J. "Avoiding Fraudulent Executive Policy: Analysis of Non-Self-Execution of the Covenant on Civil and Political Rights." *DePaul Law Review* 42 (1993): 1257–85.

———. "Self-Determination: A Definitional Focus." In *Self-Determination: National, Regional, and Global Dimensions*, pp. 3–18. Edited by Yonah Alexander and Robert Friedlander. Boulder, Colo.: Westview Press, 1980.

———. "Self-Executing Treaties." *American Journal of International Law* 82 (1988): 760–83.

Paust, Jordan J., Joan M. Fitzpatrick, and Jon M. Van Dyke. *International Law and Litigation in the U.S.* St. Paul, Minn.: West Group, 2000.

Pérez-Luño, Antonio Enrique. *La polémica sobre el Nuevo Mundo. Los clásicos españoles en la Filosofia del Dercho*, 2d ed. Madrid: Editorial Trotta, 1995.

Peterson, Nicholas, and Marcia Langton, eds. *Aborigines, Land and Land Rights*. Canberra: Australian Institute of Aboriginal Studies; distributed in North and South America by Humanities Press, 1983.

Ponting, J. Rick, and Roger Gibbons. *Out of Irrelevance: A Social-Political Introduction to Indian Affairs in Canada*. Toronto: Butterworths, 1980.

Posey, Darrell Addison, and Graham Dutlfeld. *Beyond Intellectual Property: Toward Traditional Resource Rights for Indigenous Peoples*. Ottawa, Canada: International Development Research Center, 1996.

Prucha, Francis Paul, ed. *Documents of United States Indian Policy*. 2d ed. Lincoln and London: University of Nebraska Press, 1990.

Psacharophoulos, George, and Harr. A. Patrinos. "Indigenous People and Poverty in Latin America." *Finance and Development* (March 1994): 41–43.

Rama-Montaldo, Manuel. "International Legal Personality and Implied Powers of International Organizations." *British Yearbook of International Law* 44 (1970): 111–55.

Ramcharan, B. G. "State Responsibility for Violations of Human Rights Treaties." In *Contemporary Problems of International Law: Essays in Honour of Georg Schwarzenberger on his Eightieth Birthday*, pp. 242–61. Edited by Bin Cheng and Edward Duncan Brown. London: Stevens and Son, 1988.

Ramphul, Radha Krishna. "The Role of International and Regional Organizations in the

Peaceful Settlement of Internal Disputes (With Special Emphasis on the Organization of African Unity)." *Georgia Journal of International and Comparative Law* 13 (1983): 371–84.

Reinaga, Ramiro. *Ideología y raza en América Latina.* La Paz, Bolivia: Ediciones Futuro, 1972.

Rich, Roland. "The Right to Development: A Right of Peoples?" In *The Rights of Peoples,* pp. 39–54. Edited by James Crawford. Oxford: Clarendon Press, 1988.

Riggs, Robert E., and Jack C. Plano. *The United Nations: International Organization and World Politics.* 2d ed. Belmont, Cal.: Wadsworth, 1994.

Rivera, Luis N. *A Violent Evangelism: The Political and Religious Conquest of the Americas.* Louisville, Ky.: Westminster/John Knox Press, 1992.

Rivera-Ramos, Efrén. "Self-Determination and Decolonization in the Society of the Modern Colonial Welfare State." In *Issues of Self Determination,* pp. 115–32. Edited by William Twining. Aberdeen: Aberdeen University Press, 1991.

Roberts, Adam, and Benedict Kingsbury, eds. *United Nations, Divided World: The UN's Roles in International Relations.* 2d ed. Oxford: Oxford University Press, 1993.

Rodley, Nigel S. "United Nations Non-Treaty Procedures for Dealing with Human Rights Violations." In *Guide to International Human Rights Practice,* pp. 61–84. Edited by Hurst Hannum. 3d ed. Ardsley, N.Y.: Transnational Publishers, 1999.

———. "The Work of Non-Governmental Organizations in the World Wide Promotion and Protection of Human Rights." *United Nations Bulletin of Human Rights,* no. 90/1 (1991): 90–93.

Roldán Ortega, Roque. "Adjudicación de tierras en la Amazonia: La experiencia de los países." In *Reconocimiento y demarcación de territorios indígenas en la Amazonia,* pp. 241–56. Serie Amerindia, 4. Edited by Martha Cárdenas and Hernán Darío Correa. Bogotá: CEREC, 1993.

Roldán Ortega, Roque, Gómez Vargas, and John Harold, eds. *Fuero Indígena Colombiano.* 3d ed. Santafé de Bogotá: Ministerio de Gobierno, 1994.

Ronen, Dov. *The Quest for Self-Determination.* New Haven and London: Yale University Press, 1979.

Rosas, Allan. "Internal Self-Determination." In *Modern Law of Self-Determination,* pp. 225–52. Edited by Christian Tomuschat. Dordrecht and Boston: M. Nijhoff Publishers, 1993.

Roy, Bernadette Kelly, and Gudmundur Alfredsson. "Indigenous Rights: The Literature Explosion." *Transnational Perspective* 13 (1987): 19–24.

Royal Commission on Aboriginal Peoples. *Partners in Confederation: Aboriginal Peoples, Self-Government, and the Constitution.* Ottawa: Canada Communication Group, 1993.

Ruda, José María. "The Role of the Argentine Congress in the Treaty-Making Process." *Chicago-Kent Law Review* 67 (1991): 485–94.

Ruddy, Francis S. *International Law in the Enlightenment: The Background of Emmerich de Vattel's "Le Droit des gens."* Dobbs Ferry, N.Y.: Oceana Publications, 1975.

Ryser, Rudolph C. "Between Indigenous Nations and the State: Self Determination in the Balance." *Tulsa Journal of Comparative and International Law* 7 (1999): 129–61.

Sanders, Douglas. "Collective Rights." *Human Rights Quarterly* 13 (1991): 368–86.

————. "'We Intend to Live Here Forever.' A primer on the Nisga'a Treaty." *The University of British Colombia Law Review* 33 (1999): 103–28.

Sanders, Ronald. *Lost Tribes and Promised Lands*. Boston: Little, Brown, 1978.

Sartori, Giovanni. *La Sociedad Multiétnica: Pluralismo, multiculturalismo y extranjeros*. Madrid: Taurus, 2001.

Sauceda, Guadalupe Espinoza, et al., "Los Derechos Indígenas y la Reforma Constitucional en Mexico." México D.F., Centro de Orientación y Asesoría a Pueblos Indígenas y Ce-Acatl A.C., 2001.

Shachar, Ayelet. *Multicultural Jurisdictions: Cultural Differences and Women's Rights*. Cambridge, U.K.: Cambridge University Press, 2001.

Shattuck, Petra T., and Jill Norgren. *Partial Justice: Federal Indian Law in a Liberal Constitutional System*. Oxford: Berg Publishers, 1991.

Shaw, Malcolm. *Title to Territory in Africa: International Legal Issues*. Oxford: Clarendon Press; New York: Oxford University Press, 1986.

Shelton, Dinah L. "The Inter-American Human Rights System." *Guide to Human Rights Practice*, pp. 121–34. Edited by Hurst Hannum. 3d ed. Ardsley, N.Y.: Transnational Publishers, 1999.

————. "Reparations in the Inter-American System." In *The Inter-American System of Human Rights*. Edited by David Harris and Stephen Livingston, Oxford: Clarendon Press, 1998.

Shennan, J. H. *Liberty and Order in Early Modern Europe: The Subject and the State, 1650–1800*. London and New York: Longman, 1986.

Skubiszewski, Krysztof. "Forms of Participation of International Organizations in the Law-making Process." *International Organization* 18 (1964): 790–805.

Snow, Alpheus Henry. The Question of the Aborigines in the Law and Practice of Nations. Northbrook, Ill.: Metro Books, 1972.

Soares, Guido F. S. "The Treaty-Making Process under the 1988 Federal Constitution of Brazil." *Chicago-Kent Law Review* 67 (1991): 495–513.

Sohn, Luis B. "'Generally Accepted' International Rules." *Washington Law Review* 61 (1986): 1073–80.

————. "Unratified Treaties as a Source of Customary International Law." In *Realism in Law-making: Essays on International Law in Honour of Willem Riphagan*, pp. 231–46. Edited by A. Bos and H. Siblesz. Dordrecht and Boston: M. Nijhoff Publishers; distributed in U.S. and Canada by Kluwer Academic Publishers, 1986.

Stalin, Joseph. *Marxism and the National-Colonial Question*. San Francisco: Proletarian Publishers, 1975.

Starke, Joseph Gabriel. *Introduction to International Law*. 10th ed. London: Butterworths, 1989.

Stavenhagen, Rodolfo. *The Ethnic Question: Conflicts, Development, and Human Rights*. U.N. Sales No. E.90 III.A.9. Tokyo: United Nations University Press, 1990.

————. "La Situación y los derechos de los pueblos indígenas de América." *América Indígena* 52, nos. 1–2 (1992): 63–118.

Stavenhagen, Rodolfo, and Diego Iturralde: *Entre ley y la costumbre: El Derecho consuetudinario indígena en América Latina*. México D.F., Instituto Indigenista Interamericano-Instituto Interamericano de Derechos Humanos, 1990.

Steiner, Henry J., and Philip Alston, eds. *International Human Rights in Context: Law Politics, Morals.* 2d ed. Oxford: Oxford University Press, 2000.

Stephenson, M. A., and Suri Ratnapala, eds. *Mabo: A Judicial Revolution: The Aboriginal Land Rights Decision and Its Impact on Australian Law.* St. Lucia: University of Queensland Press, 1993.

Stewart, Omer. "The Shoshone Claims Cases." In *Irredeemable America*, pp. 187–206. Edited by Imre Sutton. Albuquerque: University of New Mexico Press, 1985.

Stoelting, David. "The Challenge of UN-Monitored Elections in Independent Nations." *Stanford Journal of International Law* 28 (1992): 371–424.

Strickland, Rennard. "Trying a New Way: An Independent Assessment Report on the Self-Governance Demonstration Project." Section 2, pp. 1–56 of *The World of the People.* Sovereignty Symposium VI, June 8–10, 1993, Tulsa, Okla.

Swartz, John, and Jorge Urquillas. *Aplicación de la Política del Banco sobre Poblaciones Indígenas (OD 4.20) en América Latina (1992–1997).* Washington, D.C.: World Bank Regional Office for Latin America and the Caribbean, 1999.

Swepston, Lee. "Human Rights Complaint Procedures of the International Labour Organization." In *Guide to International Human Rights Practice*, pp. 85–118. Edited by Hurst Hannum. 3d ed. Ardsley, N.Y.: Transnational Publishers, 1999.

———. "A New Step in the International Law on Indigenous and Tribal Peoples: ILO Convention No. 169 of 1989." *Oklahoma City University Law Review*, 15 (1990): 677–714.

Taylor, Philip. *Nonstate Actors in International Politics: From Transregional to Substate Organizations.* Boulder, Colo.: Westview Press, 1984.

Thirlway, H. W. A. *International Customary Law and Codification.* Leiden: A. W. Sijthoff, 1972.

Thornberry, Patrick. "The Democratic or Internal Aspect of Self-Determination with Some Remarks on Federalism." In *Modern Law of Self-Determination*, pp. 101–38. Edited by Christian Tomuschat. Dordrecht and Boston: M. Nijhoff Publishers, 1993.

———. *Indigenous Peoples and Human Rights.* Manchester: Manchester University Press, 2002.

———. *International Law and the Rights of Minorities.* Oxford: Clarendon Press, 1991.

Toledo Maya Council and Toledo Alcaldes Association. *Maya Atlas: The Struggle to Preserve Maya Land in Southern Belize.* Berkeley: North Atlantic Books, 1997.

Tomei, Manuela, and Lee Swepston. *Indigenous and Tribal Peoples: A Guide to ILO Convention No. 169.* Geneva: International Labour Organization, 1996.

Tomuschat, Christian, ed. *Modern Law of Self-Determination.* Dordrecht and Boston: M. Nijhoff Publishers, 1993.

Transnational Law and Contemporary Problems. "Inauguration of the 'International Year of the World's Indigenous People.'" *Transnational Law and Contemporary Problems* 3 (1993): 165–222.

Trigger, David S. *Whitefella Comin': Aboriginal Responses to Colonialism in Northern Australia.* Cambridge and New York: Cambridge University Press, 1992.

Tunkin, Grigorii Ivanovich. *Theory of International Law.* Translated by William Butler. Cambridge, Mass.: Harvard University Press, 1974.

Turpel, Mary E. "Indigenous Peoples' Rights of Political Participation and Self-Determination: Recent International Legal Developments and the Continuing Struggle for Recognition." *Cornell International Law Journal* 25 (1992): 579–602.

Tushnet, Mark. *Red, White, and Blue: A Critical Analysis of Constitutional Law.* Cambridge, Mass: Harvard University Press, 1988.

Tyler, S. Lyman. *A History of Indian Policy.* Washington, Bureau of Indian Affairs: U.S. Government Printing Office, 1973.

Ullman, Walter. *Principles of Government and Politics in the Middle Ages.* London: Methuen, 1961.

Umozurike, Umozurike O. *Self-Determination in International Law.* Hamden, Conn.: Archon Books, 1972.

United Nations. *Human Rights: A Compilation of International Instruments.* U.N. Doc. ST/HR/1/Rev.6, U.N.Sales No. E.02.XIV.4 New York: United Nations, 2002.

———. *Human Rights of Indigenous Peoples: Report of the Seminar on the Draft Principles and Guidelines for the Protection of the Heritage of Indigenous Peoples.* U.N. Doc. E/CN.4/Sub.2/2000/26 (2000).

———. *Report of the Expert Seminar on Practical Experiences Regarding Indigenous Land Rights and Claims.* U.N. Doc. E/CN.4/Sub.2.AC.4/1999/6/Add.1, 4 (1996).

———. *Report of the Meeting of Experts to Review the Experience of Countries in the Operation of Schemes of Internal Self-Government for Indigenous Peoples.* U.N. Doc. E/CN.4/1992/42 (1991).

———. *Report of the Second Workshop on Multiculturalism in Africa: Peace and Constructive Group Accommodation in Situations Involving Minorities and Indigenous Peoples, Private Sector Natural Resource, Energy and Mining Companies and Human Rights.* U.N. Doc. E/CN.4/Sub.2/AC.4/2002/3 (2002).

———. *Report of the Special Rapporteur on the situation of human rights and fundamental freedoms of indigenous people, Rodolfo Stavenhagen submitted in accordance with Commission Resolution 2002/65.* U.N. Doc. E/CN.4/2003/90/Add.1 (2003).

———. *Report of the Third Workshop on Multiculturalism in Africa: Peace and Constructive Group Accommodation in Situations Involving Minorities and Indigenous Peoples.* U.N. Doc. E/CN.4/Sub.2/AC.4/2002/4 (2002).

———. *Report of the United Nations Seminar on the Effects of Racism and Racial Discrimination on the Social and Economic Relations Between Indigenous Peoples and States.* Ted Moses, special rapporteur. U.N. Doc. E/CN.4/1989/22, HR/PUB/89/5 (1989).

———. *Report of the United Nations Technical Conference on Practical Experience in the Realization of Sustainable and Environmentally Sound Self-Development of Indigenous Peoples.* U.N. Doc. E/CN.4/Sub.2/1992/31 (1992).

———. *Report of the Workshop of Indigenous Journalists.* U.N. Doc. E/CN.4/Sub.2/AC.4/1998/6 (1998).

———. *Report of the Workshop on Research and Higher Education Institutions and Indigenous Peoples.* U.N. Doc. E/CN.4/Sub.2/AC.4/1999/5/Add.1 (1999).

———. *Report of the Workshop on Traditional Knowledge and Biological Diversity,* U.N. Doc. UNEP/CBD/TKIP/1/3 (1997).

————. *Report on the Seminar on "Multiculturalism in Africa: Peaceful and Construc-tive Group Accommodation in Situations Involving Minorities and Indigenous Peoples.* U.N. Doc. E/CN.4/Sub.2/AC.5/2000/WP.3 (2000).

————. *Workshop on Indigenous Peoples, Private Sector Natural Resources, Energy and Mining Companies and Human Rights,* U.N. Doc. E/CN.4/Sub.2/AC.4/2002/3 (2002).

U.N. Centre for Human Rights and U.N. Institute for Training and Research, ed. *Manual on Human Rights Reporting.* U.N. Sales No. E.91.XIV.1. New York: United Nations, 1991.

U.N. Secretary-General. *Intellectual Property of Indigenous Peoples: Concise Report of the Secretary-General.* U.N. Doc. E/CN.4/Sub.2/1992/30 (1992).

U.N. Subcommission on Prevention of Discrimination and Protection of Minorities. *The Right to Self-Determination: Implementation of the United Nations Reso-lutions Relating to the Right of Peoples under Colonial and Alien Domination to Self-Determination.* Héctor Gross Espiell, special rapporteur. U.N. Sales No. E.79.XIV.5. New York: United Nations, 1980.

————. *The Right to Self-Determination: Historical and Current Developments on the Basis of United Nations Instruments.* Aureliu Cristescu, special rapporteur. U.N. Sales No. E.80.XIV.3. New York: United Nations, 1981.

————. *Study of the Problem of Discrimination against Indigenous Populations.* José Martínez Cobo, special rapporteur. U.N. Doc. E/CN.4/Sub.2/1986/7 and Addenda 1–4 (1986). Originally published in U.N. Docs. E/CN.4/Sub.2/476/Adds. 1–6 (1981), E/CN.4/Sub.2/1982/2/Adds. 1–7 (1982), and E/CN.4/Sub.2/1983/21/Adds. 1–7 (1983).

————. *Study on the Rights of Persons Belonging to Ethnic, Religious and Linguistic Minorities.* Francesco Capotorti, special rapporteur. Sales No. E.78.XIV.1. New York: United Nations, 1979.

————. U.N. Working Group on Indigenous Populations. *Consideration of a Permanent Forum for Indigenous People: Report of the Workshop Held in Accordance with Commission Resolution 1995/30.* U.N. Doc. E/CN.4/Sub.2/AC.4/1995/7 (1995).

————. *Consideration of a Permanent Forum for Indigenous People: Working Paper Prepared by Mrs. Erica-Irene A. Daes, Expert and Chairperson-Rapporteur of the Working Group on Indigenous Populations.* U.N. Doc. E/CN.4/Sub.2/AC.4/1995/7/Add.2 (1995).

————. *Note by the Chairperson-Rapporteur of the Working Group on Indigenous Popu-lations, Ms. Erica-Irene Daes, on Criteria Which Might Be Applied When Con-sidering the Concept of Indigenous Peoples.* U.N. Doc. E/CN.4/Sub.2/AC.4/1995/3 (1995).

————. *Protection of the Heritage of Indigenous People: Final Report of the Special Rapporteur, Mrs. Erica-Irene Daes, in Conformity with Subcommission Resolu-tion 1993/94 and Decision 1994/105 of the Commission on Human Rights.* U.N. Doc. E/CN.4/Sub.2/1995/26 (1995).

————. *Study on the Protection of the Cultural and Intellectual Property of Indigenous Peoples.* Erica-Irene Daes, special rapporteur. U.N. Doc. E/CN.4/Sub.2/1993/28 (1993).

———. *Study on Treaties, Agreements and Other Constructive Arrangements between States and Indigenous Populations: First Progress Report, Submitted by Mr. Miguel Alfonso Martínez, special rapporteur.* U.N. Doc. E/CN/.4/Sub.2/1992/32 (1992).

———. *Study on Treaties, Agreements and Other Constructive Arrangements between States and Indigenous Populations: Second Progress Report, Submitted by the special rapporteur, Mr. Miguel Alfonso Martínez.* U.N. Doc. E/CN/.4/Sub.2/1995/ 27 (1995).

———. *Study on Treaties, Agreements and Other Constructive Arrangements Between States and Indigenous Populations: Final Report by Miguel Alfonso Martínez, Special Rapporteur.* U.N. Doc. E/CN.4/Sub.2/1999/20 (1999).

U.N. Subcommission on the Promotion and Protection of Human Rights, *Indigenous People and Their Relationship to Land- Final Working Paper Prepared by the Special Rapporteur, Mrs. Erica-Irene A. Daes.* U.N. Doc. E/CN.4/Sub.2/2001/21 (2001).

U.S. Department of Justice, Office of the Attorney General. *Department of Justice Policy on Indian Sovereignty and Government-to-Government Relations with Indian Tribes.* Washington, D.C., June 1, 1995.

U.S. Department of State. *Civil and Political Rights in the United States: Initial Report of the United States of America to the U.N. Human Rights Committee under the International Covenant on Civil and Political Rights.* DOS Pub. no. 10200. Washington, D.C.: Department of State, July 1994.

Valenta, Lisa. "Disconnect: The 1988 Brazilian Constitution, Customary International Law, and Indigenous Land Rights in Northern Brazil," *Texas International Law Journal* 38 (2003): 643–62.

Valticos, Nicolas. *International Labor Law.* Deventer: Kluwer, 1979.

Van Cott, Donna Lee. *The Friendly Liquidation of the Past: The Politics of Diversity in Latin America: The Politics of Identity in Latin America,* Pittsburgh: Pittsburgh University Press, 2000.

Van Dyke, Vernon. *Human Rights, Ethnicity, and Discrimination.* Westport, Conn.: Greenwood Press, 1985.

Vattel, Emmerich de. *The Law of Nations, or The Principles of Natural Law.* Translation of the 1758 edition by Charles G. Fenwick. Classics of International Law series. Washington, D.C.: Carnegie Institution of Washington, 1916.

Vincent, Andrew. *Theories of the State.* Oxford and New York: B. Blackwell, 1987.

Victoria, Francisco de. *De indis et de ivre belli relectiones.* Translated by J. Bate. Classics of International Law series. Washington: Carnegie Institution of Washington, D.C.: 1917.

Waley, Daniel Philip. *Later Medieval Europe: From Saint Louis to Luther.* 2d ed. London and New York: Longman, 1985.

Wallace, Paul. *The Iroquois Book of Life: White Roots of Peace.* Santa Fe: Claear Light Publishers, 1994. Originally published Philadelphia: University of Pennsylvania Press, 1946.

Walters, F. P. *Historia de la Sociedad de Naciones.* Traducción de Federico Fernández de Castillejo. Madrid: Tecnos, 1971.

Watters, Mary. *A History of the Church in Venezuela, 1810–1930.* Chapel Hill: University of North Carolina Press, 1933.

Weissbrodt, David. "The Contribution of International Governmental Organizations to the Protection of Human Rights." In *Human Rights in International Law: Legal and Policy Issues*, pp. 403–38. Edited by Theodor Meron. Oxford: Clarendon Press, 1984.

Weissbrodt, David, Joan Fitzpatrick, and Frank Newman. *International Human Rights: Law, Policy and Process*. 3d ed. Cincinnati: Anderson Publishing, 2001.

Weller, Marc. Current Development Note, "The International Response to the Dissolution of the Socialist Federal Republic of Yugoslavia." *American Journal of International Law* 86 (1992): 569–607.

Westlake, John. *Chapters on the Principles of International Law*. Cambridge: University Press, 1894.

Weston, Burns H. "Human Rights." In *Human Rights and the World Community: Issues and Action*, pp. 14–30. Edited by Richard P. Claude and Burns H. Weston. 2d ed. Philadelphia: University of Pennsylvania Press, 1992.

Weston, Burns H., Robin Lukes, and Kelly Hnatt. "Regional Human Rights Regimes: A Comparison and Appraisal." In *Human Rights in the World Community*, pp. 244–55. Edited by Richard P. Claude and Burns H. Weston. 2d ed. Philadelphia: University of Pennsylvania Press, 1992.

Wexler, David. *Therapeutic Jurisprudence and Changing Conceptions of Legal Scholarship. Behavioral Sciences and the Law* 11 (1993): 17–29.

Wexler, David, and Bruce Durham Winick. *Law in a Therapeutic Key: Developments in Therapeutic Jurisprudence*. Durham, N.C.: Carolina Academic Press, 1996.

Wheaton, Henry. *Elements of International Law*. 8th ed. Edited by Richard Henry Dana, Jr. Boston: Little, Brown, 1866.

Wiessner, Siegfried. "American Indian Treaties and Modern International Law." *St. Thomas Law Review* 7 (1995): 576–602.

———. "Rights and Status of Indigenous Peoples: A Global Comparative and International Legal Analysis." *Harvard Human Rights Journal* 12 (1999): 57–128.

Wilkinson, Charles F. *American Indians, Time, and the Law: Native Societies in a Modern Constitutional Democracy*. New Haven: Yale University Press, 1987.

Williams, Robert A., Jr. "The Algebra of Federal Indian Law: The Hard Trail of Decolonizing and Americanizing the White Man's Indian Jurisprudence." *Wisconsin Law Review* 1986 (1986): 219–99.

———. *The American Indian in Western Legal Thought: The Discourses of Conquest*. New York: Oxford University Press, 1990.

———. "Encounters on the Frontiers of International Human Rights Law: Redefining the Terms of Indigenous Peoples' Survival in the World." *Duke Law Journal* (Sept.–Dec. 1990): 660-704.

———. "The Medieval and Renaissance Origins of the Status of the American Indian in Western Legal Thought." *Southern California Law Review* 57 (1983): 1–99.

Wilmer, Franke. *The Indigenous Voice in World Politics: Since Time Immemorial*. Newbury Park, Cal.: Sage, 1993.

Zeledón, Mario Rizo. "Identidad étnica y elecciones: El caso de la RAAN." *WANI* no. 8 (July–Dec. 1990): 28–51.

Zuijdwijk, Ton. *Petitioning in the United Nations*. New York: St. Martin's Press, 1982.

Table of Principal Documents

OTHER INTERNATIONAL STANDARD-SETTING
OR PROGRAMMATIC INSTRUMENTS

Table of Cases

INTER-AMERICAN COURT OF HUMAN RIGHTS

INTERNATIONAL ARBITRATION TRIBUNALS

INTERNATIONAL COURT OF JUSTICE

INTERNATIONAL LABOUR ORGANIZATION

JAPAN

NICARAGUA

PERMANENT COURT OF INTERNATIONAL JUSTICE

UNITED STATES

VENEZUELA

Index